Everyone's an Author

Everyone's an Author

WITH READINGS

FOURTH EDITION

ANDREA A. LUNSFORD
STANFORD UNIVERSITY

MICHAL BRODY

LISA EDE
OREGON STATE UNIVERSITY

JESSICA ENOCH
UNIVERSITY OF MARYLAND

BEVERLY J. MOSS
THE OHIO STATE UNIVERSITY

CAROLE CLARK PAPPER

KEITH WALTERS
PORTLAND STATE UNIVERSITY

W. W. NORTON & COMPANY
Celebrating a Century of Independent Publishing

Copyright © 2023, 2021, 2020, 2017, 2013 by W. W. Norton & Company, Inc.

Editor: Erica Wnek

Project Editor: Thea Goodrich

Assistant Editor: Serin Lee

Managing Editor, College: Marian Johnson

Managing Editor, College Digital Media: Kim Yi

Production Manager: Jane Searle

Media Editor: Joy Cranshaw

Media Project Editor: Diane Cipollone

Associate Media Editor: Jessica Awad

Media Editorial Assistants: Maria Qureshi and Juliet Godwin

Ebook Producer: Emily Schwoyer

Marketing Manager, Composition: Michele Dobbins

Design Director: Rubina Yeh

Designer: Jo Anne Metsch

Director of College Permissions: Megan Schindel

Permissions Associate: Patricia Wong

Photo Editor: Ted Szczepanski

Photo Research: Dena Betz

Composition: MPS Limited

Manufacturing: Transcontinental—Beauceville

Permission to use copyrighted material is included in the credits section of this book, which begins on p. 1035.

ISBN: **978-1-324-04527-4** (pbk)

W. W. Norton & Company, Inc., 500 Fifth Avenue, New York, NY 10110
    wwnorton.com

W. W. Norton & Company Ltd., 15 Carlisle Street, London W1D 3BS

1 2 3 4 5 6 7 8 9 0

For Lisa Ede, 1947–2021: coauthor, colleague, mentor, friend.

Preface

 **VERYONE'S AN AUTHOR** grew out of our sense—in the early years of the new millennium—that we were seeing fundamental changes in what writing means and in what it means to be a writer. Writing itself expanded exponentially, to include not only social media communication but also a host of new and emerging genres. And technology allowed students not only to write more than they ever had before but also to become *authors*, to share their ideas with audiences worldwide. In the early editions of this text, the key words of our title, "author" and "everyone," guided our efforts as we invited students to take on the authority, and the responsibility, that comes with authorship—and as we aimed to include *everyone*, all students, in this invitation.

Those goals still underpin every page of *Everyone's an Author*. But in the years since we completed the first edition over a decade ago, we have encountered even more exhilarating change and even more daunting challenges. As a result, we're tempted to begin this preface with one word: whew! Just since the last edition of *Everyone's an Author* appeared, we have lived through years of a pandemic that has affected every single teacher and student in the country, disrupting teaching and learning in ways we simply could not have imagined. We have experienced a hotly debated presidential election rife with misinformation and manipulation and violence. We've witnessed the social upheaval surrounding the killings of George Floyd, Breonna Taylor, Ahmaud Arbery—and way too many others. We have ricocheted between exhaustion, hope, and despair.

And yet. So many of us teachers of writing are still here: keeping classes going against nearly impossible odds, delivering teaching materials (and sometimes even food) to students and their families, working long hours to move to virtual teaching—and then the even longer hours required to deliver hybrid classes or to return to the classroom. And always keeping our students and their well-being uppermost in mind as they strive to adapt to today's highly varied teaching environments.

We have had this context front and center in our minds as we worked on the Fourth Edition of *Everyone's an Author*, and with it we have wanted to celebrate and support teachers and students everywhere who continue to meet these challenges with resilience, ingenuity, and determination. *Thank you*.

We have also had in mind the student authors we have been privileged to work with on this edition, who have inspired us to work harder than ever to underscore the power—and the responsibilities—that can come with authorship, along with the forces in our society that continue to discourage, or even to withhold, authorship from some. Thus we have added a new chapter, "**Language, Power, and Rhetoric**," that invites students to think about the ways in which language choices privilege some while silencing others, as well as about the validity and vibrancy of all languages and dialects—and aims to offer advice for making wise, ethical, and effective rhetorical choices regarding language use. This expanded focus on language choice echoes throughout the new edition, from coverage of critical language awareness, to expanded advice on having difficult conversations and navigating the unequal risks that accompany such situations, to new tips on using call and response, signifying, and narrative sequencing as potent strategies for supporting an argument—and many new examples throughout of authors who effectively use diverse languages and dialects.

Other additions provide guidance for the kinds of writing student authors are undertaking today. A second new chapter, "**Reflecting on Your Writing**," reviews the powerful ways in which reflection can improve writing and help ensure transfer of knowledge, offers examples of effective student reflections, and provides a roadmap for composing reflections. An updated and expanded chapter on "**Composing and Remixing across Media**" offers tips and examples for composing in various media (podcasts, infographics, social media, and more), plus advice for remixing writing into new genres and modes. And a third new chapter, "**Writing for a Public Audience**," guides students through essential considerations for engaging the public.

Because research is always evolving, so too has the research advice we provide in this edition. A new chapter, "**Conducting Research in the Field**," aims to broaden the very concept of what counts as "research" and who or what count as "sources." Throughout the Research part of *Everyone's an Author*, we take to heart—and ask student-authors to take to heart—Clint Smith's insight in his award-winning book *How the Word Is Passed* that "the best primary sources are often sitting right next to us." We hope these revisions invite students to learn from more non-Western research methodologies, such as those used by Indigenous researchers. To help make room for all that's new, we've moved chapters on "Writing and Rhetoric in the Workplace," "Assembling a Portfolio," and "Publishing Your Writing" online, where they're still available for easy reference.

But we've added much more than new chapters to this edition. You will also find many compelling new examples of writing across a wide range of media, from an annotated student literacy essay on immigrating and a visual analysis of androgynous fashion in today's WNBA to a student's public service announcement video on masking up and much more. And our newly interactive ebook now includes embedded videos as well as "Reflect & Write" prompts that get students reading actively and practicing writing as they read. Thus this new edition continues our commitment to defining and representing writing as it's done today: across media.

There is one more exciting addition with this edition: we've welcomed a new coauthor, Jessica Enoch, Director of Writing at the University of Maryland. In addition to her extensive experience as a teacher and administrator of writing and rhetoric, Jessica Enoch brings important scholarly insights on rhetoric, reflection, transfer, and much more to our project. Learn more about Jess's scholarly contributions on page 1043.

With so many new chapters and features, you may be wondering if there's anything about this book that *hasn't* changed. And indeed, there is. First and foremost is our commitment to *all* students, to making sure they see themselves in the pages of this book, to recognizing their unique strengths as users of language, and to making their voices and ideas heard. In these pages you'll find a *TikTok* campaign by community college students advertising their school's perks, a student research essay exploring the consequences of monolingual education, a student-parent's proposal for better campus policies, and many other voices reflecting diverse experiences, perspectives, and language choices.

As teachers, we have been privileged to work with generations of students, to engage technological changes to literacy and to rhetoric unimaginable to us when we entered the field, and to act and react critically in terms of the changing ways that information is created and distributed. We've continued to learn from and with students about how best to meet such challenges. As scholars, we have read widely in debates surrounding social media, artificial intelligence, and threats to privacy as well as in work that reveals how languages and images can be manipulated more easily than ever before and on the ongoing effects of linguistic racism, or "linguicism." As researchers, we have studied the changing scenes of writing with a mixture of consternation and excitement. And as always, our goal in writing this book has been to take some of the best ideas animating the field of writing and rhetoric and make them accessible to and usable by students and teachers—and to invite *everyone* to become authors, whose words—spoken, written, electronic—will help shape the world we live in.

Highlights

- *The genres students need to write:* You'll find guidelines for writing arguments, analyses, narratives, reports, reviews, proposals, summary / responses, visual analysis, literacy narratives, profiles, literature reviews—and a *NEW* chapter on reflections. Chapter 37 gives students *NEW* advice for "Composing and Remixing across Media"—when they're transforming writing into a new genre or making use of multiple modes.

- *The power of rhetoric:* From Chapter 1, "Thinking Rhetorically," to *NEW* Chapter 4 on "Language, Power, and Rhetoric," to the many prompts throughout the book that help students think about their own rhetorical situations and choices, this book helps them understand and harness the power of rhetoric.

- *Reflection:* When students pause to examine their writing choices and processes, their knowledge and skills are more likely to transfer to new situations. *NEW* Chapter 10, "Reflecting on Your Writing," helps students do just that, as do "Reflect" prompts throughout the book, and *NEW* "Reflect & Write" prompts in the ebook.

- *Argument:* Chapter 13 covers "Arguing a Position," Chapter 19 covers "Analyzing and Constructing Arguments," and Chapter 20 offers "Strategies for Supporting an Argument"—with *NEW* advice on call and response, signifying, and narrative sequencing.

- *Research:* The challenge today's students face is making sense of massive amounts of information and using it effectively in support of their own arguments. Chapters 21 to 31 cover all stages of research, from finding and evaluating sources to citing and documenting them. Guidelines for evaluating sources have been updated to help students read laterally and examine their own biases. And a *NEW* chapter covers "Conducting Research in the Field."

- *Practical and easy to use:* Roadmaps for writing, menus, directories, color-coded documentation templates, and a glossary / index make the book easy to use—and to understand. *NEW* animated videos in the ebook also reinforce challenging concepts and skills with models designed to support student learning in a variety of modalities.

- *Finding common ground:* Chapter 2, "Engaging Productively with Others," guides students in practicing empathy, listening, and being open to challenging conversations—essential for engaging with an open mind as an author.

- *Social justice:* Minimum wages, language diversity, veteran access to health care: many of the examples in this book demonstrate how people use writing in ways that strive to create "a more perfect union," a society that is just and equitable for all its members. We don't always agree on how to go about reaching those goals, and that's why rhetoric and civic discourse matter.

- *Examples and readings students will relate to—many NEW:* From a report on the effects of beauty filters and an analysis of why Beyoncé's fans' devotion doesn't fade, to a student's narrative about immigrating to the United States from Mexico and an argument for free speech on campus, we hope that all students will find examples and images that will make them smile—and inspire them to read and write and think.

Everyone's an Author is available in two versions, with and without an anthology of twenty-seven readings at the back. Readings are arranged alphabetically by author, with menus indexing the readings by genre and theme.

Resources

Ebooks, available standalone and free with all new print copies of the text, provide an enhanced reading experience with built-in highlighting and note-taking capabilities. The Fourth Edition ebook includes new embedded videos on key concepts, as well as "Reflect & Write" prompts written by new coauthor Jessica Enoch designed to get students reading actively, thinking rhetorically, and practicing writing as they read. And instructors can create their own models of engaged reading to share with their students using the instructor annotation tool. Norton Ebooks can be viewed on all devices and are born-accessible, with content and features designed from the start for all learners.

InQuizitive for Writers activities get students thinking like writers, researchers, and editors, through an interactive, low-stakes learning tool. After practicing with InQuizitive, students will be better prepared to start drafting their writing assignments, approach research projects with more focus and confidence, and edit their writing. The activities are adaptive, so students receive additional practice in the areas where they need more help, and explanatory feedback with links to *The Little Seagull Handbook* ebook offers advice precisely when it's needed. A robust activity report helps students identify challenging concepts and focus on where they can improve. The Fourth Edition includes new activities on fact-checking sources, rhetorical situations, elements of argument, thesis statements, paragraph development, critical reading strategies, and making the most of *The Little Seagull Handbook*. InQuizitive for Writers is included with all new copies of *Everyone's an Author* and can be integrated directly into most campus learning management systems.

Animated videos. New to the Fourth Edition, a collection of short, animated videos is now available in the ebook, through a campus LMS, and in new InQuizitive for Writers activities. Informed by feedback from hundreds of composition instructors, topics include the writing process, rhetorical situations, specific kinds of writing, critical reading strategies, and much more.

Everyonesanauthor.tumblr.com, a dynamic collection of online media, provides a rich, regularly updated source of readings—including articles, speeches, advertisements, and more—for inspiration, analysis, and response. Readings are sortable by theme, genre, and medium, and each reading is accompanied by a headnote and prompts that guide students to evaluate, reflect, and develop arguments. "Conversation" clusters pair multiple readings with diverse viewpoints on contemporary topics. Find a chapter-by-chapter menu of the online examples in this book by clicking "Links from the Book."

Quizzes. Short reading quizzes for each chapter and reading selection in the book hold students accountable for reading assignments so that they arrive to class ready for activities and discussion. In addition, more than 150 quizzes on topics including sentences, language, punctuation / mechanics, paragraph editing, plagiarism, and MLA and APA citation provide summative assessment opportunities for topics practiced in InQuizitive for Writers. And a plagiarism tutorial guides students through why plagiarism matters, what counts as plagiarism, and how to avoid plagiarism. Then students are asked to identify plagiarism through a short quiz to assess what they've learned.

Norton Teaching Tools. Available for the first time with the Fourth Edition, the Norton Teaching Tools site for *Everyone's an Author* is the first stop for instructors looking for creative, engaging resources to refresh their syllabus or design a new one. Written by the authors, with special contributions from instructors across the country, all of the revised contents from *A Guide to Teaching "Everyone's an Author"* can now be found here, including the comprehensive guide to teaching first-year writing as well as advice for teaching every chapter and reading in the text. The Norton Teaching Tools site is searchable and can be filtered by chapter or by resource type, making it easy to find just the right resource, download and customize it, and import it to an LMS course. New additions for the Fourth Edition include expanded sample writing assignments with corresponding peer-review templates and rubrics; worksheets, graphic organizers, and other materials for classroom and online activities; significantly revised and new chapters on diversity, equity, and inclusion; advice for teaching writing online; and more.

Author videos. Andrea A. Lunsford, Lisa Ede, Beverly Moss, Carole Clark Papper, and Keith Walters answer questions they're often asked by other instructors: about fostering collaboration, teaching multimodal writing, taking advantage of the writing center, teaching classes that include both L1 and L2 students, and more.

Resources for your LMS. All of Norton's digital resources can be easily added to online, hybrid, or lecture courses right within your campus's existing learning management system. Integration links allow for single sign-on, and graded activities can be configured to report to the LMS course gradebook.

Access all of the resources for *Everyone's an Author* at **digital.wwnorton.com /everyone4** and for *Everyone's an Author with Readings* at **digital.wwnorton .com/everyone4r**.

Acknowledgments

We are profoundly grateful to the many people who have helped bring *Everyone's an Author* into existence. In addition to the brilliant guidance of Marilyn Moller, we have been graced with the editorial skills and organizational acumen—not to mention the generosity and good humor—of our editor, Erica Wnek, who has herded this particular group of cats through a long and difficult process. We are similarly grateful to many others who contributed their talents to this book, especially Thea Goodrich and Jane Searle, for all they did to produce this book (no small undertaking). Thanks as well to Patricia Wong for her work clearing the many text permissions and to Ted Szczepanski and Dena Betz for their work finding and clearing permissions for the many images. Last but certainly not least, we thank Serin Lee for undertaking countless tasks large and small with efficiency, conscientiousness, and smarts.

Everyone's an Author is much more than a printed book, and we thank Joy Cranshaw for her guidance, inspiration, and encouragement leading the development of the many resources that contribute to this text. We're grateful to Maria Qureshi, Juliet Godwin, Jessica Awad, Diane Cipollone, Alice Garrard, Emily Schwoyer, and Kate Barnes for helping bring to life the ebook, InQuizitive, LMS resources, Norton Teaching Tools, companion website, and more.

The design of this book is something we are particularly proud of, and for that we offer our special thanks to several amazing designers. Stephen Doyle created the spectacular covers for this—and every—edition of our book. Carin Berger created the illuminated alphabet, made of text, that opens every chapter. Jo Anne Metsch and Lissi Sigillo did the lovely interior design. And Debra Morton-Hoyt, Rubina Yeh, and Michael Wood oversaw the whole thing as well as adding their own elegant—and whimsical!— touches inside and out. Best thanks to all of them.

Special thanks also to the fabled Norton Travelers, who have worked against all odds during a pandemic to contact instructors across the country about what this text and resources can offer them. And a big thank you to Michele Dobbins, Heidi Balas, and Lib Triplett for helping us keep our eye on our audience: teachers and students at colleges where rhetorics of this kind are assigned. Finally, we are grateful to Julia Reidhead, Mike Wright, Ann Shin, and Steve Dunn, who have given their unwavering support to this project for more than a decade now. We are fortunate indeed to have had the talent and hard work of this distinguished Norton team.

We are also deeply grateful to a small group of teachers who helped us look critically at how we might better address issues of diversity, equity, and inclusion in this edition and who provided invaluable response to drafts of new chapters and materials: Ronisha Browdy, North Carolina State University; Kendra N. Bryant, North Carolina Agricultural and Technical State University; Felicita Arzu Carmichael, Oakland University; Aja Y. Martinez, University of North Texas; Christine Martorana, Florida International University; Sarita Mizin, University of Wisconsin–Eau Claire; Jeannine W. Morgan, St. Johns River State College; Staci Perryman-Clark, Western Michigan University; Cristina D. Ramirez, University of Arizona; Sherita Roundtree, Towson University; Adam Sneed, Southwest Tennessee Community College; Kristen L. Snoddy, Indiana University Kokomo; Sarah Snyder, Arizona Western College; Karrieann Soto Vega, University of Kentucky; Daniel Stanford, Pitt Community College; and Missy Watson, City College of New York, CUNY.

A larger and extremely helpful group of reviewers has also helped us more than we can say. In particular, we have depended on their good pedagogical sense and advice in revising every chapter of this book. Special thanks to: Lauren Baugus, Pensacola State College; Darlene Beaman, Lone Star College–Kingwood; Logan Bearden, Nova Southeastern University; Kristin Bivens, Harold Washington College; Sidney Blaylock, Middle Tennessee State University; Kelly Blewett, Indiana University East; Susan Bosarge, Mississippi Gulf Coast Community College–Harrison County; Brenda Bryant, Lone Star College–North Harris; Alexis Butzner, Chemeketa Community College; Colin Charlton, The University of Texas Rio Grande Valley; Lisa Darling, Lone Star College–Kingwood; Christine Davis, Northern Arizona University; Karen S. Doheney, Northern Virginia Community College–Loudoun Campus; Megan Eatman, Clemson University; Heather Finch, Belmont University; Katie Chosa Franklin, University of New Orleans; David F. Green Jr., Howard University; Kimberly Greenfield-Karshner, Lorain County Community College; Andrea Holliger, Lone Star College–CyFair; Erica Jones, Northern Arizona University; Rebecca Jones, Montana State University; Steven Krause, Eastern Michigan University; Lynn C. Lewis, Oklahoma State University; Anna Maheshwari, Schoolcraft College; Joanne Mallari, University of Nevada, Reno; Tracy Ann Morse, East Carolina

University; David Moyle, South Texas College; Robin Gray Nicks, University of Tennessee; Jill Onega, Calhoun Community College; Kate Pantelides, Middle Tennessee State University; Jerry Petersen, Utah Valley University; Mary Elizabeth Rogers, Florida Gateway College; Todd Ruecker, University of Nevada, Reno; Tony Russell, Central Oregon Community College; Jordan Sanderson, Mississippi Gulf Coast Community College–Jackson County; Britni Schoolcraft, Pensacola State College; Kaia Simon, University of Wisconsin—Eau Claire; Sara Smith, Pensacola State College; Derrick Stewart, Midlands Technical College; Charlene Summers, Texas A&M International University; Michael Suwak, College of Southern Maryland; Tamara Whyte, Piedmont Virginia Community College; Amy Williams, Brigham Young University; and Tara Wood, University of Northern Colorado.

We'd also like to thank those reviewers who helped us to shape the previous editions: Forster Agama, Tallahassee Community College; Stevens Amidon, Indiana University–Purdue Fort Wayne; Georgana Atkins, University of Mississippi; Jacob Babb, Indiana University Southeast; Edward Baldwin, College of Southern Nevada; Brooke Ballard, Lone Star College–CyFair; Michelle Ballif, University of Georgia; Nancy Barendse, Charleston Southern University; Larry Beason, University of South Alabama, Mobile; Kristen Belcher, University of Colorado, Denver; Samantha Bell, Johnson County Community College; Dawn Bergeron, St. Johns River State College; Cassandra Bishop, Southern Illinois University; Kevin Boyle, College of Southern Nevada; Erin Breaux, South Louisiana Community College; J. Andrew Briseño, Northwestern State University; Elizabeth Brockman, Central Michigan University; Stephen Brown, University of Nevada, Las Vegas; Ellie Bunting, Edison State College; Vicki Byard, Northeastern Illinois University; Maggie Callahan, Louisiana State University; Laura Chartier, University of Alaska, Anchorage; Tera Joy Cole, Idaho State University; Paul Cook, Indiana University Kokomo; Adrienne J. Daly, University of Rhode Island; Beth Daniell, Kennesaw State University; James M. Decker, Illinois Central College; Anne-Marie Deitering, Oregon State University; Nancy DeJoy, Michigan State University; Debra Dew, Valparaiso University; Robyn DeWall, Idaho State University; Sara DiCaglio, Texas A&M University; Ronda Dively, Southern Illinois University, Carbondale; Patrick Dolan Jr., University of Iowa; Douglas Downs, Montana State University; Suellynn Duffey, University of Missouri, St. Louis; Anne Dvorak, Longview Community College; Beth Ebersbaker, Lee College; Maryam El-Shall, Jamestown Community College; Michael Emerson, Northwestern Michigan College; Patricia Ericsson, Washington State University; Michael

Faris, Texas Tech University; Frank Farmer, University of Kansas; Wioleta Fedeczko, Utah Valley University; Casie Fedukovich, North Carolina State University; Lindsay Ferrara, Fairfield University; Bill FitzGerald, Rutgers University–Camden; Lauren Fitzgerald, Yeshiva University; Maureen Fitzpatrick, Johnson County Community College; Kitty Flowers, University of Indianapolis; Stephanie Freuler, Valencia State College; Robin Gallaher, Northwest Missouri State University; Diana Grumbles, Southern Methodist University; Ann Guess, Alvin Community College; Michael Harker, Georgia State University; Samuel Head, Idaho State University; Tara Hembrough, Southern Illinois University; Charlotte Hogg, Texas Christian University; Jennifer Holly-Wells, Montclair State University; Emma Howes, Coastal Carolina University; Melissa Ianetta, University of Delaware; Joyce Inman, University of Southern Mississippi; Jordynn Jack, University of North Carolina, Chapel Hill; Sara Jameson, Oregon State University; David A. Jolliffe, University of Arkansas; Ann Jurecic, Rutgers University; Connie Kendall, University of Cincinnati; Debra Knutson, Shawnee State University; William Lalicker, West Chester University; Michelle S. Lee, Daytona State College; Sonja Lynch, Wartburg College; Cathy Mahaffey, University of North Carolina, Charlotte; Phillip Marzluf, Kansas State University; Richard Matzen, Woodbury University; Moriah McCracken, The University of Texas, Pan American; Mary Pat McQueeney, Johnson County Community College; Clyde Moneyhun, Boise State University; Chelsea Murdock, University of Kansas; Whitney Myers, Texas Wesleyan University; Sadeem El Nahhas, Northwestern State University; Carroll Ferguson Nardone, Sam Houston State University; Jessie Nixon, University of Alaska, Anchorage; Rolf Norgaard, University of Colorado, Boulder; Nicole F. Oechslin, Piedmont Virginia Community College; Katherine Durham Oldmixon, Huston-Tillotson University; Matthew Oliver, Old Dominion University; Gary Olson, Idaho State University; Paula Patch, Elon University; Scott Payne, University of Central Arkansas; Mary Jo Reiff, University of Kansas; Thomas Reynolds, Northwestern State University; Janice Rieman, University of North Carolina, Charlotte; Albert Rouzie, Ohio University; Alison Russell, Xavier University; Kathleen J. Ryan, University of Montana; Pamela Saunders, Suffolk University; Matthew Schmeer, Johnson County Community College; Emerson Schroeter, Northern Arizona University; Shawna Shapiro, Middlebury College; Emily Robins Sharpe, Penn State University; John Sherrill, Purdue University; Mary Lourdes Silva, Ithaca College; Marc Simoes, California State University, Long Beach; Eddie Singleton, The Ohio State University; Allison Smith, Middle Tennessee

State University; Susan Smith, Georgia Southern University; Tracie Smith, University of Indianapolis; Shannon C. Stewart, Coastal Carolina University; Emily Suh, Texas State University; Paulette Swartzfager, Rochester Institute of Technology; Deborah Coxwell Teague, Florida State University; Jason Tham, St. Cloud State University; Tom Thompson, The Citadel; Edwin Turner, St. Johns River State College; Verne Underwood, Rogue Community College; Jennifer Vala, Georgia State University; Rex Veeder, St. Cloud State University; Melanie Verner, Lee College; Emily Ward, Idaho State University; Matthew Wiles, University of Louisville; Lauren Woolbright, Clemson University; Courtney Wooten, George Mason University; Mary Wright, Christopher Newport University; Craig Wynne, Hampton University; and Vershawn Ashanti Young, University of Waterloo.

Collectively, we have taught for over 150 years: that's a lot of classes, a lot of students—and we are grateful for every single one of them. We owe some of the best moments of our lives to them, and in our most challenging moments—including some working on this edition—they have inspired us to carry on. In *Everyone's an Author*, we are particularly grateful to the student-writers whose work speaks so eloquently in this text: Crystal Aymelek, Portland State University; Annaya Baynes, Spelman College; Halle Edwards, Stanford University; Paloma Garcia, Santa Clara University; Anna Glavee, San Diego State University; Ryan Joy, Portland State University; Julia Landauer, Stanford University; Larry Lehna, University of Michigan, Dearborn; Faith Omosefe, Amherst College; David Pasini, The Ohio State University; Walter Przybylowski, Rutgers University; Melissa Rubin, Hofstra University; Katherine Spriggs, Stanford University; Manisha Ummadi, University of California, Berkeley; Gabriela Uribe, Stanford University; Saurabh Vaish, Hofstra University; Yuliya Vayner, Hunter College; and Sophia Warfield, University of Maryland, College Park. We thank, too, the small group of students who offered advice and feedback on this edition: Carlos Arze, University of Nevada, Reno; Andrew Bohen, Belmont University; Isabella Hipp, Belmont University; Jason Perez Giron, University of Nevada, Reno; and Laine Wilson, University of Nevada, Reno.

Each of us also has special debts of gratitude. Andrea A. Lunsford thanks her students and colleagues in the Program in Writing and Rhetoric at Stanford University and at the Bread Loaf School of English, along with sisters Ellen Ashdown and Liz Middleton; friends for life Marilyn Moller, Shirley Heath, Betty Bailey, Cheryl Glenn, Beverly Moss, Marvin Diogenes, Adam Banks, and William McCurdy; and beloved grandnieces Audrey and Lila.

Most especially, Andrea gives thanks for her late coauthor and friend of fifty years, Lisa Ede, whose presence she will always miss—and treasure.

Michal Brody would like to thank her partner, Mucuy Moó, and her two wonderful families in the United States and Yucatan, who so graciously support (and endure) her restless and crazy transnational life. Her conversations—both the actual and the imagined—with each and all of those loved ones provide the constant impetus to reach for deep understanding and clarity of expression. She also thanks her students in both countries, who remind her every day that we are all teachers, all learners.

Jessica Enoch would like to thank Scott, Jack, Nancy, and Teddy as well as the students and teachers in the Academic Writing Program at the University of Maryland.

Beverly Moss thanks her mother, Sarah Moss, for her love, encouragement, and confidence in her when her own wavered. In addition, she thanks her Ohio State and Bread Loaf students, who inspire her and teach her so much about teaching. She also wants to express gratitude to her colleagues in Rhetoric, Composition, and Literacy at Ohio State for their incredible support. Finally, she thanks two of her own former English teachers, Dorothy Bratton and Jackie Royster, for the way they modeled excellence inside and outside the classroom.

Carole Clark Papper would like to thank her husband, Bob, and wonderful children—Dana, Matt, Zack, and Kate—without whose loving support little would happen and nothing would matter. In addition, she is grateful for the inspiration and support over the years of teachers, colleagues, and students at Ohio State, Ball State, and Hofstra, but especially for Beverly Moss and Andrea Lunsford for launching her on this journey.

Keith Walters thanks his partner of forty years and husband of seventeen, Jonathan Tamez, for sharing a love of life, language, travel, flowers, and beauty. He is also grateful to his students in Tunisia, South Carolina, Texas, Oregon, and Palestine, who have challenged him to find ways of talking about what good writing is and how to do it.

This book is dedicated, with love, to our friend and coauthor, who died while this edition was in progress. Following are the last acknowledgments she wrote: Lisa Ede thanks her husband, Greg Pfarr, for his support, for his commitment to his own art, and for their year-round vegetable garden. Thanks as well to her siblings, who have stuck together through thick and thin: Leni Ede Smith, Andrew Ede, Sara Ede Rowkamp, Michele Ede Smith, Laurie Ede Drake, Robert Ede, and Julie Ede Campbell. She also thanks her colleagues in the Oregon State School of Writing, Literature, and Film for their encouragement and support.

Finally, we thank those who have taught us—who first helped us learn to hold a pencil and print our names, who inspired a love of language and of reading and writing, who encouraged us to take chances in writing our lives as best we could, who prodded and pushed when we needed it, and who most of all set brilliant examples for us to follow. Indeed, where we have been able to succeed, it has been because we could stand on the shoulders of giants. We thank them all.

—Andrea A. Lunsford, Michal Brody, Jessica Enoch,
Beverly Moss, Carole Clark Papper, Keith Walters

CONTENTS

Use clear and recognizable patterns of organization / Mark logical relationships between ideas / State claims explicitly and provide suitable support / Present your ideas as a response to others / Express ideas directly / Be aware of how genres and conventions vary across disciplines / Document sources using appropriate citation style

16 Reporting Information / "Just the Facts" 287

17 Writing a Review / "Two Thumbs Up" 334

PART VI Research *477*

39 Writing for a Public Audience 825

Readings 835

*New to the Fourth Edition

Bonus Ebook Chapters

digital.wwnorton.com/everyone4r

A. Writing and Rhetoric in the Workplace

B. Assembling a Portfolio

C. Publishing Your Writing

*New to the Fourth Edition

Is Everyone an Author?

E'VE CHOSEN A PROVOCATIVE TITLE for this book, so it's fair to ask if we've gotten it right, if everyone is an author. Let's take just a few examples that can help to make the point:

- A student creates a *TikTok* account that immediately finds a large audience of other interested people.

- Two friends post on *Instagram* a message of support for Ukraine that goes viral within minutes and circles the globe in less than a day.

- A professor assigns students in her class to work together to write a number of entries for *Wikipedia*, and they are surprised to find how quickly their entries are revised by others.

- A member of the Federal Reserve writes an open letter explaining the causes of recent inflation as well as the steps being taken to address the issue and publishes it in major newspapers across the country, reaching millions of readers.

- A group of Navajo students submit their special recipe for Kneel Down Bread to *foodgawker* and are thrilled at the response from other cooks.

- Five women nominated for the Academy Award for Best Actress prepare acceptance speeches: one of them will deliver the speech live before an international audience.

- You get your next assignment in your college writing class and set out to do the research necessary to complete it. When you're finished, you turn in your twelve-page argument to your instructor and class-mates for their responses—and you also post a short excerpt from it on *Twitter*.

All of these examples represent important messages written by people who probably do not consider themselves authors. Yet they illustrate what we mean when we say that today "everyone's an author." Once upon a time, the ability to compose a message that reached wide and varied audiences was restricted to a small group; now, however, this opportunity is available to anyone with access to the internet.

The word "author" has a long history, but it is most associated with the rise of print and the ability of writers to claim what they have writ-ten as property. The first copyright act, in the early eighteenth century, ruled that authors held the primary rights to their work. And while anyone could potentially be a writer, an author was someone whose work had been published. That rough definition worked pretty well until recently, when traditional copyright laws began to show the strain of their 300-year history, most notably with the simple and easy file sharing that the inter-net makes possible.

In fact, the web has blurred the distinction between writers and authors, offering anyone with access to the internet the opportunity to publish what they write. If you have access to the internet (at school, at a library, at home), you can publish what you write and thus make what you say available to readers around the world.

Think for a minute about the impact of blogs, which first appeared in 1997. When this book was first published, there were more than 156 million public blogs, and as this new edition goes to press, there are more than 518 million blogs on *Tumblr* alone. Add to blogs the rise of *Twitter*, *YouTube*, *Instagram*, *Facebook*, *TikTok*, and other social networking sites for even more evidence to support our claim: today, everyone's an author. Moreover, twenty-first-century authors just don't fit the image of the Romantic writer, alone in a garret, struggling to bring forth something unique. Rather, today's authors are part of a huge, often global, conversation; they build on what others have thought and written, they create mash-ups and remixes, and they practice teamwork at almost every turn. They are authoring for the digital age.

Redefining Writing

If the definition of "author" has changed in recent years, so has our understanding of the definition, nature, and scope of "writing."

Writing, for example, now includes much more than words, as images and graphics take on an important part of the job of conveying meaning. In addition, writing now includes sound, video, and other media. Perhaps more important, writing now often contains many voices, as information from the internet is incorporated with ease into the texts we write. Finally, as we noted above, writing today is almost always part of a larger conversation. Rather than rising mysteriously from the depths of a writer's original thoughts, a stereotype made popular during the Romantic period, writing almost always responds to some other written piece or to other ideas. If, to quote John Donne, "no [person] is an island, entire of itself," then the same holds true for writing.

Writing now is also often highly collaborative. You work with a team to produce an illustrated report, the basis of which is used by members of the team to make a key presentation to management; you and a classmate carry out an experiment, argue over and write up the results together, and present your findings to the class; a business class project calls on you and others in your group to divide up the work along lines of expertise and then to pool your efforts in meeting the assignment. In all of these cases, writing is also performative—it performs an action or, in the words of many students we have talked with, it "makes something happen in the world."

Twitter provides a case in point. In February 2022 when Russian forces entered the Ukrainian city of Henichesk, they were met by a woman armed with nothing but seeds of the Ukrainian national flower, the sunflower. She insisted that they fill their pockets with the seeds, later explaining that then "flowers would grow when they die on Ukrainian land." A video of this incident, posted on *Twitter*, went viral, drawing nearly 9 million views in a short period and helping to build Ukrainian morale and resistance.

Authors whose messages can be instantly transported around the world need to consider those who will receive those messages. Writers can no longer assume that they write only to a specified audience or that they can easily control the dissemination of their messages. We now live not only in a city, a state, and a country but in a global community as well—and we write, intentionally or not, to speakers of many languages, to members of many cultures, to believers of many creeds.

Everyone's a Researcher

Since all writing responds to the ideas and words of others, it usually draws on some kind of research. Think for a moment of how often you carry out research. We're guessing that a little reflection will turn up lots of examples: you may find yourself digging up information on the pricing of new cars, searching *Craigslist* or the want ads for a good job, comparing two new smartphones, looking up statistics on a favorite sports figure, or searching for a recipe for tabbouleh. All of these everyday activities involve research. In addition, many of your most important life decisions involve research— what colleges to apply to, what jobs to pursue, where to live, and more. Once you begin to think about research in this broad way—as a form of inquiry related to important decisions—you'll probably find that research is something you do almost every day. Moreover, you'll see the ways in which the research you do adds to your credibility—giving you the authority that goes along with being an author.

But research today is very different from the research of only a few decades ago. Take the example of the concordance, an alphabetized listing of every instance of all topics and words in a work. Before the computer age, concordances were done by hand: the first full concordance to the works of Shakespeare took decades of eye-straining, painstaking research, counting, and sorting. Some scholars spent years, even whole careers, developing concordances that then served as major resources for other scholars. As soon as Shakespeare's plays and poems were in digital form—voilà!—a concordance could be produced automatically and accessed by writers with the click of a mouse.

To take a more recent example, first-year college students not too long ago had no access to the internet. Just think of how easy it is now to check temperatures around the world, track a news story, or keep up to the minute on stock prices. These are items that you can google, but you may also have many expensive subscription databases available to you through your school's library. It's not too much of an exaggeration to say that the world is literally at your fingertips.

What has *not* changed is the need to carry out research with great care, to read all sources with a critical eye, and to evaluate sources before depending on them for an important decision or using them in your own work. What also has not changed is the sheer thrill research can bring: while much research work can seem plodding and even repetitive, the excitement of discovering materials you didn't know existed, of analyzing information in a new way, or of tracing a question through one particular historical period brings its own rewards. Moreover, your research adds to what philosopher Kenneth Burke calls "the conversation of humankind," as you build on what others have done and begin to make significant contributions of your own to the world's accumulated knowledge.

Everyone's a Student

More than 2,000 years ago, the Roman writer Quintilian set out a plan for education, beginning with birth and ending only with old age and death. Surprisingly enough, Quintilian's recommendation for a lifelong education has never been more relevant than it is in the twenty-first century, as knowledge is increasing and changing so fast that most people must continue to be active learners long after they graduate from college. This explosion of knowledge also puts great demands on communication. As a result, one of your biggest challenges will be learning how to learn and how to communicate what you have learned across wider distances, to larger and increasingly diverse sets of audiences, and using an expanding range of media and genres.

When did you first decide to attend college, and what paths did you take to achieve that goal? Chances are greater today than at any time in our past that you may have taken time off to work before beginning college, or that you returned to college for new training when your job changed, or that you are attending college while working part-time or even full-time. These characteristics of college students are not new, but they are increasingly important, indicating that the path to college is not as straightforward as it was once thought to be. In addition, college is now clearly a part of a process of lifetime learning. You are likely to hold a number of positions during and after your college career—and each new position will call for new learning.

Citizens today need more years of education and more advanced skills than ever before: even entry-level jobs now call for a college diploma. But what you'll need isn't just a college education. Instead, you'll need an education that puts you in a position to take responsibility for your own learning and to take a direct, hands-on approach to that learning. Most of us learn best by *doing* what we're trying to learn rather than just being told about it. What does this change mean in practice? First, it means you will be doing much more writing, speaking, and researching than ever before. You may, for instance, conduct research on an economic trend and then use that research to create a theory capable of accounting for the trend; you may join a research group in an electrical engineering class that designs, tests, and implements a new system; you may be a member of a writing class that works to build a website for the local fire department, writes brochures for a nonprofit agency, or makes presentations before municipal boards. In each case, you will be doing what you are studying, whether it is economics, engineering, or writing.

Without a doubt, the challenges and opportunities for students today are immense. The chapters that follow try to keep these challenges and opportunities in the foreground, offering you concrete ways to think about yourself as a writer—and yes, as an author; to think carefully about the rhetorical situations you face, about the many and varied audiences for your work, and about the choices you will make and the consequences those choices will have as you expand your writing repertoire to include new genres, new media, and new ways of producing and communicating knowledge.

Everyone's an Author

PART I

The Need for Rhetoric and Writing

CLOSE YOUR EYES and imagine a world without any form of language—no spoken or written words, no drawings, no mathematical formulas, no music—no way, that is, to communicate or express yourself. It's pretty hard to imagine such a world, and with good reason. For better or worse, we seem to be hardwired to communicate, to long to express ourselves to others. That's why philosopher Kenneth Burke says that people are, at their essence, "symbol-using animals" who have a basic need to communicate.

We can look across history and find early attempts to create systems of communication. Think, for instance, of the

Animals in ancient civilizations' art: Uffington White Horse, Oxfordshire, England (approx. 3,000 years old); Nsibidi symbols on an object from southeastern Nigeria; rock paintings, Bhimbetka, India (approx. 30,000 years old).

chalk horses of England, huge figures carved into trenches that were then filled with white chalk some 3,000 years ago. What do they say? Do they act as maps or road signs? Do they celebrate, or commemorate, or tell a story? Whatever their original intent, they echo the need to communicate to us from millennia away.

Cave paintings, many of them hauntingly beautiful, have been discovered around the world, from Africa and India to South America and Australia, some thought to be 30,000 years old. In West Africa, people communicated using pictographs, shells and seeds, painted cloths, carvings on gourds, and drumming. Nsibidi, an ancient Nigerian ideographic writing system, was in use from at least 400 CE to leave messages on houses and to decorate skin, artifacts, and items of clothing. And in the United States, New Mexico's Petroglyph National Monument is home to petroglyphs carved by Pueblo, Navajo, and Apache people, and some Spanish settlers. These carvings held sacred meanings, and continue to do so, for tribes and individual families documenting events and cultural beliefs. These symbols, carvings, and paintings all attest to the human desire to communicate—to share and to leave messages.

As languages and other symbolic forms of communication like our own alphabet evolved, so did a need for ways to interpret and organize these forms and to use them in effective and meaningful ways. And out of these needs grew rhetoric—the art, theory, and practice of communication. In discussing rhetoric, Aristotle says we need to understand this art for two main reasons: first, in order to express our own ideas and thoughts, and second, to protect ourselves from those who would try to manipulate or harm us. Language, then, can be used for good or ill, to provide information that may help someone—or to deliberately mislead.

We believe the need for understanding rhetoric may be greater today than at any time in our history. At first glance, it may look as if communication has never been easier. We can send messages in a nanosecond, reaching people in all parts of the world with ease. We can broadcast our thoughts, hopes, and dreams—and invectives—in *YouTube* videos, status updates, tweets, text messages, and a plethora of other ways.

So far, perhaps, so good. But consider the story of the Tower of Babel, told in different ways in both the Qur'an and the Bible. When the people sought to build a tower that would reach to the heavens, God responded to their hubris by creating so many languages that communication became impossible and the tower had to be abandoned. Like the languages in Babel, the means of communication are proliferating today, bringing with them the potential for miscommunication. From the struggle to sift through the

Pieter Brueghel the Elder, *Tower of Babel*, 1563.

amount of information created in a day—more than was previously created in several lifetimes—to the difficulty of trying to communicate across vast differences in languages and cultures, we face serious challenges.

But while communicating across different languages and cultures may present big challenges, it also presents an opportunity to embrace difference, to learn new ways of communicating, to value all languages and all cultures. At its best and most ethical, rhetoric provides us the means to communicate our messages to a wider range of people and to understand and value a wider range of messages from a more diverse group of people. Rhetoric creates pathways for listening, learning, and sharing.

In a time when we are constantly barraged with new (and sometimes confusing) forms of information, when we have to work hard to distinguish between legitimate information and misinformation, many of us are looking for help with crafting and disseminating our messages. So, too, are we seeking help working through all the messages that we receive through various media and devices—social media, television news networks, traditional print sources, even unsolicited robocalls and text messages.

New technologies and tools, like translation websites and apps, can certainly help us as we navigate twenty-first-century global villages. But they are not likely to reduce the need for an art and a theory that can inform our conversations—that can encourage thoughtfulness, empathy, and responsible use of such technologies. Rhetoric responds to this need. Along with writing, which we define broadly to include speaking and drawing and performing as well as the literal inscription of words, rhetoric offers you solid ground on which to build both your education and your communicative ability and style. The chapters that follow will introduce you more fully to rhetoric and writing—and engage you in acquiring and using their powers.

ONE

Thinking Rhetorically

The only real alternative to war is rhetoric.

—WAYNE BOOTH

PROFESSOR WAYNE BOOTH made this statement at a conference of scholars and teachers of writing held only months after the 9/11 attacks on the United States, and it quickly drew a range of responses. Just what did Booth mean by this stark statement? How could rhetoric—the art and practice of persuasion—act as a counter to war?

A noted critic and scholar, Booth explored these questions throughout his career, identifying rhetoric as an ethical art that begins with intense listening and that searches for mutual understanding and common ground as alternatives to violence and war. Put another way, two of the most potent tools we have for persuasion are language—and violence: when words fail us, violence often wins the day. It is language and rhetoric that provide the basis of negotiation, debate, and compromise—acts that de-escalate the kinds of confrontations that lead to divisiveness, separation, and, yes, violence. Booth sees the careful and ethical use of language as our best approach to keeping violence and war at bay.

Consider how Booth's words resonate in light of the January 6, 2021, storming of the United States Capitol that led to injuries, deaths, and ultimately the arrest of hundreds of participants. Globally, think about how Booth's words speak to the Russian war on Ukraine—ongoing as this

A mural honoring George Floyd, Breonna Taylor, Trayvon Martin, and Ahmaud Arbery, painted on a barbershop in Tampa, Florida (left). People protest COVID-19 policies using homemade signs (right).

> We didn't burn down buildings. . . . You can do a lot with a pen and pad.
>
> —ICE CUBE

book goes to print—which has led to the destruction of entire cities, and to the deaths and harm of innocent civilians trying to flee to safety. How could the careful and ethical use of rhetoric by all stakeholders have affected these events?

In many countries, including the United States, protests are effective ways of making our views known to a wider audience. Organized marchers raise their voices against or for changes in voting rights legislation, controversial topics taught in schools, and the results of an election. Mural artists celebrate the lives of Breonna Taylor, George Floyd, and others. Concerned citizens publish opinion pieces on COVID-19 policies in their local newspapers. People on social media use hashtags to amplify causes—from #prolife and #plasticfree to #metoo and #blacklivesmatter. All of these are examples of rhetoric in action.

Note that while Booth speaks of rhetoric as an "ethical art," rhetoric can also be used for unethical purposes, as Hitler and other dictators have done; in fact, rhetoric used in unethical ways can itself lead to violence. That's why Aristotle cautioned that people need to understand rhetoric—both to get their own ethical messages across *and* to be able to recognize and resist unethical messages that others attempt to use against them. We take Aristotle's point and focus in this book on how to think rhetorically both as readers and as writers. In addition, we define rhetoric as the art, theory, and practice of ethical communication—the ethical language use that Booth speaks of.

So how can you go about developing your own careful, ethical use of language? Our short answer: by learning to think and act rhetorically, that

Students use posters and conversation to protest the low wages paid to campus workers.

is, by developing habits of mind that begin with listening and searching for understanding before you decide what you yourself think, and by thinking hard about your own beliefs before trying to persuade others to listen to and act on what you say.

Learning to think rhetorically can serve you well as you negotiate the complexities of life today. For example, many of us have engaged with classmates or colleagues who hold different opinions about COVID-19 vaccines. In spite of such disagreements, we aim to communicate well enough to get things done in a responsible and ethical way. In other words, we need to come to some consensus that moves us forward toward completing a project—and maybe even saving a relationship—despite differing views.

When a group of students became aware of how little the temporary workers on their campus were paid, for example, they met with the workers and listened to gather information about the issue. They then mounted a campaign using flyers, speeches, and sit-ins—in other words, using the available means of persuasion—to win attention and convince the administration to raise the workers' pay. These students were thinking and acting rhetorically, and doing so responsibly and ethically. Note that these students worked together, both with the workers and with each other. In other words, none of us can manage such actions all by ourselves; we need to engage in conversation with others and listen hard to what they say. Perhaps that's what philosopher Kenneth Burke had in mind when he created his famous "parlor" metaphor:

> Imagine that you enter a parlor. You come late. When you arrive, others have long preceded you, and they are engaged in a heated discussion, a discussion too heated for them to pause and tell you exactly what it is about. . . . You listen for a while, until you decide that you have caught the tenor of the argument; then you put in your oar.
>
> —KENNETH BURKE, *The Philosophy of Literary Form*

In this parable, each of us is the person arriving late to a room full of animated conversation; we don't understand what is going on. Yet instead of butting in or trying to take over, we listen closely until we catch on to what people are saying. Then we join in, using language and rhetorical strategies to engage with others as we add our own voices to the conversation.

This book aims to teach you to *think and act rhetorically*—to listen carefully and respectfully and then to "put in your oar," join conversations about important issues, and develop strong critical and ethical habits of mind that will help you engage with others in responsible ways. This chapter will help you develop the habit of thinking rhetorically.

First, Listen

We have two ears and one mouth so we may listen more and talk less.

—EPICTETUS

Thinking rhetorically begins with listening, with being willing to hear the words of others in an open and understanding way. It means paying attention to what others say before—and even as a way of—making your own contributions to a conversation. Think of the times you are grateful to others for listening closely to you: when you're talking through a conflict with a family member, for instance, or even when you're trying to explain to a salesperson what you're looking for. On those occasions, you want the person you're addressing to really listen to what you say.

This is a kind of listening that rhetorician Krista Ratcliffe dubs "rhetorical listening," opening yourself to the thoughts of others and making the effort not only to hear their words but also to take those words in and fully understand what people are saying. It means paying attention to what others say as a way of establishing good will and acknowledging the importance of their views. And yes, it means taking seriously and engaging with views that differ, sometimes radically, from your own.

Rhetorical listening is what middle school teacher Julia Blount asked for in a *Facebook* post following the 2015 uprisings in Baltimore after the death of Freddie Gray, who suffered fatal spinal injuries while in police custody:

> Every comment or post I have read today voicing some version of disdain for the people of Baltimore—"I can't understand" or "They're destroying their own community"—tells me that many of you are not listening. I am not asking you to condone or agree with violence. I just need you to listen. . . . If you are not listening, not exposing yourself to unfamiliar perspectives . . . not engaging in conversation, then you are perpetuating white privilege. . . . It is exactly your ability to *not* hear, to ignore the situation, that is a mark of your privilege.
>
> —JULIA BLOUNT, "Dear White *Facebook* Friends: I Need You to Respect What Black America Is Feeling Right Now"

Hear What Others Are Saying—and Think about Why

When you enter any conversation, whether academic, professional, or personal, take the time to understand what is being said rather than rushing to a conclusion or a judgment. Listen carefully to what others are saying and consider what motivates them: where are they coming from?

Developing such habits of mind will be useful to you almost every day, whether you are participating in a class discussion, negotiating with friends over what movie is most worth watching, or studying a local ballot issue to decide how you'll vote. In each case, thinking rhetorically means being flexible and fair, able to hear and consider varying—and sometimes conflicting—points of view.

In ancient Rome, Cicero argued that considering alternative points of view and counterarguments was key to making a successful argument, and it is just as important today. Even when you disagree with a point of view—perhaps especially when you disagree with it—allow yourself to see the issue from the viewpoint of its advocates before you reject their positions. While you may be frustrated with family members who did or did not get a COVID-19 vaccine, don't dismiss their views out of hand. Listen to their concerns, try to understand their fears. Think about their perspective and how you might carefully respond.

Thinking hard about others' views also includes considering the larger context and how it shapes what they are saying. This aspect of rhetorical thinking goes beyond the kind of reading you probably learned to do in high school literature classes, where you looked very closely at a particular text and interpreted it on its own terms, without looking at secondary sources. When you think rhetorically, you go one step further and put that close analysis into a larger context—historical, political, or cultural, for example—to recognize and consider where the analysis is "coming from."

In analyzing the issue of gun control, for instance, you would not merely consider your own thinking or do a close reading of texts that address the issue. In addition to these strategies, you would look at the whole debate in context by considering its historical development over time, thinking about the broader political agendas of both those who advocate for and those who oppose stricter gun control, asking what economic ramifications adopting—or rejecting—new gun restrictions might have, examining the role of constitutional rights in the debate, and so on. In short, you would try to see the issue from as many different perspectives and in as broad a context as possible before you formulate your own stance. When you write, you draw on these sources—what others have said about the issue—to support your own position and to help you consider counterarguments to it.

REFLECT. Go to everyonesanauthor.tumblr.com *and read "The 'Other Side' Is Not Dumb" by blogger Sean Blanda, who warns that many of us gravitate on social media to those who think like we do, which often leads to the belief that we are right and that those with other worldviews are "dumb." He argues that we need to "make an honest effort to understand those who are not like us" and to remember that "we might be wrong." Look at some of your own recent posts. How many different perspectives do you see represented? What might you do to listen—and think—more rhetorically?*

What Do You Think—and Why?

Examining all points of view on any issue will engage you in some tough thinking about your own stance—literally, where you are coming from on an issue—and why you think as you do. Such self-scrutiny can eventually clarify your stance or perhaps even change your mind; in either case, you stand to gain. Just as you need to think hard about the motivations of others, it's important to examine your own motivations in detail, asking yourself what influences in your life lead you to think as you do or to take certain positions. Then you can reconsider your positions and reflect on how they relate to those of others, including your audience—those you wish to engage respectfully in conversation or debate.

In your college assignments, you probably have multiple motivations and purposes, one of which is to convince your instructor that you are a serious and hardworking student. But think about additional purposes as well: What could you learn from doing the assignment? How can doing it help you attain goals you have?

Examining your own stance and motivation is equally important outside the classroom. Suppose you are urging fellow members of a campus group to lobby for a rigorous set of procedures to deal with accusations of sexual harassment. On one level, you're alarmed by the statistics showing a steep increase in cases of rape on college campuses and you want to do something about it. But when you think a bit more, you might find that you have additional motivations. Perhaps you've long wanted to become a leader of this group. You may have just seen *The Hunting Ground*, a documentary about rape on US college campuses, and found it deeply upsetting—and persuasive. These realizations shouldn't necessarily change your mind about what action you want your group to take, but examining what you think and why will help you to challenge your own position—and to make sure that it is fair.

Do Your Homework

Rhetorical thinking calls on you to do some homework, to find out everything you can about what's been said about your topic, to **ANALYZE** what you find, and then to **SYNTHESIZE** that information to inform your own ideas. To put it another way, you want your own thinking to be aware and deeply informed, to reflect more than just your own opinion.

Maybe you've heard about dramatic school board meetings where parents and school board members yell at one another about critical race theory (CRT) being taught in K–12 schools. You've seen local and state politicians on television arguing about whether CRT should be banned. You've seen headlines about principals and teachers being fired. Rather than immediately taking a position on whether critical race theory is dangerous to young people, rhetorical thinking moves you to do some careful research to find out

TAKE A LOOK at the Jeep ad from the 2021 Super Bowl at everyonesanauthor
.tumblr.com. You'll see scenes of rural America and hear the voice of musician Bruce
Springsteen, who says, "It's no secret the middle has been a hard place to get to lately,
between red and blue, between servant and citizen, between our freedom and our
fear. . . . We just have to remember the very soil we stand on is common ground." What
kind of rhetorical thinking did the ad writers do? Who was their target audience, and
how did they go about appealing to that group? How successful do you think this was
as an ad? In other words, do you think it sold a lot of cars? If you were looking to buy
a car, what would this ad tell you about Jeeps—and what would you have to find out
from other sources?

more about the topic—and about why you want to know more. Do you have
a sibling in school whose learning could be affected? Are you thinking about
becoming a teacher? Maybe you are simply concerned about the nastiness of
the debate in your community or state.

So you get to work to find out just what critical race theory is. How did
this theory emerge, and who are the theorists behind it? What were the
historical, social, academic, and political contexts surrounding it? You'll
likely find out that it originated in legal studies at the university level, so
then you check out writing by the original theorists as well as responses
to those people and ideas over the decades. Your research will probably
lead you to learn how and where CRT has been used, and by whom. Only
after exploring such questions and understanding the rhetorical situation
can you responsibly engage with the arguments on opposing sides of the
issue. Who are the stakeholders on each side? How do stakeholders' arguments hold up when fact-checked? Are there stakeholders who have not
been heard?

This kind of rhetorical thinking prompts you to pay attention to the rhetorical strategies and appeals writers and speakers use to persuade. What kind of tone are they using? Are they using inclusive language? Are their examples factual? Are they relying on credible sources or unsubstantiated claims? Once you've read, synthesized, and analyzed all the material you've gathered, you may even talk with a classmate or friend, someone who will be a sounding board and ask tough but fair questions, as you figure out what you think. Then you will be ready to offer a well-informed opinion and to judge others' perspectives. Doing this kind of research is an example of rhetorical thinking.

Rhetorical thinking is not meant just for such weighty topics as critical race theory. In your everyday life, you make decisions that require rhetorical thinking: buying a new computer, making a decision about a job, choosing a major, considering graduate school. Each of these decisions calls on you to do your homework, to do research, to be open-minded, and to engage in careful and ethical thinking. You want to be well informed to make the best decisions and to take thoughtful positions.

Give Credit

As part of engaging with what others have thought and said, you'll want to give credit where credit is due. Acknowledging the work of others will help build your own ethos, or character, showing that you have not only done your homework but also that you want to credit those who have influenced you. The great physicist Isaac Newton famously and graciously gave credit when he wrote to his rival Robert Hooke in 1676, saying:

> What Descartes did was a good step. You have added much in several ways, and especially in taking the colours of thin plates into philosophical consideration. If I have seen a little further it is by standing on the shoulders of giants.   —ISAAC NEWTON, letter to Robert Hooke

In this letter, Newton acknowledges the work of Descartes as well as of Hooke before saying, with a fair amount of modesty, that his own advancements were made possible by their work. In doing so, he is thinking—and acting—rhetorically.

You can give credit informally, as Newton did in this letter, or you can do so formally with a full citation. Which method you choose will depend on your purpose and context. Academic writing, for instance, usually calls for formal citations, but if you are writing for a personal blog, you might embed a link that connects to another's work—or give an informal shout-out to a friend who contributed to your thinking. In each case, you'll want to be specific about what ideas or words you've drawn from others, as Newton does in referring to Hooke's consideration of the colors of thin plates. Such care in crediting your sources contributes to your credibility—and is an important part of ethical, careful rhetorical thinking.

Be Imaginative

It was rhetorical thinking that led Annette Gordon-Reed to question what she had learned in school about the history of slavery in the United States, and her thinking led to new insights about things she had always taken for granted. Read her essay on p. 901.

Remember that intuition and imagination can often lead to great insights. While you want to think carefully and analytically, don't be afraid to take chances. A little imagination can lead you to new ideas about a topic you're studying and suggest how to approach it in a way that will interest others. Such insights and intuitions can often pay off big-time. Nova Thrasher, a writing tutor in training, opened their final project on gender inclusivity and pronoun usage in college writing centers with this personal reflection:

> I wait for introductions with bated breath, hoping for and dreading what comes in the split second after "Tell everyone your name—" . . . Time drags on, suspense building in the space between exhale and inhale . . . "—and pronouns. We'll go around the room . . ." and exhale. The question has been asked, and I am theoretically safe in this room.
> —NOVA THRASHER, "Gender-Inclusivity and the Onus of Progress on the Writing Center"

This personal experience led Nova to examine writing center websites for statements on using inclusive pronouns. Before they knew it, Nova had a full-fledged research project that analyzed thirty college writing center websites, discussed writing center scholarship, and covered current debates about gender. Nova found that less than half of the thirty writing center websites addressed gender inclusive pronouns. Interested in becoming a tutor who will make the writing center safe and inviting for all, Nova conducted extremely valuable research. Like this student, you can benefit by using your imagination, reflecting on your own experiences, and listening to your intuition. You may discover something exciting and meaningful.

Put In Your Oar

So rhetorical thinking offers a way of entering any situation with a tool kit of strategies that will help you understand it and "put in your oar." When you think rhetorically, you ask yourself certain questions:

- How do you want to come across to your audience?
- What can you do to represent yourself as knowledgeable and credible?
- What can you do to show respect both for your audience and for those whose work and thinking you engage with?
- How can you show that you have your audience's best interests at heart?

This kind of rhetorical thinking will help ensure that your words will be listened to and taken seriously.

We can find examples of such a rhetorical approach in all fields of study. Take, for instance, the landmark essay by James Watson and Francis Crick deciphering the structure of DNA, published in *Nature* in 1953. This essay shows Watson and Crick to be thinking rhetorically throughout, acutely aware of their audience (major scientists throughout the world), including competitors who were simultaneously working on the same issue.

Here is Wayne Booth's analysis of Watson and Crick's use of rhetoric:

> In [Watson and Crick's] report, what do we find? Actually scores of *rhetorical* choices that they made to strengthen the appeal of their scientific claim. (Biographies and autobiographies have by now revealed that they did a lot of conscientious revising, not of the data but of the mode of presentation; and their lives were filled, before and after the triumph, with a great deal of rhetoric-charged conflict.) We could easily compose a dozen different versions of their report, all proclaiming the same scientific results. But most alternatives would prove less engaging to the intended audience. They open, for example, with
>
> > "*We wish to suggest* a structure" that has "*novel* features which are of *considerable* biological *interest*." (*My italics, of course*)
>
> Why didn't they say, instead: "We shall here demonstrate a *startling, totally new structure* that will *shatter* everyone's conception of the biological

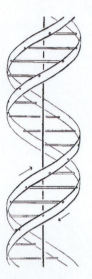

The original sketch showing the structure of DNA that appeared in Watson and Crick's article.

world"? Well, obviously their rhetorical choice presents an ethos much more attractive to most cautious readers than does my exaggerated alternative. A bit later they say

"We have made the *usual chemical assumptions*, namely . . ."

Why didn't they say, "*As we all know*"? Both expressions acknowledge reliance on warrants, commonplaces within a given rhetorical domain. But their version sounds more thoughtful and authoritative, especially with the word "chemical." Referring to Pauling and Corey, they say

"They *kindly* have made their manuscript available."

Okay, guys, drop the rhetoric and just cut that word "kindly." What has that got to do with your scientific case? Well, it obviously strengthens the authors' ethos: we are nice guys dealing trustfully with other nice guys, in a rhetorical community.

And on they go, with "*In our opinion*" (rather than "We proclaim" or "We insist" or "We have miraculously discovered": again ethos—we're not dogmatic); and Fraser's "*suggested*" structure is "*rather ill-defined*" (rather than "his structure is stupid" or "obviously faulty"—we *are* nice guys, right?).

And on to scores of other such choices.

—WAYNE BOOTH, *The Rhetoric of Rhetoric*

Booth shows in each instance that Watson and Crick's exquisite understanding of their rhetorical situation—especially of their audience and of the stakes involved in making their claim—had a great deal to do with how that claim was received. (They won the Nobel Prize!) However, Watson and Crick could have done better when it came to giving credit: scholars have pointed out that the work of Rosalind Franklin, a contemporary female scientist, greatly influenced Watson and Crick's discovery, though they did not sufficiently acknowledge or credit her.

As the example of Watson and Crick illustrates, rhetorical thinking involves certain habits of mind that can and should lead to something—often to an action, to making something happen. And when it comes to taking action, those who think rhetorically are in a very strong position. They have listened attentively, engaged with the words and ideas of others, viewed their topic from many alternate perspectives, and done their homework. This kind of rhetorical thinking will set you up to contribute to conversations—and will increase the likelihood that your ideas will be heard and will inspire real action.

The need to think rhetorically has never been more important than in today's global world. Rhetorician Jacqueline Jones Royster provides a clear guide to engaging in rhetorical thinking and acting:

> My experiences tell me that we need to do more than just talk and talk back. I believe that in this model we miss a critical moment. We need to talk, yes, and to talk back, yes, but when do we listen? How do we listen? How do we demonstrate that we honor and respect the person talking and what that person is saying, or what the person might say if we valued someone other than ourselves having a turn to speak? How do we translate listening into language and action, into the creation of an appropriate response? How do we really "talk back" rather than talk also? The goal is not, "You talk, I talk." The goal is better practices so that we can exchange perspectives, negotiate meaning, and create understanding with the intent of being in a good position to cooperate, when, like now, cooperation is absolutely necessary.
>
> —JACQUELINE JONES ROYSTER, "When the First
> Voice You Hear Is Not Your Own"

In the long run, if enough of us learn to think rhetorically, we just might achieve Royster's goals "to exchange perspectives, negotiate meaning, and create understanding" and avoid the violence and war, literal and figurative, that Booth speaks of.

REFLECT. Read the words often attributed to cultural anthropologist Margaret Mead below, and then think of at least one historical example in which a "small group of thoughtful citizens" has changed the world for the better. Then think about your own life and the ways in which you have worked with others to bring about some kind of change. In what ways were you called upon to think and act rhetorically in order to do so?

Never doubt that a small group of thoughtful committed citizens can change the world; indeed, it's the only thing that ever has.

—MARGARET MEAD

TWO

Engaging Productively with Others

HINK BACK TO early 2022 when the first Omicron variant of COVID-19 was raging across the United States. Beds in intensive care units ran low. Frontline healthcare workers were exhausted. The majority of deaths were among those unvaccinated. Fights broke out at school board meetings and in shopping centers as those who wore masks and those who didn't disagreed.

At the same time, politicians, doctors, and public health officials begged the unvaccinated to "get jabbed." The news featured heart-wrenching stories about unvaccinated individuals who had died. Many of these stories subtly or overtly sought to stigmatize those who had passed and, by extension, those who had chosen not to get vaccinated.

Elizabeth Bruenig, in an essay published in the *Atlantic* titled "Stop Death Shaming," implored those who had been vaccinated to quit doing just that. She linked heated debates about vaccination to larger issues of polarization in the United States. People seem less interested, she noted, in finding common ground than in being right, no matter the cost to themselves or others. These trying times demonstrate the sometimes extreme challenges, consequences, and, indeed, opportunities that arise when engaging productively with others.

The goal of this chapter is to encourage and guide you as you engage with others: listening to their stories and contributing to a process that may make some positive change or at least unearth some common ground. Here are some steps you can take to realize this goal.

Get to Know People Different from You

It's a commonplace today to point out that we often live and act in "silos" where we encounter only people who think like we do, who hold the same values. We increasingly choose to interact with like-minded people—online and in person. We are in what some call "filter bubbles" or "echo chambers," where we hear our views echoed back to us from every direction. In such an

atmosphere, it can be easy—and comforting—to think this is the real world, but it's not! Beyond your own bubble of posts and tweets and conversations lie countless other people with different views and values.

So one of the big challenges we face today is finding ways to get out of our own echo chambers and get to know people who take different positions, hold different values. But simply encountering people who think differently is just the start. Breaking out of our bubbles calls for making the effort to understand those different perspectives, to listen with openness and empathy, and to hear where others are coming from. All of these are habits that take practice—especially using empathy, the ability to share the feelings of someone else.

Dylan Marron is someone who shows how this can be done. As the creator and host of several popular video series on controversial social issues, Marron has gained quite a bit of attention and, he says, "a lot of hate." Early on, he tried to ignore hateful comments, but then he got interested and began visiting commenter profiles to learn about the people behind them. Doing so, he said, led him to realize "there was a human on the other side of the screen"—and prompted him to call some of these people on the phone, conversations he shares on his podcast *Conversations with People Who Hate Me.*

In one of these talks, Marron learned that Josh, who in a comment had called Marron a "moron" and said that being gay was a sin, had recently graduated from high school. When Marron asked him, "How was high

Dylan Marron, creator and host of *Conversations with People Who Hate Me*, a podcast featuring conversations between people who disagree.

school for you?," Josh replied that "it was hell" because he'd been bullied by kids who made fun of him for being "bigger." Marron shared his own experiences of being bullied too, and as the conversation progressed, listening laid the groundwork that helped them relate to each other.

Marron's work demonstrates the power of practicing empathy and how it can help us to see one another as human, even in the most negative and nasty places. In a 2018 TED talk, Marron again stressed the importance of empathy, noting, however, that "empathy is not endorsement" and doesn't require us to compromise our deeply held values but rather to acknowledge the views of "someone raised to think very differently" than we do.

Elizabeth Bruenig, author of the *Atlantic* article about understanding—not shaming—the unvaccinated, offers another example when she describes a conversation with a relative whose life is different from her own. Bruenig's uncle lives in a rural part of a conservative state, works in an auto repair shop, and hasn't been vaccinated. She called him up and posed some questions about why he declined a vaccine; she listened to what he said with an open mind. In turn, he asked her questions about information she relied on and why. She acknowledged his concerns, and she did not dispute his description of the stigma many people attach to those who were not vaccinated. Along the way, they both learned where the other was coming from, their sources of information, and the logic of each other's position. Though the conversation ended without anyone's mind being changed, Bruenig concluded: "I felt good about our talk. I want [my family] to be all right. And I believe—but cannot prove—that wanting that for someone is more persuasive" than the my-way-or-the-highway approach. She was convinced that listening to and understanding someone with a different stance was productive.

🔗 Watch Marron's TED talk and listen to his podcast by visiting everyonesanauthor.tumblr.com.

Practice Empathy

So how can you practice empathy? First comes curiosity, an interest in learning why someone feels what they feel or sees the world as they do. One way to practice empathy when talking about controversial topics, especially with someone who holds a different opinion, is to ask questions:

- Why do you think so? What has led you to that conclusion?
- How have your life experiences influenced the position you're taking?

- Why do you think others see the situation differently? Might there be value in some of their views?
- What would need to happen for you to rethink your position?
- Are there things that leave you uncomfortable or fearful about the issue we're discussing? about your own position on the issue? about other positions?
- What do you want those who disagree with you to know about you and your position? How do you think that information will help them understand you?

If you'd like to read more about Tressie McMillan Cottom's thinking, check out her essay "New Money" on p. 936.

Sociologist and writer Tressie McMillan Cottom offers another important reason to practice empathy. In her essay about empathy and COVID-19 published in the *New York Times*, Cottom says her primary concern is "what empathy does for me." And she goes on to explain that empathy gives her "the humility to keep asking questions, even when I do not like the answers. Because I value being a thinking person, I honor emotions like empathy, fear, joy and trust to guide me around the pitfalls of my ego. Ego makes for really sloppy analysis and writing." In other words, practicing empathy yields clearer thinking and better writing—important skills in college and in life.

Ted Olson, a conservative attorney who has argued before the Supreme Court sixty-five times, made a similar claim in an interview with CBS News, noting that "trying to understand both sides of an issue and being persuasive on this side, and then being persuasive on the other side" helped him improve his professional skills. He added, "In today's world, people are so polarized . . . there's not a lot of time spent trying to think the way the other side thinks, or try[ing] to express what the other side is expressing and believing," a situation he sees as unfortunate. Olson has argued all kinds of positions. For example, he defended Republican presidential candidate George W. Bush in *Bush v. Gore*, the case deliberating the results of the 2000 election. But he's also argued for "Dreamers," undocumented immigrants brought to the United States as children, in the case upholding DACA (Deferred Action for Childhood Arrivals), a program that provides some protection from deportation. Olson reports that he agreed to take on the Dreamers case, a stance many wouldn't expect of a conservative attorney, after meeting with people impacted by the policy and hearing their stories. That's the power and the promise of practicing empathy.

REFLECT. Think back to a conversation you've had with someone whose position you disagreed with and didn't understand. What did you ask that person to try to understand their position? Which of the questions above do you wish you had asked? Why? How might those unasked questions have changed the conversation?

Listen to People's Stories

Practicing empathy is about more than asking questions; it also requires listening. By listening, you learn a lot about not only a person's experiences but also the worlds they have inhabited and the events and situations that shape their positions. Good listening means withholding judgment and avoiding interrupting. Part of your task as a listener is to consider your knee-jerk responses. In this way, listening gives you a chance to learn something about yourself, too.

That's certainly what one Canadian student found when she spent a semester in Washington, DC. Shauna Vert had expected the highlights of her semester to be visiting places like the museums of the Smithsonian Institution or the Library of Congress, but her greatest experience, as she describes it in a blog post, turned out to be an "unexpected gift: While in DC, I became close, close friends with people I disagree with on almost everything." As she listened to these people's experiences, she found that they were

> funny, smart, and kind. We all really liked music. . . . We even lived together. We ate dinner together, every single night. So I couldn't look down on them. I couldn't even consider it. And when you can't look down on someone who fundamentally disagrees with you, when you're busy breaking bread, sharing your days, laughing about the weather . . . well.
> —SHAUNA VERT, "Making Friends Who Disagree with You (Is the Healthiest Thing in the World)"

↪ Read Shauna Vert's blog by visiting everyonesanauthor.tumblr.com.

During a conversation with one of her housemates, a deeply conservative Christian from Mississippi, Vert mentioned that she was "pro-choice," realizing as she did so that this was "dangerous territory." To her surprise, she met not resistance or rebuke but curiosity:

> She wanted to know more. Her curiosity fueled my curiosity, and we talked. We didn't argue—we debated gently, very gently. . . . We laughed

at nuance, we self-deprecated, we trusted each other. And we liked each other. Before the conversation, and after the conversation. To recap: Left-wing Canadian meets Bible Belt Republican. Discusses controversial political issues for over an hour. Walks away with a new friend.

This kind of careful, responsible, respectful exchange requires listening with an open mind. The point is that it's worth making the time to try to find and engage with those who hold different ideas and values than you do. And this means listening to other people's stories. It's time to shut down the echo chambers, seek out people outside of our silos, and listen with empathy.

Demonstrate Respect

"R-E-S-P-E-C-T." That spells respect. If you've never heard Aretha Franklin belt out these lyrics, take time to look her up on *YouTube*. Franklin added this now-famous line to her 1967 rendition of Otis Redding's original song, inspiring millions to expect and to demand R-E-S-P-E-C-T.

Aretha Franklin performs onstage in 1968.

Franklin's message is still a timely one today, and the strategies in this chapter will lead you to demonstrate respect. Yet, respecting others with whom we disagree has sometimes been interpreted as a call to "just be nice." While we support being civil and tolerant, we are not suggesting that you hold back your dissent when you oppose something or that you sit by silently when you see or hear injustice.

We recognize that, many times, those in subordinate positions or marginalized groups are expected to demonstrate respect while receiving little respect in return. Respect should be reciprocal. Anyone who demands respect should also give it. Black Lives Matter cofounder Alicia Garza reminds us, "You don't get far being mealy-mouthed about what you want. You just don't." If you don't receive the respect that you are owed, think and act rhetorically to demand what you deserve.

Search for Common Ground

Even children learn early on that digging in to opposing positions doesn't usually get them far: "No, you can't!" "Yes, I can!" can go on forever, without going anywhere. Rhetoricians in the ancient world understood this very well and thus argued that for conversations to progress, it's necessary to establish some COMMON GROUND, no matter how small. If "No, you can't!" moves on to "Well, you can't do that in this particular situation," then maybe a conversation can begin.

Searching for and building on common ground has helped Jewish Americans and Muslim Americans engage across difference. Writing for the *Baltimore Sun*, coauthors Sabeeha Rehman, a Muslim woman, and Walter Ruby, a Jewish man, explain how their communities are finding a way forward:

> What is different this time is that dialogue once avoided is now taking place in some communities. The ties of mutual affection we have built and the sense of solidarity and common purpose we have achieved has given us increasing confidence that we *can* have that difficult conversation about Israel-Palestine . . . and come out of that dialogue with our friendships intact. . . . Despite our very real differences over the rights and wrongs of Israel-Palestine and what is the optimum solution to the conflict, we are determined not to allow what is happening over there to imperil our success in strengthening Muslim-Jewish relations where we

live. . . . Making common cause will have the effect of further buttressing our relationship on this side of the ocean and thwart the efforts by forces who would use our differences over Israel-Palestine as a wedge to pull us apart here in the U.S.

—SABEEHA REHMAN & WALTER RUBY, "Jews and Muslims
Must Stand Together and Refuse to be Enemies"

↪ Visit everyonesanauthor .tumblr.com for tips on having difficult conversations provided by "Living Room Conversations," a group that aims to connect "people across divides."

Rehman and Ruby discuss how they personally overcame biases about the other's faith in their book *We Refuse to Be Enemies: How Muslims and Jews Can Make Peace, One Friendship at a Time*. Rehman had never met a Jewish person while growing up in Pakistan, and Ruby, growing up in the United States, had never met a Muslim until he was a young man. However, when the two met, they listened carefully to each other, asked questions, reconsidered their assumptions, and ultimately built a friendship and collaboration as writers. They found common ground where it was least expected.

Coauthors Sabeeha Rehman and Walter Ruby discuss their writing and their friendship in a virtual interview. Watch their talk by visiting everyonesanauthor.tumblr.com.

〰️ *REFLECT. Some would say it's pointless or even wrong to try to find common ground with people whose views you find problematic. Based on your own experiences, what do you think—and why? What do you think the writers featured in this chapter would say?*

Examine Your Own Positions

If your goal is to interact with others in ways that might move them—or you—to look at things differently, then you'll need to think deeply about how who you are and what you've experienced influence your views. Consider these questions in order to build that awareness:

- Why is this issue important to me? What's my stake in it?
- What emotions, memories, or experiences come up for me when this topic is raised? when someone disagrees with my stance? What experiences have shaped my understanding?
- Do I identify with a "side" on this issue?
- What information am I relying on to support my position? Is it reliable?
- When it comes to this topic, what am I certain about? What am I unsure about?
- What is my biggest fear about what could happen in a conversation about this topic?
- How can I respond with curiosity, rather than judgment, to positions different from my own?

These questions invite you to investigate ideas and reactions that you may have taken for granted. The examples in this chapter all show people open and curious about their own views, which helped them engage more deeply with others. Building self-awareness won't always be comfortable, but it is sure to be productive.

Be Open to Challenging Conversations

Well before the dramatic events of the past few years, many have sought to help Americans engage in important conversations on difficult topics. By engaging with those who see the world differently than we do, all of us can build shared understandings that will benefit us as individuals and as a society. That's exactly what happened when residents of Nashua, New Hampshire, came together for a series of conversations about race and law enforcement, starting in 2015 and continuing today. The stakes are high and the conversations difficult, as community members and police officers gather regularly in small groups to discuss bias, use of force, and community policing, among other topics. The police chief, Michael Carigan, and Jordan Thompson, founder of Black Lives Matter Nashua, agree the conversations aren't easy and aren't a cure-all; according to Thompson, they "disagree on things all the time," but "it's a great thing that we're able to come together at the same table and say, okay, we disagree on these things, but we agree on other things." And Carigan believes these talks actually "further the minimization of the implicit biases" in the community.

Difficult conversations like these are never entered lightly, and many groups have developed techniques to increase the likelihood that everyone involved can be safe. A common practice for such conversations is to begin by reviewing a set of principles like the ones below that all have agreed to work toward:

- Stay engaged
- Listen to understand, rather than thinking of what you'll say next
- Allow time between speakers
- Disagree with someone's *ideas* but avoid criticizing or demeaning the speaker
- Let others speak if you have already spoken
- Be willing to do things differently
- Be open to some discomfort
- Expect no clean resolution; listening and thinking is enough

Many issues are messy and different groups and cultures have different preferred ways of interacting. Some cultures may invite vigorous public debate while others prefer engaging through questions. Working to respect what everyone brings to the table, and being open to following their lead and doing things differently, helps put everyone on an equal footing.

Communicating across difference about hot-button topics is often going to leave all involved a little uncomfortable because you're listening to others whose experience and views are different from, even contradictory to, your own. As Dylan Marron reminds us, practicing empathy in those moments doesn't mean you agree with the opinions you hear but that, rather, you acknowledge others see the world differently for reasons that, at least to them, seem sound. It is an acknowledgment that our society—and the world—is bigger and more diverse than you had realized it was.

Join the Conversation: Collaborate! Engage! Participate!

Especially in times of deep societal divisions, it may be tempting to retreat, to put our heads in the sand and hope that, somehow, things will get better. But don't give in to that temptation. Your voice is important, your thoughts are important, and you can best make them heard if you engage and join with other people. That may mean working with groups of like-minded people to speak out—for or against—on issues such as immigration bans, gun rights, or environmental policies. That kind of civic engagement and participation is important in a democracy. But there are smaller ways, too, like looking beyond those who think as you do, seeking to collaborate with them, listening with empathy, understanding their reasons for thinking as they do—and then looking hard for a shared goal that you can work toward together.

As a country, as a world, we have a lot riding on our willingness to reach across barriers, work together for the common good, and keep on trying even in the most difficult circumstances. As writers, readers, and thinkers, we all have much to offer in this endeavor. So let's get going!

REFLECT. Look back through the examples in this chapter of people working out disagreements or finding ways to empathize with one another. Then think about your own experiences interacting with people who think differently than you do or with whom you disagree. How did you handle those encounters? Were you satisfied with the results? What would you do differently if you could replay them? What will you try to do differently next time? How can you apply this advice when engaging with the ideas of others in writing?

THREE

Rhetorical Situations

uring her second semester in college, Lucia gave a virtual presentation, complete with slides, to seniors in her former high school about differences between high school and college—and then fielded questions from the audience. The same week, Lucia and two friends designed a flyer to advertise a dance-a-thon their Spanish club was sponsoring to raise funds for the club's tutoring program. The flyer, posted around campus and on social media, attracted 150 students to the event, raising enough money to fund the program for another year.

Lucia's projects required that she negotiate multiple, diverse contexts—or rhetorical situations—as an author and speaker. She moved from one to another, each with a different purpose and audience and each calling for different genres, mediums, languages, and so on. Shifting from one rhetorical situation to another is common; we do it all the time, especially as college students. For Lucia's virtual presentation, she speaks to an audience in a different location—an important part of her rhetorical situation. The geographical location, audience, topic, and technology, as well as Lucia's status as a college student are all part of the rhetorical situation. In a different rhetorical situation,

Three different rhetorical situations: a lone writer texting (top left); a student giving an oral presentation in class (right); and members of a community group collaborating on a project (bottom left).

Lucia collaborates with others, using a visual medium (a flyer), presented on social media and in print, to communicate with a large group of college classmates about their club's fundraising event. Think about how this situation—creating a flyer—is different from the first one—giving a presentation. The flyer needs to attract attention with bright colors and bold, catchy headlines in Spanish and English to reach the broadest audience and persuade them to attend while also providing information about the event. The high school presentation requires a computer with a camera, a quiet setting, and informative, well-designed slides to present at a *Zoom* meeting.

In each of these scenarios, an author is writing (or speaking) in a different set of specific circumstances—addressing certain audiences for a particular purpose, using certain technologies, and so on. So it is whenever we write. Whether we're texting a friend, outlining an oral presentation, or writing an essay, we do so within a specific rhetorical situation. We have a purpose, an audience, a stance, a genre, a medium, a design—all of which exist in some larger context. This chapter covers each of these elements and provides prompts to help you think about some of the choices you have as you negotiate your own rhetorical situations.

Every rhetorical situation presents its own unique constraints and opportunities, and as authors, we need to think strategically about our own situation. Adding to a class discussion thread presents a different challenge from writing an in-class essay exam, putting together a résumé and cover letter for a job, or working with fellow members of a campus choir to draft a grant proposal to the student government requesting funding to go on tour. A group of neighbors developing a proposal to present at a virtual community meeting will need to attend to both the written text they will submit and the oral arguments they will make. They may also need to create slides or other visuals to support their proposal.

The workplace creates still other kinds of rhetorical situations with their own distinctive features. Reporters, for instance, must always consider their deadlines as well as their ethical obligations—to the public, to the persons or institutions they write about, and to the story they are reporting. A reporter working for six months to investigate corporate

Barack Obama delivers a virtual commencement speech to high school students around the United States (top left); a group of students work on an in-class writing project (bottom left) a panel gives a talk on climate change to college students (right).

wrongdoing faces different challenges from one who covers local sports day to day. The medium—print, video, radio, podcast, social media feed, or some combination of these or other media—also influences how reporters write their stories. Take a look at the three images on the previous page and think about the rhetorical situation each presents. What do the images suggest about what the speakers / writers needed to keep in mind about their rhetorical situations?

Think about Your Own Rhetorical Situation

It is important to start thinking about your rhetorical situation early in your writing process. As a student, you'll often be given assignments with very specific guidelines—to follow the conventions of a particular genre, in a certain medium, by a specific date. Nevertheless, even the most fully developed assignment cannot specify every aspect of any particular rhetorical situation.

Effective writers—whether students, teachers, or journalists—know how to analyze their rhetorical situations. They may conduct this analysis unconsciously, drawing on the rhetorical common sense they have developed as writers, readers, speakers, and listeners. Particularly when you are writing in a new genre or discipline—a situation that you'll surely face in college—it can help to analyze your rhetorical situation more systematically.

Jose Antonio Vargas risked everything by revealing his status as an undocumented immigrant. See how he navigated that rhetorical situation on p. 999.

THINK ABOUT YOUR PURPOSE

- *How would you describe your own motivation for writing?* To fulfill a course assignment? To meet a personal or professional commitment? To express your ideas to someone?

- *What is your primary goal?* To inform your audience about something? To persuade them to think a certain way? To call them to action? To entertain them? Something else?

- *How do your goals influence your choice of genre, language, medium, and design?* For example, if you want to persuade neighbors to recycle, you may choose to make colorful posters for display in public places. If you want to inform a corporation about what recycling programs accomplish, you may want to write a report using charts and data.

THINK ABOUT YOUR GENRE

- *Have you been assigned a specific genre?* If not, do any words in the assignment imply a certain genre? "Evaluate" may signal a review, for example, and "explain why" could indicate a causal analysis.

- *If you get to choose your genre,* consider your **PURPOSE**. If you want to convince readers to recycle their trash, you would probably write an argument. If, however, you want to explain how to recycle food waste into compost, your purpose would call for a process analysis.

- *Does your genre require a certain organization?* A process analysis, for instance, is often organized **CHRONOLOGICALLY**, whereas a visual analysis may be organized **SPATIALLY** —and an annotated bibliography is almost always organized alphabetically.

- *How does your genre affect your* **TONE**? A lab report, for example, generally calls for a more matter-of-fact tone than a film review.

- *Are certain* **DESIGN** *features expected in your genre?* You would likely need to include images in a review of an art show, for instance, or be required to use a standard typeface for a research paper.

THINK ABOUT YOUR AUDIENCE

- *Who is your intended audience?* An instructor? A supervisor? Classmates? Members of a particular organization? Visitors to a website? Who else might see or hear what you say?

- *How are members of your audience like and unlike you?* Consider demographics such as age, gender, religion, income, education, occupation, and political attitudes.

- *What's your relationship with your audience?* An instructor or supervisor, for example, holds considerable authority over you. Other audiences may be friends, coworkers, or even strangers. What expectations about the text might they have because of your relationship?

- *If you have a choice of* **MEDIUM**, which one(s) would best reach your intended audience?

- *What do you want your audience to think or do* as a result of what you say? Take your ideas seriously? Reflect on their beliefs? Respond to you? Take some kind of action? How will you signal to them what you want?

- *Can you assume your audience will be interested* in what you say, or will you need to get them interested? Are they likely to resist any of your ideas?

- *How much does your audience know about your topic?* How much background information do they need? Will they expect—or be put off by—the use of technical jargon? Will you need to define any terms?

- *Will your audience expect a particular* GENRE*?* If you're writing about Mozart for a music class, you might analyze a piece he composed; if, however, you're commenting on a music video posted on *YouTube*, you'd be more likely to write some kind of review.

- *What about audience members you don't or can't know?* It goes without saying that you won't always know who could potentially read your writing, especially if you're writing on a site that anyone can access. The ability to reach hundreds, even thousands, of readers is part of the internet's power, but you will want to take special care when your writing might reach unknown audiences. Remember as well that anything posted on the internet may easily be shared and read out of context.

THINK ABOUT YOUR STANCE

- *What's your attitude toward your topic?* Objective? Strongly supportive? Mildly skeptical? Amused? Angry?

- *What's your relationship with your* AUDIENCE*?* Do they know you, and if so, how? Are you a student? a friend? a mentor? an interested community member? How do they see you, and how do you want to be seen?

- *How can you best convey your stance in your writing?* What TONE do you want it to have? How will your stance and tone be received by your audience? Will they be drawn in by both?

THINK ABOUT THE LARGER CONTEXT

- *What else has been said about your topic,* and how does that affect what you will say? What would be the most effective way for you to add your voice to the conversation?

- *Do you have any constraints?* When is this writing due and how much time and energy can you put into it? How many pages (or minutes) do you have to deliver your message?

- *How much independence do you have as a writer* in this situation? To what extent do you need to meet the expectations of others, such as an instructor or a supervisor? If this writing is an assignment, how can you approach it in a way that makes it matter to you?

THINK ABOUT YOUR LANGUAGE

- *What language does the rhetorical situation invite?* If Lucia's presentation to high school seniors included students from diverse language backgrounds, she probably spoke English. However, if all the students were bilingual, Spanish-speaking students, she could have given the presentation in Spanish or some combination of English and Spanish. Choose the language that best fits your situation.

- *What dialect does the rhetorical situation encourage / require?* Does the assignment specify a dialect? If you get to choose, it can be tricky. Most people think of standardized English as the default choice—or what's expected—in American classrooms and workplaces. But this assumption isn't always correct, and another dialect may be more effective or necessary to connect with your audience and achieve your purpose.

- *What level of formality and tone does your rhetorical situation call for?* Does it suggest a serious tone and formal stance? Something more lighthearted and informal? What will your audience expect in terms of tone and formality?

THINK ABOUT YOUR MEDIUM AND DESIGN

- *If you get to choose your medium,* which one will work best for your audience and purpose? Print? Spoken? Digital? Some combination?

- *How will the medium determine what you can and cannot do?* For example, if you're submitting an essay online, you could include video, but if you were writing the same essay in print, you'd only be able to include a still shot from the video.

- *Does your medium favor certain conventions?* Paragraphs work well in print, but presentation slides usually rely on images or bulleted phrases instead. If you are writing online, you can include links to sources and background information.

- *What's the best look for your writing given your* RHETORICAL SITUA-
TION*?* Plain and serious? Warm and inviting? What design elements
will help you project that look?

- *Should you include visuals?* Would any part of your text benefit from
them? Will your audience expect them? What kind would be suitable—
photographs? videos? maps? Is there any statistical data that would be
easier to understand as a table, chart, or graph?

- *If you're writing a spoken or digital text,* should you include sound? still
images? moving images?

*REFLECT. Make a list of all the writing you remember doing in the last
week or two—including everything from texts and posts to formal academic or work
writing. Choose the two pieces that seem most different from each other and then
describe the rhetorical situation you faced for each one, using the guidelines in this
chapter. Conclude with a bit of analysis: which piece do you think is more successful at
addressing the rhetorical situation, and why?*

FOUR

Language, Power, and Rhetoric

So, if you really want to hurt me, talk badly about my language.
Ethnic identity is twin skin to linguistic identity—I am my language.
Until I can take pride in my language, I cannot take pride in myself.

—GLORIA ANZALDÚA

YOU MIGHT REMEMBER being told when you were a child that words do not matter, that "sticks and stones may break your bones, but words will never hurt you." But even as we heard those words, most of us knew they weren't true. Words matter. We can all point to instances when words have been so powerful that they have changed what we think, angered or hurt us, or moved us to action—or when we have used words in the same ways ourselves, for good or for ill.

That was the case for Chicana scholar and author Gloria Anzaldúa, who recalled that when she was growing up in south Texas in the 1950s, she got slapped on the knuckles with a sharp ruler if she was caught speaking Spanish. When she tried to tell the teacher how to pronounce her name, she was sent to the corner for "talking back." Years later, Anzaldúa, along with all Chicana / Chicano students at University of Texas–Pan American at that time, was required to take two speech classes in order to "get rid of [their] accents."

Anzaldúa's experiences were not unusual. Even today, interactions like this happen in the United States, not only for speakers of languages besides English but also for speakers of the many dialects that differ from "standardized English," the variety of language generally used in US schools, newspapers, mainstream media broadcasts, and most textbooks, including this one. African American studies professor Vershawn Ashanti Young refers to these varieties as "undervalued dialects," which include Black English, the Chicano English mentioned by Anzaldúa, signed language, and many other social and regional dialects. And it's not just the dialects that are undervalued; their speakers are often subjected to acts of intolerance, as Anzaldúa recounts. In short, the words we choose can sometimes do harm.

This chapter invites you to reflect on your attitudes about language (including your own ways of communicating) and to consider how to use your full repertoire of languages and dialects in ways that are effective and also fair, just, and equitable for everyone concerned, including yourself. Thinking rhetorically will be a key tool for achieving these goals.

Gloria Anzaldúa, who asserted, "I am my language."

REFLECT. Have you had experiences of being "corrected" for something you said or the way you said it? Was it about your pronunciation? word choice? grammar? Who made the comment? Why did they do so? On the other hand, can you think of any times when you were praised or rewarded for your language use? How do you think those experiences have contributed to the ways you use language today?

How Does Language Relate to Power—and Privilege?

It's our job as ethical authors to understand how our language choices are connected to power and privilege. "Power" is the ability to control or influence, while "privilege" refers to advantages or benefits available to some but not to others. Language is one engine through which power and privilege operate. Think for a moment about whether you've ever witnessed someone mocked for the way they speak or write—or maybe you have experienced this yourself.

This is exactly what talk show host and South Carolina native Stephen Colbert experienced when he decided at a young age that he didn't want to have a Southern accent. In an interview on *60 Minutes*, Colbert explained, "When I was a kid watching TV, if you wanted to use a shorthand that someone was stupid, you gave them a Southern accent. And that's not true. Southern people are not stupid." What Colbert says shows how self-conscious people can become when the way they speak is considered in some way inferior, and how entire groups of people may be ostracized for the way they use language. And it's about more than just feelings: a 2018 study by urban policy professor Jeffrey Grogger found that people with identifiable Southern accents earned lower wages than those without the

Stephen Colbert, on the set of his late-night TV show.

same accent. In other words, Colbert wasn't imagining things; research shows evidence of discrimination.

As these examples suggest, language plays a key role in establishing—and maintaining—power and privilege. With so many languages and dialects spoken in the United States (one in six Americans reports using a language other than English daily!), it's important to understand how words and language grant privileges to some, hinder others, and offer opportunities for us all. Doing so is an important step in understanding the **CONTEXT** for our language choices. Whatever else language is all about, it is certainly about power and privilege.

Look into Your Own Attitudes about Language

Attitudes—how we think and feel about something—affect our lives at every turn. But what do attitudes have to do with language? We all have attitudes toward particular languages or dialects, pronunciations, and other ways of using words. If a certain accent strikes you as comforting, snooty, or unsophisticated, those reactions are based on feelings, even unconscious ones, that can affect how you relate to people—or even to yourself. So our attitudes about languages can have consequences. For example, linguists John Rickford and Sharese King analyze how, in the George Zimmerman trial for the murder of Trayvon Martin, the testimony of key prosecution witness Rachel Jeantel was largely dismissed by jurors because of her use of African American Vernacular English:

> Not only was Jeantel's vernacular pivotal in the disregard of her critically important testimony in this case, but in numerous other cases in the United States and around the world in which witnesses and defendants use a vernacular rather than the mainstream variety, they tend to be misunderstood or discredited, and encounter dialect unfamiliarity or prejudice in courtrooms and potentially unfair judicial outcomes.
> —JOHN RICKFORD & SHARESE KING, "Language and Linguistics on Trial: Hearing Rachel Jeantel (and Other Vernacular Speakers) in the Courtroom and Beyond"

Research confirms that the linguistic discrimination pointed out by Rickford and King plays a role in the judicial system as well as in housing, education, and employment opportunities.

Anna Glavee describes some language attitudes—including her own—that have affected her life and her identity. Read her essay on p. 891.

So how can you go about examining your own language attitudes? Changing how we think and feel can be a long process. What you can do right now, though, is be more aware of your responses to language—stop to think through your automatic reactions and examine your beliefs and assumptions. You can also consider how language, power, and privilege are at work around you, which is called practicing **CRITICAL LANGUAGE AWARENESS**. Developing the habit of checking your own language attitudes will prepare you to make better-informed choices as an author.

Let's take a look at how such language awareness works—or doesn't work! In 2021, sports commentator Stephen A. Smith caused quite a stir when he made on-air comments about Los Angeles Angels baseball star and Japanese native Shohei Ohtani, who uses an interpreter during media interviews. Smith said:

> The fact that you've got a foreign player that doesn't speak English . . . contributes to harming the game to some degree. . . . I don't think it helps that the number one face [of baseball today] is a dude that needs an interpreter so you can understand what the hell he's saying.
>
> —STEPHEN A. SMITH, *First Take*

During that same broadcast, Smith used his airtime to demean the "unpronounceable" names of members of the Nigerian basketball team after they defeated Team USA. Though he later apologized on-air for the offensive remarks, saying, "I messed up and I hurt people with my words," Smith

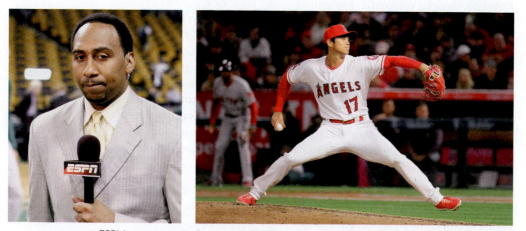

ESPN commentator Stephen A. Smith (left) and baseball superstar Shohei Ohtani (right).

initially showed a lack of language awareness. We can do better than Smith and go beyond apologies to ask where our assumptions about language come from, and to intentionally practice language awareness rather than language discrimination.

REFLECT. Are there any ways of speaking that you find irritating? How about ones that you really like a lot? Where do your own ways of speaking fall on this spectrum? Do you have any general opinions about the users of the languages that came to mind? Examine those reactions to check if any stereotypes slipped in. Would the speakers or users of that variety agree with your assessments? Upon reflection, do you think your judgments are accurate and fair?

What Is Standardized English?

We can't discuss language, power, and rhetoric without considering the variety of English widely used in US schools, government, businesses, and industries: the variety we call standardized English. It's the variety we use in this textbook and one your rhetorical situation will likely point you toward during your college and professional careers. Understanding some of the controversy and debate about standardized English is important as you consider your own language choices. There is no single, universally accepted name for this variety; it also goes by "academic English," "White mainstream English," and "dominant English." The authors and editors of this book have chosen "standardized English" because it emphasizes the fact that this isn't a naturally occurring, organic variety. Further, "standardized" signals that this variety of English is always (slowly) shifting and changing rather than being a fixed "standard."

Some form of standardization exists for every language that has an active writing and publishing tradition. And some standardization is useful, for example, by allowing published works to reach the broadest possible audiences. Some argue that using standardized English in certain contexts can open doors—especially in professional worlds. As high school English teacher Jasmine Lane puts it, she would never "discount the impact that my command of Standard English has had on my success."

But you might wonder why the standardized English we know today is the way it is. Why, for example, is it so close to how many upper- and upper-middle-class people in the United States speak? In almost all languages, the dialect chosen to be the "standard" has been the one generally used by social elites. Over time, the standardized variety comes to be used in most public contexts—like in government and education. Many come to see it as the "best," "most proper," or "correct" form of the language, which can result in all other dialects being viewed as "less than."

At the same time, resistance to standardization has always existed, not only among those who speak other dialects in the United States but also among artists, activists, and educators—people who use a variety of resources to champion linguistic justice. And today, there are many examples of "standards" being up for intepretation. As rhetoric and composition professor Asao Inoue points out, we can see such variation at work in the standards guiding highway speed limits, which dictate 65 mph in Arizona, 70 in Michigan and Mississippi, and 80 in South Dakota. Is it really safer to go 80 in South Dakota just over the border from Iowa, where the standard is 65? Inoue goes on to consider how such standards apply to language:

> Standards are decisions made by people for particular reasons, but they are not universal, nor are they infallible. This goes for language standards too. They may very well be capricious and cause some people undue harm. They are just the rules we have inherited today, made by people who had the power to do so yesterday.
>
> —ASAO INOUE, *Above the Well: An Antiracist Literacy Argument from a Boy of Color*

Inoue's example points out what scholars of language have argued for a long time: considering one "standard" variety of a language better than all others is a mistake. Or as the University of Michigan's Linguistics Department puts it, "no language is superior or inferior to another." In other words, every language, and every variety of language, is vital, valid, and can be used effectively—including standardized English and all the many varieties and languages beyond it. And you can judge what will be most effective by analyzing your **RHETORICAL SITUATION**.

We know, however, that not every variety is welcome in every setting. An academic setting like the college classroom is one place where a standardized version is often still expected. Many scholars and instructors of writing have worked for change around language standards in American English classes. One notable attempt occurred in 1974.

Students' Right to Their Own Language. In 1974, the Conference on College Composition and Communication, a professional organization for teachers of college writing, adopted a statement called "Students' Right to Their Own

Language." It began: "We affirm the students' right to their own patterns and varieties of language—the dialects of their nurture or whatever dialects in which they find their own identity and style." This statement sounded a call for teachers of writing to be more critically aware of language, and to recognize that the dominant "standard" being taught was just one variety of English—one that had too often left out or suppressed many student voices. The Students' Right statement urged teachers to recognize this discrepancy and to honor linguistic diversity in their classrooms.

Demand for Black Linguistic Justice. Since issuing the 1974 statement, that same professional organization has issued more than a dozen statements and resolutions on topics related to linguistic diversity, awareness, and justice. In 2020, a special committee released a position statement titled "This Ain't Another Statement! This is a DEMAND for Black Linguistic Justice!," which demands, among other things, that "teachers stop using standard English as the accepted norm, which reflects White Mainstream English." In 2021, the organization issued another statement, with the resolution: "We reaffirm our commitments to linguistic diversity and to the multiple languages and linguistic histories of our students and communities."

Although the organization's statements are clear and strong, many still seek practical guidance for how to ensure that the rights these statements recognize can be met. In the past, teaching standardized English was a tidy way to approach a wide range of languages and dialects in one course. But as you've seen, this approach can also present barriers. What if standardized English were instead expanded and enlarged, making space within it so that many varieties could be recognized and appreciated?

REFLECT. Did you ever consider that the language you use is something you have "rights" about? Would those rights include only what you say, sign, and write, or could they also include what you hear, see, or read? How might you describe or explain your language rights?

What's an Author to Do?

Today, debates about standardized English and other powerful ways of communicating are a hot topic. In such a time, what's a college student to do? How can you navigate language expectations? How can you make careful language choices in all the writing, speaking, and listening that you do?

Missy Watson, a composition instructor, has a lot more to say about standardized English. Read her essay on p. 1016.

How can you make the most of all your language abilities while negotiating any risks? In short, how can you become a just, effective, and responsible communicator?

Answering these questions is a tall and complex order. There are no easy solutions, but we can offer some guiding thoughts and questions to consider, which all begin with practicing language awareness—keeping in mind the social, political, and ideological contexts of all language choices.

- *Understand your* RHETORICAL SITUATION. What are your AUDIENCES' expectations? What is your PURPOSE and how can your language choices help you achieve it? Does your CONTEXT or GENRE come with certain language expectations? How will your STANCE be most clearly stated? What's at stake for you when making decisions about how to respond to your specific rhetorical situation?

- *Navigate language expectations.* You might be thinking, "No one language or dialect is better than another, but there is still this thing called standardized English and expectations or requirements to use it." You're right, there is and there are. So, what if you're most comfortable communicating in a dialect that's not standardized English? How do you, as a writer, create a space for yourself, and set yourself up for success, in a setting that values or requires standardized English? Believing that standardized English is not superior to other dialects doesn't eliminate the power that standardized English has, particularly in classrooms or boardrooms. And using it is neither "bad" nor "good"; it's all about assessing which language choices will best help you achieve your goals.

  For example, it's no coincidence that this textbook is written in standardized English. We could use a different dialect to communicate our writing advice effectively; however, the rhetorical situation we've assessed—a writing textbook for a broad audience of college writers across the United States, multiple coauthors from diverse language and cultural backgrounds, and the expectations of an American textbook publisher, to name a few factors—figured in our decision. You, too, will need to make decisions by analyzing your RHETORICAL SITUATION, what's expected, and your own values and goals.

- *Explore all the language resources you bring with you* from your community, your family, and your life experience (multiple languages, several dialects). Consider how power and privilege may be at play in the choices you make but remember also that your resources are strengths you can consider drawing on. (See Chapter 33 for suggestions on mixing languages and dialects in your writing.)

- **REFLECT** *on the language choices you're making,* why you're making them, and how those choices help you take control of your writing. Reflect, too, on the times you may want to resist expectations—of a particular genre or rhetorical situation—and when you may choose to accept and conform to them.

- **REFLECT** *on your own attitudes about language.* What beliefs do you have about English and its relationship to other languages and dialects? Where do these beliefs come from?

- *Consider how you use different varieties of language* to communicate and/or to position yourself inside or outside of a group. Have you been in a situation where someone has used language to position you as an outsider? Have you used language in order to position yourself as an insider?

- *Observe how others act on their attitudes toward language.* What do you notice about how individuals and groups use language to establish bonds with others? to create or reinforce identity? to support others? to put others down?

- *Listen and read carefully* to understand and engage with speakers and writers from diverse language backgrounds. Use social media as a resource for getting acquainted with people who use language differently than you do. Be open-minded and pay attention to check any knee-jerk reactions you have to someone's language or dialect. Examine what assumptions or biases are behind any immediate reactions to see if you're being fair.

We've all read writers, listened to songs, and viewed advertisements in which a dialect of English different from the standardized version was used. We've probably all admired writers who push the boundaries of language expectations. If no one pushes back against established power structures, what chance is there to challenge the privileges that leads to inequity? Yet, we recognize that you, as college students, are in precarious positions and that pushing back against language expectations may threaten your academic success. We invite you to understand the challenges, risks, and benefits of using standardized English and other varieties in college classrooms and then make informed choices. If you're interested in doing more, consider these further steps:

- **Ask** your instructor if your class can have discussions about language expectations, linguistic diversity, equity, and rhetoric. These kinds of discussions are sure to benefit everyone.
- **Explore and learn** about research on the history of specific language practices in your home and community.
- **Develop,** as best you can, proficiency in a variety of dialects and languages, appreciating the power and value of all your language tools.
- **Think** about how you as a writer can effect changes toward a more equitable and just world through your writing. This is, perhaps, the most important step you can take.

REFLECT. *Professor of anthropology and African American studies H. Samy Alim poses two questions that prompt language awareness: "How can language be used to maintain, reinforce, and perpetuate existing power relations?" and "Conversely, how can language be used to resist, redefine, and possibly reverse these relations?" How would you answer these questions based on your own experiences? Write a brief description of a time when you used language either to maintain or to resist existing power relations. Reflect on why you made the choices you did.*

FIVE

Understanding College Expectations

"It's Like Learning a New Language"

ELLEN MacNAMARA ARRIVED AT COLLEGE excited but anxious. She had grown up in a small rural town with an almost all-White population and attended a school that offered few options in terms of learning languages or taking Advanced Placement classes, where most students sought employment right after high school. The first person in her family to go to college, she wondered what she was in for.

Andrei Alexandrescu arrived at college from his home in Brasov, Romania, also excited and anxious. Andrei grew up speaking the country's official language, Romanian, but he also learned Hungarian and English, with a smattering of French. He had learned enough from his high school studies to be aware that different languages value different styles, and that his US college might well expect him to practice ways of speaking and writing and reading that he was not very familiar with. Would he succeed in this new environment?

Luis Garcia arrived at college from his home in Brownsville, Texas, where his grandparents immigrated from Mexico in the 1960s. With family on both sides of the border, Luis grew up speaking Spanish and a Tex-Mex dialect, only using English in school. A strong student throughout high school, Luis received a local scholarship—and he too was excited but nervous about what college would expect of him.

Like Ellen, Andrei, and Luis, millions of students enter college wondering what the campus and their instructors will expect of them, how well they will "fit in," and perhaps also how well they want to "fit in" to the culture they will find there. One student we know described arriving at college and getting to know the lingo and what's expected by saying, "It's almost like learning a new language!"

Habits for Success

While every college campus has its own unique culture, its own ways of doing things, there are some general expectations that hold across campuses, so we can suggest some habits to help you understand and navigate those expectations. Your ability to evaluate the expectations at your own school will also be of major importance. Practicing these habits in your coursework will put you on a path toward success as you work to become an active, engaged writer and thinker.

- *Be curious.* Inquire, investigate, poke, and pry until you discover or create something new. Ask a lot of questions: Why are the parking lots or dorms on campus so far away from the academic buildings? How does the distance affect students who don't have bikes, for instance, or those with physical disabilities? Who makes these decisions, and why?

- *Be creative.* Take a risk investigating an idea or topic outside your comfort zone. Try methods, approaches, or styles that are new to you. Try looking at your topic from different points of view or conduct an imaginary interview with your subject. Perhaps use a different medium for representing an idea or mix languages and/or dialects in making your point to a broad audience. If you think about your favorite school endeavors, you may find that creativity played an important role: the decision you made to create hip-hop lyrics to illustrate a point in a history essay, for example.

- *Be open & flexible.* Work hard at looking at all sides of any issue, especially those that seem strange or incorrect to you. Listen carefully to opposing views. In a discussion about campus safety, for example, listen and try to put yourself in the position of people with different perspectives—perhaps an older faculty member, or a student who works in a lab late at night, or someone who identifies with a different gender category than you do.

- **Be engaged.** Grapple with the ideas of others, responding to them and looking for connections between them. Seek out something in every course or assignment that really interests you, even if the course is not your favorite. A student we know was taking a course on ancient religious texts, primarily to fulfill a requirement, but when they read the Samson and Delilah story in different traditions, they used a big interest in comics to create a graphic narrative of one version. A seemingly boring topic suddenly became pretty exciting, thanks to this student's creative and engaged thinking!

- **Be persistent.** Keep at it. Follow through. Take advantage of opportunities to redo and improve. Keep track of what's challenging or hard for you—and talk with your instructor or a writing center consultant (or a good friend!) to look for ways to overcome those obstacles. Or keep asking why these obstacles exist: Where do they come from? What about them is in your power to change? A student searching for information on a distant relative who had played a role in the civil rights movement kept coming up empty-handed and was tempted to give up on the project and change topics. Persistence paid off, though, when she decided to have one more conversation with her grandmother's cousin, who remembered a name she was able to trace to an ancestry website—a crucial piece of information that led to a big breakthrough.

- **Be responsible.** Hold yourself responsible for making the most of your education—own it. And be a responsible participant in academic conversations by acknowledging the words and ideas of others and engaging with them thoughtfully and fairly. At the same time, take responsibility for holding your college, your instructors, and other students accountable. You may see major unfairness at work, for example, in the process of inviting students into honor societies, or the way financial aid is awarded. When you note such inequities, step up and work with others to confront them.

- **Think about the way you think.** Take time to reflect on how you learn and think. Such purposeful **REFLECTION** provides a snapshot of you as a thinker, a snapshot you can learn from as you identify obstacles to your learning and create ways to overcome them.

- **Be true to yourself.** While you, like almost all students, will change during college, developing intellectually and emotionally, acquiring a great deal of new knowledge, and growing more surely into the person you want to become, that definitely does not mean leaving behind core values or cultures or languages. You may come to question some of your earlier values or revise them; you may add an understanding of other cultures and languages—but you have the right, and perhaps the responsibility, to do so while also honoring your own.

REFLECT. Think about how you felt before coming to college. Then make notes on what you have found since you've been in college about what your college and your instructors expect of you. Talk your findings over with several classmates and then choose one expectation that has been most important to you and explain why: Is it an expectation you agree with and want to meet? Is it one you do not agree with and want to resist? What are the risks involved in these choices—and what are your options?

Expectations for Joining Academic Conversations

You are going to find yourself engaged in a great many conversations in college, both in and out of the classroom. In most of these situations, you will likely need to address, and perhaps sometimes negotiate, the following expectations:

You're expected to respond. In some cultures, students are penalized if they attempt to read established texts critically or disagree with authorities or state their own views. In such cases, this kind of response can be rude—or risky. In most US campus classrooms, however, your take on what you are reading and learning, your views and ideas, are not only encouraged but expected. Such response demonstrates your active engagement with what you are reading and learning and your ability to articulate your ideas, to add your voice to the academic conversation.

Remember, however, that the kind of engagement instructors want is not hostile or combative; it's not about showing off by beating down the ideas of others. It's fine to express strong opinions, but it's also important to remember—and acknowledge—that there is value in perspectives other than your own. Remember, too, that you can negotiate expectations for response: just because you are not talking a lot in class doesn't mean you are not engaging; you may be thinking!

Academic writers at work in (clockwise from top left) India, Chile, Burkina Faso, the United States, Thailand, and Italy.

You're expected to ask questions. One way to build your own knowledge base and your own authority is to ask questions. In other words, don't assume you have to figure everything out for yourself. While you want to take responsibility for your own learning in as many ways as possible, you will also gain by asking questions—of your instructors during class or office hours—about what you don't understand, especially on specific assignments. In addition, taking responsibility for your own learning means questioning texts or ideas or concepts that seem unfair, wrong, or harmful.

You're expected to say what *you* think. As you gain new knowledge and understanding, you will likely move from relying on or just accepting the thoughts of others to formulating your own ideas and arguments on a topic. One good way to help make this move is to engage in rigorous dialogue with other students and instructors. Your teachers are probably not simply expecting you to express a "right" answer or idea but rather to articulate your own ideas and provide adequate support for your own point of view.

REFLECT. How does your own home culture fit with these three expectations? What will be easy—or hard—for you in accepting or meeting these expectations?

CHARACTERISTIC FEATURES

No list of characteristics can describe all the kinds of texts you'll be expected to write in college, particularly given the differences among disciplines. But there are certain things you're generally expected to do in college writing:

- Use clear and recognizable patterns of organization. (p. 55)
- Mark logical relationships between ideas. (p. 56)
- State claims explicitly and provide suitable support. (p. 56)
- Present your ideas as a response to others. (p. 57)
- Express your ideas directly. (p. 58)
- Be aware of how genres and conventions vary across disciplines. (p. 58)
- Document sources using the appropriate citation style. (p. 59)

Use Clear and Recognizable Patterns of Organization

Academic writing is often organized in a way that's clear and easy for readers to recognize. In fact, writers generally describe the pattern explicitly early in a text by including a **THESIS** sentence that states the main point and says how the text is structured.

At the paragraph level, the opening sentence generally serves as a **TOPIC SENTENCE**, which announces what the paragraph is about. Readers of academic writing expect such signals for the text as a whole and within each paragraph, even in shorter texts like essay exams. Sometimes you'll want to include headings to make it easy for readers to locate sections of text.

Readers of academic writing look for organization not only to be clear but also to follow some kind of logical progression. For example:

- Beginning with the simplest ideas and then moving step by step to the most complex ideas
- Starting with the weakest claims or evidence and progressing to the strongest ones
- Treating some topics early in the text because readers must have them as background to understand ideas introduced later
- Arranging the text chronologically, starting with the earliest events and ending with the latest ones

Some academic documents in the sciences and social sciences require a specific organization known as **IMRAD** for its specific headings: introduction, methods, results, and discussion. Although there are many possible logical patterns to use, readers will expect to be able to see that pattern with little or no difficulty. Likewise, they generally expect the **TRANSITIONS** between sections and ideas to be indicated in some way, whether with words like "first," "next," or "finally," or even with full sentences like "Having considered three reasons to support this position, I will now present some alternative positions."

Finally, remember that you need to conclude your text by somehow reminding your readers of the main point(s) you want them to take away. Often, these reminders explicitly link the conclusion back to the thesis statement or introduction.

Mark Logical Relationships between Ideas

John Maeda weaves together ideas and information from many areas. Part of what makes his writing so interesting and successful is how well he signals the transitions and logical relationships between them. Check out his essay on p. 925.

Academic writers usually strive to make clear how the ideas they present relate to one another. Thus, in addition to marking the structure of the text, you'll want to mark the links between ideas and to do so explicitly. If you say in casual conversation, "It was raining, and we didn't go on the picnic," listeners will interpret "and" to mean "so" or "therefore." In academic writing, however, you have to help readers understand how your ideas are related to one another. For this reason, you'll want to use **TRANSITIONS** like "therefore," "however," or "in addition." Marking the relationships among your ideas clearly and explicitly helps readers recognize and appreciate the logic of your arguments.

State Claims Explicitly and Provide Suitable Support

One of the most important conventions of academic writing is to present **CLAIMS** explicitly and support them with **EVIDENCE**, such as examples or statistics, or by citing authorities of various kinds. Notice the two distinct parts: presenting claims clearly and supporting them suitably. In academic writing, authors don't generally give hints; instead, they state what is on their minds, often in a **THESIS** statement. If you are from a culture that communicates by hinting or by repeating proverbs or telling stories to make a point, check to be sure that you have stated your claims explicitly in your academic writing. Doing so will help readers from different cultural backgrounds follow along.

Qualify your statements. Note that being clear and explicit doesn't mean being dogmatic or closed-minded. You'll generally want to moderate your claims by using qualifying words like "frequently," "often," "generally," "sometimes," or "rarely" to indicate how strong a claim you are making. Note as well that it is much easier to provide adequate support for a qualified claim than it is to provide support for a broad unqualified claim.

Choose evidence your audience will trust. Whatever your claim, you'll need to use **EVIDENCE** that will be considered trustworthy and persuasive by your audience. And keep in mind that what counts as acceptable and suitable evidence in academic writing often differs from what works in other contexts. Generally, for example, you probably wouldn't cite from uncorroborated social media posts for academic arguments. In addition, writers today need more than ever to act as fact-checkers, making certain that their sources are accurate and credible rather than based on misinformation or lies.

Consider multiple perspectives. You should be aware that your readers may have a range of opinions on any topic, and you should write accordingly. Thus, citing only sources that reflect one perspective won't be sufficient in most academic contexts. Be sure to consider and acknowledge COUNTER-ARGUMENTS and viewpoints other than your own.

Organize information strategically. One common way of supporting a claim is by moving from a general statement to more specific information. When you see words like "for example" or "for instance," the author is moving from a more general statement to a more specific example.

In considering what kind of evidence to use in supporting your claims, remember that the goal is not to amass and present large quantities of evidence but instead to sift through all the available evidence, choose the evidence that will be most persuasive to your audience, and arrange and present it all strategically. Resist the temptation to include information or ANECDOTES that do not contribute to your argument.

Present Your Ideas as a Response to Others

Strong academic writers do more than just make well-supported claims. They present their ideas as a response to what else has been said (or might be said) about their topic. One common pattern, introduced by English professors Gerald Graff and Cathy Birkenstein, is to start with what others are saying and then to present your ideas as a response. If, as noted earlier in this chapter, academic writing is a way of entering a conversation—of engaging with the ideas of others—you need to include their ideas with your own.

In fact, providing support for your claims will often involve SYNTHESIS : weaving the ideas and even the words of others into the argument you are making. And since academic arguments are part of a larger conversation, all of us are always responding to and borrowing from others, even as we are developing our own individual ideas.

Express Your Ideas Directly

Be specific in your language. You'll want to **DEFINE** terms you use, both to be sure readers will not be confused and to clarify your own positions. Clarity of expression in academic writing also means being direct and concise. Academic writers in the United States tend to avoid elaborate sentence structures or flowery language, and they don't let the metaphors and similes they use get the best of them either, as this author did:

> Cheryl's mind turned like the vanes of a wind-powered turbine, chopping her sparrowlike thoughts into bloody pieces that fell onto a growing pile of forgotten memories.

In fact, this sentence was the winner of an annual "bad writing" contest in which writers try to write the worst sentence they can. It's easy to see why this one was a winner: it has way too much figurative language—chopping wind turbines, bleeding sparrows, thoughts in a pile, forgotten memories—and the metaphors get in the way of one another. Use metaphors carefully in academic writing, making sure they add to what you're trying to say. Here's one way the prize-winning sentence might be revised to be clearer and more direct: "Cheryl's mind worked incessantly, thought after thought piling up until she couldn't keep track of them all."

Be Aware of How Genres and Conventions Vary across Disciplines

As you are no doubt discovering, academic disciplines have their own sets of conventions: the use of first person is "conventional" in some humanities courses, for instance, but in the sciences—not so much. Passive voice verbs are preferred in the sciences, while writers in the humanities often go for active verbs. The social sciences generally use the conventions of the documentation system endorsed by the American Psychological Association (APA); those in the humanities the systems endorsed by the Modern Language Association (MLA) or *The Chicago Manual of Style* (Chicago); those in the sciences the system endorsed by the Council of Science Editors (CSE). As you choose a major and enter a discipline, reading articles and books in the field and composing assignments, you will learn more and more about the particular conventions—and you will have a chance to decide which you want to accept and follow, and which you may want to resist or reject.

One of the authors of this text, for instance, objected strenuously to the conventional MLA practice of citing only the name of the first author (followed by the Latin "et al.") in cases where there are more than three authors. Arguing that this practice erased the contributions of people who deserve credit for producing the article or book, she decided not to adhere to this convention—and she protested to the MLA and urged other scholars to follow her lead. In this and other ways, disciplinary conventions shift and change over time; they are not carved in stone forever. You will want, then, not only to understand what your discipline's conventions are but also to think carefully about how they can be made more useful, more inclusive, or even more fair.

Despite the significant differences in genres across academic disciplines, you'll also find that there are some common rhetorical moves you'll likely make in much of the academic writing you do. You'll find that academic essays and research articles generally open with three such moves:

- First, you give the **CONTEXT** or general topic of whatever you are writing. Frequently, you will do this by discussing the existing research or commentary on the topic you are writing about.

- Second, you point out some aspect of this topic that merits additional attention, often because it is poorly understood or because there is a problem that needs to be solved: that is, you'll show there is a problem or gap of some kind in our understanding.

- Finally, you'll explain how your text addresses that problem or fills that gap. This explanation often happens within the first paragraph or two of the text.

Document Sources Using the Appropriate Citation Style

Finally, academic writers credit and **DOCUMENT** all sources carefully. Understanding how Western academic culture defines intellectual property and **PLAGIARISM** is complicated. Although you never need to provide a source for common knowledge that no one disputes (for example, that the US Declaration of Independence was approved by Congress on July 4, 1776, in Philadelphia), you will need to document words, information, or ideas that you get from others, including, of course, any content (words or images) you find on the internet.

What else do you need to know about academic writing? It's important to note that the academic expectations, moves, and conventions discussed in this chapter are solidly set in Western traditions of language and thought, ways of knowing and of persuading that have long been associated with the dominant, often elite, culture in the United States as well as with the dialect of standardized English. Throughout our history, this dialect—along with Western academic conventions—have been thought to provide a common ground for communication, something everyone could learn and use. But "everyone" has turned out to leave a lot of people out. Thus, as noted in Chapter 4, resistance to such "standard" practices has a long history in the United States, and today many aspects of Western academic conventions, including standardized English, are under careful scrutiny as writers push the envelope of academic discourse to make room for more expansive methods of research, means of organization, languages and dialects, and styles. As professor of literacy studies Elaine Richardson says, learning to use academic styles today needs to allow for experimentation and inclusivity and must not "lock us into evaluating students' cultures. Curricula must be conceived in such a way that students are trained to discern, appreciate, and master diverse styles."

Taking such a flexible approach is now characteristic of many college writing programs as well as much of the best writing occurring today. This mindset recognizes that there's usually more than one effective way to say or write something. And while the use of Western forms of academic discourse and standardized English is one way (and still the dominant way in most academic writing), it's not better or worse than other ways. As you negotiate college expectations for writing, your audience and purpose should ultimately guide the choices you make.

REFLECT. What has been your experience with using the academic conventions discussed in this chapter, or with using standardized English? How did you learn these conventions? Has doing so in some ways cramped your own style or affected your ability to communicate? Has it in some ways helped you to communicate more effectively? Spend some time talking these questions over with one or two classmates and then write a brief summary of your thoughts.

PART II

Reading Processes

DO YOU REMEMBER the first word you learned to read? For many people, that first word is their own name: you learn to print it and you do this over and over again and—suddenly, as if by magic—you can read it! Those first reading moments are miraculous because they open up entire new worlds to us. And as this example suggests, writing and reading are reciprocal processes: writing evokes reading and reading evokes writing, as if the two are intertwined in a seamless dance.

Like writing, many of us take reading for granted: it's something we have been able to do for so long that it seems run-of-the-mill, almost like breathing. But reading turns out to be a complicated process, and one with a long history. The word comes down to us from Old English, "rœdan": to advise, counsel, guess, learn by reading—and, as early as 1610, "to make out the character of a person." Sojourner Truth, a nineteenth-century abolition advocate and formerly enslaved person, surely knew this definition of "read" when she said, "I don't read such small things as letters; I read men and nations." This early sense of the word "read" is still with us: we "read" situations, we "read" people, we "read" images, and so on. We also read with eyes, ears, and fingers: those with low vision read by listening or by tracing braille, for example, while people who are hard of hearing might use closed captions while watching television.

One aim of the following chapters is to do what ethnographers recommend to spark new ideas: make the familiar strange. We want to make the processes and practices of everyday, commonplace reading "strange" in order to call attention to them, to get you to look at them with fresh and creative eyes, and to think carefully—about what you are doing when you read, about different ways of reading, and about the processes that reading demands of you.

The chapters that follow will introduce you to the concept of reading rhetorically—that is, reading a text with clear intention and attention and putting that text, whether written, oral, visual, or digital, in its context. This kind of reading will help you read and understand the texts you encounter during your college career and well beyond. In addition, we'll focus on particular processes of reading, from annotating and summarizing a text to the point where reading meets writing in the responses you compose to what you have read. And last but certainly not least, we'll focus on drawing careful distinctions among facts, misinformation, and lies—and provide ways in which you can identify, understand, and engage productively with each category, practicing what we call "defensive reading."

Reading is a profoundly social act: it connects us to other people and places and times and at its best can be an act of empathy, helping us to walk in other people's shoes. As novelist Jean Rhys says, "Reading makes immigrants of us all. It takes us away from home, but more important, it finds homes for us everywhere."

SIX

Reading Rhetorically

HANCES ARE, YOU READ MORE than you think you do. You read print texts, of course, but you probably also read regularly on a phone, tablet, or computer. Reading is now, as perhaps never before, a basic necessity. In fact, if you think that reading is something you learned once and for all in childhood, think again.

Reading calls for strategic effort. In his book *The Economics of Attention*, rhetorician Richard Lanham explains: "We're drowning in information. What we lack is the human attention needed to make sense of it all."

When so many texts are vying for our attention, which ones do we choose? In order to decide what to pay attention to, we need to practice what media critic Howard Rheingold calls "infotention," a word he came up with to describe a "mind-machine combination of brain-powered attention skills and computer-powered information filters." Rheingold is talking primarily about reading online, but we think that infotention is important for reading any kind of text because it calls for synthesizing and thinking rhetorically about the enormous amount of information available to us in both print and digital sources. And while some of us can multitask, most of us are not good at it and must learn to focus our attention when we read.

In other words, we need to learn to read rhetorically. Reading rhetorically means attending carefully and intentionally to a text. It means being open-minded to that text. And it means being an active participant in understanding and thinking about and responding to what is in

So many texts vying for our attention!

the text. As Nobel laureate Toni Morrison says, "The words on the page are only half the story. The rest is what you bring to the party."

So how do you learn to read rhetorically and to practice infotention? Some steps seem obvious: especially for high-stakes reading, like much of what you do for school, you need to find space and time in which you can really focus—turn off social media and put down your phone. Beyond such obvious steps, though, you can improve your reading by approaching texts systematically. This chapter and the chapter that follows will guide you in doing so, beginning with tips for considering your rhetorical situation and motivating yourself to engage actively with texts.

THINKING ABOUT YOUR RHETORICAL SITUATION

Before jumping into a text, consider your **RHETORICAL SITUATION** ; doing so will help you get straight where the author—and you—are coming from. Following are some questions to consider when approaching a text:

- What's the **PURPOSE** for your reading? To learn something new? To fulfill an assignment? To prepare for a test?

- Who's the intended **AUDIENCE** ? What words or images in the text make you think so? Are you a member of this group? If not, there may be unfamiliar terms or references that you'll need to look up.

- What's the **GENRE**? An argument? Report? Review? Proposal? Knowing the genre will tell you something about what to expect.
- How might the **MEDIUM** affect how you will read the text? Is it a written print text? An oral text? A visual or multimedia text, such as an infographic? How will you go about attending carefully to different media elements?
- What do you know about the larger **CONTEXT** of the text? What do you know about the topic? What do you need to find out? What resources can you draw on for the information you will need?
- What is your own **STANCE** on the topic? Are you an advocate? a critic? an impartial observer?

Setting your rhetorical bearings prepares you for your first job as a reader: making sure you understand what you read. Chapter 7 offers guidance on other essential strategies for understanding texts: previewing, annotating, and summarizing. The rest of this chapter focuses on how to be a motivated, engaged, and persistent reader.

BECOMING AN ACTIVE, ENGAGED READER

"Engagement" is one of the habits of mind scholars see as crucial to success in college, and it's certainly crucial to any reading you do there. You're "engaged" in reading when you are invested in the text. Sounds good in theory, right? But just how can you get yourself "invested" in something you've been assigned to read, especially if it's a text you wouldn't choose to read otherwise? There's no magic wand you can wave to make this happen, but we can offer some advice:

- *Find your comfort zone,* someplace where you'll be able to concentrate. A comfy lounge chair? A desk chair with back support? Starbucks? Some students tell us they like to be a little *uncomfortable* because it keeps them on their mental toes.
- *Choose a device that helps you focus.* Some like print texts best for taking notes, while others like reading on a device without internet distractions.
- *Make it social.* In the case of difficult texts, two heads are usually better than one—and discussing a text with someone else will help you both to engage with it. Try to explain something in the text to a friend; if you can get across the major points, you've surely understood it!

- *Start with what's easy, then tackle what's difficult.* The introduction may be easy to read, so begin there and make sure you understand before moving on to more difficult material. If the text is short, read it all the way through once, marking the hard parts. Then return to the tricky parts without spending too much time; you'll probably find they are easier to understand once you've read through the entire text once.

- *Annotate as you read.* The following chapter will give you guidelines for using annotation to understand, engage, and respond to what you read.

FAST—AND SLOW—READING

Do you feel like you are always rushing? Running or scrolling to the next thing, and the next, and the next? We seem to like everything fast—fast cars, fast videos, fast food—and often, fast reading. We're not talking about speed reading, which advocates claim can allow you to read up to 1,500 words a minute, but rather about the kind of skimming and scanning that most of us do online.

And there are good reasons to skim texts, particularly when you are looking for specific information. You can skim across passages looking for keywords that signal information you need, or you can read the first sentence of a paragraph to get the gist. Reading expert Louise Rosenblatt calls this kind of reading "efferent," reading that's aimed at getting into a text and extracting key information in the swiftest and most effective way possible. She uses the example of a parent whose child has swallowed a dangerous substance: the parent is looking for the antidote and needs only one piece of information—fast!

The opposite of such fast reading is, logically enough, slow reading. There are lots of "slow" movements with loyal participants today: slow travel, slow media, slow fashion, and even slow reading. Some colleges now offer courses in slow reading. In his book *The Art of Slow Reading*, English professor Thomas Newkirk describes five "slow" practices we believe are helpful for the kind of reading you're expected to do in college:

- *Make a mark.* Annotate what you notice as key parts of a text, what stands out to you as central or important to remember.

- *Find problems.* Stop to note a problem or confusion in the text and try to come up with a strategy for solving it. Such problem finding can work especially well if you are reading with someone else, someone you can talk with about the problem or confusion.

- *Read like a writer,* asking yourself about the decisions or moves the writer is making: Why shift topics here? Why introduce a particular piece of evidence at this point? Why choose this word?
- *Elaborate,* going beyond the text by comparing and contrasting it with other texts or drawing out unstated implications from the text.
- *Memorize short bits.* Learning key terms and phrases by heart can help you understand and remember what you are reading. This can be especially helpful for reading literature, though less applicable in other fields and disciplines.

Slow reading, then, doesn't refer simply to speed. Rather, it's about attending carefully to the text, taking responsibility for your reading practices.

READING UNFAMILIAR OR DIFFICULT TEXTS

You'll surely encounter subject matter and texts that are hard to understand. Most often these will be texts that you're reading not for pleasure but to learn something. You'll want to slow down with such texts—and you might find this easier to do with print texts, where paragraphs and headings and highlighted features help you see the various parts and find key information. Here are some other tips for making your way through difficult texts:

- On your first reading, read for what you can understand, and simply mark places that are confusing or where you don't understand.
- Then choose a modest amount of material to read—a chapter, say, or even part of a chapter. Look it over to figure out how it is organized and see its main points—look at headings, for example, as well as any THESIS and TOPIC SENTENCES.
- Check to see if there's a summary at the beginning or end of the text. If so, read it very carefully.
- Re-read the hard parts. Slow down, and focus.
- Try to make sense of the parts: "this part offers evidence," "that paragraph summarizes an alternative view," "here's a signal about what's coming next."
- If the text includes visuals, what do they contribute to the message?
- Resist highlighting: better to take notes in the margins.

READING ON-SCREEN AND OFF

Once upon a time "reading" meant attending to words on paper. But today we often encounter texts that convey information in images and in sound as well—and they may be on- or off-screen. When you approach such texts, think carefully about how the medium of delivery may affect your understanding, engagement, and response.

Researchers have found that we often take shortcuts when we read online, searching and scanning and jumping around in a text or leaping from link to link. This kind of reading is very helpful for finding answers and information quickly, but it can blur our focus and make it difficult to attend to the text carefully and purposefully. Here are a few tips to help you when you're reading on-screen:

- Be clear about your purpose for reading. If you need to understand and remember the text, remind yourself to read carefully and avoid skimming or skipping around.

- Close pages or tabs that may distract you from reading.

- Learn how to take notes in PDFs, *Word* documents, and *Google Docs*. Then you can make notes as you read on-screen, just as you would when reading a print text. Or take notes on paper.

- Look up unfamiliar terms as you read, making a note of definitions you may need later.

- If it increases your focus, consider printing out the text to read.

The pervasiveness of reading on-screen may suggest that many readers prefer to read that way. But current research suggests that most students still prefer to read print, especially if the reading is important and needs to be internalized and remembered. Print texts, it's worth remembering, are easy to navigate—you can tell at a glance how much you've read and how much you still have to go, and you can easily move back and forth in the text to find something important.

In addition, researchers have found that students reading on-screen are less likely to reflect on what they read or to make connections and synthesize in ways that bind learning to memory. It's important to note, however, that studies like these almost always end with a caveat: reading practices are changing and technology is making it easier to read on-screen.

It's important to note that online texts often blend written words with audio, video, links, charts and graphs, and other elements that you can attend to in any order you choose. In reading such texts, you'll need to make decisions carefully. When exactly should you click on a link, for example? The first moment it comes up? Or should you make a note to check it out later since doing so now may break your concentration—and you might not be able to get back easily to what you were reading? In addition, scrolling seems to encourage skimming and to make us read more rapidly. In short, reading on-screen can make it harder to stay on task. So you may well need to make a special effort with digital texts—to read them attentively and to pay close attention to what you're reading.

We are clearly in a time of flux where reading is concerned, so the best advice is for you to think very carefully about why you are reading. If you need to find information quickly, to follow a conversation on *Twitter*, or to look for online sources on a topic you're researching, reading on-screen is the way to go. But if you need to fully comprehend and retain the information in a text, you may want to stick with print.

Reading Visual Texts

Take a look at the Thistle advertisement on the following page. You may know that Thistle is a subscription-based meal delivery service for "plant forward" foods; if not, a quick look at the company's website will fill in this part of the ad's **CONTEXT**. This *Twitter* ad may be tweet-size, but there's a lot going on in terms of its rhetorical situation. It combines several elements— all very spare and minimal—in order to capture the attention of *Twitter* users, who tend to scroll quickly through content.

Thinking through the rhetorical situation tells you something about the ad's purpose and audience. Of course its major **PURPOSE** is to sell as many meals as possible, but you can tell right away that Thistle isn't trying to compete with McDonald's, say, or Burger King. Its appeal is to a much more exclusive **AUDIENCE**. What clues can you gather about who the intended audience really is? What might that audience want?

Reading a visual begins, then, with studying the purpose, audience, message, and context. We need to examine all the elements and how they each contribute to a coherent whole. This visual combines a color photo with just a few brief sentences. The short, snappy **TONE** conveys information

Take a look at the excerpt from Alison Bechdel's graphic memoir on p. 857. You could read only the words in the narrative boxes and get a good sense of the story she tells about her father, but how much more deeply do you understand her narrative from viewing the drawings?

Thistle 🌱
@ThistleCo

Eat well. Save time. Feel amazing. Get plant-forward, gluten-free meals, delivered. thistle.co

quickly, and the message hits three important values of many young adults: nutrition, time management, and health. Three more important bits of information appear: plant-forward, gluten-free, and delivered—all there in one tidy package. In addition to the company's *Twitter* handle—an obligatory element—the ad also includes Thistle's URL.

Then there's the photo. What you see is a viewed-from-above image of a square container holding some kind of colorful salad. The salad is held in someone's lap, with their frayed jeans visible. We can also see this person's hand, seemingly holding the device that snapped the photo. It resembles the kind of quick photo anyone might take and post to show off their own healthy lunch, if only they had the perfect food to show. Is this food meant to be savored, combined with delightful conversation in a glamorous setting? Not likely. This is a meal eaten alone and quickly by a busy person, a person who can pay for premium-priced, high-nutrition meals that require zero effort to prepare.

In short, this Thistle ad is skillfully designed and placed in a strategic **CONTEXT** where its intended audience of high-income, career-driven, and probably single people will encounter it and absorb its message in the second or two that it takes to scroll across the screen.

"Reading" Spoken Texts

Spoken texts need to be "read" in a different way, by listening to what speakers are saying while you view images they project on a screen or provide in a handout. If the presentation is a really good one, these elements will complement each other, joining together to get their message across. Still, you may need to learn to split your attention, making sure you are not focusing so much on any slides or handouts that you're missing what the speaker is saying—or vice versa. Remember, too, that you'll be a better audience member if you look at the speaker and any visuals, rather than staring at your laptop or looking down at the desk.

READING ACROSS GENRES

Genres affect how we read and can help guide our reading. Knowing the characteristic features of a genre, therefore, can help you read more attentively and more purposefully. When you read REPORTS, for example, you expect information you can trust, and you look for signs that the authors know what they are writing about and have cited authoritative sources. When you read a REVIEW, you expect to find some judgment, along with reasons and evidence to support that judgment. And you know to question any ARGUMENT that fails to acknowledge likely counterarguments. In other words, what you know about common genres can help you as a reader. Knowing what features to expect will help you read with a critical eye, and just recognizing a genre can help you adjust your reading as need be (reading directions more slowly, for example).

READING ACROSS ACADEMIC DISCIPLINES

Differences in disciplines can make for some very difficult reading tasks, as you encounter texts that seem almost to be written in foreign languages. As with most new things, however, new disciplines and their texts will become familiar the more you work with them. The more you read such texts, the more familiar they will become to you until, eventually, you will be able to "talk the talk" of that discipline yourself.

Pay attention to terminology. It's especially important to read rhetorically when you encounter texts in different academic fields. Take the word "analysis," for instance. That little word has a wide range of definitions across fields. In philosophy, analysis has traditionally meant breaking down a topic into its parts in order to understand them—and the whole—more completely. In the sciences, analysis often involves the scientific method of observing a phenomenon, formulating a hypothesis, and experimenting to see whether the hypothesis holds up. And in business, analysis usually refers to assessing needs and finding ways to meet them. When you're assigned to carry out an analysis, then, it's important to know what the particular field of study requires you to do and to ask your instructors if you aren't sure.

Know what counts as evidence. Beyond attending to what particular words mean from field to field, you should note that what counts as effective EVIDENCE can differ across disciplines. In literature and other fields in the humanities, textual evidence is often the most important: your job as a reader is to focus on the text itself. For the sciences, you'll most often focus on evidence gathered through experimentation, on facts and figures. Some of the social sciences also favor the use of "hard" evidence or data, while others are more likely to use evidence drawn from interviews, oral histories, or even anecdotes. As a strong reader, you'll need to be aware of what counts as credible evidence in the fields you study.

Be aware of how information is presented. Finally, pay attention to the way disciplines format and present information. You'll probably find that articles and books in the fields of literature and history present their information in paragraphs, sometimes with illustrations. Physics texts present much important information in equations, while those in psychology and political science rely more on charts and graphs of quantitative data. In art history, you see extensive use of images, while much of the work in music relies on notation and sound.

So reading calls for some real effort. Whether you're reading words or images or bar graphs, literary analysis or musical notation, in a print book or on a screen, you need to read rhetorically—attentively and intentionally and with an open mind. And on top of all that, you need to be an active participant with what you read, just as Toni Morrison says: "The words on the page are only half the story. The rest is what you bring to the party."

REFLECT. The next time you're assigned to read a text online, pay attention to your process. Take some notes on just how you read: Do you go straight through, or do you stop often? Do you take notes? Do you take breaks while reading to attend to something else? What do you do if you don't understand a passage? How long can you read at a stretch and maintain full concentration? Then answer the same questions the next time you're assigned to read a print text. What differences do you notice in the way you read each text? What conclusions can you draw about how to be a more effective reader, both on- and off-screen?

SEVEN

Annotating, Summarizing, Responding

OW DO YOU read when the stakes are high, when you really need to understand and remember what you're reading? One student we know, who chooses to read hard copy whenever possible, keeps a highlighter and a stack of sticky notes on hand in order to talk back to the text. Another student makes comments using a note-taking app. And still another takes photos of lecture slides and annotates them in a *Google Doc* while in class. These students are all using strategies they've developed for reading purposely and attentively, strategies that suit their own needs.

Like these students, you've likely already developed reading strategies that work for you, and you'll surely be developing new strategies as you encounter new kinds of texts and disciplines, from reports in a plant science course to executive summaries in business management. This chapter offers guidance on three key strategies that will help you engage actively and productively with all kinds of texts. **ANNOTATING**—the process of taking notes, underlining important information, and marking passages of a text that strike you as important—helps you focus and attend carefully to what you read. **SUMMARIZING** helps you synthesize the ideas in what you are reading, consolidate your understanding, and remember important points. And responding gives you an opportunity to engage the text directly, talking back and joining the conversation.

"We may have the same books, but we highlight entirely different passages."

Each of these strategies marks a point where reading and writing intersect: reading leads to writing (annotating, summarizing, responding), and writing about what you've read often leads you to re-read.

ANNOTATING

Annotating might sound simple: you just mark up the text as you read, right? Keep in mind, however, that what you annotate should be driven by your purpose for reading. Whatever that purpose, annotating will help you read actively—thinking, questioning, and responding as you go. Like Hansel and Gretel sprinkling bread crumbs in the forest, it's also a way of leaving a trail you can revisit later if you need to review concepts for an exam or find a quote for an essay. Taking the following steps will help you annotate purposefully and productively.

Think about your purpose for reading. If you're reading a biology textbook to prepare for an exam, you might highlight key concepts, summarize theories to be sure you understand them, and respond to the chapter's review questions. When reading a treatise by Aristotle to prepare for discussion in a philosophy class, however, you may mark passages that are hard to understand, write out questions to ask in class, and highlight statements to remember. Consider the following questions:

- *Why are you reading this text?* As a model for writing you'll be expected to do? So that you'll learn about a certain topic?

- *What do you need to be able to do with this text?* Apply concepts? Respond to the author's argument? Cite it in something you're writing?

Preview the text. Rather than plunging right in, skim the text first to get a sense of what it's about and how it's organized. Jot down what you notice.

- *What do you already know (and think) about the topic?* Do you have any personal experience with the subject? What do you want or expect to learn?

- *Who are the authors or sponsors?* Where do you think they're coming from? Might they have a particular agenda or purpose?

- *Who published the text,* and what does that tell you about its intended audience and purpose?

- *What does the title tell you?* If there's a subtitle, does it indicate the author's argument or stance?

- *If there's an abstract,* read it. If not, read the introduction. What new information do you learn?

- *Scan any headings* to see what's covered, and look at any text that's highlighted. How will the design help you read the text?

- *What is your initial response* to the text based on your preview of it?

Annotate as you read. Annotate the text as a way of talking back to it—marking what the author is saying, how the author is getting their message across, and how you are reacting to what you're reading.

Why not try your hand at annotating now? The report by Richard Alba, Morris Levy, and Dowell Myers on p. 837 is a good one for practice.

WHAT'S THE TEXT SAYING?

- What claims does the text make? Underscore the **THESIS** statement. If there's no explicit thesis, what key questions and issues does the text address?

- What **REASONS** and **EVIDENCE** does the author provide? Are they sufficient?

- Does anything surprise you or make you feel skeptical? Mark any facts or statements that seem questionable.

- Note any **COUNTERARGUMENTS**. Does the author represent and respond to them fairly? Are any other perspectives missing?

- Identify any key terms (and look them up if necessary). This can be especially important if you're reading a text in an unfamiliar discipline. Define important terms and concepts in your own words.
- Do you understand graphs, charts, or other visual elements? These often play an important role in the sciences and social sciences.

WHO'S THE INTENDED AUDIENCE?

- Who do you think the author is addressing? Students like you? Other scholars? The general public? Mark words that make you think so. Are you included in that group? If not, does that affect your response?
- What do you know about the audience's values? Highlight words that suggest what the author thinks the audience cares about.

WHAT DO YOU KNOW ABOUT THE AUTHOR?

- Who wrote the text? Is the author credible and reliable? What makes you believe that this is the case? Note places in the text where the author demonstrates **AUTHORITY** to write on the topic. Is the author a scholar? a popular commentator? To learn more about the author, search their name in sources you trust.
- What is the author's **STANCE**? Objective? Passionate? Something else? Mark words that indicate the author's stance.
- How would you describe the author's **STYLE** and **TONE**? Formal? Casual? Serious? Humorous? Mark any words or passages that establish that style and tone.
- What kinds of **LANGUAGE** choices does the author make? Do they use language their audience likely expects? Do they use language in surprising or especially effective ways? Mark language choices that you find interesting.

HOW IS THE TEXT DESIGNED?

- How does the design affect the way you understand the text?
- Note headings, sidebars, or other design features that add emphasis.
- If the text includes visuals, what do they contribute to the message?

WHAT ARE YOUR REACTIONS?

- Mark places in the text where you agree, disagree, or both. Note why.
- Note any claims, facts, or other things you find surprising—and why.

We bet you'll have a lot to say when you annotate Clyde McGrady's analysis of cancel culture on p. 929.

- Note any passages you find confusing or difficult to understand. What questions do you have?
- Jot down any possible counterarguments or conflicting evidence that you need to check out.
- If a passage reminds you of a past experience, memory, or strong emotion, note it.
- While noting your reactions, consider what experiences, beliefs, or biases inform your responses. Do you need to check any of your gut reactions to be sure you're staying fair and open-minded?

If you're reading a particularly important text, read it more than once, paying attention to different elements each time. For example, to prepare for a class discussion you might first focus on the argument and then re-read focusing on how the writer supports that argument. With long or dense texts, you may want to annotate by summarizing paragraphs or sections as you go.

Since you likely read on-screen often, take the time to learn one of the many free programs that make it easy to annotate digital texts. *Hypothesis* and *Adobe Acrobat Reader* are two programs that allow you to add notes, highlight, insert URLs and images, and more. In fact, the ebook version of this book includes annotation tools to mark up what you're reading right now!

↪ To read—and annotate—a digital version of this book, visit digital.wwnorton.com/everyone4r.

So annotating keeps you active and helps you engage more deeply with what you read. Annotating also helps you approach reading as a social activity, bringing you into conversation with writers, engaging them and their ideas actively. Sometimes, especially for a research project, you'll be assigned to write formal annotations in the form of an **ANNOTATED BIBLIOGRAPHY**. That's a reading (and writing) situation with its own characteristic features. For now, focus on making annotating a habit—especially when you read academic texts.

Online or on a printed page, there are many methods and tools for annotating as you read. Try a few to find the ones that work best for you.

A Sample Annotated Text

Here's the opening of an essay by Katherine Spriggs on shopping locally, along with annotations by YULIYA VAYNER, a former Hunter College student who read and annotated this piece for a summary/response essay assignment.

AMERICANS TODAY CAN eat pears in the spring in Minnesota, oranges in the summer in Montana, asparagus in the fall in Maine, and cranberries in the winter in Florida. In fact, we can eat pretty much any kind of produce anywhere at any time of the year. But what is the cost of this convenience? In this essay, I will explore some answers to this question and argue that we should give up a little bit of convenience in favor of buying local.

Thesis statement

"Buying local" means that consumers choose to buy food that has been grown, raised, or produced as close to their homes as possible ("Buy Local"). Buying local is an important part of the response to many environmental issues we face today (fig. 1). It encourages the development of small farms, which are often more environmentally sustainable than large farms, and thus strengthens local markets and supports small rural economies. By demonstrating a commitment to buying local, Americans could set an example for global environmentalism.

I wonder what she means exactly by "buying local."

This paragraph states her stance: strongly in favor of sustainable farming and buying local.

But what about people who don't have access to locally produced food or who can't afford to buy it?

In 2010, the international community is facing many environmental challenges, including global warming, pollution, and dwindling fossil fuel resources. Global warming is attributed to the release of greenhouse gases such as carbon dioxide and methane, most commonly emitted in the burning of fossil fuels. It is such a pressing problem that scientists estimate that in the year 2030, there will be no glaciers left in Glacier National Park ("Global Warming Statistics"). The United States is especially guilty of contributing to the problem, producing about a quarter of all global greenhouse gas emissions, and playing a large part in pollution and shrinking world oil supplies as well ("Record Increase"). According to a CNN article published in 2000, the United States manufactures more than 1.5 billion pounds of chemical pesticides a year that can pollute our water, soil, and air (Baum). Agriculture is particularly interconnected with all of these issues. Almost three-fourths of the pesticides produced in the United States are used in agriculture (Baum). Most produce is

Here comes some evidence. Looks like she's done research to inform her argument.

I want to check out this source: I'm a little suspicious of what she says here.

Fig. 1. Shopping at a farmers' market is one good way to support small farms and strengthen the local economy. Timothy Mulholland. *Dane County Farmers' Market on the Square Madison Wisconsin.* 2008, Alamy.

> *Farmers' markets are expensive. Many people—including me!—can't afford to shop at them.*

shipped many miles before it is sold to consumers, and shipping our food long distances is costly in both the amount of fossil fuel it uses and the greenhouse gases it produces.

> *She's serious about this issue and is making a strong case. Including these researched facts lends credibility, but I'm waiting to see if she acknowledges the fact that many people can't afford or easily get to locally grown food.*

✍ REFLECT. *Find something you've read and annotated recently. What kinds of annotations did you make? Calling out keywords, ideas, and claims? Strategies the writer used? Areas of confusion? Points you agree or disagree with? Your own personal connections? Try highlighting your annotations in different colors for a visual breakdown by type. What do these annotations tell you about your reading process? Looking back at the prompts in this section, are there types of annotations that you didn't make but would have proved useful? Re-read the text and add them!*

SUMMARIZING

Summarizing a text helps you understand and engage with it—and internalize and remember what you read. When you summarize, you're boiling a text down to its central ideas, claims, and theories in your own words. One student we know writes summaries in the margins as a strategy for making sure she understands the most important concepts, especially in textbooks. These summaries, along with additional annotations throughout the chapters, help her prepare for exams. Besides helping you understand what you read, summarizing is also essential for weaving the viewpoints of others into your own writing. Both at work and at school, you'll be expected to summarize something—the plot of a short story, the results of a scientific study, takeaways from a meeting. The following advice will help you craft strong summaries in academic and professional writing.

Read the text carefully—and annotate. Read the text to figure out its main message, idea, or argument. Annotate as you read, marking key ideas and claims as well as supporting points such as anecdotes, supporting evidence, and counterarguments. When you identify a sentence or paragraph that states a main point, try restating it in your own words. A pair of highlighters can help; try using different colors to distinguish the main ideas from the supporting points.

When you summarize something other than a printed text—a music video, a printed advertisement, a speech—practice the same careful reading. Observe your subject and take note of the main message as well as the supporting details that lead you to draw this conclusion.

Be brief, stating the main points while leaving out minor supporting details. Summaries are generally brief, stating the main ideas while leaving out the supporting evidence and anecdotes that aren't necessary for understanding. A summary serves as a stand-in for readers who aren't familiar with the full text, so your aim is to get readers up to speed on the main points without getting lost in the details.

Be fair and accurate, using neutral language. Think of a summary as stating the facts, not sharing your opinion. Use neutral language to present the author's main ideas with evenhandedness and respect, not judgment or criticism. Imagine the author reading your summary of their work. Would they find it accurate? Have you left out an important point? Would the writer find it fair? Have your opinions snuck in?

Use SIGNAL PHRASES to present what the author says as distinct from what you say—and use quotations in moderation. Summarizing calls for boiling down information and presenting it in your own words and sentence structure. Use signal phrases such as "she concludes" or "the report states" to indicate that you're summarizing someone else's ideas and claims, not your own. At the start of a summary, state the author's name, credentials, and the title of the work so it's clear what you're referring to. While you may quote notable phrases or key terms, your summary should be made up of mostly your own unique language and sentence structure. And any text you summarize should be documented in a list of works cited or references.

Consider visuals. Not all summaries are written text: summaries can also be presented visually. In scientific, technical, or social science writing, charts, graphs, or maps often summarize key information and data from other sources. For example, the following map from the US Census Bureau shows the most-used language other than English or Spanish in each of the fifty states. The colorful visual presents the information in a way that's easier to understand (and more compact) than if the same data were presented using only words or lists.

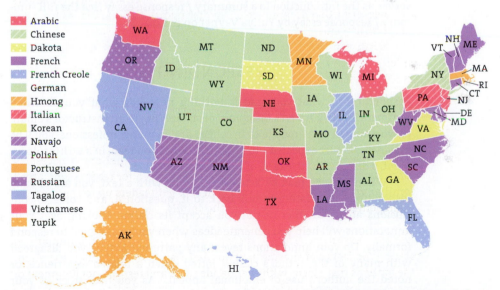

Source: U.S. Census Bureau's American Community Survey

A colorful US map shows each state's most commonly spoken language beyond English or Spanish, helping readers see regional trends and main takeaways at a glance.

A Sample Summary

Here is a summary of Katherine Spriggs's essay "On Buying Local" (see her full essay on p. 186):

> In her essay "On Buying Local," college student Katherine Spriggs argues that consumers should purchase food grown locally whenever possible. After demonstrating the environmental and practical reasons for doing so, Spriggs shows that buying local can offer an alternative to destructive mass farming, help small farmers and their families, build sustainable agricultural models, reduce the cost of shipping food from faraway places, and avoid the exploitation of workers, especially in third-world countries. In spite of a few drawbacks (local food may be more expensive, and seasonal variation may reduce the number of choices available), she concludes that shopping local is an easy lifestyle change that will make a big difference to our environment.

This is a fair and accurate summary of Spriggs's essay. It begins by stating the author's name and the title of the work and includes only the main points of the argument, restated in the writer's own words. This summary serves as the introduction to a summary / response essay (see the full summary / response essay by Yuliya Vayner on p. 87).

RESPONDING

Responding to what you read is nothing new—it's what you do when commenting on a friend's *Instagram* post, replying to an instructor's email, or weighing in on a group text. In college and in many professions, you'll be assigned—or just expected—to respond to what you read, in a written document, a discussion, an exam, or a presentation.

Whenever you read by actively engaging with a text, you are already responding—annotating to talk back to it, question it, and come to conclusions about whether or not you accept its claims. Looking over your annotations will help you generate ideas when you're assigned to respond formally. Do your annotations reveal any patterns? Maybe you disagreed with many of the author's claims, jotted down a related experience, or noted the author's use of emotional appeals. As you take stock of your annotations, consider which of the following ways you'll respond to what you've read: argue with what the text says, analyze the way it says it, or reflect on its ideas.

Respond to what a text says, agreeing or disagreeing with its position—or both. However you respond, you'll be making an **ARGUMENT** for what you say. Before you come to any final conclusions, keep an open mind by saying "yes," "no," and "maybe" to the text. First say "yes" by making an effort to understand the way the author sees the topic and where they're coming from. Doing so can be especially important if you find yourself strongly disagreeing with the author's position. Then say "maybe" to any passages that seem confusing or poorly supported—and consider why. Finally, look for anything to which you feel obligated to say "no," and think about why it seems unacceptable or just plain wrong. Here are some questions to consider when you're responding to what a text says:

- What does the text **CLAIM**, and what **REASONS** and **EVIDENCE** does the author provide?
- Do you agree or disagree with the author's position? Why?
- Does the author acknowledge any other positions? If so, are they treated fairly? What other perspectives should be addressed?
- Has the author overlooked anything?
- Is it clear why the topic matters, why anyone should care?
- What's the larger **CONTEXT**? How does the text fit into the larger conversation on the topic? Is the author's point corroborated by what others have said, or is it a claim that hardly anyone else agrees with?

Analyze the way a text is written to figure out how it works, what makes it tick. Here are some questions to consider when you're analyzing how a text is written:

- What does the text **CLAIM**? Is it stated explicitly—and if not, should it be? Has it been carefully qualified—and if not, does it need to be?
- Look for and assess the **REASONS** and **EVIDENCE** provided in support of the claim. Are you persuaded? If not, what other kinds of evidence would help?
- Does the author use emotional, ethical, or logical appeals? Do you notice any logical **FALLACIES**?

- Has the writer mentioned any **COUNTERARGUMENTS** or alternative points of view? If so, are they described respectfully and fairly? And how does the writer respond—by acknowledging that other writers have a point? Refuting what they say?

- How does the author use **LANGUAGE**? Do they meet or challenge their audience's expectations? Do they take risks with language? How effective are their language choices?

- How has the author established **AUTHORITY** to write on this topic? Do you think the text is trustworthy and fair?

- What design elements help convey the text's main message?

Reflect on a text's ideas by drawing connections to your own personal experiences, beliefs, or ways of thinking. Maybe the text leads you to see a topic in a new light, question your assumptions and biases, or wonder about how your beliefs influenced your reaction. Here are some questions to consider when you're reflecting on a text's ideas:

- What impact has the reading had on you—as a student, scholar, citizen, and researcher? What are the big takeaways for you personally?

- Did any parts of the text make you feel uneasy, laugh, or cry? Investigate why.

- Which past experiences or memories did you recall while reading the text? Can you relate to anything in the text? Why or why not?

- Does the text challenge or uphold any of your beliefs? Or cause you to question some of your assumptions and biases?

- What other texts, images, videos, recordings, etc., does the text remind you of?

- What lessons, insights, or ideas has the text taught you? How might you apply those lessons in your own writing or thinking?

SUMMARY / RESPONSE ESSAYS

A summary / response essay demonstrates that you have engaged with a text, understand its main message, and have something to say as a result. This assignment is common in first-year writing classes because of the focus on critical reading and supporting a position with evidence. Unless the assignment names other requirements, your summary / response should cover the following ground.

A Fair, Accurate, and Concise Summary

A fair and objective summary of the text to which you are responding is essential. To make your subject crystal clear, begin by stating the author, title, and author's credentials. And keep the following points in mind:

- Include the main claims and primary supporting points of the text, and exclude examples or supporting ideas that aren't essential to the text's main message.
- Use an even and objective **TONE**. Would the author of the text find your summary fair and accurate?
- Be concise. Most summaries of full texts are 100 to 125 words, giving readers enough information to understand what you're responding to without unnecessary details.
- Make it clear that you are summarizing someone else's text by using **SIGNAL PHRASES** like "according to X." Words such as "asserts," "argues," and "examines" are also good signals—just be sure they are neutral. Include quotations only when keywords and phrases are central to the overall argument.

A Clear Response, Supported by Evidence

Your response is the meat of a summary / response essay. There's more than one way to respond to a text. See if you're being asked to respond in a particular way—for example, to "assess the author's argument and take a stance" or "analyze how effectively the text addresses its intended audience." If the assignment isn't specific, think about what you're most interested in doing: responding to what the text says, analyzing how the text works, reflecting on the text's ideas, or some combination. No matter how you respond, support your position with evidence.

- If you're responding to what the text says, take a position—agreeing, disagreeing, or both. State your position explicitly in a **THESIS STATEMENT**.

Support your position with evidence from the text and from outside sources, if necessary. Facts, statistics, anecdotal evidence, and textual evidence can serve as support. Think about and address any **COUNTERARGUMENTS** to your position.

- If you're analyzing how the text works, you'll describe both what the text is saying and the strategies used to convey the message. You might analyze a text's organization, **DICTION**, language choices, use of appeals, design, or other elements. Include evidence from the text to demonstrate the features or strategies you're analyzing. Be sure you state your main takeaway in an explicit thesis statement. Why did you choose to analyze what you did and why does it matter?

- If you're reflecting on the text's ideas, you'll likely explain some way in which the text impacted you personally or evoked a particular emotion, memory, or idea. Passages from the text that prompted your response should be cited as evidence. And your own beliefs, experiences, or emotions might serve to support and explain your personal response. Boil down your main point in a thesis statement—even a reflection should tell readers what you're saying and why it matters.

A Logical Organization

A summary / response can be organized in different ways, and your assignment may ask for a specific structure. Here are some general ways of structuring a summary / response to help you get started:

- Summarize first, and then respond: introduce and summarize the text, then state your thesis (this might all fall in the first paragraph). Then respond to the text, providing supporting points for your thesis. End by summing up your response and its implications.

- Summarize and respond point-by-point: introduce the text and state your thesis. Then summarize a claim or strategy from the text and respond to it. Do this for as many supporting points as you have to develop and defend your thesis. End by summing up your response and its implications.

YULIYA VAYNER, a former Hunter College student, summarizes and responds to Katherine Spriggs's essay "On Buying Local" in the following example. You can read Spriggs's full essay on page 186. Vayner primarily responds to what the text says—taking a position that both agrees and disagrees with Spriggs's argument. This essay is organized around several counterarguments that Vayner says Spriggs does not address.

The Higher Price of Buying Local

YULIYA VAYNER

IN HER ESSAY "On Buying Local," Katherine Spriggs argues that consumers should purchase food grown locally whenever possible. After demonstrating the environmental and practical reasons for doing so, Spriggs shows that buying local can offer an alternative to destructive mass farming, help small farmers and their families, build sustainable agricultural models, reduce the cost of shipping food from faraway places, and avoid the exploitation of workers, especially in third-world countries. Though Spriggs acknowledges that buying local can be inconvenient (local food may be more expensive, and seasonal variation may reduce the number of choices available), she argues that the benefit outweighs the inconvenience and concludes that shopping local is an easy lifestyle change that will make a big difference to our environment.

Begins with a concise summary.

But is buying local truly an "easy step" that "everyone can take"? Is inconvenience the only drawback? There are at least two

Articulates a key question that motivates and grounds the analysis.

additional challenges to buying local that Spriggs doesn't acknowledge in her analysis: cost and access. It's clear that buying locally
grown food benefits the environment, but because cost and access limit some people from being able to buy local, it is not a habit
everyone is equally able to practice.

Spriggs makes a convincing argument that giving up a bit of
convenience in return for a healthier environment is a worthy
trade. In discussing polyculture farming (producing a variety of
crops from the same land—an approach small farms tend to prefer), Spriggs juxtaposes personal convenience and environmental
benefits. She concedes that being unable to buy whatever produce
we want whenever we want is less convenient than most consumers are used to but suggests this sacrifice would allow farmers
to harvest from healthier soil and foster a healthier environment.
Spriggs explains that while monoculture farms (producing a small
number of single crops—the approach large mass-production
farms use) provide the convenience of year-round access to
produce, they do so by resorting to "modern fertilizers, herbicides, and pesticides [that] allow farmers to harvest crops from
even unhealthy land" (190). By giving up the convenience of eating strawberries at any time of year, Americans could begin to
rely less on chemical treatments that damage the environment
and more on natural resources through what Spriggs calls "dual
usage"—like using pigs to plow blueberry fields and putting cows
to pasture in last year's cornfields. Considering the environmental
damage that large-scale farming causes, sacrificing convenience is
a small price to pay for a healthier land and atmosphere.

However, Spriggs doesn't acknowledge that some people
would be giving up more than just evergreen strawberries in an
attempt to buy local. For many, lack of access to any fresh produce at all is an issue, making the sacrifice of buying produce
that's locally sourced unaffordable. According to a recent report
by the US Department of Agriculture's Economic Research Service, an estimated 1 in 8 Americans or 40 million people experienced food insecurity, which is defined as "a lack of consistent
access to enough food for an active, healthy life" in 2017 ("What
Is Food Insecurity?"). So when Spriggs argues that there's little
reason to ship strawberries from California all over the United

---

A thesis statement offers a clear position.

Agrees with part of Spriggs's argument and explains why.

Summarizes Spriggs's argument in her own words.

Quotes specific details from Spriggs's essay.

Quotes a key term and defines it in her own words.

Notes an argument that Spriggs does not address: how will people who live in food deserts access locally produced foods?

States when they can easily be grown closer to the customers who want to eat them, she fails to acknowledge that there are areas that can't readily access or grow fresh produce (190). These areas are sometimes called food deserts: areas that have limited access to affordable and nutritious food, forcing residents to rely on food sold at convenience stores or fast-food chains, which is often highly processed and of limited nutritional value ("Why Low-Income and Food-Insecure People"). These food deserts exist overwhelmingly in low-income areas, and studies have shown that "both poverty and race matter when it comes to having healthy food options" (Brooks). So, although Spriggs does not mention these issues, buying local is also a question of access—which is impacted by race and income level rather than being purely one about convenience and ease.

Time becomes an issue of access as well: for some a long drive to a grocery store is merely inconvenient. For others, there simply aren't enough hours in a day to make an extended trip for fresh, local produce. People living below the poverty line tend to work multiple jobs (Sherman); in addition, they may also be responsible for household errands and family care. Lower-income families are not only less likely to have places nearby that sell locally grown food, they are also less likely to have the time and the means to visit them ("Why Low-Income and Food-Insecure People"). Even when locally grown food can be found within a reasonable distance, it may still be out of reach for those living on a limited income.

Here's another argument Spriggs doesn't cover.

This adds yet another aspect to the challenge of buying local that Spriggs doesn't address: low-income individuals are significantly less likely to be able to afford the extra expense of locally sourced food, which Spriggs explains as only slightly pricier. Yet, "slightly more expensive than 'industrially grown' food" (Spriggs 192) is subjective. Not only would buying local potentially strain the budgets of those struggling to get by, it could also make it more difficult to make use of government assistance, especially since farmers' markets have struggled to obtain the necessary equipment to process SNAP, a government assistance program that provides a monthly supplement for purchasing nutritious foods (Andrews). So for many, buying local is not just an

A third counterargument Spriggs doesn't cover: the financial expense of buying local.

inconvenience, it's not a financial possibility. Furthermore, the price gap seems wider than Spriggs admits; a journalist for *The Washington Post* reports that in 2016 "cage-free eggs, cheese, mushrooms, salad mix and both organic and conventional strawberries" came to be $64.62 at the local market in Richmond, Virginia—"I could have bought them all from Kroger for $31.37" (Hise). At nearly double the price, this difference is far from Spriggs's claim that buying local is only "slightly more expensive" (192). The price increase that comes with buying local is not a mere inconvenience but rather a question of affordability for many.

Concludes by summarizing her own argument in response to Spriggs.

While Spriggs succeeds in showing that buying local can contribute to a healthier environment, in addressing the obvious drawback of inconvenience she considers only one aspect of a complex issue involving race, income level, and access. The inconvenience of buying local comes at a much higher price for some people, a fact Spriggs leaves out. People who are struggling to make ends meet cannot always afford this social and economic privilege, nor do they always have access to this privilege. To many, industrially grown food is a necessity rather than, as Spriggs suggests, a convenience.

Works Cited

Andrews, Michelle. "Technical Difficulties May Jeopardize Food
Stamps at Farmers Markets." *NPR*, 5 Nov. 2018, www.npr
.org/sections/thesalt/2018/11/05/662322655/technical
-difficulties-may-jeopardize-food-stamps-at-farmers
-markets.

Brooks, Kelly. "Research Shows Food Deserts More Abundant
in Minority Neighborhoods." *Johns Hopkins Magazine*,
10 Mar. 2014. *The Hub*, Johns Hopkins U, hub.jhu.edu
/magazine/2014/spring/racial-food-deserts/.

Hise, Phaedra. "Why Does a Strawberry Grown Down the Road
Cost More than One Grown in California?" *The Washington
Post*, 21 June 2016, www.washingtonpost.com/lifestyle
/food/why-local-food-costs-more-a-strawberry-case
-study/2016/06/20/c7177c56-331f-11e6-8ff7-7b6c1998b7a0
_story.html.

Sherman, Erik. "More People Probably Work Multiple Jobs than
the Government Realizes." *Forbes*, 22 July 2018, www
.forbes.com/sites/eriksherman/2018/07/22/more-people
-probably-work-multiple-jobs-than-the-government-realizes.

Spriggs, Katherine. "On Buying Local." *Everyone's an Author*, by
Andrea A. Lunsford et al., W. W. Norton, 2022, pp. 186–94.

"What Is Food Insecurity in America?" *Hunger and Health*,
Feeding America, hungerandhealth.feedingamerica.org
/understand-food-insecurity/.

"Why Low-Income and Food-Insecure People Are Vulnerable to
Poor Nutrition and Obesity." *Food Research & Action
Center*, www.opportunityhome.org/wp-content/uploads
/2018/04/frac_org.pdf.

REFLECT. *Think about something you were recently assigned to read. What was your purpose for reading? What strategies from this chapter, if any, did you use to achieve that purpose? Re-read the text again, this time preparing to write a brief 250- to 500-word summary / response. Practice annotating, summarizing, and responding using the guidelines in this chapter. How did reading in preparation to respond change your reading process? What did you find challenging—and not so challenging—about writing a brief summary / response?*

EIGHT

Distinguishing Facts from Misinformation

POPE FRANCIS Says 'God Has Instructed Me to Revise the Ten Commandments.'" "Palestinians Recognize Texas as Part of Mexico." "Canada Bans Beyoncé after Her Super Bowl Performance." Really? Well, actually, no. While these are actual headlines, not one is anywhere near true. But being false hasn't kept them from being widely shared—and not as jokes but as facts. With people spreading misinformation, unsubstantiated claims, and even outright lies, it can be hard to know whom and what to trust or whether to trust anything at all. The good news is that you don't have to be taken in by such misinformation. This chapter provides strategies for navigating the choppy waters of news and information so that you can make confident decisions about what to trust—and what not to.

Defining Facts and Misinformation

Some say we are living in a "post-truth" era, when the loudest voices take up so much airtime that they can sometimes be seen as telling the truth no matter what they say. A 2018 study by MIT scholars examined tweets about every major contested news story in English across the ten years of *Twitter*'s existence and came to the conclusion that satirist Jonathan

Swift was right: "the truth simply can't compete with hoax and rumor." In fact, the study says, "fake news and false rumors reach more people, penetrate deeper into the social network, and spread much faster than accurate stories."

It's worth asking why misinformation outperforms real news. While it is notoriously difficult to establish airtight cause-and-effect relationships, these researchers suspect that several reasons account for the "success" of

Try these tips to help you distinguish fact from fake.

false stories. First, they're often outlandish in a way that attracts attention. Second, the content of such stories is often negative and tends to arouse strong emotions. Third, they use language that evokes surprise or disgust, as compared to accurate tweets, which, the researchers found, use words associated with trust or sadness rather than surprise or disgust: as they note, "the truth simply does not compete." For all these reasons, misinformation tends to attract attention and spread quickly.

Lies and misinformation are nothing new. What's new is that anyone with an internet connection can post whatever they think (or want others to think) online, where it can easily reach a wide audience. And unlike traditional newspapers and other publications, it can go out without being vetted by editors or fact-checkers.

Perhaps it's time to step back, take a deep breath, and attend to some basic definitions. Just what is a "fact"? What's "misinformation"? And what about "disinformation"? Both misinformation and disinformation are untrue statements; what makes them different is the motive behind each. Misinformation is factually incorrect, but the error may not be intentional; disinformation, on the other hand, is purposely misleading and designed to cause harm. The person who spreads disinformation intends to deceive the audience; it's not an innocent mistake. And "fake news," a form of disinformation, is fabricated information presented as authentic news. It's a common method for spreading conspiracy theories or deliberate hoaxes, and the more bizarre the better: "The FBI planned and executed the January 6 Capitol riot!," "Ocasio-Cortez: 'If Food Runs Scarce, It's Okay to Eat Pets.'" While some people may dismiss anything they don't like or agree with as fake, we know that facts can be independently verified and supported by reliable evidence.

Think about Your Own Beliefs

It's one thing to be able to spot unsubstantiated claims and exaggerations in the words of others, but it's another thing entirely to spot them in your own thinking and writing. So you need to take a good look at your own assumptions and biases (we all have them!).

ATTRIBUTION BIAS is the tendency to think that your motives for believing, say, that the Environmental Protection Agency (EPA) is crucially important for keeping our air and water clean are objective or good while the motives of those who believe the EPA is not at all necessary are dubious or bad. We all have this kind of bias naturally, tending to believe that what we think must be right. When you're thinking about an argument you strongly disagree with, then, it's a good idea to ask yourself why you disagree—and why you believe you're right. What is that belief based on? Have you considered that your own bias may be keeping you from seeing all sides of the issue fairly, or at all?

CONFIRMATION BIAS is the tendency to favor and seek out information that confirms what we already believe and to reject and ignore information that contradicts those beliefs. Many studies have documented this phenomenon. For example, a Stanford University experiment gathered forty-eight students, half of whom favored capital punishment and thought it was a deterrent to crime and half of whom opposed capital punishment. Researchers then asked students to respond to two studies: one provided data that supported capital punishment as a deterrent to crime; the other provided data that called this conclusion into question. Sure enough, the

students who were in favor of capital punishment rated the study that showed evidence that it was a deterrent as "more highly credible," while the students who were against capital punishment rated the study that showed evidence that it did not deter crime as "more highly credible"—in spite of the fact that both studies had been made up by the researchers. Moreover, by the end of the experiment, each side had doubled down on its original beliefs.

That's confirmation bias at work, and it works on all of us. It affects the way we search for information and what we pay attention to, how we interpret it, and even what we remember. So don't assume information is trustworthy just because it confirms what you already think. Ask yourself if you're seeing what you want to see. And look for confirmation bias in your sources; do they acknowledge viewpoints other than their own?

Read Defensively and Find the Good Stuff

Well over two thousand years ago, the philosopher Aristotle said that one reason people need rhetoric is self-defense, for making sure that we aren't being deceived, manipulated, or lied to. Today, the need for such caution may be more important than ever when false stories often look authentic and appear right next to accurate, factual information online. These times call, then, for what we think of as defensive reading—the kind of reading that doesn't take things at face value, that questions underlying assumptions, that scrutinizes claims carefully, and that does not rush to judgment. This is the kind of reading that media and technology critic Howard Rheingold calls "crap detection." Crap, he says sardonically, is a "technical term" he uses to describe information "tainted by ignorance or deliberate deception." He warns us not to give in to such misinformation:

> Some critics argue that a tsunami of hogwash has already rendered the web useless. I disagree. We are indeed inundated by online noise pollution, but the problem is soluble. The good stuff is out there if you know how to find and verify it.
>
> —HOWARD RHEINGOLD, "Crap Detection 101"

As Rheingold and many others note, there is no single foolproof way to identify misinformation. But we can offer some advice, along with some specific strategies.

Triangulate—and use your judgment. Find three different ways to check on whether a story can be trusted. Google the author or the sponsor. Check *FactCheck.org* or *Snopes*. Look for other sources that are reporting the same story, especially if you first saw it on social media. If it's true and important, you should find a number of other reputable sources reporting on it. But however carefully you check, and whatever facts and evidence you uncover, it's up to you to sort the accurate information from the misinformation— and to use your own judgment.

Before reading an unfamiliar source, determine whether it's trustworthy. History professor Sam Wineburg and his research team have found that professional fact-checkers don't even start to read an unfamiliar website until they've determined that it's trustworthy. They practice LATERAL READING, or going outside of the source and opening new tabs to investigate it instead of scrutinizing only the source itself. Here are some ways to do so:

- Open a new tab and do a search about the author or sponsor. What's the author's expertise? Be wary if there's no author. Does the author belong to any organizations you don't know or trust? Look up any unfamiliar organizations to see what reliable sources have to say. And do a search about the site's sponsor. If the website is run by an organization you've never heard of, find out what it is—and whether it actually exists. What do reliable sources say about it? Read the site's About page, but check up on what it says. As Wineburg says, "If an organization can game what they are, they can certainly game their About page!"

- Check any links to see who sponsors the site and whether they are trustworthy sources. Do the same for works cited in print sources.

- Be careful of over-the-top headlines, which often serve as clickbait to draw you in. Check to see that the story and the headline actually match. Question any exaggerated words like "amazing," "epic," "incredible," or "unbelievable." (In general, don't believe anything that's said to be unbelievable!)

- Pay attention to design. Be wary if it looks amateurish, but don't assume that a professional-looking design means the source is accurate or trustworthy. Those who create fake news sites often design them to look like real news sites.

- Recognize satire! Remember that some authors make a living by writing satirical fake news articles. Here's one: "China Slaps Two-Thousand-Per-Cent Tariff on Tanning Beds." This comes from Andy Borowitz, who writes political satire in the *New Yorker*, which tips us off not to take it seriously by the label "not the news." The *Onion* is another source that pokes fun at gullible readers. Try this: "Genealogists Find 99% of People Not Related to Anyone Cool." This one's silly enough that it can't possibly be true. But if you're not sure, better check.

Ask questions, and check evidence. Double-check things that too neatly support what you yourself think.

Jia Tolentino's review of *Coco* on p. 973 was originally published in the *New Yorker*, a magazine with an excellent reputation for fact-checking. But for some practice, go ahead and do some fact-checking of the statements and facts Tolentino includes about the movie.

- What's the **CLAIM**, and what **EVIDENCE** is provided? What motivates the author to write, and what's their **PURPOSE** —to provide information? make you laugh? convince you of something?
- Check facts and claims using nonpartisan sites that confirm truths and identify lies. *FactCheck.org*, *Snopes*, and *AllSides* are three such sites. Copy and paste the basics of the statement into the search field; if it's information the site has in its database, you'll find out whether it's a confirmed fact or lie. If you use *Google* to check on a stated fact, keep in mind that you'll need to check on any sources there—and that even if the statement brings up many hits, that doesn't make it accurate.
- Don't assume a story or an image must be true—especially if it seems outrageous. Do research on stories; if they are true, they will be widely reported. On the other hand, double-check stories that confirm your own beliefs; assuming they're true might well be **CONFIRMATION BIAS** at work.
- Look up any research that's cited. You may find that the research has been taken out of context or misquoted—or that it doesn't actually exist. Is the research itself reliable? Pay close attention to quotations: who said it, and when? Is it believable? If not, copy and paste the quotation into *Google* or check *FactCheck.org* to verify that it's real.
- Check the comments. If several say the article sounds fake, it may well be. But remember that given the presence of trolls and people with malicious intent, comments can't be taken at face value, either.

Fact-Check Photos and Videos

Is a picture really worth a thousand words? In some cases, but only if the picture is an accurate depiction. It's never been easier to falsify photographs. Look at the image below of a pilot leaning from the cockpit of a commercial airliner to snap a selfie as the plane departs. While his tie blowing in the wind might seem authentic, look again: airspeed at that altitude would have sucked him out and into the engine. Besides, in his original caption he

Brazilian pilot Daniel Centeno used *Photoshop* to superimpose a selfie over a photo of a plane in flight. See the airport runway reflected in his sunglasses.

noted: "Photoshop mode ON!" Be vigilant and examine images (and information) closely!

There are no simple, foolproof ways to identify doctored photos, but
experts in digital forensics recommend various steps we can take. There are
numerous webpages with tips and techniques for spotting fake photos; run
a search and bookmark one or two that you like for future reference. Here's
advice from Hany Farid, a computer science professor at the University of
California at Berkeley:

- Do a reverse image search, using *Google Images* or *Tin Eye*, to see if an
  image has been recirculated or repurposed from another website. Both
  sites allow you to drag an image or paste a link to an image into a search
  bar to learn more about the image's source and see where else the image
  appears online.

- Check *Snopes*, where altered images are often identified, by typing a
  brief description of the image into the *Snopes* search box.

- Look carefully at shadows and reflections: an image may have been
  altered if you find shadows where you don't expect them or don't see
  them where you do expect them.

Farid goes on to say that the best defense against fabricated photos is "to
stop and think about the source"—especially before you share it with others.
After a shooter killed seventeen people at a Florida school in 2018, an altered
photo of Emma González, one student survivor who advocated for stronger
gun laws, went viral, showing her tearing up a page of the US Constitution.
In fact, she was actually tearing up a shooting target as part of her advocacy
for gun control.

The same advice holds true for researching suspicious video, which
is also easy to falsify. Videos that flicker constantly or that consist of just
one short clip are often questionable, as are videos of famous people doing
things that are highly suspicious. The example that follows is one of many
tweets posted from numerous accounts supposedly capturing a frenzied
rush by Afghans trying to flee Kabul in August 2021. The video clip was
actually first tweeted by a sports journalist in January 2019, and it shows
Dallas Cowboys fans rushing into AT&T Stadium for an NFL game, as you
can see in the second image. This fake video was exposed by Reuters Fact
Check, a good resource to remember.

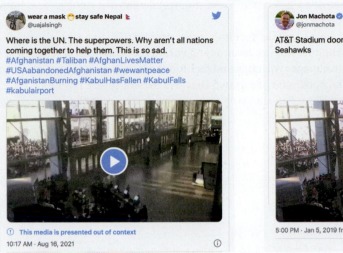

People trying to flee Afghanistan or rushing into an NFL stadium? It's the latter, though at least one tweet claimed this video showed a Kabul airport.

Such fabricated videos and deepfakes proliferate, especially on *YouTube*. The *Guardian* warns that "advances in artificial intelligence and computer graphics . . . allow for the creation of realistic looking footage of public figures appearing to say, well, anything." Using the fact-finding and defensive-reading strategies described in this chapter, we hope you'll become able to sort out fact from fiction and determine with confidence who and what you can trust in all the kinds of reading you do—from keeping up with the news and scanning your friends' social media posts to conducting research for a project at school or work.

PART III

Writing Processes

IMAGINE THAT YOU are living in the Middle Ages and that you know how to write (a rare skill at that time). Now imagine the processes you have to engage in to do that writing. You might well begin by making the surface you need to write on, probably parchment or vellum made from animal skins—a process that takes several days.

Once you have something to write on, you make lines across the page to "rule" it and guide your writing. When at last you're ready to begin to write, you do so with a quill pen crafted out of a feather that had its end sharpened into a "nib" with a slit in the middle through which the ink

The medieval equivalent to a blank *Word* document: writers began by making their own writing surfaces, first soaking animal skins to remove the fur, then stretching and scraping them until they were the right thickness.

flows onto the parchment. Woe to you if you make a mistake, for correction is exceedingly difficult—or impossible. And once the writing is done, you still might not be finished if you need to illustrate the manuscript, as in the "illuminated" page from *The Canterbury Tales* on the facing page.

Because the process was so complicated, writing often demanded a team approach. In fact, "book" is defined in an early German encyclopedia as a "work of many hands."

With the advent of the printing press and subsequent technological developments, such material aspects of the writing process became easier, so much so that they became somewhat invisible: writers simply *wrote*. The focus, especially in schools, shifted to the final product, one composed by individual students; any concern with the process, as well as with writing's collaborative aspects, disappeared entirely. And so for many years, the emphasis on the final or "published" piece kept us from seeing the many other processes of writing, from generating ideas to hypothesizing, drafting, revising, and more. Writing involves far more than putting words down on a page and checking punctuation. For any important piece of writing,

"The Knight's Tale." An illuminated page from *The Canterbury Tales*, circa 1410.

the author must think the message through in many ways to understand and communicate it to an audience. As researcher Janet Emig has concluded, writing is a unique form of learning, and understanding it calls for understanding the complex processes involved.

In studying just how those processes work, researchers have lately returned to the medieval notion that a piece of writing is the "work of many hands," recognizing that almost all writing is highly social, created by one or more writers in conversation with many others, from those who have influenced us in the past to those who read and respond to our work. By the end of the twentieth century, the popular image of a writer as a solitary figure (almost always a man) holed up in a tiny room struggling to create an individual work of great genius began to give way to that of a writer as part of an elaborate network, what author Steven Johnson called "connected minds."

The kind of networking now available through the internet and especially through social media surely does involve "connected minds." English poet John Donne's insight that no one "is an island, apart from the main" has never been more true than it is today, as writers around the globe collaborate on everything from a *Google Doc* to a flash mob to a protest movement like Black Lives Matter.

The chapters that follow invite you to think hard about the processes you engage in when you write and about how those processes involve other writers (those you write with and those you write to). We hope that such thinking will not only make you more aware of how, when, and where you write but also help to make your writing processes more efficient—and more fun!

NINE

Managing the Writing Process

THINK OF SOMETHING YOU LIKE TO DO: ride a bike, play a certain video game, do Sudoku. If you think about it, you'll see that each of these activities involves learning a process that took some effort to get right when you first started doing it. But eventually, the process became familiar, and now you do it almost automatically.

Writing is much the same. It, too, is a process: a series of activities that takes some effort to do well. And as with any process, you can manage the writing process by approaching it in parts. This chapter introduces the various stages of the writing process—from generating ideas and coming up with a topic to drafting and revising—and provides strategies that will help you make the most of the many writing demands you'll encounter at school, at work, and elsewhere.

One important aspect of becoming comfortable with the writing process is figuring out what works best for you. No single process works for every author or every writing task, so work instead to develop a repertoire of strategies that will enable you to become an efficient, productive, and effective writer.

Develop writing habits that work for you. Think about how you usually approach a writing task. Do you draw up extensive outlines? Do you

Writing involves complex processes and often the "work of many hands."

organize visually or use note cards? Do you write best at a particular time of the day? Do you write best with solitude and quiet—or do you like to have music playing? Think carefully about what habits seem to help you produce your best work.

WRITING PROCESSES / A Roadmap

Whatever processes you find most productive, following are some tips that provide general guidance. If and when you decide on a particular genre, you'll find genre-specific guidance in the Roadmaps in Chapters 13–18.

Understand your assignment. If you're writing in response to an assignment, make sure you understand what it asks you to do. Does it specify a topic? a theme? a genre? Look for words like "argue," "evaluate," and "analyze"—words that specify a GENRE and thus point you to approach your topic in a certain way. An assignment that asks you to analyze, for example, lets you know that you should break down your topic into parts that can then be examined closely. If your assignment doesn't name a genre, think about which genre will best suit your rhetorical situation.

Come up with a topic. If you get to choose your topic, think of things you are particularly interested in and want to know more about—or something that puzzles you or poses a problem you'd like to solve or that gets you fired up. If your topic is assigned, try to find an aspect or angle that interests you. Looking for a particular angle on a topic can help you to narrow your focus, but don't worry if the topic you come up with right now isn't very specific: as you do research, you'll be able to narrow and refine it.

Consider your RHETORICAL SITUATION. Whether you're writing an argument or a narrative, working alone or with a group, you'll have an audience, a purpose, a stance, a genre, a medium and design, and a context. You'll also make choices about language. These are all things you should be considering as you move through your writing process.

- *Audience.* Whom are you addressing? What do they likely know or believe about your topic? What do you want them to think or do in response to your writing?

- *Purpose.* What is your goal in writing? What has motivated you to write, and what do you wish to accomplish?

- *Stance.* What is your attitude toward your topic? What perspective do you offer on it? What's your relationship with your audience, and how do you want to be seen by them?

- *Genre.* Have you been assigned a specific genre? If not, which genre(s) will best suit your purpose and audience?

- *Medium and design.* What medium or media will best suit your audience, purpose, and message? What design elements are possible (or required) in these media?

- *Context.* Consider the conversation surrounding your argument. What has been said about your topic, and how does that affect what you say? What about your immediate context—when is your writing due, and are there any other requirements or constraints?

- *Language.* What are your audience's expectations for language and style? Do you want to meet those expectations? challenge them? What do you want your language to say about you? What risks might you be willing to take with your language?

Schedule your time. Think about how to fit your writing project into your schedule. Taking a series of small steps is easier than doing it all at once. So schedule periodic goals for yourself: meeting them will build your confidence and reinforce good writing habits.

Generate ideas. Writing can help us explore a topic and can even lead us to new ideas. Here are some activities that can help you sort out what you already know about your topic—and come up with new ideas about it:

- *Brainstorming* is a way to generate ideas without worrying about whether they're useful or not. Take a few minutes to focus on your topic or thesis (or a broad idea you want to develop into a specific topic or thesis) and list, using words or phrases, everything that occurs to you about this subject. Then review what you have written, looking for ideas that seem promising and relationships that you can develop. Remember: there are no right answers at this point!

- *Clustering* is a strategy for generating and processing ideas visually. Take a sheet of paper and write a word or phrase that best summarizes or evokes your topic. Draw a circle around this word. Now fill in the page by adding related words and ideas, circling them and connecting them to the original word, forming clusters. Then look at all the clusters to see what patterns you can find or where your ideas seem to be leading.

- *Freewriting* is a strategy for writing ideas down quickly, without stopping. To freewrite, simply write about whatever comes into your head in relation to a particular idea or topic for several minutes. Be careful not to censor yourself: let your ideas flow as freely as possible. You may

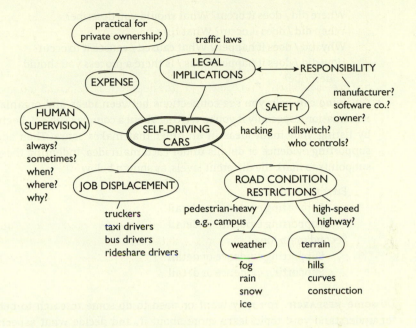

be surprised at the complexity and power of the ideas that you can develop through this process.

- *Looping* is an extended and more focused kind of freewriting. Begin by establishing a subject and then freewrite for several minutes. Look at what you've written. Identify the most important or interesting or promising idea and write a sentence summarizing it. Use this sentence to start another "loop" of freewriting. Repeat this process as many times as necessary.

- *Drawing or sketching a picture of your topic* can help spark and guide your thinking about it. See if creating a series of sketches can help you figure out the structure of an essay you're writing.

- *Questioning* is an especially good way of exploring a topic. Starting with questions can help you discover what you already know about your topic—and, just as important, what you don't know and need to learn. Try starting with the questions "Who?" "What?" "Where?" "When?" "Why?" "How?"

    Who was / is involved? What can you say about them?
    What happened / happens?

Where did / does it occur? What should you describe?

When did / does it occur? What time?

Why did / does it happen? What caused / causes it to occur?

How did / does it happen? Was / is there a process you should describe?

- *Outlining* can help you see connections between ideas and organize information, especially if you're writing about a complex subject. Begin by listing your main ideas in an order that makes sense. Then add supporting evidence or details under each main idea, indenting these subpoints to mark the different levels, as shown below:

First main idea
    Supporting evidence or detail
    Supporting evidence or detail
Second main idea
    Supporting evidence or detail
    Supporting evidence or detail

Do some RESEARCH. You may want or need to do some research to better understand your topic, learn more about it, and decide what aspects of it you want to explore further. This could mean reading about your topic, **INTERVIEWING** experts about it, conducting surveys and informal interviews, observing something firsthand, or some combination of those methods. Learning what others have said about a topic is an important step to figuring out what you want to say—and to joining the conversation.

Notice how Dennis Baron weaves together observations of current language use and trends with historical research. Find his essay on p. 844.

Come up with a tentative THESIS, a statement that identifies your topic and the point you want to make about it. You'll rarely, if ever, have a final thesis when you start writing, but establishing a tentative one will help focus your thinking and any research you may do. Here are some prompts to get you started.

1. *What point do you want to make about your topic?* Try writing it out as a promise to your audience: "In this essay, I will present reasons for people to limit their social media use."

2. *Try plotting out a tentative thesis in two parts,* the first stating your topic, the second making some claim about the topic:

    ⌐———— **TOPIC** ————⌐———— **CLAIM** ————⌐
Limiting your social media time will improve your self-esteem, provide

real-life social opportunities, and reduce vulnerability to hacking.

3. *Ask some questions about what you've written.* Will it engage your intended audience? What's your claim? Is it debatable? There's no point in staking a claim that is a fact, or one that no one would disagree with.

4. *Do you need to narrow or* QUALIFY *your thesis?* Can you do what you say you will, given the time and resources available? You don't want to overstate your case—or make a claim that you'll have trouble supporting. Adding words such as "could," "might," "likely," or "potentially" can qualify what you say: "Limiting the time you spend on social media might provide more real-life social opportunities, and it could improve self-esteem as well as reduce vulnerability to hacking."

5. *Is the thesis clear and focused?* Will it tell readers what's coming? And will it help keep you (and your readers) on track?

Keep in mind that at this point in your process, this is a tentative thesis, one that could change as you research, write, and revise. Continue to explore your topic. Don't stop until you feel you've reached a full understanding of your topic. As you learn more about it, you may well find that you want to revise your thesis. This is a good thing! Your position on your topic should change (even in the smallest ways) as you learn and think about it more.

Once you're satisfied that your thesis makes a clear claim that you can support, and one that will interest your readers, gather together the notes from your research. This is the information you'll draw from as support for your thesis.

ORGANIZE your ideas. Whether you like to write out an outline or prefer to do most of your planning on note cards or sticky notes (or in your head!), you'll want to think about how best to organize your text before beginning to write. Writing about events generally works best when told in CHRONOLOGICAL ORDER. And facts, data, and other EVIDENCE are usually most effective when stated in order of importance, starting with the information that's most crucial to your argument before stating the less important information. If you're describing something, you might organize your information SPATIALLY, beginning at one point and moving from left to right, or top to bottom. There's no one way to organize your writing; the order in which you present your points will depend on the topic and what you have to say about it.

Write out a draft. Keep your tentative thesis statement and any other notes and outlines close by as you start writing. A complete draft will include an introduction, a body, and a conclusion, though you may not necessarily draft them in that order.

- *The* **INTRODUCTION** is often the most difficult part to write, so some authors decide to write it last. But just as a well-crafted opening can help guide your readers, it can also help you get started writing. A good introduction should grab readers' attention, announce your topic and your claim, and indicate how you plan to proceed. A provocative question, an anecdote, a startling claim: these are some of the ways you might open an essay.

- *The body* of an essay is where you will develop your argument, point by point, paragraph by paragraph. Strategies such as **COMPARISON**, **DESCRIPTION**, **NARRATION**, and others can help you develop paragraphs to present **EVIDENCE** in support of your **THESIS**.

- *The* **CONCLUSION** should sum up your argument in a way that readers will remember. You might end by restating your claim, discussing the implications of your argument, calling for some action, or posing further questions—all ways of highlighting the significance of what you've said.

Be flexible, and make changes if you need to. Even the most well-planned writing doesn't show its true shape until you've written a full draft, so don't be surprised if you find that you need to reorganize, do additional research, or otherwise rethink your argument as you go. Be flexible! Rather than sticking stubbornly to a plan that doesn't seem to be working, use each draft and revision as an opportunity to revisit your plan and to think about how you can strengthen your argument or your appeal.

The ancient Greeks had a word for thinking about the opportunities presented by a particular rhetorical situation. They called it "kairos," and it referred to the ability to seize an opportune and timely moment. Kairos was the ancient Greek god of opportunity and perfect timing, qualities every author needs. He was often depicted as a young man running, and it was said that you must seize the forelock of his hair as he passes by; once he's passed, there's nothing to cling to because the back of his head is completely bald—you've missed your opportunity.

This is a concept that can be especially helpful when you're drafting—and that can also help you revise. As you work, think of each paragraph and sentence as an opportunity to add (or eliminate) detail, to reorganize, or to improve your point in some other way. Think about how your sentences and

Kairos

paragraphs might be received by your audience—and about how you can get readers to pay attention to and value what you say.

Get responses from others—from your instructor, a classmate, a writing center tutor. Be sure to tell them about any questions or concerns you have about the draft, and ask for their advice. But remember: you don't have to take all the advice you get, just what you consider helpful. You're the author!

Look at your draft with a critical eye and revise. You'll find genre-specific guidelines for reading a draft carefully and revising in the chapters on **ARGUMENTS**, **NARRATIVES**, **ANALYSES**, **REPORTS**, **REVIEWS**, and **PROPOSALS**. For more general advice, following are some prompts to help you read over a draft, either your own or one you're peer-reviewing for a fellow writer.

- How does the **INTRODUCTION** capture readers' attention and make them want to read on? Does it indicate that (or why) the topic matters? How else might it begin?

- How do you as the author come across—as well-informed? passionate? serious? something else?

- Is it clear what motivated you to write? Consider the larger **CONTEXT**: what else has been said about the topic, and have you considered perspectives other than your own?

- Is there an explicit **THESIS**? If not, does there need to be? If so, does it make clear what you are claiming about the topic?

- Is there sufficient support for the thesis? What **REASONS** and **EVIDENCE** do you provide? Will they be persuasive for the intended audience?

- Is the draft **ORGANIZED** in a way that is easy to follow? Check to see how each paragraph supports the thesis, and whether it is developed fully enough to make its point. Are there headings—and if not, should there be? Is there any information that would be easier to follow if set off as a list? Are there explicit **TRANSITIONS** to help readers follow the text—and if not, are they needed?

- What **LANGUAGE** and **STYLE** choices have you made? How are your choices meeting or challenging the expectations of your audience and context? How might your language and style choices do more to enliven your writing, engage your audience, and reflect your persona as an author?

- How does the text **CONCLUDE**? What does it leave readers thinking? How else might it conclude?

- Is there a title? If so, does it tell readers what your topic is and make them want to read on? If not, think in terms of **KAIROS**: the title is your first opportunity to indicate that this is a text about something that matters and that readers should care about.

Edit and proofread. Now's the time to pay close attention to the details. Review each sentence and edit so that every word (and punctuation mark!) supports the message you want to convey. Finally, take the time to proofread. Read with an eye for typos and inconsistencies. Make sure all your sentences are complete. Run a spell checker, but be aware that it is no substitute for careful proofreading.

An important part of your writing process is to reflect on it: examining the processes you've used, weighing the success of those processes, and identifying practices you want to keep—and those you want to drop or change. Chapter 10 provides advice on reflecting and the ways it can help you gain more awareness of your writing processes and yourself as a writer. For now, try the following prompt to get started.

REFLECT. Take some time to think about your writing process. What works well? What tends to be a struggle? What do you want to try to do differently? Think about the various ways and places in which you've been able to do good writing. Are you able to make them a regular part of your writing process?

Approach Your Writing Pragmatically

Even if you have a writing process that works well for you, that doesn't mean you complete all writing tasks the same way—or that you should. It's just common sense that you spend more time and take more care with your writing process for a fifteen-page research paper that counts for 40 percent of your final grade than you do for a much briefer, less formal essay that counts for 10 percent of that grade. Approach your writing pragmatically: consider how important your task is, what time constraints you face, what else you may have to do, what the nature of the task itself requires, and how well prepared you feel to complete it. Then, make realistic decisions. What do you *need* to do to complete an assignment effectively—and what *can* you do?

TEN

Reflecting on Your Writing

**A**T **HIS HIGH** school graduation, Akash Bobba spoke to his classmates, reflecting on what they had endured: "From unthinkable loss fueled by a pandemic, to civil unrest sparked by the death of George Floyd, . . . this last year has undoubtedly been painful and difficult for us as Pirates. . . ." But Bobba didn't stop there. In light of the strains he and his peers have faced, he went on to consider what's next, offering this advice:

> We live in an age where simplicity reigns supreme, where 30-second TikToks and 280-character tweets define our identities. This . . . willingness to simplify even the most complex narratives into sensational tidbits perpetuates misinformation and in the process divides the communities, families, and relationships we cherish. What's the solution, you might ask? Seek discomfort. If there's anything South [High School] has taught us, it's that the answers we deserve demand discomfort. From solving polynomials in Algebra II to breaking down Jacksonian democracy in [AP US History], our quest for understanding was often complex and difficult, challenging us to think past the superficial.

It is through reflecting—taking stock of the circumstances and contemplating what comes next—that Bobba imagines ways forward.

Big life moments—graduations, milestone accomplishments, the loss or gain of a loved one, moving to a new place—prompt us all to step back, make sense of what's happened, and plan for what's next. But you likely practice such reflection more regularly, too, maybe as you exercise, listen to music, or fall asleep at night. Jotting down what you're thinking can even enable it. You might have seen—or used—a journal with daily prompts to appreciate meaningful moments. Writing helps you pause, consider more deeply, and sometimes come away with new knowledge. So reflecting is powerful: it helps you unpack why things are the way they are, gain a deeper understanding of what you think about them, and even come up with ideas for change.

Print journals and apps, like *The Five-Minute Journal* (left) and *Reflectly* (right), help make reflection a daily habit.

⟳ *REFLECT. Think about moments in your life, or even just in the past day, when you've paused to reflect—on how something went, on what you wish you'd done differently, etc. What prompted you to stop and think? How did you go about doing it—were you lost in thought for a few moments? scribbling notes in a journal? talking it out with a friend? What did you realize or learn as a result of reflecting?*

Reflecting as a Writer

So writing fosters reflection, but what does reflection do for writing—and for you as a writer? A lot! Reflection can help you better understand the writing strategies and processes you use, why you make certain decisions, and, ultimately, how you might become a more effective author. That's why many writing teachers assign reflection: it prompts writers to study what they've written with the goal of identifying what worked, what didn't, and how to improve. This chapter offers strategies for developing that self-awareness as a writer and guidelines for writing reflections. Here are the main kinds of reflection you can practice.

Reflect to assess your past experiences as a writer. Try this before jumping into a new writing task to help you see how previous experiences have affected the way you approach writing now. Consider assignments, courses, and writing done outside of school—the good and the bad—that've

THINK BEYOND WORDS

↪ *WATCH A VIDEO of three high school students reflecting on writing award-winning essays for the* New York Times *annual student editorial contest. What do these writers say they've learned about themselves and their writing? How might their reflections be different if written instead of spoken into a camera? What does the format make possible that you'd miss if relying on print or audio alone? Go to* everyonesanauthor .tumblr.com *to watch the video.*

shaped the way you think about writing. Reflecting in this way might result in a **LITERACY NARRATIVE**, like Paloma Garcia's on page 217, in which she describes her love of reading and how facing language discrimination detracted from her confidence for a time. Such narratives offer opportunities for you to take stock of your relationship to writing and to see how your practices shift across circumstances.

Reflect to identify your processes and strategies. No two writers use the same process. Like any skill that takes practice, writing requires experimenting to see what works. Through reflection, you can break down the steps you took. For an essay assignment, maybe you brainstormed topics, freewrote to narrow your stance, outlined for organization, talked about your project with a friend, wrote a full draft before visiting the writing center, and revised along the way. Or maybe you sat down and finished a draft in one go. Reflection gives you the space to see all the steps you took and to evaluate them. Start by listing what you did without judging if a step was good or bad. Then assess each strategy. What helped move the project forward and what led to a dead end or took more time than it was worth? You'll see the practices you want to keep as they are, to keep but improve, or to eliminate. Take a look at how Annie Schmittgens, a student at DePaul University, identified peer-review as an integral step in her writing process:

> I now understand that peer reviewing is the most important component to my writing process. . . . Peer reviewing has helped me become a more attentive reader, expanded my outlook, and strengthened my writing. It's also made me a better reader because I quickly learned that skimming was not effective. When reviewing a classmate's paper, each word and sentence has to be carefully considered. Becoming a deliberate reader has . . . also helped my reading outside of English class, as well as my writing. When it's time to edit, I look at each word and each sentence and make sure I am expressing my thoughts clearly.

In order to understand her current financial situation and approach to money, Tressie McMillan Cottom reflects on childhood experiences and memories. Read her narrative on p. 936.

Reflect to understand your decisions. Effective writing is all about smart choices based on your **RHETORICAL SITUATION** —what best suits your audience, purpose, and context. Reflecting offers one way to make sense of those decisions by studying the piece of your writing itself. Once you've got a draft, take stock of the choices you made. What motivated those choices and how did they play out? What **GENRE** did you choose and why? Did it help achieve your purpose or reach your audience? Why did you choose a particular writing **STRATEGY** (narrative, description, compare/contrast, etc.)? How did you decide on the **STYLE** or language variety you used? Aim to identify the important decisions you made and interrogate the reasons behind your choices.

This kind of reflection can also help you transfer effective strategies from one context to another. For example, what you perfected in writing lab reports for general chemistry could be useful when you're assigned to analyze data in microeconomics. When faced with a new writing task, consider how strategies you already know might work in this unfamiliar context. Analyze your rhetorical situation, compare it to those you've been in before, and reflect on how you might draw on your existing skills. You might find that some skills and strategies should *not* carry over. That's good to know, too!

Reflect to plan out what's left to do. Try reading a draft once over with an eye toward what you're liking so far and what you want to work on. Pausing to take stock while you write is the key to **REVISING** and improving your work. You might use this moment to recall a strategy you've learned about and want to try in this piece of writing. Through reflection, you can identify what you still need to do and make a plan to get it done. Maybe you need to conduct more research, revisit your introduction, replace a weak example, or experiment with language choices. You'll end up with a to-do list and maybe even a revision plan.

Reflect to grow and improve. All of these practices create the space for you to see what's working and what's not, which habits are leading to success or holding you back, and how you can improve along the way. Ultimately, reflection offers you the opportunity to deepen your writing knowledge and awareness so that you can make smarter choices in the future. You might even take a moment in your reflection to map a path forward, noting the practices you plan to take along as you move on to new projects.

Make Reflecting a Habit

You may have noticed that this book includes "reflect" prompts throughout, which invite you to think about how the concepts covered relate to your experiences and your writing. These brief activities can help you make connections, to see how the writing practices being discussed are ones you've encountered before, and to consider how they relate to your current writing assignments. By making connections, it's more likely information will "stick" because you're taking a moment to apply this new knowledge by building on previous experiences. We also hope these prompts get you in the habit of pausing to assess your reading, writing, and learning experiences— a practice that will surely benefit you as a student and as an author.

REFLECT. Think about a time when you've taken a writing strategy (addressing counterarguments, citing evidence, defining terms, etc.) you already knew and used it in a different context—from one course to another, or from school to work. Maybe you took what you learned about using stories to hold people's attention in a writing course and applied it in an article for the school newspaper or in a TikTok video. Why did you use this strategy? What skills or practices did you transfer? What about the new situation called for it? How did it go?

WRITING A REFLECTION / A Roadmap

While reflecting doesn't always require writing, you may be assigned to document your reflective observations. In many cases, the key to reflective writing is to identify what you've learned about yourself and to explain how it's changed the way you work, using specific examples as evidence. The following guidelines will help you compose a reflection.

Understand your assignment. You'll usually receive a prompt to guide your reflection. For example, your instructor might ask you to compose a **LITERACY NARRATIVE** about one writing experience or to **ANALYZE** your revisions for a specific assignment. You might be asked to submit a **PORT-FOLIO** in which you collect and then reflect on pieces of your writing in a letter to your instructor. Or maybe you're prompted to write brief, informal reflections in a journal or on a discussion board. Inspect the prompt carefully and focus your reflection accordingly. What kind of reflection does the prompt ask you to take on? What texts or experiences should you reflect on? How are you expected to deliver your reflection? What details and examples are you asked to include? What writing strategies or processes should take center stage?

↪ Visit the ebook at digital.wwnorton .com/everyone4r for a bonus chapter of advice on assembling a portfolio.

Consider your rhetorical situation

Identify your AUDIENCE. A key audience for your reflection is *you*, since one goal is to discover something about yourself as a writer. Your instructor is also likely part of your audience, and your peers might be, too. Consider these questions about your audience: Who are you trying to reach and why? What are they expecting to learn from your reflection? What topics are important to them? Revision work? Decision making? Previous writing experience? Processes?

Think about your PURPOSE. Why are you writing this reflection? To explain your revisions? consider your growth as a writer? examine your process? analyze how you transferred writing knowledge from one situation to another? What do you want your audience to know and understand after reading your reflection?

Examine the larger CONTEXT. What background information do you need to provide? How, for instance, does the writing you're reflecting on fit into your larger coursework? You might provide materials for your audience to reference, like an original draft. Offering context could also mean connecting your writing decisions to concepts discussed in class, like argument strategies or source integration. If you're explaining how you've transferred a practice from one context to another, what do you need to say about each situation so readers can follow?

Consider your GENRE, MEDIUM, and DESIGN. Reflective writing can take many forms, from memos and letters to literacy narratives and analyses. Let your prompt and your purpose guide you. You'll also want to consider which STRAT-EGIES are best suited to your genre and purpose, like DESCRIPTION (what you did in your writing), ANALYSIS (examining your writing), and EVALUATION (assessing your writing). Finally, how can your medium and design convey your points most clearly? If you're submitting a portfolio or you refer to other pieces of writing, think about how best to represent those artifacts. And, if you're providing reference materials, how will you signal what readers should focus on? You might highlight important passages or use the "comment" function to add notes in the margins.

Think about your LANGUAGE. You likely use a number of DIALECTS—and maybe even languages—in your everyday life, which means you have many options for composing a reflection. Which option will be most effective for what you're trying to accomplish? Will your audience expect a certain kind of language or style? Do you want to meet those expectations? challenge them? What do you want your language to say about you? What risks might you be willing to take? See Chapters 4 and 33 for more advice about language choices.

Explore your writing and reflect

Gather the materials you're reflecting on, which can include pieces of your writing (essays, drafts, etc.), artifacts that represent your writing process (notes; outlines; instructor, peer, or tutor feedback), or any related documents (assignment prompts, brainstorming doodles, emails, etc.). Depending on your focus, you might need all your writing for a single course or just the writing and notes from one assignment. Do you have revised versions you can compare to original drafts to see what changed? Grab anything that helps you see evidence of your writing choices and processes.

　　　Think about how to organize what you've gathered. Will you create a folder on your laptop and view everything on-screen? Do you prefer to print files and store them in a physical folder? What storage system will help you to curate (and find!) all the writing artifacts you need?

Re-read and take notes. Once you've gathered your materials, review them with the goals of your assignment in mind. Take notes to keep track of what you notice, especially any memories, thoughts, and feelings that aren't visible on the page. Consider the following questions:

- What do you remember about your writing process? What trends do you see in your writing over the course of a project or a semester?
- What do you like most about this piece of writing—a particular section, a sentence, a passage that reflects your personality—and why?
- Where do you see successful writing, and how did you make it happen? Did you have any "aha!" moments when an idea or writing strategy clicked?
- What struggles did you encounter while drafting, and how did you work through them? Which strategies, texts, or ideas gave you trouble, and why?
- What decisions changed the direction of your work? How did peer or instructor feedback shape your writing?
- Did you experiment with language or try different media (text, photos, audio, video)? Why or why not? What were the intended effects?

Generate ideas. FREEWRITING will help jog your memory and pinpoint what stands out to you most and therefore could become the focus of your reflection. The following questions can help get your creative juices flowing:

- What important steps and thinking happened off the page but influenced your project? What circumstances helped or impeded your writing? Did a morning run clear your mind or a noisy roommate make composing difficult?
- Consider your emotional responses. What kinds of writing have excited and interested you? When have you felt challenged as a writer? What emotions emerged as you composed, received feedback, and revised? How did these emotional responses shape your work?

Identify significant patterns and major decisions. After you've reviewed your materials, taken notes, and generated ideas, step back and identify the patterns and themes in your writing and writing process. Focus on your most substantive observations—the ones that most significantly impacted you and your writing. What you come up with should help you craft a thesis.

- What common trends do you notice in your writing or process? Maybe anecdotes are your primary form of evidence or peer feedback always prompts your heaviest revisions. Are there issues that pop up frequently?
- What were your greatest successes (and obstacles)? What are you most proud of? What do you want to do differently or better?
- What decisions were most impactful on your writing and process? Maybe it made a big difference when you switched topics early or chose to get feedback even when the draft felt final.
- What were the major changes you made as you revised?

Organize and start writing

As you draft, consult your freewriting and your notes. Remember your rhetorical situation, and if you're responding to a specific assignment, return to the prompt to be sure you're addressing it.

Draft a THESIS. Some, though not all, reflective writing includes a central claim or thesis. Your thesis should focus on the key insights you've gained from reflecting on your writing and signal the main points to follow. As you consider your thesis, pinpoint the important takeaways you arrived at as you reflected on your writing. The work you did to identify significant patterns and major decisions will be a big help.

Craft and ORGANIZE supporting paragraphs or sentences. While your thesis statement concisely identifies the focus of your reflection, your paragraphs or sentences should support your main claim by providing evidence. If you're writing a full essay, each paragraph might center on one of those significant patterns or decisions you uncovered. Think about how best to arrange your supporting points: which observations about your writing should come first, last, or somewhere in between?

Include EVIDENCE from your writing to develop each point. If you're highlighting your use of instructor and peer feedback, you might quote directly from a note you received. If you're analyzing your use of language varieties, show a passage from your writing as an example. Consider which examples from your writing offer the clearest insights to the decisions you've made. Think, too, about which revisions show how you've experimented with new ideas or strategies. Such examples help your readers see what your reflective takeaways are based on.

Explain why and how. Strong reflective writing explains *how* your decisions and experiences have affected you as a writer and *why* you've made the choices you have. In other words, you want to make clear the significance of your decisions and experiences so that readers see the meaning these choices hold for you and your writing. These explanations help your readers—and you!—understand the awareness you've gained about your writing. One way to ensure you're including the "how" and "why" is by using "because" statements: "I made this decision because" or "I experimented with this writing strategy because." Aim to answer the following questions: Why did I make these decisions, take up these practices, or experience writing in this way? What effect have specific decisions, practices, or experiences had on my writing and on me as a writer? How do particular decisions and experiences show my writing awareness or growth?

Identify plans for future writing. You can use reflection not only to look back at what you've done but also to look ahead, mapping out the kind of writer you want to be and the writing processes you want to use in the future. For example, you might realize that draft workshops are central to your writing process, so you plan to visit the writing center more regularly. Consider the practices that have held you back, too, and strategize ways to overcome them. How will you employ strategies that work for you in the future? Looking forward, how will you address areas that give you trouble?

Draft an OPENING. Your introduction should orient your readers to the main ideas and concerns you'll focus on as well as the kind of reflection you're undertaking—a specific assignment, all of the assignments for a term or course, your writing process, a significant writing experience, or a combination of these. Provide any background information your audience may need. This is where your thesis will likely go.

Draft a CONCLUSION. Use your conclusion to consider the big picture: What were the major takeaways that your reflection helped you realize? Why do those takeaways matter to you? Your conclusion is a great place to describe your future writing plans given what you've learned through reflection.

Look critically at your draft, get responses—and revise

Read your draft slowly and carefully to see whether your reflection responds to the prompt and that it delivers on the reflective work you set out to do. Make sure you've composed a clear thesis and supporting paragraphs that include examples to help readers see what you've learned. Then ask others to read and respond to your draft. Here are some questions that can help you or others read over a draft of reflective writing.

- *Is your* THESIS *clear?* Do you make a specific claim about your writing or writing process? Does the thesis center readers' attention on significant writing strategies and decisions?

- *How does the* OPENING *preview the work of your reflection?* Does it focus readers' attention on the aspects of reflection most important to you? Does it provide relevant background information?

- *How do the supporting sentences or paragraphs develop the ideas discussed in your thesis and opening?* Do they center on major writing concerns instead of minor issues? Does each point support your thesis?

- *What details and examples do you provide?* Where might you add details to clarify a point? Do you include examples of your own writing?

- *Where do you explain your plans for future writing tasks,* given the knowledge you've gained through this reflection?

- *How does your reflection* CONCLUDE*?* Does it explain what you've learned and why it matters?

Revise your draft in light of your own observations and any feedback from others—keeping your audience and purpose firmly in mind, as always.

ANNAYA BAYNES wrote the following essay when prompted to reflect on their growth as a writer while attending Spelman College. Baynes reflects on completing a first-year writing assignment, describing a more rigorous process than the one they used in high school.

Becoming the Writer I Am: A Reflection on My First-Year Composition Class

ANNAYA BAYNES

BEFORE ATTENDING SPELMAN college, I excelled in my writing classes without being pushed past my intellectual boundaries. In high school, I would often hastily throw together papers without much purpose. My first-year composition course at Spelman, however, prepared me for the rest of my career as a college student. I learned to write papers that were intellectually curious; in the process, my writing became better, and I learned more about myself as a writer. In high school, my teachers taught me the mechanics of writing, but my composition professor taught me how to *write* by pushing me and my peers to ask more complex questions of texts and of ourselves. I learned that revision can include developing ideas rather than focusing on mechanics. By reflecting on the writing and revision process for my first paper in a college writing course, I saw how this course helped improve my writing overall. In this essay, I describe the changes I made to my writing process as a result of one assignment in my first-year writing course.

> Opens with important context: a description of the writer in high school so readers can gauge their changes as a first-year writing student.

> Sets out a thesis for the reflection.

Background information about the class and the assignment being discussed.

A description of the author's writing process and how it compares to what they did in high school.

Pinpoints a significant moment that prompted a change in the author's writing practice.

Considers the effects of not sharing their work with others previously.

Explains an important realization: sharing work with others can improve one's writing.

Highlights another major change in their writing process: getting feedback from their instructor.

As I entered college, I knew that I would have to change my work ethic to be a successful student, but I had no clue what writing at a college level meant. Thus, when my writing instructor assigned our first essay topic—to explore Black love in Tera W. Hunter's text *Bound in Wedlock: Slave and Free Black Marriage in the Nineteenth Century* and to put Hunter's ideas in conversation with Plato's *Phaedrus* and *The Symposium*—I had the sense that I needed to do something different; I just didn't know what. I started by going about my usual process. I gathered salient quotes from the texts assigned and organized them into potential body paragraphs. Then I just sat down to write, starting with the introduction, and I knocked out the paper in one sitting. I read it once to find any errors and then submitted it. When I received my grade for the essay, I was shocked. The lowest grade I'd ever received for a paper was an A-, but my first collegiate essay earned a B. That was the wake-up call that showed me I needed to rethink my writing process to uphold the standard I set for myself. My professor gave the class the opportunity to revise, so I decided to take the time to develop a more intellectually rigorous paper.

In high school, I was too protective of my writing. I never wanted anyone (besides the teacher, but only once submitted) to see my work. I placed a lot of pressure on myself to be a perfect writer, and I saw any constructive criticism as an attack on my intelligence and character. Therefore, I retreated to work alone rather than be vulnerable and allow others into my editing and revision process. With my first college writing assignment, I realized that I did not have all the answers to improve my writing. I needed help. I paid attention to the professor's notes on my paper, and I revised as best I could. Then, I took a big step and showed my friend the revised draft. She pointed out moments where she could not follow my line of thinking and where my argument was not developed fully. I revised the essay again with her notes in mind, and then took an even bigger leap: I met with my instructor.

In talking with my instructor about my essay and revision ideas, I gained clarity not only on this one essay's weaknesses but also on what I needed to work on as a writer. I was anxious before the meeting because I felt like I failed in the original essay. The meeting itself was not as scary as I had feared. We went over my revised paper, and my instructor highlighted areas for improvement. For example, my paragraphs were disjointed with no transition sentences, and my instructor suggested ways that I could more effectively move from idea to idea. I realized that just because my thoughts made perfect sense to me did not mean that the reader would always follow my logic. Working alone, without feedback, had prevented me from considering a reader's experience of my essay.

An example of how a new process (getting feedback) led to a specific improvement: stronger transitions.

Further, I realized I also had difficulty making my essay cohesive. I had so many ideas, but I needed to be more economical in choosing what to include. My instructor suggested I assess each argument—and even each sentence—and question how it was supporting my thesis. I applied this approach to the following passage, which appeared in my first draft:

5

Another writing practice the author learned: evaluating and choosing the strongest arguments.

> Whites tried to exert control over black bodies through rape, but enslaved black people rejected this attempt by forming their own consensual relationships. Enslavers had the power to force copulation but not attachment. Black people were the only ones capable of forming those bonds for themselves. Before emancipation, marriages for African Americans combatted white supremacy by illustrating just how powerless enslavers truly were in the face of romantic relationships between enslaved people.

This section took too many words to state my point. In revising, I condensed this point into two sentences: "Whites tried to impose control over black bodies through rape, but enslaved people rejected this attempt by forming their own consensual relationships. Before emancipation, African American marriages helped combat white supremacy by illustrating just how powerless enslavers were in the face of romantic relationships between enslaved people." By focusing my point, I was able to dedicate more space to developing my argument. Previously, I viewed writing as a single action instead of a process; I'd think "just sit down, write the essay, and get it done." Now, I understand that

As evidence, the author compares examples from their original and revised essay and explains the rationale behind a revision.

writing is as much about the initial draft as the constant revision that follows.

I also sharpened my language choices while revising. For example, in the original essay, I wrote, "For the reasons listed previously, marriage was not merely the consummation of a romantic relationship for black people." I revised this sentence to read: "The ability to marry was important not only as a consummation of love but also as a tool to combat white supremacy." The initial sentence states that marriage had some importance beyond romance for Black people, but it does not say what that importance is. The latter sentence makes explicit that marriage was also "a tool to combat white supremacy."

I am now a junior, but I haven't forgotten all I learned in freshman composition. On the contrary, I have successfully taken these lessons into all my courses and writing since. In fact, I am also now a writing center tutor, and a lot of the advice I give pushes students to think more deeply about their writing in the same way I learned to in my composition course. Being open and receptive to feedback from peers and my instructor helped develop my writing style and process. I no longer hoard my writing away from critical eyes like a literary dragon. I rely on my community to offer feedback on my work. Also, my writing contains considerably less fluff, as I always evaluate whether what I am writing (at the argument and sentence level) reinforces my thesis. Of course, my writing is not perfect, but it now has the quality that I searched for but could not find at the start of my college career. My strengths and weaknesses are clear to me. Without the work I did in my composition course my first year of college, I would not be the writer I am today.

REFLECT. Reflect on a writing project that you especially enjoyed or that you found rewarding. What made the project successful? How did you move through your writing process? What parts of that process could you carry forward to future assignments? Let reflection help you feel good about what you've achieved and take time to appreciate your successes and your strengths!

ELEVEN

The Need for Collaboration

"Here Comes Everybody!"

ERE COMES EVERYBODY is the title of NYU professor Clay Shirky's book about "what happens when people are given the tools to do things together, without needing traditional organizational structures" to do them. Put another way, Shirky's book is about how technology has led to connectivity and how connectivity has led to easy and innovative collaborations. Here's what we mean:

- A group of students creates a *Wikipedia* entry devoted to manga, a genre of Japanese comic books. Within hours, others from around the world have joined in, helping to expand and refine the entry.

- A budding essayist uses the blogging platform *Medium* to publish their writing and interact with readers and other writers. They find that the online community is full of authors who want to collaborate and discuss their ideas.

- Assigned to write an essay about the dangers faced by independent war journalists, a student starts by researching what has been written on this topic (reading current news magazines, online news sites, and *Twitter* feeds and blogs kept by the journalists themselves). When he writes the essay, he weaves the views of others (carefully cited) in with his own, adding his voice to the conversation about that topic.

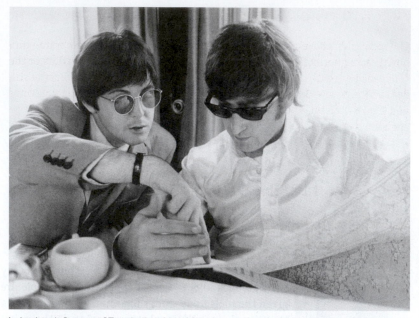

In his book *Powers of Two*, Joshua Wolf Shenk argues that the real genius of the Beatles and their best work grew out of the collaborative nature of the Lennon-McCartney partnership.

Even the student mentioned above, researching alone at his computer, depends on others. In short, writers seldom—if ever—write alone. Collaboration has always been inevitable and essential, and our digital connectivity makes working together easier—and more interesting—than ever. This chapter will help you think about the role that collaboration plays in your life, and especially how it affects the work you do as an author and a reader.

REFLECT. Think about reading and writing that you do regularly online— posts, articles, comments—everything. In what ways are you an author, and in what ways are you a member of an audience? To what extent does each activity involve collaboration with others, and how would it be different if there were no collaboration at all?

What Collaboration Means for Authors—and Audiences

The examples above show some of the ways that authors collaborate—and how they sometimes even trade places with their audiences. Readers of the *Wikipedia* entry on manga can take on the role of editors or authors; the student writer using *Medium* becomes an audience for their readers' suggestions and ideas; the student reading and writing about independent war reporters is an audience for those authors whose work he reads and then an author when he responds to their views in his own essay. Authors and audiences shift roles and collaborate constantly.

Once upon a time, newspapers reported information and events; today, they maintain social media accounts and blogs that serve as forums for discussing, challenging, and updating information. Readers who were once passive consumers of the news can now be active participants in responding to and sharing that information with others. As media professor Henry Jenkins puts it, ours is "a world where no one knows everything, but everyone knows something." Putting those somethings together is what happens when we collaborate.

To take another familiar example, players of the first video games were an audience for stories that were written by the games' designers. That's not the case in many of today's games, however, in which the players / audience members customize their characters and write their own story—very often in collaboration with other players. Consider, for example, multiplayer online games such as *Fortnite*, in which a large number of people play as a group, or the more serious video game *World without Oil*, in which almost 2,000 individuals from twelve countries collaborated over the course of a month to imagine how to deal with a global oil crisis. Such games don't merely offer opportunities for collaboration; it's actually impossible for any one player to play alone.

Collaboration is an everyday matter. We collaborate for fun, as when a flash mob suddenly appears and starts dancing to Queen or singing the "Hallelujah Chorus" and then just as suddenly disappears. And we collaborate for more serious purposes, as when many people contribute over time to develop a *Wikipedia* entry or when people in countries as far-flung as the United States, Malaysia, Germany, Nigeria, and dozens more collaborate on a dance project such as One Billion Rising. In his book *Net Smart*, digital communications scholar Howard Rheingold argues that collaboration is today's tool for social engagement: "Knowing the importance of

**THINK
BEYOND
WORDS**

TAKE A LOOK *at some favorite flash mobs* at *everyonesanauthor.tumblr.com.*
*Some promote a cause, others sell a product, still others celebrate something or
someone. The picture above is from a flash mob in the Netherlands to raise awareness
of the exploitation of women. Inspired by One Billion Rising, performances like this
one take place around the world every February to shine light on violence against
women and to demand change. What ideas do you have for an effective flash mob?
In what ways would a flash mob accomplish your goal better than a piece of writing?*

participation and how to participate has suddenly become not only an individual survival skill but a key to large-scale social change." For these and
other purposes, collaboration is a necessity.

What Collaboration Means for You as a Student

As a student, you'll have many occasions to collaborate, from a simple class
discussion to a full-fledged team project in which you work with peers to
research and write a report, carry out and write up an experiment, or build
a website.

As a writer, you'll be in constant collaboration with others, from teachers and classmates who read and respond to your drafts to the audience
you're addressing—and don't forget those whose work you read and cite.

Academic writing in particular calls on you to engage with the ideas of others—to listen to and think about what they say, to respond to views you don't agree with, and to weave the ideas of others (those you agree with and those you don't) into your own arguments. Very often you'll want to present your own views as a direct response to what others say—in fact, when you think about it, the main reason we make arguments at all is because someone has said or done something that we want to respond to. And one reason we make academic arguments is to add our voices to conversations about topics that we're studying, things that matter to us.

And consider your nonacademic writing, particularly the writing you do online. Whether you're posting or following others on *TikTok* or viewing or contributing to *Wikipedia* or *YouTube*, these kinds of writing assume and make possible a back-and-forth—a collaboration. You might be an author, an audience, or both. These are all ways that we regularly communicate—and collaborate—with others.

✎ *REFLECT. Go to* Wikipedia *and work with several classmates to choose an entry that interests you and then revise or add to it. Or, if you don't find what you're looking for, create a new entry yourselves. Revisit your entry in a few days to see what others may have added (or removed).*

Collaboration with a Writing Tutor

Speaking of collaboration in your academic writing, have you heard of your school's writing center? Most schools have one, and it's a place where you can go (online or physically) to consult with a trained tutor on any aspect of a class assignment. All writers need good readers, and a tutor can work with you at any stage of the process—brainstorming ideas, organizing the sequence of information, polishing, clarifying, documenting your sources. And the good news is that the writing center probably doesn't charge a cent for what it offers. Or rather, you've already paid for it as part of your tuition and fees, so you might as well take advantage.

The more prepared you are for your writing center session, the more you'll get out of it. First, figure out what you'd like to accomplish in your session and share that information with your tutor early. Discuss your ideas, goals, doubts, and questions. Your tutor may suggest a different focus for your session; be open and flexible to such suggestions and reasoning. Let the session be a collaboration. A lot of ideas and information will be discussed during your session, so it's important that you take good notes in order to be able to remember it all. You may want to sit down immediately after your session and add more details to your notes while your memory is still fresh. Finally, write out a plan of action for what you'll do next; this plan will guide you when you get back to your assignment. We also recommend that you schedule your next appointment before leaving the writing center, as having an appointment can be a soft deadline for advancing your project.

Collaboration at Work

The collaborative projects described by Taté Walker deal with agriculture rather than writing, but think about the level of good, clear communication that each project requires. Read the report on p. 1009.

Collaboration almost certainly plays a role in your work life. Indeed, teamwork is central to most businesses and industries. Engineers work in teams to design power plants; editors and designers work together to publish books and magazines; businesses from Google to Taco Bell rely on teams to develop and market new products. Whatever work you do—whether it is that of an engineer, health-care worker, bookstore owner, chemist, or teacher—you will find yourself continually communicating with others. The effectiveness of these communications will depend to a large extent on your ability to collaborate effectively.

The social distancing required by the COVID-19 pandemic prompted workers in settings all over the world to rethink how they could collaborate virtually instead of in person. As we all acclimated to "*Zoom* life," articles published in the *New York Times*, *Forbes*, and *Harvard Business Review* offered specific suggestions for running effective and inclusive online meetings so that work collaborations continued and thrived. In her article published on the *TED* website, social psychologist Dolly Chugh suggests that leaders of virtual meetings not only provide an agenda and designate a notetaker to keep discussion on track, but that meeting leaders should also create opportunities for all attendees to make their voices heard by inviting participants to contribute in the "chat" and by creating breakout rooms for small group conversations. She argues that a key to effective breakouts is to have one participant from each group share an important point from their smaller group discussion when the larger group reconvenes. Just like collaborating in person, online meetings are most effective, helpful, and fun when you hear and learn from people with different ideas, views, and backgrounds. These guidelines are key to effective professional collaboration, as virtual meetings are now a staple in many work environments.

An employee working remotely participates in a virtual team meeting.

As a student, you're likely well prepared for these kinds of virtual collaborations from your experiences learning and interacting online. Think about the online classes you've taken or the virtual meetings you've participated in: How have collaborations, class discussions, or group writing projects taken shape? What strategies did your instructor, your peers, or you put in place to make them effective? How might these strategies carry over to a collaborative working environment?

REFLECT. Create a brief guide for how to collaborate well in online meetings by writing ten short suggestions that lead to working together effectively. Base your tips on your own experience of what helps foster good conversation in virtual gatherings—and maybe some research into what experts suggest.

Some Tips for Collaborating Effectively

Sometimes your class collaborations will be fleeting and low risk—for example, to work with a group to respond to questions about a reading and then to share the group's ideas with the class. Other collaborations are more extended and high risk, as when you pick lab partners for the whole term or have a major group project that will count for a significant percentage of everyone's final grade.

Extended collaborative assignments can be a challenge. Members of the group may have differing goals—for instance, two members will accept nothing less than an A and others are just hoping for a C. Domineering members of the team may try to run the show; others won't participate at all. And the logistics of collaborating on a major project can be a challenge. Here are some tips that can help ensure efficient, congenial, and productive team relationships when you are working on an extended collaborative project.

- *Find ways of recognizing everyone.* For example, all group members could talk about a strength that they can contribute to the project.

- *Listen carefully*—and respectfully—to every group member.

- *Establish some ground rules.* Whether online or face-to-face, the way your group runs its meetings can make or break your collaborative effort. Spend part of your first meeting exploring your assignment and figuring out how often the group will meet, the responsibilities of each member, and the general expectations you have of one another.

- *Make an effort to develop trust and group identity.* To get started, members could share some pertinent information, such as their favorite spots for writing or their typical writing processes. Remember, too, that socializing can play an important role in the development of group identity. Sharing a pizza while brainstorming can pay off down the road. However, remember to stay focused on the project.

- *Get organized.* Use an agenda to organize your meetings, and be sure that someone takes notes. Don't count on anyone's memory, and don't leave all the note-taking to one person! You may want to take turns developing the agenda, reminding everyone of upcoming meetings via email or text message, maintaining written records, and so on.

- *Develop nonthreatening ways to deal with problems.* Rather than stating that a member's ideas are unclear, for instance, you might say, "I'm having trouble making the connection between your suggestion and my understanding of what we're discussing." Just a simple shift from "your" to "my" can defuse difficult situations. And remember that tact, thoughtfulness, and a sense of humor can go a long way toward resolving any interpersonal issues.

- *Build in regular reality checks* to nip any potential problems in the bud—for example, reserve some time to discuss how the group is working and how it could be better. Try not to criticize anyone; instead, focus on what's working and what could be improved.

- *Encourage the free play of ideas,* one of the most important benefits of working collaboratively. Think carefully about when your group should strive for consensus and when you should not. You want to avoid interpersonal conflicts that slow you down, yet remain open and consider everyone's ideas.

- *Expect the unexpected.* Someone's computer may crash, interlibrary loan materials may arrive later than expected, someone may be sick on the day when they were supposed to write a key section of the text. Try to build in extra time for the unexpected, and help each other out when extra teamwork is needed.

- *Be flexible about how you meet.* If getting together in person poses problems, go virtual with *Zoom* or collaborate asynchronously on *Google Docs*. Use your school's course management system for discussion forums, wikis, and file-sharing folders—all of which will prove helpful for collaborative work.

Remember that when you engage in group work, you need to attend to both the task and the group. And keep in mind that each member of the group should be valued equally and that the process should be satisfying to all.

PART IV

Genres of Writing

WHEN YOU WERE A KID, did you have certain kinds of clothes you liked to wear? Six-year-old Maya describes her choices this way: "I have school clothes—they're okay, I guess. And I have a couple of dress-up things, like for when I go to church or a birthday party. But my favorites are my make-believe clothes for when I dress up as Moana, Tiana, and Shuri from *Black Panther*—they're my favorites!" What Maya displays here is a fairly sophisticated sense of genres, ways that we categorize things. You see genres everywhere—in literature (think poetry, fiction, drama), in sports (baseball, basketball, volleyball), or in dance (tap, hip-hop, jazz). And when we talk about writing, we often talk in terms of genres too: narratives, lab reports, project proposals, movie reviews, argument essays, and so on. Like all genres, those associated with writing are flexible: they expand and change over time as writers find new ways to communicate and express themselves.

In the ancient world, for example, personal communication involved carving symbols into clay tablets or, a bit later, having a scribe record your message on papyrus. For communicating with speed, couriers memorized letters and raced to deliver them orally. Once paper was available and letters were less costly and easier to produce, they evolved into multiple subgenres: the business letter, the personal letter, the condolence letter, the thank-you letter, and so on. Today, letters have further evolved into electronic forms—emails, social media messages, texts. It's hard to predict how these genres of communication will evolve in the future, but when they do, we know they will stretch to accommodate new modes and new media, as genres always do. In short, genres reflect current expectations while also shaping—and sometimes even changing—them.

Instructors will often ask you to use particular genres, most likely including the ones taught in this book: arguments, narratives, analyses, reports, reviews, and proposals. You may need to write a rhetorical analysis of a speech, for instance, or to analyze the causes of the increased frequency of wildfires in California. In either case, knowing the characteristic features of an analysis will be helpful. And you may want or need to combine genres—to introduce an analysis with a short narrative or to conclude it with a proposal of some kind.

Of course, you may not always be assigned to write in a particular genre. Your instructor may give you a topic to write about in whatever way you choose. In this case, you'll need to think carefully about what genre will be best suited to addressing that topic—and Chapter 12 will help you choose a genre when the choice is yours.

The chapters that follow introduce most of the genres you'll be assigned to do in college. Each chapter explains the genre's characteristic features; discusses how, when, where, and why you might use the genre; provides a roadmap to the process of writing in that genre; and includes several example essays. We hope that you'll use these chapters to explore these common academic genres—and to adapt them as needed to your own purposes and goals.

Communication throughout the ages, from clay tablets to couriers delivering messages to tweets and texts.

TWELVE

Choosing Genres

OMICS HAVE MANGA, superheroes, and fantasy. Music has hip-hop, country, and folk. Internet aesthetics? Think cottagecore, dark academia, and e-girl. How about restaurants? Try Italian, Vietnamese, Tex-Mex, vegan, or southern soul food. Or movies: sci-fi, thrillers, drama, comedy. These are all genres, and they are one important way we structure our world.

Genres are categorizations, ways of classifying things. The genres this book is concerned with are kinds of writing, but you'll find genres everywhere you look.

In fact, rhetorician and researcher Carolyn Miller has been tracking the use of the word "genre" and has found it everywhere, including on many of the sites you visit every day. *Netflix* lists nineteen film genres, from action and drama to sports and thrillers—and thousands of subgenres within each of these. The video game review site *GameSpot* sorts games into sixty-eight genres, and *Spotify*'s algorithm draws from over 5,000 distinct genres as this book goes to press. You can even see new genres developing on *YouTube*, including microgenres like "cute babies" or "cats being mean." Indeed, there is now such a proliferation of genres that they've become the subject of parody, with comedians mixing musical genres to make new ones, like honky tonk and techno to make "honky techno" or folk and dubstep to make "folk step." To get a sense of the result, just take a look at the cartoon on the next page.

In this cartoon, Roz Chast comes up with her own new movie genres: sci-fi/Western, musical/self-help, sports/horror, and documentary/romance. What new hybrid movie genre can you suggest?

What You Need to Know about Genres of Writing

Genres are kinds of writing that you can use to accomplish a certain goal and reach a particular audience. As such, they have well-established features that help guide you in your writing. However, they're not fill-in-the-blank templates; you will adapt them to address your own rhetorical situations.

Genres have features that can guide you as a writer and a reader. Argument essays, for instance, usually take a position supported by reasons and evidence, consider a range of perspectives, and so on. These features help guide you as an author in what you write—and they also set up expectations for you as a reader, affecting the way you interpret what you read. If something's called a report, for instance, you are likely to assume that it presents information—that it's in some way factual.

This book covers those genres that are most often assigned in school—ARGUMENTS, ANALYSES, REPORTS, NARRATIVES, REVIEWS, PROPOSALS, and ANNOTATED BIBLIOGRAPHIES—and some subgenres: VISUAL ANALYSES, PROFILES, LITERACY NARRATIVES, LITERATURE REVIEWS, and PROJECT PROPOSALS. These are kinds of writing that have evolved over the years as a useful means of creating and sharing knowledge. As you advance in a major, you will become familiar with the most important genres and subgenres in that field. Especially when you are new to a genre, its features can serve as a kind of blueprint, helping you know how to approach an assignment. Knowing these features helps you organize a text and guides your choices in terms of content.

Genres are flexible. Keep in mind that genres can be both enabling and constraining. Sometimes you'll have reason to adapt genre features to suit your own goals. One student who was writing an analysis of a sonnet, for example, wanted to bend the analysis genre just a little to include a poem that experimented with the sonnet form. He checked with his teacher, got approval, and it worked. You might not want to stretch a lab report in this way, however. Lab reports follow a fairly set template, covering purpose, methods, results, summary, and conclusions to carry out the goals of the scientific fields that use them; they would not be fitting (or effective) in a creative writing class.

See how Dana Canedy's narrative about a conversation with her son makes an argument on p. 868.

You may also have occasion to combine genres—to tell a story in the course of arguing a position or to conclude a report with a proposal of some kind. If you ever decide to adapt or combine genres, think hard about your rhetorical situation: what genres will help you achieve your purpose? reach the audience you're addressing? work best in the medium you're using?

Genres evolve. While it is relatively easy to identify some characteristic genre features, such features are not universal rules. Genres are flexible, and they evolve across time and in response to shifting cultural contexts. Letters, for example, followed certain conventions in medieval Europe (they were handwritten, of course, and they were highly formal); by the twentieth century, letters had developed dozens of subgenres (thank-you notes, letters to the editor, application letters). Then, in the 1990s, letters began to morph into email, adapting in new ways to online situations. Today, text messages, tweets, and social media posts may be seen as offshoots of the letter genre.

And as with all genres and subgenres, letters, email, text messages, and social media posts have developed their own conventions and features, ones that guide you as a writer and a reader.

REFLECT. Think about a favorite song, movie, or game, and then decide what genre or subgenre it fits into. How do you know? List the features that help you identify it as belonging to a particular genre. What do you know about that genre? Name a few other examples of that genre, and then think about what features they have in common.

Deciding Which Genres to Use

Sometimes you'll be assigned to write in a particular genre. If that's the case, think about what you know about the genre and about what it expects of you as a writer, then turn to the corresponding chapter in this book for guidance. But other times your assignments won't make the genre perfectly clear. The following advice can help determine which genre(s) to use when the choice is yours. In all cases, remember to consider your **PURPOSE** for writing and the **AUDIENCE** you want to reach in deciding which genres would be most useful.

Look for clues in the assignment. Even without a clearly assigned genre, your assignment should be your starting point. Are there any keywords that suggest one? "Discuss," for example, could indicate a **REPORT** or an **ANALYSIS**. And you might also need to consider how such a keyword is used in the discipline the assignment comes from—"analyze" in a chemistry assignment doesn't likely mean the same thing as in a literature assignment. In either case, you should ask your instructor for clarification.

Consider this assignment from an introductory communications course: "Look carefully at letters to the editor in one newspaper over a period of two weeks, and write an essay describing what you find. Who are the letter writers? What issues are they writing about? How many different perspectives are represented?" Though this assignment doesn't name a genre, it seems to be asking students for a report: to research a topic and then report on what they find.

But what if this were the assignment: "Look carefully at letters to the editor in one newspaper over a period of two weeks, and write an essay describing what you find. Who are the letter writers? What issues are they writing about? How many different perspectives are represented? What rhetorical strategies do the writers use to get their points across? Draw some conclusions based on what you find." This assignment also asks students to research a topic and report on what they find. But in asking them to identify rhetorical strategies and draw some conclusions based on their findings, it is also prompting them to do some analysis. As you look at your own assignments, look for words or other clues that will help you identify which genres are expected.

If an assignment doesn't give any clues, here are some questions to ask in thinking about which genre may be most effective:

- *What discipline is the assignment for?* Say you're assigned to write about obesity and public health. If you're writing for a journalism course, you might write an op-ed essay **ARGUING** that high-calorie sodas should not be sold in public schools. If, on the other hand, you're writing for a biology class, you might **REPORT** on experiments done on eating behaviors and metabolic rates.

- *What is the topic?* Does it call for a specific genre? If you are asked, for example, to write about the campaign speeches of two presidential candidates, that topic suggests that you're being asked to **ANALYZE** the speeches (and probably **COMPARE** them). On the other hand, if you're writing about an experiment you conducted, you're probably writing a **REPORT** and should follow the conventions of that genre.

- *What is your purpose in writing?* If you want to convince your readers that they should "buy local," for example, your purpose will likely call for an **ARGUMENT**. If, however, you want to explain what buying local means, your purpose will call for a **REPORT**.

- *Who is the audience?* What interests and expectations might they have? Say you're assigned to write about the collective-bargaining rights of unions for a first-year seminar. There your audience would include other first-year students, and you might choose to write a **NARRATIVE** about the father of a friend who lost his job as a non-union high school teacher. Imagine, however, writing on the same topic for a public policy course; there you would be more likely to write an essay **ANALYZING** the costs and benefits of unionized workers in the public sector.

- *What style and/or language does your assignment call for* and how does that affect your choice of genres? What style (formal or informal, humorous or serious, academic or conversational) will your audience expect you to use in the genre you choose? Do you want to meet those expectations—or perhaps challenge them in some way? What do you want your choice of style and/or language to reflect about you? What risks might you be willing to take with your language? For an analysis of a current film for your intro to film studies course, as you **ARGUE** that 2020's *Time*, directed by Garrett Bradley, was hands down the year's best documentary, you might choose fairly formal standardized English only—or you might decide to use Black language since that's what your instructor (and you) use in class discussions about movie screenings, it's how some characters in the film speak, and you see ways to make your points most effectively using this language.

- *What medium will you use?* Are there certain genres that work well—or not—in that medium? If you are assigned to give an oral presentation, for example, you might consider writing a **NARRATIVE** because listeners can remember stories better than they are able to recall other genres. Even if you decide to write an analysis or a report, you might want to include some narrative.

If the assignment is wide open, draw on what you know about genres. Sometimes you may receive an assignment so broad that not only the genre but even the topic and purpose are left up to you. Consider, for example, a prompt one of the authors of this book encountered in college: in an exam for a drama class, the professor came into the room, wrote "Tragedy!" on the blackboard, and said, "You have an hour and a half to respond." We hope you don't run into such a completely open-ended assignment, especially in a timed exam. But if you do, your knowledge of genre can help out. If this assignment came in a Shakespeare course, for example, you might **ARGUE** that *Hamlet* is Shakespeare's most complex tragedy. Or you could perhaps **ANALYZE** the role of gender in one of his tragedies.

Luckily, such wide-open assignments are fairly rare. It's more likely that you will encounter an assignment like this one: "Choose a topic related to our course theme and carry out sufficient research on that topic to write an essay of eight to ten pages. Refer to at least six sources and follow MLA citation style." In this instance, you know that the assignment calls for some kind of research-based writing and that you need a topic and thesis that can be dealt with in the length specified. You could write an **ARGUMENT**, taking a position and supporting it with the research you have done. Or you could write a **REPORT** that presents findings from your research. But you might also choose to write a **NARRATIVE** that presents your research in story form. At this point, you would be wise to see your instructor to discuss your choices. Once you have decided on a genre, turn to the corresponding chapter in this book (Chapters 13–18) to guide your research and writing.

When an assignment is wide open, try using what you know about genres as a way to explore your topic:

- What are some of the **POSITIONS** on your topic? What's been said or might be said? What controversies or disagreements exist? What's your own perspective?

- What stories— **NARRATIVES** —could you tell about it?

- How might you **ANALYZE** your topic? What are its parts? What caused it—or what effects might it have? Does it follow a certain process?

- What information might be important or interesting to **REPORT** on?

- How can your topic be evaluated, or **REVIEWED** ?

- What problems does your topic present for which you can **PROPOSE** a solution?

- In our current remix culture, you might decide to do some **REMIXING** of your own, taking something written in one genre and transforming it for a different genre altogether. A **REPORT** on internet access across your campus might become a **PROPOSAL**, an **ARGUMENT**, or even a **NARRATIVE** aimed at closing the "access gap" that your report demonstrated. See Chapter 37 for more on remixing your writing.

❦○ *REFLECT. Look at three writing assignments you have been given for any of your classes. Did the assignments specify a genre? If so, what was it? If not, what genres would you say you were being asked to use—and how can you tell?*

THIRTEEN

"This Is Where I Stand"
Arguing a Position

SO WHAT'S YOUR POSITION ON THAT?" This familiar phrase pops up almost everywhere, from talk radio to social media, from political press conferences to classroom seminars. In fact, much of the work you do as an author responds, in some way, to this question.

After all, taking a position is something you do many times daily: you talk with your academic advisor to explain your reasons for dropping a course; you text a friend the reasons she should see a certain film with you; in an economics class discussion, you offer your own position on consumer spending patterns in response to someone else's; you survey research on electric vehicle charging stations and then write a letter to the editor of your local newspaper advocating (or protesting) the installation of new charging stations in your town. In all these cases, you're doing what philosopher Kenneth Burke calls "putting in your oar," taking and supporting positions of your own in conversation with others around you.

Look around, and you'll see other positions being articulated all over the place. Here's one we saw recently on a T-shirt:

Work to eat.

Eat to live.

Live to bike.

Bike to work.

The central argument here is clear: bike to work. One of the reasons it's so effective is the clever way that the last sentence isn't quite parallel with the others. (In the first three, "to" can be replaced by "in order to"; in the last case, it can't.) Another reason it works well is the form of the argument, which is a series of short commands, each beginning with the same word that the previous sentence ends with.

This chapter offers guidelines for writing an academic essay that takes a position. While taking a position in an academic context often differs in crucial ways from doing so in other contexts, many of the principles discussed will serve you well when stating a position generally.

〰️ *REFLECT. Stop for a moment and jot down every time you remember having to take a position on something—anything at all—in the last few days. The list will surely soon grow long if you're like most of us. Then take an informal survey, noting and writing down every time in one day someone around you takes a position. This informal research should convince you that the rhetorical genre of taking a position is central to many of your daily activities.*

Across Academic Disciplines

Position papers are written in many fields, and a number of disciplines offer specific guidelines for composing them. In philosophy, a position paper is a brief persuasive essay designed to express a precise opinion about some issue or some philosopher's viewpoint. In computer science, a position paper considers a number of perspectives on an issue before finally offering the writer's own position. In political science, a position paper often critiques a major argument or text, first summarizing and analyzing its main points and then interpreting them in the context of other texts. Many college courses ask students to take a position in response to a course reading, specifying that they state their position clearly, support it with evidence and logical reasons, and cite all sources consulted. So one challenge you'll face when you're asked to write a position paper in various disciplines will be to determine exactly what is expected of you.

Across Media

Different media present different resources and challenges when it comes to presenting your position. Setting up a website that encourages people to take action to end animal abuse gives you the ability to link to additional information, whereas writing a traditional essay advocating that position for a print magazine requires that you provide all the relevant evidence and reasons on the page. It is very easy to incorporate color images or video clips in the webpage, but the magazine's budget may not allow for color at all. If you make the same argument against animal abuse in an oral presentation, you'll mostly be talking, though you may use slides to help your listeners follow your comments, to remind them of your main points, and to show graphs or photos that will appeal to their sense of reason or their emotions.

　　Remember that persuasion is always about connecting with an audience, meeting them where they are, and helping them see why your position is one they should take seriously or even adopt. To achieve that goal, you have to convey your position in a medium your audience will be receptive to—and can access. Different media serve different purposes, and you will want to consider your own goals as well as your audience's expectations.

THINK BEYOND WORDS

📤 *TAKE A LOOK at the website of Mutt Love Rescue, a dog adoption organization in Washington, DC, where you can see photos of available dogs, find out about fostering a dog, and more. Click on "Saving a Life" to see the organization's appeal for donations, along with photos of some of the "lucky pups." How compelling do you find the organization's argument? How does the use of words and images contribute to its appeal—is one more important? How would you revise this site to make it more effective—add video? audio? statistics? testimonials? more written information (or less)? Go to* everyonesanauthor.tumblr.com *to access the site.*

Across Cultures and Communities

Taking a position in cultures or communities other than your own poses special challenges. Advertising—a clear case of taking a position—is full of humorous tales of cross-cultural failure. When Pepsi first sought to break into the Chinese market, for example, its slogan, "Pepsi Brings You Back to Life," got mangled in translation, coming out as "Pepsi Brings Your Ancestors Back from the Grave."

Far more problematic than questions of translation are questions of STANCE. When taking a position in American academic contexts, you're almost always expected to state your position explicitly while showing your awareness of other possible positions. In contrast, in some cultures and communities, you would generally avoid stating your opinion directly; rather, you would hint at it. In yet others, you would be expected to state your mind forthrightly, paying little attention to what others think about the issue or to how your words might make them feel. So as an author, you always need to understand and respect the cultural context you are writing in.

But cultures and communities are not monolithic. Remember, then, that how people are expected to frame positions they take may well vary within a community, depending on their place in the social hierarchy as supervisor or employee, teacher or student, ruler or governed. To complicate matters, the expectations with respect to outsiders are almost always different from those for the locals. Most people might be quick to criticize their own government among friends, but they don't necessarily grant outsiders the same privilege. A word to the wise: humility is in order, especially when taking a position in communities or cultures of which you're not a member. Don't assume that what works at home will work elsewhere. A safe first step is to listen and observe carefully when in a new context, paying special attention to how people communicate any positions they are taking.

Across Genres

Arguing a position, as we've pointed out, is something that we do, in small ways or large, almost every day—and even across a range of genres. You might, for instance, write a letter to the editor of your local newspaper lamenting the closure of the local library—and setting forth your POSITION that it must be kept open at all costs. Similarly, a company's annual REPORT would likely set out its position that collective bargaining with suppliers will improve the company's bottom line. After taking in a highly anticipated film, you might post a brief REVIEW, arguing that it wasn't as good as you'd expected. In each case, the text states a position.

See how video game publisher Activision-Blizzard states its position on esports in its 2017 annual report. Go to everyonesanauthor.tumblr.com and scroll to p. 15 of the report.

REFLECT. Look to see where and how positions are expressed around you, considering posters, editorials, songs, social media posts, blog entries, and so on. Then choose one that most interests you—or that most irritates you—and spend some time thinking about how it presents its position. How does it appeal to you—or why does it fail to appeal? What kinds of words, images, or sounds does it offer as support for its position? If you were going to revise it for a different audience, what would you do? If you were going to create it in another medium, how would it be different?

CHARACTERISTIC FEATURES

Given the many different forms of writing that take a position, no one-size-fits-all approach to composing them is possible. We can, however, identify the following characteristic features common to writing in which the author is arguing a position:

- An explicit position (p. 158)
- A response to what others have said or done (p. 160)
- Useful background information (p. 161)
- A clear indication of why the topic matters (p. 164)
- Good reasons and evidence (p. 166)
- Attention to more than one point of view (p. 168)
- An authoritative tone and stance (p. 170)
- An appeal to readers' values (p. 170)

An Explicit Position

Stating a position explicitly is easier said than done, since the complexity of most important issues can make it hard to articulate a position in a crystal-clear way. But it's very important to do so insofar as possible; nothing will lose an audience faster than drowning your position in a sea of qualifications. At the same time, in most academic contexts (as well as many others), a position stated baldly with no qualifications or nuances may alienate many readers.

In an article published by *Forbes*, Michelle Greenwald, a professor of marketing and CEO of several networking and innovation companies, begins her argument about *TikTok*'s growing influence this way:

TikTok will grow and broaden its appeal . . . for 4 key reasons:
- Its algorithm and data set, currently second to none, will keep getting better
- It's the easiest platform algorithm for users to train to feed them content they love
- It's highly accurate at targeting and connecting micro-cultures with content users crave
- For creators, barriers to entry are low and they can gain followers more quickly than on any other platform
> —MICHELLE GREENWALD, "Audience, Algorithm and Virality:
> Why TikTok Will Continue to Shape Culture In 2021"

Greenwald's position is clear and explicit: *TikTok* will continue to grow and be highly influential. Although such a strong position may alienate some readers, all readers have a clear understanding of where Greenwald stands.

There are times, however, when you will want to **QUALIFY** your position by using words like "many," "some," or "maybe"—or writing "could" rather than "will." Not every position you take can be stated with absolute certainty, and a qualified claim is generally easier to support than an unqualified one. When LeBron James announced that he would leave the Cleveland Cavaliers to join the Los Angeles Lakers, many argued that this move would be a great boon to the LA economy. See how one writer for *Fortune* was careful to qualify that position:

> LeBron James' move to Los Angeles is expected to have more than just an impact on the Lakers—a once-dominant team that has sagged in recent years. His move might also boost the local economy. According to a study conducted by legal document website FormSwift in February, LeBron James will likely have a positive economic impact on the food and drink industries in Los Angeles based on data from the previous cities he's called home, including Cleveland and Miami, before and after he left.
> —SARAH GRAY, "Why LeBron James' Move to
> Los Angeles Could Boost the City's Economy"

Gray's position is clear—LeBron James's move to Los Angeles will have a positive effect on the economy—but she is careful to qualify that claim so as not to overstate it. Note that she says James's move is "expected" to have an impact, "might" improve the LA economy, and "will likely" add growth to the local food and drink industries.

Keep in mind that while it may be useful, even necessary, to qualify a statement, you should be careful not to overdo it. You don't want to sound unsure of your position. In this case, Gray's position turned out to be correct. Even during the COVID-19 pandemic, James's stardom helped keep LA going strong: in addition to keeping the Lakers franchise in good shape, James starred in *Space Jam: A New Legacy*, which brought more revenue into the community.

A Response to What Others Have Said or Done

Crucially, position papers respond to other positions. That is, they are motivated by something that has been said or done by others—and are part of an ongoing conversation. In the *Forbes* example, Greenwald responds to critics who have argued *TikTok*'s influence is declining.

In some cases, the position the author is responding to becomes part of the argument. The music video "Immigrants (We Get the Job Done)," produced by Lin-Manuel Miranda, uses this strategy. Viewed more than 8 million times on *YouTube*, the video features four well-known rappers from around the world responding to the vilification of immigrants by making a case for how much immigrants contribute to the United States. The video begins by acknowledging the debate and the lyrics are punctuated throughout by a chorus with a clear position: "Immigrants, we get the job done. Look how far I come." The video's argument is an explicit response to those who think that

THINK BEYOND WORDS

IMMIGRANTS

≋ ★ WE GET THE JOB DONE ★ ≋

HAMILTON ★ MIXTAPE

▶ *WATCH THE VIDEO of "Immigrants (We Get the Job Done)." Consider how the medium—video, with the addition of music by diverse performers, a radio voice-over at the start, and images of immigrant experiences—contributes to the power of the argument. Find the link to view the full video at* everyonesanauthor.tumblr.com.

"immigrant" is a "bad word." In fact, Lin-Manuel Miranda even described the video as "musical counterweight" to the xenophobia and criticism of immigrants at the time it was written.

Later in this chapter, you will meet Katherine Spriggs, who staked out a position on "buying local" in an essay written for one of her college courses. In this brief excerpt from her essay, she responds directly to those who say buying local will have negative environmental effects:

> It has also been argued that buying locally will be detrimental to the environment because small farms are not as efficient in their use of resources as large farms. This is a common misconception and actually depends on how economists measure efficiency. Small farms are less efficient than large farms in the total output of one crop per acre, but they are more efficient in total output of all crops per acre (McCauley).
>
> —KATHERINE SPRIGGS, "On Buying Local"

In a short space, Spriggs identifies an argument that others have made about the position she is taking and then responds to it explicitly. In academic position papers, authors are expected to acknowledge and address other positions directly in this way. That is often not the case when you take a position in other contexts and in some cultures. In online writing, for instance, it's not unusual for authors to simply provide a brief mention with a link to refer readers to another position within an ongoing conversation.

🖎 *REFLECT. Think about your writing as part of a larger, ongoing conversation. Examine something that you have recently written—an email, a social media post, an essay for a class—that expresses a position about an issue that matters to you. Check to see whether it makes clear your motivation for writing and the position(s) to which you were responding. If these aren't clear, try revising your text to make them more explicit.*

Useful Background Information

The amount of background information needed—historical background, definitions, contextual information—will vary widely depending on the scope of your topic, your audience, and your medium. If you are preparing a position paper on the effects of global warming for an environmental group, any background information provided will represent extensive, often detailed, and sometimes highly technical knowledge. If, on the other hand, you are preparing a poster to display on campus that summarizes your position on an increase in tuition, you can probably assume your audience will need little background information—for which you will have only limited space anyway.

As a music video partly intended to entertain, the "Immigrants (We Get the Job Done)" video provided no background information other than the radio voice-over that sounds like a news broadcast indicating "you know, and it gets into this whole issue of border security" and "we've got the House and the Senate debating this issue." The video's creators assume the viewers will know about the context of the video's message—how immigrants and refugees were being talked about and treated in the United States when the video was made. In online writing, links can often do much of the work of filling readers in on background information; they are especially convenient because readers have the option of clicking on them or not, depending on how much information they need or want.

In academic contexts, writers are generally expected to provide a great deal of background information to firmly ground their discussion of a topic. When the president of Rensselaer Polytechnic Institute, Shirley Ann Jackson, spoke at a symposium celebrating women in science and engineering, she argued that while the number of women graduating with degrees in STEM fields has increased, major obstacles still stand in the way of women academics in the sciences at research universities. To make this argument, she first provided background information about the number of women PhDs leaving the research science track:

> Writing for the *New York Times*, Steven Greenhouse noted that, based on a University of California, Berkeley, study, "Keeping Women in the Science Pipeline," women are far more likely than men to "'leak' out of the research science pipeline before obtaining tenure at a college or university." After receiving a PhD, married women with young children are 35 percent less likely to enter a tenure-track position in science than are married men with young children and PhDs in science. According to the report from the University of California, "women who had children after becoming postdoctoral scholars were twice as likely as their male counterparts to shift their career goals away from being professors with a research emphasis—a 41 percent shift for women versus 20 percent for men." And a 2005 report from Virginia Tech found a disproportionate share of women made up "voluntary departures" from the faculty. Although women represented one-fifth of the faculty, they accounted for two-fifths of departures.

At every step along the way—from entering college as a science or engineering major to graduating with a technical degree, from entering graduate school to exiting successfully, to getting a postdoc, to succeeding as faculty, to attaining tenure—we need to provide women with bridges to the next level. As is clear from the studies I mentioned, the unequal burden of family life turns the gaps in the road into chasms. Help with childcare, which has been provided at MIT, and the establishment of parental childbirth leave, which has been provided at Rensselaer, can help. But there is more to be done.

—SHIRLEY ANN JACKSON, "Leaders in Science and Engineering: The Women of MIT"

Hearing about specific research studies helps Jackson's audience see that a disproportionately high number of women scientists are "shift[ing] their career goals away from being professors with a research emphasis"—and supports her argument that universities must do more to ease the "unequal burden of family life" that young women scientists bear.

Background information is not always statistical and impersonal, even in academic contexts. In an essay written for *Academe*, a publication

Many women are earning degrees in STEM fields, and universities need to do more to help young women scientists balance the demands of family life and scientific research.

of the American Association of University Professors, Randall Hicks, a professor of chemistry at Wheaton College, argues that it is harder for working-class students to become professors than it is for children of college-educated parents. The background information he provides is startlingly personal:

> "I'll break his goddamned hands," my father said. I wonder if he remembers saying it. Nearly twenty-five years later, his words still linger in my mind. My father had spent the entire day in the auto body shop only to come home and head to the garage for more work on the side. I may have finished my homework, and, tired of roughhousing with my brother, gone out to help him scrape the paint off his current project, some classic car that he was restoring. "It's okay for a hobby, but if somebody tells me that he's thinking of doing it for a living, I'll break his goddamned hands." Although we had no firm plans and little financial means to do so, he was telling me that he expected me to get an education.   —RANDALL HICKS

Note how this story provides readers with important background information for Hicks's argument. Immediately, we learn relevant information about Hicks and the environment that shaped him. Thus, we understand part of his passionate commitment to this topic: he learned, indirectly, from his father to put a high value on education, since doing so in his father's view would allow Hicks to get a job that would be better than something that is just "okay for a hobby."

A Clear Indication of Why the Topic Matters

No matter the topic, one of an author's tasks is to demonstrate that the issue is real and significant—and thus to motivate readers to read on or listeners to keep listening. Rarely can you assume your audience sees why your argument matters.

As a student, you'll sometimes be assigned to write a position paper on a particular topic; in those cases, you may have to find ways to make the topic interesting for you, as the writer, although you can assume the topic matters to the person who assigned it. On other occasions, you may take it upon yourself to write about something you care deeply about, in which case you will need to help your audience understand why they should care as well.

See how Mellody Hobson, CEO of the first Black-owned mutual fund in the United States and chairwoman of Starbucks, tells a personal story in a conversation with journalist Jonathan Capehart that illustrates why being the "first and only [Black person] is not enough." Opening with "it's a true story," she tells Capehart,

> Harold Ford was running for the U.S. Senate, and he called me one day. We were very good friends, and are. And he said, "You know, Mellody, I need some national press. Do you have any ideas?" We're just like pip-squeaks. But I had a friend who was a major, major person, one of the biggest media companies in the world, and so I reached out to her and I told her what we were trying to accomplish. And she said, "Why don't you come and do editorial board lunch? . . .
>
> [Harold and I] were wearing our best suits. You know, we looked like shiny, new pennies. We were so excited for this opportunity. And we get upstairs, and the receptionist says, "Follow me." . . . And all of a sudden, we enter this room completely stark, empty. And she turns and looks at us and she says, "Where are your uniforms?"
>
> And we were like stunned, I mean, just really stunned. And all of a sudden, my friend runs in, because she knew we were taken to the wrong place, clearly. We were the lunch. And all of the color drained out of her face. And I joked with her. I looked at her and I said, "Now, don't you think this is the reason why we need more than one Black person in the U.S. Senate?" because at that time we only had Barack Obama.
>
> —MELLODY HOBSON, *Washington Post Live* interview

Mellody Hobson, the first Black woman to chair the Economic Club of Chicago.

By sharing this story about how she and Ford were assumed to be kitchen workers on the basis of their race, Hobson establishes in a vivid way why it matters that business and government entities go well beyond having a "first and only" Black person, so that such inaccurate and injurious assumptions can no longer be so readily made.

The creators of the "Immigrants (We Get the Job Done)" video certainly believed immigrants matter, as demonstrated in the values they appealed to and the range of people they included in the video. Similarly, Michelle Greenwald certainly thinks understanding *TikTok*'s growing influence is important. When she writes that "an estimated 56% of U.S. consumers under 24 were on the platform" in 2020 and "on average, they spent 52 minutes per day," which is "more than Netflix or YouTube" for some demographics, these striking facts and comparisons convey a sense of urgency. In all these cases, the writers share the conviction that what they're writing about matters not just to them but to us all, and they work hard to make that conviction evident.

REFLECT. Examine something you've written that takes a strong position. Catalog the specific ways you make clear to your readers that the topic matters to you—and that it should matter to them.

Good Reasons and Evidence

Positions are only as good as the reasons and evidence that support them, so part of every author's task in arguing a position is to provide the strongest possible reasons for the position, and evidence for those reasons. Evidence may take many forms, but among the most often used, especially in academic contexts, are facts; firsthand material gathered from observations, interviews, or surveys; data from experiments; historical data; examples; expert testimony (often in the form of what scholars have written); precedents; statistics; and personal experience.

See how Barbara Ehrenreich went about getting firsthand information in order to write about low-wage workers in Florida, p. 873.

In an essay from the *New York Times* Opinions page, Jennifer Delahunty, dean of admissions at Kenyon College, seeks to explain to her own daughter why one of her daughter's college applications had been rejected. Delahunty's explanation—the position her essay takes—is that the rejection was due at least in part to the fact that young women, even accomplished ones, face particular challenges in getting into prestigious colleges:

She had not . . . been named a National Merit Finalist, dug a well for a village in Africa or climbed to the top of Mount Rainier. She is a smart, well-meaning, hard-working teenage girl, but in this day and age of swollen applicant pools that are decidedly female, that wasn't enough. . . .

Had she been a male applicant, there would have been little, if any, hesitation to admit. The reality is that because young men are rarer, they're more valued applicants. Today, two-thirds of colleges and universities report that they get more female than male applicants, and more than 56 percent of undergraduates nationwide are women.

—JENNIFER DELAHUNTY, "To All the Girls I've Rejected"

Delahunty offers two related reasons that her daughter had not been admitted. First, for all her daughter's accomplishments, they were not as impressive as those of other applicants. Here she provides specific evidence (her daughter was not a National Merit finalist, nor had she "dug a well for a village in Africa or climbed to the top of Mount Rainier") that makes the reason memorable and convincing.

The second reason focuses on the fact that male applicants in general have a better chance than female applicants of getting into many schools. This time her evidence is of a different sort; she uses statistics to show that "young men are rarer" and therefore "more valued applicants." Note that Delahunty expects readers to share her knowledge that something seen as valuable takes on additional value when it is rare.

The scientific community typically takes the long view in terms of gathering evidence in support of the positions it takes. That certainly seems to have been the case with the slow accumulation of evidence to suggest cow's milk may not be as good for us as we once thought. Until recently, US dietary guidelines recommended drinking three glasses of milk a day. But over time, scientists questioned this guideline (heavily promoted by the milk industry), showing in numerous studies that too much milk harms both people and the planet. In a report published by *The New England Journal of Medicine*, Harvard professor of epidemiology and nutrition Walter Willett and Harvard professor of pediatrics David Ludwig make the following case:

> For adults, the overall evidence does not support high dairy consumption for reduction of fractures, which has been a primary justification for current U.S. recommendations. Moreover, total dairy consumption has

not been clearly related to weight control or to risks of diabetes and car-
diovascular disease. High consumption of dairy foods is likely to increase
the risks of prostate cancer and possibly endometrial cancer but reduce
the risk of colorectal cancer.

—WALTER C. WILLETT & DAVID LUDWIG, "Milk and Health"

In this case, the researchers analyzed evidence gathered over many years
before reaching their conclusion.

Attention to More than One Point of View

Considering multiple, often opposing, points of view is a hallmark of any
strong position paper, particularly in an academic context. By showing that
you understand and have carefully evaluated other viewpoints, you show
respect for the issue's complexity and for your audience, while also showing
that you have done your homework on your topic.

In a journal article on human-caused climate change, Naomi Oreskes
takes a position based on a careful analysis of 928 scientific articles published in well-known and respected journals. Some people, she says, "suggest
that there might be substantive disagreement in the scientific community
about the reality of anthropogenic climate change. This is not the case." Yet
in spite of the very strong consensus on which Oreskes bases her claim, she
still acknowledges other possible viewpoints:

> Admittedly, [some] authors evaluating impacts, developing methods, or
> studying paleoclimatic change might believe that current climate change
> is natural. . . . The scientific consensus might, of course, be wrong. If
> the history of science teaches anything, it is humility, and no one can be
> faulted for failing to act on what is not known.
>
> —NAOMI ORESKES, "Beyond the Ivory Tower:
> The Scientific Consensus on Climate Change"

Oreskes acknowledges that the consensus she found in the articles she
examined might be challenged by other articles she did not consider and
that any consensus, no matter how strong, might ultimately prove to be
wrong. The most recent United Nations Intergovernmental Panel on Climate Change offers no such qualifications, however, reporting that human-
influenced climate change is "widespread, rapid, and intensifying." The

conclusion reached by 234 scientists (and over 500 other contributing authors) from sixty-six countries, based on an analysis of more than 14,000 studies and over 80,000 statements by international experts, is what the report's authors call "an unequivocal consensus."

Sometimes you'll want to both acknowledge and reply to other viewpoints, especially if you can answer any objections persuasively. Here is college admissions officer Jennifer Delahunty, noting—and ruling out—the possible criticism that college admissions officers do not give careful consideration to all applicants:

> Rest assured that admissions officers are not cavalier in making their decisions. Last week, the 10 officers at my college sat around a table, 12 hours every day, deliberating the applications of hundreds of talented young men and women. While gulping down coffee and poring over statistics, we heard about a young woman from Kentucky we were not yet ready to admit outright. She was the leader/president/editor/captain/ lead actress in every activity in her school. She had taken six advanced placement courses and had been selected for a prestigious state leadership program. In her free time, this whirlwind of achievement had accumulated more than 300 hours of community service in four different organizations.
>
> Few of us sitting around the table were as talented and as directed at age 17 as this young woman. Unfortunately, her test scores and grade point average placed her in the middle of our pool. We had to have a debate before we decided to swallow the middling scores and write "admit" next to her name.
>
> —JENNIFER DELAHUNTY, "To All the Girls I've Rejected"

Delahunty provides evidence from a specific case, demonstrating persuasively that the admissions officers at her college take their job seriously.

Even bumper stickers can subtly acknowledge more than one position, as does this one from late 2008:

> I Support Our Troops / I Question Our Policies

This bumper sticker states two positions that initially might seem contradictory, arguing that supporting a country's troops and questioning a government's foreign policies are not mutually exclusive.

An Authoritative Tone and Stance

Particularly in academic contexts, authors make a point of taking an authoritative tone. Even if your goal is to encourage readers to examine a number of alternatives without suggesting which one is best, you should try to do so in a way that shows you know which alternatives are worth examining and why. Likewise, even if you are taking a strong position, you should seek to appear reasonable and rational. The 1964 surgeon general's report on the consequences of smoking does not waver: smoking causes cancer. At the same time, in taking this position, it briefly outlines the history of the issue and the evidence on which the claim is logically based, avoiding emotional language and carefully specifying which forms of smoking ("excessive" cigarettes) and cancer (lung) the claim involves.

Jennifer Delahunty establishes her authority in other ways. Her description of ten admissions officers putting in twelve-hour days going through hundreds of applications and "poring over statistics" backs up her forthright assertion, "Rest assured that admissions officers are not cavalier in making their decisions." Later in the essay, acknowledging her own struggles to weigh issues of fairness to highly qualified young women against the need to maintain gender balance in incoming classes, Delahunty not only demonstrates that she knows what she is writing about but also invites readers to think about the complexity of the situation without offering them any easy answers. In short, she is simultaneously reasonable and authoritative.

An Appeal to Readers' Values

Implicitly or explicitly, authors need to appeal to readers' values, especially when taking a strong position. The creators of the "Immigrants (We Get the Job Done)" video clearly appealed to a number of cultural values Americans hold dear, such as work ethic and opportunity (with references to the demanding kinds of work immigrants do to survive—picking oranges, sewing textiles, nursing the ill, constructing buildings) as well as equality, justice, and hope (depictions of harrowing migration journeys and confrontations with border agents). The refrain "Immigrants, we get the job done" is itself a strong appeal to the audience's sense of fairness and democratic ideals.

Freeman A. Hrabowski III, president of the University of Maryland, Baltimore County (UMBC) from 1992 to 2022, appeals to values of honesty, hard work, resilience, and grit in a conversation on *The Innovating Together Podcast* series, produced by the University Innovation Alliance. About success, he says,

> It's not just reaching the goal line. It is about how we get there, and that means showing people that in stressful times, we need to think about being supportive of each other, to keep a kind of calmness, to bring honesty to the work but to be able to say things in a way that we can hear each other. We talk about "retriever courage"—at UMBC our [mascot's] a Chesapeake Bay retriever—and that's the courage to look in the mirror and not only be honest with self, but to listen to the other voices. Whether it's about the fears that people have about this disease right now [COVID-19] or it's about the challenges involving racism, the question is: how can we show, not only through what we say but through our actions, that we are committed to making the place better, to addressing the issues and concerns that people bring up, and most important that we have a vision that tomorrow can be better than today? . . .
>
> And the more we get knocked down, as we get knocked down by health or by these other challenges and we get back up, the stronger we can be. And that's probably the most important lesson. . . . And we use the word at UMBC "grit." When we see that word, grit, that hard work, that resilience, and never giving up—now is the time we in America, in the world, and at UMBC *must* use that word and show it through our actions. Grit: it's very important.
>
> —FREEMAN A. HRABOWSKI III, *The Innovating Together Podcast*

Freeman A. Hrabowski III

Hrabowski appeals to readers' patriotic values of hard work and of pulling together for the common good. In this conversation he goes on to call for listening carefully and respectfully to one another about partisan health-related issues and for leaders everywhere to "set a tone" that says "we are all in this together."

RUSSEL HONORÉ wrote this essay for *This I Believe*, a not-for-profit organization that sponsors "a public dialogue about belief, one essay at a time." The essay was later broadcast on NPR's *Weekend Edition* on March 1, 2009. Honoré is a retired lieutenant general in the US Army who has contributed to response efforts to Hurricanes Katrina and Rita in 2005 and other natural disasters.

Work Is a Blessing

RUSSEL HONORÉ

Background information.

GREW UP IN Lakeland, Louisiana, one of 12 children. We all lived on my parents' subsistence farm. We grew cotton, sugarcane, corn, hogs, chickens and had a large garden, but it didn't bring in much cash. So when I was 12, I got a part-time job on a dairy farm down the road, helping to milk cows. We milked 65 cows at 5 in the morning and again at 2 in the afternoon, seven days a week.

A position taken in response to another position.

In the kitchen one Saturday before daylight, I remember complaining to my father and grandfather about having to go milk those cows. My father said, "Ya know, boy, to work is a blessing."

Admitting his own slowness to understand what his father meant contributes to his authoritative tone.

I looked at those two men who'd worked harder than I ever had—my father eking out a living on that farm and my grandfather farming and working as a carpenter during the Depression. I had a feeling I had been told something really important, but it took many years before it sunk in.

Going to college was a rare privilege for a kid from Lakeland, Louisiana. My father told me if I picked something to study that I liked doing, I'd always look forward to my work. But he also added, "Even having a job you hate is better than not having a job at all." I wanted to be a farmer, but I joined the ROTC program to help pay for college. And what started out as an obligation to the Army became a way of life that I stayed committed to for 37 years, three months and three days.

Citing his father, Honoré shows his attention to more than one point of view about work.

In the late 1980s, during a visit to Bangladesh, I saw a woman with a baby on her back, breaking bricks with a hammer. I asked a Bangladesh military escort why they weren't using a machine, which would have been a lot easier. He told me a machine would put that lady out of work. Breaking those bricks meant she'd earn enough money to feed herself and her baby that day. And as bad as that woman's job was, it was enough to keep a small family alive. It reminded me of my father's words: To work is a blessing.

Reasons and evidence for how the author came to see work as a blessing.

Serving in the United States Army overseas, I saw a lot of people like that woman in Bangladesh. And I have come to believe that people without jobs are not free. They are victims of crime, the ideology of terrorism, poor health, depression and social unrest. These victims become the illegal immigrants, the slaves of human trafficking, the drug dealers, the street gang members. I've seen it over and over again on the U.S. border, in Somalia, the Congo, Afghanistan and in New Orleans. People who have jobs can have a home, send their kids to school, develop a sense of pride, contribute to the good of the community, and even help others. When we can work, we're free. We're blessed.

Specific examples indicate why the topic matters and show the author's awareness of his audience's values.

I don't think I'll ever quit working. I'm retired from the Army, but I'm still working to help people be prepared for disaster. And I may get to do a little farming someday, too. I'm not going to stop. I believe in my father's words. I believe in the blessing of work.

The author concludes by stating his position explicitly.

Listen to the audio essay at everyonesanauthor .tumblr.com. You'll hear someone who sounds like he grew up on a farm in Louisiana, a fact that contributes to Honoré's authority: this guy knows what he's talking about.

REFLECT. *Choose a short piece of writing on a website such as* Salon *that takes a position on an issue you care about. Look at the list of characteristic features on page 158 and annotate your text to point out the ones that are represented in it, using Honoré's essay as a model. Make a list of any features that are not included as well. (While not every effective position paper will include all of the characteristic features, many of them will.) Then consider whether including those features might have improved the text—and if so, how.*

ARGUING A POSITION / A Roadmap

Choose a topic that matters—to you, and to others

If you get to select your topic, begin by examining your own interests and commitments in light of the context you are writing for. Global warming might be a fitting topic for a course in the life sciences or social sciences, but it's probably not going to serve you well in a course in medieval history unless you can find a direct link between the two topics. You might consider focusing on some issue that's being debated on campus (Are those new rules for dropping classes fair?), a broader political or ethical issue (Is eating meat by definition unethical?), or an issue in which you have a direct stake (Does early admission penalize those who need financial aid?).

Lynda Barry thinks arts education is really important. See how she makes us think the same in "The Sanctuary of School," p. 851.

If you've been assigned a topic, do your best to find an aspect of it that interests you. (If you're bored with your subject, you can be sure your readers will be.) If, for example, you're assigned to write about globalization in an international studies course, you could tailor that topic to your own interests and write about the influence of American hip-hop on world music.

Be sure that your topic is one that is arguable—and that it matters. Short of astounding new evidence, it's no longer worth arguing that there is no link between smoking and lung cancer. It's a fact. But you can argue about what responsibility tobacco companies now have for tobacco-related deaths, as recent court cases demonstrate.

One sure way to find out whether a topic is arguable is to see if it *is* being debated—and that is a good first step as you explore a topic. You can probably assume that any topic that's being widely discussed matters—and of course you'll want to know what's being said about it in order to write about it. Remember that your essay is part of a larger conversation about your topic: you need to become familiar with that conversation in order to contribute to it.

Be careful to keep an open mind. A good, arguable topic will surely trigger at least several different points of view. Keeping an open mind and considering those points of view fairly and carefully at the start is always a good idea. And it will make your argument stronger by showing that you can be trusted to consider all sides of an issue, especially those you may not agree with.

Consider your rhetorical situation

Looking at your audience, your purpose, and other aspects of your rhetorical situation will help you to think carefully about how to achieve your goals.

Focus on your AUDIENCE. Who are you trying to reach, and what do you hope to persuade them to think or do?

- What are they likely to know about your topic, and what background information will you need to provide?

- How are they like or unlike you—and one another? Consider such things as age, education, gender, abilities and disabilities, cultural and linguistic heritage, and so on. How will such factors influence the way you make your argument?

- What convictions might they hold about the topic you're addressing—and how sympathetic are they likely to be to your position?

If you're trying to convince your fellow business majors of the virtues of free-market capitalism, your task is quite different than if you're trying to convince members of the campus socialist organization. In the first case, you would almost surely be preaching to the choir, whereas in the second, you would likely face a more skeptical audience.

Keep in mind that there's always danger in speaking only to those who already agree with you; if you keep audiences with differing values and viewpoints in mind, you will be more likely to represent all views fairly and hence encourage others to consider your position seriously. Keeping your audience in mind, then, means thinking in terms of who may respond to your position, how they will likely respond, and why.

Think hard about your PURPOSE. Why are you arguing this position? What has motivated you to write on this topic? What do you hope to learn by writing about it? What do you want to convince your audience to think or do? How can you best achieve your purpose or purposes?

Think about your STANCE. Start by asking yourself where you are coming from in regard to this topic. What about the topic captured your interest, and how has that interest led you to the position you expect to take on it? Why do you think the topic matters? How would you describe your attitude toward the topic: are you an advocate, a critic, an observer, or something else? How do you want to be seen as an author—as forceful? thoughtful? curious? How can you establish your own authority in writing on this topic?

Consider the larger CONTEXT. What are the various perspectives on the issue? What have others said about it? If you're writing about the use of ethanol as a fuel source, for instance, you'll need to look at what circumstances led to its use, at who's supported and opposed it (and why), and at the economic ramifications both of producing ethanol for fuel and of not doing so. As you come to understand the larger context, you'll become aware of various positions you'll want to consider, and what factors will be important to consider as you develop your position.

Consider your LANGUAGE. Almost any argument can be presented in a number of ways. Regardless of how many languages and dialects you use in your everyday life, you have many options to consider in taking a position. Will your audience expect a certain kind of language or style? Do you want to meet those expectations? challenge them? What do you want your language choices to say about you? What risks might you be willing to take with your language? How will your choice of medium and the larger context limit or expand the language options available to you? (You may want to consult Chapters 4 and 33 for more information about language options.)

Consider your MEDIUM. Will your writing take the form of a print essay? Will it appear as an editorial in a local paper? on a website? as an audio essay to be broadcast on a local radio station or posted as a podcast? as an oral or multimedia presentation for a class you are taking? The medium you choose should be one that suits both your purpose and your audience.

Consider matters of DESIGN. Think about the "look" you want to achieve and how you can format your text to make it easy to follow. Do you need headings? illustrations? any other graphics? color? Does the discipline you're writing in have any conventions you should follow? Does your medium allow for certain elements such as audio or video links that will help you achieve your purpose?

Research your topic

Begin exploring the topic by looking at it from different points of view. Whatever position you take will ultimately be more credible and persuasive if you can show evidence of having considered other positions.

Begin by assessing what you know—and don't know—about the topic. What interests you about the topic, and why? What more do you want or need to find out about it? What questions do you have about it, and where might you go for answers? To answer these questions, you might try **BRAINSTORMING** or other activities for **GENERATING IDEAS**.

What have others said? What are some of the issues that are being debated now about your topic, and what are the various positions on these issues? What other **POSITIONS** might be taken with respect to the topic? Remember, too, to seek out sources that represent a variety of perspectives.

Where should you start your research? Where you start and what sources you consult depend upon your topic and what questions you have about it. If you are focusing on a current issue, turn to news media and to websites, listservs, *Twitter*, or other online groups devoted to the issue. If you are investigating a topic from the distant past, be sure to look for both older sources and more recent scholarship on the topic. For some issues, you might want to interview everyday folks, local experts, or community-based sources—or conduct other sorts of **FIELD RESEARCH**.

Do you need to cut your topic down to size? Few among us know enough to make strong general claims about climate change. While that fact does not and should not keep us from having opinions about the issue, it suggests that the existence of global warming is much too broad a topic to be well suited to a five-page essay. Instead, you'll need to focus on some aspect of that topic for your essay. What angle you take will depend on the course you're writing for. For a geology class, you might focus on the effects of rising temperatures on melting glaciers; for an international relations course, you could look at climate shift and national security debates. Just remember that your goal is to take an informed position, one that you can support well.

Formulate an explicit position

Once you have sufficient information about your topic and some understanding of the complexity of the issue, you'll need to formulate a position that you can state explicitly and support fully. Let's say you decide to take a position on a current controversy among scientists about climate change. Here's how one author formulated a position:

Many scientists have argued that climate change has led to bigger and more destructive hurricanes and typhoons. Other researchers, however, have countered by saying that climate change is not linked causally to an increase in hurricane strength. After reviewing both sides of this debate, I see two strong reasons why changes in our climate have not necessarily led to more severe hurricanes.

—SOFI MINCEY, "On Climate Change and Hurricanes"

These three sentences articulate a clear position—that climate change is not necessarily to blame for bigger hurricanes—and frame that position as a response to an existing debate. Notice also how the writer qualifies her claim: she does not claim definitively that climate change has not led to bigger hurricanes; rather, she promises to present reasons that argue for this view.

By arguing only that the claims of many scientists *may* be wrong, she greatly increases the likelihood that she can succeed in her argument, setting a reasonable goal for what she must achieve. Note that her position still requires support: she needs to present reasonable evidence to challenge the claim that climate change has "necessarily" led to bigger hurricanes.

State your position as a tentative THESIS. Once you formulate your position, try stating it several different ways and then decide which one is most compelling. Make sure the position is stated explicitly. Your statement should let your audience know where you stand and be interesting enough to attract their attention.

Then think about whether you should QUALIFY your position. Should you limit what you claim—is it true only sometimes or under certain circumstances? On the other hand, does it seem too weak or timid and need to be stated more forcefully?

Remember that a good thesis for a position paper should identify your specific topic and make a CLAIM about that topic that is debatable. The thesis should also give your audience your reasons for making this claim. Consider the following thesis statement from two scholars at a public policy institute:

The case against raising the minimum wage is straightforward: A higher wage makes it more expensive for firms to hire workers.

—KEVIN A. HASSET & MICHAEL R. STRAIN,
"Why We Shouldn't Raise the Minimum Wage"

Hasset and Strain's claim about raising the minimum wage is explicitly stated (they are "against" it), as is a major reason for that position.

Come up with REASONS and EVIDENCE. List all the reasons supporting your position that you discovered in your research. Which ones will be most persuasive to your audience? Then jot down all the evidence you have to support those reasons—facts, quotations, statistics, examples, testimony, visuals, and so on. Remember that what counts as evidence varies across audiences and disciplines. Some are persuaded by testimonials, while others want statistical data. In some cases, NARRATIVES can underscore or illustrate the importance of your argument. Finally, look for any FALLACIES or weak reasons or evidence, and decide whether you need to do further research.

Identify other positions. Carefully consider COUNTERARGUMENTS and other points of view on the topic and how you will account for them. At the very least, you need to acknowledge other positions that are prominent in the larger conversation about the topic and to treat them fairly. If you disagree with a position, you need to offer reasons why and do so respectfully.

Organize and start writing

Once you have a fair sense of how you will present your position, it's time to write out a draft. If you have trouble getting started, it might help to think about the larger conversation about the topic that's already going on—and to think of your draft as a moment when you get to say what *you* think.

Be guided by your THESIS. As you begin to organize, type it at the top of your page so that you can keep looking back to it to be sure that each part of your text supports the thesis.

Give REASONS for your position, with supporting EVIDENCE. Determine an order for presenting your reasons, perhaps starting with the one you think will speak most directly to your audience.

Don't forget to consider COUNTERARGUMENTS. Acknowledge positions other than your own, and respond to what they say.

Draft an OPENING. Introduce your topic, and provide any background information your audience may need. State your position clearly, perhaps as a response to what others have said about your topic. Say something about why the issue matters, why your audience should care.

Draft a CONCLUSION. You might want to end by summing up your position and by answering the "so what" question: why does your topic matter—and who cares? Make sure you give a strong takeaway message. What are the implications of your argument? What do you want readers to remember or do as a result of reading what you've written?

Look critically at your draft, get responses—and revise

Go through your draft carefully, looking critically at the position you stake out, the reasons and evidence you provide in support of it, and the way you present them to your audience. For this review, play the "doubting game" with yourself by asking "Who says?" and "So what?" and "Can this be done better?" at every point.

Being tough on yourself now will pay off by showing you where you need to shore up your arguments. As you work through your draft, make notes on what you plan to do in your revision.

Next, ask some classmates or friends to read and respond to your draft. Here are some questions that can help you or others read over a draft of writing that takes a position.

- *Is the position stated explicitly?* Is there a clear THESIS sentence—and if not, is one needed? Does it need to be qualified, or should it be stated more strongly?

- *What positions are you responding to?* What is the larger conversation?

- *Is it clear why the topic matters?* Why do you care about the topic, and why should your audience care?

- *How effective is the* OPENING*?* How does it capture your audience's interest? How else might you begin?

- *Is there sufficient background information?* What other information might the audience need?

- *How would you describe the* STANCE *and* TONE—do they reflect your purpose and appeal to your audience?

- *What* REASONS *do you give for the position, and what* EVIDENCE *do you provide for those reasons?* What are the strongest reasons and evidence given? the weakest? What other evidence or reasons are needed to support this position?

- *How trustworthy are the sources you've cited?* Are **QUOTATIONS**, **SUMMARIES**, and **PARAPHRASES** smoothly integrated into the text—and is it clear where you are speaking and where (and why) you are citing others?

- *What other positions do you consider, and do you treat them fairly?* Are there other **COUNTERARGUMENTS** you should address as well? How well do you answer possible objections to your position?

- *How is the draft organized?* Is it easy to follow, with clear **TRANSITIONS** from one point to the next? Are there headings—and if not, would they help? What about the organization could be improved?

- *Does the* **STYLE** *fit with your purpose and appeal to your audience?* Could the style—choice of words, kinds of sentences—be improved in any way?

- *How effective is your text* **DESIGN** *?* Have you used any visuals to support your position—and if so, have you written captions that explain how they contribute to the argument? If not, what visuals might be helpful? Is there any information that would be easier to follow if it were presented in a chart or table?

- *How does the draft* **CONCLUDE** *?* Is the conclusion forceful and memorable? How else might you conclude?

- *Consider the title.* Does it make clear what the text is about, and does it make a reader want to read on?

- *What is your overall impression of the draft?* Will it persuade your audience to accept the position—and if not, why? Even if they don't accept the position, would they consider it a plausible one?

Revise your draft in light of your own observations and any feedback from others—keeping your audience and purpose firmly in mind, as always.

ℜ *REFLECT. Once you've completed your essay, let it settle for a while and then take time to* **REFLECT***. How well did you argue your point? What additional revisions would you make if you could? Research shows that such reflections help "lock in" what you learn for future use.*

How Colleges Tell Student-Parents They Don't Belong

NICOLE LYNN LEWIS

OVER THE PAST five years, Yoslin Amaya would return home most days in the early-morning hours from her night shift as a janitor to her in-laws' house in Rockville, Maryland, where she lived in a bedroom with her husband and two sons, Andrew and James. Though she was often exhausted, her long days were not over. While her family slept, she would crack open a laptop to finish assignments for her classes, first at Montgomery College, and later at the University of Maryland. She was pursuing a bachelor's degree in government and politics with a minor in public leadership. Her dream: to one day "be on Capitol Hill, making decisions about what bills get passed or not. I see myself as an advocate for change."

Amaya's story mirrors that of nearly 4 million college students across the country who are parents. A 2017 study found that, after completing work and household responsibilities, college students with preschool-aged children had about 50 percent fewer hours left for things like studying and sleeping than their nonparent classmates. And national data show that student-parents are 10 times less likely to complete a bachelor's degree within five years than nonparents.

NICOLE LYNN LEWIS is founder and CEO of Generation Hope, a nonprofit devoted to supporting teen parents who are pursuing a college education. A former teen parent herself, Lewis worked while earning her degree from the College of William & Mary, and now advocates for millions of student-parents. Author of *Pregnant Girl*, published in 2021, Lewis and her husband are the parents of five children.

America's higher-education system is not set up for student-parents to succeed. In many ways, classes and campus life are designed for those who come to college right out of high school and who aren't parenting or working full-time. Though this kind of student is often portrayed in American culture as typical, 74 percent of undergraduates in this country don't wholly fit that profile. They are parents like Amaya (single or married), working full-time while going to school, paying for college on their own, attending school part-time, or older than 25, or they have earned a GED. This stereotype of the "typical" college student is damaging, because it obscures the needs of those who don't fit that mold. When four-year institutions require that all freshmen live on campus, that creates challenges for students who need to live at home to take care of their family. When campus offices, such as financial aid or student affairs, are not open in the evenings, students who have to work during the day can't access important services that could help them stay in school.

Student-parents, who make up nearly a quarter of the U.S. college population, are particularly vulnerable to this blind spot because caregiving comes with a unique set of challenges. Parenting responsibilities rule schedules, and financial need extends beyond tuition and books to child care and housing costs. Student-parents are also more likely than nonparents to be people of color, women, low-income, older than 30, and first-generation college students, adding layer upon layer of obstacles to degree completion. Even prior to the coronavirus pandemic, nearly 70 percent of student-parents reported that they were housing-insecure. Forty percent of all Black female undergraduate students are mothers. As a young child, Amaya emigrated from El Salvador with her mother. She is a Deferred Action for Childhood Arrivals recipient, which means that on top of being a parent in college, a Latina student, and a first-generation college student with few resources, she also had to navigate her uncertain immigration status.

As a former young mother in college—at 19, I possessed both a beautiful 5 infant daughter and an acceptance letter to the prestigious William & Mary but no clear path to my degree—I have a firsthand understanding of the various ways in which college is not built for student-parents. Sometimes the hurdles were subtle, such as not being able to register for the classes I needed for my major because they were offered at times when I had to be home with my daughter, or being unable to attend group-project meetings in the evenings because they were past her bedtime. Other times, the hurdles were so significant that they threatened my ability to stay enrolled.

Take the never-ending challenge of finding affordable and reliable child care as a single mother, or how afraid I was to disclose to professors that I had a child, because the culture made clear that being a parent was an inconvenience that would not be accommodated. (Once, a professor told me that if I did not show up for class in the middle of winter, when my 2-year-old had walking pneumonia, she would fail me. So I bundled up my daughter and took her with me to class despite how miserable she was.)

Twenty years later, some colleges—many of them community colleges, which have the largest share of parenting students—have launched programs to support student-parents on their campuses. The City University of New York has invested in creating child-care options for students with daytime and evening hours, parenting workshops, and connections to community resources. In Atlanta, Morehouse College, the world's only historically Black four-year liberal-arts college for men, has developed its Fathers to the Finish Line Initiative to help student-fathers complete their degrees by providing "academic support, mentorship, professional development, leadership training . . . and access to financial resources." Although people might think this issue affects only mothers, fathers also need support in graduating. (In fact, Black fathers drop out at higher rates than any other student-parent group.) The Single Parent Scholar Program at Wilson College, in Pennsylvania, provides family-friendly on-campus housing year-round to single student-parents and their children. This is a rarity—just 8 percent of all U.S. colleges and universities offer on-campus housing for student-parents. In the fall of 2020, Wilson dropped its housing fee for participants in that program.

These examples are encouraging but do not represent the offerings of most colleges and universities. Even the federal Child Care Access Means Parents in School Program, which provides funding to establish child-care centers on college campuses, was serving only 1 percent of parenting college students who qualified 11,000 students—as of 2019, according to estimates from the Institute for Women's Policy Research. If more colleges were to do things like this, student-parents would have far easier roads to their degrees, giving them the ability to build a better life for themselves and their children. But a truly inclusive college environment for parents would require schools to consider them in all aspects of campus life, not just housing and child care. To have a broader impact, institutions would need to include student-parents in their diversity and equity efforts, and address how every step of getting into college and attaining a degree might present challenges, from enrollment practices to financial-aid procedures to everyday treatment in the classroom.

Amaya graduated this month from the University of Maryland, beating tremendous odds. But despite having a higher GPA on average than their peers, 52 percent of student-parents like her leave college within six years without completing their degree. If more colleges and universities could widen their vision of who their students are—and who they could be—that number could change, preventing millions from having to decide between going to college and raising a family.

Thinking about the Text

1. Why do you think Nicole Lynn Lewis chose to open her argument with a **NARRATIVE**?

2. What does Lewis do to establish her own **CREDIBILITY** and credentials for writing about this topic?

3. How would you describe Lewis's **STANCE** and **TONE**? Identify a spot where the tone shifts and explain what you think accounts for this shift.

4. What pieces of **EVIDENCE** did you find most persuasive in this essay, and why?

5. Near the end of her essay, Lewis argues that "To have a broader impact, institutions would need to include student-parents in their diversity and equity efforts, and address how every step of getting into college and attaining a degree might present challenges, from enrollment practices to financial-aid procedures to everyday treatment in the classroom" (7). Do a little research on how student-parents are included in policies and procedures on your campus and write a couple of paragraphs explaining your own **POSITION** on this issue, using local examples as evidence.

On Buying Local

KATHERINE SPRIGGS

AMERICANS TODAY can eat pears in the spring in Minnesota, oranges in the summer in Montana, asparagus in the fall in Maine, and cranberries in the winter in Florida. In fact, we can eat pretty much any kind of produce anywhere at any time of the year. But what is the cost of this convenience? In this essay, I will explore some answers to this question and argue that we should give up a little bit of convenience in favor of buying local.

"Buying local" means that consumers choose to buy food that has been grown, raised, or produced as close to their homes as possible ("Buy Local"). Buying local is an important part of the response to many environmental issues we face today (fig. I). It encourages the development of small farms, which are often more environmentally sustainable than large farms, and thus strengthens local markets and supports small rural economies. By demonstrating a commitment to buying local, Americans could set an example for global environmentalism.

In 2010, the international community is facing many environmental challenges, including global warming, pollution, and dwindling fossil fuel resources. Global warming is attributed to the release of greenhouse gases such as carbon dioxide and methane, most commonly emitted in the burning of fossil fuels. It is such a pressing problem that scientists estimate that in the year 2030,

---

KATHERINE SPRIGGS wrote this essay for a writing course she took in her first year at Stanford University.

Fig. 1. Shopping at a farmers' market is one good way to support small farms and strengthen the local economy. Timothy Mulholland. *Dane County Farmers' Market on the Square, Madison, Wisconsin. 2008, Alamy.*

there will be no glaciers left in Glacier National Park ("Global Warming Statistics"). The United States is especially guilty of contributing to the problem, producing about a quarter of all global greenhouse gas emissions, and playing a large part in pollution and shrinking world oil supplies as well ("Record Increase"). According to a CNN article published in 2000, the United States manufactures more than 1.5 billion pounds of chemical pesticides a year that can pollute our water, soil, and air (Baum). Agriculture is particularly interconnected with all of these issues. Almost three-fourths of the pesticides produced in the United States are used in agriculture (Baum). Most produce is shipped many miles before it is sold to consumers, and shipping our food long distances is costly in both the amount of fossil fuel it uses and the greenhouse gases it produces.

A family friend and farmer taught me firsthand about the effects of buying local. Since I was four years old, I have spent every summer on a 150-acre farm in rural Wisconsin, where my family has rented our 75 tillable acres to a farmer who lives nearby. Mr. Lermio comes from a family that has farmed the area for generations. I remember him sitting on our porch at dusk wearing his blue striped overalls and dirty white T-shirt, telling my parents about all of the changes in the area since he was a kid. "Things sure are different around here," he'd say. He told us that all the farms in that region used to milk about 30 head of cattle each. Now he and the other farmers were selling their herds to industrial-scale farms milking 4,000 head each. The shift came when milk started being processed on a large scale rather than at small local cheese factories. Milk is now shipped to just a few large factories where it is either bottled or processed into cheese or other dairy products. The milk and products from these factories are then shipped all across the country. "You see," Mr. Lermio would tell us, "it's just not worth shipping the milk from my 20 cows all the way to Gays Mills. You just can't have a small herd anymore." Farming crops is also different now. Machinery is expensive and hard to pay off with profits from small fields. The Lermio family has been buying and renting fields all around the area, using their tractors to farm hundreds of acres. Because they can no longer sell locally, Mr. Lermio and many other rural farmers have to move towards larger-scale farming to stay afloat.

Fig. 2. A small polyculture farm. *Crops Growing on a Farm*. 2013, iStock.

Buying local could help reverse the trend towards industrial-scale farming, 5 of which the changes in Wisconsin over Mr. Lermio's lifetime are just one example. Buying local benefits small farmers by not forcing them to compete with larger farms across the country. For example, if consumers bought beef locally, beef cattle would be raised in every region and their meat would be sold locally rather than shipped from a small number of big ranches in Texas and Montana. Small farms are often polycultures—they produce many different kinds of products (fig. 2). The Lermios' original farm, for example, grew corn, hay, oats, and alfalfa. They also had milking cattle, chickens, and a few hogs. Large farms are often monocultures—they raise only one kind of crop or animal (fig. 3). The Lermio family has been moving towards becoming a monoculture; they raise only three field crops, and they don't have any animals. Buying local, as was common in the first half of the twentieth century, encourages small polyculture farms that sell a variety of products locally (McCauley).

For environmental purposes, the small polyculture farms that buying local encourages have many advantages over industrial-scale monoculture farms because they are more sustainable. Small farmers tend to value local natural

Fig. 3. A large monoculture farm. *Aerial Mid-Summer Farm Surrounded by Cornfields.* 2013, *iStock.*

resources more than industrial-scale farmers do and are therefore more conscientious in their farming methods. Small farms are also intrinsically more sustainable. As mentioned, small farms are more likely to be polycultures—to do many different things with the land—and using a field for different purposes does not exhaust the soil the way continually farming one crop does. Rotating crops or using a field alternately for pasture and for crops keeps the land "healthy." On small farms, sometimes a farmer will pasture his cattle in the previous year's cornfield; the cattle eat some of the stubble left from last year's crop and fertilize the field. The land isn't wasted or exhausted from continuous production. I've even seen one organic farmer set up his pigpen so that the pigs plow his blueberry field just by walking up around their pen. This kind of dual usage wouldn't be found on a large monoculture farm. Most big farms use their fields exclusively either for crops or for pasture. Modern fertilizers, herbicides, and pesticides allow farmers to harvest crops from even unhealthy land, but this is a highly unsustainable model. Farming chemicals can pollute groundwater and destroy natural ecosystems.

Not only are small farms a more sustainable, eco-friendly model than big commercial farms, but buying local has other advantages as well. Buying local, for example, would reduce the high cost of fuel and energy used to transport food across the world and would bring long-term benefits as well. It is currently estimated that most produce in the United States is shipped about fifteen-hundred miles before it is sold—it travels about the distance from Nebraska to New York ("Why Buy Local?"). Eighty percent of all strawberries grown in the United States are from California ("Strawberry Fruit Facts"). They are shipped from California all around the country even though strawberries can be grown in Wisconsin, New York, Tennessee, and most other parts of the United States. No matter how efficient our shipping systems, shipping food thousands of miles is expensive—in dollars, in oil, and in the carbon dioxide it produces (fig. 4). One of the main reasons that produce is shipped long distances is that fruits and vegetables don't grow everywhere all year around. Even though strawberries grow in a lot of places during the early summer, they grow only in Florida in the winter, or in California from spring to fall (Rieger). Americans have become accustomed to being able to buy almost any kind of produce at any time of the year. A true commitment to buying local would accommodate local season and climate. Not everything will grow everywhere, but the goal of buying local should be to eliminate all unnecessary shipping by buying things from as close to home as possible and eating as many things in season as possible.

Fig 4. Interstate trucking is expensive financially and ecologically. *Interstate Traffic with Trucks.* 2012, *iStock.*

Some argue that buying local can actually have negative environmental effects; and their arguments add important qualifiers to supporting small local farms. Alex Avery, the director of research and education at the Center for Global Food Issues, has said that we should "buy food from the world region where it grows best" (qtd. in MacDonald). His implication is that it would be more wasteful to try to grow pineapples in the Northeast than to have them shipped from the Caribbean. He makes a good point: trying to grow all kinds of food all over the world would be a waste of time and energy. Buying local should instead focus on buying *as much as possible* from nearby farmers. It has also been argued that buying locally will be detrimental to the environment because small farms are not as efficient in their use of resources as large farms. This is a common misconception and actually depends on how economists measure efficiency. Small farms are less efficient than large farms in the total output of one crop per acre, but they are more efficient in total output of all crops per acre (McCauley). When buying locally, the consumer should try to buy from these more efficient polyculture farms. Skeptics of buying local also say that focusing food cultivation in the United States will be worse for the environment because farmers here use more industrial equipment than farmers in the third world (MacDonald). According to the Progressive Policy Institute, however, only thirteen percent of the American diet is imported

("98.7 Percent"). This is a surprisingly small percentage, especially consider-ing that seafood is one of the top imports. It should also be considered that as countries around the world become wealthier, they will industrialize, so exploiting manual labor in the third world would only be a temporary solution (MacDonald). The environmental benefits now, and in the long run, of buying local outweigh any such immediate disadvantages.

Critics have also pointed to negative global effects of buying local, but buy-ing local could have positive global effects too. Speaking with the *Christian Science Monitor*, John Clark, author of *Worlds Apart: Civil Society and the Battle for Ethical Globalization*, argues that buying local hurts poor workers in third world countries. He cites the fact that an estimated fifty thousand children in Bangladesh lost their jobs in the garment industry because of the 1996 Western boycott of clothing made in third world sweatshops (qtd. in MacDonald). It cannot be denied that if everyone buys locally, repercussions on the global market seem unavoidable. Nonetheless, if the people of the United States demonstrated their commitment to buying local, it could open up new conversations about environmentalism. Our government lags far behind the European Union in environmental legislation. Through selective shopping, the people of the United States could demonstrate to the world our commitment to environmentalism.

Arguments that decentralizing food production will be bad for the national 10 economy also ignore the positive effects small farms have on local economies. John Tschirhart, a professor of environmental economics at the University of Wyoming, argues that buying locally would be bad for our national economy because food that we buy locally can often be produced more cheaply some-where else in the United States (qtd. in Arias Terry). This seems debatable since most of the locally grown things we buy in grocery stores today aren't much more expensive, if at all, than their counterparts from far away. In New York City, apples from upstate New York are often cheaper than the industrial, waxed Granny Smiths from Washington State or Chile; buying locally should indeed save shipping costs. Nonetheless, it is true that locally grown food can often be slightly more expensive than "industrially grown" food. Probably one of the biggest factors in the difference in price is labor cost. Labor is cheap in third world countries, and large U.S. farms are notorious for hiring immigrant laborers. It is hard to justify the exploitation of such artificially cheap labor. While the case for the economic disadvantages of buying local is dubious, buy-ing local has clear positive economic effects in local communities. Local farms hire local workers and bring profits to small rural communities. One study of pig farmers in Virginia showed that, compared to corporate-owned farms, small farms created ten percent more permanent local jobs, a twenty percent higher increase in local retail sales, and a thirty-seven percent higher increase in local per capita income (McCauley).

Buying locally grown and produced food has clear environmental, social, and economic advantages. On the surface it seems that buying local could constitute a big personal sacrifice. It may be slightly more expensive, and it wouldn't allow us to buy any kind of produce at any time of the year, a change that would no doubt take getting used to. But perhaps these limitations would actually make food more enjoyable. If strawberries were sold only in the summer, they would be more special and we might even enjoy them more. Food that is naturally grown in season is fresher and also tends to taste better. Fresh summer strawberries are sweeter than their woody winter counterparts. Buying local is an easy step that everyone can take towards "greener" living.

Works Cited

Arias Terry, Ana. "Buying Local vs. Buying Cheap." *Conscious Choice: The Journal of Ecology and Natural Living*, Jan. 2007, www.alternet.org /story/342/buying_local_vs._buying_cheap. Accessed 27 Apr. 2011.

Baum, Michele Dula. "U.S. Government Issues Standards on Organic Food." *CNN*, 20 Dec. 2000, www.cnn.com/FOOD/specials/2000 /organic.main/story.html. Accessed 25 Apr. 2011.

"Buy Local." *Sustainable Table*. Grace Communications Foundation, Jan. 2007, www.sustainabletable.org. Accessed 27 Apr. 2011.

"Global Warming Statistics." *Effects of Global Warming*, 2007, www .effectofglobalwarming.com/global-warming-statistics.html.

MacDonald, G. Jeffrey. "Is Buying Local Always Best?" *Christian Science Monitor*, 24 July 2006, www.csmonitor.com/2006/0724/p13s02-lifo.html.

McCauley, Marika Alena. "Small Farms: The Optimum Sustainable Agriculture Model." *Oxfam America*, 2007, oxfamamerica.org /whatwedo/where_we_work/united_states/news_publications /food_farm/art2570.html. Accessed 27 Apr. 2011.

"98.7 Percent of Imported Food Never Inspected." *Progressive Policy Institute*, 7 Sept. 2007, www.ppionline.org/ppi_ci.cfm?knlgAreaID=85&subsecID =108&contentID. Accessed 25 Apr. 2011.

"Record Increase in U.S. Greenhouse Gas Emissions Reported." *Environment News Service*, 18 Apr. 2006, ens-newsire.com/ens/apr2006/2006-04 -18-02.asp.

Rieger, Mark. "Strawberry—*Fragaria X ananassa*." *Mark's Fruit Crops*, 2006, fruit-crops.com/strawberry-fragaria-x-ananassa.

"Strawberry Fruit Facts Page." *Grown in California*, Gourmet Shopping Network, grownincalifornia.com/fruit-facts/strawberry-facts.html. Accessed 25 Apr. 2011.

"Why Buy Local?" *LocalHarvest*, localharvest.org/buylocal.jsp. Accessed 23 Apr. 2011.

Thinking about the Text

1. It's clear that this is a topic that matters to Katherine Spriggs. Has she convinced you that it matters—and if so, how? How does Spriggs establish the importance of her topic?

2. What **COUNTERARGUMENTS** or positions other than her own does Spriggs consider—and how does she respond in each case?

3. Choose a section of Spriggs's essay that you find especially effective or ineffective. Referring to the genre features listed on page 158, describe what makes this part of her argument persuasive—or not.

4. Spriggs includes several photos in her essay. How do they contribute to her argument?

5. Consider your own response to Spriggs's position. Write an essay in response to one of the issues she raises. State your **POSITION** explicitly, and be sure to consider arguments other than your own.

FOURTEEN

"Here's What Happened"
Writing a Narrative

"**S**O, TELL ME WHAT HAPPENED." Anytime we ask someone about an incident at work or an event at school, we are asking for a narrative: tell us about what happened. Narratives are stories, and they are fundamental parts of our everyday lives. When we tell someone about a movie we've seen or a basketball game we played in, we often use narrative. When we want someone to understand something that we did, we might tell a story that explains our actions. When we post to *Instagram*, we often write about something we've just done or seen.

If you wrote an essay as part of your college applications, chances are that you were required to write a narrative. Here, for instance, are instructions from two colleges' applications:

> Describe a personal moral or ethical dilemma and how it impacted your life. —HAMPTON UNIVERSITY

> Describe a meaningful event or experience and how it has changed or affected the person you are today. —HOFSTRA UNIVERSITY

Each of these prompts asks applicants to write a narrative about some aspect of their lives. In each case they need to do more than just tell a good story; they need to make a clear point about why it matters.

Narrative is a powerful way to get an audience's attention. Telling a good story can even help establish your authority as a writer. Take a look, for example, at the opening to Lynda Barry's narrative of a childhood experience in her essay "The Sanctuary of School":

> I was 7 years old the first time I snuck out of the house in the dark. It was winter and my parents had been fighting all night. They were short on money and long on relatives who kept "temporarily" moving into our house because they had nowhere else to go.

You can read Barry's full essay on p. 851.

That grabbed your attention, didn't it? You want to keep reading, to know what happened to that child, where she went, what she did outside in the winter dark. (Spoiler alert: she went to her school, where she always felt safe. And she grew up to become an award-winning author and cartoonist.)

Images, too, can tell stories. Before 2020, the following image would have made no sense. It would have been puzzling, maybe even creepy or distressing. Two women (one of whose face mask is visible) wearing coats, separated by a large sheet of plastic hung from above, are awkwardly

Relatives hug through a plastic drop cloth, hung from a clothesline, in May 2021. It was their first physical contact since the COVID-19 pandemic began, fourteen months earlier.

embracing on either side of the barrier. Seeing the image today, though, we have a pretty good idea about what's going on. We can see (and feel) the extraordinary lengths that people will go to in order to hug a loved one during a dangerous pandemic. We can admire the creativity, sense the urgency and warmth, and shake our heads a little in sadness and awe at the human condition—our condition.

Think about some of the powerful personal narratives you've read, perhaps the *Narrative of the Life of Frederick Douglass* or Anne Frank's *Diary of a Young Girl*. We could, of course, read about their lives on *Wikipedia*, but a good narrative provides more than just the facts; it gives us a well-told story that captures not only our attention but also our imagination.

So what exactly is a narrative? For our purposes, narrative is a kind of writing that presents events in some kind of time sequence with a distinct beginning, middle, and ending (but not necessarily in strict chronological order) and that is written for the purpose of making a point. That is, to write a narrative it is not enough to simply report a sequence of events ("this happened, then that happened"), which is often what children do when they tell stories. Narrative essays, especially in college, are meaningful ways of making sense of our experiences, of what goes on around us—and of illustrating a point, making an argument, or writing about the lives of others.

〰◎ *REFLECT. Think about some stories that are told in your favorite songs or music videos, that you hear in sermons, or that your older relative tells. Make a list of the stories that you hear, read, see, or tell in one day and the subjects of those stories. You'll begin to see how narratives are an important way that we communicate with each other.*

Across Academic Disciplines

The narrative essay is a common assignment in the humanities and increasingly in other academic fields as well. In a composition class, you may be asked to write a literacy narrative about early memories of reading or writing, or a personal narrative about an important person or experience in your life. In a history class, you may be asked to take data from archives and construct a narrative about a particular historical event. (Some think that historians focus on dates and facts about incidents from the past, but actually they are generally piecing together narratives that provide a context for interpreting what those dates and facts mean.) In medicine, patient

↪ Visit the Digital Archive of Literacy Narratives (thedaln .org), a site sponsored by Ohio State and Georgia State where you can read literacy narratives as well as post your own.

accounts and medical histories play a key role in diagnosis and treatment. In the sciences, lab reports tell the story of how researchers conducted an experiment and interpreted the data they collected. Since narratives take different forms across disciplines, one challenge you'll face will be to determine which narrative elements are valued or even required in a particular situation.

Across Media

The medium you use makes a big difference in the way you tell a story. Video, for example, presents a wide range of possibilities. *TikTok* is full of mini-stories told through video in a variety of ways, and anyone can participate. TV broadcasts of football games cut between shots of players, coaches, and fans. Commentators review key plays in slow motion or from multiple angles, diagram plays on the screen, and pull up player statistics—all of which combine to tell the story of what's happening on the field. These same stories will be told differently in print, with written words, still photos, and tables of statistics to show how the players performed.

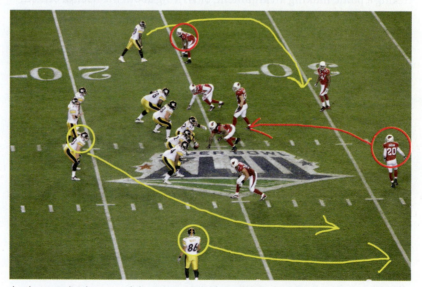

Analysts circle players and draw arrows to show those watching the game on TV what just happened.

When you're writing a narrative, you'll want to think about what media will best suit your audience and purpose. But you won't always have a choice. If you're assigned to work in a specific medium, think about whether a narrative would help get your message across. Well-told stories are a good way to engage your audience's attention in an oral presentation, for instance, and to help them remember what you say.

꙰ *REFLECT. Compare narratives in different media. From the many kinds of narratives you encounter in one day—in books or magazines, on YouTube and TikTok or in video games, in textbooks or conversations with friends—choose two narratives on the same topic from different media that you find most interesting. Think about the similarities and differences between the ways the two stories are told. What would change about each narrative if it were presented in a different medium?*

Across Cultures and Communities

What makes a good story often depends on who's telling the story and who's listening. Not only is that the case for individuals, but different communities and cultures also tell stories in unique ways and value particular things in them.

Many Native American tribes consider narrative an important tradition and art form, so much so that storytellers hold a place of honor. In much of West Africa, the griots are the official storytellers, entrusted with telling the history of a village or town through recitation and song. And in many Appalachian communities, storytelling functions as a way to pass down family and community history. As in West Africa, good storytellers enjoy high status in Appalachia.

In many cultures and communities, stories are the way that history is passed down from generation to generation. Think about the ways that family histories are passed down in your family or community—through oral stories? photo albums? home videos?

Precisely because stories provide a strong foundation for history and for belief systems, it's worth adding a caution here about what author Chimamanda Ngozi Adichie calls "the danger of a single story." When one story is told about a people or a place, it tends to become *the* story. As Adichie points out, "The single story creates stereotypes. And the problem with stereotypes is not that they are untrue, but that they are incomplete. They make one story become the only story." As a writer, you'll want to make sure that the story you tell isn't simply a variation of "the single story."

↪ Watch Adichie's TED talk in which she warns against the danger of a single story by visiting everyonesanauthor .tumblr.com.

➦ *GO TO itgetsbetter.org, the award-winning site of the It Gets Better Project, begun in 2010 to show LGBTQ+ youths that life will get better "if they can just get through their teen years." There you'll find thousands of videos, including many personal narratives from adults who tell how their lives got better. There's also a button to submit your story, in video or writing. Watch a few of the videos that are already there. Which one do you find most powerful, and why?*

Across Genres

Narrative is often a useful strategy for writers working in other genres. For example, in an essay **ARGUING A POSITION**, you may use a narrative example to prove a point. In a **REVIEW** of a film, in which evaluation is the main purpose, you may need to tell a brief story from the plot to demonstrate how the film meets (or does not meet) a specific evaluative criterion. These are only two of the many ways in which narrative can be used as part of a text.

CHARACTERISTIC FEATURES

There is no one way to tell a story. Most written narratives, however, have a number of common features, revolving around the following characteristics and questions:

- A clearly identified event: What happened? Who was involved? (p. 201)
- A clearly described setting: When and where did it happen? (p. 202)

- Vivid, descriptive details: What makes the story come alive? (p. 203)
- A consistent point of view: Who's telling the story? (p. 204)
- A clear point: Why does the story matter? (p. 207)

A Clearly Identified Event: What Happened? Who Was Involved?

Narratives are based on an event or series of events, presented in a way that makes audiences want to know how the story will turn out. Consider this paragraph by Mike Rose, in which he narrates how he, as a marginal high school student with potential, got into college with the help of his senior-year English teacher, Jack MacFarland:

> My grades stank. I had A's in biology and a handful of B's in a few English and social science classes. All the rest were C's—or worse. MacFarland said I would do well in his class and laid down the law about doing well in others. Still the record for my first three years wouldn't have been acceptable to any four-year school. To nobody's surprise, I was turned down flat by USC and UCLA. But Jack MacFarland was on the case. He had received his bachelor's degree from Loyola, so he made calls to old professors and talked to somebody in admissions and wrote me a strong letter. Loyola finally accepted me as a probationary student. I would be on trial for the first year, and if I did okay, I would be granted regular status. MacFarland also intervened to get me a loan, for I could never have afforded a private college without it. Four more years of religion classes and four more years of boys at one school, girls at another. But at least I was going to college. Amazing.
>
> —MIKE ROSE, *Lives on the Boundary*

It's not the actual facts that make this narrative worth reading; rather, it's the way the facts are presented—in other words, the way the story is told.

The narrator grabs our attention with his first sentence ("My grades stank"), then lays out the challenges he faced ("turned down flat by USC and UCLA"), and ends with a flourish ("Amazing"). He could have told us what happened much more briefly—but then it would have been just a sequence of facts; instead, he told us a story. As the author of a narrative, you'll want to be sure to get the facts down, but that won't be enough. Your challenge will be to tell about "what happens" in a way that gets your audience's attention and makes them care enough to keep on reading.

A Clearly Described Setting:
When and Where Did It Happen?

Narratives need to be situated clearly within time and space in order for readers to understand what's going on. For that reason, you will generally arrange your story in **CHRONOLOGICAL ORDER** starting at the beginning and moving straight ahead to the end. There are times, though, when you may choose to present a narrative in reverse chronological order, starting at the end and looking back at the events that led up to it—or with a flashback or flash-forward that jumps back to the past or ahead to the future. Whether you tell your story in chronological order or not, the sequence of events needs to be clear to your audience.

Also important is that your audience get a clear idea of the place(s) where the events occur. Time and space work together to create a scene that your audience can visualize and follow, as they do in the following example from student Minh Vu's essay "Dirty Nails," which documents growing up in his family's nail salon.

> I was born in my family's nail salon. It was in the waxing room, and my first swaddle was made up of giant waxing strips. Normally, they're used to tear the hair off people. For me, they were warmth and protection.
>
> I was raised within glass doors kept shiny with diluted Windex, among towering boxes of acetone, and atop giant pedicure thrones. Such was my childhood kingdom. Alphabet blocks were replaced by white Arial stickers I used to spell out "JEL MANICURE" and "BIKIKNEE WAX" on the price board. Instead of bicycles I rode bumper cars with the pedicure stools. And the rest of my time I spent trying to fit my toddler toes into the pastel foot separators that looked like mini combs. . . . The pallor of peeling plaster was rolled over with a deep textured azure, like the ocean [my grandma] immigrated across in the 1970s. Dim overhead lights were torn down and replaced with a crystal chandelier that, albeit fake, brought illumination in a time of immigrant loneliness. And red leather diner stools from the space's past life were refurbished into sleek manicure chairs.
>
> The nail salon was my world. It was where all of life existed.
>
> —MINH VU, "Dirty Nails"

Minh Vu establishes the setting by providing vivid, descriptive language of the nail salon that makes up the center of his story. His first statement—"I was born in my family's nail salon"—establishes the setting of the story, but it's the details that come after that that paint a picture for readers: "giant pedicure thrones" and "pastel foot separators." These details help readers, especially those who have been to nail salons, visualize where and how the writer grew up.

Vivid, Descriptive Details: What Makes the Story Come Alive?

You may remember English teachers telling you that good writers "show rather than tell." It's an old adage that applies to narratives in particular. Vivid, descriptive detail makes the people, places, and events in a narrative come alive for an audience, helping them see, hear, smell, taste, and feel "what happened." In the following example from an extensive *New Yorker* report on the fall 2020 California fire season, author Dave Eggers calls his friend KC while a wildfire is burning close by. KC is at home, her neighborhood enveloped in smoke.

> "I just heard from a friend," she says. "She woke up at three-thirty this morning and she felt a strange hot wind. So she got up, but figured it was nothing and went back to bed. Half an hour later, she woke up again. She looked out her window and the sun was coming up already. She looked at the clock and it said four. She woke up her husband and called 911. It was a big orange ball of fire coming over the hillside."
>
> This is a familiar story. The fire always comes from behind a hill or treeline. Always it resembles a sunrise.
>
> —DAVE EGGERS, "All That Could Burn"

The narrative is vivid and frightening, even though the details are passed along from the friend to KC, to Eggers, and finally, to us. Some of the details are felt and seen—"strange hot wind" and "big orange ball of fire." Other details lead us to think, "Wait. Does the sun come up at 4 A.M.?" And then we read Eggers's no-frills generalization: "always comes from behind a hill," "always it resembles a sunrise." The evocative image of a lovely sunrise turns to something ominous, dangerous.

Think about how much detail and what kind of detail your narrative needs to "come to life" for your audience. Remember that you are likely

A wildfire comes up and over the hills of a California suburb.

writing for readers (or listeners) unfamiliar with the story you are telling. That means that you need to choose details that help them get a vivid picture of the setting, people, and events in the narrative. When deciding whether to include direct quotations or dialogue, ask yourself if doing so would paint a scene or create a mood more effectively than a summary would.

A Consistent Point of View: Who's Telling the Story?

A good narrative is generally told from one consistent point of view. If you are writing about something that happened to you, then your narrative should be written from the first-person point of view (I, we). First person puts the focus on the narrator, as Georgina Kleege does in the following example, which recounts the opening moments of one of her classes:

> I tell the class, "I am legally blind." There is a pause, a collective intake of breath. I feel them look away uncertainly and then look back. After all, I just said I couldn't see. Or did I? I had managed to get there on my own—no cane, no dog, none of the usual trappings of blindness. Eyeing me askance now, they might detect that my gaze is not quite focused.

My eyes are aimed in the right direction but the gaze seems to stop short of touching anything. But other people do this, sighted people, normal people, especially in an awkward situation like this one, the first day of class. An actress who delivers an aside to the audience, breaking the "fourth wall" of the proscenium, will aim her gaze somewhere above any particular pair of eyes. If I hadn't said anything, my audience might understand my gaze to be like that, a part of the performance. In these few seconds between sentences, their gaze becomes intent. They watch me glance down, or toward the door where someone's coming in late. I'm just like anyone else. Then what did I actually mean by "legally blind"? They wait. I go on, "Some people would call me 'visually challenged.'" There is a ripple of laughter, an exhalation of relief. I'm making a joke about it. I'm poking fun at something they too find aggravating, the current mania to stick a verbal smiley-face on any human condition which deviates from the status quo. Differently abled. Handicapable. If I ask, I'm sure some of them can tell jokes about it: "Don't say 'bald,' say 'follicularly challenged.'" "He's not dead, he's metabolically stable." Knowing they are at least thinking these things, I conclude, "These are just silly ways of saying I don't see very well."

—GEORGINA KLEEGE, "Call It Blindness"

Notice how the first-person point of view—and the repetition of "I"—keeps our attention focused on Kleege. Like the students in her class, we are looking right at her.

If your narrative is about someone else's experience or about events that you have researched but did not witness, then the narrative should probably be written in third person (he, she, it, they). Unlike a first-person narrative, a third-person narrative emphasizes someone or something other than the narrator. Historical and medical narratives are usually written in third person, as are newswriting and sportswriting. Look at the following description of a play by tennis star Roger Federer:

The ball comes toward Federer and, as he sees it, his body is suddenly in the air, turning effortlessly, his arms unfurling like two waves moving in opposite directions, and he hits his one-handed backhand. As he extends through the shot, his chest opens wide and his arms keep reaching, away, and the movement ripples down through his fingers, which are so relaxed that they look weightless, fluttering briefly in the breeze, and it is beautiful so beautiful.

—CHLOÉ COOPER JONES, "Champion Moves"

Roger Federer stretches to make a one-handed backhand at the Australian Open.

Notice how Jones's narration puts the action in slow motion, allowing readers to notice every detail of the motion of Federer's body—arms, chest, fingers.

Compare the points of view of Georgina Kleege's first-person narrative and Chloé Cooper Jones's third-person one. Notice that there is one consistent point of view in each example. As an author, you will have to determine whether your narrative is most effective told from the first-person or third-person point of view. No matter what you may have been taught in high school, the first person is acceptable in many (though not all) academic contexts. Whatever point of view you use, however, do so consistently. That is, if you refer to yourself in the narrative, do not switch between first (I, we) and third (he, she, they) person. (Rarely is a narrative told from a second-person—"you"—point of view.)

Part of maintaining a consistent point of view is establishing a clear time frame. Notice Chloé Cooper Jones's use of present-tense verbs in the example about Federer. By consistently narrating the actions in the present tense, Jones places the reader in the moment of the story being told. Using a consistent verb tense situates the actions of the event within a clear time frame.

A clear time frame does not mean that every verb in the narrative has to be in the same tense, only that the writer establishes one primary tense—usually present or past—for the main action of the story. In the example by Mike Rose on page 201, most of the verbs are in the past tense: "said," "made," "talked." But other tenses are used to indicate events that, in relation to the main action of the narrative, occurred earlier ("He had received his bachelor's degree from Loyola") or might occur later ("I would be granted regular status").

A Clear Point: Why Does the Story Matter?

Good narratives tell stories that matter. In academic writing in particular, narratives are told to make a point. Whether they begin by stating the point explicitly in a thesis or build toward a point that is expressed at the end, the purpose of the narrative needs to be clear to the audience. Nothing irritates an audience more than reading or listening to a story that has no point. Even if a story is interesting or entertaining, it will most likely be deemed a failure in an academic context if it does not make clear why the events matter. Consider how the late author and English professor bell hooks makes a point about learning to value work:

See how Zeynep Tufekci's personal narrative gives an ordinary trip to the post office a whole new perspective on p. 995.

> "Work makes life sweet!" I often heard this phrase growing up, mainly from old black folks who did not have jobs in the traditional sense of the word. They were usually self-employed, living off the land, selling fishing worms, picking up an odd job here and there. They were people who had a passion for work. They took pride in a job done well. My Aunt Margaret took in ironing. Folks brought her clothes from miles around because she was such an expert. That was in the days when using starch was common and she knew how to do an excellent job. Watching her iron with skill and grace was like watching a ballerina dance. Like all the other black girls raised in the fifties that I knew, it was clear to me that I would be a working woman. Even though our mother stayed home, raising her seven children, we saw her constantly at work, washing, ironing, cleaning, and cooking (she was an incredible cook). And she never allowed her six girls to imagine we would not be working women. No, she let us know that we would work and be proud to work.
>
> —BELL HOOKS, "Work Makes Life Sweet"

Professor hooks opens with her main point, that "work makes life sweet!" In the sentences that follow, she explains how she learned this lesson from "old black folks who did not have jobs in the traditional sense." Through specific examples, she illustrates how they "took pride in a job done well" and passed on this pride in their work to hooks and her sisters. The explicit restatement of the point in the final sentence—that hooks and her six sisters learned from their mother that they would "work and be proud to work"—recasts the notion of "working woman" in a unique and engaging way.

In contrast to bell hooks, author and activist Roxane Gay, in a speech to publishers, withholds her main point even after announcing to the audience that she had anticipated what topic she would be asked to address:

> When I received the invitation to speak at Winter Institute, I knew, even before I got the details, that I would be asked to talk about diversity in some form or fashion. This is the state of most industries, and particularly contemporary publishing. People of color are not asked about our areas of expertise as if the only thing we are allowed to be experts on is our marginalization. We are asked about how white people can do better and feel better about diversity or the lack thereof. We are asked to offer "good" white people who "mean well" absolution from the ills of racism.
>
> —ROXANE GAY, speech to *Publishers Weekly*'s Winter Institute, 2017

Rather than announcing her main point right away, Gay provides a bit of context on the word "diversity," including the current state of discussions about diversity. After giving this background and making a bold admission, she *then* states her main point:

> The word diversity has of late become so overused as to be meaningless. In a 2015 article for *The New York Times Magazine,* Anna Holmes wrote about the dilution of the word diversity, attributing its loss of meaning to "a combination of overuse, imprecision, inertia, and self-serving intentions."
>
> The word diversity is, in its most imprecise uses, a placeholder for issues of inclusion, recruitment, retention and representation. Diversity is a problem, seemingly without solutions. We talk about it and talk about it and talk about it and nothing much ever seems to change. And here we are today, talking about diversity yet again.

I am so very tired of talking about diversity.

Publishing has a diversity problem. This problem extends to absolutely every area of the industry. I mean, look at this room, where I can literally count the number of people of color among some 700 booksellers. There are not enough writers of color being published. When our books are published, we fight, even more than white writers, for publicity and reviews. People of color are underrepresented editorially, in book marketing, publicity, and as literary agents. People of color are underrepresented in bookselling. On and on it goes.

Gay states her main point—"Publishing has a diversity problem"—and provides further clarification and evidence of the problem. She makes the main point even more visible by focusing on the lack of diversity in the audience. In contrast to hooks, Gay moves more slowly toward her main point, describing her reaction to both the speaking invitation and the topic she was asked to cover before offering her main message outright: "People of color are underrepresented in bookselling."

As an author, don't assume that your readers will recognize the point you're trying to make. No matter how interesting you think your story is, they need to know why they should care. Why is the story important? State your main point as bell hooks and Roxane Gay do.

⬙ *REFLECT. Look at a narrative in a newspaper or magazine article or on a blog or other website to see what main point it makes and how it does so. Is the main point explicitly stated in a thesis, or is it only implied? Does the narrative make clear to readers why the story is important or why they should care about it?*

RAYA ELFADEL KHEIRBEK is a professor at the University of Maryland School of Medicine in Baltimore, Maryland. She has served in several roles within the Department of Veterans Affairs. This 2017 essay was originally published in *Health Affairs*, an American journal about national and global health policy and research issues.

At the VA, Healing the Doctor-Patient Relationship

RAYA ELFADEL KHEIRBEK

The title suggests what the narrative is about: resolving a conflict between doctor and patient.

THE MAN'S VOICE over the phone was angry: "The VA provides terrible care!" I had promised the Veterans Affairs (VA) Medical Center's Patient Advocate office that I would connect with the man, Mr. Davis, who had called three times before to complain about his care. I was warned beforehand that he was displeased, to say the least.

Opens with an attention-grabbing quote and introduction to a central person in the story. And the author sets the scene—the Veterans Affairs (VA) Medical Center.

With him on the line, I took a deep breath and began to look up his records. "I am sorry to hear this, Mr. Davis," I said. "Would you please tell me specifically what is bothering you? I am covering for your doctor and will do my best to help."

Mr. Davis needed to have an MRI for his right shoulder, as was recommended by his military doctor before he separated from the service. He also was having back pain and wasn't exercising enough. He had gained twenty pounds in six months and asked if we offered liposuction.

The author provides details about Mr. Davis's medical condition, necessary background information for readers.

He had met his primary care clinician, Dr. Kumar, for the first time a couple of weeks earlier and was very uncomfortable when he saw her. To him, there was great insensitivity in the VA's decision to assign him a doctor who he believed was originally from the Middle East.

"Those people wanted to kill me," he remarked to me on the phone, "and I do not appreciate having a doctor who is one of them."

"If you had a woman who was subjected to repeated rape, would you let her be examined by a male doctor?" he continued.

I knew that our policy would allow him to switch doctors, but I had no idea what to say. I had been practicing medicine for a couple of decades and naturally had encountered many types of unusual behavior. Yet I had never heard this type of comment from a patient. I composed myself and quietly explained to Mr. Davis that Dr. Kumar's family came from India. Dr. Kumar herself was born and raised in Pennsylvania and had no connection to the Middle East whatsoever.

But Mr. Davis was insistent on having a doctor who looked like him.

And he was angry.

"I am not your typical patient," he fired back. "I am smart, educated, and highly trained. I do not need your opinion. I have lived in my body for three decades. I know what I want, and your job is to deliver."

I told him that I wanted to meet with him to help resolve these issues and blocked off an hour the following week to meet during my administrative time. He was excited that I would be able to see him quickly, given what he referred to as the long wait time to get an appointment in the VA. He added that, based on our conversation, I seemed to be a good doctor.

While I was determined to meet and help Mr. Davis, a potential challenge loomed. I am of Middle Eastern origin. I wondered if I should reveal this information after coordinating his care and give him another opportunity to seek a different clinician. My colleagues advised me to stand tall and not give him that choice. To them, his views represented bigotry.

---

5 *Even more details that contribute to making Mr. Davis a compelling character.*

A consistent point of view. The story is told through the author's eyes—with lots of dialogue between her and Mr. Davis.

10 *Direct quotes support the author's claims.*

The author provides important details about herself.

A Veterans Affairs health care center in Phoenix, Arizona—similar to the one where Mr. Davis and Dr. Kheirbek met.

Yet Mr. Davis was not the only one struggling with the past. For me, encountering Mr. Davis brought back painful memories and forced me to stop and reflect on my years of service in the VA, my belief system, and my biases. I wondered if his "bigotry" was really so alien to the human nature in us all.

An Occupational Hazard

Details about the author's experience move the story along.

As a primary care physician working in the VA, I have heard countless stories from soldiers reliving their experiences in war zones. As an Arab American immigrant, I had followed the Iraqi war and—later—the promising start of the Arab Spring and then watched them both spiral into the chaos of death and destruction, including a civil war in my native country, Syria. I felt privileged to be a physician and an American, especially as violence took hold overseas. I could have been back home, along with everyone I worried about. I could be dead. Feeling powerless, I forced myself to watch and listen to the news. The least I could do was to be aware.

Meeting Mr. Davis

I introduced myself to Mr. Davis on a Tuesday in March 2017, less 15
than a week after our initial phone conversation. A white man in
his early thirties, he was tall and well built, with a rectangular face;
a defined, slightly pointed chin; and a sturdy jaw line. He had light
brown hair, small blue eyes, and a straight nose. The jacket he
wore over his broad shoulders had neatly polished buttons and
was slightly frayed in places. Part of his right hand was missing. He
glanced at me with a smile. I am a white woman with green eyes
and brown hair.

Reestablishing the timeline makes the progression of events clear.

Vivid details paint a picture of Mr. Davis's physical appearance.

"I am very happy you were able to make it to this meeting,"
I said with a big smile.

He nodded in silence and avoided making eye contact.

"I had a chance to review your chart. I think I can help with
your physical needs," I added. "But I am also suspecting there are
mental health issues that might need to be addressed."

Given his sentiments about Middle Eastern doctors, I thought
he had a plausible PTSD diagnosis. When I began to suggest as
much, he cut me off.

"This is all stereotyping," he asserted. "I did what I was sup- 20
posed to do. I will heal through going back to work and being
productive."

Dialogue makes us feel as if we're witnessing the conversation.

I caught him looking at my name badge.

"I understand," I said. "Thank you for clarifying."

I asked how he had ended up in the military. He said he'd signed
up simply because college was "so damn expensive." He was not
a "military brat" and didn't enlist out of a sense of obligation. He
was not angry or in need of some form of revenge. It's not that he
felt enlisting was brave or important.

Mr. Davis had been in three combat deployments—Iraq in
2010 and Afghanistan in 2011 and 2013—as a member of the US
Army Special Forces. He'd been involved in multiple close-range
blasts, traumatic jumps, and firefights. Many of the people he had
served with had been killed. Since his return to the United States,
he had been having constant pain in his right shoulder. He had
nightmares one or two times a week, and recently they'd become
more frequent.

Details establish the intensity of Mr. Davis's combat experiences.

"What kept you going during all the deployments?" I asked.　25

A turning point signals the growing bond between doctor and patient.

"I closed my eyes while hiding from fire and remembered family trips skiing with my little sister and laughing on the slopes of Jackson Hole." He looked up and smiled. I saw a glimpse of the little boy in his face and knew he was in pain. I wanted to reach out and touch his hand, but I was afraid he would not welcome my gesture.

I asked if he'd had any good experiences in Iraq. Yes, he said. It touched him to see families with young children walking for many miles to collect American parachutes to help build houses. The local people found something useful to do with even the trash that Americans had left. All his memories, however, were haunted by the killings he had witnessed and the poverty of the places he had been.

I felt it was then time to address his comments about Dr. Kumar. I said: "You know, Mr. Davis, you are a man of tremendous courage. It is not easy to share your experiences with someone else, especially experiences of this nature."

He looked out the window.

"You mentioned to me in our phone conversation last　30 week that you were uncomfortable with a doctor from the Middle East."

I paused, then continued. "I want you to be comfortable, and I am very happy we met today. I want to thank you for allowing me into your life and for the opportunity to help. I owe to you the knowledge that I was born and raised in Syria."

The few seconds of silence that ensued felt like an eternity.

Then Mr. Davis abruptly got to his feet and raised his severed hand. "I am so sorry I was being a jerk. I would really like you to be my physician—unless you do not feel comfortable caring for me, based on my earlier comments."

I stood up and extended my hand to him. "It was important for us to talk. Please keep doing so, as it's the only way for us to deal with such emotions."

A resolution follows a tense moment.

His face broke out into a wide smile. He was absolutely thrilled　35 at the prospect of us working together. I was, too.

Healing Takes Time

Though I have served in the VA for many years and in different roles, my focus has always been on patients. The sacred time spent with patients in an exam room is the only lasting truth in medicine. In this large bureaucratic system, all else can wait. Yet many priorities compete for our attention during a single visit. It might not be possible to spend the needed time on each important issue. While a slew of mandatory screenings for diseases has improved our medical care, it is equally crucial to take the time to develop a relationship with the patient, exploring his or her service history and the lived experiences that may come with that. It is not always easy. In my work, I know what it is like to be discriminated against, and what it is like to have stereotypes of my own. Yet an admission of our own vulnerability and opening the door to a conversation about self-care, compassion, understanding, and human connection is how we attend to all aspects of our patients' suffering—and perhaps some of our own.

> *The conclusion tells the significance of the two meeting, why the story matters.*

REFLECT. *Analyze a short nonfiction narrative that you find in a magazine or on a website. Look at the list of five characteristic features of narratives on pages 200–201 and annotate the essay to point out these features, using Kheirbek's essay as a model. Then look at your annotations and the parts of the text they refer to and evaluate how well your chosen narrative illustrates the characteristic features. For example, is the setting clearly described? How vivid are the details?*

LITERACY NARRATIVES

Literacy narratives focus on meaningful experiences involving some kind of reading or writing: stories, music, computer code, learning a foreign language, and so on. The focus on learning and literacy makes this sort of narrative a common assignment in first-year writing classes. Professional writers also use the genre to reflect on their craft. Literacy narratives can serve various purposes, but they generally have the following characteristic features.

A Well-Told Story

Whether you're writing about the joys or struggles (or both) of learning to do something or why you've always loved a certain book or song, there are some tried-and-true storytelling techniques that can help your literacy narrative interest readers. If you write about something you struggled to learn, for instance, readers will want to know how your struggle turned out, how the story ends. And whatever your topic, make sure your narrative has a clear arc, from a beginning that engages your audience to a conclusion that leaves them understanding why the experience you wrote about matters to you.

A Firsthand Account, Often (but Not Always) about Yourself

You'll want to write about an experience that you know firsthand, not one that you've only read about. Writing about your own experience is the most common way of achieving this close perspective, but you may also reflect on the experiences of others. Perhaps you've observed or had a hand in helping someone else learn to read or write and are able to speak about it firsthand. This, too, could be a productive topic for a literacy narrative.

An Indication of the Narrative's Significance

Readers quickly lose patience with stories that seem to have no point, so you need to make clear what significance your narrative has for those involved. Sometimes you may have an explicit **THESIS** that makes the point clear from the start; other times, you may prefer to let the narrative play out before explaining its significance.

PALOMA GARCIA was a student at Santa Clara University when she wrote this literacy narrative for her Literacy and Social Justice class, which was then published by the Digital Archive of Literacy Narratives (thedaln.org). Today she is chief of staff at New York University's Metropolitan Center for Research on Equity and the Transformation of Schools.

First Day of School

PALOMA GARCIA

IT WAS A WARM MORNING at *el ranchito*, and a special one, too—it was the opening of my day-school, and my first day as a teacher, or so I liked to think. Although at the time I was only seven years old, I knew I wanted to be a teacher and help others learn. Ironically, even though I was never read to at home, I loved reading, and I especially loved (and still do) going to school and learning as much as I could from my teachers. I would go home from school and tell my mom what I had learned in class, an everyday ritual she and I shared. This daily report of what I learned helped me see that I wanted to share knowledge and teach others. This is how I got the idea to become a teacher, and before my mother knew my brilliant plan, half the kids in our neighborhood were knocking on our door, anxiously waiting for me to come outside and begin class.

> The compelling opening draws readers in by setting up a surprise: the "teacher" is only seven years old.

I began class by reading my first and favorite book: *Pulgarcito*, or *Tom Thumb* in English. I can still see the look in my friends' faces; they seemed to be so engaged in the story, very attentive,

A strong sensory detail brings the narrative to life.

and extremely quiet. I could hear my own breathing and feel my heart beat at times. After I finished reading, I would ask what my "students" had learned, what they had most liked, and what did not interest them much. Then came "*las clases de escritura*," or the writing classes, as I would call them. I would go over vowels and the whole alphabet, giving a brief explanation and an example word for each letter. Despite my young age, I felt I was truly helping my students, and I loved how they sometimes called me "*maestra*," or teacher, even if they only did so playfully or to tease me. To me, it was real. I knew I was their teacher.

The author sprinkles in some Spanish words, usually with an English translation. The Spanish disappears, however, when she shifts to narrate her experiences in the US.

Soon enough, I wanted to teach something to everyone that I encountered, especially family and friends who visited our home. I grew confident and proud of my improved reading and writing skills, my ability to address large groups without overwhelming fear, and my knack for talking and connecting with others no matter their age or gender. Unfortunately, this was all soon to change, and it happened when I least expected it.

A clear shift signals a significant turning point is coming.

One day when I arrived home from school, my mother didn't welcome me with a hug and kiss like she usually did, and I knew something was wrong. I was told we were immigrating to *El Norte*, or the North. I knew my life was never going to be the same. We made the move, and on my first day at my new school, Los Padres Elementary, I cried and begged my mom to take me back to our old home. I knew I was going to be at a disadvantage for not knowing a single word in English.

A firsthand account, told from a first-person point of view.

Only because of my mom's assurances and blessings, I gathered my strength and walked into Ms. Camaney's third-grade classroom. About a month or so into class, Ms. Camaney asked several students to read aloud, and my worst fear was realized: she asked if I could continue reading the story—in English, of course. I felt my face turn red hot with embarrassment, and I asked to be excused from reading, since I still wasn't comfortable with English, especially reading it out loud to the rest of the class. But Ms. Camaney insisted. I began reading with my heavy accent, mispronouncing almost every word, while my classmates laughed.

5

This anecdote includes details that vividly illustrate the author's new circumstances.

It was an enormous challenge to be so young in a foreign place with no knowledge of the language, and incidents like the read aloud debacle at school made me feel like I was living through a war where I was wounded and defeated constantly as everything and everyone plotted against me. Although I tried to continue to read—something that gave me comfort before—no words came out. Instead, tears would stream down my cheeks. Here I was, scared but hopeful for a helping hand and an opportunity to try my best, but instead I was laughed at and ridiculed for trying.

This incident in Ms. Camaney's class marked a turning point in my life; I began to lose my interest in and passion for reading, and I wasn't interested in learning English. Now I was afraid of being laughed at and humiliated for mispronouncing a word or stumbling through a sentence. My fear overwhelmed my love of learning and killed my interest in practicing a new language. I began to isolate myself from others, avoiding any social interactions that required English, since I felt inferior to my fluent classmates.

The author shifts from recounting a specific event to reflecting on its impact.

As I reflect on these years of my childhood, I know that this experience with language, reading, and education affected both my self-esteem and my academic performance and ambition. I went from a kid who loved reading and writing and dreamed of becoming a teacher to a student who lacked confidence and dreaded school. Humiliation and discrimination turned into fear, and fear kept me from participating in class, from asking questions, and ultimately, from believing in my own abilities and strengths to excel as a student. As time passed in my new life in the US, however, I learned to believe in my own will power and to reconnect with my passion for language, learning, and teaching. Incidents of language discrimination were painful; they have also shaped me, in part, into the person I'm proud to be today: bold, determined, and not afraid to speak up for my beliefs and ideals. My passion for reading and teaching others slowly returned and is stronger than ever because I learned how precious and fragile our relationships to language and education can be.

A clear contrast between "before" and "after" points to the story's larger significance.

The conclusion indicates why this story is so meaningful—and why it matters to the author.

✺ **REFLECT** *on your own experiences as a reader, writer, or language learner. Identify one experience that played a key role in your developing literacy. What did you learn, and how? What impact has it had on your life?*

WRITING A NARRATIVE / A Roadmap

Choose a topic that matters—to you, and to others

Whether you write a narrative for personal reasons or in response to an assignment, choose your own topic or work with an assigned topic, try to write about something that matters to you—and try to make sure that it will matter to your audience as well.

If you are writing a personal narrative, choosing a topic can be difficult. You will need to choose an experience or event that you feel comfortable sharing, in some detail, with an audience. Be sure that the experience is not only important to you but also of enough general interest to engage your audience.

If your narrative is not a personal one, you still want it to be compelling. Narratives that aren't personal are often part of a larger conversation about an event, or some topic that the event represents, which gives the story significance. For example, if you are writing a narrative about how specific students' academic performances changed when their school began participating in a school lunch program, you need to recognize that such stories are part of an ongoing educational and political debate about the effectiveness and public benefit of such programs. You may need to do some research to understand this debate and how your narrative fits into it.

Consider your rhetorical situation

Whenever you write a narrative (or anything, for that matter), you need to consider the following elements of your rhetorical situation:

Think about your AUDIENCE. Who will be reading what you write, and what's your relationship with them?

- Will your audience have any knowledge about your topic? Will you need to explain anything or provide any background information?
- How are they like or unlike you? Consider age, gender, income, cultural heritage, political beliefs, and so on. How will such factors affect how you tell the story?

- Can you assume they'll be interested in what you write? How can you get them interested?
- How are they likely to react to your narrative? What do you want them to think or do as a result of reading what you say?

Think about your PURPOSE. Why are you writing this narrative? What is the significance of this story, and what do you hope it will demonstrate to your readers? Remember that your narrative needs to do more than just tell an engaging story; it needs to make a point of some kind.

Think about your STANCE. Are you telling a story that is very personal to you, or is it one you have some distance from? How do you want to present yourself as the narrator? Do you want to come across as witty and amusing, if you're telling a humorous family story? As knowledgeable but impersonal, if you're recounting historical events for a political science essay? Whatever your stance, how can you make your writing reflect that stance?

Consider your LANGUAGE. Almost everything can be said in a variety of ways. Regardless of how many dialects or languages you use in your everyday life, you have many options for your narrative. Will your audience expect a certain kind of language or style? Do you want to meet those expectations? challenge them? What do you want your language to say about you? What risks might you be willing to take with your language? How will the medium and larger context limit or expand the language options that are available to you? (You may want to consult Chapters 4 and 33 for more advice about language options.)

Consider the larger CONTEXT. What broader issues are involved in your narrative? What else has been said and written about this topic? Even if your narrative is personal, how might it speak to some larger topic—perhaps a social or political one? Considering the larger context for your narrative can help you see it from perspectives different from your own and present it in a way that will interest others.

Consider your MEDIUM. If you have a choice, think about which medium best suits your goals and audience. The kinds of details you include, the language you use, the way you present materials from sources, and many other things depend on the medium. The conventions of a print essay, for instance, in which you can use written words and images, differ markedly from those of an audio essay (in which you can use sounds but no written words or images).

Consider matters of DESIGN. Does your narrative need headings? Is there anything in the story that could be conveyed better with a photograph than with words alone? Will embedded audio or video clips help you engage your audience? Often in academic writing, you may have to conform to a specific design format. If you can determine the look of your text, though, remember that design has a powerful impact on the impression your narrative makes.

Explore your topic and do any necessary research

If you are writing a personal narrative, write down all that you remember about your topic. Using FREEWRITING or other activities for GENERATING IDEAS, write down as many specific details as you can: sounds, smells, textures, colors, and so on. What details will engage your audience? Not all the details that you jot down in this exploratory stage will make it into your essay. You'll need to choose the ones that will engage your audience and support your main point. In addition to sensory details, try to write down direct quotations or dialogue you can remember that will help bring your story to life.

If your narrative is not a personal one, you'll likely need to conduct RESEARCH so that you can provide accurate and sufficient details about the topic. Whether your research takes you to sources in the library or online, or into the community to conduct interviews, it's important to get the what, when, and where of the narrative right, and consulting sources will help you do that.

Decide on a point of view

The subject that you choose to write about will usually determine the point of view from which you write. If you're telling a story in which you are a central participant, you will usually use the first person (I, we). In some academic disciplines, however, or if you're narrating a story that is not personal, the third person (he, she, they) may work better.

Also think about what verb tense would be most effective for establishing the point of view in your narrative. Most personal narratives that are arranged in chronological order are written in the past tense ("When I <u>was</u> twelve, I <u>discovered</u> what I <u>wanted</u> to do for the rest of my life"). However, if you want readers to feel like they are actually experiencing an event, you may choose to use the present tense, as Georgina Kleege and Chloé Cooper Jones do in examples earlier in this chapter.

Organize and start writing

Once you've chosen a subject and identified your main point, considered your rhetorical situation, come up with enough details, and decided on a point of view (not necessarily in this order), it's time to think about how to organize your narrative.

Keep your main point in mind. As you begin to draft, type out that point as a tentative THESIS and keep your eye on it as you write; you can decide later whether you want to include it in your text.

Organize your information. What happened? Where? When? Who was there? What details can you describe to make the story come alive? Decide whether to present the narrative in CHRONOLOGICAL ORDER, in reverse chronological order, or in some other order.

Draft an OPENING. A good introduction draws your audience into the story and makes them want to know more. Sometimes you'll need to provide a context for your narrative—to describe the setting and introduce some of the people before getting on with what happened. Other times you might start in the middle of your story, or at the end—and then circle back to tell what happened.

Draft a CONCLUSION. However you organize your narrative, make sure your readers see the point of your story; if you haven't made that clear, you might end by saying something about the story's significance. Why does it matter to you? What do you want readers to take away—and remember?

Look critically at your draft, get responses—and revise

Read your draft slowly and carefully. Try to see it as if for the first time: Does the story grab your attention, and can you follow it? Can you tell what the point is, and will your audience care? If possible, get feedback from others. Following are some questions that can help you or others examine a narrative with a critical eye:

- *How does the* OPENING *capture the audience's interest?* Is it clear why you're telling the story, and have you given readers reason to want to find out what happened? How else might the narrative begin?

- *Who's telling the story?* Have you maintained a consistent POINT OF VIEW?

- *Is the setting of your story clear?* Have you situated the events in a well-described time and place?

- *Is the story easy to follow?* If it's at all confusing, would TRANSITIONS help your audience follow the sequence of events? If it's a lengthy or complex narrative, would headings help?

- *Are there enough vivid, concrete details?* Is there a good balance of showing and telling? Have you included any dialogue or direct quotations—and if not, would adding some help the story come alive?

- *Are there any visuals?* If not, would adding some help bring the narrative to life?

- *How do you establish* AUTHORITY *and credibility?* How would you describe the STANCE and TONE? Do they reflect your purpose and appeal to your audience?

- *Does the story have a clear point?* Is the point stated explicitly—and if not, should it be? If the main point is implied rather than stated, is the significance of the narrative still clear?

- *How satisfying is the* CONCLUSION*?* What does it leave the audience thinking? How else might the narrative end?

- *Does the title suggest what the narrative is about,* and will it make an audience want to read on?

Revise your draft in light of any feedback you receive and your own critique, keeping your purpose and especially your audience firmly in mind.

REFLECT. Once you've completed your narrative, let it settle for a while and then take time to REFLECT. *How well did you tell the story? What additional revisions would you make if you could? Research shows that such reflections help "lock in" what you learn for future use.*

They Called Me a Girl before Anyone Else Did

CHARLOTTE CLYMER

WHILE MAKING PUBLIC REMARKS at a school board meeting for Loudoun County in Virginia, Tanner Cross, an elementary school physical education teacher in the district, stated he would not use the authentic pronouns for trans and non-binary students under his care.

This was in response to the school board implementing non-discrimination protections for LGBTQ students following the Virginia state legislature passing broad legislation banning discrimination against all LGBTQ people in the state.

In return, the district rightly suspended Cross for his remarks, and then, a circuit court judge ordered his reinstatement. The district is now in the process of appealing that decision to Virginia's Supreme Court, and Cross has become a cause célèbre among social conservatives who are obsessed with the bodies of trans children in a way that is entirely creepy.

In his remarks, Cross said he wouldn't "affirm that a biological boy can be a girl and vice versa because it's against my religion. It's lying to a child; it's abuse to a child—and it's sinning against our God."

Leaving aside the fact that the discussion of transgender people in the Bible is quite murky (and rather fascinating)—and thus, as more than a few social conservatives have admitted to me, it's unclear being transgender is a so-called

5

CHARLOTTE CLYMER is a Texan, a military veteran, and—in her own words—"a proud trans woman." Her political and social commentary has appeared in the *Washington Post* and *GQ,* among other national publications. This 2021 essay is from her Substack, *Charlotte's Web Thoughts*. She tweets from @cmclymer.

"sin"—we're still left with a public employee charged with the welfare of children stating before God and Creation that he refuses to treat certain children with respect and dignity. That, in fact, is abusive.

I'm not going to unpack all the myriad reasons why this is clownish in itself because I want to focus on something that hit me when this story popped up.

I don't personally know Tanner Cross other than what I've read in the news. I've never met him, and I don't know anyone who knows him.

And yet, I feel like I've known Tanner Cross all my life. He hits all the same marks as so many men I've known in positions of authority, particularly in sports and the military.

I grew up in a conservative environment in Central Texas. I played high school football. I went to an evangelical church in my late teens (where, unsurprisingly, my political views were not warmly received). And I served in the military—and not just in the military but in the testosterone-saturated U.S. Army Infantry.

For most of my life, I have been around men like Tanner Cross. They have   10
strong opinions about what men should be (and what women should be) and tend to make those opinions known.

I am a proud trans woman, but for the first 30 years of my life, I was in the closet and navigating these spaces. Around these men.

And without fail, men like Tanner Cross would—in some way, shape, or form—call me a girl. They weren't just the first people to call me a girl. They were the only people to call me a girl or woman before I came out.

Like my 8th grade football coach who really loved calling us "ladies" during practice.

Like my freshman football coach who never seemed to tire of telling us that we "hit like girls" if he felt we weren't going at full speed.

Like the assistant football coach during my junior year of high school who,   15
on more than a few occasions, said some choice words about how we should try out for the girls volleyball team instead. Oh, and this mocking inquiry toward one of my teammates: "Did your mother teach you how to throw?"

Like during minute one of hour one of day one in basic training when I heard a drill sergeant scream at all of us to "get the sand out of your pussies." And that was probably one of the more tame things I heard along these lines during my time in the military.

I heard that all my life in male environments, and that's to say nothing of the numerous ways in which society communicates to boys that they shouldn't cry, shouldn't appear weak, be the "man of the house," etc.

That's what I've been thinking about over the past two months as this situation unfolds in Loudoun County, Virginia (which, by the way, is a lovely place with no shortage of wonderful people).

I've been thinking of all the school coaches and P.E. teachers who I saw throughout my childhood call boys and young men "ladies" and "girls" as a way of, uh, "motivating" them and now claim that using the correct pronouns for trans kids goes against their religion. I call it the Male Coach Gender Paradox.

These are the same men. Truly.   20

Do I have proof that Tanner Cross has done that? I do not. But I'm right. I know I'm right. Call it hard-earned instinct.

These men always betray themselves by their fear of women. They seem unable to maintain any sort of consistency in following their own views. Because it was never about religion or respect for God. It was always about their profound discomfort with women.

In their minds, women are weaker and less worthy of respect. They jab their fingers in the direction of girls and women and yell at the boys and young men under their control: *Do you want to grow up and be that? Small and weak? Then get your shit together and man up.*

I'm sometimes asked by the occasional cis man why there's far more support for trans women among cis women than cis men, since it's cis women, social conservatives falsely claim, who have the "most to lose" from trans equality.

I think there are a lot of reasons, but two stick out for me personally, one   25
for women and one for men.

The first is that I believe the vast majority of cis women understand deeply what it means to have your body controlled in service to a forced gender identity and expression.

The second is that these particular cis men absolutely feel they have the most to lose. Not materially or spiritually, despite the claims of Tanner Cross. They feel they have the most to lose because when they already benefit substantially from a social framework that supposedly prescribes in detail what "manhood" should be, why cave in to that internal fear in the pit of their stomach that they're not really being themselves but a carbon copy of the fearful neuroses of all the men who came before them?

Why would these cis men admit that gender is incredibly complex and fluid? They're scared of the answer to that question—the possibility that they don't know their true selves and it's so much safer to stick with the devil they know than the one they don't.

Ironically, these cis men live in fear of their own gender reveals.

I'm not saying they're secretly transgender and in denial. I'm saying that gen- 30
der identity and expression are so directly structured that these cis men are
terrified of a world in which "manhood" may encompass the full spectrum of
gender expression and they find themselves doing things they've always been
told men don't do.

And yes, hashtag not all cis men—I knew so many wonderful cis men growing up, men who I looked up to, men who wouldn't use their religion as an
excuse to abuse trans children.

Men who respect me as a woman now.

Thinking about the Text

1. How does Charlotte Clymer's life experience of living in both genders
    contribute to her POINT OF VIEW in the essay? Would her argument
    have been as effective if she had omitted disclosing her own experi-
    ences as a high school football player and US Army infantryman? Why
    or why not?

2. Clymer uses the phrase "hashtag not all cis men" (31). Was it surpris-
    ing to read the phrase spelled out? Did you immediately understand
    it? Why or why not? Should she have written a more conventional sen-
    tence in order to express the same idea? In responding, consider her
    PURPOSE and AUDIENCE.

3. Clymer makes a CLAIM that men who refuse to use "the authentic pro-
    nouns for trans and non-binary students" are the same coaches, train-
    ers, and drill sergeants who call their players and trainers "ladies" and
    "girls" in order to "motivate" them. How well does Clymer establish this
    argument? Is it persuasive? Why or why not?

4. Clymer writes with passion and uses elements of EMOTIONAL APPEAL
    in her essay. But there are also plenty of ETHICAL APPEALS. Which do
    you think is more effective in this essay? Why? Point to specific exam-
    ples to support your conclusion.

5. Clymer's essay may not fit perfectly into the description of a NARRATIVE
    that we lay out in this chapter. Which of the characteristic features
    listed on pages 200–201 does it include? Which does it leave out? Do you
    consider it an effective narrative? Why or why not?

The Look

LARRY LEHNA

IFEAR THAT I CARRY FAR MORE BAGGAGE than the typical college student. Unlike Frank Sinatra, regrets I have more than "a few," and even if I do not mention them they weigh heavily upon me. I sometimes regret my wasted life. Then I stop and wonder if it was really wasted. There are so many things I did not accomplish. However, I helped to raise a fine son and he was almost through college before my downfall. My step-daughters were seven and sixteen when I was sent to prison. Yet they both wrote to me for the full eleven years. At different times they have both told me that I am the only real father they have known. Each of them now has children of her own whom I dote upon. So even among the regrets is a modicum of satisfaction.

Always present are my scars, both physical and mental. Mine was not an easy life. I carry many memories. The burning pain of bullet wounds (they really do burn). The agony of stitches going into a fresh knife wound. The nearly immobilizing ache of broken ribs. But most of all I carry emotions. The anguish of being arrested. The despair over lost loves. The disappointment of unfulfilled dreams. I am an emotional cauldron. There is a reason for this.

For eleven years I could not show any emotion. When you go to prison you put on a mask called a "Marquette," the name of Michigan's toughest prison.

LARRY LEHNA is a writer whose work has been published in the *Detroit Metro Times* and *Quail Bell Magazine,* an online feminist magazine that publishes "real and unreal stories." Lehna was a student at University of Michigan–Dearborn at the time that he wrote this essay for a narrative journalism class.

The look says, "I'm tough, I like to fight, and I would just love to hurt you. So mess with me if you dare." When I was in jail awaiting my sentencing I spent hours glaring into the mirror trying to perfect the look, but what gazed back at me was a look that said instead, "I'm constipated." I concluded I would never achieve that look. Little did I know that it would come naturally.

When I was sentenced to ten to thirty years in prison I was stunned. I wanted to cry. I wanted to be hugged. I wanted my mommy. I wanted to hurt someone, but I knew I should not show any emotion. That is when the look appeared on my face. When I got back to the cell-block I noticed a new-found wariness from the other prisoners. They kept their distance. When I went to the bathroom I glanced in the mirror. There it was: the look I would wear for over eleven years, the look that acted like a stopper in the bottle of my emotions. Nothing could faze me, and nothing did. It was more than a look; it was an attitude that was much more severe than mere stoicism. No emotions in, no emotions out.

Over the course of my first year that attitude became ingrained. Part of it 5 was always expecting the worst. I learned to never anticipate anything good from my fellow prisoners or from the institution. When they denied my first attempt at parole, after ten years, I received the information with the same deadpan expression as if they were handing me a pair of socks.

When I finally received my parole I wore the same look. I assumed they would take my parole away, and they did postpone it six months because I had once assaulted a thieving bunkmate. Another bit of news that had no visible effect. I no longer had to try to hide my feelings; I no longer felt any.

When I was released I was sent to a halfway house in Pontiac, one of the few cities in the country in worse shape than Detroit. There were absolutely no job prospects. Add to this the fact that a minimum of three days a week I had to report to either parole, or one of their programs, such as their Job Shop. What a joke. They acted as if they actually spoke with the people offering the jobs. They never did. They found the ads online and printed them. It did not bother these people to send us miles away to apply only to find out that the employer would not even consider a felon. Meanwhile, the amount they spent on counseling and other programs was enormous. It would have been enough to offer a parolee a fresh start, with a car and an apartment and a little bit of a chance at success. But let's not cloud this issue with logic.

The programs, too, were miles away in different directions. It was winter when I was released. I plodded through the snow wearing my cheap state shoes and the look. Whatever they got, I could take it. I only had 90 days to make something happen, and then I had to leave the halfway house. With less than a week left I told my parole officer that I had nowhere to go. When she suggested the homeless shelter, I took her response with a simple nod of my head and the look. With one day to spare I found a place where I could work for my room and board; I was glad to avoid the shelter, but I don't recall a feeling of happiness.

Once ensconced in my palatial new digs, I found my room was actually smaller than my prison cell, but it was all mine. No bunkie for me, but otherwise I continued on as I had done for the past eleven years. I was existing. I had learned that if I applied for a FAFSA [Free Application for Federal Student Aid] educational grant they would pay for my schooling and give me whatever was left over in a check. I applied, was accepted and I made an appointment to see a counselor at Oakland Community College. I expected resistance, having experienced nothing but rejection for the last eleven years. The Secretary of State made it almost impossible to get a driver's license once they saw my prison ID card. Society did not like me; they too had a look when they learned of my past. That was just fine; I didn't like them in return. The pressure was building up like Mount St. Helens.

I arrived for my appointment at OCC less than two weeks before classes were to begin. They ushered me into the office of a woman named Noreen Ruehs. I was fully prepared for her to adopt the look and I was ready to set the counselor straight about how little I cared about her and her fancy college job.

When I told her about my past she raised her eyebrows, nodded and said, "Well, you have some catching up to do. Let's see what kind of degree would suit you best." She proffered a few small pamphlets and suggested I look over the one for General Studies. She asked if I knew about computers. When I admitted my ignorance she recommended a Computer Literacy class. She asked about my typing skills and suggested a keyboarding class. We soon had my whole schedule full and all of it at very convenient times. Her kindness had a remarkable effect. There were times when I had to look at the floor and blink several times before I could speak. Kindness was unexpected and I got choked up. I was starting to believe that I could do this. She asked how I planned to pay for college. I told her about my Pell grant. When she said it could be too late for the summer semester, I know she saw my disappointment.

The counselor picked up the phone. "Have you got a minute or two right now? It's important," she said into the handset. Together we walked to the financial aid office and went straight to the supervisor. Noreen asked the woman if she could rush my paperwork through to get me into the coming semester, adding, "Please do this as a personal favor to me."

"Okay, I will handle this myself," said the supervisor. As we left the office I couldn't speak. I just nodded dumbly. The same thing happened in the enrollment office—straight to the supervisor. The problem was that my financial aid had not been processed and I did not have my transcripts from the 1960's at Henry Ford Community College.

Noreen also asked this woman for a personal favor. "Please, just get him enrolled and make sure he gets these classes," she said. "I guarantee the financial aid will come through and we will have his transcripts in here tomorrow." My eyes were blinking like a strobe light to keep the tears at bay. This woman had spent two hours helping me pick my classes and asking for personal favors on my behalf.

"Well, you're all set. Now it is up to you," she said. I reached out to shake her hand, but she gave me a hug instead and went in to counsel the next student. I was unprepared for a physical demonstration of warmth. I had not been hugged by a woman in eleven years. I walked to the parking structure in a daze. It was darker inside with very few people. By the time I got to my car tears were streaming down my cheeks. When someone walked by I would duck down in the seat. After twenty minutes I managed to slap my mask back on.

But when I walked into my room the mask slipped again. It didn't just slip, the damn thing fell off. This time it was not just tears. My body convulsed in guttural sobs. I fell on the bed, and all of the anguish of the lost years came pouring out. I gagged and gasped and howled. It lasted a good thirty minutes, until I cried myself to sleep. When I woke up an hour later the pillow was wet with tears and drool, and my mustache was stuck to it with dried snot. I got up and washed my face, and afterward I felt remarkably good. I knew I would excel at school. That counselor had given me a new outlook on life. I knew from then on things would change, and they did. But one lingering symptom has refused to go away.

When something good happens to me I get choked up. When someone gives me a compliment I get choked up. While typing this I have used two paper towels just from remembering the counselor's kindness. I blubber through any movie or TV show. It's the same with books. It does not have to be a heart-wrenching scene. If someone succeeds I get tears. If anything good happens I get tears. I sometimes tear up just thinking about good things in my life. There is no returning to what was once my emotional normal. I have turned into a real wuss. Even so, I believe I am a better person now. My look has vanished, but I still get the opposite looks on occasion from people who know about my past. Those looks are the least of my worries; you can't argue with the ignorant.

Noreen Ruehs called Susan Cushner at the University of Michigan–Dearborn and helped me transfer there. I'll graduate in a few weeks with "high distinction" and one of the five Chancellor's Medallions that are awarded to the best in the class. I have tried to thank Noreen but she says that I am the one who did all the work. She has no idea what she did for me. Of course I am wiping tears now.

Thinking about the Text

1. What is Larry Lehna's point in telling this story? Where does he make that point clear?

2. How would you describe the organization of Lehna's narrative? Chronological? Reverse chronological? Some other order? Where does the story start and end, and how effective is this structure?

3. Lehna talks about a look he sometimes receives from "people who know about my past" (17), a look that tells him that "society did not like me" (9) and that people doubted his character. We're willing to bet you feel quite differently after reading his story. How does Lehna connect with his **AUDIENCE** in this piece and establish his **CREDIBILITY**?

4. This essay was written for a course in narrative journalism, a genre that uses individual stories to illuminate public issues. Imagine that Lehna told this story as part of an essay on the need for prison reform for a political science course. How might the essay be different for that **PURPOSE**?

5. Identify an experience from your own life that sheds light on a social, political, cultural, or economic issue. Perhaps you were bullied in middle school, for instance—a deeply personal experience that has broader significance. Write a **NARRATIVE** essay in which you bring your own experience to life while also making the broader significance clear.

FIFTEEN

"Let's Take a Closer Look"
Writing Analytically

**NALYSIS IS A NECESSARY STEP** in much of the thinking that we do, and something that we do every day. What should you wear today? T-shirt and flip-flops? A sweatshirt? Your new red sweater? You consider the weather forecast, what you will be doing, the people you will be with, and then decide based on those factors. You may not consciously think of it as analysis, but that's what you've done.

When you analyze something, you break it down into its component parts and think about those parts methodically in order to understand it. Since our world is awash in information, the ability to read it closely, examine it critically, and decide how—or whether—to accept or act on it is essential. To navigate this sea of information, we rely on our ability to analyze.

Case in point: you want new headphones, but how do you choose? Do you want earbuds? over-the-ear? noise canceling? Bluetooth? As you consider your options, focus your analysis with questions: What's most important to you—sound quality? comfort? price? look? When will you most often be wearing your headphones—at the gym? on your daily bus commute? while playing video games? You could ask your music-loving friends for their opinions, or you might check websites, like *RTINGS.com*, that provide expert analysis as well as price comparisons. Analyzing your options will enable you to understand what each offers and decide based on your goals.

You've probably analyzed literary texts in English classes. In many college classes, you'll be expected to conduct different kinds of analyses—of texts, and also of events, issues, arguments, and more. Analysis is critical to every academic discipline and useful in every professional field. This chapter provides guidelines for conducting an analysis and writing analytically, with specific advice for rhetorical, causal, discourse, process, data, and visual analysis.

REFLECT. How many decisions—large and small—have you made in the last week? in the last month? in the last year? From small (what to have for breakfast) to major (which college to attend), make a chart listing a sample of these decisions and what areas of your life they affected. Then note the information you gathered in each case before you came to a final decision. What does this chart tell you about your interests, activities, and priorities? You've just completed an analysis.

Across Academic Disciplines

Some form of analysis can be found in every academic discipline. In a history class, you may be asked to analyze the causes of the US Civil War. In biology, you might analyze how the body responds to exercise. In economics, you might analyze the trade-off between unemployment and inflation rates. In a technical communication course, you might analyze a corporate website. In your composition course, you'll analyze your own writing for many purposes, from thinking about how you've appealed to your audience to deciding how you need to revise a draft. So many courses require analysis because looking closely and methodically at something—a text, a process, a philosophy—helps you discover connections between ideas and think about how things work, what they mean, and why.

Across Media

Your medium affects the way you present your analysis. In print, you'll be writing mostly in paragraphs, and you might include photos, tables, graphs, diagrams, or other images to make your analysis clear. If you're making an oral presentation, you might show information on slides or handouts. A digital text allows you to blend words, images, and audio—and you can link to more information elsewhere. In an analysis of Serena Williams's tennis serve published on *TheTennisBros.com*, note how the authors use links to videos so readers can see specific moves for themselves. If publishing in print, they might have included an image like the one below.

> Whilst Serena is clearly a very complete tennis player, there is one shot in particular that stands out as her most lethal weapon. Her serve. . . . Serena has one of the most powerful serves out there, recording the 3rd fastest ever official serve by a woman at the 2013 Australian Open of 128.6 MPH. . . . Her trophy position is perfect and she is able to generate a lot of easy power using her pinpoint stance. She places her weight on her front foot as she steps up to serve behind the baseline, then rocks back on to her back foot to create more momentum before she brings both feet together and drives up into her serving motion.
>
> —THETENNISBROS.COM, "Serena Williams Serve Analysis"

Serena Williams serving at the French Open in 2021.

↪ *WATCH THE VIDEO of 2005 Female Beatbox Battle World Champion Antoinette Clinton, who goes by the stage name Butterscotch, defining and explaining beatboxing in thirteen levels of complexity. Her video pairs verbal explanation with visual and auditory demonstrations for the moves of each "instrument" she's mimicking. How do the visuals and sounds contribute to this analysis? Go to* everyonesanauthor.tumblr.com *to watch the video.*

Across Cultures and Communities

Communicating with people from other communities or cultures challenges us to examine our assumptions and think about our usual ways of operating. Analyzing and understanding beliefs, assumptions, and practices that we are not familiar with may take extra effort. We need to be careful not to look at things only through our own frames of reference.

Sheikh Jamal Rahman, Pastor Don Mackenzie, and Rabbi Ted Falcon put in this extra effort in writing their book, *Getting to the Heart of Interfaith: The Eye-Opening, Hope-Filled Friendship of a Pastor, a Rabbi and a Sheikh*. In this book they take on the challenge of working toward interfaith understanding, saying that religion today "seems to be fueling hatred rather than expanding love" and that in order to heal the divisions, we must "find ways of entering into conversation with those different from us." And they say that analysis—what they call "inquiring more deeply"—is essential to their ongoing journey toward understanding issues central to each faith.

All three agree that it is critical to discuss the difficult and contentious ideas in faith. For the minister, one "untruth" is that "Christianity is the only way to God." For the rabbi, it is the notion of Jews as "the chosen people." And for the sheikh, it is the "sword verses" in the Koran, like "kill the unbeliever," which when taken out of context cause misunderstanding.

Their book embodies cultural sensitivity and describes the process of practicing analysis that's respectful of difference. Reading a sentence that the sheikh had written about the security wall in Israel, the rabbi responded, "If that line is in the book, I'm not in the book." Then they analyzed and discussed the sentence, and Sheikh Rahman revised the wording to be "respectful of [both] their principles."

Having respect for the principles, values, and beliefs of others means recognizing and being sensitive to differences among cultures. The best way to demonstrate cultural sensitivity is to use precise language that avoids negative words or stereotypes about gender, religion, race, ethnicity, and such—in short, by carefully selecting the words you use.

Across Genres

Seldom does any piece of writing consist solely of one genre; in many cases, writers draw on multiple genres as the situation demands. Analysis is a crucial step in writing for many purposes. To **ARGUE A POSITION** on an issue, you'll need to analyze that issue before you can take a stand on it. To compose a **REPORT**, you sometimes have to first analyze the data or the information that the report will be based on. And a **REVIEW**—whether it's of a film, a website, a book, or something else—depends on your analyzing the material before you evaluate it. Likewise, you might use a short **NARRATIVE** as an introductory element in a process or causal analysis.

REFLECT. Look for analysis in everyday use. Find two websites that analyze something you're interested in—laptops, cell phones, sneakers, places you want to go, things you want to do. Study the analyses and decide which one is more useful. What makes it better? Is it the language? the images? the amount of detail? the format? Keep these observations in mind as you write and design your own analyses.

CHARACTERISTIC FEATURES

While there are nearly as many different kinds of analysis as there are things to be analyzed, we can identify five common elements that analyses share across disciplines, media, cultures, and communities:

- A question that prompts you to take a closer look (p. 239)
- Some description of the subject you are analyzing (p. 240)
- Evidence drawn from close examination of the subject (p. 242)
- Insight gained from your analysis (p. 252)
- Clear, precise language (p. 254)

A Question That Prompts You to Take a Closer Look

Look at the examples cited earlier in this chapter, and note that each is driven by a question that doesn't have a single "right" answer. What should you wear today? Which set of headphones best meets your needs? How can we begin to achieve interfaith understanding? Each question requires some analysis. While an author may not explicitly articulate such a question, it will drive the analysis—and their writing. In this essay examining the capitalization of "White" when referring to race, see how sociologist Eve L. Ewing provides a prompt that requires taking a closer look:

> Multiple well-respected journalistic outlets have announced to much fanfare that, having reflected on the rapidly shifting American racial landscape, they will be capitalizing "Black" as designations for people and cultures. Some have also clarified why they're not capitalizing "white." . . . I haven't always capitalized "White" in my own writing, but I do now. Here's why.
>
> Whiteness is not only an absence. It's not a hole in the map of America's racial landscape. Rather, it is a specific social category that confers identifiable and measurable social benefits. . . . As long as White people do not ever have to interrogate what Whiteness is, where it comes from, how it operates, or what it does, they can maintain the fiction that race is other people's problem, that they are mere observers in a centuries-long stage play in which they have, in fact, been the producers, directors, and central actors.

Other than the demonstrably untrue idea that White "merely" describes skin color, there are other interesting arguments to consider for keeping it lowercase. For instance, many Black people I know say that they capitalize Black as a show of respect, pride, and celebration, and they don't want to afford the same courtesy to Whiteness. But we frequently capitalize words for reasons other than respect—words like Holocaust, or Hell, which can be capitalized to indicate specificity or significance. When we ignore the specificity and significance of Whiteness—the things that it is, the things that it does—we contribute to its seeming neutrality and thereby grant it power to maintain its invisibility.

Some outlets have also noted that White supremacist hate groups capitalize White, so we shouldn't. To that, I respond with an ancient African American proverb: *I ain't studdin' them.*

—EVE L. EWING, "I'm a Black Scholar Who Studies Race. Here's Why I Capitalize 'White.'"

Even though Ewing doesn't pose an explicit question, her early statement—"I haven't always capitalized 'White' in my own writing, but I do now"—invites readers to consider why she's changed her mind. Then she takes a closer look, providing an analysis of the social conditions that support her stance, as well as an analysis of counterarguments. You might not always start an analytical essay by asking an explicit question, but your analysis will always be prompted by a question of some kind.

Some Description of the Subject You Are Analyzing

To be sure your audience fully understands your analysis, you need to first describe what you are analyzing, focusing on the elements that support your claims. How much description you need depends on your subject, your audience, and your medium. For example, if you're analyzing gender roles in the *Fantastic Four* film franchise for your contemporary film course, you can assume most of your audience will be familiar with your subject. However, if you're analyzing the success of the same films for your marketing class, you will have to describe the elements that make the franchise so successful. See how marketing strategist Shimoli Pandya does so in a piece published on *Medium* that tackles the question: "What Makes the Marvel Cinematic Universe So Successful?":

A collage featuring some of the Marvel Cinematic Universe's vast world of characters.

> The Marvel Cinematic Universe currently comprises 23 films, span-
> ning 11 years over three "phases," each of the movies' story lines con-
> nected to each other. The MCU is the highest earning film franchise of all
> time with revenue of $21.4 billion. The 22nd movie, *Avengers: Endgame*,
> became the highest grossing film of all time at $2.79 billion. . . . Producing
> a series of movies that span an entire decade demands many things: a
> sense of consistency, being able to reinvent yourself in terms of the nar-
> rative, planning, and marketing.
>
> —SHIMOLI PANDYA, "What Makes the MCU So Successful?"

Writing for this site, Pandya rightly assumes that some of the audience may
know little about Marvel, and thus she includes background information as
well as an explanation of what draws fans to watch film after film. The author
goes on to provide subheads identifying the five major contributors to the movies' success. Throughout these sections, she provides examples and details
about how Marvel's universe operates that give readers a sense of the epic films.
These details support her claim that Marvel became the "highest earning film
franchise of all time" due to a variety of critical factors—perhaps chief among
them Marvel's "storytelling genius" and its "universe of characters that mirrors
our own [world] . . . [dealing with] problems that many of us face in real life."

When you're composing a text that will be read by an audience that may
not know your topic well, you'll also need to provide necessary description

and details. You might also include an image, embed a video, or include a link to a site offering more information if the medium you're writing in allows it.

Evidence Drawn from Close Examination of the Subject

Examining the subject of your analysis carefully and in detail and then thinking critically about what you find will help you discover key elements, patterns, and relationships—all of which provide you with the evidence on which to build your analysis. For example, if you are analyzing a poem, you might examine word choice, rhyme scheme, figurative language, repetition, and imagery. If you are analyzing an ad in a magazine, you might look at the use of color, the choice of typefaces, and the placement of figures or logos. Each element contributes some part of the message being conveyed. The kinds of elements you examine and the evidence you draw from them will depend on the nature of your subject as well as the kind of analysis you are conducting. Following are discussions and examples of five common kinds of analysis: rhetorical analysis, discourse analysis, process analysis, causal analysis, and data analysis.

Rhetorical analysis. This kind of analysis can focus on a written text, a visual text, an audio text, or one that combines words, images, and sound. All of these are rhetorical analyses; that is, they all take a close look at how authors, designers, or artists communicate a message to an audience. Whether they are using words or images, adjusting typeface sizes or colors, they all are trying to persuade a particular audience to have a particular reaction to a particular message—theirs.

See how the following example from an article published on *Branding Strategy Insider*, a blog about brand strategy, analyzes Nike's thirtieth anniversary Just Do It campaign and the company's choice to feature Colin Kaepernick, a former NFL quarterback who sat and knelt during the national anthem at 49ers games in the 2016 season as a protest against the oppression of Black people and people of color:

> Is the new Kaepernick 30th Anniversary Just Do It Campaign a smart move for the Nike brand? . . . Perhaps the first question to ask about this campaign from a brand planner's perspective is: *What is it about Colin Kaepernick's character that Nike finds so important to attach it to the Nike brand?*
>
> Developing brand character has many things in common with screenwriting and the attempt to develop relatable characters for film

and TV. Relatable characters are . . . sympathetic heroes on a mission to achieve worthy goals. They're often created as original, attractive, intelligent and provocative, and definitely not cliché, predictable or superficial. They have a definite point of view and a convincing way of getting it across. . . . Above all, relatable characters get people talking about them.

In Nike's current campaign, Kaepernick has certainly demonstrated that he has character, conviction about his beliefs, concern for social justice and he certainly has people talking about him. But, is he really a sympathetic hero? To segments of society struggling with [or sympathetic to] experiences of social injustice he definitely is. . . . To [others] . . . he carries strong and negative emotional associations.

Risk or Reward? In launching this new campaign Nike is risking alienating a huge segment of its U.S. consumer base, perhaps as much as half. Why would they do that? Perhaps they are thinking that it will tighten the tribe with millennials, who tend to be involved in protest movements, particularly when political leaders and other authority figures are not aligned with their feelings and values. They see Kaepernick as a champion of individual rights, fighting for a sense of social justice. . . .

This campaign will [also] scatter parts of the Nike tribe. . . . These people see not standing for the national anthem at a sporting event as an outward sign of disrespect for the idea of America and all the sacrifices made in the name of the nation. They see the gestures taken by Colin Kaepernick as a sign of questionable character. They see his public gestures as inappropriate and out of place.

—JEROME CONLON, "Analyzing Nike's Controversial
Just Do It Campaign"

In the rest of the article, Conlon goes on to analyze how two different and opposing audiences are likely to react to the ad: those who will "like that Nike is supporting individual athlete rights, acts of moral conscience, conviction and protest," and those who will see the choice as disrespectful to the American values they embrace. As a former director of marketing for Nike, Conlon also analyzes the advertisement—and its likely impact—by looking at the history of the Just Do It campaign, which was designed to celebrate "the joy of all kinds of sports and fitness activities . . . for everyone, pro sports athletes to fitness amateurs, young and old, men and women, people in America, people around the world. No one was excluded."

🡆 To see Nike's Just Do It campaign videos and posters, go to everyonesanauthor .tumblr.com.

Nike's Just Do It ad campaign featuring former football quarterback Colin Kaepernick. About his controversial gesture, Kaepernick explained, "I am not going to stand up to show pride in a flag for a country that oppresses black people and people of color."

Conlon concludes with a prediction and wider implications of the ad: "Short-term pain for Nike's brand, but long-term gain. The social discussion around the campaign will elevate public understanding of the greatness of America and the need for more respect and regard for all people, of all colors and classes." Note how the author begins with a question and then presents evidence by analyzing the ad's tone, stance, context, and how all of these elements will play with specific audiences.

In the following example from her study of a literacy tradition in African American churches, rhetorician Beverly Moss uses direct quotations from her field notes to illustrate a key rhetorical pattern she noticed in one preacher's sermons.

> One of the patterns that leapt out at me as I sat in the pew during all the sermons and as I listened to tapes and reviewed fieldnotes was the high level of participation in the sermons by the congregation. . . . It is a pattern that almost any discussion of African American

preaching addresses. Just as in the three churches highlighted [earlier], in this church, the congregation and Reverend M. engaged in a call-and-response dialogue. At times during the revival sermons, the feedback from the congregation was so intense that it was impossible to separate speaker from audience. Consider the following exchange. . . .

> When you shout before the battle is over (Preach!)
> It puts things in a proper perspective (Yeah!)
> It puts you in a posture of obedience (Yeah!)
> And it puts things in a proper perspective
> But finally
> When you shout before the battle is fought
> It puts the enemy in confusion (Yeah! That's right!)

The parenthetical expressions, responses from the congregation, do not appear on separate lines because there was little or no pause between the minister's statement and the congregation's response. Often, the congregation's response overlapped with the minister's statement. This type of feedback was typical in the sermons Reverend M. preached to this congregation, as was applause, people standing, cheering, and so on. Practically every sermon Reverend M. preached ended with the majority of the congregation on their feet clapping and talking back to Reverend M.

—BEVERLY MOSS, *A Community Text Arises*

Members of a congregation move and shout in response to the preacher's words.

Moss analyzes and presents evidence from a spoken text. Because she was writing a print book, she could not include the actual audio of the sermon, but still she presents evidence in a way that demonstrates a key point of her analysis: that the closeness of the preacher's "call" and the congregation's "response" made it almost "impossible to separate speaker from audience." This quoted evidence shows a specific example of how the congregation's response becomes a part of the sermon, filling the church with "applause, people standing, cheering."

Discourse analysis. This kind of analysis can focus on any spoken or written language used in a particular social context. Discourse analysis often entails analyzing the communication practices of a specific community—people who share basic values, practices, and goals. For example, a community of scholars such as the teachers at your school all likely value education, believe in helping students grow intellectually, and practice their profession by providing instruction to enable students to achieve their goals. You've probably noticed that most of your teachers—especially those in a particular discipline or department—share a specific vocabulary. This holds true for any field, any profession, any group of people with shared interests; they develop ways of interacting and communicating most effectively with each other. In order to analyze how a specific group communicates, you'll examine that community's practices, an effort that requires careful observation and even immersion when possible.

Discourse analysis might even scrutinize elements as tiny as periods and commas. Check out Jessica Wildfire's examination of online punctuation on p. 1024.

Look at the following example by Alberta Negri, a student at the University of Cincinnati, that analyzes the communication practices of a local group of bikers. Note how the introduction draws you in with a brief narrative and specific sensory details before offering background information. The author moves from common misperceptions of bikers to her specific subject, a group she refers to as the "Shell Station Squad." Note that Negri gives a rationale for focusing on this group; she tells readers why it matters.

It's 8:56 p.m. on a Tuesday evening, and from my third-floor dorm room, I can once again hear the aggressive growls of 600-pound motorcycles as they roll into the parking lot of the Shell station across the street. The riders meet every night around 9:00 and face the usual apprehensive looks from bystanders. . . . Few investigations have been done from within the biking community; even fewer have examined the inner workings of the communication among members. . . . The following research makes the effort to peek into this unexplored group and discuss the less action-packed qualities, including its status as a discourse community, the process of club enculturation, and how a member's new identity can complicate their previous social roles.

—ALBERTA NEGRI, "Underneath the Leather Jackets and Chrome Pipes: Research into a Community of Local Bikers"

Negri goes on to explain the methods used to conduct her research—including firsthand observation—and then she begins her analysis:

> What do these men have in common? The riders of the Shell Station Squad have separate personal lives: full-time gunsmith, engineering firm representative, college student and *Call of Duty* gamer among them, but they all plan to meet every night and anticipate their 9 p.m. ride all day. Their passion to ride is often their only unifying characteristic. There is no need for them to begin each ride with a preface, stating the goals for the ride for the night, or what they hope to accomplish as a team. There is a simple, unspoken understanding that if you pull into that gas station parking lot, you're there for the chance to revel in the thrill of weaving through streets on a motorcycle, while flocking as a group to make the experience a little safer for all involved. . . .
>
> Their primary mode of correspondence is *Facebook*; they use social media to create a private group for discussing matters such as driving routes and safety updates. . . . There is no clear pecking order. The peer-appointed leader never dominated the discourse. More often, he would push for more interaction from those who were recently recruited: addressing questions to them to get individual opinions and inviting them to special weekend rides. [This leader] went as far as directly introducing new riders, saying, "Guys: new kid with us tonight. Thomas is a student at [the university], new rider, let's make sure to make him feel welcome tonight, alrite? Good kid, i think" [sic] (Lucius). His digital diction was a tad gentler in these interactions compared to his brash joking with the more experienced riders.

Negri analyzes the shared motivations and passions that build kinship among the group members—"the thrill of weaving through streets on a motorcycle"—and acknowledges what sets them apart from one another, too: their personal lives outside of biking. She goes on to examine the group's way of communicating and building community, in person and online, in order to understand how the community operates. To conduct her analysis,

↷ Visit everyones anauthor.tumblr .com for a link to Negri's complete analysis.

Negri relies on interviews with group members as well as primary texts: text messages, *Facebook* posts, and hand signals.

Process analysis. Analyzing a process requires you to break down a task into individual steps and examine each one to understand how something works or how something is done. Thus there are two kinds of process analyses: **INFORMATIONAL**, showing how something works; and **INSTRUCTIONAL**, telling how something is done. An analysis of the chemistry that makes a cake rise would be informational, whereas an analysis of how to make a cake would be instructional.

The following example analyzes the process of how skaters make high-speed turns. This is the most critical element in speed skating, for being able to consistently make fast turns without slipping can be the difference between winning and losing. This analysis from *Science Buddies*, a website for students and parents, closely examines the key steps of the process. Note how the author provides some information about the basic physics of speed and turns and then systematically explains how each element of the action—speed, angle, push-back force from the surface—contributes to the total turn.

Whether it's ice, wood, or a paved surface, the science that governs a skater's ability to turn is essentially the same. It's based on a couple of basic laws of physics that describe speed and the circular motion of turns. The first is Newton's *law of inertia* that says a body in motion will stay in motion unless there is some outside force that changes it. To skaters hoping to make a turn after they speed down the straightaway, that means the force of inertia would tend to keep them going straight ahead if there wasn't a greater force to make them change direction and begin turning.

The force that causes the change in direction comes from the skater's blades or wheels as they cross over at an angle in front of the skater leaning to make a turn. Newton's *law of reaction* explains that the push from the skater's skates generates an equal but opposite push back from the ice or floor. This push back force draws the skater in towards the track and is described as a "center seeking" or *centripetal* type of force. It's the reason why turns are possible in any sport. The wheels of a bicycle, for example, also angle into the road surface when the cyclist leans to begin a turn. As the road pushes back on both bike and rider, it supplies the inward centripetal force to generate the turning motion.

The more a skater leans into a turn, the more powerful the push from the skate, and the greater centripetal force produced to carry the skater through the turn. Leaning in also creates a smaller arc, or tighter

Skaters from around the world competing in the 2021 Short Track Speed Skating World Cup.

turn, making for a shorter distance and a faster path around the turn. However, there's a catch. As the skater leans more and more into the track, the balancing point of the body, or the skater's *center of gravity*, also shifts more and more to the side. If it shifts too far, the skater no longer can maintain balance and ends up splayed out onto the rink rather than happily heading round the turn to the finishing line.

So success in turns, especially fast ones, means skaters must constantly find their center of gravity while teetering on the edge of their skates. To make the turn at all requires that the skater push the skates against the ice with sufficient power to generate enough inward centripetal force to counter the inertia of skating straight ahead. And to keep up speed in a race, a skater must calculate and execute the shortest, or tightest, turns possible around the track.

—DARLENE JENKINS, "Tightening the Turns in Speed Skating: Lessons in Centripetal Force and Balance"

To read the full analysis and see a video analysis, go to everyonesanauthor .tumblr.com.

This kind of close examination of the subject is the heart of analysis. Darlene Jenkins explains the key elements in the process of making a high-speed turn—speed, angle, push-back force—and also examines the relationships among these elements as she describes what happens in minute detail, revealing how they all combine to create the pattern of movement that leads to a successful high-speed turn. By including a photograph that shows skaters leaning into a turn, blades and bodies angled precariously, Jenkins shows what the process entails, and readers can actually see what's being described.

Causal analysis. Why is the Arctic ice pack decreasing in volume? What causes extreme droughts in California? These and other questions about why something occurs or once occurred call on you to analyze what caused a certain event, the possible effects of an event, or the links in a chain of connected events. Put most simply, causal analyses look at why something happened or will happen as a result of something else.

Go to everyones
anauthor.tumblr
.com to link to the
full article, "The
Cry Embedded
within the Purr."

Behavioral ecologist Karen McComb, who studies communication between animals and humans, wanted to understand why cat owners so often respond to purring cats by feeding them. To answer this question, McComb and a team recorded a number of domestic cats in their homes and discovered what the team termed "solicitation purring"—an urgent high-frequency sound, similar to an infant's cry, that is embedded within the cats' more pleasing and low-pitched purring and that apparently triggered an innate nurturing response in their owners. In an article presenting their findings, the team provided quantitative data about the pitch and frequency of different kinds of purring to support their conclusion about what the data showed: that the similarities in pitch and frequency to the cries of human infants "make them very difficult to ignore."

Using data like these to support an analysis is common in science classes, while in the humanities and social sciences, you're more likely to write about causes that are plausible or probable than ones that can be measured. In a literature class, for example, you might be asked to analyze the influences that shaped F. Scott Fitzgerald's creation of Jay Gatsby in *The Great Gatsby*—that is, to try to explain what caused Fitzgerald to develop Gatsby the way he did. In a sociology class, you might be asked to analyze what factors contributed to a population decline in a certain neighborhood. In both cases, these causes are probabilities—plausible but not provable.

Data analysis. Some subjects will require you to examine data. **QUANTITATIVE** analysis looks at numerical data; **QUALITATIVE** analysis looks at data that's not numerical.

When Beverly Moss analyzed the rhetoric of three ministers, she worked with qualitative data: transcripts of sermons, personal testimonies, her own observations from the church pews. Her data came mostly in the forms of words and text, not statistics.

Now see how blogger Will Moller analyzes the performances of ten major-league baseball pitchers using quantitative data—baseball statistics, in this case—to answer the question of whether New York Yankees pitcher Andy Pettitte is likely to get into baseball's Hall of Fame.

I prefer to look at Andy versus his peers, because simply put, it would be very odd for 10 pitchers from the same decade to get in (though this number is rather arbitrary). Along that line, who are the best pitchers of Andy's generation, so we can compare them?

	Wins	Win%	WAR	ERA+	IP	K	K/BB	WAR/9IP
Martinez	219	68.7%	89.4	154	2827	3154	4.15	0.28
Clemens	354	65.8%	145.5	143	4917	4672	2.96	0.27
Johnson	303	64.6%	114.8	136	4135	4875	3.26	0.25
Schilling	216	59.7%	86.1	128	3261	3116	4.38	0.24
Maddux	355	61.0%	120.6	132	5008	3371	3.37	0.22
Mussina	270	63.8%	85.6	123	3563	2813	3.58	0.22
Smoltz	213	57.9%	82.5	125	3473	3084	3.05	0.21
Brown	211	59.4%	77.2	127	3256	2397	2.66	0.21
Pettitte	240	63.5%	66.9	117	3055	2251	2.34	0.20
Glavine	305	60.0%	67.1	118	4413	2607	1.74	*0.14*

The above table tells the story pretty well. I've bolded the numbers that are particularly absurd, and italicized one in particular which should act as a veto. Though I imagine most of the readers of this blog know full well what these statistics mean at this point, for those of you who don't, a primer:

WAR stands for Wins Above Replacement, and is a somewhat complicated equation which estimates the true value of a pitcher, taking into account league, ERA, park effects, etc. For instance, a pitcher that wins a game but gives up 15 earned runs has probably lost value in their career WAR, even though they get the shiny addition to their win-loss record. We like WAR around these parts.

ERA+ is a normalized version of ERA centered on 100, basically showing how much better or worse a pitcher was compared to their league average (by ERA). 110, for example, would indicate that the pitcher's ERA was 10% better than average. 95, on the other hand, would be roughly 5% worse than average. This is a good statistic for comparing pitchers between different time periods—a 4.00 ERA in 2000 doesn't mean the same thing as a 4.00 ERA in 1920, for example.

K/BB is how many strikeouts a pitcher had per walk. More is better, less is worse.

As you can see, the above table doesn't do Andy any favors. He's 6th in wins and 5th in winning percentage, but he's 9th in ERA+ and dead last in WAR. His K/BB beats only Tom Glavine, who comes off looking pretty bad on this list. The only thing he has going for him is his playoff record—and frankly, the team he was on won a whole bunch of playoff games while he was on the team, even when he wasn't pitching. Besides, we're pretty much past the point of taking W/L record as a good indication of pitcher skill—why is it that when we slap the word "postseason" onto the statistic, we suddenly devolve 10 years to when such things seemed to matter?

—WILL MOLLER, "A Painful Posting"

Moller's guiding question, "Should Andy Pettitte be in the Hall of Fame?," is unstated in this excerpt, but it is made clear earlier in the piece. He presents the data in a table for readers to see—and then walks us through his analysis of that data. It's critical when using numerical data like these not only to present the information but also to say what it means. That's a key part of your analysis. Using a table to present data is a good way to include numerical evidence, but be careful that you don't just drop the table in; you need to explain to readers what the data mean and to explain any abbreviations that readers may not know, as Moller does. Though he does not state his conclusions explicitly here, his analysis makes clear what he thinks.

Insight Gained from Your Analysis

One key purpose of an analysis is to offer your audience some insight on the subject you are analyzing. As you examine your subject, you discover patterns, data, specific details, and key information drawn from the subject—which will lead you to some insight, a deeper understanding of the subject you're analyzing. The insight that you gain will lead you to your thesis. When the sheikh, pastor, and rabbi mentioned earlier in this chapter analyzed a sentence in their book that offended the rabbi, each gained insight into the others' principles that led them to further understanding. In "I'm a Black Scholar Who Studies Race. Here's Why I Capitalize 'White.',"

Eve L. Ewing makes clear the insights she derived from analyzing the reasons for and against capitalizing "White" and especially why she believes it's an important topic:

> Ultimately, it's good that we're having this public conversation. Plenty of other scholars who study race and racism will disagree with me on this, and that's fine. In fact, I disagree with myself from two years ago. . . . I might change my mind again. Language and racial categories have some important things in common: They are fluid, they are inherently political, and they are a socially constructed set of shared norms that are constantly in flux as our beliefs and circumstances change.
>
> The terms we use, and the ways we write them, are less about saying or doing the "correct" thing, the thing that will prevent you from getting flamed on Twitter or earning an eye roll in a staff meeting. Rather, it's about what we want words to do for us and the arguments we're trying to make about ourselves and the world through the words we choose.
>
> —EVE L. EWING, "I'm a Black Scholar Who Studies Race. Here's Why I Capitalize 'White.'"

Ewing makes clear that the words we use—and how we style them—are powerful tools for reflecting and engaging with the world around us.

Summarizing the study of the way humans react to a cat's purr, Karen McComb and her team note parallels between the isolation cry of domestic cats and the distress cry of human infants as a way of understanding why the "cry embedded within the purr" is so successful in motivating owners to feed their cats. They conclude that the cats have learned to communicate their need for attention in ways that are impossible to ignore, ways that prompt caring responses from people. Thus, their work suggests that much can be learned by studying animal-human communication from both directions, from animals to humans as well as the reverse.

Remember that any analysis you do needs to have a purpose—to discover how cats motivate their owners to provide food on demand, to understand the power behind word and style choices, to explain why a favorite baseball player's statistics probably won't get him into the Hall of Fame. In writing up your analysis, your point will be to communicate the insight you gain from the analysis.

Clear, Precise Language

Since the point of an analysis is to help an audience understand something, you need to pay extra attention to the words you use and the way you explain your findings. You want your audience to follow your analysis easily and not get sidetracked. You need to demonstrate that you know what you are talking about. You've studied your subject, looked at it closely, thought about it—*analyzed* it; you know what to say about it and why. Now you have to craft your analysis in such a way that your readers will follow that analysis and understand what it shows. Andy Pettitte doesn't just rank low by his statistics; "he's 9th in ERA+ and dead last in WAR." It's not just that White people don't have to think about their race while others do: "White people get to be only normal, neutral, or without any race at all, while the rest of us are saddled with this unpleasant business of being racialized." Like Moller and Ewing, you should be precise in your explanations and in your choice of words.

Analyzing an intricate process or a complicated text requires you to use language that your audience will understand. The analysis of speed skating turns earlier in this chapter was written for an audience of young people and their parents. The language used to describe the physics that govern the process of turning works well for such an audience—precise but not technical. When the author refers to Newton's law of inertia, she defines "inertia" and then explains what it means for skaters. The role of centripetal force is explained as "the more a skater leans into a turn, the more powerful the push from the skate." Everything is clear because the writer uses simple, everyday words—"tighter turn," "teetering on the edge of their skates"—to convey complex science.

You need to consider what your audience knows about your topic and what information you'll need to include to make sure they'll understand what you write. You'll also want to be careful to state your conclusions explicitly—in clear, specific language.

SHAAN SACHDEV wrote this article in 2021 analyzing why Beyoncé enjoys such enduring success. It was published by *Slate*, an online magazine and podcast network that offers "analysis and commentary about politics, news, business, technology, and culture."

The Key to Beyoncé's Lasting Success

SHAAN SACHDEV

FIFTY THOUSAND PEOPLE—more Black and brown than white, more gay than straight—comprise a studious frenzy. Sure, there are some in the crowd who chatter amongst themselves as Beyoncé successively runs through "Mine," "Baby Boy," "Hold Up," and "Countdown," in one of the more exhilarating mid-concert medleys in modern pop history, but this show is neither for casual spectators nor about casual spectatorship. It's about memorizing and mirroring her choreography in the stadium's narrow aisles. It's about obeying her commands, six times per song, that everyone "sing!", these interruptions the only sign her pristine vocals are live and not lip-synched. It's about ecstasy, tears, and breathlessness. The least breathless person in the stadium, it seems, is Beyoncé. . . .

> *The author begins by describing the energy of Beyoncé's performances.*

As Beyoncé turns 40, her legacy might already be cemented even as it is evolving. So perhaps it is opportune to point to precisely what distinguishes her from the glittery cadre of millennial pop

Beyoncé performing at New Jersey's MetLife Stadium.

The driving question behind this analysis: what makes Beyoncé so captivating to her audience?

princesses (Rihanna, Lady Gaga, Britney Spears, Ariana Grande, Katy Perry, Pink, and yes, Mariah Carey, Jennifer Lopez, and Madonna too)—making her "the result, the logical end point, of a century-plus of pop," as Jody Rosen wrote in 2013.

The answer lies in her live performances.

Stadium-sized live concerts are the closest things we have to the artistic mass ritual. But the burden of a hundred thousand eyes and ears is so taxing that the superstars who bear them often crack, fizzle, or are simply conceded lowered expectations.

Here's the insight that the analysis will develop.

Because Beyoncé approaches her performances with the sort of ferocious discipline more commonly associated with professional athletes than with pop stars—she practices until her feet bleed— she is our most physically capable living superstar.

She brings her music and visions to life with the force and glitz of a cultural deity. None of the aforementioned pop princesses— and no one else in our constellation of arena-filling performers— can sing and dance in six-inch heels for two and a half hours with the same unremitting vocal wattage and choreographic mastery. Her musical athleticism is unrivaled. And for atheists, agnostics, 5 queers, and aesthetes, what is a deity, a goddess, if not a buxom diva striking a silhouetted posture of superlative womanhood — and then *embodying* it —before millions of congregants around the world?

Critics, scholars, and professors of voice performance tend to name just five virtuosos in the history of pop music who rival Beyoncé's strenuous showmanship. Or rather, whom *she* rivals, since four of the five are dead, and the only one still alive, the fabulous Tina Turner, is now over 80. After Tina and Sammy Davis Jr. and James Brown and Prince, the experts usually settle upon one name.

"I think she is, in some ways, the inheritor of Michael Jackson's legacy—the truest inheritor that we have today," says Jason King, Chair of NYU's Clive Davis Institute of Recorded Music. Jackson was crowned "King of Pop" precisely because of his supernatural aura on stage, a dazzling amalgam of dance, vocals, and visual effects. But the resemblance between the two stars has its limits—Jackson's legacy has since been clouded by abuse allegations in ways Beyoncé's has not. . . .

Quoting an expert provides evidence for the author's analysis.

Perhaps it isn't altogether surprising that Beyoncé's father, Matthew Knowles, is sometimes compared to Michael Jackson's father, Joe Jackson. But where Joe Jackson was a violent martinet, tales of Knowles portray more of a drill sergeant who'd wake a young Beyoncé early in the morning, along with the other founding members of Destiny's Child, and make them jog for miles around Houston's Hermann Park *while singing*.

Background information provides context and supports the author's claim of Beyoncé's athleticism.

Beyoncé eventually confirmed the stories to the *Times of India*, and years later, celebrity trainer Mark Jenkins told Insider Magazine that he'd similarly have Beyoncé sing an entire album while running in the Georgia heat—and "make it sound good." The result? Some of the best breath control on the Billboard Hot 100—and "bionic" onstage execution.

When Beyoncé says, "I've worked harder than probably anyone I know, at least in the music industry," she sounds more matter-of-fact than arrogant. While Michael Jackson was scarred by his father's tyrannical exploitations, Beyoncé fired her father, took possession of the torch, and kept on perfecting.

"One of the reasons I connect to the Super Bowl is that I approach my shows like an athlete," she told *GQ* in 2013, finally

10

using the A-word. "You know how they sit down and watch who-ever they're going to play and study themselves? That's how I treat this."

Beyoncé's own words are included to illustrate the main point.

She wasn't overstating. When she's on tour, Beyoncé said she watches a recording of the show she's just performed every night before bedtime, handing her dancers, bandmates, and crew pages of notes the next day. Her 2016 VMA and 2016 BET Awards performances, both amid her Formation World Tour, supplied the national airwaves with outrageously incontrovertible evidence that her method was working.

Additional examples—Beyoncé's performance, the crowd's reaction, and her musical ability—are offered as further evidence.

"I promise I will always give you a hundred percent of myself," she said to 185,000 fans at the end of her 2011 Glastonbury set (to their—and George Michael's—roaring approval). It was less a "thank you for coming" and more a declaration of her creed. . . .

"A Broadway show is about the show. Even if there's a celebrity in it, it's still about the context of the show itself," says King. "With Beyoncé, it's really about the cult of her celebrity and the kind of deification of her on stage working very hard on *our* behalf, not even just her behalf. There's an element of this power and ferocity that is a kind of martyrdom. You have to leave it all on stage. You have to give it all up." . . .

If her songs sounded like those of Lady Gaga or Katy Perry, her performances would be campy and fun, but she'd qualify neither as a queen nor a genius. Her musical athleticism, in other words, would be moot if her songs didn't merit this divine breath of life. 15

Thankfully, Beyoncé's music is pretty damn good. Lyrical simplicities aside, her songs are weird, distinctive, beautiful, ranging, and complicated. She can do maternal power pop and outlandish anthems, rap and eerie ballads. No superstar pays more attention to production. "Countdown" might be the strangest R&B song of the new millennium, while "Love on Top" might number among the most difficult to sing live. (Linda Balliro even shows Beyoncé's performance of "Love on Top" at the 2011 MTV Music Awards to her students at Berklee as an exemplar of stamina and energy, likening the four key changes to running a marathon.)

Prince may have lost the "black-queen vote"—or at least Hilton Als's faith—in the 80s, but Beyoncé continues to win the pop-queen vote because she inspirits an identification that is much more viscerally thrilling than genuine political subversiveness. She also wins the critical and celebrity vote. As a matter of fact, she is the celebrity of celebrities—the rare untouchable who makes Oscar winners nervous and giddy, talk show hosts grill guests about their interactions with her, comedians speechless, rappers gush, musicians gush, other singers gush, the old guard applaud, and First Ladies want to trade places.

Perhaps it's not only queens, misfits, and artists who identify with Beyoncé as she transforms from woman to goddess—a singular amplified voice and spectacle, serenading the masses' desire for straightforward rhapsodic pleasure. Goddesses, after all, give us energy, glory, beauty, and joy. Most of us wouldn't mind *being* divine, if it didn't take so much damn practice, stamina, and lung power. Instead we exalt, and we are deified vicariously.

Widespread recognition and appreciation of Beyoncé's excellence drives home the main point.

The author concludes by reiterating the main elements of his analysis and connecting with his audience by identifying himself as a fan.

REFLECT. *Find a short analytical article online or in a newspaper or magazine. Look at the list of five characteristic features of analysis on page 239 and, using Sachdev's essay as a model, annotate the article to point out these features. Then evaluate how successful the article's analysis is. For example, can you identify the question that drove the analysis? Has the author provided enough description for you to follow the analysis? Is the language clear and precise? Has the author clearly stated the insight the analysis led to? Does the author provide evidence to support that insight?*

VISUAL ANALYSIS

Photos, cartoons, ads, movies, *YouTube* videos, *TikToks*—all are visual texts, ones that say something and, just like words alone, make some kind of claim that they hope we will accept. When you analyze a visual, you ask the same questions you would of any text: How does it convey its message? How does it appeal to audiences? To answer such questions for a visual text, you'd begin by considering each of its elements—its use of color, light, and shadow; its perspective; any words or symbols; and its overall composition. Visual analysis takes various forms, but it generally includes the following features.

A Description of the Visual

Include an image of the visual in your analysis, but if that's not possible—in a print essay analyzing a video, for instance—you'll need to describe it. Your description should focus on the most important elements and those you'll point to in your analysis. What draws your eye first, and why? What's most interesting or seems most important? Does any use of contrast affect what you see? Consider the cartoon below. Your eyes were probably first drawn to the road signs because they come at the top and use capital letters. Then you may have noticed Uncle Sam next, the only human figure included, wearing red, white, and blue clothing that stands out against the white road.

Some Contextual Information

You'll need to provide contextual information about your subject. What's its purpose, and who's the target audience? Is there any historical, political, or cultural context that's important to describe? Such factors are important to think about—and to describe in your analysis. The Uncle Sam at a crossroads cartoon by John Darkow appeared in the *Columbia Missourian*, a local newspaper in Columbia, Missouri, in 2021 and reflects the concern many had at the time about political divisions and extremism in the United States.

Attention to Any Words

If the visual includes any words, what do they add to its message? Whatever the words—the name of a sculpture, a caption beneath a photo, a slogan in an ad, the words in a speech balloon—you'll want to discuss how they affect the way we understand the visual. The same is true of the typography: words in boldface are likely ones the author wants to emphasize; the typefaces affect the tone. If you were analyzing the Uncle Sam cartoon, for instance, you might point out that the signs containing all-capitalized words suggest that both fascism and authoritarianism oppose the traditional path of the United States since those two signs point one way while the "democracy" sign points in the opposite direction.

Close Analysis of the Message

What elements are most important in conveying the message? Probably the most compelling in the Uncle Sam cartoon is the placement of Uncle Sam himself, a figure often used as a traditional symbol of the United States. What does his posture suggest? He's still, hands at his sides, baggage in tow, looking in democracy's direction and not at the signs above. The fact that he's showing little emotion, other than his stillness, might be read as his own concern and deliberation—worry that the direction he chooses could be terribly important and thus worthy of serious consideration. You might also note that the sun seems to be setting—or is it rising?—on the land labeled as "democracy."

Insight into What the Visual "Says"

Your analysis of the visual will lead you to an understanding of what it's saying. In the Uncle Sam cartoon, the character's position and posture at a literal crossroads suggests the country is at a pivotal moment when a path other than democracy might take us into the future. Whenever you analyze a visual—a cartoon, an advertisement, a slogan on a sign or T-shirt—you know it's trying to persuade you to take an action, to have an emotional response, to desire—and perhaps purchase—something. When you analyze visuals, you need to think about how the image makes you feel. What is it suggesting you think or do? And what techniques does it use to draw that reaction from you?

Precise Language

It's especially important to use precise words in writing about a visual. Saying that the Uncle Sam cartoonist "places a symbol of the United States at a crossroads" doesn't say much. Better: "the vivid red, white, and blue of Uncle Sam's clothes are in contrast to the stark crossroads he stands on—all while he looks ahead and into the sun, which might be rising or setting on democracy." When you write about a visual, you need to use language that will help readers see the things that matter.

THINK BEYOND WORDS

⤴ *TAKE A LOOK at "Paradise, Paved,"* a photo essay about travelers spending the night in Walmart parking lots. Click through the images and read the surrounding text. Then pick one image to analyze. How are the people in the image portrayed? How is the image itself composed? If this photo essay had a thesis, what would it be? Go to everyonesanauthor.tumblr.com to access the entire piece.

FRANKIE DE LA CRETAZ teaches writing at GrubStreet, a creative writing center in Boston, and writes about sports, gender, culture, and queerness for publications including the *New York Times*, *Sports Illustrated*, and *Teen Vogue*. They wrote this piece in 2018 for *Elle* magazine.

Serena Williams's Tennis Outfits Defy the Norms Female Athletes Face

FRANKIE DE LA CRETAZ

SERENA WILLIAMS CALLED IT her Black Panther suit. Custom designed with Nike to prevent blood clots—the health condition that nearly killed Williams after she gave birth to her daughter—Williams said the full-length black catsuit made her "feel like a superhero."

The French Tennis Federation called it disrespectful. In an interview with Tennis Magazine . . ., FTF president Bernard Giudicelli announced they will be changing the French Open's dress code going forward. "Serena's outfit this year, for example, would no longer be accepted," he said. "One must respect the game and the place."

Williams, for her part, seems unbothered. Responding to the comments . . ., Williams said she has a good relationship with Giudicelli and is confident they would come to an understanding. "If they know that some things are for health reasons, then there's no way they wouldn't be okay with it," she said. . . .

Williams's singular on-court style often feels like a metaphor for all the other ways she is singular: the world's best player and the black star of an overwhelmingly white, historically exclusionary

> A description of one subject of the analysis.

sport. So to fans and observers, the catsuit ban was the latest instance of Williams facing racial discrimination within a sport she has single-handedly propelled forward. From racist slurs at Indian Wells to disproportionate drug testing to comments comparing her to an animal or a man, the sport continually sends the message that Williams doesn't belong. Her strong black body—now uncovered by a skirt—seems to be perceived as a threat to tennis' status quo.

The FTF's updated dress code reflects a troubling desire to   5
uphold ideas about respectability and femininity—white feminin-ity, specifically—in women's sports, a tradition that dates back more than a century in the US. In the beginning of the twentieth century, women's participation in sports was dictated by the "skirt theory": the only sports acceptable for women were ones they could play without wearing pants. The 1914 Olympic Committee opposed "women taking part in any event in which they could not wear long skirts." Sports like golf, archery, and croquet were most popular, but women managed to play baseball in full-length skirts, as well as ice skate. In the 1870s, then women's college Vassar's baseball team, the Resolutes, played the game in the era's cumbersome fashion.

As long as women continued to play in skirts, the thinking went, white men didn't need to fear white women had abandoned

*Contextual information
and precise language
analyzing what's behind
these rules more broadly.*

their feminine duties to live like men. We see remnants of this thinking today: just last year, Toronto Blue Jays manager John Gibbons responded to what he perceived as a "softening" of baseball rules by saying that his team might as well "come out wearing dresses" next game. His commentary ties into patriarchal ideas about femininity and weakness, yes, but also the notion that anyone who plays in skirts could not also be considered a serious athlete.

Direct quotations support the author's claims.

Women took it upon themselves to shorten their skirts, giving them the freedom of movement to compete at higher levels. In the 1920s, Norwegian figure skater Sonja Henie scandalized the skating community when she shortened her skirt to her knees, allowing her to spin and jump like the male skaters did. When the All-American Girls Professional Baseball League came around in 1943, women were again required to wear skirts to play baseball— though they were much shorter now. Still, the skirts were not ideal for sliding, a problem made famous by the film *A League of Their Own*. But the short skirt or skort became entrenched as the female uniform for sports—in spite of the obvious impracticality. Until recently, even female boxers were asked to wear skirts.

Historical evidence reinforces the author's points.

Today, dress codes for many women's sports are being policed by two seemingly opposed forces—modesty and objectification. Either cover up your body because it's inappropriate or a distraction, or reveal almost all of it because female athletes are primarily here for men's pleasure. Ever since women's sports began to be televised (though, it should be noted, still at a rate far less than men's sports), the age-old demand for female modesty was met with a new demand to draw in audiences.

Forced sexiness is no less sexist than forced modesty. In sports like track and field, gymnastics and volleyball, skimpy uniforms can prevent players who dress modestly, like Muslim athletes, from participating. It was 2004 before the International Skating Union did away with the rule that "ladies must wear skirts" and in 2012, the International Volleyball Federation finally stopped requiring that female volleyball players wear bikinis, which many people saw as a sexist rule. Meanwhile, women in culturally conservative sports like tennis and golf must try to walk the line between attracting audiences and distracting them.

These dress codes are not so different than the controversial 10 school dress codes in place for girls. They use arbitrary moral standards to control women's bodies and expression—privileging onlookers' opinions over those of the women wearing the clothes. Last year, the LPGA released a new dress code that has been criticized as slut-shaming. It includes guidelines like "Length of skirt, skort, and shorts MUST be long enough to not see your bottom area. . . . at any time, standing or bent over" and "plunging necklines are NOT allowed." Rarely, in discussing women's dress codes, do we discuss what's distracting for the athletes.

When it comes to sports, safety and function need to come into play when choosing uniforms. But all too often morals and prejudice are the deciding factors. Williams was not the first female tennis player to attempt to buck tradition with a bodysuit. In 1985, Anne White wore a white, full-length version to Wimbledon. Her opponent complained, she was not allowed to wear it again the next day, and news coverage was dominated by stories about her clothing. . . .

Calling Williams's catsuit "disrespectful" harkens back to racist and sexist ideas about what female athletes should be: white, feminine, and unserious. When athletes don't conform to these

The author's insight: what they think the long-term impacts of these regulations are.

ideals that still dominate the sports landscape, they are criticized or, as in Williams's case, accused of not honoring the culture of the game. But Williams's influence, her outspokenness, and her on-court performances are the biggest selling points the sport of tennis has. Tennis has Williams—considered by many to be the greatest athlete ever—to thank for all the headlines generated by her talent and her personality.

By banning her catsuit, the powers that be sent the message that upholding the status quo matters more than respecting their star athlete. By winning 6-4, 6-0 in a headlinemaking tutu—black-designed, over-the-top feminine, and dead serious—Williams reminded us why she's still the star.

A conclusion that restates the result of the author's analysis: women athletes' success is not related to clothing choices.

REFLECT. *Were you aware of the history surrounding women athletes' clothing? Why do you think Frankie de la Cretaz chose this topic to analyze? What do you think their main point was in writing this piece? The piece was published on* Elle *magazine's website. How do you think this essay might have been different if published elsewhere—on* ESPN.com? *your campus or local city newspaper? a personal website or blog?*

WRITING ANALYTICALLY / A Roadmap

Find a topic that matters—to you, and to others

Whether you can choose your topic or have to respond to a specific assignment, find an angle that appeals to you—and to your audience. Write about something that you care about, that engages you. No audience will want to hear about something that you are not interested in writing about.

If you can choose your topic, begin by considering your interests. What do you like to do? What issues do you care about? If you are a dedicated follower of Billie Eilish, you might analyze her musical influences or how her approach has changed over her career. If you are interested in sports, you might examine statistical data on a favorite athlete or analyze the process of doing something in a particular sport (as Darlene Jenkins does).

If you've been assigned a topic, say to conduct a rhetorical analysis of the Gettysburg Address, find an angle that interests you. If you're a history buff, you might research the particular occasion on which Lincoln spoke and look at how his words were especially fitting for that audience and event. Or perhaps your interests lie more in current politics, in which case you might compare Lincoln's address to the speeches politicians make today.

Make your topic matter to your audience. Some topics matter to everyone, or nearly everyone; you might be able to identify such topics by checking the media for what's being debated and discussed. But when you're writing about something that may not automatically appeal to a wide audience, it's your responsibility as the writer to tell them why they should care about it. Frankie de la Cretaz does this in their piece about Serena Williams's tennis outfits by demonstrating the long-term negative impact of sexist assumptions.

Consider your rhetorical situation

Keep in mind the elements of your particular situation—your audience, your specific purpose, your stance, and so on—and how they will or should influence the choices you make in your writing.

Identify your AUDIENCE. Whom do you want to reach, and how can you shape your analysis so that you get through to them? Karen McComb's analysis of cat purring was for an audience of scientific peers, whereas Shimoli Pandya wrote about the Marvel Cinematic Universe on *Medium*, a venue for the general public. Very different audiences, very different purposes—very different analyses. You, too, should think carefully about whom you are trying to reach.

- What do you know about them—their age, gender, cultural and linguistic background?
- What are they likely to know about your subject, and what background information will you need to provide?
- How might they benefit from the analysis and insight you offer?
- Will your subject matter to them—and if not, how can you make them care about it?

If you are writing for the internet, you will likely reach a broad audience whose characteristics you can't predict, so you need to assume a range of readers—just as Will Moller does in his blog post about Andy Pettitte. Even though his primary audience is Yankees fans, he knows that some readers won't know much about statistics, so he provides the definitions they need to understand his analysis.

Articulate your PURPOSE. Even if you're writing in response to an assignment, here are some questions that can help you narrow your focus and articulate some more specific purposes:

- What are you analyzing? A text? A community? A process? Causes? Data? A visual?
- What's motivated you to write? Are you responding to some other text or author?
- What do you want to accomplish by analyzing this subject? How can you best achieve your goals?
- What do you want your audience to take away from your analysis?

Think about your STANCE. How do you want to come across as an author? How can your writing reflect that stance? If your subject is surfing and you're writing on a surfers' blog about how to catch a wave for an audience of beginners, your stance might be that of an experienced surfer or a former beginner. Your language would probably be informal, with little or no surfing jargon. If, on the other hand, you're writing an article for *Surfing Magazine* analyzing the process Laird Hamilton developed to ride fifty-foot waves, your stance might be that of an objective reporter, and your language would need to be more technical for that well-informed audience. No matter what your stance or target audience, you need to consider what kind of language will work best, what terms need to be defined, and how you can establish your authority as an author.

Consider the larger CONTEXT. If you are analyzing an ad in a composition class, you will want to look at relevant information about its original context. When was the ad created, and who was the target audience? What were the social, economic, and political conditions at the time? All of that is contextual information. If you are preparing a load analysis for an engineering class, you'll need to consider factors such as how, when, and where the structure will be used. Other contextual information comes from what others have said about your subject, and your analysis adds to the conversation.

Consider your LANGUAGE. Almost any analysis can be presented in a number of ways. Regardless of how many languages and dialects you use in your everyday life, you have many options to consider in crafting an analysis. Will your audience expect a certain kind of language or style? Do you want to meet those expectations? challenge them? What do you want your language choices to say about you? What risks might you be willing to take with your language? How will your choice of medium and the larger context limit or expand the language options available to you? (You may want to consult Chapters 4 and 33 for more information about language options.)

Consider MEDIA. Will your analysis be delivered in print? on a website? in an oral presentation? Are you writing for an online class? a blog? your campus newspaper? If you get to choose your medium, the choice should depend on how you can best present your subject and reach your intended audience. Do you need to be able to incorporate visuals, or audio or video, or to speak directly to your audience in person? Whether you have a choice or not, the media you use will affect how you design and deliver your analysis.

Consider matters of DESIGN. Think about how to best present your information and whether you need to follow any disciplinary conventions. Does your analysis include data that is easiest to understand in a chart or graph? Would headings help readers follow your analysis? Would illustrations make your point clearer?

Analyze your subject

What kind of analysis is needed for your subject and purpose? You may be assigned to conduct a certain kind of analysis, or you may be inspired by a question, as Shaan Sachdev was in analyzing the reasons for Beyoncé's enduring popularity. But sometimes you may be asked simply to "analyze x"—an ad, a game, a historical event, profiles of several companies—in which case you'll need to determine what kind of analysis will work best. The kind of analysis you need to do—rhetorical analysis, discourse analysis, process analysis, causal analysis, data analysis, visual analysis—will determine the way you study your subject.

If you're analyzing rhetoric, you need to look at what the text you're examining says and how it supports its claims.

- What question are you asking about this text? What specifically are you looking for?
- What CLAIM is the text making—and what REASONS and EVIDENCE does the author provide for the claim? Do they convince you?
- Does the writer acknowledge or respond to COUNTERARGUMENTS or other opinions? If so, are they presented fairly?
- Are there any words that indicate what the author thinks—or wants you to think?
- How does the author establish AUTHORITY to address the topic?
- Does the text use any EMOTIONAL APPEALS? If so, how?

If you're analyzing a discourse community, you're trying to understand the community whose language practices you are focusing on. And you'll want to be clear about both your reasons for choosing a particular community and the questions you're striving to answer about your subject.

Are you primarily concerned with how a given community creates cohesion through its discourse practices? Or are you interested in narrowing your focus to a particular type of exchange, focusing on vocabulary choices, figurative language, rhetorical elements, or preferred types of argument?

Are you interested in understanding how the community establishes its social relationships through language? Or do you want to chart this particular community's similarities to and differences from other groups? Or perhaps you want to focus on how a given individual manages the discourses of multiple communities: an engineering student who is also a birder and a church choir member. Enacting one's identity in multiple communities requires using language at least somewhat differently in each. The following questions can guide your research and analysis:

- Why have you chosen this particular community? Or this specific discourse?
- What questions are you trying to answer about your subject?
- What existing texts—written, visual, recorded—can you draw on for background information?
- What kinds of research will you need to do to observe your subject's communication practices? Textual analysis? Data collection? Interviews?
- Do you observe any patterns or habits? Does what you observe match your expectations or surprise you?
- Can you observe your subject firsthand? Who might help you access the community you're interested in? Will you need permissions from your subjects or your university?

If you're analyzing a process, you'll need to decide whether your analysis will be **INFORMATIONAL** (how something works) or **INSTRUCTIONAL** (how to do something). Writing about how solar panels convert sunshine to energy would be informational, whereas writing about how to install solar panels would be instructional—and would need to explicitly identify all materials needed and then tell readers step-by-step exactly how to carry out the process. Once you've determined the kind of analysis, you might then consider questions like these:

- What question is prompting your analysis?
- If the process is instructional, what materials are needed?
- What are the steps in the process? What does each step accomplish?
- What order do the steps follow? Whether a process follows a set order (throwing a curveball, parallel parking a car) or not (playing sudoku), you'll need to present the steps in some order that makes sense.

If you're analyzing causes, you're looking for answers to why something happened. Why, for instance, are Americans waiting longer to get married? Is it because more people—especially young women—are putting their educations and careers first? Or because more young people have seen their parents divorce? Or because they are less financially able to spend on a large event than previous generations?

Questions about causes can rarely be answered definitively, so you'll usually be **ARGUING** that certain causes are the most plausible or the primary ones, and that others are less likely or secondary. In addition, although an immediate cause may be obvious, less obvious long-term causes may also have contributed. You'll need to consider all possible causes and provide evidence to support the ones you identify as most plausible.

As you determine which causes are more or less likely, be careful not to confuse coincidence with causation. That two events—such as higher divorce rates in older people and later marriages in younger people—occurred more or less simultaneously, or even that one event preceded the other, does not prove that one *caused* the other.

You'll often need to do some **RESEARCH** to understand all the possible causes and whether they are primary or contributing, immediate or long-term causes. The following questions can guide your research and analysis:

- What question is prompting your analysis?
- List all the causes you can think of. Which seem to be the primary causes and which are contributing or secondary causes? Which are immediate causes and which are long-term causes?
- Might any of the causes on your list be merely coincidences?
- Which causes seem most plausible—and why?
- What research do you need to do to answer these questions?

If you're analyzing data, you're trying to identify patterns in information that you or someone else has gathered in order to answer a question or make an argument. The information collected by the US Census is quantitative data. Social scientists looking for patterns to help them make arguments or predictions about population trends might analyze the data on numbers of families with children in urban areas.

Although the mathematical nature of analyzing **QUANTITATIVE DATA** can often make it more straightforward than other kinds of analysis, identifying statistical patterns and figuring out their significance can be challenging. Finding and interpreting patterns in QUALITATIVE data can also be tricky, especially as the data is more free-form: words, stories, photographs, and so on. Here are some questions to consider when analyzing data:

- What question are you trying to answer?
- Are there any existing data that can help answer your question? If so, will they provide sufficient information, or do you need to conduct any RESEARCH of your own to generate the data you need?
- If you're working with existing data, who collected the data, using what methods, and why? How do the data relate to the analysis you're conducting?
- Do the data show the full picture? Are there other data that tell a different story?
- Can you identify patterns in the data? If so, are they patterns you expected, or are any of them surprising?

If you're analyzing a visual, how do specific visual elements convey a message or create an effect?

- What draws your eye first, and why? What seems most interesting or important?
- What's the PURPOSE of this visual, and who's its target AUDIENCE?
- Is there any larger historical, cultural, or political CONTEXT to consider?
- Are there any words, and what do they tell you about the message?
- What's the overall ARGUMENT or effect? How do you know?

Determine what your analysis shows

Once you've analyzed your subject, you need to figure out what your analysis shows. What was the question that first prompted your analysis, and how can you now answer that question? What have you discovered about your subject? What have you found that interests you—and how can you make it matter to your audience?

State your insight as a tentative THESIS. Once you've determined what insight your analysis has led to, write it out as a tentative thesis, noting what you've analyzed and why and what conclusions or insights you want to share. Your thesis introduces your point, what you want to say about your subject. Let's say you're writing a rhetorical analysis of the Gettysburg Address. Here's how you might introduce an analysis of that speech:

> Following Edward Everett's two-hour oration, President Lincoln spoke eloquently for a mere two minutes, deploying rhetorical devices like repetition, contrast, and rhythm in a way that connected emotionally with his audience.

This sentence tells us that the writer will describe the event, say something about the length of the speech, and explain how specific words and structures resulted in an eloquently simple but profoundly moving speech.

As you formulate your thesis, begin by thinking about your **AUDIENCE** and how you can make your analysis most compelling to them. What aspects of your analysis will they care most about? How might it apply to them? Does your analysis have important implications beyond the immediate subject, as Eve L. Ewing's analysis of a single word does?

Then list the evidence you found that supports your analysis— examples, quotations, significant data points, and so forth. What of all your evidence will best support your point, and what will your audience find most persuasive?

Organize and start writing

Start with your tentative thesis, being sure that it identifies what you're analyzing, what insights you have to offer, and why it is significant. As you write, be sure you're supporting your thesis—and that it's working. That said, don't hesitate to revise it if you have difficulty supporting it.

Give EVIDENCE that supports your thesis. Depending on the kind of analysis, evidence could include examples, statistics, quotations, definitions, and so on.

Cite other sources, but remember that this is *your* analysis. Your audience wants to hear your voice and learn from your insights. At the same time, don't forget to acknowledge other perspectives.

Draft an OPENING. You might begin by describing what you're analyzing and why, explaining what question prompted you to take a closer look at your topic. Provide any background information your audience might need. State your thesis: what are you claiming about your subject?

Draft a CONCLUSION. You might reiterate what you've learned from your analysis and what you want your audience to understand about your subject. Make sure they know why your analysis matters, to them and to you.

Look critically at your draft, get responses—and revise

Read your draft slowly and carefully to see whether you've made your guiding question clear, described your subject sufficiently, offered enough evidence to support your analysis, and provided your audience with some insight about your subject.

Then ask others to read and respond to your draft. If your school has a writing center, try to meet with a tutor, bringing along any questions you have. Here are some questions that can help you or others read over a draft of analytic writing:

- *Is the question that prompted your analysis clear?* Is it a question worth considering?

- *How does the* OPENING *capture the audience's interest?* Does it indicate why this analysis matters? How else might you begin?

- *Is the point of your analysis clear?* Have you stated the point explicitly in a THESIS —and if not, do you need to?

- *Is the subject described in enough detail for your audience?* Is there any other information they might need in order to follow your analysis?

- *What* EVIDENCE *do you provide to support your point?* Is it sufficient?

- *What insights have you gained from the analysis?* Have you stated them explicitly? How likely is it that readers will accept your conclusions?

- *If you've cited any sources, are they credible and convincing?* Have you integrated them smoothly into your text—is it clear what you are saying yourself and where (and why) you are citing others? And have you DOCUMENTED any sources you've cited?

- *Have you addressed other perspectives?* Do you need to acknowledge possible COUNTERARGUMENTS ?

- *How would you describe the* TONE, *and does it accurately convey your* STANCE *?* Is the tone well suited to your audience and purpose?

- *How is the analysis organized?* Is it easy to follow, with clear TRANSITIONS from one point to the next? Are there headings—and if not, would adding them help? If you're analyzing a process, are the steps in an order that your audience will be able to follow easily?

- *Consider* STYLE. Look at the choice of words and kinds of sentences—are they fitting for the audience and purpose? Could the style be improved in any way?

- *How effective is the* DESIGN *?* Have you included any images or other visual elements—and if so, how do they contribute to the analysis? If not, is there any information that might be easier to understand if presented in a table or chart or accompanied by an image?

- *How does the draft* CONCLUDE *?* Is the CONCLUSION forceful and memorable? How else might the analysis conclude?

- *Consider the title.* Does it make clear what the analysis is about, and will it make your audience interested in reading on?

Revise your draft in light of your own observations and any feedback you get from others, keeping your audience and purpose firmly in mind. But remember: *you* are the analyst here, so you need to make the decisions.

REFLECT. Once you've completed your analysis, let it settle for a while and then take time to REFLECT. *How well did you analyze your subject? What insights did your analysis lead to? What additional revisions would you make if you could? Research shows that such reflections help "lock in" what you learn for future use.*

Google Home vs. Alexa:
Two Simple User Experience Design Gestures
That Delighted a Female User

JOHNA PAOLINO

A YEAR AGO, MY BOYFRIEND got an Amazon Echo. I remember first using the product, dazzled at its ability to process requests from across the room. *Alexa, play us some music.*

As the year progressed, the wow factor faded quickly.

The product features continued working to their full effect, but I felt very unsettled. I found myself constantly agitated as I observed my boyfriend bark commands at this black cylinder.

Alexa, turn off the lights. Alexa, set my alarm for 8am.

This declarative speech was so incongruous with how he interacts with me, with how he interacts with any human.

Was it how he was asking? Was it that she was female? Was I jealous?

As a user experience designer, I am constantly questioning the emotional effect technology has on me. Perhaps I was taking too much of my day job into my personal life. I decided to mute this awareness until this holiday season when

---

JOHNA MANDEL (née Paolino) is a product designer at *Instagram*. Previously she designed digital tools for the *New York Times* newsroom. She has published articles on user experience and design; this piece appeared on *Medium* in 2017.

I unwrapped my very own Google Home. I configured the device, hesitantly looking forward to some of the features my apartment had been missing over the past year.

Ok Google, play NPR news. Hey Google, set my alarm for 8am.

Why did these interactions suddenly feel so natural? They felt appropriate. In fact, I was delighted by my new Google Home.

Although product features differ slightly, the root cause of my emotional shift had nothing to do with these capabilities. All the feelings I had for Alexa came down to two simplistic user experience design differences.

The Naming of the Products

I've learned throughout my career that the most significant UX performance gains often come down to microcopy. This could not be more true here. Amazon is the name of a pioneering e-commerce platform and revolutionary cloud computing company. Echo is its product name, first to market of its kind. Alexa? Alexa is just the name of a female that performs personal tasks for you in your home. 5

Apple and Siri set a precedent for this. Was there a need to rename the voice component of these products? Why isn't it Echo or Amazon? Why not Apple? By doing this, we've subconsciously constrained the capabilities of a female. With the Echo, we've even gone as far as to confine her to a home.

The voice component of the Google Home, however, is simply triggered with "Google." Google, a multinational, first-of-its-kind technology company. Suddenly a female's voice represents a lot more. This made me happy.

Conversational Triggers

Alexa responds to her name only. Google's product must be triggered with a "hey Google" or "ok Google." By requiring these introductory words as triggers, Google has forced an element of conversation. The experience difference here is huge! When I return to Alexa now I feel authoritative.

The advancement of feminism requires awareness from both genders. It isn't isolated to how men treat women, but extends to how women treat each other. I am constantly making an effort to change my behaviors towards other women, and in this effort certainly prefer how I am asked to greet Google.

The smallest of user experience details matter. My entire emotional experience   10
between these products can be boiled down to: "Hey," "Ok," and a name. I want to thank Google. Thank you for paying closer attention to the details, and to the female users.

We have a responsibility as designers and technologists. We can make these systems model how we want the world to be—let's take steps forward not backward.

Thinking about the Text

1. With her title, Johna Paolino immediately establishes that this will be a contest: Google Home against Alexa. How does she establish her **AUTHORITY** to write on this topic?

2. Where does Paolino indicate the question driving her analysis?

3. Who is Paolino's **AUDIENCE**? Point to specific places where she uses language to establish a connection with readers. How would you describe her **TONE**?

4. Since Paolino doesn't include any photographs or audio clips (just her own original drawing of her subjects), the analysis largely depends on her **DESCRIPTION** of the two smart speakers. What **EVIDENCE** does Paolino provide to support her stance? What details or evidence might you add to make her argument even stronger?

5. Following the guidelines in this chapter, write an **ANALYSIS** of two competing tech products you have experience using—perhaps an Android phone and an iPhone, two fitness tracking apps, or competing social media platforms. Be sure to state the question you're exploring, the insight you gain, and the evidence supporting your stance.

Advertisements R Us

MELISSA RUBIN

ADVERTISEMENTS ARE WRITTEN to persuade us—to make us want to support a certain cause, buy a particular car, drink a specific kind of soda. But *how* do they do it? How do they persuade us? Since the beginning of modern consumer culture, companies have cleverly tailored advertisements to target specific groups. To do so, they include text and images that reflect and appeal to the ideals, values, and stereotypes held by the consumers they wish to attract. As a result, advertisements reveal a lot about society. We can learn a great deal about the prevailing culture by looking closely at the deliberate ways a company crafts an ad to appeal to particular audiences.

This ad that appeared in the August 1950 *Coca-Cola Bottler* magazine, a trade magazine for Coca-Cola bottlers (fig. 1), features a larger-than-life red Coca-Cola vending machine with the slogan "Drink Coca-Cola—Work *Refreshed*" (Advertisement for Coca-Cola). Set against a bright blue sky with puffy white clouds, an overlarge open bottle of Coke hovers just to the right and slightly above the vending machine, next to the head of "Sprite Boy," a pixie-ish character and onetime Coke symbol, who sports a bottle cap for a hat. Sprite Boy's left hand gestures past the floating Coke bottle and toward a crowd congregating before the vending machine. The group, overwhelmingly

---

MELISSA RUBIN wrote this analysis when she was a student at Hofstra University using an early draft of this chapter. She has taught creative writing and composition at Hofstra University and Touro College.

Fig. 1. 1950 ad from *Coca-Cola Bottler* magazine. Advertisement for Coca-Cola.

male and apparently all white, includes blue-collar workers in casual cloth-ing, servicemen in uniform, and businessmen in suits in the foreground; the few women displayed are in the background, wearing dresses. The setting is industrialized and urban, as indicated by the factory and smokestacks on the far left side of the scene and by the skyscrapers and apartment building on the right.

Practically since its invention, Coca-Cola has been identified with mainstream America. Born from curiosity and experimentation in an Atlanta pharmacy in 1886, Coke's phenomenal growth paralleled America's in the industrial age. Benefiting from developments in technology and transportation, by 1895 it was "sold and consumed in every state and territory in the United States" ("Coca-Cola Company"). In 2010, Diet Coke became the second-most-popular carbonated drink in the world . . . behind Coca-Cola (Esterl). In the immediate postwar world, Coke became identified with American optimism and energy, thanks in part to the company's wartime declaration that "every man in uniform gets a bottle of Coca-Cola for 5 cents, wherever he is, and whatever it costs the Company" ("Coca-Cola Company"). To meet this dictate, bottling plants were built overseas with the result that many people other than Americans first tasted Coke during this war that America won so decisively, and when peace finally came, "the foundations were laid for Coca-Cola to do business overseas" ("Coca-Cola Company").

Given the context, just a few years after World War II and at the beginning of the Korean War, the setting clearly reflects the idea that Americans experienced increased industrialization and urbanization as a result of World War II. Factories had sprung up across the country to aid in the war effort, and many rural and small-town Americans had moved to industrial areas and large cities in search of work. In this advertisement, the buildings surround the people, symbolizing a sense of community and the way Americans had come together in a successful effort to win the war.

The ad suggests that Coca-Cola recognized the patriotism inspired by the war and wanted to inspire similar positive feelings about their product. In the center of the ad, the huge red vending machine looks like the biggest skyscraper of all—the dominant feature of the urban industrial landscape. On the upper right, the floating face of Coca-Cola's Sprite Boy towers above the scene. A pale character with wild white hair, hypnotic eyes, and a mysterious smile, Sprite Boy stares straight at readers, his left hand gesturing toward the red machine. Sprite Boy's size and placement in the ad makes him appear god-like, as if he, the embodiment of Coca-Cola, is a powerful force uniting—and refreshing—hardworking Americans. The placement of the vending machine in the center of the ad and the wording on it evoke the idea that drinking Coca-Cola will make a hardworking American feel refreshed while he (and apparently it was rarely she) works and becomes part of a larger community. The text at the bottom of the ad, "A welcome host to workers—*Inviting you to the pause that refreshes with ice-cold Coca-Cola*"—sends the same message to consumers: Coke will refresh and unite working America.

The way that Coca-Cola chooses to place the objects and depict men and women in this ad speaks volumes about American society in the middle of the twentieth century: a white, male-dominated society in which service-men and veterans were a numerous and prominent presence. The clothing that the men in the foreground wear reflects the assumption that the target demographic for the ad—people who worked in Coca-Cola bottling plants—valued hard workers and servicemen during a time of war. White, uniformed men are placed front and center. One man wears an Army uniform, the one next to him wears a Navy uniform, and the next an Air Force uniform. By placing the servicemen so prominently, Coca-Cola emphasizes their important role in society and underscores the value Americans placed on their veterans at a time when almost all male Americans were subject to the draft and most of them could expect to serve in the military or had already done so. The other men in the foreground—one wearing a blue-collar work uniform and the other formal business attire—are placed on either side of and slightly apart from the soldiers, suggesting that civilian workers played a valuable role in society, but one secondary to that of the military. Placing only a few women dressed in casual day wear in the far background of the image represents the assumption that women played a less important role in society—or at least in the war effort and the workforce, including Coke's.

The conspicuous mixture of stereotypical middle-class and working-class attire is noteworthy because in 1950, the US economy had been marked by years of conflict over labor's unionization efforts and management's opposition to them—often culminating in accommodation between the two sides. The ad seems to suggest that such conflict should be seen as a thing of the past, that men with blue-collar jobs and their bosses are all "workers" whom Coca-Cola, a generous "host," is inviting to share in a break for refreshments. Thus all economic classes, together with a strong military, can unite to build a productive industrial future and a pleasant lifestyle for themselves.

From the perspective of the twenty-first century, this ad is especially interesting because it seems to be looking backward instead of forward in significant ways. By 1950, the highly urban view of American society it presents was starting to be challenged by widespread movement out of central cities to the suburbs, but nothing in the ad hints at this profound change. At the time, offices and factories were still located mostly in urban areas and associated in Americans' minds with cities, and the ad clearly reflects this perspective. In addition, it presents smoke pouring from factory smokestacks in a positive light, with no sign of the environmental damage that such emissions cause, and that would become increasingly clear over the next few decades.

Another important factor to consider: everyone in the ad is white. During the 1950s, there was still a great deal of racial prejudice and segregation in the United States. Coca-Cola was attuned to white society's racial intolerance and chose in this ad to depict what they undoubtedly saw as average Americans, the primary demographic of the audience for this publication: Coca-Cola employees. While Coke did feature African Americans in some ads during the late 1940s and early 1950s, they were celebrity musicians like Louis Armstrong, Duke Ellington, Count Basie, or Graham Jackson (the accordion player who was a huge favorite of Franklin Delano Roosevelt) or star athletes like Marion Motley and Bill Willis, the first men to break the color barrier in NFL football ("World"). The contrast between these extremes underscores the prejudice: "ordinary" people are represented by whites, while only exceptional African Americans appear in the company's ads.

In 1950, then, the kind of diversity that Coke wanted to highlight and appeal to was economic (middle-class and working-class) and war-related (civilian and military). Today, such an ad would probably represent the ethnic diversity missing from the 1950 version, with smiling young people of diverse skin colors and facial features relaxing with Cokes, probably now in cans rather than bottles. But the differences in economic, employment, or military status or in clothing styles that the 1950 ad highlighted would be unlikely to appear, not because they no longer exist, but because advertisers for products popular with a broad spectrum of society no longer consider them a useful way to appeal to consumers.

While initially the ads for Coca-Cola reflected the values of the time, their enormous success eventually meant that Coke ads helped shape the American identity. In them, Americans always appear smiling, relaxed, carefree, united in their quest for well-deserved relaxation and refreshment. They drive convertibles, play sports, dance, and obviously enjoy life. The message: theirs is a life to be envied and emulated, so drink Coca-Cola and live that life yourself.

Works Cited

Advertisement for Coca-Cola. *Vintage Ad Browser*, 1950, www
.vintageadbrowser.com/coke-ads-1950s/6#adjjm2v0hc7efog6.
"The Coca-Cola Company Heritage Timeline." *Coca-Cola History*, Coca-Cola
Company, www.coca-colacompany.com/history/.
Esterl, Mike. "Diet Coke Wins Battle in Cola Wars." *The Wall Street Journal*,
17 Mar. 2011, p. B1.
"The World of Coca-Cola Self-Guided Tour for Teachers. Highlights: African
American History Month." *World of Coca-Cola*, www.worldofcoca-cola
.com/wp-content/uploads/sites/3/2013/10/aahhighschool.pdf.

Thinking about the Text

1. What insight does Melissa Rubin offer about the Coca-Cola ad she analyzes, and what **EVIDENCE** does she provide to support her analysis? Has she persuaded you to accept her conclusions? Why or why not?

2. What historical **CONTEXT** does Rubin provide, and what does that information contribute to her analysis?

3. Rubin's analysis is driven by this question: what can we learn about the culture in which a given ad is created by closely examining how that ad appeals to particular audiences? What other questions might you try to answer by analyzing an ad?

4. Rubin looks closely at the men and women in this ad and makes certain assumptions about them. What sorts of details does she point out to identify who these people are? Do you think she's represented them accurately? If not, how might you identify them differently, and why?

5. Write an **ANALYSIS** of a current ad, looking specifically at how it reflects American values in the twenty-first century. Be sure to include the ad in your essay.

SIXTEEN

"Just the Facts"
Reporting Information

REPORTS HAVE PROBABLY played an important role in your life for a long time: remember all those report cards sent home—often requiring a guardian's signature? Those cards offered a summing up of how you were doing in school, and they could be encouraging— or just the opposite. Or think of the reports you received after taking the SAT or ACT or any other tests, including your driver's license exam, if you drive. If you've had medical checkups, you've likely received reports on the state of your health. And you've no doubt written your share of reports, beginning in elementary school with reports on what you read over summer break or on a book your class was reading, and moving to lab reports in middle school science classes—and on and on.

Reports contain information that is factual in some way. As you no doubt realize, separating what is factual from what is opinion can be a challenge, especially when the topic is controversial.

The primary goal of a report is to present factual information to educate an audience in some way. The stance of those who write reports is generally objective rather than argumentative. Thus, newspaper and television reporters—note the word—in the United States have traditionally tried to present news in a neutral way. Writers of lab reports describe as carefully and objectively as they can how they conducted their experiments and what they found. Perhaps even more than authors in other

This cartoon shows a familiar moment for many students who may wish to redact, or edit out, portions of their report cards.

genres, therefore, writers of reports aim to create an **ETHOS** of trustworthiness and reliability.

This chapter offers guidelines for composing reports, including profiles, a kind of report often assigned in college. As you'll see, writing effective reports requires you to pay careful attention to your purpose, audience, and stance as well as to whatever facts you're reporting.

REFLECT. Think about reports you've read, heard, seen, or written recently, and make a list of them. Your list may include everything from a lab report for a biology class, to a documentary film, to a PowerPoint presentation that you and several classmates created for a course. What features do these reports share—and how do they differ?

Across Academic Disciplines

Reports are found everywhere in academic life. You're certainly familiar with book reports, and you're probably familiar with lab reports from science courses. Students and practitioners in most fields in the physical sciences, social sciences, and applied sciences regularly write reports, generally based on experiments or other kinds of systematic investigation.

Many scientific reports share a common format—often labeled IMRAD (introduction, methods, results, and discussion)—and a common purpose: to convey information. The format mirrors the stages of inquiry: you ask a question, describe the materials and methods you used to try to answer it, report the results you found, and discuss what your results mean in light of what you and others already know.

Another kind of report students often write, especially in courses that focus on contemporary society in some way, is the profile, a firsthand report on an individual, a group, an event, or an institution. A profile of a person might be based on an interview, perhaps with an American soldier who served in Afghanistan, for example, or the first woman professor to receive tenure in your college's economics department. Similarly, a profile of an institution might report on the congregation of a specific house of worship, an organization, or a company; such reports often have a specific audience in mind, whether it is donors, investors, members, or clients.

Across Media

When reporting information, you'll find that different media offer you radically different resources. Throughout this chapter, we'll refer to reporting on Simone Biles's Yurchenko double pike vault, an especially challenging gymnastics move involving a round-off, a back handspring, and a somersault with a double twist. Just before the 2020 Summer Olympics, Biles successfully completed this move—the first and only athlete ever to do so in women's gymnastics—and reports of her maneuver appeared across media. It was the subject of numerous reports in news outlets from *Wired* magazine, the *Los Angeles Times*, and *Women's Health* to the *Washington Post*, the *Philadelphia Inquirer*, and *ESPN.com*. Biles's feat was the subject of a podcast on *GymCastic: The Gymnastics Podcast*, and videos of her landing the move circulated on *Twitter* through the Team USA account as well as Biles's own feed. These reports used images, diagrams, and video, as well as spoken and written words.

In studying these reports, you'll get a clear idea of the ways medium influences not only how information is reported but also what kinds of information can be covered. For example, consider *Twitter*: how would you report on Biles's Yurchenko double pike vault in 280 characters or fewer?

Across Cultures and Communities

Wherever you find formal organizations, companies, and other institutions, you'll find reports of various kinds. For example, a school board exploring new models for bilingual education will surely rely on information in reports written by education researchers, parents' organizations, community groups, teachers' unions, or outside consultants. Odds are that the reports from each of these groups would differ in focus, tone, and even language. Some of these reports might be based primarily on research and statistical data while others might feature personal testimonies. Those created by outside consultants would likely be very formal and data-driven and might include a presentation to the school board followed by a question-and-answer period. In contrast, a report from a parents' group could include a homemade video consisting primarily of conversations with students.

And, of course, the language you choose is an important consideration for report writing. For example, the report on the following page about

THINK BEYOND WORDS

↪ *WATCH THE VIDEO of US Olympic gymnast Simone Biles performing the Yurchenko double pike vault. Then read the* Philadelphia Inquirer *article on the physics of gymnastics flips, including Biles's unique move. Pay attention to how some of the technical terms are defined (and keep in mind that in the video, definitions may include images as well as words). Describe the Yurchenko double pike vault using words alone. Then add an image. Do you need to alter your original description once you add the image? Go to* everyonesanauthor.tumblr.com *to access the video and article.*

San Antonio's Independent School District's revised bilingual immersion program is available in both English and Spanish, so that community members who read in either (or both!) of these languages can learn more. Even the English-language version demonstrates the value of a bilingual community by weaving in some Spanish. The report concludes this way: "For a long time now, the societal marketplace of this city has been calling for a bilingual education program that produces bilingual and multicultural individuals who can run our social systems and take them boldly into the future. . . . Today, that call is stronger than ever, and San Antonio [Independent School District] has taken a wonderful opportunity to respond to it loudly, decisively *y con mucho orgullo* [and with much pride]."

En una ciudad bilingüe como San Antonio, la educación de lenguaje dual es clave

 by **Olivia Hernández** and **Esmeralda Alday**
September 27, 2021

This *San Antonio Report* article, "In a bilingual city like San Antonio, dual language education is key," is available in Spanish and English to reach those most interested in the city's dual language programs.

As a student, you'll be working in various academic communities, and you will need to pay attention to the way information is reported across disciplines and communities—and to what is expected of you in any reports that you write.

Across Genres

Josh Trujillo and Levi Hastings incorporate numerous elements of a report in their graphic argument about blood donation rules in the United States. See how they've used maps, statistics, and more on p. 978.

While reports are a common genre of writing, you'll also have occasion to report information in other genres. **NARRATIVES**, **ANALYSES**, **REVIEWS**, **ARGUMENTS**, and many other kinds of writing contain factual information often presented as neutrally as possible—and you will often report factual evidence to support your claims.

On the other hand, some documents that are called reports present more than facts alone and cross the line to **ANALYZE** and interpret the information presented or go on to make a **PROPOSAL** that offers recommendations for the future. These recommendations, though, should follow carefully reported information (as well as considerable analysis of that information).

REFLECT. Analyze the purposes of the reports that you listed (see p. 288). Who is the intended audience for each? To what degree does each simply report information, and to what degree does each use information to serve some larger goal, for example, to take a position on an issue? Can you distinguish clearly between a report that only presents information and one that presents information and also argues a point?

CHARACTERISTIC FEATURES

While you can expect differences across media and disciplines, most of the reports you will write share the following characteristics:

- A topic carefully focused for a specific audience (p. 293)
- Definitions of key terms (p. 297)
- Trustworthy information (p. 299)
- Effective organization and design (p. 300)
- A confident, informative tone (p. 301)

A Topic Carefully Focused for a Specific Audience

The most effective reports have a focus, a single topic that is limited in scope by what the audience already knows and what the author's purpose is. For example, *Sierra* magazine, published by the Sierra Club, puts out an annual report on the "greenest" US colleges. The opening of the 2019 edition outlines some criteria for the rankings and the scope of the report:

> For 13 years, *Sierra* has been ranking colleges according to which ones offer the best sustainability-focused courses, ecofriendly cafeteria provisions, and carbon-neutral land and energy policies, as well as the most opportunities to engage with the environmental movement. Since 2007, sustainability measures that once seemed cutting-edge have become the norm, and we've seen schools effect real change across their communities, regions, and states. This year [2019], a record 282 schools vied to become the eco-savviest in all of academia. Please join us in congratulating the tremendously cool—and diverse—schools topping their class in the most crucial subject of all.

The report goes on to showcase the top 20 "coolest" of 2019, elaborating on the environmental programming and opportunities at schools like the University of Illinois at Urbana-Champaign, University of New Hampshire, and Colorado State University. Visuals add depth and specificity to the innovative work happening at these institutions, offering photographic evidence—like the University of California, Merced's community garden program, the University of Dayton's state-of-the-art solar power system, and Chatham University's greenhouse.

The authors of the "cool schools" report assume they're writing for people who care about the environment and who are interested in the ways colleges and universities—as well as their students—contribute. A high school student aspiring toward a career in environmental studies might use the report to help them decide where to apply. A current university student might also consult this report to consider ways their institution could improve. And yet another student might search to see if or where their college falls in the 282 schools ranked. It's also important to note that the report was published through *Sierra* magazine, so their regular readers, who have a general interest in the environment, would also likely see value in this report.

6. University of California, Merced
Score: 83.68 | Merced, California

11. Sterling College
Score: 80.86 | Craftsbury Common, Vermont

14. Chatham University
Score: 79.01 | Pittsburgh, Pennsylvania

19. University of Dayton
Score: 76.12 | Dayton, Ohio

Images provide examples of the sustainable programs at four of the top 20 "greenest" schools ranked in *Sierra* magazine's report.

In their 2018 annual report for Oakland Promise, a nonprofit group striving to ensure that all children in Oakland, California, graduate from high school with access to the resources required to succeed in college, the authors have a different focus with three clear purposes. First, they aim to showcase the successes over the past year by using attractive infographics detailing the number of children and families served in the organization's programs. Second, the authors inform readers of the short- and medium-range goals of each program through more infographics. Third, the authors demonstrate the ample and enthusiastic community support the initiative receives by including a long list of elected officials, institutions both public and private, and individuals who advise, volunteer, and donate. The report is sprinkled with photos showing the activities and success stories of the programs. These images add life to what might otherwise be a dry recitation of names and numbers; the photos connect to the readers' emotions and ethics in reminding them of Oakland Promise's mission as well as its success.

In composing this report, the authors were obviously thinking about their primary audience: those who have participated in and donated to Oakland Promise in the past and those who might do so in the future, and who want to be informed about the work the initiative does—what it accomplishes and how economically it does so.

In both the Sierra Club and Oakland Promise reports, the topic is carefully focused, and the authors approach their task with a keen eye toward the intended audiences and their organization's goals. You'll want to do the same in the reports that you write: to consider carefully whom you're addressing, what they know about your topic, and what information they expect.

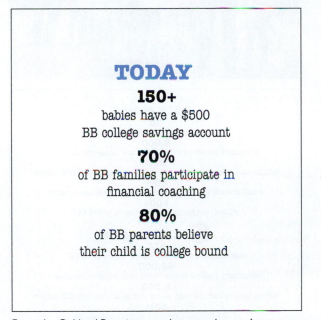

From the Oakland Promise annual report, the year's acccomplishments of the Brilliant Baby (BB) program.

"When we visited UC Berkeley, the whole idea of college became real. We could actually picture the campus and see ourselves there. Everything changed!"
—K2C Parent

2018 goals

50
elementary schools implementing K2C

8,000
elementary students awarded $100 early college scholarships

500
families have opened their own college savings account with K2C support

80%
of K2C students and families report a strong college-bound identity

500+
students and families visit a college as part of K2C

2025 targets

ALL
Oakland public elementary schools implementing K2C

40,000
elementary students awarded $100 early college scholarships

5,000
families have opened their own college savings account with K2C support

80%
of ALL Oakland elementary students and families
report strong college-bound identity

From the Oakland Promise annual report, a photo of a college visit (top) and the short- and medium-range goals of the Kindergarten to College (K2C) program (bottom).

Definitions of Key Terms

Effective reports always define key terms explicitly. These definitions serve several functions. Some audience members may not understand some of the technical terms. And even those familiar with the terms pay attention to the definitions for clues about the writer's stance or assumptions.

Tom Avril and Ellen Dunkel's *Philadelphia Inquirer* report on Simone Biles's Yurchenko double pike vault is full of definitions their readers might need. As newspaper journalists, they write for a general audience, and they don't assume readers will know much about biomechanics, which are important to understanding Biles's move. Avril and Dunkel break down Biles's vault into two major pieces: the "run up" and the "redirection," and they spend a good deal of time defining "redirection," since most readers who are nonspecialists in both biomechanics and gymnastics won't be familiar with this concept. Here's how Avril and Dunkel define redirection:

> **Redirection**. Next, Biles transfers her horizontal momentum into new directions. She pitches forward into a cartwheel-like move called a round-off, flipping once around until she returns to an upright position. From there, she drives her feet forcefully into the springboard, launching herself upward into a back handspring—using her hands to propel herself off the vaulting table.
>
> —TOM AVRIL & ELLEN DUNKEL, "How Simone Biles Lands Her Signature Move, the Yurchenko Double Pike"

Note that within this definition of redirection, Avril and Dunkel clarify another term: a "round-off" is "a cartwheel-like move."

Avril and Dunkel know too that readers will want to know why this move is called a "Yurchenko" vault, so the authors define this term as well: "the Yurchenko family of vaults" is "named for former Soviet gymnast Natalia Yurchenko, now a coach in Chicago." They explain that while there are various forms of Yurchenko vaults, they differ by virtue of the "types of twists and turns that the gymnast executes after hitting the table." And this, Avril and Dunkel make clear, is how Biles "distinguishes herself among the women": "No one else has done 2½ rotations, much less in the L-shaped 'pike' position (though male gymnasts have done so)."

The authors go on to offer yet another definition when explaining the biomechanics of Biles's redirection. They write that the key to this move "is a physics concept called the moment of inertia—loosely speaking, a measure of how the mass of a rotating object is spread out along its length." To help readers understand how inertia works, the authors offer two sports-related examples. They note first that "baseball players exploit this phenomenon when choking up on a bat—gripping it higher on the handle so that the bat is effectively shorter, allowing them to swing faster." And then they apply inertia to Biles's Yurchenko double pike: "Biles is doing the opposite [of what happens in baseball], extending herself into a longer L-shape, requiring herself to work even harder to whip around 2½ times."

Avril and Dunkel rely on words to explain Biles's Yurchenko double pike, but they also know that readers will understand the move better when words are complemented by visuals. The authors incorporate a video of Biles completing the vault and a six-step diagram that helps readers see the move in slow motion. Since Biles completes her vault in mere seconds, this step-by-step visual clarifies each move. Through all of these strategies of providing definitions, Avril and Dunkel help readers to understand what the Yurchenko double pike is and why Biles has been designated as the greatest gymnast of all time because she can complete it (along with a

Simone Biles' Yurchenko Double Pike Vault. Step 2: The Roundoff. She plants her hands on a mat, propelling her muscular 4'8" frame. Amy Junod.

number of other amazing moves). Notice too that the authors neither quote from a dictionary nor use the formula "the definition of X is Y"—instead they offer memorable and relatable examples (like baseball) to help readers understand the subject.

Trustworthy Information

Effective reports present information that readers can trust to be accurate. In some cases, writers provide documentation to demonstrate the veracity of their information, including citations of published research, the dates of interviews they have conducted, or other details about their sources.

In a report for a writing class at Chapman University, Kelley Fox presents information in ways that lead readers to trust the details she offers and, ultimately, the author herself. The report describes how Griffin, Simon, and Andy, three roommates in Room 115 of her dorm, create their identities. Beginning with Muhammad Ali's line "Float like a butterfly, sting like a bee," which is the caption on a large poster of Ali on Griffin's wall, Fox seeks to characterize Griffin as someone who floats at "the top of the pecking order" and who seems "invincible":

> In a sense, Griffin is just that: socially invincible. A varsity basketball athlete, Griffin has no shortage of friends, or of female followers. People seem to simply gravitate toward him, as if being around him makes all their problems trivial. Teammates can often be found in his room, hanging out on his bed, watching ESPN. Girls are certainly not a rarity, and they usually come bearing gifts: pies, CDs, even homework answers. It happens often, and I have a feeling this "social worship" has been going on for a while, although in myriad other forms. Regardless, the constant and excessive positive attention allows Griffin to never have to think about his own happiness; Griffin always seems happy. And it is because of this that, out of the three roommates, it is easiest to be Griffin.
>
> —KELLEY FOX, "Establishing Identities"

Fox's description demonstrates to readers that she has spent considerable time in or around Room 115 and that she knows what she is writing about. Her use of specific details convinces us that Griffin is real and that the things she describes in fact occur—and on a regular basis.

Dennis Baron provides a lot of historical facts that likely would not be in the general knowledge of most people, but he presents the information in a matter-of-fact manner and backs it up with detailed references to his sources. See how he does it on p. 844.

In a report on early language development in children written for a linguistics class at Portland State University, Katryn Sheppard demonstrates the trustworthiness of her information differently, citing both published research and her own primary research on a speech transcript of one-year-old Allison.

> One feature of Allison's utterances that did adhere to what is expected for a typical child at this age was related to her use of negatives. Although she used only one negative word—"no"—the word was repeated frequently enough to be the fourth most common category in the transcript. Her use of "no" rather than any other negative conformed to Brown's (1973) finding that other forms of negation like "not" and "don't" appear only in later stages (Santelmann, 2014). In Allison's very early stage of linguistic development, the reliance on "no" alone seems typical.
>
> —KATRYN SHEPPARD, "Early Word Production"

By citing both published research and examples from her own primary research, Sheppard demonstrates that she has spent considerable time researching her topic and can thus make informed observations about Allison's speech. These citations not only let readers know that Sheppard can support her claims but they also indicate where readers can go to verify the information if they so choose; both strategies demonstrate trustworthiness.

Although Fox and Sheppard use different techniques, both of them convince readers that the information being presented and the writers themselves can be trusted.

Effective Organization and Design

There is no single best strategy for organizing the information you are reporting. In addition to **DEFINING** (as Tom Avril and Ellen Dunkel do), you'll find yourself **DESCRIBING** (as Kelley Fox does), offering specific **EXAMPLES** and data (as the report from Oakland Promise does), **ANALYZING CAUSES AND EFFECTS** (as *Sierra* magazine does), and so on. The specific organizational strategies you'll use will depend on the information you want to report.

In many cases, you'll want to include visuals of some sort, whether photographs, charts, figures, or tables. See, for example, the diagram explaining Biles's Yurchenko double pike vault. Displaying information visually helps deepen the impact of the sentence-level descriptions and definitions in the report. And as noted on page 295, Oakland Promise also uses color photos to make the report more interesting and appealing.

Sometimes the way you organize and present your information will be prescribed. If you're writing a report following the **IMRAD** format, you will have little choice in how you organize and present information. Everything from the use of headings to the layout of tables to the size of typefaces may be dictated.

Some disciplines specify certain format details. Students of psychology, for example, are expected to follow **APA STYLE**. On the other hand, a report for a composition class may have fewer constraints. For example, you may get to decide whether you will need headings and whether to use personal examples. Ask your instructor about the format they'd like you to use.

A Confident, Informative Tone

Effective reports have a confident tone that assumes the writer is presenting reliable information rather than arguing or preaching. The authors of the Oakland Promise and Sierra Club reports both sound like they know what they're writing about. In both these cases, we as readers are getting the facts about the subject, though it is apparent the authors have clear convictions about student academic success and encouraging colleges to take up environmental activism.

The line between informing and arguing can become fuzzy, however. If you read reports on any number of hot-button issues—voting rights, the economy, transgender rights, abortion—you'll find that they often reflect some kind of position or make recommendations that convey a stance. But the authors of such reports usually try to create an informative tone that avoids indicating their own opinions.

You may sometimes find yourself struggling with this line, working to present information while stopping short of telling readers what to think about or how to feel about a topic. Here we can offer two pieces of advice. First, keep in mind that you're aiming to explain something to your audience clearly and objectively rather than to persuade them to think about it a certain way. You'll know you've succeeded if someone reading a draft of your report can't tell exactly what your own position on the topic is. Second, pay special attention to word choice because the words you use give subtle and not-so-subtle clues about your stance. Referring to "someone who eats meat" is taking an objective tone; calling that person a "carnivore" is not.

WIKIPEDIA, the free online encyclopedia that "anyone can edit," has become one of the most-visited sites on the internet since its launch in 2001. Like any encyclopedia, the primary purpose of *Wikipedia* is to report information. Below is an example from the entry on gender, as it appeared on December 17, 2021. This article demonstrates how authors negotiate the challenges of reporting information fairly and from an unbiased perspective. *Wikipedia* provides many examples of reporting on controversial topics, and the site has explicit policies and guidelines for authors to follow. Documenting the sources of information is an important tool for maintaining the reliability of information. This lengthy article, for example, has 180 citations, principally from academic journals in the physical and social sciences.

Gender
WIKIPEDIA

A definition of the term followed by several ways that the term may be applied.

GENDER IS THE RANGE OF CHARACTERISTICS pertaining to, and differentiating between, femininity and masculinity. Depending on the context, these characteristics may include biological sex, sex-based social structures (i.e., gender roles), or gender identity. [1][2][3] Most scholars agree that gender is a central characteristic for social organization. [4] Most cultures use a gender binary, having two genders (boys/men and girls/women); [5] those who exist

The tone is confident and informative and avoids indicating a specific stance or opinion.

outside these groups fall under the umbrella term non-binary or genderqueer. Some societies have specific genders besides "man" and "woman", such as the hijras of South Asia; these are often referred to as third genders (and fourth genders, etc.).

Sexologist John Money introduced the terminological distinction between biological sex and gender as a role in 1955. Before his work, it was uncommon to use the word gender to refer to anything but grammatical categories.[1][2] However, Money's meaning of the word did not become widespread until the 1970s, when feminist theory embraced the concept of a distinction between biological sex and the social construct of gender. Today, the distinction is followed in some contexts, especially the social sciences[6][7] and documents written by the World Health Organization (WHO).[3] Both physiologists and biologists agree that gender is distinct from sex.[8]

Underlining signals links to more information in Wikipedia entries.

In other contexts, including some areas of the social sciences, gender includes sex or replaces it.[1][2] For instance, in non-human animal research, gender is commonly used to refer to the biological sex of the animals.[2] This change in the meaning of gender can be traced to the 1980s. In 1993, the US Food and Drug Administration (FDA) started to use gender instead of sex.[9] Later, in 2011, the FDA reversed its position and began using sex as the biological classification and gender as "a person's self representation as male or female, or how that person is responded to by social institutions based on the individual's gender presentation."[10] . . .

Notice the overall organization of the entry: definition and explanation first, brief historical context of the term's application, and amplification of the categories that the term encompasses.

Categorizing males and females into social roles creates a problem, because individuals feel they have to be at one end of a linear spectrum and must identify themselves as man or woman, rather than being allowed to choose a section in between.[31] Globally, communities interpret biological differences between men and women to create a set of social expectations that define the behaviors that are "appropriate" for men and women and determine women's and men's different access to rights, resources, power in society and health behaviors.[32] Although the specific nature and degree of these differences vary from one society to the next, they still tend to typically favor men, creating an imbalance in power and gender inequalities within most societies.[33] Many cultures have different systems of norms and beliefs based on gender, but there is no universal standard to a masculine or feminine role across all cultures.[34] Social roles of men and women in relation to each other is based on the cultural norms of that society, which lead to the creation of gender

Go to everyones
anauthor.tumblr
.com to link to
the full *Wikipedia*
article.

*Footnotes link to evidence
that demonstrates the
trustworthiness of the
information.*

systems. The gender system is the basis of social patterns in many societies, which include the separation of sexes, and the primacy of masculine norms.[33] . . .

Some societies have historically acknowledged and even hon- 5
ored people who fulfill a gender role that exists more in the middle of the continuum between the feminine and masculine polarity. For example, the Hawaiian māhū, who occupy "a place in the middle" between male and female,[44][45] or the Ojibwe *ikwekaazo*, "men who choose to function as women",[46] or *ininiikaazo*, "women who function as men".[46] In the language of the sociology of gender, some of these people may be considered third gender, especially by those in gender studies or anthropology. Contemporary Native American and FNIM people who fulfill these traditional roles in their communities may also participate in the modern, two-spirit community,[47] however, these umbrella terms, neologisms, and ways of viewing gender are not necessarily the type of cultural constructs that more traditional members of these communities agree with.[48]

REFLECT. *Analyze a* Wikipedia *entry on a topic of your choice to see how focused the information is, how key terms are defined, and how the entry is organized. How trustworthy do you find the information—and what makes you trust it (or not)? How would you characterize the tone—informative? informative but somewhat argumentative? something else? Point to words that convey that tone.*

PROFILES

Profiles provide firsthand accounts of people, places, events, institutions, or other things. Newspapers and magazines publish profiles of interesting subjects; college websites often include profiles of the student body; investors may study profiles of companies before deciding whether or not to buy stock. If you're on *Instagram* or *LinkedIn*, you have likely created a personal profile saying something about who you are and what you do. Profiles take many different forms, but they generally have the following features.

A Firsthand Account

In creating a profile, you're always writing about something you know firsthand, not merely something you've read about. You may do some reading for background, but reading alone won't suffice. You'll also need to talk with people or visit a place or observe an event in some way. Keep in mind, however, that while a profile is a firsthand account, it should not be autobiographical. In other words, you can't profile yourself. Lucy Diavolo opens her *Teen Vogue* profile on climate activist Greta Thunberg by narrating the moments leading up to their first meeting (and including her regret for not being better environmentally prepared):

> I'm on the subway headed to Manhattan to meet Greta Thunberg, the 16-year-old Swedish climate activist who pioneered the climate strike movement, and I'm absolutely kicking myself for forgetting my travel mug. The iced coffee I'm sipping is in a single-use plastic cup—straw and all—and here I am on my way to meet arguably the most visible climate activist in the world.
>
> —LUCY DIAVOLO, "Greta Thunberg Wants You—Yes,
> You—to Join the Climate Strike"

Once she gets over her embarrassment, Diavolo settles in to her meeting with Thunberg, and the profile proceeds with Diavolo considering how Thunberg is both disrupting and confirming the expectations Diavolo had of the activist.

Having completed a transatlantic journey by sailboat, Greta is scheduled to speak at the United Nations General Assembly's Climate
Action Summit, another chance she'll have to make her no-nonsense
appeal to world leaders about the urgent necessity of international
action on the climate crisis. She's famous for being ruthlessly frank
with the global elite, so when I meet her in a midtown conference
room on a recent Friday morning, I'm surprised to find a reserved
young woman who speaks softly after carefully considering each
question I ask.

What's less surprising is the steadfast confidence and grave serious-
ness that emanates from this teenager who has given voice to an entire
generation's existential fear and energized a worldwide movement
demanding everything necessary and possible to save our planet.

Diavolo's in-person meeting and interview enables her to gain insight on
Thunberg and share that insight with readers. That we're reading a profile
through Diavolo's eyes is clear: Diavolo notes her embarrassment for for-
getting her travel mug, and she marks her "surprise" at Thunberg's soft-
spokenness, when her previous knowledge of Thunberg was that the young
woman was "urgent," "frank," and "no-nonsense." Though the profile offers
factual information, it is enriched by Diavolo's firsthand account of her
interactions with Thunberg.

Detailed Information about the Subject

Profiles are always full of details—background information, descriptive
details (sights, sounds, smells), anecdotes, and dialogue. Ideally, these details
help bring the subject to life—and persuade your audience that whatever
you're writing about is interesting, and worth reading about. What makes
the *Teen Vogue* profile so successful is the kind of details about Thunberg
the author provides. Diavolo zeroes in on Thunberg's experiences with
both Asperger's syndrome and depression and includes quotations from
Thunberg to help readers gain a keen sense of Thunberg's ideas on these
topics. For instance, Thunberg explains to Diavolo the importance of listening to people who "think a bit outside the box and who can see things from
a different, new perspective." Diavolo then includes a longer quotation so
readers can learn more directly from Thunberg:

We need these people, especially now, when we need to change things and we can't see it just from where we are. We need to see it from a bigger perspective and from outside our current systems. . . . That's why people who are different are so necessary: because they contribute so much. Therefore we need to really look after the people who may not be heard. We need to listen to those and to look after each other.

These inspirational words enable readers to grasp Thunberg's understanding of difference and the role of difference in activism. The author also includes more mundane yet still compelling details that help readers come to know Thunberg. Diavolo reports that when she asked how Thunberg has

Greta Thunberg holds a protest sign that says *Skolstrejk för klimatet*, Swedish for "School strike for climate." School strikes were Thunberg's early form of activism.

liked her visit to the States and especially New York City, Thunberg replies that she has been "keeping up her routine of unwinding with long walks by strolling through Central Park and visiting New York's museums." Diavolo notes that it's especially "fitting" that Thunberg's favorite museum is the American Museum of Natural History—a specific detail that adds even more nuance to the picture Diavolo draws for readers.

Another way that writers of profiles bring their subjects "to life" is by including photos, letting readers see their subjects in action. In the photo on the previous page (which was featured in the *Teen Vogue* profile), Thunberg is in her element, holding a protest sign with a solemn expression on her face, letting us see some of what Diavolo describes.

An Interesting Angle

The best profiles present a new or surprising perspective on whatever is being profiled. In other words, a good profile isn't merely a description; rather, it captures something essential about its subject from an interesting angle, much as a memorable photo does. When you plan a profile, try to come up with an angle that will engage readers. This angle will dictate what information you include. In addition to the smaller details that bring to life Thunberg's personality throughout Diavolo's profile, the author takes an interesting angle in the concluding paragraphs when she reflects on the importance of "perspective," which came up several times in conversation with Thunberg. Diavolo considers how this term resonates for herself and for people interested in supporting Thunberg's activism:

> The fact that "perspective" came up twice during our interview doesn't surprise me, nor does it surprise me that Greta talks about the view of the stars from her sailboat or the way she views Asperger's as her superpower. Youth climate activists have a way of giving those of us who might be older and more jaded the perspective to see the potential for a future without crisis, but meeting Greta affirms that this is more than just hijacking youthful activism. It is about welcoming the perspective of a generation that is fighting for its own future—for the right to live.

BILL LAITNER covers local news for the *Detroit Free Press*, specializing in social and political issues and human interest stories like the one below. The following profile, published in the *Free Press* in January 2015, inspired a nationwide response.

Heart and Sole:
Detroiter Walks 21 Miles in Work Commute

BILL LAITNER

L EAVING HOME IN DETROIT at 8 a.m., James Robertson doesn't look like an endurance athlete.

Pudgy of form, shod in heavy work boots, Robertson trudges almost haltingly as he starts another workday.

But as he steps out into the cold, Robertson, 56, is steeled for an Olympic-sized commute. Getting to and from his factory job 23 miles away in Rochester Hills, he'll take a bus partway there and partway home. And he'll also walk an astounding 21 miles.

Five days a week. Monday through Friday.

It's the life Robertson has led for the last decade, ever since his 1988 Honda Accord quit on him.

Every trip is an ordeal of mental and physical toughness for this soft-spoken man with a perfect attendance record at work. And every day is a tribute to how much he cares about his job,

The profile opens with descriptive details that introduce readers to the subject—and make us want to read on.

5

James Robertson commutes twenty-three miles to and from his job every day—most of it on foot.

Placing Robertson's challenging commute in the context of the struggles faced by other Detroiters gives it an interesting and meaningful angle.

his boss and his coworkers. Robertson's daunting walks and bus rides, in all kinds of weather, also reflect the challenges some metro Detroiters face in getting to work in a region of limited bus service, and where car ownership is priced beyond the reach of many.

But you won't hear Robertson complain—nor his boss.

Another interesting angle: Robertson's extraordinary work ethic in spite of the challenging circumstances.

"I set our attendance standard by this man," says Todd Wilson, plant manager at Schain Mold & Engineering. "I say, if this man can get here, walking all those miles through snow and rain, well I'll tell you, I have people in Pontiac 10 minutes away and they say they can't get here—bull!"

Interviews with Robertson and his coworkers provide detailed firsthand information.

As he speaks of his loyal employee, Wilson leans over his desk for emphasis, in a sparse office with a view of the factory floor. Before starting his shift, Robertson stops by the office every day to talk sports, usually baseball. And during dinnertime each day, Wilson treats him to fine Southern cooking, compliments of the plant manager's wife.

"Oh, yes, she takes care of James. And he's a personal favorite of the owners because of his attendance record. He's never

10

missed a day. I've seen him come in here wringing wet," says Wilson, 53, of Metamora Township.

With a full-time job and marathon commutes, Robertson is clearly sleep deprived, but powers himself by downing 2-liter bottles of Mountain Dew and cans of Coke.

"I sleep a lot on the weekend, yes I do," he says, sounding a little amazed at his schedule. He also catches zzz's on his bus rides. Whatever it takes to get to his job, Robertson does it.

"I can't imagine not working," he says.

"Lord, Keep Me Safe"

The sheer time and effort of getting to work has ruled Robertson's life for more than a decade, ever since his car broke down. He didn't replace it because, he says, "I haven't had a chance to save for it." His job pays $10.55 an hour, well above Michigan's minimum wage of $8.15 an hour but not enough for him to buy, maintain and insure a car in Detroit.

As hard as Robertson's morning commute is, the trip home is even harder.   15

At the end of his 2–10 p.m. shift as an injection molder at Schain Mold's squeaky-clean factory just south of M-59, and when his coworkers are climbing into their cars, Robertson sets off, on foot—in the dark—for the 23-mile trip to his home off Woodward near Holbrook. None of his coworkers lives anywhere near him, so catching a ride almost never happens.

Instead, he reverses the 7-mile walk he took earlier that day, a stretch between the factory and a bus stop behind Troy's Somerset Collection shopping mall.

"I keep a rhythm in my head," he says of his seemingly mechanical-like pace to the mall.

At Somerset, he catches the last SMART bus of the day, just before 1 a.m. He rides it into Detroit as far it goes, getting off at the State Fairgrounds on Woodward, just south of 8 Mile. By that time, the last inbound Woodward bus has left. So Robertson foots it the rest of the way—about 5 miles—in the cold or rain or the mild summer nights, to the home he shares with his girlfriend.

"I have to go through Highland Park, and you never know what   20
you're going to run into," Robertson says. "It's pretty dangerous.
Really, it is dangerous from 8 Mile on down. They're not the type
of people you want to run into.

"But I've never had any trouble," he says. Actually, he did get
mugged several years ago—"some punks tuned him up pretty
good," says Wilson, the plant manager. Robertson chooses not
to talk about that.

So, what gets him past dangerous streets, and through the cold
and gloom of night and winter winds?

"One word—faith," Robertson says. "I'm not saying I'm a
member of some church. But just before I get home, every night,
I say, 'Lord, keep me safe.' "

The next day, Robertson adds, "I should've told you there's
another thing: determination."

A Land of No Buses

Robertson's 23-mile commute from home takes four hours. It's   25
so time-consuming because he must traverse the no-bus land of
rolling Rochester Hills. It's one of scores of tri-county communities
(nearly 40 in Oakland County alone) where voters opted not to
pay the SMART transit millage. So it has no fixed-route bus service.

> Detailed information about Robertson's commute, including a graphic with time stamps, helps readers understand it more clearly—and why it's so incredible.

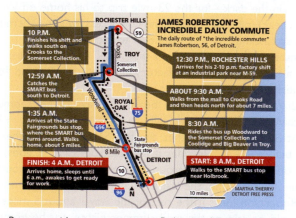

Buses provide sparse service on Robertson's long work
commute, leaving him to walk most of the way on foot.

Once he gets to Troy and Detroit, Robertson is back in bus country. But even there, the bus schedules are thin in a region that is relentlessly auto-centric.

"The last five years been really tough because the buses cut back," Robertson says. Both SMART and DDOT have curtailed service over the last half decade, "and with SMART, it really affected service into Detroit," said Megan Owens, executive director of Transportation Riders United.

Detroit's director of transportation said there is a service Robertson may be able to use that's designed to help low-income workers. Job Access and Reverse Commute, paid for in part with federal dollars, provides door-to-door transportation to low-income workers, but at a cost. Robertson said he was not aware of the program.

Still, metro Detroit's lack of accessible mass transit hasn't stopped Robertson from hoofing it along sidewalks—often snow-covered—to get to a job.

The local angle on this story as an example of the struggles many face in Detroit leads Laitner to include information about the city's transportation services.

At Home at Work

Robertson is proud of all the miles he covers each day. But it's taking a toll, and he's not getting any younger.   30

"He comes in here looking real tired—his legs, his knees," says coworker Janet Vallardo, 59, of Auburn Hills.

But there's a lot more than a paycheck luring him to make his weekday treks. Robertson looks forward to being around his coworkers, saying, "We're like a family." He also looks forward to the homemade dinners the plant manager's wife whips up for him each day.

"I look at her food, I always say, 'Excellent. No, not excellent. Phenomenal,' " he says, with Wilson sitting across from him, nodding and smiling with affirmation.

Although Robertson eats in a factory lunchroom, his menus sound like something from a Southern café: Turnip greens with smoked pork neck bones, black-eyed peas and carrots in a brown sugar glaze, baby-back ribs, cornbread made from scratch, pinto beans, fried taters, cheesy biscuits. They're the kind of meal that can fuel his daunting commutes back home.

Though his job is clearly part of his social life, when it's time   35
to work this graduate of Northern High School is methodical.
He runs an injection-molding machine the size of a small
garage, carefully slicing and drilling away waste after removing each finished part, and noting his production in detail on
a clipboard.

Strangers Crossing Paths

Robertson has walked the walk so often that drivers wonder:
Who is that guy? UBS banker Blake Pollock, 47, of Rochester,
wondered. About a year ago, he found out.

Pollock tools up and down Crooks each day in his shiny black
2014 Chrysler 300.

"I saw him so many times, climbing through snow banks. I saw
him at all different places on Crooks," Pollock recalls.

Last year, Pollock had just parked at his office space in Troy as
Robertson passed. The banker in a suit couldn't keep from asking
the factory guy in sweats, what the heck are you doing, walking
out here every day? They talked a bit. Robertson walked off and
Pollock ruminated.

From then on, Pollock began watching for the factory guy. At   40
first, he'd pick him up occasionally, when he could swing the time.
But the generosity became more frequent as winter swept in.
Lately, it's several times a week, especially when metro Detroit
sees single-digit temperatures and windchills.

"Knowing what I know, I can't drive past him now. I'm in
my car with the heat blasting and even then my feet are cold,"
Pollock says.

Other times, it's 10:30 or 11 p.m., even after midnight, when
Pollock, who is divorced, is sitting at home alone or rolling home
from a night out, and wondering how the man he knows only as
"James" is doing in the frigid darkness.

On those nights, Pollock runs Robertson all the way to his
house in Detroit.

"I asked him, why don't you move closer" to work. "He said
his girlfriend inherited their house so it's easy to stay there,"
Pollock said.

On a recent night run, Pollock got his passenger home at 11 p.m.   45
They sat together in the car for a minute, outside Robertson's house.

"So, normally you'd be getting here at 4 o'clock (in the morning), right?" the banker asks. "Yeah," Robertson replies. Pollock flashes a wry smile. "So, you're pretty early, aren't you?" he says. Robertson catches the drift.

> Laitner notes details such as Pollock's "wry smile" and "sheepish laugh" that signal that he is providing details from conversations he heard, adding credibility to his writing.

"Oh, I'm grateful for the time, believe me," Robertson says, then adds in a voice rising with anticipation: "I'm going to take me a bath!"

After the door shuts and Pollock pulls away, he admits that Robertson mystifies him, yet leaves him stunned with admiration for the man's uncanny work ethic and determination.

"I always say to my friends, I'm not a nice guy. But I find myself helping James," Pollock says with a sheepish laugh. He said he's picked up Robertson several dozen times this winter alone.

Has a Routine

At the plant, coworkers feel odd seeing one of their team numbers always walking, says Charlie Hollis, 63, of Pontiac. "I keep telling him to get him a nice little car," says Hollis, also a machine operator.   50

> The conclusion brings up another interesting angle to Robertson's story: how he connects his walking to a strong work ethic he inherited from his parents.

Echoes the plant manager Wilson, "We are very much trying to get James a vehicle." But Robertson has a routine now, and he seems to like it, his coworkers say.

"If I can get away, I'll pick him up. But James won't get in just anybody's car. He likes his independence," Wilson says.

Robertson has simple words for why he is what he is, and does what he does. He speaks with pride of his parents, including his father's military service.

"I just get it from my family. It's a lot of walking, I know."

REFLECT. Bill Laitner profiles an ordinary person whose extraordinary commute brought nationwide attention to the challenges of getting to work without a car or public transportation. Think about someone you know whose story might prove significant in this way. If you were to profile this person, what details would bring the person to life and what angle would make their story matter to others?

REPORTING INFORMATION / A Roadmap

Choose a topic that matters—to you, and to others

If you get to select your topic, begin by considering topics that you know something about or are interested in learning more about. Whatever your topic, be sure it's one you find intriguing and can be objective about. If you're a devout Catholic and believe that the church is wrong—or right—in its stance on birth control, you're likely to have trouble objectively sticking to the facts, which is necessary for writing a good report.

The more controversial the topic, the more challenging it may be to report fairly and accurately on it because the facts themselves likely will be the subject of controversy. So if you're going to write about a controversial topic, you might consider reporting on the controversy itself: the major perspectives on the issue, the kinds of evidence cited, and so on.

If you've been assigned a topic, find an aspect of it that is both interesting and focused. Unless you've been specifically instructed to address a broad topic (for example, the consequences of World Bank policies for third-world economies), focus on a narrower aspect of the topic (take a single developing country that interests you and report on the consequences of World Bank policies for that economy). Even when you are asked to report on a broad topic, see if it is possible to start out with a specific case and then move to the broader issue.

Consider your rhetorical situation

Analyzing your audience, purpose, and other elements of your rhetorical situation will help you to make the decisions you'll face as you write.

Think about the best way to address your AUDIENCE. If you're writing a report for an audience you know—your classmates, your instructor—you can sometimes assume what they will and won't know about your topic. But if you're writing for a broader audience—all students on campus, readers of a blog—you'll probably be addressing people with different levels of knowledge. Your challenge will be to provide enough information without including irrelevant details. For example, Tom Avril and Ellen Dunkel didn't explain what gymnastics is or waste their readers' time by including information not directly relevant to their topic. Here are some questions that might guide you in considering your audience:

- What do you know about your audience? To what extent are they like or unlike you—or one another?

- What background information will your audience need on your topic? Will their knowledge of it vary?

- What terms need to be defined or illustrated with examples? What sorts of examples will be most effective for your audience?

- What interest does your audience have in your topic? If they're not already interested in it, how can you get them interested—or at least to see that it matters?

Be clear about your PURPOSE. Consider why you are writing a report on this topic for this particular audience. Odds are that you want your report to do more than merely convey information. If you're writing it for a course, you want to learn something and to get a good grade. If the report is part of a large project—a campaign to encourage composting on campus, for example—a lot may be riding on the quality of your work. What short-term goals do you have in writing, and do they relate to any longer-term goals?

Consider your STANCE. Think about your own attitudes toward your topic and your audience: What about this topic captured your interest? Why do you think it matters—or should matter—both in general and to your audience? How can you establish your authority on the topic and get your audience to trust you and the information you provide? How do you want them to see you? As a fair, objective reporter? As thoughtful? serious? curious? something else?

Consider your LANGUAGE. Almost everything can be said in a variety of ways. Regardless of how many dialects or languages you use in your everyday life, you have many options for your report including, for example, your level of formality. Which option will be most suitable and effective for what you are trying to accomplish? Will your audience expect a certain kind of language or style? Do you want to meet those expectations? challenge them? What do you want your language to say about you? What risks might you be willing to take with your language? How will the medium and larger context limit or expand the language options that are available to you? You may want to consult Chapters 4 and 33 for more advice about language options.

Consider the larger CONTEXT. What are the various perspectives on the topic, and what else has been said about it? What larger conversations, if any, is this topic a part of? For a report that's part of a campaign to encourage composting on campus, for example, you'd need to become familiar with how such programs have been conducted at other schools, and what the main challenges and arguments have been.

Think about MEDIA. As the reports on Biles's Yurchenko double pike vault make clear, the medium you use plays a big role in determining the message you convey. If you have a choice, will your text be presented in print? online? as an oral report? via a podcast? Which will be most effective for your subject and audience? If you've got audio of an interview, can you embed it in an online report or incorporate it into an oral report? If your report will be in print, can you summarize or quote from the interview? If your report will be oral, should you prepare slides to help your audience follow your main points?

Think about DESIGN. Consider what design elements are available to you and will help you convey your information in the clearest, most memorable way. For example, much of the effectiveness of Oakland Promise's annual report comes from the large color photos and testimonials from students, parents, and teachers. Think about whether your report will include any elements that should be highlighted. Do you need headings? Would photos, charts, tables, or other visuals help you convey information more effectively than words alone? Do you have the option of using color in your text—and if so, what colors will set the right tone?

Research your topic

Your goal in researching your topic is first to get a broad overview of what is known about it and second to develop a deeper understanding of the topic. While most high school reports discuss the research of others, those you write in college may call on you to gather data yourself and then write about the data in light of existing research.

LAB REPORTS, for example, describe the results of experiments in engineering and the natural sciences, and reports based on ethnographic observation are common in the social sciences. And whatever your topic or field, reading SECONDARY SOURCES will help you see how your findings relate to what people already know.

Thus, your first task is to read broadly enough to get a feel for the various issues and perspectives on your topic so that you know what you're talking about and can write about it authoritatively.

Begin by assessing what you know—and don't know—about the topic. What aspects of your topic do you need to learn more about? What questions do you have about it? What questions will your audience have? To answer these questions, you might try BRAINSTORMING or other activities for GENERATING IDEAS. Such activities may help you focus your topic and also discover areas you need to research further.

Find out what others say. You can research others' POSITIONS and perspectives in many different ways. If your topic is a local one, such as alcohol use at your college, you may want to conduct a student survey, interview administrators or counselors who deal with campus drinking problems, or do a search of local newspapers for articles about alcohol-related incidents. But it would also be a good idea to look beyond your own community, in order to gain perspective on how the situation at your school fits into national patterns. You could consult books and periodicals, databases, websites, or online forums devoted to your topic. If your topic doesn't have a local focus, you will likely start out by consulting sources like these. You may also interview people at your school or in the community who are experts on your topic.

Decide whether you need to narrow your topic. What aspect of your topic most interests you, and how much can you cover given the constraints of your assignment? If your political science professor has assigned a five-minute oral report on climate-change legislation, for example, you will need to find a more specific focus than you would for a twenty-page written report on the same general topic.

Organize and start writing

Once you've narrowed your topic and have some sense of what you want to say about it, you need to think about how you can frame your topic to appeal to your audience and how you can best organize the information you have collected. As you draft, you may discover that you need to do some additional research as new questions and ideas arise. But for now, just get started.

Come up with a tentative thesis. State your topic and the gist of what you have to say about it in a tentative THESIS statement, trying to make it broad enough to cover the range of information you want to share with your audience but limited enough to be manageable—and keeping in mind that your goal is to report information, not to argue a position.

Organize your information. Make a list of the information you want to convey, and think about what details you want to include. You'll find that you need various strategies for presenting information— DESCRIPTION, DEFINITION, ANALYSIS, EXAMPLES, and so on.

Then consider how to arrange your material. Some topics call for a CHRONOLOGICAL structure, moving from past to present, maybe even projecting into the future. Or you may find that a SPATIAL ORGANIZATION works well—if you're reporting on the design of a new building, for instance— moving from exterior to interior or from top to bottom. There are any number of ways to organize a report in addition to these; you'll just need to work out a structure that will help your audience understand your topic in a systematic way.

Don't be surprised if you find that you do not need to use all of the information that you have collected. Authors often gather far more information than they finally use; your task is to choose the information that is most relevant to your thesis and present it as effectively as possible.

Draft an OPENING. Why do you care about your topic, and how can you get your audience interested in it? You will want to open by announcing your subject in a way that makes your audience want to know more about it. Consider opening with an intriguing example or a provocative question. Perhaps you have a memorable anecdote. It's usually a good idea also to include the thesis somewhere in the introduction so that your audience can follow from the outset where your report is heading and don't have to figure this out for themselves.

Draft a CONCLUSION. What do you want your audience to take away from your report? What do you want them to remember? You could end by noting the implications of your report, reminding them why your topic matters. You could summarize your main points. You could even end with a question, leaving them with something to think about.

Look critically at your draft, get responses—and revise

Try re-reading your draft several times from different perspectives and imagining how different readers will experience your text. Will readers new to the topic follow what you are saying? Will those who know about the topic think that you have represented it accurately and fairly? If possible, get feedback from a classmate or a tutor at your school's writing center. Following are some questions that can help you and others examine a report with a critical eye:

- *How does the report* OPEN*?* Will it capture your audience's interest? How else might it begin?

- *Is the topic clear and well focused?* Are the scope and structure of the report set out in its opening paragraphs? Is there an explicit THESIS statement—and if not, would it help to add one?

- *Is it clear why the topic matters*—why you care about it and why others should?

- *How does the draft appeal to your* AUDIENCE*?* Will they be able to understand what you say, or do you need to provide more background information or define any terms?

- *How do you establish your* AUTHORITY *on the topic?* Does the information presented seem trustworthy? Are the sources for your information credible, and have you provided any necessary DOCUMENTATION?

- *Is the* TONE *suited to your audience and purpose?* If it seems tentative or timid, how could you make it more confident? If it comes across as argumentative, how could you make it focus on the facts alone?

- *How is the information organized?* Past to present? Simple to complex? Some other way? Does the structure suit your topic and MEDIUM? What strategies have you used to present information— COMPARISON, DESCRIPTION, NARRATION?

- *What* MEDIA *will the report be presented in,* and how does that affect the way it's written? You might consider, for example, including photos in a print report, videos and links in an online report, or slides to go along with an oral presentation.

- *Is the report easy to follow?* If not, try adding TRANSITIONS or headings. If it's an oral report, you might put your main points on slides.

- *If you've included illustrations,* are there captions that explain how they relate to the written text? Have you referred to the illustration in your text? Is there information in your text that would be easier to follow in a chart or table?

- *Is the* STYLE *effectively engaging your audience?* How are you speaking to their language backgrounds and expectations? How might you challenge those expectations and for what purpose? Consider choice of words, level of formality, and so on.

- *How effective is your* CONCLUSION *?* How else might you end?

- *Does the title tell readers what the report is about,* and will it make them want to know more?

Revise your draft in response to any feedback you receive and your own analysis, keeping in mind that your goal is to stick to the facts.

REFLECT. Once you've completed your report, let it settle for a while and then take time to REFLECT *. How well did you report on your topic? How successful do you think you were in making the topic interesting to your audience? What additional revisions would you make if you could? Research shows that such reflections help "lock in" what you learn for future use.*

How Digital Beauty Filters Perpetuate Colorism

TATE RYAN-MOSLEY

WHEN LISE WAS A YOUNG TEENAGER in Georgia, her classmates bullied her relentlessly. She had moved with her family from Haiti a few years earlier, and she didn't fit in with the other students. They teased her about her accent, claimed she "smelled weird," and criticized the food she ate. But most often they would attack her with remarks about her dark complexion. Sometimes teachers would send her home from school because she couldn't stop crying. "I remember going home and I would take those copper wire things that you scrub dishes with," she says. "I would go to the bathroom and I would take my mom's bleach cream and scrub my skin with it."

And it wasn't just white classmates. Black students harassed her too—for being an outsider, for being too different. She remembers them asking, "Why is she so dark?"

Just when she thought it couldn't get worse, the phone in her palm became an endless stream of pictures of beautiful, lighter-skinned women getting dozens, hundreds, or even thousands of likes and affirming comments. She slowly began to notice that the world wanted parts of her—like her curves and her lips—but not things like her dark skin or her hair. Not her whole self, all together.

TATE RYAN-MOSELY is a reporter for *MIT Technology Review*, where she writes about the social impact of new technologies. Ryan-Mosely's articles for *MIT Technology Review* have focused on police use of facial recognition, internet shutdowns, artificial intelligence, and disinformation. This report was published in August 2021.

As she struggled to cope with the abuse, Lise convinced herself that the darkness of her skin was to blame. And social media platforms and the visual culture of the internet suggested the same thing.

Even among those closest to her, the undesirability of her darkness was reinforced. She grew to realize that her mom, aunts, and friends all used the skin-lightening creams she'd borrowed after school, many of which contain toxins and even carcinogens. It was confusing: her community fought hard against racism, but some of the prejudice she experienced came from Black people themselves.

And social media was just making it worse.

The prejudice Lise experienced—colorism—has a long history, driven by European ideals of beauty that associate lighter skin with purity and wealth, darker tones with sin and poverty. Though related to racism, it's distinct in that it can affect people regardless of their race, and can have different effects on people of the same background. . . .

These prejudices have been part of the social and media landscape for a long time, but the advent of digital images and Photoshop created new ways for colorism to manifest. In June 1994, notoriously, *Newsweek* and *Time* both ran cover images of O.J. Simpson's mug shot during his murder trial—but on *Time*'s cover, his skin was markedly darker. The difference sparked outrage: *Time* had darkened the image in what the magazine's photo illustrator claimed was an attempt to evoke a more "dramatic tone". But the editing reflected that the darker the man, the more criminal the American public assumes him to be.

This association has very real consequences. A 2011 study from Villanova University found a direct link between the severity of sentences for 12,000 incarcerated women and the darkness of their complexion.

And today, thanks to the prevalence of selfies and face filters, digital colorism has spread. With *Snapchat*, *Instagram*, *TikTok*, and *Facebook* a part of billions of people's everyday lives, many of us find that people see far more pictures of us than ever before. But there are biases built into these systems. At a basic level, the imaging chips found in most personal cameras have pre-set ranges for skin tones, making it technically impossible to accurately capture the real variety of complexions.

And the images that do get taken are often subject to alteration. *Snapchat* reports that over 200 million people use its filter product, Lenses, every day. Some of them use it to lighten their skin tone; other filters and automatic enhancing features can do the same on *Instagram* and *TikTok*. Photo technologies and image filters can do this in ways that are almost imperceptible. Meanwhile, social

Snapchat filters alter a user's skin tone.

media algorithms reinforce the popularity of people with lighter skin to the detriment of those with darker skin. Just this week, *Twitter*'s image-cropping algorithm was found to prefer faces that are lighter, thinner, and younger.

Selfie-Esteem

. . . The [filter] phenomenon has led to the concept of the "Instagram face," a particular look that's easily accessible through the proliferation of editing tools. Photos reflecting this look, with a small nose, big eyes, and fuller lips, attract more comments and likes, leading recommendation algorithms to prioritize them. We also interviewed researchers who say beauty ideals are narrowing even more dramatically and quickly than they expected—with especially profound effects on the way young girls, in particular, see themselves and shape their identity.

But it could be particularly catastrophic for women with darker complexions, says Ronald Hall, a professor at Michigan State University and an expert on colorism. As more European looks are increasingly held up as an ideal, "these young girls imitate these behaviors, and those who are super dark-complected see no way out," he says. "Those are the ones who are most at risk for harming themselves."

That harm can involve bleaching or other risky body treatments: the skin-lightening industry has grown rapidly and is now worth more than $8 billion worldwide each year. But beyond physical risks, researchers and activists have also begun documenting troubling emotional and psychological effects of online colorism.

Amy Niu researches selfie-editing behavior as part of her PhD in psychology at the University of Wisconsin, Madison. In 2019, she conducted a study to determine the effect of beauty filters on self-image for American and Chinese women. She took pictures of 325 college-aged women and, without telling them, applied a filter to some photos. She then surveyed the women to measure their emotions and self-esteem when they saw edited or unedited photos. Her results, which have not yet been published, found that Chinese women viewing edited photos felt better about themselves, while American women (87% of whom were white) felt about the same whether their photos were edited or not.

Niu believes that the results show there are huge differences between cultures when it comes to "beauty standards and how susceptible people are to those beauty filters." She adds, "Technology companies are realizing it, and they are making different versions [of their filters] to tailor to the needs of different groups of people."

This has some very obvious manifestations. Niu, a Chinese woman living in America, uses both *TikTok* and *Douyin*, the Chinese version (both are made by the same company, and share many of the same features, although not the same content). The two apps both have "beautify" modes, but they are different: Chinese users are given more extreme smoothing and complexion lightening effects.

She says the differences don't just reflect cultural beauty standards—they perpetuate them. White Americans tend to prefer filters that make their skin tanner, teeth whiter, and eyelashes longer, while Chinese women prefer filters that make their skin lighter.

Niu worries that the vast proliferation of filtered images is making beauty standards more uniform over time, especially for Chinese women. "In China, the beauty standard is more homogeneous," she says, adding that the filters "erase lots of differences to our faces" and reinforce one particular look.

"It's Really Bad"

Amira Adawe has observed the same dynamic in the way young girls of color use filters on social media. Adawe is the founder and executive director of

Beautywell, a Minnesota-based nonprofit aimed at combating colorism and skin-lightening practices. The organization runs programs to educate young girls of color about online safety, healthy digital behaviors, and the dangers of physical skin lightening.

Adawe says she often has to inform the girls in her workshops that their skin is being lightened by social media filters. "They think it's normal. They're like, 'Oh, this is not skin lightening, Amira. This is just a filter,'" she says. "A lot of these young girls use these filters and think, 'Oh my God, I look beautiful.'"

It's so easy to do—with a few clicks, users can make their appearance more similar to everyone else's ideal—that many young women end up assuming a lighter-skinned identity online. This makes it easier to find acceptance in the digital world, but it can also make it harder for them to identify with their real complexion.

When Adawe explains how using a face filter can be part of a cycle of colorism, she is often met with resistance. The filters have become essential to the way some girls see themselves.

"It's really bad," she says. "And it's contributing to this notion that you're not beautiful enough."

And it's complicated regardless of your skin tone.   25

Halle, a single biracial woman in her mid-20s, thinks a lot about her own racial identity. She says most people would use the term "ambiguous" to describe her appearance. "I have whiter features," she says. "My skin complexion is lighter than some other mixed-race girls', and my hair is less curly." She also used to be a regular user of dating apps. And from conversations with her friends who have darker complexions, she realized that her experience on dating apps was very different from theirs.

"Quite candidly, we compare matches and number of matches," she says. "That is where I started to realize: wait a minute, there's something going on here. My friends who identify as Black or Afro-Latina don't get as many matches.". . .

Halle says her experience on these apps reflects the wider world, too. "This is deeply rooted in racism, colorism, and everything that's happening in our society," she says. The experience became so frustrating for her that she deleted all her dating apps. *MIT Technology Review* has reached out to many dating sites to ask whether they use beauty-scoring algorithms for matches, but none will confirm or deny. . . .

Meanwhile, platforms including *TikTok* have been accused of intentionally "shadow-banning" content from some Black creators, especially those discussing the Black Lives Matter movement or racism in general. That diminishes their reach, and the cycle reinforces itself further. (In a statement, a *TikTok* spokesperson said "We unequivocally do not moderate content or accounts on the basis of race.")

Michigan State's Ronald Hall says he's "extremely worried" about the impact   30 on women of color in particular: "Women of color are constantly bombarded with these messages that you gotta be light in order to be attractive."

Adawe, meanwhile, thinks the only solution is an all-out ban on filters that lighten faces. She says she has emailed *Snapchat* asking for just that. "Social media companies keep [creating] filters because the demand is so high," she says. "But to me, I think they're promoting colorism, whether they realize it and whether it's intentional or not."

A spokesperson for Snap told *MIT Technology Review,* "Our goal is to build products that are fully inclusive of all Snapchatters, and we've put in place a number of processes and initiatives to help us do that. Our guidelines for all Snapchatters—which also apply to Lens submissions—prohibit discrimination and the promotion of stereotypes, and we have an extensive review process in place for Lenses, which includes testing them on a wide range of skin tones."

The company says it is partnering with experts for advice, and earlier this year it launched an initiative to build an "inclusive camera," which is meant to be better at capturing a broader range of skin tones.

A Completely Different Lens

Lise, who now lives in Minnesota, struggled with the effects of colorism for a long time. She went to therapy, watched endless *YouTube* tutorials on photo editing, and even bought a $600 camera that she hoped would make her look less dark in photos. Eventually she came to realize how harmful it had been.

"Now I just view everyone's social media page with a completely different   35 lens," she says. . . .

She says she wants to see more raw photos online that show beautiful women who look like her. She no longer edits her skin color in photos, and she tries hard to stop the negative thoughts in her head, though it can be hard. "Oh, I'll be darned if I see someone saying anything to a beautiful dark-skinned woman," she says. "I don't care if it's online, I don't care if it's in person—I'm going to call you out. I just can't be quiet about it anymore. . . ."

Thinking about the Text

1. How does Tate Ryan-Mosley **DEFINE** the term "colorism"? Where in the text does this definition appear? What other terms or concepts does she define? Are there other terms you think ought to be defined?

2. This report begins and ends with a **NARRATIVE** about one person's painful experience with beauty filters. What other examples and **EVIDENCE** does Ryan-Mosley provide? Do you find the evidence trustworthy? Why? How do examples help the author convey why this topic matters?

3. Effective reports use a confident **TONE** that informs rather than argues. Does Ryan-Mosley's satisfy this criterion? Cite examples from the article to support your answer.

4. This report was published in *MIT Technology Review*, a magazine and website dedicated to identifying and analyzing new technologies. Who do you think is the primary **AUDIENCE** for this publication? What strategies does Ryan-Mosley use to reach this audience? What other audiences might be interested?

5. Ryan-Mosley's report describes the harmful, and unequal, effects that digital technologies like photo-editing tools have on users, and how some technology companies are responding. She quotes a *Snapchat* representative who says, "Our goal is to build products that are fully inclusive of all Snapchatters, and we've put in place a number of processes and initiatives to help us do that. Our guidelines for all Snapchatters . . . prohibit discrimination and the promotion of stereotypes, and we have an extensive review process in place for Lenses, which includes testing them on a wide range of skin tones" (32). Do your own research into what companies with beauty filter features are doing in response to the information Ryan-Mosley reports. Do these companies have a responsibility to ensure their products don't promote discrimination? If so, are these companies doing enough? Write an essay that takes a **POSITION** on these questions.

This article has been edited specifically for this textbook. The original article can be found online at https://www.technologyreview.com/.

The Right to Preach on a College Campus

RYAN JOY

FREE SPEECH ON COLLEGE CAMPUSES has recently become a hotly contested issue in both the popular press and academic circles. The question of whether incendiary speech abides by university guidelines and constitutional protections raises important and fraught questions for both students and the administrators who arbitrate disputes over what qualifies as protected free expression.

Last month, in an area of campus on Park Avenue called the Park Blocks, a street preacher aggressively ministered to the students of Portland State University (PSU) in service to his religious beliefs. On a number of occasions over about a week, he harangued passersby, even instigating verbal altercations with students. The man seems to have been unaffiliated with any student group or organization.

In seeking to understand the significance of such an event, we come to a better comprehension of the larger issue of how college administrators seek to foster a safe and secure environment for students without running afoul of laws protecting the right to freedom of expression.

The question of whether informal public preaching falls within the First Amendment's definition of protected religious speech becomes more

RYAN JOY graduated from Lewis and Clark College with a degree in religious studies and went on to study economics at Portland State University. A version of this article was first published in 2015 in the *Portland Spectrum*, a student magazine at Portland State.

complicated when considering a few of the comments this preacher made to specific people. For example, he is purported to have called one woman a "slut" and to have asked others intrusive, personal questions.

When deciding on issues of free speech, administrators must balance the competing interests of a student's right to attend class free of harassment with someone else's right to voice his or her views unimpeded. Indeed, it is often the most objectionable views that require the most steadfast protection. Generally, the Supreme Court disallows speech restrictions that discriminate on the basis of content, and religious speech has been notoriously difficult to proscribe. 5

Legal precedent has something to say on the subject: in *McGlone v. Cheek, et al.*, a 6th U.S. Circuit Court of Appeals decided against the school after the administration sought to bar an itinerant preacher from speaking publicly on campus. Although the preacher, John McGlone, appears to have been moderately respected in the community (the PSU preacher struck many observers as unstable at best), the precedent set by the *McGlone* decision starkly illustrates how our courts balance rival interests in such disputes.

In *McGlone*, the preacher successfully reversed a lower court ruling and affirmed his right to preach on the basis of a rule known as the "vagueness doctrine," a legal test founded in the due process clause of the Fifth and Fourteenth Amendments that requires that laws must be clearly comprehensible and allow for uniform enforcement ("Vagueness Doctrine"). The judge who wrote the opinion in *McGlone* remarked that First Amendment cases must apply the vagueness doctrine stringently. Thus, since John McGlone contends that the university gave him conflicting information about his right to preach on campus, the 6th Circuit Court overturned the lower court's decision to uphold the university's rule barring public speech absent formal permission from a registered student organization or a current student.

Extrapolating from this court's decision, one may wonder whether a clear, unambiguous rule banning unaffiliated speakers would pass constitutional muster if instituted at PSU. As it stands, the university has no restrictions against people wandering onto campus and expounding on their topic of choice. While it is true that PSU has instituted and assiduously promoted its safety guidelines, PSU's codes of conduct stay largely silent on the type of on-campus conflicts that might occur between a student and those unaffiliated with the university— the types of conflicts that are abundant on a downtown college campus.

In response to an emailed list of questions concerning whether PSU might successfully restrict the presence of such visitors, Phillip Zerzan, PSU's chief of campus public safety, confirmed that "the ability to regulate or control speech in the Park Blocks is guided by the First Amendment" and that while the preacher appears to have harassed students, such "non-physical, generally directed harassment speech is still protected speech."

"There is much case law confirming [that the regulation of speech] must be content neutral," Zerzan added, recognizing that speech restrictions are difficult if not impossible to institute when they restrict speech on a certain topic, especially religion. Even religiously motivated hate-speech enjoys the same protections as more benign forms of expression. "The preachers are a common event on campus, and we encourage students to engage in this conversation in a constructive manner, or otherwise ignore the speech," Zerzan concluded.

David Johns, a PSU professor of political science, corroborates this reading of the law as it applies to the preacher, who technically was preaching on public, city-owned property. According to Johns, as long as someone in the Park Blocks is not drawing noise complaints, engaging in disorderly conduct, or specifically threatening students, "they can pretty much say what they want."

To be sure, there are categories of speech that courts have exempted from First Amendment protections. Speech that presents an imminent danger to public health, for instance, and that which intends to do harm enjoy no legal immunity. In the landmark 1942 Supreme Court case *Chaplinsky v. New Hampshire*, the "fighting words" doctrine limited the First Amendment's protection of certain types of speech, including "the lewd and obscene, the profane, the libelous, and the insulting or 'fighting' words—those which by their very utterance inflict injury or tend to incite an immediate breach of the peace" (United States, Supreme Court).

This category may not apply to street preachers, however, regardless of the illicit questions they might pose to students. And while the courts may have once been sympathetic to the notion that large categories of speech deserved little in the way of First Amendment protections, as of the late twentieth century, courts have begun to roll back such exemptions and have granted First Amendment protection to all types of speech. As Johns notes, "although *Chaplinsky* has never been overturned directly . . . its effect has been considerably reduced."

The current Supreme Court seems more inclined than ever to give preference to those claiming immunity under the First Amendment, often invoking the reasoning that more speech equals more freedom. PSU, for one, is in no danger of stifling freedom of expression. Recently, PSU has witnessed a flourishing display of ideas, and while certain visitors may strike some as unworthy of careful consideration, it is the principle that allows them to continue that many consider worthy of protection.

Works Cited

United States, Court of Appeals for the Sixth Circuit. *McGlone v. Cheek, et al.* Docket no. 12-5306, 2 Aug. 2013. *United States Court of Appeals for the Sixth Circuit*, www.ca6.uscourts.gov/opinions.pdf/13a0710n-06.pdf. PDF download.

United States, Supreme Court. *Chaplinsky v. State of New Hampshire*. 9 Mar. 1942. *Legal Information Institute*, Cornell Law School, www.law.cornell.edu/supremecourt/text/315/568.

"Vagueness Doctrine." *Legal Information Institute*, Cornell Law School, www.law.cornell.edu/wex/vagueness_doctrine.

Thinking about the Text

1. A good report generally does not take sides on an issue and instead presents a balanced discussion of the major viewpoints in play. What key positions does Ryan Joy identify in the controversy over the rights of the campus preacher? How fairly does he represent each side?

2. Examine the way that Joy introduces the issue in the first few paragraphs of his report. What kind of background information does he provide? Do you think he should have provided any additional background information or definitions—and if so, why?

3. Joy wrote this report for the *Portland Spectrum*, a student publication about campus issues, yet he addresses a controversy that has wide significance. How does Joy make his report applicable to **AUDIENCES** beyond the Portland State community?

4. What types of **EVIDENCE** does Joy rely on to develop his discussion of the two sides of this issue? How does the range of evidence affect Joy's **CREDIBILITY** as an author?

5. Choose an important campus issue that you want to explore. Research the issue by reading what others have written, speaking to people in your campus community, conducting a survey, or some other method of gathering information. Write a **REPORT** that presents a balanced view of all sides of the issue. Consider submitting the report to a school publication.

SEVENTEEN

"Two Thumbs Up"

Writing a Review

RESTAURANTS, CELL PHONES, BOOKS, movies, TV shows, cars, toaster ovens, employees—just about anything can be reviewed. Many people don't buy a new product or try a new restaurant without first checking to see what others have said about it online—and even posting their own thoughts on it afterward.

You've probably given casual reviews of this sort yourself. If a friend asks what you think of the TV series *The Handmaid's Tale*, your response would probably constitute a brief review: "It mostly lived up to the hype. The acting was really impressive, but sometimes the plot lagged. I guess I'll keep watching since people are talking about it." Even this offhand opinion includes two basic elements of all reviews: a judgment ("impressive," "lagged") and the criteria you used to arrive at that judgment, in this case the quality of the performances, the script, and the show's popularity.

Reviews can vary a good deal, however, as you can see in these examples from other reviews of *The Handmaid's Tale*.

> Gilead may be the creation of religious patriarchy grown monstrous, but "The Handmaid's Tale" is a creation shaped by the female gaze. Reed Morano, who directed the first three episodes, establishes a visual language that plays as important a role in this series as the dialogue. Her lush cinematography latches onto the hazy nightmarishness of Offred's tenuous existence.

A still from *The Handmaid's Tale*.

Gilead is a place of shadowed interiors, where costume designer Ane Crabtree's creations remind us with elegant subtlety of the place's sinister caste system. The aquamarine dress of the commander's wife pops into the fore in dim hallways, the dove gray worn by the Marthas and Aunts demarcates the border between light and shadow, and the handmaids' scarlet dresses mark them as targets as well as silent, compliant objects of desire. . . .

And [Elizabeth] Moss' acting style works in concert with Morano's direction. She devastatingly conveys Offred's seething exasperation with shock darting through slightly widened eyes or tiny curls of defiance dancing around the edge of her lips. Those milliseconds of honesty make the viewer's adrenaline spike along with the character's.

—MELANIE McFARLAND, "'The Handmaid's Tale': A Dystopian Tale of Female Subjugation That Hits Close to Home"

Melanie McFarland's review, published on *Salon*, makes clear her criteria: the show's cinematic qualities, on the one hand, and its actors' performances, on the other. McFarland is able to elaborate on these criteria with vivid examples like the costumes and acting methods she describes above.

On the other hand, *Metacritic.com* gives ratings by gathering numerical scores from multiple sources and calculating an average—92 out of 100 in the case of this series, on the high end of "Universal Acclaim." The site also provides excerpts and links to full reviews, and lets visitors add their own reviews. On *Metacritic.com*, everyone can be a reviewer.

This chapter provides guidelines for writing reviews—whether an academic book review for a political science class, a product review on *Amazon*, or a movie review in your campus newspaper.

REFLECT. Think about reviews you've read. All reviews evaluate something, and they do so using relevant criteria. Someone reviewing a movie, for instance, would generally consider such factors as the quality of the script, acting, directing, and cinematography. Think about a product you are familiar with or a performance you have recently seen. Develop a list of criteria for evaluating it, and then write an explanation of why these criteria are well suited to your subject. What does this exercise help you understand about the process of reviewing?

Across Academic Disciplines

Reviews are a common genre in all academic disciplines. As a student, you will often be assigned to write a review of something—a book, a work of art, a musical performance—as a way of engaging critically with the work. While students in the humanities and social sciences are often asked to write book reviews, students in the performing arts may review a performance. In a business course, you may be asked to review products or business plans.

In each of these cases, you'll need to develop criteria for your evaluation and to support that evaluation with substantial evidence. The kind of evidence you show will vary across disciplines. If you're evaluating a literary work, you'll need to show evidence from the text (quotations, for example), whereas if you are evaluating a proposed tax policy for an economics class, you're probably going to be required to show numerical data demonstrating projected outcomes.

Across Media

Reviews can appear in many media—from print to digital, online to television and radio. Each medium offers different resources and challenges. A television film critic reviewing a new movie can intersperse clips from the film to back up their points, but their own comments will likely be brief. A different critic, writing about the same film for a print magazine, can develop a fuller, more carefully reasoned review, but will be limited to still images rather than video clips.

The same choices may be available to you when you are assigned to review something. For instance, if you give an oral presentation reviewing an art show, you might create slides that show some of the art you discuss. Perhaps your review could be a video that includes not only images of the art but also footage of viewers interacting with it. If you get to choose media, you'll need to think about which one(s) will allow you to best cover your subject and reach your audience.

THINK BEYOND WORDS

⤴ *LOOK AT this photo of Immersive Van Gogh, a traveling art exhibit that immerses visitors in the Impressionist artist's famous works. A similar photo was included in Keisha Raines's review of the exhibition in LA, published on Thrillist.com. According to Raines, "The artist's works are brought to life in a production that includes 60,600 frames of captivating video totaling 90 million pixels and 500,000+ cubic feet of projections set to original song compositions." The brief review, which you can see at everyonesanauthor.tumblr.com, includes several photos. How else could a review published online take advantage of the medium—with maps? music? video? interviews? What else?*

Across Cultures and Communities

Conventions for reviewing vary across communities and cultures. In most US academic contexts, reviews are quite direct, explicitly stating whether something is successful or unsuccessful and why. Especially online, reviews are often very honest, even brutal. In other contexts, reviewers have reason to be more guarded. When the *Detroit News* reviews a new car, for instance, its writers have to keep in mind the sensitivities of the community, many of whom work in the auto industry, and of the company that produces that car, which may be a major advertiser in the newspaper. *Consumer Reports* might review the same car very differently, since it is supported not by advertisers but by subscribers who want impartial data and information that will help them decide whether or not to purchase that car.

Across Genres

Evaluation is often used as a strategy in other genres. **PROPOSALS** offer solutions to problems, for example, and in that process they must consider— and review and evaluate—various other solutions. Evaluation and **ANALYSIS** often go hand in hand as well, as when *Consumer Reports* analyzes a series of smartphones in order to evaluate and rank them for its readers. Even **ARGUMENTS** sometimes call for some type of review.

REFLECT. Look for several reviews of a favorite movie. You're likely to find many reviews online, but try also to find reviews in print sources or online versions of print publications. How do the reviews differ from one medium to the next? What, if anything, do the online reviews have that the print versions do not? Then check out some fan sites or social media posts about the same movie. How does the medium affect the decisions that a reviewer makes about content, length, style, and design?

CHARACTERISTIC FEATURES

Whatever the audience and medium, the most successful reviews share most of the following features:

- Relevant background information about the subject (p. 339)
- Criteria for the evaluation (p. 341)

- A well-supported evaluation (p. 344)
- Attention to the audience's needs and expectations (p. 346)
- An authoritative tone (p. 348)
- Awareness of the ethics of reviewing (p. 351)

Relevant Background Information about the Subject

The background information needed in a review may entail anything from items on a restaurant menu to a description of the graphics of a video game to the plot summary of a novel or movie. What information to include—and how much—depends on your rhetorical situation. In the case of an academic review, your instructor may specify a length, which will affect how much information you can provide. What's needed in nonacademic reviews varies depending on the audience and publication. Someone reviewing a new album by an indie group for *Rolling Stone* may not need to provide much background information since readers are already likely to be familiar with the group. This would not be the case, however, if the same author were writing a review for a more general-interest magazine, such as *Time*.

Reviews of books and films (and other narratives) often provide background information about the subject matter, the research process, or the story (depending on the genre of the work being reviewed). See how Viveca Novak's review of the book *From Warsaw with Love: Polish Spies, the CIA, and the Forging of an Unlikely Alliance* opens with background information to help readers appreciate how unprecedented the work is:

> Cold War spy tales abound, but few true-to-life accounts of espionage that occurred in the last two decades have emerged—in large part due to the CIA's highly methodical declassification process.
>
> But former *Washington Post* reporter John Pomfret went the shoe-leather route—interviewing dozens of current and former government officials and intelligence operatives on both sides of the Atlantic and mining declassified files in Poland—to put together his fascinating story of the Polish-U.S. intelligence relationship.
>
> The book's title, *From Warsaw With Love*, grows from a story Pomfret dug up in 1995, while posted in eastern Europe. Soon after Poland's first

Geoffrey Pullum's essay on emoji use is more a rebuttal than a review, but notice how his essay employs many of the same characteristic features. Read what he has to say about "the stupidest story about language this week" on p. 959.

post-Communist, freely-elected prime minister took office in 1990, the Polish and U.S. spy agencies began working together. Polish operatives came to the U.S. for training; the U.S. provided millions of dollars in cash and equipment, Pomfret reports.

—VIVECA NOVAK, "Spies on Opposite Sides of the Cold War Unite in 'From Warsaw with Love'"

In this NPR review, Novak provides information on the author's research methods ("shoe-leather route—interviewing dozens of current and former government officials") including about Pomfret's access to information ("grows from a story Pomfret dug up in 1995, while posted in eastern Europe"). Not only does Novak provide insight that gives the author credibility as a researcher but she also situates the genre of the book in the first sentence by introducing it as a "Cold War spy tale" that is "true-to-life."

Now look at Diep Tran's review of Alice Childress's 1955 play *Trouble in Mind,* in which the author provides necessary context for the significance of the work's 2021 debut on Broadway:

In 1955, Childress's play *Trouble in Mind* premiered off Broadway and was well-received critically. The play was optioned for Broadway with a caveat: Childress had to tone down her play about racism in the American theatre and make it more comfortable for the ostensibly white audience that would be seeing it. Childress refused, and *Trouble in Mind* was relegated to the footnotes of American theatre history, never achieving the kind of mainstream success that it deserved. Until now, when it has been given its much-delayed Broadway debut 66 years later.

Childress's contemporaries included Lorraine Hansberry and her play *A Raisin in the Sun.* While Hansberry's play dealt with the overt, capital-R racism of housing discrimination, Childress's dealt with a common, insidious form of racism, that of well-meaning liberals—those who Dr. Martin Luther King Jr. called the white moderates, "more devoted to 'order' than to justice."

—DIEP TRAN, "'Trouble in Mind' Review— The Kind of Good Trouble Broadway Needs"

Tran offers this important historical information to provide the context in which *Trouble in Mind* appears on Broadway in 2021 as a revival of a play that was implicated in racial politics in 1955. Had Childress acquiesced to the pressure to "tone down her play," she would have been the first African

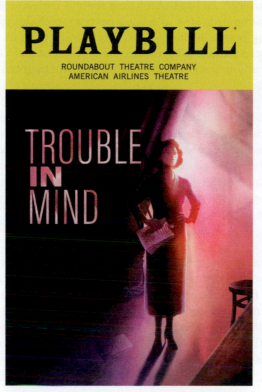

2021 Broadway playbill for *Trouble in Mind*.

American woman playwright to have her work produced on Broadway. Instead, that honor went to Lorraine Hansberry. Tran felt it was necessary for readers to have this information to understand the place of Childress's play in American theater history and in current news.

Criteria for the Evaluation

Underlying all good reviews are clear criteria. As an author, then, you'll need to establish the criteria for any review you write. Sometimes, the criteria are obvious or can be assumed: criteria for reviewing cars, for example, would almost assuredly include price, style, comfort, performance, safety, gas mileage, and so on. Often, however, you may want to shape the criteria for specific purposes and audiences. Now see how *Consumer Reports*, a non-profit publication dedicated to product reviews, provides specific criteria for evaluating bicycle helmets. First, they specify that "fit, comfort, and durability are important factors when you choose a helmet." Then, they use those same criteria to review, rate, and recommend their top pick, the Giro Register MIPS:

> This adult bike helmet is one of the best CR has tested. It rates Excellent for absorbing impact forces in a crash. And it includes a multidirectional impact protection system (MIPS), a promising technology designed to reduce the risk of concussion. This relatively lightweight, easy-to-use helmet also provides excellent ventilation. Its one less-than-stellar quality concerns fit adjustability: It comes in a universal size and not all the straps are adjustable.
>
> —CONSUMER REPORTS, "Giro Register MIPS Bike Helmet"

Consumer Reports presents their review in multiple formats. For readers who are very familiar with helmets already or want just the highlights, they offer a "ratings scorecard" and a list of "highs" and "lows." For readers who may want a bit more detail or need background information, *Consumer Reports* provides a narrative explanation as well as verified users' reviews. In this case, the criteria are flexible enough that they work for these different audiences and formats.

Consumer Reports rating scorecard for the GIRO Register MIPS bike helmet.

However, **QUALITATIVE** criteria can be as persuasive as **QUANTITATIVE** criteria, and many reviews combine both. For example, that's often what you'll find when examining reviews of colleges and universities. Student-written and alumni evaluations of colleges and universities tend to be qualitative. Consider this brief review from a Spelman College alumna published on the college profile website *Niche* (which offers both qualitative and quantitative reviews):

> We are women who serve. Attending Spelman empowered me in a way that would not have been possible at any other institution. I have a community or family of Spelman sisters that will be with me forever. I wish I could have my college experience one more time to take advantage of more opportunities presented to me at that fine establishment. Black women being educated and supporting one another is beautiful and powerful.
>
> —SPELMAN COLLEGE ALUMNA, Review on *Niche*
> (© Niche.com, Inc. 2022)

This reviewer uses qualitative criteria such as personal feelings and values ("Spelman empowered me" and "I have a community or family") to signal the strengths of this college. This qualitative review complements the following quantitative assessment of Spelman that appeared in *U.S. News & World Report*. Note the rankings process that this publication uses, relying on numerical ranking rather than qualitative experience:

> Spelman College Rankings: See where this school lands in our other rankings to get a bigger picture of the institution's offerings:
>
> #54 in National Liberal Arts Colleges (tie)
>
> #24 in Best Undergraduate Teaching (tie)
>
> #90 in Best Value Schools
>
> #7 in Most Innovative Schools (tie)
>
> #4 in Top Performers on Social Mobility (tie)
>
> #1 in Historically Black Colleges and Universities
>
> #33 in Study Abroad (tie)
>
> #9 in Learning Communities (tie)
>
> #21 in Service Learning (tie)
>
> —U.S. NEWS & WORLD REPORT, "Spelman College Rankings"

As you consider writing reviews, keep in mind how the criteria you use presents a particular story about what you are reviewing. Think about both your subject and the discipline you're writing within to help determine how you'll use qualitative and quantitative criteria.

A Well-Supported Evaluation

The foundation of every review is a clear evaluation, a claim that something is good or bad, right or wrong, useful or not. Whatever you're reviewing, you need to give reasons for what you claim and sufficient evidence to support those reasons. And because rarely is anything all good or all bad, you also need to acknowledge any weaknesses in things you praise and any positives in things you criticize. Also, remember to anticipate and acknowledge reasons that others might evaluate your subject differently than you do. In other words, you need to consider other possible perspectives on whatever you're reviewing.

Journalist Amy Goldwasser approached a number of passengers on a New York subway and asked them for impromptu reviews of what they were reading. She then collaborated with the illustrator Peter Arkle to compose graphic reviews for the *New York Times Book Review*. Here's what two readers had to say:

MARIAH ANTHONY, 18, high school senior, on p.133 of THE KITE RUNNER, by Khaled Hosseini (paperback)

I read every day. Every. Day. I'm not a novel-reader. I'm more self-help and psychology. But this is an **amazing** book. You should read it. The author went way into depth. Where I'm at, the main character's 18. He and his father moved to San Francisco from Kabul...they were **refugees** who had to be smuggled into the States. He had to travel *inside an oil tank* to be here. I don't think I can exactly relate, but it's about how people go through things. It's **beautiful**.

DON SHEA, 70, fiction writer, on p. 214 of LIT, by Mary Karr (paperback)

This is her third book. I've read the first two. She's a poet.... I've been struck by the **wonderful** metaphors. I'm always surprised when poets really write superb prose. It gets a little draggy in the rehab part. She just keeps **slipping and slipping**. But it's good—all her stuff is good.

Both readers clearly stated what they thought of the books they were reading ("an amazing book," "it's good"). And then they gave reasons ("the author went way into depth," "all her stuff is good") and evidence to support those reasons ("he had to travel *inside an oil tank* to be here," "wonderful metaphors"). Note as well that one of the readers, Don Shea, acknowledges one weakness in Mary Karr's book ("It gets a little draggy in the rehab part").

When you're writing a review for a college class, you'll need to be more systematic and organized than these off-the-cuff reviews—with an explicitly stated evaluation, for one thing. See how *Salon*'s Melanie McFarland opens her review of the 2021 movie *Dune* by offering a clear evaluation. She acknowledges the failed attempts of other directors who tried—unsuccessfully—to adapt this popular novel to the screen. Her opening also sets up a contrast between those lackluster previous attempts and the 2021 adaptation.

> Adapting Frank Herbert's "Dune" for the screen has proven to be somewhat akin to ingesting the potentially fatal sandworm bile known as the Water of Life. Men may not have died in the attempt, but those who tried failed to adequately transmute Herbert's full vision.
>
> That alone is reason enough to appreciate Denis Villeneuve's mesmerizing interpretation of this sci-fi masterpiece, the release of which was delayed due to the pandemic. His take on "Dune" isn't merely fascinating and narratively coherent. It is a gorgeous sensory immersion that holds us in its spell for hours, with an ending that sparks yearning to see what comes next.
>
> —MELANIE McFARLAND, "'Dune' is the masterful adaptation of Frank Herbert's epic we've been waiting for"

McFarland states her evaluation explicitly as part of her praise of the director's skill (his "mesmerizing interpretation") in bringing Herbert's sci-fi novel to the big screen. McFarland's effusive, yet specific praise continues as she notes the director's skillful approach to transforming the story from book to film.

> Villeneuve mitigates the novel's perilous complexity by presenting it as a two-part journey instead of trying to jam the entire tapestry into a single pass. This approach invites us to consider this movie as the world-building chapter of what could, and should, become a franchise chronicling Timothée Chalamet's youthful Paul Atreides' maturity from an uncertain youth tossed into the wilderness into a messiah who threatens to rearrange the social order.

A still from *Dune* (2021).

Read McFarland's full review at everyonesanauthor .tumblr.com.

McFarland's full review includes all the characteristic features introduced earlier in this chapter on pages 338–39. It offers detailed, necessary background information about the book and the challenges of turning it into a film, explicit criteria for evaluating the movie, and evidence from the film to support the evaluation—including details that readers need about characters, plot, and potential sequels. Equally important is McFarland's credibility as a reviewer, which she demonstrates through her knowledge of *Dune*'s history as a book and a film, and of the detailed discussion of filmmaking elements that good reviewers of this medium tend to display.

Attention to the Audience's Needs and Expectations

All authors need to consider what their audience expects from them. But this consideration plays a particularly important role in the case of reviews. In many situations, some audience members will be familiar with what you're reviewing, whereas others will need a detailed summary or description; some will need an explicit statement of the criteria for the evaluation, while others will know what the criteria are without being told. When in doubt about audience knowledge, provide criteria and more details.

Audience considerations can also influence the criteria that reviewers identify as most crucial for their evaluation. Consider, for instance, reviews of video games. Gamers might expect one set of criteria, perhaps focusing on the games' playability and entertainment value. Parents and teachers might want entirely different criteria, ones that call attention instead to any violence and strong language.

Here, for instance, is an excerpt of a review of *Pokémon Brilliant Diamond and Shining Pearl* from *GameSpot*, a website for news and reviews serving the gaming community. This review was clearly written for an audience familiar with previous versions of the game. Even though the reviewer, Steve Watts, provides a bit of background in the second paragraph for those newer to the Pokémon universe, he assumes his audience knows the history of the game, previous critiques, and some other similar games (note the Mario reference at the end of the second paragraph).

> Even in the context of a series that regularly receives criticism for feeling formulaic, Pokémon Brilliant Diamond and Shining Pearl are particularly familiar. As remakes of the fourth-gen titles Diamond and Pearl, these are homages to an era of Pokémon when the series was just starting to settle into a comfortable niche. Not only that, but these are extremely faithful remakes, right down to the visual style and classic combat mechanics. . . .
>
> Even those who haven't spent the last few decades repeatedly catching "em" all know the gist by now. You're a plucky kid who goes on a grand cross-country adventure training pocket monsters and ultimately becoming world champion. It's recognizable in the same way that you basically already know that Mario is going to have to save the princess, and has a certain level of simplistic appeal.
>
> That same brand of simplicity is present in the mechanical underpinnings. Diamond and Pearl hailed from a simpler era of Pokémon, before full 3D became the norm. Instead, they harkened back to the series' roots as an overhead, sprite-based RPG. . . . While your character has a full range of movement in the world and the geometry isn't terribly blocky, there are some obvious anachronisms—how NPCs always move at right angles, for example, or how floor tiles are sized to fit your character perfectly. It's only mildly distracting and, for the most part, is just charming.
>
> —STEVE WATTS, "Pokémon Brilliant Diamond / Shining Pearl Review"

Watts assumes the readers are gamers who will know what an "overhead, sprite-based RPG" is or understand the suggestion that "there are some obvious anachronisms—how NPCs always move at right angles." Writing for a gaming website, Watts takes some liberties in assuming a fairly knowledgeable audience. However, like all good reviews, this one provides a clear evaluation using explicit criteria and demonstrating detailed knowledge of this game and video games in general.

REFLECT. Find two reviews of the same subject (a movie, a band, whatever) from two different sources: Yelp *and* Travel + Leisure, *perhaps, or* Salon *and* Time. *Look over each source and decide what kind of audience each one addresses. Young? Affluent? Intellectual? A general audience? Then study each review. How much prior knowledge does each one expect of its readers? How much space is devoted to describing the subject and how much to evaluating it? Do the two reviews use the same criteria—and if not, what might account for the difference? What does this analysis suggest about the role that audience plays in the way reviews are written?*

An Authoritative Tone

As important as the reviews themselves is the credibility of the reviewers. Authors of reviews establish their authority and credibility in a variety of ways, including demonstrating their knowledge of the subject, balancing praise and critique, and establishing a relationship with the audience early on. Note how *Washington Post* TV critic Inkoo Kang connects the HBO docuseries *Black and Missing* to another widely known story in the news at the time.

> In March 2014, 8-year-old Relisha Rudd, who had been living with her family at a homeless shelter in Washington, D.C., went missing. The second-grader was last seen alive on the day of her disappearance: Cameras caught her entering a motel room with 51-year-old Kahlil Tatum, a janitor at the shelter who had served long stints in prison. . . .
>
> Her case . . . was assiduously covered by the local media but hardly registered on the national consciousness. Gabby Petito-style news coverage has traditionally been reserved for girls and women who look like Gabby Petito, and Rudd did not.

Rudd's disappearance is one of several explored in the HBO docu-series "Black and Missing." Part of a steady drip of programming attempt-ing to reform the fire hose of true-crime entertainment, the two-night, four-part series profiles the sisters-in-law founders of the Maryland-based Black and Missing organization—and attests to why their work of circulating the names, photos and identifying details of Black missing people is regrettably necessary.

True crime, as we know it today, is a White genre, focusing over-whelmingly on White victims and White perpetrators, with a tendency to ally with law enforcement and uphold the prison-industrial complex. That gives its consumers a distorted sense of the world, as the factors that lead to missing girls and women—poverty, mental illness, domes-tic violence and police indifference—disproportionately impact Black (and Native) Americans. One of the primary aims of the docuseries is to redirect the media spotlight on the groups most likely to suffer victimization.

—INKOO KANG, "'Black and Missing' attempts a much-needed reform of true-crime storytelling. It mostly succeeds."

The dramatic, horrifying opening example and comparison to a well-known news story captures readers' attention while demonstrating Kang's deep knowledge of the subject. In addition, the review's title: "'Black and Miss-ing' attempts a much-needed reform of true-crime storytelling. It mostly succeeds."—particularly the final statement—previews Kang's critical stance. Readers can trust Kang is a credible reviewer.

In another example, Hephzibah Anderson, reviewing Ann Patchett's col-lection of essays *These Precious Days* in the *Guardian*, creates an authorita-tive tone through her demonstrated knowledge of nonfiction recently published by other women writers:

At first brush, *These Precious Days* seems [an] incongruous addition to the sizeable stack of recently published essays by female writers. Though not devoid of joy, titles such as Lavinia Greenlaw's *Some Answers Without Questions* or Lucy Ellmann's *Things Are Against Us* are unabashed polemics; they grapple with the gritty, they rail and they fulminate. Patchett's, in contrast, is characterised by sun-dappled beneficence.

—HEPHZIBAH ANDERSON, "*These Precious Days* by Ann Patchett review"

Finally, here is the introduction to a review of Steven Spielberg's 2021 adaptation of *West Side Story* written by University of California, Berkeley, student Joy Diamond and published in the *Daily Californian*, the independent student-run newspaper at her university:

> "West Side Story" has an outstanding legacy. The original musical, with lyrics by Stephen Sondheim, won two Tony Awards and marked a turning point in musical theater with its dark themes and emphasis on social problems. The 1961 film adaptation was nominated for 11 Oscars and won 10, including the Academy Award for Best Picture, and the film has been deemed "culturally, historically or aesthetically significant" by the Library of Congress. Needless to say, the 2021 film adaptation of "West Side Story" has some large dancing shoes to fill—but equally obvious is its inability to do so.
>
> —JOY DIAMOND, "Devoid of Spark, 'West Side Story' Is Rough, Unfortunate Film Adaptation"

This introduction shows that the reviewer is knowledgeable about *West Wide Story*'s history and accolades.

If you get to choose your subject, select a topic that you know (and care) about, and share some of what you know in your introduction. Telling your audience something interesting about your subject and giving some sense that it matters will help establish your credibility and make them want to know more.

Scenes from *West Side Story*, the 1961 film (left) and the 2021 adaptation (right).

Awareness of the Ethics of Reviewing

Depending on context and purpose, a review can have substantial—or minimal—consequences. When the late, widely syndicated film reviewer Roger Ebert gave a Hollywood movie a thumbs-up or thumbs-down, his judgment influenced whether the movie was shown in theaters across America or went immediately to DVD. Those reviewing Broadway plays for publications like the *New York Times* hold similar powers. And reviews in *Consumer Reports* influence the sale of the products they evaluate.

By comparison, a review of a local high school musical will not determine how long the musical will run or how much money it will make, but an especially negative review, particularly if it is unjustified, will certainly wound the feelings of those involved in the production. And a movie review on the *Internet Movie Database* (*IMDb*) that gives away key elements of a plot without including a "spoiler alert" will ruin the film for some of the audience. So an ethical reviewer will always keep in mind that a review has power—whether economic, emotional, or some other kind—and take care to exercise that power responsibly. An ethical reviewer also considers how their background influences their evaluation. How might your previous experiences factor into your review? For example, your background as a veteran will likely be a filter through which you review a military-oriented video game or film. That background may help you identify inaccuracies, but it may also make you less open to experiences different from your own. Think about how best to be fair-minded.

Considering the likely effect of your review on those who created whatever you're reviewing is part of the ethics of reviewing as well. It's one thing to criticize the latest episode of *The Handmaid's Tale* (the creators of that series can likely afford to laugh all the way to the bank) but quite another when you're reviewing a new restaurant in town. It's not that you should hold back criticism (or praise) that you think the subject deserves, but you do need to think about the effect of your judgments before you express them.

How you express them is also important. In academic contexts, remember this responsibility especially when reviewing other students' drafts. Don't avoid mentioning problems just because you might make the writer feel bad, but be sure that any criticisms are constructive. Be sure to mention strengths as well as weaknesses and offer suggestions and encouragement for overcoming those weaknesses if you can.

TIM ALAMENCIAK is communications manager for Reep Green Solutions, an environmental charity based in Ontario. He previously wrote for the *Toronto Star*, a widely read newspaper in Canada, where this book review was published in 2015.

Monopoly: The Scandal behind the World's Favorite Board Game

TIM ALAMENCIAK

Opening with a mysterious but clever statement that turns out to be about a game many readers will know establishes an authoritative tone; the promise of a good story makes us want to read on.

SOMETIMES THE IRONIES OF THE WORLD are stranger than fiction. That a game based on wheeling and dealing was born of wheeling and dealing writ large is a prime example of this.

Mary Pilon's *The Monopolists* unearths and charts the fascinating history of the popular board game Monopoly and the court battle fought by Ralph Anspach, a quixotic professor trying to save his own game. It's a story rife with controversy and scandal.

The book hitches its narrative on the tale of Anspach, the professor who took umbrage with Monopoly's capitalist focus and created Anti-Monopoly. His move so rankled Parker Brothers, the then-owner of the original game, they started a legal action that unfolded over decades of hearings and appeals.

Providing background information.

Once thought to be the brainchild of a man named Charles Darrow, who profited immensely from the game's success, the history is much more complicated than that.

A woman named Elizabeth Magie originally invented "The Landlord's Game" to teach students about Henry George's "single

5

tax" concept—a notion that all land should be owned by the public and simply rented by the occupants. She patented it in 1903—three decades before Darrow attempted to sell the game.

Magie was a prolific advocate for the rights of women but remained hidden for decades—overshadowed by the story Parker Brothers included with every game about Darrow, a down-on-his-luck man during the depression who invented a game for his kids.

Magie made waves in other ways after inventing the game. Finding it difficult to support herself on a stenographer's wage and frustrated with the way things were, she took out an ad in the paper offering herself for sale as a "young woman American slave." The satirical ad spread like wildfire and Magie was eventually hired as a newspaper reporter.

Alamenciak summarizes the history told in Pilon's book (without giving too much away) and provides relevant background information.

Meanwhile, her game had taken on a life of its own and was being passed around from family to family across the country. While still obscure, its fans were devoted and eager to teach it to others.

The board went through some transformations as others picked up the game and copied it for themselves. The original game was anti-capitalist, with an alternate set of rules to teach the difference. Pilon meticulously charts the path the design took from Magie's hands to Atlantic City, where Quakers penned the famous street names that exist to this day, then to the living room of Darrow.

Words like "meticulously" and "compelling" (in the following paragraph) establish Alamenciak's criteria for evaluation.

The book is a compelling look at history through the lens of Monopoly. Pilon paints Magie as a heroine long forgotten who contributed more than just a game but also then-rebellious writing that advanced the cause of women.

10

Pilon's book is full of interesting historical info, but rather than unfolding as a cohesive narrative that follows Anspach's quest to keep Anti-Monopoly alive, it reads more like a book divided into two parts. The reader is provided the true biography of Monopoly and then is asked to accompany Anspach as he uncovers the revelations that were just delivered.

More could have been done to weave the two together and bring the reader with Anspach throughout the text.

Alamenciak acknowledges the book's limitations, but he also notes its strengths. In considering both and phrasing his criticisms fairly, he shows he is aware of the ethics of reviewing.

That said, Pilon's writing is on-point and the historical information she's uncovered is fascinating. She is not writing about Monopoly; she is writing about American history intertwined with games.

An explicit statement of another criterion for evaluation.

Quotes and specific
examples from the book
provide evidence for
Alamenciak's claims.

"Games aren't just relics of their makers—their history is also told through their players," writes Pilon. "And like Lizzie's original innovative board, circular and never-ending, the balance between winners and losers is constantly in flux."

This is not just a book for Monopoly fans. It's a great read for anyone who likes to know the quirky, interesting history of board games in twentieth century America. Even discussions on trademarks and brands—which are frequent in the book—are made interesting by Pilon's well-reported examples.

She chronicles the fight by Parker Brothers to keep the sport of ping-pong known as Ping-Pong, their brand name, rather than table tennis. In 1933, the United States Table Tennis Association was formed to oversee the sport.

"It's hard to say just how much money Parker Brothers lost after control of the game slipped out of its grasp, meaning it now produced the game alongside a fleet of competitors," writes Pilon.

Alamenciak concludes
by stating his overall
evaluation of the book in
a way that is useful to his
audience.

This is a great book for anyone who likes a good historical read. It moves quickly and provides lots of interesting bits of history, wrapped together in a fascinating package that tells the true story of Monopoly.

REFLECT. *Study a review on a subject that interests you and evaluate it, using the list of characteristic features of reviews on pages 338–39. Annotate the text you have chosen, noting which of the features are included and which are not. For any features you find missing, consider whether including them might have improved the review.*

WRITING A REVIEW / A Roadmap

Choose something to review and find an interesting angle

If you get to choose your topic, pick a subject you're interested in and know something about. Perhaps you're an artist or art lover who is interested in the works of Van Gogh and therefore choose to review the *Immersive Van Gogh* exhibit for your school paper. Or maybe you love mountain biking: you could review three best-selling bikes. Remember that many things can be reviewed—shoes, appliances, restaurants, books, music. Choose a topic you want to learn more about.

If your topic is assigned, try to tailor it to your interests and to find an angle that will engage your audience. For instance, if your assignment is to review a specific art exhibit, see if you can focus on some aspect of the work that intrigues you, such as the use of color or the way the artist represents nature. If you are assigned to review a particular book, try to center your review on themes that you find compelling and that might interest your audience.

Consider your rhetorical situation

Once you have a tentative topic, thinking about your audience and the rest of your rhetorical situation will help you focus on how you can best address it.

Think about what your AUDIENCE knows and expects. If your review is for an assignment, consider your instructor to be your primary audience (unless they specify otherwise) and know what's expected of a review in your discipline. If, however, you're writing for a specific publication or another audience, you'll have to think about what's expected in that situation. Here are some things to consider:

- Who are you trying to reach, and why?
- In what ways are they like or unlike you? Are they likely to agree with you?
- What do they probably know about your subject? What background information will you need to provide?
- Will the subject matter to your audience? If not, how can you persuade them that it matters?
- What will they be expecting to learn from your review? What criteria will they value?

Think about your PURPOSE. Why are you writing this review? If it's for a class, what motivations do you have beyond getting a good grade? To recommend a book or film? evaluate the latest smart device? introduce your classmates to a new musical group? What do you expect your audience to do with the information in your review? Do you want them to go see something? buy something (or not)? just appreciate something? How can you best achieve your purpose?

Consider your STANCE. Think about your overall attitude about the subject and how you want to come across as an author. Are you extremely enthusiastic about your subject? firmly opposed to it? skeptical? lukewarm? How can you communicate your feelings? Think also about how you want your audience to see you as author. As well-informed? thoughtful? witty? How can your review reflect that stance?

Think about the larger CONTEXT. What, if any, background information about your subject should you consider—other books on the same subject or by the same author? movies in the same genre? similar products made by different companies? What else has been said about your subject, and how will you respond to it in your review?

Consider your LANGUAGE. Almost any review can be presented in a number of ways. Regardless of how many languages and dialects you use in your everyday life, you have many options to consider in crafting an analysis. What variety of language or dialect will best suit your audience and help you achieve your goals as a writer? Will your audience expect a certain kind of language or style? Do you want to meet those expectations? challenge them? What do you want your language choices to say about you? What risks might you be willing to take with your language? How will your choice of medium and the larger context limit or expand the language options available to you? See Chapters 4 and 33 for more information about language options.

Consider MEDIA. Whether or not you have a choice of medium—print, spoken, or electronic—you need to think about how your medium will affect what you can do in your review. If you're presenting it online or to a live audience, you may be able to incorporate video and audio clips of a film or a concert. If your review will appear in print, can you include still photos? And most important of all: if you get to choose your medium, which one will best reach your audience?

Consider matters of DESIGN. If you are writing for an academic assignment, be sure to follow the format requirements of the discipline you're writing in. If you're writing for a particular publication, you'll need to find out what design options you have. But if you have the option of designing your text yourself, think about what will help readers understand your message. Should you include illustrations? Are you including any information that would be best presented in a list or a graph? Product reviews, for example, often display data in a table so that readers can compare several products.

Evaluate your subject

Think about your own first impressions. What about the subject got your interest? What was your first reaction, and why? What is the first thing you would tell someone who asked your opinion on this subject?

Examine your subject closely. If you're reviewing a performance, take notes as you're watching it; if you're reviewing a book, read it more than once. Look for parts of your subject that are especially powerful, or weak, or unexpected to mention in your review.

Do any necessary RESEARCH. Your subject will be your primary source of information, though you may need to consult other sources to find background information or to become aware of what else has been written about your subject. Would learning more about a book's author or a film's director help you evaluate your subject? If you're writing an academic review, do you need to find out what else has been said about your subject?

Determine the CRITERIA for your evaluation. Sometimes these are obvious: film reviews, for instance, tend to focus on criteria like acting, directing, script, and so forth. At other times, you'll need to establish the criteria that will guide your review. If you're unsure what criteria are most well suited to your subject, look up reviews others have written on a similar topic. What criteria do those models use effectively?

Make a judgment about your subject. Based on the criteria you've established, evaluate your subject. Remember that few things are all good or all bad; you will likely find some things to praise, and others to criticize. Whatever you decide, use your criteria to examine your subject carefully, and look for specific EVIDENCE you can cite—lines or scenes from a movie, particular features of a product, and so on.

Anticipate other points of view. Not everyone is going to agree with your evaluation, and you need to acknowledge COUNTERARGUMENTS to what you think. Even if you don't persuade everyone in your audience to accept your judgment, you can demonstrate that your opinion is worth taking seriously by acknowledging and responding respectfully to those other perspectives.

Think about your mix of DESCRIPTION or SUMMARY and EVALUATION. You need to describe or summarize your subject enough so that readers will understand it, but remember that your primary goal is to evaluate it. The balance will depend on your purpose. Some reviews are expected to give a simple star rating, or a thumbs-up (or thumbs-down). Others require more complex judgments.

Organize and start writing

Once you've determined your overall evaluation of your subject, compiled a list of its strengths and weaknesses, and assembled EVIDENCE you can draw upon to support that evaluation, it's time to organize your materials and start writing. To organize your review, think about what you want to tell readers about your subject, what your evaluation of it is, and why.

Come up with a tentative THESIS. What major point do you want to make about your subject? Try writing this point out as a tentative thesis. Then think about whether the thesis should be stated explicitly or not. Also consider whether to put the thesis toward the end of your introduction or save it for the conclusion.

DESCRIBE or SUMMARIZE the subject you're reviewing, and provide any background information your audience may need.

Evaluate your subject. Using the CRITERIA you identified for your review, present your subject's strengths and weaknesses, generally in order of importance. Provide REASONS and specific EVIDENCE to back them up. Don't forget to acknowledge other points of view.

Draft an OPENING. Introduce your subject in a way that makes clear what you're reviewing and why your audience should care about it—and shows that you know what you're talking about!

Draft a CONCLUSION. Wrap up your review by summarizing your evaluation. If you have any recommendations, here's where to make them.

Look critically at your draft, get responses—and revise

Once you have a complete draft, read it over carefully, focusing on your evaluation, the reasons and evidence you provide as support, and the way you appeal to your audience. If possible, ask others—a writing center tutor, classmate, or friend—for feedback. Be sure to give your readers a clear sense of your assignment or purpose and your intended audience. Here are some questions that can help you or others respond:

- *Is the evaluation stated explicitly?* Is there a clear THESIS—and if not, is one needed?

- *How well does the introduction capture the audience's interest?* How well does it establish your AUTHORITY as a reviewer? Does it make clear what the review is about? How will it engage your audience's interest? How else might it begin?

- *Is the subject* DESCRIBED *or* SUMMARIZED *sufficiently for your audience?* Is any additional description or background information needed?

- *How much of the review is* DESCRIPTION *and how much is* EVALUATION— and does the balance seem right for the subject and purpose?

- *What are the* CRITERIA *for the evaluation?* Are they stated explicitly— and if not, should they be? Do the criteria seem suitable for the subject and audience? Are there other criteria that should be considered?

- *What good* REASONS *and* EVIDENCE *support the evaluation?* Will your audience be persuaded?

- *What other viewpoints do you consider,* and how well do you respond to these views? Are there other views you should consider?

- *How would you describe the* STANCE *and* TONE *?* Are they authoritative? What words or details create that impression?

- *How is the draft organized?* Is it easy to follow, with clear TRANSITIONS from one point to the next?

- *What about* DESIGN *?* Should any material be set off as a list or chart or table? Are there any illustrations—and if not, should there be?

- *Is the* STYLE —choice of words, kinds of sentences, level of formality— well suited for the intended audience?

- *How does the draft* CONCLUDE *?* Is the conclusion decisive and satisfying? How else might it conclude?

- *Is this a fair review?* Even if readers do not agree with the evaluation, will they consider it fair?

REFLECT. *Once you've completed your review, let it settle for a while and then take time to* REFLECT. *How well did you argue for your evaluation? How persuasive do you think your readers will find your review? Will those who do not agree with your evaluation consider it fair? What additional revisions would you make if you could? Research shows that such reflections help "lock in" what you learn for future use.*

Respect: Aretha's Music Carries This Biopic

K. AUSTIN COLLINS

I CAN'T SAY I ENVY the task of trying to bring Aretha Franklin—one of the most enduring artists of the 20th century (and beyond), with a voice so singular that most other singers have been wise enough to spare her the flattery of genuine imitation—to the big screen. And for the Queen of Soul herself to have picked Jennifer Hudson to play the part must, for Hudson, have been a daunting honor, second only to being asked to sing a tribute to Franklin at the icon's 2018 funeral.

Respect, in which Hudson stars, doesn't—*can't*—entirely do justice to such a vast talent, not least because Franklin's life had an equally vast historical reach. This is a woman whose life and upbringing didn't merely touch on the issues of her era; she was born of them, tied to them. Her father, C. L. Franklin, was a renowned pastor and civil rights leader whose home saw guests as estimable as the major Black recording artists of the moment, like Dinah Washington and Sam Cooke (or "Aunt" Dinah and "Uncle" Sam, as a young Aretha calls them in the movie), and whose civil rights activism would encourage a friendship with

---

K. AUSTIN COLLINS is a film critic who has reviewed films for *Rolling Stone, Vanity Fair,* the *Ringer,* and the *Los Angeles Review of Books.* He is also a crossword contributor for the *New York Times* and the *New Yorker.* His review of *Respect* appeared in *Rolling Stone* in 2021.

Martin Luther King Jr. himself, with whom Aretha—armed with that legendary voice—toured and fundraised on behalf of the movement.

Add to that the other particulars—the death of Franklin's mother when she was 10; childhood sexual abuse that would, as some of the movie's clumsier but well-meant moments imply, haunt her for the rest of her life; battles with alcoholism, domestic abuse, and the less-tragic (but no less stultifying) rule of her father—and what you have is, well, the stuff from which biopics are made.

What other films of this kind *don't* have, not even when they're about legends as incomparable as the incomparable Ray Charles, is music that rips through the spirit quite as thoroughly as Aretha's. It doesn't necessarily go without saying that many of the best scenes in *Respect* are those focused on the queen's music; the movie could easily have botched the job, in that regard. But director Liesl Tommy and writer Tracey Scott Wilson have—with the further input of Hudson, who as executive producer had the authority to make sure the "right songs" were in the film and that they were largely performed in full—given us a generous sampling of Franklin's music, less in terms of the number of songs than in terms of the production's attentive efforts to capture their power.

Though the movie's already been accused of being a cookie-cutter biopic, 5 the power of those songs is hardly mitigated by the film's fairly straightforward approach. *Respect* chronicles Franklin's life and career from her Detroit childhood, in which the young prodigy was dragged out of bed on Saturday nights to sing for her father's famous guests, to her recording of the timeless 1972 gospel album *Amazing Grace*: Franklin's career-bestselling work and, as the movie frames it, a return to the singer's church roots that, after a low period in her life, nearly saved her. Musically, this means that the movie covers Franklin's middling Columbia Records years and her megastar Atlantic years under Jerry Wexler, with a due nod to her first contract at Detroit's J.V.B. Records. Personally, it means we get a story that is by and large anchored in Franklin's struggles against the control of the men in her life, namely her first two managers: her father, played by Forest Whitaker, and her first husband, Ted White (Marlon Wayans).

Under the thumb of her father, Franklin (who's played, as a child, by Skye Dakota Turner) grows into a woman whose meek politeness is hard to square with the powerhouse we know the artist to be—which, it seems, is the point. After the death of her mother (played, too briefly, by Audra McDonald) and a pair of barely-teen pregnancies that the queen herself was not eager to discuss publicly (but which the film pointedly traces back to that childhood abuse), young Aretha practically goes silent. It's a move that allows the film to begin tracing the arc of the demons that would later overcome her, from which she would, with *Amazing Grace*, save herself. But it also gives the power of Franklin's voice a peculiar dramatic charge that races through the length of the film.

Before her death, Franklin's mother reminds her that her father does not own her voice; later, as he's showing her off in the offices of Columbia Records's John Hammond (Tate Donovan), it would appear that the Reverend Franklin hasn't gotten this memo. It's the way young Aretha is pulled out of her silence, not entirely of her own will, that's striking. She doesn't, in these early moments, sing because she wants to; she sings because she's told to—and she happens to not only love it but also be a genius at it. . . .

But she does, indeed, get bigger, and bolder, and the lack of self-assurance she displays early on—the forward, upfront star power that Hudson has to surgically subtract from her own persona, as if with a scalpel, in order to play a queen who doesn't yet realize that she is one—eventually morphs, for a time,

Jennifer Hudson performing as Aretha Franklin in *Respect*.

into the powerhouse personality we associate with her hits from the era, the Aretha who spelled out, letter by letter, what she demanded of the rest of us. Then comes the other Aretha—the monster with her demons, her distaste for rivals, her eventual hollowing out to the point of needing a reckoning. But this last phase is curtailed, usefully and not. By the time it arrives, so much has already happened—the movie's runtime approaches two and half hours—that you can see why the story caps itself off triumphantly, with a hint of the lurking difficulties (and, by many accounts, difficult-*ness*) that would come in the proceeding half-century.

This stuff all makes for good enough, watchable drama. But *Respect* is never better—Hudson is never better—than when the movie sets aside the bullet points to delve into the talent, on the one hand, with some meager but fruitful drips of Franklin's politics, on the other. The scene in Muscle Shoals, with her backing band full of white Alabamians who by all indications, being good Southern boys, have little interest in collaboration at first, is one of the best things in the movie. . . . The scene is a jam session. Plotwise, the narrative bullet point at stake—that this collaboration would prove to be, as Aretha herself said in the Muscle Shoals documentary from 2013, a turning point in the legend's career—is a straightforward high point among biopics' usual highs.

But the chemistry is something else: watching these expert talents build 10 their way toward something, working their way through a rendition that's onto something, but too close to outright gospel at first, then gradually finding a groove and, with it, mutual respect. We get a healthy dose of the sense of Franklin and the gang's *process*, of the ways they worked as artists—the kind of insight that films about artists curiously tend to shortchange.

That song, by the way, though nearly unrecognizable at first, blooms into what we know to be Franklin's brilliant, funky stroll of a first hit: "I Never Loved a Man (The Way I Love You)." And the scene of its recording is matched, if not outdone, by a similar scene in which Franklin and her sisters, Erma (Saycon Sengbloh) and Carolyn (Hailey Kilgore), the latter of whom wrote the song, work—Muscle Shoals boys in tow—toward a timeless rendition of "Ain't No Way." Both of these scenes, which are well-directed and edited to give us the right reaction shots at the right time to infuse them with just the right amount of subtext, are as much about Franklin wresting control over her path through her music as they are about obstructions in the way of that path—namely, Ted. The cut to Ted's face when Aretha belts out "Stop trying to be someone you're not," nearly ascending in her seat as she grows with the song, says more than a dramatization of that idea could say, by a long shot. It's the fact that she feels the line so hard that everyone, including Ted, cannot help but notice.

Of course, any scene in which Franklin sings further doubles as a chance for the Oscar-winning Hudson to prove herself worthy of the role. Dramatically, the movie doesn't always know what to do with her, even as the arc it traces for Franklin as a character is very clear. But in scenes like these (another standout: Aretha and her sisters jamming their way, at 3 a.m., toward that stunning rendition of Otis Redding's—but, really, Aretha's—"Respect"), Hudson, who sang live on set and is not lip-syncing to a prerecorded track, does her best acting. This isn't new news; Hudson has often proven herself more a natural actor while performing a song than in the more turgid dramatic scenes she's sometimes had to muscle her way through. This, too, is a benefit of how generous *Respect* is with Franklin's music, even as it doesn't offer a deep dive into her catalog, and even as the songs that do appear here feel overly tied to the arc of the plot. It isn't that she sounds like Aretha when she sings, or that she's even trying to pull off a plain imitation. It's that, while finding ways to approach Aretha's sound while tamping down some of her own, different style, she digs to the root of the songs, their feelings, in ways that tell us what the movie— what the songs—are all really about.

No wonder, then, that the film ends with *Amazing Grace*, that unmatched set of live January sessions at L.A.'s Missionary Baptist Church, under the choral direction of Reverend James Cleveland (a great Tituss Burgess), whose Southern California Community Choir is no mere crew of backup musicians. "Amazing Grace," itself, is given all the holy aura the song and Hudson's performance deserve. The path there is a little long, and not always as exciting or dangerously complex as the film's subject. And some of the hints dropped along the way, about Franklin's political life—her admiration for Angela Davis, for example, and the ideological rift at stake in disagreeing with her nonviolence and MLK-worshipping father—entice us with avenues of inquiry into the Queen of Soul that are well worth exploring, more so than some of what's here. But the movie, which has been released a few days short of the second anniversary of Franklin's death, is a solid vessel for Franklin's music, why it still moves us, why—even hearing renditions in the movie—her accomplishments as an artist remain jaw-dropping. As for Franklin herself, the best we can say is that she's a little fuller, a little less mysterious, than she was at the start of the movie. Her music blows the movie out of the water—and the movie, at its best, is wise to let itself get blown away.

Thinking about the Text

1. Write a one-paragraph SUMMARY of K. Austin Collins's review. Be sure to identify his criteria for evaluation and the extent to which he claims the movie did or did not satisfy them.

2. In the OPENING of his review, Collins previews his stance and approach. What expectations does Collins establish in the first two paragraphs? How do those paragraphs contribute to Collins's authoritative TONE ?

3. How does Collins establish his CREDIBILITY as a reviewer? Point to specific rhetorical choices Collins makes that suggest readers should trust his judgment. Are there rhetorical choices that Collins makes that take away from his credibility?

4. Collins's review is not all positive; he offers some criticism of this biopic. What EVIDENCE does Collins provide for the elements of the film he argues could be stronger? Do you see Collins as an ethical reviewer? Why or why not?

5. Collins alludes, in this review, to the challenge of making a film about an icon like Aretha Franklin. Identify a film (biopic, documentary, or docudrama) or book about a real-life iconic figure that you find compelling. After reading the book or viewing the film, write a REVIEW of it. Identify the evaluative CRITERIA that you will use to guide your review. Be sure to use specific EVIDENCE, as Collins does, to support your claims. Think about how you will establish your AUTHORITY and CREDIBILITY. Consider what kind of information your AUDIENCE will need.

Indie Gem *Please Knock on My Door* Expertly Captures Mental Illness

MANISHA UMMADI

FOR SOMEONE WHO NEVER personally experienced the crippling effects of mental illness, the idea of climbing into the complex mind of an afflicted individual may seem like a daunting experience. But as Swedish indie developer Michael Levall proves through his new story-driven, top-down adventure game *Please Knock on My Door*, investigating depression and anxiety at a personal level may be the key to understanding the inner mechanisms of our own minds.

Built around Levall's own experiences with depression, *Please Knock on My Door* gives the player control over the daily life of an individual navigating depression and social anxiety—the player takes on the responsibility of getting the unnamed protagonist through the routine of eating, working, sleeping, and tending to his other needs as he progresses through the workweek. Yet what begins as an inconsequential life simulator quickly escalates to an emotionally grueling daily battle against both time and the darker voices in the protagonist's head.

Please Knock on My Door features a thoughtfully minimalistic art style reminiscent of an old-school, two-dimensional, top-down game—even the game's protagonist is depicted as a simple Minecraft-esque being, devoid of any detail except for his expressive eyes. Yet the game uses extensive narration and written

---

MANISHA UMMADI is an infectious disease research specialist at the University of California, San Francisco, where she studies coronaviruses. As an undergraduate, she wrote for the student-run *Daily Californian*, where this review appeared in 2017.

text in the form of text boxes and journal entries to construct a thorough narrative that delves into the deep roots of the protagonist's most vulnerable feelings.

Consistent with its art style, most of the game takes place in the protagonist's darkened apartment. . . . Throughout the game, the player is also led to make decisions that determine the protagonist's interpersonal relationships and job performance each workday.

But embedded in these deceivingly simple daily interactions is a robust system 5 of rewards and consequences that factors the player's every decision into the protagonist's mental well-being and physical health—making the decision to forsake sleep or work in order to appease the protagonist's all-encompassing thoughts affect his emotional engagement and the end result of his journey.

As the game progresses and the protagonist increasingly falls victim to his own headspace, completing even the simplest sequence of tasks within the limited time frame each day becomes a near-impossible challenge. Learning from the player's decisions, the game attempts to push and pull the protagonist against the will of the player, leaving the player to painfully fight the game itself to just survive through each increasingly difficult day.

Yet despite the inevitably heavy subject matter that *Please Knock on My Door* tackles, the game manages to approach mental illness with a sense of realistic optimism—for every isolating interaction the protagonist experiences within his own headspace, the game presents a support system in the form of friends and coworkers, each with a particular personality, that reminds both the protagonist and the player that healing is as much an aspect of mental illness as the symptoms themselves. In fact, Levall adds an utterly human dimension to the gameplay by using the game's unique endings to explore the direct effects of reaching out and seeking help in the face of even the most debilitating mental challenges.

. . . *Please Knock on My Door* uses its quirky gameplay to masterfully radiate an unwavering sense of authenticity. . . . The game's basis in Levall's own struggle with depression undoubtedly feeds into its hauntingly realistic nature, developing the game itself into an extremely personal journey of varying interpretation depending on the player. Indeed, no two playthroughs of the game are remotely identical to one another, adding to the game's replay value.

As the protagonist perpetually struggles through the symptoms of depression and anxiety that cloud his days, the player cannot help but reciprocate his raw feelings of helplessness and frailty. Placing the player in the darkest corner of the protagonist's mind, *Please Knock on My Door* manages to do the unthinkable and force the player into not just observing but experiencing the indescribable effects of mental illness. Through every aspect of the game,

Levall showcases his prowess as an interactive storyteller, affirming that video games as a genre can be used to tell rich stories that carry emotional weight, rather than being confined to a series of mind-numbing shooters. *Please Knock on My Door* undeniably cements itself as an indie gem bent on changing the way in which narratives are delivered to the player, making the experience of interacting with a game a highly personal matter.

 . . . The game undoubtedly bestows a level of profound insight upon all— 10 some may experience a mind-shattering introspective epiphany by the end of the game, some may not—but at the very least, the player will walk away with a more nuanced understanding of mental illness.

Thinking about the Text

1. How does Manisha Ummadi establish her **AUTHORITY** and credibility as a reviewer? How does her **INTRODUCTION**, for instance, contribute to her credibility? How would you describe her **TONE**? Point to specific words and passages that contribute to that tone.

2. What is Ummadi's **EVALUATION** of this video game, and what evidence does she offer in support of her views? How persuasive do you find her evaluation? What **CRITERIA** do Ummadi use as a basis for her evaluation? How does she make these criteria clear? Point out specific passages from the text that support your response.

3. Mental illness is an unusual subject for a video game to address, and it poses challenges for those reviewing the video game as well. What strikes you as particularly helpful and relevant in Ummadi's comments on mental illness in the review? How does Ummadi work to build her **AUDIENCE**'s interest on this topic?

4. Imagine that you, like Ummadi, wanted to tell your classmates about a book, performance, game, podcast, or artist that you like—or don't like—in a piece that will be published in your campus newspaper. Write a **REVIEW** to persuade other students to check it out—or not. Take care to introduce your subject, establish criteria for your evaluation, and show evidence from the subject to support what you say.

EIGHTEEN

"Here's What I Recommend"

Making a Proposal

 ILL YOU MARRY ME? There is no clearer proposal than the one this question represents. It proposes something that at least one person thinks ought to occur. Proposals are just that: recommendations that something be done, often to bring about some kind of change or to solve a problem. You'll likely have occasion to write proposals for various purposes; and if you're reading this chapter now, you've probably been assigned to write one for a composition class.

You might propose better financial aid options, a more efficient way of recycling, a possible solution to housing insecurity among students. Like a marriage proposal, each suggests change; unlike a marriage proposal, however, each of these cases addresses a problem and calls for careful analysis of several possible courses of action. While it may be obvious to your beloved that you are the one, it's less obvious how a more flexible borrowing plan can ease the burden of student debt, how to motivate people to recycle, or how to respond to a problem as complex as housing insecurity. Proposals of this kind argue for clear solutions to specific problems; and as with any argument, they build a convincing case that what they recommend should be considered—and even acted on.

This chapter provides guidelines for writing proposals that will be taken seriously, ones that say, "Here's what I recommend—and why you should take my advice."

REFLECT. Proposals are part of daily life, but some are more compelling than others. Find a proposal that interests you, perhaps an op-ed on a social issue such as gun rights or free speech or a GoFundMe *campaign. How does the proposal convince—or fail to convince—you that it's important and that the recommended solution is worth your support?*

Across Academic Disciplines

When you're assigned to write a research paper, chances are your instructor will ask you to present a proposal before you begin researching and drafting the paper. Such proposals ensure that your topic and plan of action are suitable for the assignment. You'll likely have occasion to write these and other kinds of proposals in many courses. For an engineering course, you may be asked to create a new product, explaining the need it fills and how it'll work. In a public policy course, you might work with a group to analyze a specific policy—perhaps your city's policy of providing incentives to encourage the use of solar power—and to propose changes. In each case, you'll need to think about what's expected, given the topic and the discipline.

Across Media

Authors of proposals often use multiple media to present their recommendations. Crowdfunding sites like *Kickstarter* may use video to show their projects in action or bring audiences face-to-face with their cause. Op-ed columnists writing for newspapers rely on carefully crafted words to make their points, but online versions of the papers include links to supporting materials. If you're presenting a proposal as a part of an oral presentation, slides can help illustrate what you're recommending—and you may be asked to provide a print document to elaborate on what you propose.

Across Cultures and Communities

Proposals of various sorts are common in the United States. At your school, for example, students might band together to propose more effective campus policies to prevent sexual assault. In business, many companies encourage employees at all levels to share ideas for improving the company's products or services. And in many states, voters can propose a ballot initiative to change existing laws.

↪ CROWDFUNDING SITES *are filled with proposals. Take a look at the proposal that former flight attendant Robin Wearly created on Kickstarter for a disabled passenger transfer sling (ADAPTS) that permits air travelers who use wheelchairs to get off the plane quickly and safely in case of evacuation. It states a problem and proposes a solution. Go to* everyonesanauthor.tumblr.com *to see the full proposal. Note how the campaign page uses written text, images, and videos. Imagine how Wearly might present this proposal in a meeting with potential investors. What information would be best presented as speech, on slides, as an embedded video, or in a handout? What additional information might investors want that the website does not contain?*

Proposals are common in cultures and industries that thrive on open discussion and innovation, but not every community is receptive to input from just anyone. Many governments, organizations, and households around the world value the judgment of authorities and community leaders, and proposals from others may be seen as disrespectful. So be aware of the context you're writing in and the audience you are speaking to, not just to avoid offending someone but also to determine how to present your ideas so they'll have the greatest chance of succeeding.

Across Genres

Proposals occur in many kinds of writing. REVIEWS sometimes end with proposals for how something could be improved, and many REPORTS, especially those on pressing social issues, conclude by proposing a course of action to address the issue.

A fully developed proposal is based on a detailed **ANALYSIS** of a problem or situation. It requires **REPORTING** trustworthy information, and often involves **NARRATING** one or more past events as part of that reporting.

REFLECT. Find two proposals that address the same issue, perhaps one students are currently debating on your campus. How does each proposal define the issue, what solutions does each of them offer, and what evidence does each provide to show that its solutions will work? Which of the two proposals do you find more persuasive, and why?

CHARACTERISTIC FEATURES

Although there will be variation depending on the topic, you'll find that nearly all strong proposals share the following characteristics:

- A precise description of the problem (p. 373)
- A clear and compelling solution to the problem (p. 375)
- Evidence that your solution will address the problem (p. 377)
- Acknowledgment of other possible solutions (p. 378)
- A statement of what your proposal will accomplish (p. 380)

A Precise Description of the Problem

The goal of all proposals is to offer a solution for some problem, so most of them begin by explicitly stating the problem and establishing that it is serious enough that it needs a solution. Some problems are obvious—that there's a water shortage in California, for instance, or your campus needs more resources to support mental health—so you won't have to say much to convince your audience that they matter. In other cases, though, you'll need to describe the problem in detail and provide data, examples, and other evidence to convince readers that it's serious enough to require a solution.

For example, see how Grace DeLallo, writing for the University of Pittsburgh's daily student newspaper, the *Pitt News*, begins her proposal by clearly describing a problem familiar to many of the paper's readers:

Congress estimated in a 2017 report that the global fashion industry is worth a whopping $2.5 trillion, with Americans spending $380 billion to the market that year alone. . . . But money doesn't seem to be the only thing driving the fashion industry. Inclusive sizing and affordable pricing would improve clothing brands' reach and, most likely, their profits. Yet, for most brands, these seem secondary to deep-seated disdain for fat people and the poor.

One size does not fit all, and it never will. Genetics, diet, ethnicity, and cultural norms all shape how our bodies look and grow. The assortment of people's shapes and sizes should illustrate our sublime diversity, but instead often prompts critical speculation on who is worthy of having quality clothing that fits.

The fashion industry has cultivated an image of what this deserving man or woman should look like—non-binary and genderfluid folks aren't even a consideration most of the time. . . . The average American woman wears between a size 16 and 18, but the "ideal woman" is only meant to comfortably fit within the constraints of a size zero. . . . I've cried over the cookie cutter shapes not fitting my physique. It distorted how I viewed my body and made me feel uncomfortable in my own skin whenever my growing body gained weight—an anguish millions of women experience.

The same stores that sell single-cut items are also the ones that don't sell sizes large enough for average people to fit into. Even when they do sell the sizes, the clothes are ill-fitting and unflattering. This perpetuates the feeling that midsized and large bodies aren't supposed to be fashionable.

—GRACE DeLALLO, "The Fashion Industry Hates Fat People and the
Lower Class More Than It Loves Money"

In the opening paragraphs of her proposal, DeLallo provides a statistic demonstrating the significance and reach of the fashion industry and then offers examples that will resonate with readers' experiences, thereby establishing why this serious problem needs a solution.

Robin Wearly, author of the *Kickstarter* proposal illustrated on page 372, begins her proposal by stating the problem in terms that appeal to readers' emotions and logic in a culture that values individual responsibility and thinking ahead: "Emergencies happen. What if you or a loved one rely on a wheelchair? What's the plan?" She then provides a series of brief but vivid scenarios that confront readers with the reality of the problem:

Wheelchairs are checked in cargo on airplanes. Elevators are shut down in hotel emergencies. So did you ever wonder how wheelchair travelers escape a burning airplane, a derailed train, a bus accident, a cruise ship disaster, or hotel room when told to evacuate? What if they can't wait for rescue personnel and their only hope is the crew or kindness of strangers? What if you have less than 90 seconds to make it to an emergency exit? Will a trapped person leave both your lives in peril? Here's how ADAPTS comes to the rescue!

—ROBIN WEARLY, "ADAPTS, the First Evacuation Sling for Wheelchair Users"

These descriptions remind readers, especially able-bodied ones, of things that can go wrong and the consequences of such situations for wheelchair users. These high-stakes scenarios define the problem that the proposal will then address.

In any proposal, it's important to identify the problem clearly and in a way that sets up the solution you'll be recommending. Defining the problem precisely can also help make your solution realistic: preventing emergencies that endanger individuals with various mobility impairments is a tall order, while creating a tool that helps people with physical disabilities get to safety more easily in an emergency seems doable.

A Clear and Compelling Solution to the Problem

Successful proposals offer a compelling solution to the problem at hand. That is, it isn't sufficient merely to have a good idea; in a proposal, you'll have to convince readers that your idea squarely addresses the problem as you've defined it.

You'll want to explain the solution succinctly but in enough detail to make a clear and confident case for it. See how the Interdisciplinary Group on Preventing School and Community Violence offers a research-based proposal to respond to gun violence in schools and communities. While acknowledging the need for security measures—a common response to such acts of violence—the group proposes a more focused solution: "a change in mindset and policy," that is, focusing on preventing such events in the first place. They frame the issue as a public health problem and detail specific steps to achieve the needed shift in mind-set and policy:

> A public health approach to protecting children as well as adults from gun violence involves three levels of prevention: (1) universal approaches promoting safety and well-being for everyone; (2) practices for reducing

Check out the simple and concise solutions that Huma Farid proposes for making menstrual products more accessible and affordable. Find her proposal on p. 887.

risk and promoting protective factors for persons experiencing difficulties; and (3) interventions for individuals where violence is present or appears imminent.

—INTERDISCIPLINARY GROUP ON PREVENTING SCHOOL AND
COMMUNITY VIOLENCE, "Call to Action to Prevent Gun Violence"

In the paragraphs that follow, the group then explains what each level of prevention would require of various stakeholders—from Congress and social service agencies to students and parents. The number and detail of the proposed actions along with logical appeals make a strong and clear case why, if the country carried out these actions, gun violence in schools and communities would be greatly reduced.

Now consider a proposal for a policy that would provide more affordable housing in Portland, Oregon, from an article by a member of that city's city council written for *Street Roots*, a weekly newspaper often sold by people who are experiencing homelessness:

> We can't require developers to build affordable housing; state law prevents it. But we can encourage those who want to build here to be part of the solution. . . . The city currently provides "density bonuses" to developers for including certain public benefits in their projects—meaning they can build taller buildings or get more floor space than would normally be allowed in exchange for including features like eco-roofs or bicycle parking.
>
> Now is the time to restructure our density bonus regulations to prioritize affordable housing development. . . .
>
> Under a proposal that will go before the council on July 9, developers seeking a density bonus must either provide affordable housing within their development or pay a fee into a fund for the creation and preservation of affordable housing. This proposal . . . would require them to contribute to the creation of affordable housing in order to receive the maximum density that our zoning currently allows.
>
> —DAN SALTZMAN, "Incentive for Developers
> Would Spur Affordable Housing"

Saltzman's proposal describes a solution that addresses the problem clearly: to build the largest permissible buildings (and hence make more money), developers will have to include affordable units in the development *or* contribute to a fund for creating affordable housing. In return for something a developer wants, the city gets something it wants: more affordable housing.

Evidence That Your Solution Will Address the Problem

A proposal is convincing when the evidence it provides shows that the solution being proposed will, in fact, address the problem. The kind of evidence that will be convincing will vary depending on what it is you're proposing and to whom. If you're pitching a new business venture to potential investors, your evidence would include numbers showing the projected returns on investment. If you're proposing a new honor code at your school, your evidence would likely include testimonies and examples of how it would improve the learning environment. In his article on the Portland affordable housing proposal, Dan Saltzman provides data projecting what the proposal could accomplish:

> This "affordable housing incentive zoning proposal" could result in as many as 60 additional units of affordable housing a year on top of those already being developed by the city, or it could mean an additional $120 million to $200 million in funds for affordable housing over the next 20 years.
>
> This proposal alone will not solve our affordable-housing crisis but is a critical step to ensuring more affordable housing in our city.

By acknowledging that this proposal will not totally solve the problem of affordable housing but demonstrating its potential benefits—more affordable housing or funds to create such housing—Saltzman limits his solution to one that Portland will be able to address at the time, thus making a persuasive case that what he is suggesting is feasible.

Another example comes from Appleton, Wisconsin, a city facing the challenge of redesigning its streets and transit systems to accommodate pedestrians and bicyclists. In an eighty-page proposal laying out a twenty-year plan to improve such access, the city's designers offer plenty of evidence to support their ideas: diagrams showing how specific roads will be reconfigured to include bike lanes, charts of costs and funding sources, and a timetable for completing the project over the twenty-year construction period. Some of this evidence illustrates that the proposed changes will achieve the city's goal; other evidence shows that they will do so in a feasible manner.

Acknowledgment of Other Possible Solutions

English has a pronoun problem, according to Dennis Baron. See how he calmly explains all of the proposed solutions (including the status quo) before arguing for his preferred course of action on p. 844.

Part of crafting a persuasive proposal is making it clear that your solution is the best course of action—and hence better than other options. To do so, you need to account for other possible solutions and demonstrate the comparative advantages of the solution you're suggesting.

In his article proposing that junk food has the best potential to end obesity, David Freedman describes in detail what those in the "wholesome food" camp suggest—and then points out why what they advocate is not so good after all. Here he visits his local Whole Foods store, where he finds many "wholesome" items:

> One that catches my eye . . . is Vegan Cheesy Salad Booster . . . whose package emphasizes the fact that it is enhanced with spirulina, chlorella, and sea vegetables. The label also proudly lets me know that the contents are raw—no processing!—and that they don't contain any genetically modified ingredients. What it does contain, though, is more than three times the fat content per ounce as the beef patty in a Big Mac . . . and four times the sodium.
>
> —DAVID FREEDMAN, "How Junk Food Can End Obesity"

Later in his article, he does acknowledge that some of the arguments on behalf of "wholesome food" are accurate:

> For the purpose of this article, let's simply stipulate that wholesome foods are environmentally superior. But let's also agree that when it comes to prioritizing among food-related public-policy goals, we are likely to save and improve many more lives by focusing on cutting obesity—through any available means—than by trying to convert all of industrialized agriculture into . . . small organic farms.

Notice that in each case Freedman first describes something others have proposed (or might propose)—and then points out its shortcomings.

Other situations call for proposals that consider several possible solutions at the same time, as in the case of the one for creating bicycle and pedestrian access in Appleton, Wisconsin. Because there's no one-size-fits-all solution that will work for every street in the city, the authors of this proposal suggest several possible configurations, including those shown in Figures 18.a and 18.b.

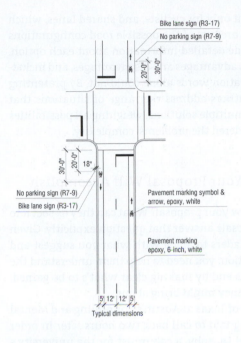

Bike lane sign (R3-17)
No parking sign (R7-9)
20'-0"
30'-0"

30'-0"
20'-0"
18"
No parking sign (R7-9)
Bike lane sign (R3-17)

Pavement marking symbol &
arrow, epoxy, white

Pavement marking
epoxy, 6-inch, white

5' 12' 12' 5'
Typical dimensions

Fig. 18.a BIKE LANE

Description/Purpose: Marked space along length of roadway for exclusive use of cyclists. Bike lanes create separation between cyclists and automobiles.

Advantages

- Provides bicycle access on major through streets
- Clarifies lane use for motorists and cyclists
- Increases cyclists' comfort through visual separation

Disadvantages

- Space requirements may preclude other possible uses like parking or excess travel lane width

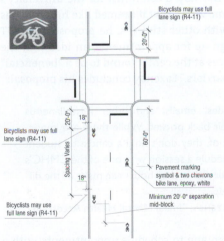

Bicyclists may use full
lane sign (R4-11)
20'-0"

Bicyclists may use full
lane sign (R4-11)
20'-0"
18"
60'-0"
Spacing Varies
18"
Pavement marking
symbol & two chevrons
bike lane, epoxy, white
Minimum 20'-0" separation
mid-block
Bicyclists may use
full lane sign (R4-11)

Fig. 18.b SHARED LANE

Description/Purpose: Shared roadway pavement markings, or "sharrows," are markings used to indicate a shared lane environment for bicycles and automobiles. Sharrows identify to all road users where bicycles should operate on a street where a separated facility is not feasible.

Advantages

- Helps cyclists position themselves in lanes too narrow for a motor vehicle and a bicycle to travel side by side
- Provides pavement markings where bike lanes are not possible

Disadvantages

- Maintenance requirements
- Not as effective as a separated bicycle facility

—WISCONSIN DEPARTMENT OF TRANSPORTATION, *City of Appleton On-Street Bike Plan*

Bike lanes, which are meant only for cyclists, and shared lanes, which are shared by bicycles and cars, are two of the possible road configurations the authors explore. They provide detailed information about each option, describing its purpose, listing its advantages and disadvantages, and including visuals that provide information words alone could not. By presenting multiple design options, the authors address the range of situations that exist. In situations that call for multiple solutions, weighing all possibilities shows that you have fully considered the problems' complexity.

A Statement of What Your Proposal Will Accomplish

So what if readers decide to follow your proposal? What can they expect it to accomplish? The strongest proposals answer that question explicitly. Given that your goal is to persuade readers to agree with what you suggest and perhaps to take some kind of action, you need to help them understand the likely outcomes. Many proposals end by making clear what's to be gained, what outcomes large and small they might bring about.

After calling the University of Texas at Austin's Counseling and Mental Health Center (CMHC) and being told to call back two hours later in order to speak with someone, Michael Lazenby, a columnist for the university's student newspaper, the *Daily Texan*, wrote that it seemed like his problems "didn't matter." After speaking with other students, he proposed that UT create an app where students sign up for appointments, an idea that the associate director of clinical services at the center found to be a "beneficial" and "feasible" way to "reduce . . . barriers." Lazenby concludes his proposal:

> Students have access to grades, emails, and other miscellaneous announcements from UT in their back pocket. While these are important for students to keep track of, they don't hold a candle to student mental health. Being able to schedule a session with one of the CMHC's counselors in a matter of seconds rather than hours can make all the difference for a student seeking help.
>
> —MICHAEL LAZENBY, "Make Mental Health Accessible"

By comparing the usefulness of an app to schedule appointments with a counselor to other online campus communications that, in a time of crisis, are far less important, Lazenby makes clear what his proposal will accomplish in a compelling and persuasive way.

EMILY BURACK works as deputy managing editor at *Alma*, a Jewish culture publication online. Her writing about sports, culture, and books has been published in *Teen Vogue*, *Marie Claire*, and on *Alma*'s website. Burack wrote this piece for *Teen Vogue* in 2021. Visit everyonesanauthor.tumblr.com to access the links (underscored here) as you read.

The Olympics Devastate Host Cities and Need a Permanent Location

EMILY BURACK

THE OLYMPICS ARE BROKEN. Nowhere is this clearer than in Tokyo, where polls have indicated more than 80% of Japanese citizens oppose the [2020] Summer Games and the Japanese government has declared a state of emergency [due to COVID-19]. There's never been an Olympics so deeply unpopular with a host city—and so dangerous to hold—and yet by all indications, the Tokyo Games will go on as scheduled.

A direct statement of the problem, with statistical evidence in support of canceling the Olympics.

Even without a pandemic, the impact of the Olympics on host cities has become too devastating to ignore.

A broader argument for why the problem matters, which the following paragraphs support with data.

It's hard not to feel the hype during an Olympics. Held every two years since 1992, it's an absorbing competitive spectacle featuring the world's best athletes. Plus, female athletes, disabled athletes, and athletes from sports who typically don't get media coverage are given a well-deserved and long overdue turn in the spotlight.

Acknowledges a stance that runs counter to the big problem.

"The Olympics are very popular, as long as they're not happening in your city," political scientist Jules Boykoff, who has written extensively on the Olympics, explains to *Teen Vogue*. "While the

Quoting an expert reinforces the author's claim.

Olympics tend to bring out the very best in athletes, they also tend to bring out the very worst in host cities."

In host cities, the games have displaced residents, sped up 5 gentrification, and increased policing and the militarization of the public sphere. Before the 2008 Beijing Olympics, 1.5 million Chinese residents were evicted from their homes. In preparation for Rio 2016, countless neighborhoods were destroyed—an estimated 60,000 Brazilians lost their homes—to make way for Olympics infrastructure. Ahead of the Tokyo Games this summer, some residents of the Kasumigaoka apartment complex in Tokyo were evicted to make way for the main stadium. Communities across the city saw "severe gentrification," according to Ayako Yoshida, a member of Hangorin No Kai, the Japanese anti-Olympics activist organization. "Under the banner of so-called neighborhood 'redevelopment,' we witnessed private corporations kick people out of their homes and transform neighborhoods for their own profit," she told *Teen Vogue*.

Examples give a precise description of the problem, and explain why it matters.

Seven years out from the 2028 Games in Los Angeles, the local community is already seeing this pattern of displacement and gentrification. "For the Olympics, [what's] going to drive people to be displaced out of rent-stabilized housing is the construction of new hotels, which are being built in now-gentrifying neighborhoods around Olympic sites in downtown and South L.A., which are predominantly communities of color," NOlympics L.A. organizer Gia Lappe, tells *Teen Vogue*. Lappe points to the Ellis Act, a loophole in state law, that allows landlords of affordable housing to evict tenants if the landlord is planning to "change the use" of the building, i.e., make that property a hotel. She speculated that displacement, like the recent clearing of a homeless community in Echo Park Lake, is happening now in preparation for the Games.

Cites an opposing perspective, one that argues there's no problem at all.

When reached for comment, the International Olympic Committee (IOC) told *Teen Vogue* that their sustainability efforts include only building new sports venues in host cities that don't have them. "If a host does not need a new permanent sports venue, its leaders will not be asked to build one," they said. "This has significantly reduced the costs of organizing the Games while

ensuring their fundamental values of universality and diversity."
When asked about the redevelopment ahead of Tokyo and Los
Angeles Games, specifically, they referred *Teen Vogue* to the local
city organizing committees, stating, "LA28 games are a no-build
Games with a master plan specifically designed to use the city's
existing sports venues. There's no connection to Echo Park."

Yet, every two years in cities all across the world, poor communities seem to pay the price of hosting the Olympic Games. As Yoshida
explained, "The sacrifice will be burdened by everyday people, who
are often poor or in the most vulnerable position in society."

A clear solution to the disastrous impact of the Games is a
permanent location. On an emotional level, athletes may not care
where the Olympic Games are held—they simply want to compete in the Olympics. And there could be something meaningful
about competing in the same spot where champions played years
before.

It makes sense economically too as the Games have evolved   10
into a money-losing endeavor for host cities. Economist Victor
A. Matheson told *Teen Vogue* that "no possible understanding of
the benefits could possibly cover the cost of a typical Olympic
Games these days." In a study published in 2016, Matheson and
coauthor Robert A. Baade found that hosting the Olympics is not
economically viable for most cities. Indeed, the Tokyo Olympics,
which originally anticipated would cost about $7 billion in 2013,
was on track in 2018 to cost upwards of $30 billion, according to
the *Washington Post*—and that was prior to COVID. "This was
at least a $25 billion debacle, even before COVID added to the
problems," Matheson said. There will be a significant one-time
investment with a permanent location as the necessary athletic
infrastructure is constructed and then continued upkeep cost,
which would be much lower, he explained.

Even if the Olympics doesn't find one permanent home, rotating
between a few locations would still be a more sensible alternative.
A study published last month in the journal *Nature Sustainability*
proposed a few options to improve the Games: downsizing the
event, having the IOC implement an independent body to monitor its promise of "sustainability," or, critically, rotating the event

The author responds to the opposing view, citing an expert for support.

Succinctly states a clear solution to the problem.

Evidence for how the solution addresses the problem.

Acknowledges other possible solutions.

among the same few cities, so the Games "could be hosted with minimal social and ecological disruption and at minimal cost." Imagine that the infrastructure built in Olympic cities didn't go to ruin, but was reused again and again. Imagine an eco-friendly Olympic Village ready to host athletes and coaches, and serving as dorms and temporary housing in the Games' off years.

It's easy to imagine, but it all rests on the IOC, an organization that many critics see as having no incentive to reform. The IOC was founded in 1894 under the name the Olympic Congress. According to a 2015 article in the *European Journal of International Relations*, the non-governmental sports organization has no real oversight, and seemingly, no pressure to change the way things have been done. Some of its members have reportedly benefited greatly from the Olympics. In 2014, *Slate* described the IOC as having "diva-like demands for luxury treatment," including what Norwegian media reported as the creation of separate lanes on public roads, ceremonial greetings, and more, prompting the Norwegian capital of Oslo to drop its bid for the 2022 Games. The IOC's members include royalty, corporate executives, and many wealthy individuals, who are likely accustomed to receiving lavish benefits.

Details the major obstacles to the proposed solution.

"Fundamentally, their job is a very enviable one: They own the rights to a sporting event that draws billions of eyeballs every two years. And yet, they're actually responsible for very little," explained Chris Dempsey, who co-led the No Boston Olympics movement. Though it may be the only sustainable way to continue holding an Olympics, Dempsey doesn't believe the IOC will ever move to a permanent location. He theorized they simply risk losing too much money in broadcasting rights.

Cites additional proposals for combating opposition.

Boykoff takes a similarly pessimistic view on any possibility of IOC reform. "The International Olympic Committee has to be one of the most pervasive, yet least accountable organizations in the world, sports-related or otherwise," he said. "Until we get [some] hook where we can hold them accountable, it's going to be dificult to change. That means we're only left with the athletes to stand up and speak out, break rules, and maybe even challenge the Olympic system, the corporate sponsors to back out, or the broadcasters to say, 'This isn't worth our money anymore.'"

After the end of the first modern Olympics in Athens in   15
1896, the Greek king viewed it as such a success that he asked
the IOC to consider making Athens the permanent home of the
Olympics. In a toast, King George I of Greece said he hoped
"foreigners . . . will remember Athens as the peaceful meeting
place of all nations, as the tranquil and permanent seat of the
Olympic Games." Soon after, the U.S. Olympic team at the time
endorsed his idea, writing that due to the existing infrastructure,
Greece's "competent" administration, and the historical legacy,
"these games should never be removed from their native soil." If
only the world had listened.

> Concludes reiterating the proposed solution, this time with the support of a memorable anecdote from history.

REFLECT. *Find a proposal in a campus publication or local newspaper. Read it first to see if you find it persuasive. If not, why not? Then annotate it as we've done with Burack's proposal to see if it includes all the features listed on page 373. If not, would it be improved by adding any of the features it's lacking or by elaborating on any it doesn't demonstrate well?*

PROJECT PROPOSALS

You may be asked to write a project proposal to explain your plans for a large or long-term assignment: what you intend to do, how you'll go about doing it, and why the project is important. Like any proposal, a project proposal makes an argument, demonstrating that the project is worth doing and feasible given the available time and resources. Unless the assignment names other requirements, your proposal should cover the following ground:

An Indication of Your Topic and Focus

Explain what your topic is, giving any necessary background information. In some cases, you might be required to do some background research and to include a **LITERATURE REVIEW** summarizing what you find, including any issues or controversies you want to investigate. Say what your research focus will be, with the **RESEARCH QUESTION** you plan to pursue and a tentative **THESIS**. Finally, say why the topic matters—so what, and who cares?

An Explanation of Why You're Interested in the Topic

Briefly explain what you already know about your topic and why you've chosen to pursue this line of inquiry. You might describe any coursework, reading, or experience that contributes to your knowledge and interest. Also note what you don't yet know but intend to find out.

A Plan

Explain how you will investigate your research question. What types of sources will you need, and what will your research methods be? If you plan to do **FIELD RESEARCH**, how will you conduct your study? And what **GENRE** and **MEDIUM** will you use to present your findings? What steps will be required to bring it all together into the final document?

A Schedule

Break your project into tasks and make a schedule, taking into account all the research, reading, and writing you'll need to do. Include any specific tasks your instructor requires, such as handing in a draft or an **ANNOTATED BIBLIOGRAPHY**. Be sure also to leave yourself time to get feedback and revise.

DAVID PASINI wrote this project proposal for a first-year writing course at The Ohio State University on the theme of sports in American society.

The Economic Impact of Investing Public Funds in Sports Franchises

DAVID PASINI

SINCE THE 1960s, local governments have provided increased funding and subsidies for professional sports franchises. Tax-payer money has gone toward facilities like stadiums and arenas, and many cities have offered tax exemptions and other financial incentives to keep a team in town that has threatened to relocate. Proponents of public funding for privately owned sports franchises argue that cities gain more from the arrangement—namely jobs, status, and tourist dollars—than they lose. Opponents argue that using public funds for these purposes results in long-term financial drains on local governments and point out that many communities have been abandoned by teams even after providing substantial benefits.

Writing in *The New York Times*, Ken Belson gives an example of one such government-funded project: "The old Giants Stadium, demolished to make way for New Meadowlands Stadium, still carries about $110 million in debt, or nearly $13 for every New Jersey resident, even though it is now a parking lot" (Belson). The image included here shows the governor of New Jersey looking over a

> The introduction announces the topic and summarizes a controversy the project will focus on.

Fig. 1. Left to right: The governor of New Jersey, William T. Cahill; the owner of the Giants, Wellington Mara; and chairman of the New Jersey sports authority, Sonny Werblin, admire a drawing of Giants Stadium. Neal Boenzi, 1971. "As Stadiums Vanish, Their Debt Lives On," by Ken Belson. *The New York Times*, 8 Sept. 2010, p. A1.

drawing of the Giants Stadium, which was completed in 1976 and destroyed in 2010 (fig. 1).

An explicit statement of his research questions.

Given the high stakes involved—and particularly the use of taxpayer dollars—it seems important, then, to ask what these sports franchises contribute (or do not contribute) to their cities and wider metropolitan areas. Do these teams "generate positive net economic benefits for their cities," or do they "absorb scarce government funds" that would be better spent on programs that have "higher social or economic payoff" (Noll and Zimbalist 55)? My research project will investigate these questions.

A statement of why this topic matters, and to whom.

Pasini explains his interest in the topic and his current knowledge of it.

The question of public funding for sports is important to any resident of a community that has a professional sports franchise or is trying to lure one, as well as to any citizen who is interested in local economic and political issues. I am in the latter group, a nonfan who is simply interested in how public monies are being used to support sports, and whose knowledge about the issues is primarily in the economic domain. At this point, I am neither a proponent nor an opponent of investing in sports, but I think that it's important to consider how much professional sports contribute to the economic well-being of the government that funds them. How much of the money that teams generate supports local businesses, school districts, or other entities that benefit all citizens? How much of it stays in the owners' pockets? Do the franchises "give back" to their communities in tangible or intangible ways? The franchises themselves should consider these questions, since the communities that invest in their success have a right to expect something in return.

More focused research questions, leading to a tentative thesis statement.

To learn more about investment in sports teams and the teams' economic impact, I will consult business and sports management journals and appropriate news sources, both print and digital. I will also interview stakeholders on both sides of the debate as well as experts on this topic. I will consider the many factors that must be taken into account, such as the benefits of tourism and the costs of "creating extra demand on local services" (Crompton 33). As a result of my research, I hope to offer insight on whether public funds are in fact put to good use when they are invested in major sports franchises.

A research plan, including kinds of sources he'll consult and field research he plans to conduct.

The conclusion restates why this research matters.

Proposed Schedule

A schedule that allows time for research, writing, and revising—and lists assignment deadlines.

Do library and internet research	April 6–20
Submit annotated bibliography	April 20
Schedule and conduct interviews	April 21–25
Turn in first draft	May 10
Turn in second draft	May 18
Turn in final draft	May 25

Pasini uses MLA style for
a preliminary list of works
consulted.

Preliminary Works Consulted

Belson, Ken. "As Stadiums Vanish, Their Debt Lives On." *The New York Times*, 8 Sept. 2010, p. A1.

Crompton, John L. "Economic Impact Analysis of Sports Facilities and Events: Eleven Sources of Misapplication." *Journal of Sport Management*, vol. 9, no. 1, 1995, pp. 14-35.

Noll, Roger G., and Andrew Zimbalist, editors. *Sports, Jobs, and Taxes: The Economic Impact of Sports Teams and Stadiums.* Brookings Institution Press, 1997.

Robertson, Robby. "The Economic Impact of Sports Facilities." *The Sport Digest,* vol. 16, no. 1, 2008, www.thesportdigest .com/archive/article/economic-impact-sports-facilities.

REFLECT. If you're reading about project proposals, you've probably been assigned to write one. Analyze what your assignment is asking for, comparing it with the features listed on page 373. What does this exercise help you appreciate about how such a proposal works? What you can learn from doing one?

WRITING A PROPOSAL / A Roadmap

Think of a problem you can help solve

If you get to select the topic, identify an issue you know something about. You'll find it easiest—and most rewarding—to tackle an issue on which you can have some real impact. Try choosing a topic you have authority to speak on and one that is narrowly focused or local enough that your suggestions may be heard. You can't expect to solve all the problems of body-shaming in America's fashion industry, but you can help by raising awareness among your peers as consumers.

If you've been assigned a topic, consider ways that you can make it interesting to you and your readers. This may mean finding an interesting angle on the topic you've been assigned, or, if the assignment is framed in general terms, finding a specific aspect that you can address with a specific solution.

Consider your rhetorical situation

Once you have a topic, thinking about your rhetorical situation will help you focus on how to proceed.

Think about your AUDIENCE. Who do you want your proposal to reach, and why? If you're proposing changes to a campus policy, you would do so differently if you're writing to school administrators in charge of that policy than if you're writing a piece for the newspaper. Here are some things to consider:

- What do you know about your audience? In what ways are they like or unlike you—and one another?
- What will they likely know about your topic? What background information will you have to provide?
- What interest or stake are they likely to have in the situation you're addressing? Will you need to convince them that the problem matters— and if you do, how can you do so?
- What sorts of evidence will they find most convincing?
- How likely are they to agree with what you propose?

Be clear about your PURPOSE. Odds are that you'll have multiple purposes— everything from getting a good grade, to demonstrating your understanding of a situation, to making your community a better place for everyone.

The more you understand your own motivations, the clearer you can be with your audience about what is at stake.

Be aware of your STANCE. What is your attitude about your topic, and how do you want to come across to your audience? How can your choice of words help convey that stance? When David Freedman, writing about food, refers to those he disagrees with as the "let-them-eat-kale" crowd, his dismissive language tells us as much about him as it does about those he is criticizing.

Examine the larger CONTEXT. What do you know about the problem you're tackling? What might you need to learn? How have others addressed it? What solutions have they proposed and how well have they worked?

Consider your LANGUAGE. Almost any proposal can be presented in a number of ways. Regardless of how many languages and dialects you use in your everyday life, you have many options to consider in crafting a proposal. What variety of language or dialect will best suit your audience and help you achieve your goals as a writer? Will your audience expect a certain kind of language or style? Do you want to meet those expectations? challenge them? What do you want your language choices to say about you? What risks might you be willing to take with your language? How will your choice of medium and the larger context limit or expand the language options available to you? See Chapters 4 and 33 for more information about language options.

Think about MEDIA. If the choice is yours, what medium will best reach your audience and suit your purpose? If you're assigned to use a particular medium, how can you use it best? If, for example, you're giving an oral presentation, slides can help your audience follow the main points of your proposal, especially if you're presenting quantitative data.

Think about DESIGN. If you have the option of designing your proposal, think about what it needs. If it's lengthy or complex, should you use headings? Is there anything in your proposal that would be hard to follow in a paragraph—and easier to read in a chart or a graph?

Study the situation

Whatever the problem, you have to understand it in all its complexity and think about the many ways in which different parties will likely understand it.

Begin by thinking about what you know about the situation. What interests you about the issue, and why do you care? What more do you need to find out about it? To answer these questions, try BRAINSTORMING or other activities for GENERATING IDEAS.

Be sure you understand the problem. To do so, you'll surely need to do some RESEARCH. What CAUSED this problem, and what are its EFFECTS? How serious is it? Who cares about it? What's been said about it? What efforts have already been made to address the problem, and how have they succeeded? How have similar problems been handled, and what insights can you gain from studying them?

Consider how you can best present the problem for your AUDIENCE. If they're aware of the problem, how much do they care about it? Does it affect them? If they're not aware of it, how can you make them aware? What kind of evidence can you provide to make them recognize the potential consequences? Why do you think the issue matters, and how can you persuade others to take it seriously?

For example, if you were writing about the need for a program to raise awareness of the effects of hate speech on campus, you might open with an anecdote about hateful things that have been said about others to make those not otherwise concerned with the topic aware of the issue. And you could then appeal to their goodwill and concern for fellow students to understand why it's a problem that needs to be tackled.

Determine a course of action

Once you've got a thorough understanding of the problem and what others think about it, you can start thinking about possible solutions.

Come up with some possible solutions. Start by making a list of options. Which ones seem most feasible and most likely to solve the problem? Is there one that seems like the best approach? Why? Will it solve the problem entirely, or just part of it?

If, for example, you're proposing a program to raise awareness about hate speech on campus, what are the options? You could suggest an open forum, or a teach-in. Maybe you could get an outside speaker to visit campus.

Decide on the best solution. Determine which of the options would be feasible and would work the best. Then think about how far it would go toward actually solving the problem. Hate speech is not easily solved, so this might well be a case when you can realistically only raise awareness of the problem.

These are some of the questions you'll need to ask and answer as you determine the best solution to propose.

Organize and start writing

Once you've clearly defined the problem, figured out a viable solution, and identified evidence to support your proposal, it's time to organize your materials and start drafting.

Come up with a tentative THESIS that identifies the problem it proposes to solve. Use this statement to guide you as you write.

Provide EVIDENCE showing that the problem in fact exists, that it is serious enough to demand a solution, and that your proposed solution is feasible and the best among various options.

Acknowledge other possible solutions. Decide how and at what point in your proposal you will address other options. You might start with them and explain their shortcomings, or you could raise them after presenting your own solution, comparing your solution with the others as a way of showing that yours is the most feasible or the most likely to solve the problem.

Draft an OPENING. Identify and describe the problem, making clear why the issue matters—and why the problem needs a solution.

Draft a CONCLUSION. Reiterate the nature of the problem and the solution you're proposing. Summarize the benefits your proposal offers. Most of all, remind readers why the issue matters, why they should care, and why they should take your proposal seriously (and perhaps take action).

Look critically at your draft, get responses—and revise

Once you have a complete draft, read it over carefully, focusing on how you define the problem and support the solution you propose—and the way you appeal to your audience. If possible, ask others to read it over as well. Here are some questions to help you or others read over the draft with a critical eye:

- *How does the proposal* OPEN*?* Will it capture readers' interest? Does it make clear what problem will be addressed and give some sense of why it matters? How else might it begin? Does the title tell readers what the proposal is about, and will it make them want to know more?

- *Is the problem* DESCRIBED *in enough detail?* Will any readers need more information to understand that it's a problem that matters? Have you said anything about its CAUSES and consequences—and if not, do you need to?

- *Is the proposed solution explicit and compelling?* Have you provided enough EVIDENCE to show that it's feasible and will address the problem—and that it's better than other possible solutions? Is there an explicit statement of what it will accomplish?

- *Have other possible solutions been acknowledged fairly?* How well have you responded to them? Are there any other solutions to be considered?

- *Is the proposal easy to follow?* If not, try adding TRANSITIONS or headings.

- *How have you established your* AUTHORITY *to write on this topic?* Does the information seem trustworthy? How do you come across as an author—passionate? serious? sarcastic?—and how does this tone affect the way the proposal comes across to readers?

- *How would you characterize the* STYLE*?* Is it fitting for your intended audience? Consider the choice of words, the level of formality, and so on.

- *How about* DESIGN*?* Are there any illustrations—and if so, how do they contribute to the proposal? If not, is there any information that would be easier to show with a photo or in a chart? What about the typeface: is it right for a proposal of this kind? Is the design well suited to the MEDIUM?

- *How does the proposal* CONCLUDE*?* Will it inspire the change or action you're calling for? How else might it conclude?

Revise your draft in response to any feedback you receive and your own analysis.

REFLECT. Once you've completed your proposal, let it settle for a while and take time to REFLECT. *How well did you define the problem? How thoroughly did you support your proposed solution? How persuasively have you demonstrated the feasibility of your solution? How fairly did you acknowledge and respond to other possible solutions? Research shows that such reflections help "lock in" what you learn for future use.*

Guaranteed Income Can Solve U.S. Poverty

MARY KING

WE COULD ERADICATE POVERTY and raise the incomes of U.S. families in the bottom half of the income distribution by providing a guaranteed income through the tax system, according to a proposal from a team led by Naomi Zewde and Darrick Hamilton. The impact would be enormous, dramatically reducing homelessness, hunger, killer stress and despair, as well as racial disparities and the severe economic insecurity of single-mother households.

The reduction in child poverty alone would be transformative. America stands alone among wealthier nations in keeping people in poverty, with by far the highest rates, especially for people in extreme poverty and for children. All other wealthy countries lift many more of their families out of the poverty created by their economies, and especially target child poverty. They know that poverty is the most important influence on children's future education, earnings and health, as well as their odds of avoiding future poverty, unemployment, early child bearing, substance abuse and incarceration.

MARY KING, emerita professor of economics at Portland State University, is vice president of the Oregon Center for Public Policy and a columnist for *Street Roots*, the publication in which this essay was published in 2021. A weekly newspaper, *Street Roots* is sold in Portland, Oregon, by people experiencing homelessness "as a means of earning an income with dignity." Go to everyonesanauthor.tumblr.com to access the links (underscored here) as you read.

Hasn't This Idea Been Around for a Long Time?

Yes, and across the political spectrum! Dr. Martin Luther King Jr. called for eliminating poverty, including "a secure and adequate income for all" in the Economic Bill of Rights promoted by the Poor People's Campaign. Before him, conservative economist and Nobel Laureate Milton Friedman called for a "negative income tax," to create a guaranteed income for all. The Black Panthers, several women's groups including the National Welfare Rights Organizations and the International Association for Feminist Economics, the Movement for Black Lives and the renewed Poor People's Campaign, now led by Reverends Barber and Theoharis, have all called for a guaranteed income. A network of "Mayors for a Guaranteed Income" supports the idea, and some cities, including Stockton, California, have implemented successful pilot projects.

How Would the Guaranteed Income Work?

The Zewde team's proposal would eliminate poverty as officially defined and also lift a number of families from the near poor or working poor into the middle class. The program would pay the most to households with the lowest incomes and taper off to nothing for single-adult families with annual incomes of $50,000 or more and two-adult families with $70,000 or more a year.

As outlined in their recent policy paper, Zewde and her co-authors call for the IRS to make monthly payments that total $12,500 a year for each adult and $4,500 for each child to households with zero income. That would raise them above the poverty line. Slightly smaller payments would be made to single-adult families with incomes above $10,000 a year and two-adult families with incomes above $15,000, and continue to decline until nothing would be paid to families in the upper half of the income distribution. Families would always be better off if they can earn some income by work, and may be able to earn more if they use some of their guaranteed income for training or to pay for child care.

The table below illustrates how the distribution of income among American households would change with a guaranteed income refund, by showing what percent of U.S. families would fall into five income categories defined by their

U.S. families with incomes of different multiples of the federal poverty line, with and without proposed guaranteed income refund (percent of all households).

Family Income	Now	With Guaranteed Income
Below poverty line	11%	0%
Poverty line to double poverty line	16%	12%
Double poverty line to triple poverty line	20%	28%
Triple poverty line to 5 times the poverty line	22%	29%
More than 5 times the poverty line	31%	31%

This table lists U.S. families with incomes of different multiples of the federal poverty line, with and without proposed guaranteed income refund. The first figure is the percentage of households that meet that definition now; the second figure is the percentage of households under the proposed guaranteed income.... SOURCE: Naomi Zewde, Kyle Strickland, Kelly Capatosto, Ari Glogower and Darrick Hamilton. May 2021. "A Guaranteed Income for the 21st Century." The New School Institute on Race and Political Economy.

relationship to the poverty line. The poverty line is complex, being defined for each family depending on the number of people in the household and their ages. For that reason, looking at multiples of the poverty line is the most straightforward way to see the impact on income distribution of this guaranteed income proposal.

How Much *Is* the Federal Poverty Line?

Most people think the federal poverty line is set too low. Poverty researchers often double the federal poverty line when talking about poor households. A family of four, with two adults and two children, isn't considered poor if their total income is over $26,246. For a single senior citizen, it's just over $12,000 a year. In Portland, most people have to pay more than $12,000 a year in rent alone, even for a studio apartment—which would leave nothing for food, transportation, medicine or anything else.

What's more, that's before paying any taxes! What people don't realize is that poor people in this country pay more than a quarter of their income in taxes, when you consider all the taxes that people pay, not just income taxes. Berkeley economists Emmanuel Saez and Gabriel Zucman show, in their book, "The Triumph of Injustice," that the very wealthiest people in the country pay the smallest slice of their incomes for all taxes combined. The wealthy like to call themselves "makers" and the rest of us "takers," but the opposite is true.

For this reason, the Zewde team calls for adding a guaranteed income to our other anti-poverty efforts because housing, food aid and health programs will still be needed.

What Would This Guaranteed Income Program Cost?

Paying a guaranteed income to half of U.S. families would cost $876 billion a 　10 year, just 4% of our national income. That's all it would take to move every household in the country above the poverty line, while also lifting the incomes of another 23 million families so that they were at least double the poverty line.

To put that in perspective, the federal government has wasted more than one-fifth of that much each year on the Trump tax cuts for the wealthy and another two-fifths each year to fight the wars in Iraq and Afghanistan. As predicted by many, neither effort delivered on any of its promises.

Why Should We Create a Guaranteed Income Program?

The free market alone will never eradicate poverty. Markets create wealth, but concentrate it in very few hands. The U.S. is one of the richest countries in the world, but the number of people who don't even have shelter and enough to eat keeps growing.

All of the countries with lower poverty rates rely on the government to put a much higher proportion of their national income toward raising the living standards by providing public housing, public child care, national health care and pursuing different strategies for a guaranteed income. The U.S. ranks 30th among nations, when it comes to the proportion of its national income spent on cash benefits. A guaranteed income is essential to ensuring a better future for our children; to economic, race and gender justice; to creating community resilience and economic mobility; and to assuring a dignified life for all.

Thinking about the Text

1. What specific problem does Mary King focus on in this essay? What **EVIDENCE** does she provide to explain the extent of the problem and to support her proposed solution?

2. In the third paragraph, King elaborates on the recognition of the problem by several major historical figures and national organizations. How compelling do you find this tactic? How else does King establish her **CREDIBILITY** to propose solutions on this topic?

3. How does King make clear the extent and impact of the problem she addresses? Are you convinced it's a problem that needs solving?

4. This piece was published in *Street Roots*, a publication self-described as "Portland, Oregon's award-winning weekly street newspaper for those who can't afford free speech." Which strategies does King use to reach and appeal to the **AUDIENCE** for this publication?

5. Choose an ongoing problem that matters to you and offer a **PROPOSAL** that addresses some aspect of that problem. You might start by observing issues around you, but you'll likely find that you need to do some research to precisely define the problem and propose a solution. Use the features on page 373 as a guide for developing your proposal.

To Unite a Divided America, Make People Work for It

JONATHAN HOLLOWAY

IF WE AMERICANS listened to one another, perhaps we would recognize how absurd our discourse has become. It is our own fault that political discussions today are hotheaded arguments over whether the hooligans storming the halls of the Capitol were taking a tour or fomenting an insurrection; if we broadened our audiences, perhaps we would see the fallacy of claims that all Republicans are committed to voter suppression and that all Democrats are committed to voter fraud.

It seems like an easy challenge to address, but we lack the incentives to change our behavior. We are all, regardless of where we sit on the political spectrum, caught in a vortex of intoxication. We have fooled ourselves into thinking that our followers on social media are our friends. They aren't. They are our mirrors, recordings of our own thoughts and images played back to us, by us and for us. We feel good about ourselves, sure, but do we feel good as citizens? Do we feel good as Americans? Are we better off? Is America?

There are many problems in America, but fundamental to so many of them is our unwillingness to learn from one another, to see and respect one another, to become familiar with people from different racial and ethnic backgrounds

JONATHAN HOLLOWAY is an American historian, the president of Rutgers University, and the author of several books on race in America—most recently *The Cause of Freedom: A Concise History of African Americans* (2021). This essay was published in the *New York Times* in 2021 as part of a series dedicated to "exploring bold ideas to revitalize and renew the American experiment."

and who hold different political views. It will take work to repair this problem, but building blocks exist. A good foundation would be a one-year mandatory national service program.

Nearly 90 years ago, in response to the Great Depression, President Franklin Roosevelt created the Civilian Conservation Corps, what was then America's largest organized nationwide civilian service program. About 30 years later, President Lyndon Johnson brought to fruition President John Kennedy's "domestic Peace Corps" initiative, the Volunteers in Service to America program, known as VISTA. Today, domestic civilian service is dominated by AmeriCorps and nongovernmental programs like Teach for America.

Taken together, these programs have been enormously successful at putting people to work, broadening the reach of basic social services related to education, health and welfare. Most important, they have helped citizens see the crucial role that they can play in strengthening our democracy. Given that we know service programs can be so effective in shoring up the nation in moments of crisis, the time has come for a broader initiative, with higher aspirations and goals. The time has come for compulsory national service for all young people—with no exceptions.   5

Universal national service would include one year of civilian service or military service for all adults to be completed before they reach the age of 25, with responsibilities met domestically or around the world. It would channel the conscience of the Civilian Conservation Corps and put young people in the wilderness repairing the ravages of environmental destruction. It would draw on the lessons of the Peace Corps and dispatch young Americans to distant lands where they would understand the challenges of poor countries and of people for whom basic health and nutrition are aspirational goals. It would draw on the success of our military programs that in the past created pathways toward financial stability and educational progress for those with limited resources while serving as great unifiers among America's races, religions and social classes.

These are but three examples. A one-year universal national service program could take many other forms, but it is easy to imagine that it could be a vehicle to provide necessary support to underserved urban and rural communities, help eliminate food deserts, contribute to rebuilding the nation's infrastructure, enrich our arts and culture, and bolster our community health clinics, classrooms and preschools.

Furthermore, because service would be mandatory, it would force all of our young people to better know one another, creating the opportunities to learn about and appreciate our differences. Speaking as an educator, I know that we get better answers to complex problems when we assemble teams from a wide range of backgrounds. Once these teams realize that they have a common purpose, their collective differences and diversity in race, gender, expertise, faith, sexual orientation and political orientation start to emerge as a strength. If you look at the state of our civic culture, it is clear that we have a long way to go before we can claim that we are doing the best that we can. The kind of experiential education I am advocating could change a life, could open a mind and could save a democracy.

A sensible system of compulsory national service would build bridges between people and turn them into citizens. It would shore up our fragile communities and strengthen us as individuals and as a nation. Compulsory national service would make us more self-reliant and at the same time more interdependent. It would help us to realize our remarkable individual strengths and would reveal the enormous collective possibilities when we pull together instead of rip apart.

At its core, we need to heed the call for citizenship. We need to take the 10 natural inclination to help out our friends and families and turn it into a willingness to support strangers. We need to inspire people to answer the call to serve because in so doing, they will discover ways to have their voices heard and their communities seen and respected.

This is neither a new nor a partisan idea. This call to serve and inspire is written into the preamble of the United States Constitution. When the founders sought to "form a more perfect union, establish justice, ensure domestic tranquility, provide for the common defense, promote the general welfare, and secure the blessings of liberty," they were talking about establishing an ethos of citizenship and participation.

Compulsory national service is not a panacea, but neither is it a mere placebo. It could be a very real solution to a very real problem that already has wrought havoc on our democracy and that threatens our future as a nation, our viability as a culture and our very worth as human beings. This nation and its democratic principles need our help. We can and must do better.

Thinking about the Text

1. In his first two paragraphs, Jonathan Holloway signals that he wants to "unite a divided America." What problem does he define, and what solutions does he **PROPOSE** to solve that problem? Why do you think Holloway holds off proposing his solution until paragraph three?

2. Given that this essay was published in the *New York Times*, what strategies does the author use to establish his **CREDIBILITY** with that publication's **AUDIENCE**? How might this proposal be different if it were written instead for a campus or local newspaper?

3. What **COUNTERARGUMENTS** does Holloway acknowledge? Do you find them convincing? Try to come up with some additional objections and respond to them yourself.

4. What **EVIDENCE** does Holloway offer to show that his proposal will adequately address the problem he identifies?

5. Write an essay responding to Holloway—agreeing, disagreeing, or both. Take a **STANCE** in response to Holloway's proposal and back up your **ARGUMENT** with evidence. Raise any questions you think need to be considered and provide suggestions about how to apply or adapt Holloway's proposal on your campus or in your community.

PART V

The Centrality of Argument

CHANCES ARE THAT your first attempt to communicate was an argument. When you cried as a baby, that is, you were arguing that you were hungry or sleepy or wanted to be held. Later, you could use words or signs to indicate what you wanted: "More!" "No!" "Cookie!" All arguments. So if you think that argument is just about disputes or disagreements, think again. In rhetorical terms, argument refers to any way that human beings express themselves to try to achieve a particular purpose—which, many would say, means any way that people express themselves at all.

If you think about the kinds of writing covered in this book, for example, it is easy to understand that an opinion article taking a position on a political issue or a TV critic's rave review of a new series is "arguing" for or against something. An editorial cartoon about the issue or an ad for the movie is making an obvious argument, too. But even when you post on *TikTok* about something you just did, you're implicitly arguing that it will be intriguing or important or perhaps amusing to your audience, those who follow you on *TikTok*. Even when you write a lab report, you'll describe and interpret the results of an experiment, arguing that your findings have certain implications.

In fact, you are immersed in argument. Try counting the number of arguments you either make or encounter in just one day, starting with the argument you may have with yourself over what to wear, moving on to the barrage of posters asking you to support certain causes or attend various concerts, to a biology lecture where the professor explains the conflicting arguments about climate change, then the flood of claims and arguments you scroll through in your social media feed, and ending only when you and a friend agree to disagree about who's better, Kevin Durant or LeBron James. We bet you'll be surprised by how many arguments you encounter in a day.

The point we want to make is simple: you are the author of many arguments and the target of many more—and you'll be a better reader and writer of your own arguments if you understand how they work.

It's important to mention as well that arguments today most often consist of more than just words, from the signs encouraging you to wear a mask in public, to a big "thumbs up," to an ad for McDonald's. These familiar images demonstrate how words and images can make strong visual arguments.

Words, graphics, and images can be combined to make strong visual arguments.

It's also worth noting that arguments today are more seductive than ever. A fifteen-second sound bite sways millions of voters; a song you loved as a twelve-year-old now boosts sales of soft drinks; celebrities write op-ed essays on issues they care about. Even your school mounts arguments intended to attract prospective students—and, later, to motivate alumni to give generously. Check out your school's social media accounts, and you'll find appeals intended to attract applications and contributions.

Perhaps you think that such arguments are somewhat manipulative, intended to trick you into buying a product or contributing to a cause. But arguments are always trying to achieve some purpose, so it is up to you both as a reader and as a writer to distinguish the good from the bad. And arguments can, of course, be used for good (think of Martin Luther King Jr.'s powerful arguments for human rights) or ill (think of Hitler's diabolical but hypnotic speeches). They can be deceptive, even silly—does that gorgeous woman holding a can of cleanser really mean to claim that if you buy the cleanser, you'll look just like her?

In fact, argument is about many things and has many purposes. Of the many purposes we might name, here are just a few:

to explore

to understand

to seek consensus

to make decisions

to convince or persuade

Keep in mind, however, that arguments are always embedded in particular **CONTEXTS** —and that what is persuasive can vary from one context to another, or from one culture to another. The most persuasive evidence in one community might come from religious texts or the knowledge of revered elders; in another, from facts or statistics. Especially when arguments so often take place online, reaching people all around the world, it's important to be aware of such differences.

In 2021, the world's #2 ranked women's tennis player and highest-earning female athlete, Naomi Osaka, announced her withdrawal from the French Open after being fined for declining to participate in press conferences. Citing the "huge waves of anxiety" such encounters caused her, along with ongoing struggles with depression, Osaka said that withdrawing would allow her to concentrate on her mental well-being.

Worldwide response was swift, with support coming from other players like Coco Gauff and Billie Jean King, who tweeted "It's incredibly brave that Naomi Osaka has revealed her truth about her struggle with depression." Others strongly disagreed, arguing that for their sky-high paychecks, athletes should answer press questions, and that mental health issues are no excuse to opt out. Player Andrew Castle called her actions "completely wrong" and a British sportswriter described her actions as "diva behavior." Piers Morgan, former host of *Good Morning Britain*, called her an "arrogant spoiled brat." Still others noted that the opinions being aired in the media varied in some predictable ways, with women generally expressing understanding and solidarity and men generally delivering barbs. And ethnicity may well have played a role in some cases; reactions in Japan were mixed, with some fans cheering Osaka on and others complaining that she was not "really Japanese" or didn't speak Japanese very well. It's no surprise that opinions vary from culture to culture or from one group to another, but writers and speakers need to be especially aware of such variability and question what assumptions and beliefs underlie these opinions as well as how the particular context shapes how they are understood and received.

Naomi Osaka scores a point during the 2019 French Open.

Martin Luther King Jr. in a jail cell in Birmingham, Alabama.

During his lifetime, Martin Luther King Jr. did not have the benefit of the internet, but the arguments he made eventually reverberated around the world. In his "Letter from Birmingham Jail," King was responding to a statement written in 1963 by eight White Alabama clergymen who had urged him to stop his campaign of civil disobedience to protest racial discrimination. This particular context—the US South at the height of the civil rights struggle—informs his argument throughout. And while King's argument remains the same, having been republished countless times, its interpretation varies across time and cultures. When the letter first appeared, it responded point by point to the statement by the eight clergymen, and it was read as an answer to their particular charges. Today, however, it is read as a much more general statement about the importance of civil rights for all people. King's famous conclusion to this letter sums up his argument and consciously addresses an audience that extends far beyond the eight clergymen:

> Let us all hope that the dark clouds of racial prejudice will soon pass away and the deep fog of misunderstanding will be lifted from our fear-drenched communities, and in some not too distant tomorrow the radiant stars of love and brotherhood will shine over our great nation with all their scintil- lating beauty.   —MARTIN LUTHER KING JR., "Letter from Birmingham Jail"

As with all arguments, the effectiveness of King's letter has always varied according to the context in which it is read and, especially, the audience that is reading it. In most of his letter, King addresses eight specific people, and they are clearly part of his primary audience. But his use of "us" and "our" in the passage above works to broaden that audience and reaches beyond that time and place to many other readers and listeners.

King's letter was a written text and meant to be read. But like his spoken texts, it can also be heard—what Nicole Furlonge, author of *Race Sounds: The Art of Listening in African American Literature*, calls "listening in print." This kind of listening calls on us to concentrate on the soundscape of a text, what we can hear in our aural imagination that can add a great deal of richness to what we are seeing with our eyes. Imagine King speaking this text and listen for his pacing, his cadences, and his strong baritone voice.

Because arguments are so central to our lives, it's important to understand how they work—and to learn how to make effective arguments of your own, remembering that you can do so only by paying very careful attention to your purpose, your intended audience, and the rest of your rhetorical situation. The next two chapters focus on how good arguments work and on strategies for supporting the arguments that you make.

NINETEEN

Analyzing and Constructing Arguments

Those You Read, Those You Write

 HE CLOTHES YOU CHOOSE TO WEAR argue for your own sense of style; the courses your college requires argue for what educators consider important; the kind of transportation you take, the food you eat (or don't eat)—almost everything represents some kind of argument. So it is important to understand all these arguments, those you encounter and those you create. Consider a couple of everyday examples.

What's in a social media handle? An email address? You may not have thought much about the argument that these chosen titles make, but they certainly do make a statement about you. One student we know chose the email address 2hot2handl@gmail.com. But when it came time to look for meaningful employment, he began to think about what that address said about him. As a result, he chose an address he felt was more fitting for the image he wanted to convey: DavidSmythe494@gmail.com.

If you need to think about what arguments you may be making yourself, it's also important to understand the arguments that come from others. Take a look, for example, at the two images on the next page, both of which appeared after events protesting against or rallying for the Texas legislative bill banning abortions after six weeks of pregnancy. The first image shows people holding signs arguing that abortion unnecessarily takes the lives of children, saying that it is the child that matters, not the

Protesters' signs make decidedly different arguments about abortion rights in America.

choice. The second image shows protesters arguing that abortion saves the lives of women and that they have a right to bodily autonomy. These two images make radically different arguments about the role of abortion in our society, arguments that call on us to think very carefully before we respond. Note that these events took place after the Supreme Court upheld a Texas law banning abortion after six weeks in 2021 and as other abortion-related cases were being appealed to the high court. Like all arguments, then, these exist in a larger **CONTEXT**; they always involve more than just the person or group making the argument on one specific day or time.

Arguments, in short, don't appear out of thin air: every argument begins as a response to some other argument—a statement, an event, an image, or something else. From these images we see how important it is to analyze any argument you encounter—and consider the other side—before deciding where you yourself stand. That goes for arguments you read and for ones you write. Either way, all arguments are part of a larger conversation. Whether you're responding to something you've read, discussing a film you've seen, or writing an essay that argues a position, you enter into a dialogue with the arguments of others.

This chapter will help you analyze the arguments you encounter and compose arguments of your own.

WHERE'S THE ARGUMENT COMING FROM?

As a reader, you need to pay special attention to the source of an argument— literally to where it is coming from. It makes a difference whether an argument appears in the *New Pittsburgh Courier* or a school newspaper, in

Physics Review or on the *Twitter* feed of someone you know nothing about, in an impromptu speech by a candidate seeking your vote or in an analysis of that speech done by the nonpartisan website *FactCheck.org*. And even when you know who's putting forward the argument, you need to dig deeper to find out where—what view of the world—that source itself is "coming from."

For example, see the homepage of the website of Public Citizen, a nonprofit organization founded in 1971 by consumer advocate and social critic Ralph Nader. So what can we tell about where this argument is coming from? We might start with the image in the upper-left corner of Lady Liberty holding up her torch right next to the headline "PUBLIC CITIZEN." Below that is the menu bar and a statement of the organization's goal:

> We fight for you and take on corporate power. Corporations have their lobbyists. The People need advocates too.

Based on its website and its stated goal, we can surmise, then, that Public Citizen supports the rights of ordinary citizens and liberal democratic values and opposes the influence of corporations on government. Indeed,

The homepage of Public Citizen's website.

if we look a bit further, to the About page, we will find the following statement:

> Public Citizen is a nonprofit consumer advocacy organization that champions the public interest in the halls of power. We defend democracy, resist corporate power and work to ensure that government works for the people—not for big corporations. Founded in 1971, we now have 500,000 members and supporters throughout the country.
>
> We don't participate in partisan political activities or endorse any candidates for elected office. We take no government or corporate money, which enables us to remain fiercely independent and call out bad actors—no matter who they are or how much power and money they have.

Together, these images and statements tell us a lot about Public Citizen's stance, where the organization is coming from. Checking a few other trustworthy sources confirms this stance, since they call Public Citizen a "progressive" and "liberal" organization that practices "lobbying and advocacy." As savvy readers, we then have to assess the claims Public Citizen makes on its website and elsewhere in light of this knowledge: knowing where an organization is coming from and how it is seen by others affects how willing or skeptical we are to accept what it says.

Or consider a more lighthearted example, this time from political pundit David Brooks:

> We now have to work under the assumption that every American has a tattoo. Whether we are at a formal dinner, at a professional luncheon, at a sales conference or arguing before the Supreme Court, we have to assume that everyone in the room is fully tatted up—that under each suit, dress or blouse, there is at least a set of angel wings, a barbed wire armband, a Chinese character or maybe even a fully inked body suit. We have to assume that any casual anti-tattoo remark will cause offense, even to those we least suspect of self-marking.
>
> —DAVID BROOKS, "Nonconformity Is Skin Deep"

David Brooks

What can we know about where Brooks is coming from? For starters, a quick *Google* search will bring up photos showing a middle aged White man, and other sources describing Brooks as a conservative journalist whose work appears in many publications across the political spectrum and who often appears as a television commentator on the *PBS NewsHour*. We also know that this passage comes from one of his opinion columns for the *New York Times*. His professional photo on the *Times* website presents him in jacket and tie.

What more can we tell about where he's coming from in the passage itself? Probably first is that Brooks is representing himself here as somewhat old-fashioned, as someone who's clearly an adult and a member of what might be called "the establishment" in the United States (note his off-handed assumption that "we" might be "at a formal dinner" or "arguing before the Supreme Court"). He's someone who almost certainly does not have a tattoo himself. He's also comfortable using a little sarcasm ("everyone in the room is fully tatted up") and exaggeration ("every American has a tattoo") to make a humorous point. Finally, we can tell that he is a self-confident—and persuasive—author and that we'll need to be on our toes to understand the argument that he's actually making.

As an author, you should always think hard about where *you* are coming from in the arguments you make. What's your **STANCE**, and why? How do you want your audience to perceive you? As reasonable? knowledgeable? opinionated? curious? something else?

How can you convey your stance? Through your choice of words, of course—both *what* you say and *how* you say it—but also through any images you include and the way you design your text. The words you choose not only convey your meaning, they reveal a lot about your attitude—toward your subject and your audience. Introducing a quotation with the words "she insists" indicates a different attitude than the more neutral "she says."

WHAT'S THE CLAIM?

You run into dozens of claims every day. Your brother says that Shang-Chi is the best Marvel superhero ever; your news feed predicts that the Brooklyn Nets will win the NBA championship; a friend texts to say it's a waste of time and money to eat at Power Pizza. Each of these statements makes a claim and argues implicitly for you to agree. The arguments you read and write in college often begin with a claim, an arguable statement that must then be supported with good reasons and evidence.

In 2021, famed Broadway singer and actor Billy Porter, shown below in a luscious gold and orange sequined gown, announced he would play Cinderella's fairy godmother in a remake of the classic story. Porter is well known for pushing boundaries of all kinds in his work. For example, in 2019 he won an Emmy for his role in the series *Pose*, making him the first openly gay Black man to win that prize for lead actor in a drama series. About his decision to play a genderless fairy godperson, Porter took the director's challenge that "it's time to shake it up" seriously. Noting that "magic has no gender," Porter says he is happy playing this powerful genderless role, making a "classic fairytale for a new generation"; he believes "the new generation is really ready. The kids are ready. It's the grownups that are slowing stuff down." So what's the claim? Porter's role as a fairy godperson whose gender is indeterminate—depicted below in the character's signature outfit—suggests that gender doesn't have a role to play in helping make dreams true.

Billy Porter as Cinderella's fairy godperson.

The easiest claims to identify are those that are stated directly as an explicit **THESIS**. Look, for instance, at the following paragraph from a journal article by civil rights activist W. E. B. Du Bois in 1922. As you read each sentence, ask yourself what Du Bois's claim is.

> Abraham Lincoln was a Southern poor white, . . . poorly educated and unusually ugly, awkward, ill-dressed. He liked smutty stories and was a politician down to his toes. Aristocrats—Jeff Davis, Seward and their ilk—despised him, and indeed he had little outwardly that compelled respect. But in that curious human way he was big inside. He had reserves and depths and when habit and convention were torn away there was something left to Lincoln—nothing to most of his contemners. There was something left, so that at the crisis he was big enough to be inconsistent—cruel, merciful; peace-loving, a fighter; despising Negroes and letting them fight and vote; protecting slavery and freeing slaves. He was a man—a big, inconsistent, brave man.
>
> —W. E. B. DU BOIS, "Abraham Lincoln"

We think you'll find that the claim is difficult to make out until the last sentence, which lets us know in an explicit thesis that the contradictions Du Bois has been detailing are part of Lincoln's greatness, part of what made him "big" and "brave." Take note as well of where the thesis appears in the text. Du Bois holds his claim for the very end.

Here is a very different example, from a newspaper column about legendary dancer Judith Jamison. Note that it begins with an explicit thesis stating a claim that the rest of the passage expands on—and supports:

> Judith Jamison is my kind of American cultural icon. . . . She has many accolades and awards—among them the National Medal of Arts, the Kennedy Center Honors and an Emmy. . . .
>
> But when I met her . . . she said with a huge smile, "Yes, honey, but you know I still have to do the laundry myself, and no one in New York parts the sidewalk 'cause I am comin' through!"
>
> I like icons who are authentic and accessible. I think our country benefits from that. It can only serve to inspire others to believe that they can try to do the same thing.
>
> —MARIA HINOJOSA, "Dancing Past the Boundaries"

Notice that although Hinojosa's claim is related to her own personal taste in American cultural icons, it is not actually about her taste itself. Her argument is not about her preference for cultural icons to be "authentic and accessible." Instead, she's arguing that given this criterion, Judith Jamison is a perfect example.

Judith Jamison — 1987 "Revelations"   ©Jack Mitchell

Judith Jamison dancing with the Alvin Ailey American Dance Theater.

As an author making an argument of your own, remember that a claim shouldn't simply express a personal taste: if you say that you feel lousy or that you hate the New York Yankees, no one could reasonably argue that you don't feel that way. For a claim to be *arguable*—worth arguing—it has to take a **POSITION** that others can logically have different perspectives on. Likewise, an arguable claim can't simply be a statement of fact that no one would disagree with ("Violent video games earn millions of dollars every year"). And remember that in most academic contexts, claims based on religious faith alone often cannot be argued since there are no agreed-upon standards of proof or evidence.

In most academic writing, you'll be expected to state your **CLAIM** explicitly as a **THESIS**, announcing your topic and the main point(s) you are going to make about that topic. Your thesis should help readers follow your train of thought, so it's important that it state your point clearly. A good thesis will also engage your audience's interest—and make them want to read on.

Be careful, however, not to overstate your thesis: you may need to **QUALIFY** it with words like "some," "might," or "possible"—for example, that "Recent studies have shown that exercise has a limited effect on a person's weight, so eating less may be a better strategy for losing weight than exercising more." By saying that dieting "may be" more effective than exercise, the author of this thesis has limited her claim to one she will be able to support.

In most US academic contexts, authors are expected to make claims directly and get to the point fairly quickly, so you may want to position the thesis near the beginning of your text, often at the end of the introduction or the first paragraph. When your claim is likely to challenge or surprise your audience, though, you may want to build support for it more gradually and hold off stating it explicitly until later in your argument, as Du Bois does. In other situations, you may not need to make a direct statement of your claim at all. But always make sure in such cases that your audience has a clear understanding of what the claim is.

WHAT'S AT STAKE?

Figuring out the answer to this question takes you to the heart of the argument. Rhetoricians in ancient Rome developed what they called stasis theory, a simple system for identifying the crux of an argument—what's at stake in it—by asking four questions in sequence:

1. What are the facts? What happened?
2. How can the issue be defined?
3. How much does the issue matter, and why?
4. What actions should be taken as a result?

Together these questions help determine the basic issues at stake in an argument. A look at the arguments that swirled around Hurricane Katrina, one of the deadliest and costliest hurricanes to hit the United States, and its effects can illustrate how these questions work.

What are the facts? What happened? Certainly the hurricane hit the Gulf Coast squarely in 2005, resulting in almost unimaginable damage and loss of life, especially in New Orleans, where levees failed along with the city's evacuation plan. Many arguments about the disaster had their crux (or stasis) here, claiming that the most important aspect of "what happened" was not the hurricane itself but the lack of preparation for it and the response to it.

How can the issue be defined? In the case of Katrina, the question of definition turned out to be crucial for many arguments about the event: it was easy enough to define the storm itself as a "category 4 hurricane" but much more difficult to classify the disaster beyond that simple scientific tag. To what extent was it a national disaster or a local one? A natural disaster or a man-made one? Was it proof of corruption and incompetence on the part of local and state officials? of FEMA and the Bush administration? Something else?

How much does the issue matter, and why? In addition to questions of fact and definition, ones about how serious the event was also produced many arguments in the wake of Katrina. In the first week or so after the storm hit, the mayor of New Orleans argued that it was the most serious disaster ever to strike that city and that up to 10,000 lives would be lost. Others argued that while the storm represented a huge setback to the people of the region, they could and would overcome their losses and rebuild their cities and towns.

What actions should be taken as a result? Of all the stasis questions, this one was the basis for the greatest number of arguments. From those arguing that the federal government should be responsible for funding reconstruction, to those arguing that the government should work with insurance agencies and local and state officials, to those arguing that the most damaged neighborhoods should not be rebuilt, thousands of proposals were offered and debated.

Such questions can help you understand what's at stake in an argument—to help you figure out and assess the arguments put forth by others, to identify which stasis question lies at the heart of an argument—and then to decide whether or not the argument answers the question satisfactorily.

As an author, you can use these questions to identify the main point you want to make in an argument of your own. In the Katrina example, for instance, working through the four stasis questions would help you see the disaster from a number of different perspectives and then develop a cogent argument related to them. In addition, these questions may help you decide just what **GENRE** of argument you want to make: a question of fact might lead you to write a **NARRATIVE**, explaining what happened, while the question of what action(s) should be taken might lead you to compose a **PROPOSAL**.

MEANS OF PERSUASION: EMOTIONAL, ETHICAL, AND LOGICAL APPEALS

Aristotle wrote that good arguments should make use of "all the available means" of persuading an audience and named three in particular, which he labeled emotional appeals (to the heart), ethical appeals (about credibility or character), and logical appeals (to the mind). These universal appeals must always, however, be looked at—and used—in context: what is effective as an emotional appeal in one time and place may be quite different in another. In other words, all appeals exist in specific cultural contexts.

Emotional Appeals

Emotional appeals (also referred to as "pathos") stir feelings and often invoke values that the audience is assumed to hold. The paragraph on Lincoln on page 417, for example, offers a strong appeal to readers' emotions when it represents Lincoln as "big" and "brave," invoking two qualities Americans traditionally value. Images can make especially powerful appeals to our emotions, such as the one on the following page from the 2021 earthquake in Haiti. This image pulls at our heartstrings, leading us to empathize with the plight of children left injured and homeless by forces of nature. Here a young boy is in a makeshift medical space outside a badly damaged hospital, with heavily bandaged wounds. His eyes, staring straight into the camera, compel us to connect to this child's human experience and want to ease his suffering. Such images can speak volumes to viewers, encouraging them to empathize and to support relief efforts. As a reader, you'll want to consider how any such emotional appeals support an author's claim.

As an author, you should consider how you can appeal to your audience's emotions and how such appeals may work to support your claim and your purpose for your audience. But whatever you decide, remember that the line

Jia Tolentino uses an emotional appeal when she describes her boyfriend's "delirium of happy, wistful tears" after seeing the movie *Coco*. See her review of the film on p. 973.

In the wake of a disastrous earthquake in Haiti in 2021, a young boy recuperates in a makeshift hospital. This image appeals directly to our hearts and our desire to help those in need.

between persuasion and coercion is easily crossed, so work hard to avoid using images that are manipulative.

Ethical Appeals

Ethical appeals (also referred to as "ethos") invoke the credibility and good character of whoever is making the argument. See how the website for the Interfaith Youth Core, a nonprofit organization building common ground between people with different beliefs, includes information intended to establish founder Eboo Patel's credibility and integrity. Here is part of Patel's "bio" page from the site:

> [Eboo] is inspired to build this bridge by his identity as an American Muslim navigating a religiously diverse social landscape.
>
> For over 15 years he has worked with governments, social sector organizations, and college and university campuses to help make interfaith cooperation a social norm. Named by *U.S. News & World Report* as one of America's Best Leaders of 2009, Eboo served on President Obama's Inaugural Faith Council and is the author of *Acts of Faith, Sacred Ground,*

Interfaith Leadership: A Primer, and *Out of Many Faiths: Religious Diversity and the American Promise.* He holds a doctorate in the sociology of religion from Oxford University, where he studied on a Rhodes scholarship.

These days, Eboo spends most of his time on the road, doing what he loves: meeting students, educators, and community leaders to talk about the complex landscape of religious diversity and the power of interfaith cooperation in the 21st century. —INTERFAITH YOUTH CORE, "Eboo Patel"

All of this information, including Patel's numerous degrees and publications and his position advising the US president helps establish his credibility and helps readers decide how much stock they can put in his words and the work of the organization he founded.

Citing scholarly achievements and national positions of influence is only one way of establishing credibility. Here Patel uses another approach during a *PBS NewsHour* interview when he responds to a question about "hostile racial divisions" on campus:

I'm on 25 college campuses a year. I have probably visited something like 130 in the past eight or 10 years. It's not like things don't ever get

Interfaith leader Eboo Patel delivering a talk on religious diversity and the American promise at Dickinson University.

tense, but what I read about in the news on college campuses is foreign to me, right, which is to say it is by definition sensational.

How am I not going to be optimistic, really? . . . The beautiful thing is, there's lots of us that feel this way. There's this whole growing network of college student interfaith leaders on American campuses basically saying, where's the divide? Let me bridge it. That's the future of America, or we have no future at all.

—EBOO PATEL, *PBS NewsHour* Interview, "To Narrow Toxic Divides, Students Build Bridges between Faiths"

In his comments, Patel lets listeners know that he is basing his claim on a lot of personal experience. And his informal tone suggests that he has a simple, direct message to give to his audience. His extensive experience gives him confidence to talk with conviction about why he's optimistic in the face of deep differences.

↪ Visit everyones anauthor.tumblr .com to find Patel's full interview.

Building common ground. Patel's use of simple, everyday language helps establish credibility in another way: by building common ground with his audience. He is not "putting on airs" but speaking directly to them; the concerns so many feel, he seems to say, are his concerns. He also uses ANALOGIES, especially those associated with bridges, which can bring people of different views together. Given Patel's goals and the aims of the organization he founded, it's no surprise that he seeks to build common ground with his audience.

While building common ground cannot ensure that your audience is "on your side," it does show that you respect your audience and their views and that you've established, with them, a mutual interest in the topic. Both parties care about the issues that you are addressing. Thus, building common ground is a particularly important part of creating an effective argument. Especially if you are addressing an audience unlikely to agree with your position, finding some area of agreement with them, some common ground you can all stand on, can help give the argument a chance of being heard.

No global leader in recent history has been more successful in building common ground than Nelson Mandela, who became the first Black president of South Africa in 1994 after the country's harsh apartheid system of racial segregation ended. In *Playing the Enemy: Nelson Mandela and the Game That Made a Nation*, the basis for the 2009 film *Invictus*, author John Carlin recounts hearing Mandela say that "sport has the power to change the world . . . the power to unite people in a way that little else does" and that "it is more powerful than governments in breaking down racial barriers."

Carlin uses this quotation as an example of Mandela's singular ability to "walk in another person's shoes" and to build common ground even where none seems possible. He goes on to detail the ways in which Mandela used White South Africans' love of rugby to build common ground between them and the country's Black majority, which had long seen the almost all-White national rugby team, the Springboks, as a symbol of White supremacy:

> He explained how he had . . . used the 1995 Rugby World Cup as an instrument in the grand strategic purpose he set for himself during his five years as South Africa's first democratically elected president: to reconcile blacks and whites and create the conditions for a lasting peace. . . . He told me, with a chuckle or two, about the trouble he had persuading his own people to back the rugby team. . . . Having won over his own people, he went out and won over the enemy.
>
> —JOHN CARLIN, *Playing the Enemy*

Mandela understood, in short, that when people were as far apart in their thinking as Black and White South Africans were when apartheid ended, the only way to move forward, to make arguments for the country's future that both groups would listen to, was to discover something that could bring them together. For Mandela—and for South Africa—rugby provided the common ground. His personal meetings with the Springboks players and his support for the team paid off to such an extent that when they won a stunning upset victory in the 1995 World Cup final in Johannesburg, the multiracial crowd chanted his name and the country united in celebration. And establishing that common ground contributed to Mandela's extraordinary ethical appeal—which he put to good use in the difficult arguments he had to make in the transition to a post-apartheid South Africa.

In all the arguments you encounter, you'll want to consider how much you can trust the author. Do they seem knowledgeable? represent opposing positions fairly (or at all)? do anything to build common ground?

As an author, you need to establish your own AUTHORITY: to show that you know what you're talking about by citing trustworthy sources; to demonstrate that you're fair by representing other positions even-handedly and accurately; and to work toward establishing some common ground with your audience. Remember, though, that on some occasions finding common ground may not be possible. In these cases, it's most important that you remain true to your values, representing them as clearly and as fairly as possible.

President Nelson Mandela, wearing a Springboks cap and shirt, presents the Rugby World Cup to South African captain Francois Pienaar in June 1995.

Logical Appeals

Appeals to logic (also referred to as "logos") were long regarded in the Western world as the most important of all the appeals, following Aristotle's definition of humans as rational animals. Recent research has made it increasingly clear, however, that people seldom make decisions based on logic alone and that emotion often plays a larger role in our decision making than does logic. Nevertheless, in US academic contexts, logical appeals still count for a lot. When we make an argument, we need to provide **REASONS** and **EVIDENCE** to support our claims. Such evidence may include facts and statistics, data from surveys and questionnaires, direct observations, interviews, testimony, experiments, personal experience, visuals, and more.

Facts and statistics. Facts and statistics are two of the most commonly used kinds of evidence. Facts are claims that have been proven to be true—and that an audience is likely to accept without further proof. Statistics are research-based numerical data. Here *Men's Health* editor David Zinczenko offers facts and statistics as support for an argument in the *New York Times* about the effects of fast foods on Americans:

> Before 1994, diabetes in children was generally caused by a genetic disorder—only about 5 percent of childhood cases were obesity-related, or Type 2 diabetes. Today, according to the National Institutes of Health, Type 2 diabetes accounts for at least 30 percent of all new childhood cases of diabetes in this country.
>
> Not surprisingly, money spent to treat diabetes has skyrocketed, too. The Centers for Disease Control and Prevention estimate that diabetes accounted for $2.6 billion in health care costs in 1969. Today's number is an unbelievable $100 billion a year.
>
> Shouldn't we know better than to eat two meals a day in fast-food restaurants? That's one argument. But where, exactly, are consumers—particularly teenagers—supposed to find alternatives? Drive down any thoroughfare in America, and I guarantee you'll see one of our country's more than 13,000 McDonald's restaurants. Now, drive back up the block and try to find someplace to buy a grapefruit.
>
> —DAVID ZINCZENKO, "Don't Blame the Eater"

The facts about the proliferation of fast-food chains compared to the relative lack of healthier options will be obvious to Zinczenko's readers, and most of his statistics come from respected health organizations whose authority adds to the credibility of his argument. Statistics can provide powerful support for an argument, but be sure they're accurate, current, from reliable sources—and relevant. And if you base an argument on facts, be sure to take into account all the relevant information. Realistically, that's hard to do—but be careful not to ignore any important available facts. Also, remember that "facts" can be manufactured online and then spread like a virus, so you need to verify your facts. The advice in Chapter 8 will further help you distinguish facts from dis- or misinformation.

Surveys and questionnaires. You have probably responded to a number of surveys or questionnaires, and you will often find them used as evidence in support of arguments. When a college student wondered about the kinds of reading for pleasure her dormmates were doing, she decided to gather information through a survey and to present it in a pie chart.

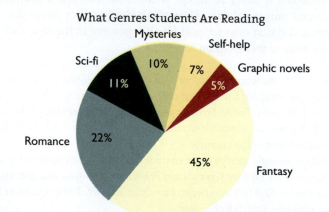

What Genres Students Are Reading

The information displayed in the chart offers evidence that fantasy is the most-read genre, followed by romance, sci-fi, mysteries, self-help, and graphic novels. Before accepting such evidence, however, readers might want to ask some key questions: How many people were surveyed? What methods of analysis did the student use? How were particular works classified? (For example, how did she decide whether a particular book was a "romance" or a "mystery"?) Whether you're reacting to survey data in an essay or a lecture, or conducting a survey of your own, you need to scrutinize the methods used and findings. Who conducted the survey, and why?

(And yes, you need to think about that even if you conducted it.) Who are the respondents, how were they chosen, and are they representative? What do the results show?

Observations. A 2011 study reported in *Science News* demonstrates the way direct observations can form the basis for an argument. In this study, researchers in Uganda observed the way young chimpanzees play, and their findings support arguments about the relative importance of biology and socialization on the way children play.

> A new study finds that young females in one group of African chimpan-zees use sticks as dolls more than their male peers do, often treating pieces of wood like a mother chimp caring for an infant. . . .
>
> Ape observations, collected over 14 years of field work with the Kanyawara chimp community in Kibale National Park, provide the first evidence of a nonhuman animal in the wild that exhibits sex differences in how it plays, two primatologists report in the Dec. 21 *Current Biology*. This finding supports a controversial view that biology as well as society underlies boys' and girls' contrasting toy preferences.
>
> —BRUCE BOWER, "Female Chimps Play with 'Dolls'"

A young chimp holds a stick in imitation of a mother caring for her child.

As this study suggests, observations carried out over time are particularly useful as evidence since they show that something is not just a onetime event but a persistent pattern. As a college student, you probably won't have occasion to spend fourteen years observing something, but in most cases you'll need to observe your subject more than once.

Interviews & informal conversations. Reporters often use information drawn from interviews to add authenticity and credibility to their articles. For an article on the danger concussions cause to athletes and the number of such unreported injuries, Kristin Sainani, a professor of health policy, interviewed Stanford neuroscientists conducting research on concussions as well as one athlete who had suffered several. Here is basketball star Toni Kokenis describing the effects her concussions had on her:

> "I felt withdrawn from everything. It was like I was there, but in slow motion," she says. "I didn't feel comfortable shooting three-pointers because I couldn't focus on the basket long enough to know that the ball was actually going to go near the hoop."
>   —KRISTIN SAINANI, "Damage Control"

Sainani also cites information she learned from researcher David Camarillo, whose lab is at work on understanding concussions—a science, he says, that is still in its infancy. Preventing concussions won't be possible, he tells us, until we understand them. Camarillo then goes on to describe, in everyday language, what happens during a concussion: "You've got this kind of gelatinous blob in a fluid floating in a sealed pressure vessel. A concussion occurs when the brain is sloshed and bounced around in this fluid."

Unfortunately, he tells Sainani, wearing a helmet does little to prevent concussions, and so his lab is conducting research to "change the industry standards" for protective equipment.

Throughout this article, Sainani uses evidence drawn from interviews to engage readers and convince them that equipment to protect against concussions "needs to be better." As an author, be sure that anyone you interview is an authority on your subject whom your audience will consider trustworthy.

You may also gather important and useful information through informal conversations. Especially in cultures or communities where formal, scripted interviews might not be accepted—or could be offensive—consider alternative possibilities. Two Navajo students, for example, wanted to gather information about how elders in their home community had managed to cope early during the COVID-19 pandemic. They did so by asking to visit each elder in their home. Rather than arriving with a list of set questions, they arrived with a gift for the elder and expressed a desire to join the elder in some activity (sometimes cooking, sometimes gardening, sometimes walking), during which time they shared information about their lives during the pandemic and listened actively and respectfully to what the elder said in response.

Testimony. Most of us depend on reliable testimony to help us accept or reject arguments: a friend tells us that *High on the Hog* is a great documentary series, and likely as not we'll watch it at least once. Testimony is especially persuasive evidence when it comes from experts and authorities on a topic. When you cite authorities to support an argument, you build your own credibility as an author; readers know that you've done your homework and are aware of the different perspectives on your topic. In the example on page 429 about gender-linked behavior among chimpanzees, for example, the *Science News* report notes testimony from the two scientists who conducted the research.

Good testimony doesn't have to come from experts. See how Barbara Ehrenreich uses the testimony of coworkers in her essay about blue-collar working conditions, on p. 873.

Experiments. Evidence based on experiments is especially important in the sciences and social sciences, where data is often the basis for supporting a claim. In arguing that multitaskers pay a high mental price, Clifford Nass, a professor of communications, based his claims on a series of empirical studies of college students who were divided into two groups, those identified as "high multitaskers" and those identified as "low multitaskers." In the first studies, which measured attention and memory, Nass and his fellow researchers were surprised to find that the low multitaskers outperformed high multitaskers in statistically significant ways. Still not satisfied that low multitaskers were more productive learners, the researchers designed another test, hypothesizing that if high multitaskers couldn't do well in the earlier studies on attention and memory, maybe they would be better at shifting from task to task more quickly and effectively than low multitaskers.

> Wrong again, the study found.
>   The subjects were shown images of letters and numbers at the same time and instructed what to focus on. When they were told to pay attention to numbers, they had to determine if the digits were even or odd. When told to concentrate on letters, they had to say whether they were vowels or consonants.
>   Again, the heavy multitaskers underperformed the light multitaskers.

"They couldn't help thinking about the task they weren't doing," the researchers reported. "The high multitaskers are always drawing from all the information in front of them. They can't keep things separate in their minds." —ADAM GORLICK, "Media Multitaskers Pay Mental Price"

As Gorlick notes, these researchers had evidence to support their hypothesis. Nevertheless, they realized the dangers of generalizing from one set of students to all students. Whenever you use data drawn from experiments, you need to be similarly cautious not to overgeneralize.

Personal experience can provide powerful support for an argument since it brings "eyewitness" evidence, which can establish a connection between author and audience. In an interview published in British fashion and culture magazine *The Face*, Raquel Willis, director of communications for the Ms. Foundation for Women, talks about the role personal stories play in her memoir, where she argues for the importance of Black trans lives.

I'm excited to be working on this book and releasing it because I feel like we don't tell our stories enough. We can never share our insights enough, and for me as a Black trans woman from Augusta, Georgia, it is important for me to elevate the ways that my life has been impacted by systems of oppression, but also the ways that I have figured out how to come up from under the thumb of oppression. And then also the way that the stories of the spaces and the movements I've been in and the relationships that I've had are complicated. I'm talking about the way that gender and identity is messy. The ways that our movements are messy, the ways that being empowered and successful is messy. I'm excited to put all that out there.

—RAQUEL WILLIS, "Why Activist Raquel Willis Believes
in Black Trans Power"

In your own writing, your personal experience can often provide important and relevant support for your argument, so make use of it when you can, remembering that personal stories can make a strong impact on your audience.

Charts, images, and other visuals. Visuals of various kinds often provide valuable evidence to support an argument. Pie charts like the one showing the literary genres favored in a college dorm, photographs like the one of the female chimpanzee cradling a stick, and many other kinds of visuals—including drawings, bar and line graphs, cartoons, screenshots, videos, and advertisements—can often make it easier for an audience to see certain kinds of evidence. Imagine how much more difficult it would be to take in the information shown in the pie chart about the genres read by students in the dorm had the data been presented in a paragraph. Remember, though, that visual evidence usually needs to be explained—photos need captions, and any visuals need to be referenced in the accompanying text.

As an author, keep in mind that the MEDIUM you're using affects the kind of EVIDENCE you choose and how you present it. In a print text, evidence has to be in the text itself; in a digital medium, you can link directly to statistics, images, and other information. In a spoken text, any evidence needs to be said or shown on a slide or a handout—and anything you say should be simple, direct, and memorable. In every case, any evidence drawn from sources needs to be fully DOCUMENTED.

Are There Any Problems with the Reasoning?

Some kinds of appeals use reasoning that some may consider unfair, unsound, or demonstrating lazy or simpleminded thinking. Such appeals are called fallacies, and because they can often be very powerful and per-suasive, it's important to be alert for them in arguments you encounter—and in your own writing. Here are some of the most common fallacies.

Ad hominem (Latin for "to the man") arguments make personal attacks on those who support an opposing position rather than addressing the posi-tion itself: "Of course council member Acevedo doesn't want to build a new high school; she doesn't have any children herself." The council member's childlessness may not be the reason for her opposition to a new high school, and even if it is, such an attack doesn't provide any argument for building the school.

Bandwagon appeals simply urge the audience to go along with the crowd: "Join the millions who've found pain relief through Weleda Migraine Remedy." "Everybody knows you shouldn't major in a subject that doesn't lead to a job." Such appeals often flatter the audience by implying that making the popular choice means they are smart, attractive, sophisticated, and so on.

Begging the question tries to support an argument by simply restating it in other language, so that the reasoning goes around in circles. For example, the statement "We need to reduce the national debt because the government owes too much money" begs the question of whether the debt is actually too large, because what comes before and after "because" say essentially the same thing.

Either-or arguments, also called false dilemmas, argue that only two alternatives are possible in a situation that actually is more complex. A candidate who declares, "I will not allow the United States to become a defenseless, bankrupt nation—it must remain the military and economic superpower of the world," ignores the many possibilities in between.

Faulty analogies are comparisons that do not hold up in some way crucial to the argument at hand. Accusing parents who homeschool their children of "educational malpractice" by saying that parents who aren't doctors wouldn't be allowed to perform surgery on their children, so parents who aren't trained to teach shouldn't be allowed to teach their children makes a false analogy. Teaching and surgery aren't alike enough to support an argument that what's required for one is needed for the other.

Here's a doozy: emoji are ruining people's grasp of English because young people rely on them to communicate. See how Geoffrey Pullum debunks this fallacy on p. 959.

Faulty causality, the mistaken assumption that because one event followed another, the first event caused the second, is also called post hoc, ergo propter hoc (Latin for "after this, therefore because of this"). For example, a mayor running for reelection may boast that a year after their administration began having the police patrol neighborhoods less frequently, the city's crime rate has dropped significantly. But there might be many other possible causes for the drop, so considerable evidence would be needed to establish such a causal connection.

Hasty generalizations draw sweeping conclusions on the basis of too little evidence: "Both of the political science classes I took were deadly dull, so it must be a completely boring subject." "You shouldn't drink so much coffee—that study that NPR reported on today said it causes cancer." Many hasty generalizations take the form of stereotypes about groups of people, such as men and women, young and elderly, and ethnic or religious groups. It's difficult to make arguments without generalizing, but they always need to be based on sufficient evidence and qualified with words like "most," "in many cases," "usually," "in this state," "in recent years," and so on.

Paralipsis (from the Greek for "omission") statements provide information after claiming such information won't be included. For example, during Socrates's trial for supposedly corrupting the youth of Athens (by inviting them to think!), the philosopher is believed to have said, "I will not mention here my grieving wife and children," and thereby of course, mentions them. That is an example of paralipsis, saying what you supposedly will not say. Former president Donald Trump is infamous for his use of paralipsis, as is Robert Downey Jr.'s character in *Iron Man*, who said: "I'm not saying I'm responsible for this country's longest run of uninterrupted peace in thirty-five years!"

Setting up a straw man misrepresents an opposing argument, characterizing it as more extreme or otherwise different than it actually is, in order to attack it more easily. The misrepresentation is like an artificial figure made of straw that's easier to knock down than a real person would be. For example, critics of the Affordable Care Act often attacked it as a "federal takeover of health care" or a "government-run system." In fact, although the legislation increased the government's role in the health-care system, it still relied primarily on private systems of insurance and health-care providers.

Slippery slope arguments contend that if a certain event occurs, it will (or at least might) set in motion a chain of events that will end in disaster, like a minor misstep at the top of a slick incline that causes you to slip and then slide all the way to the bottom. For example, opponents of physician-assisted suicide often warn that making it legal for doctors to help people end their lives would eventually lead to an increase in the suicide rate, as people who would not otherwise kill themselves find it easier to do so, and even to an increase in murders disguised as suicide. Slippery slope arguments are not always wrong—an increasingly catastrophic chain reaction does sometimes grow out of a seemingly small beginning. But the greater the difference is between the initial event and the predicted final outcome, the more evidence is needed that the situation will actually play out in this way.

WHAT ABOUT OTHER PERSPECTIVES?

In any argument, it's important to consider perspectives other than those of the author, especially those that would not support the claim or would argue it very differently. As a reader, you should question any arguments that don't acknowledge other positions, and as a writer, you'll want to be sure that you represent—and respond to—perspectives other than your own. Acknowledging other arguments, in fact, is another way of demonstrating that you're fair and of establishing your credibility—whereas failing to consider other views can make you seem closed-minded or lazy, unfair or manipulative. Think of any advertisements you've seen that claim, "Doctors recommend drug X."

The famous Got Milk? ads, run for decades by the milk industry, often suggested that milk was the secret ingredient of good health, strength, and athletic achievements, as this video ad featuring milk-drinker and pro climber Kai Lightner does. Lightner drinks a glass of milk before scaling a rock-climbing wall atop a thirty-story building. We might note, though, that these ads, funded and produced by the US milk industry, routinely omit any mention of alternative points of view—for example, that milk is a major source of saturated fats in American diets or that many people, including athletes, are lactose intolerant.

 Visit everyonesanauthor .tumblr.com to watch the video.

Got Milk? ad, 2021.

Compare such partial or one-sided arguments with the following detailed discussion of contemporary seismology:

Jian Lin was 14 years old in 1973, when the Chinese government under Mao Zedong recruited him for a student science team called "the earthquake watchers." After a series of earthquakes that had killed thousands in northern China, the country's seismologists thought that if they augmented their own research by having observers keep an eye out for anomalies like snakes bolting early from their winter dens and erratic well-water levels, they might be able to do what no scientific body had managed before: issue an earthquake warning that would save thousands of lives.

In the winter of 1974, the earthquake watchers were picking up some suspicious signals near the city of Haicheng. Panicked chickens were squalling and trying to escape their pens; water levels were falling in wells. Seismologists had also begun noticing a telltale pattern of small quakes. "They were like popcorn kernels," Lin tells me, "popping up all over the general area." Then, suddenly, the popping stopped, just as it had before a catastrophic earthquake some years earlier that killed more than 8,000. "Like 'the calm before the storm,'" Lin says. "We have the exact same phrase in Chinese." On the morning of February 4, 1975, the seismology bureau issued a warning: Haicheng should expect a big earthquake, and people should move outdoors.

At 7:36 p.m., a magnitude 7.0 quake struck. The city was nearly leveled, but only about 2,000 people were killed. Without the warning, easily 150,000 would have died. "And so you finally had an earthquake forecast that did indeed save lives," Lin recalls. . . .

Lin is now a senior scientist of geophysics at Woods Hole Oceanographic Institution, in Massachusetts, where he spends his time studying not the scurrying of small animals and fluctuating electrical current between trees (another fabled warning sign), but seismometer readings, GPS coordinates, and global earthquake-notification reports. He and his longtime collaborator, Ross Stein of the U.S. Geological Survey, are champions of a theory that could enable scientists to forecast earthquakes with more precision and speed.

Some established geophysicists insist that all earthquakes are random, yet everyone agrees that aftershocks are not. Instead, they follow certain empirical laws. Stein, Lin, and their collaborators hypothesized that many earthquakes classified as main shocks are actually aftershocks, and they went looking for the forces that cause faults to fail.

Their work was in some ways heretical: For a long time, earthquakes were thought to release only the stress immediately around them; an earthquake that happened in one place would decrease the possibility of another happening nearby. But that didn't explain earthquake sequences like the one that rumbled through the desert and mountains east of Los Angeles in 1992. . . .

Lin and Stein both admit that [their theory] doesn't explain all earthquakes. Indeed, some geophysicists, like Karen Felzer, of the U.S. Geological Survey, think their hypothesis gives short shrift to the impact that dynamic stress—the actual rattling of a quake in motion—has on neighboring faults.

—JUDITH LEWIS MERNIT, "Seismology: Is San Francisco Next?"

As this example shows, Lin and Stein's research supports the claim that earthquakes can be predicted some of the time, but they—and the author of the article about them—are careful not to overstate their argument or to ignore those who disagree. The author responds to other perspectives in three ways. She acknowledges the "all random" theory held by "some established geophysicists"; she provides evidence (not shown here) to refute the idea that "earthquakes release only the stress immediately around them." And in the last paragraph she accommodates other perspectives by qualifying Lin and Stein's claim and mentioning what some critics see as a weakness in it.

As an author, remember to consider what other perspectives exist on your topic—and what COUNTERARGUMENTS someone might have to your position. You may not agree with them, but they might lead you to QUALIFY your thesis—or even change your position. Whatever you think about other viewpoints, be sure to acknowledge them fairly and respectfully—and to accommodate or refute them as possible. And carefully investigate your reactions to opposing positions to be sure you aren't falling prey to CONFIRMATION BIAS or ATTRIBUTION BIAS. They will help you to sharpen your own thinking, and your writing can only improve as a result.

WAYS OF STRUCTURING ARGUMENTS

You can organize arguments in several ways. You may decide to approach a controversial or surprising argument slowly, building up to the claim but withholding it until you have established plenty of evidence to support it, as in this introductory paragraph from an essay about sports injuries:

> The flood of media attention highlighting damaged brains, dementia, and suicides in retired NFL players has made concussions synonymous with football. That attention was greatly needed: the debilitating consequences of brain injuries in football players of all ages has been severely overlooked. But the focus of this controversy has been far too narrow. It's true that young players need better equipment and stricter safety standards on the gridiron. But in many of the most popular sports, boys aren't the ones most likely to be afflicted by concussions. Girls are.
>
> —MARJORIE A. SNYDER, "Girls Suffer Sports Concussions at a Higher Rate Than Boys. Why Is That Overlooked?"

On the other hand, you may choose to start right off with the claim and then build support for it piece by piece by piece, as in this opening from an essay in the *Atlantic* about François Poulain de la Barre, a very early advocate of women's rights who argued that the labor of motherhood should be fairly compensated and other way-ahead-of-his-time ideas:

> What if I told you that the first modern feminist was a man, lived in the 17th century, and was a priest? I'm guessing you'd be especially skeptical about the priest part, so I'll add that when this father of feminism wrote his vindications of women's rights, he wasn't a priest yet. He became one later, probably because he was broke.
>
> —JUDITH SHULEVITZ, "I Found the Feminism I Was Looking for in the Lost Writings of a 17th Century Priest"

Another common way to begin is to note what others have said about your topic and then to present your own ideas—your claim—as a response. Whether you agree, disagree, or both, this is a way of adding your voice to the larger conversation. See how libertarian journalist Radley Balko uses this technique to begin an essay on government policies on obesity:

> This June, *Time* magazine and ABC News will host a three-day summit on obesity [that] promises to be a pep rally for media, nutrition activists, and policy makers—all agitating for a panoply of government anti-obesity initiatives. . . . In other words, bringing government between you and your waistline. . . .

This is the wrong way to fight obesity. Instead of manipulating or intervening in the array of food options available to American consumers, our government ought to be working to foster a sense of responsibility in and ownership of our own health and well-being.

—RADLEY BALKO, "What You Eat Is Your Business"

This toy store display argues that if you loved the movies, you should buy Minions-themed products.

Whatever the approach, arguments are inherently social, involving an author and an audience. They always have certain purpose(s) and make debatable claims that the author presents as true or beneficial. In addition, they all provide reasons and evidence as support for their claims, though what counts as good evidence varies across fields and communities. And finally, arguments almost always rely on assumptions that may not be explicitly stated but that the audience must agree with in order to accept the argument. For example:

Claim: Colleges should not rely on standardized tests for admission.

Reason: Such tests are socioeconomically biased.

Evidence: The disparity in test scores among various groups has been linked to cultural biases in the types of questions posed on such tests.

Assumption: Questions that favor any group are inherently unfair.

Now let's consider four ways of approaching and structuring an argument: **CLASSICAL**, **TOULMIN**, **ROGERIAN**, and **INVITATIONAL**.

Classical Arguments

Originating in the ancient Greek law courts and later refined by Roman rhetoricians, the system of argumentation often referred to as "classical" is still favored by writers in different fields. Throughout a classically structured argument, you'll rely on **ETHICAL**, **EMOTIONAL**, and **LOGICAL** appeals to your audience. Ethical appeals (those that build your credibility) are especially effective in the introduction, while logical and emotional appeals are useful anywhere.

The introduction engages the interest and attention of its audience by establishing the importance of the issue, establishing **COMMON GROUND** with the audience and showing how they are affected by the argument, and establishing the author's **CREDIBILITY**. To engage the audience, you might begin with an anecdote, ask a provocative question, or state the issue explicitly. Most writers taking a classical approach state the **CLAIM** in the introduction; students making an academic argument do so in an explicit **THESIS** statement.

The body of the argument provides any necessary background information, followed by **REASONS** and **EVIDENCE** in support of the claim. In addition, this section should make clear how the argument you're making is in the best interests of the audience. Finally, it should acknowledge possible **COUNTERARGUMENTS** and alternative points of view, presenting them fairly and respectfully and showing how your own argument is preferable.

The conclusion may summarize your argument, elaborate on its implications, and make clear what you want those in your audience to do in response. Just as it's important to open in a way that will engage their attention, you'll want to close with something that will make them remember your argument—and act on it in some way.

Let's suppose you've been assigned the topic of free speech on campus, and you believe that free speech must always be protected. That's a fairly broad topic, so eventually you decide to focus on the trend at many colleges to withdraw invitations to speakers holding controversial viewpoints. You might begin your introduction with a provocative statement, followed by some facts that will get your readers' attention (both ways of appealing to emotions) and culminating in a statement of your claim:

> Our most cherished American freedom is under attack—and not from abroad. On numerous campuses in recent years, an increasing number of invited speakers have been disinvited or cancelled or driven to decline because various members of the campus community find it offensive to hear from people who hold beliefs or positions that they or others disagree with. However, true freedom of speech requires us to encounter ideas and even language we don't like, don't agree with, or find offensive. As students, we need to wrestle with ideas that challenge us, that make us think beyond our personal beliefs and experiences, and that educate us in and out of the classroom.

You might then introduce some background information about this issue, identifying points you'll develop later as support for your claim. Here you might note examples of disinvitation campaigns. Using specific examples will make your argument more credible:

> According to the Foundation for Individual Rights in Education (FIRE), 465 college campus speakers have been disinvited between 1999 and 2020, and most often conservative speakers. As noted by Isaac Chotiner in the *New Republic*, such campaigns indicate "rising levels of intolerance, which is good for neither university campuses nor the truly shun-worthy people in our midst."

And then you might provide support for your claim by noting specific instances when invitations to speak have been withdrawn or speeches have been derailed by hecklers and giving reasons that free speech applies to everyone:

Conservative media pundit Ann Coulter, former secretary of state Condoleezza Rice, author and political commentator Michael Eric Dyson, former vice president Mike Pence, and actress and political activist Jane Fonda have been uninvited and/or silenced by hecklers as they attempted to speak or even before they had the opportunity to speak on campus. When we accept only speakers whose political philosophies are ones no one would disagree with, free speech becomes "free only if you agree with me" speech. And then we may as well give up the notion of independent thought.

Acknowledging and responding to counterarguments or other viewpoints strengthens your argument by showing you to be well informed, fair, and open-minded:

Of course, some resistance may well be justified, as when many attendees of CPAC, the Conservative Political Action Conference, protested the 2020 appearance of musician Young Pharaoh, who had posted anti-Semitic and conspiracy theory tweets (for example, that the pandemic had been "staged"). Moreover, the focus on disinvitations and cancellations ignores the fact that many controversial figures continue to speak without protest: economist Jeffrey Sachs compiled a long list on *Twitter* of schools where controversial speeches took place without incident. And in an essay for *Deseret News*, Jacob Hess offers other examples of schools that do not give in to protests for cancellations, including this one about a commencement speaker at Utah Valley University: "After getting pressure by activists on and off campus to cancel Sister [Wendy] Nelson's speech because of her traditional views on marriage and sexuality, university leaders did something brave. They stuck with their plans."

And then in your conclusion you might reiterate the major points of your argument and rephrase your claim:

We should strive to accept diverse voices and viewpoints on campus. Our conversations should challenge us to question our own long-held beliefs and closely examine those of others. We can do so only if we protect and truly embrace the right to freedom of speech—for one and all.

Toulmin Arguments

British philosopher Stephen Toulmin developed a detailed model for analyzing arguments, one that has been widely used for writing arguments as well.

The introduction presents a CLAIM, one that others will find debatable. If need be, you'll want to carefully QUALIFY this claim using words like "often" or "it may be" that limit your argument to one you'll be able to support.

Huma Farid's essay about period equity could be considered a Toulmin argument. See her essay on p. 887 and try to identify all the components.

The body of the argument presents good REASONS and EVIDENCE (which Toulmin calls "grounds") in support of the claim and explains any underlying assumptions (Toulmin calls these "warrants") that your audience needs to agree with in order to accept your argument. You may need to provide further evidence (which Toulmin calls "backing") to illustrate the assumptions. Finally, you'd acknowledge and respond to any COUNTERARGUMENTS.

The conclusion restates the argument as strongly and memorably as possible. You might conclude by discussing the implications of your argument, saying why it matters. And you'll want to be clear about what you want readers to think (or do).

For example:

> *Claim:* Our college should ban vape pens.
>
> *Qualification:* The ban should be limited to public places on campus.
>
> *Good reasons and evidence:* Vape pens contain some of the same toxins as cigarettes; research shows that they are a hazard to health.
>
> *Underlying assumptions:* Those who work and study here are entitled to protection from the harmful acts of others; the US Constitution calls for promoting "the general welfare" of all citizens.
>
> *Backing for the assumptions:* Other colleges and even some cities have banned vape pens; highly respected public health advocates have testified about their ill effects.
>
> *Counterarguments:* Vape pens are less harmful than traditional cigarettes; smokers have rights too. However, this argument limits the ban to public spaces, which means smokers can still use vape pens in their homes and other private places.

Conclusion: Our school should ban the use of vape pens in public places to protect the health of all who work and study here.

Now let's see how an argument about free speech on campus would work using Toulmin's model. You'd begin with your claim, carefully qualified if need be. The underlined words in the following example are qualifiers:

> To be successful as college students, to truly develop into independent thinkers, we need to wrestle with ideas that challenge us and that make us think beyond our personal beliefs and experiences, both in and out of the classroom. Such intellectual challenges are being diminished at <u>many</u> colleges as <u>some</u> on campus decide that ideas they or others disagree with are more threatening than educational. On numerous campuses in recent years, a number of invited speakers have been disinvited or driven to decline because some on campus find it offensive to hear from those who hold beliefs different from theirs.

You would then follow that claim with the reasons and evidence that support your claim:

> Education requires exposure to multiple points of view, at least according to Aristotle and Martin Luther King Jr. Aristotle notes in his *Metaphysics* that "it is the mark of an educated mind to be able to entertain a thought without accepting it." More than 2,000 years later, King defined the purpose of education as enabling a person to "think incisively and to think for one's self . . . [and not to] let our mental life become invaded by legions of half truths, prejudices, and propaganda."

Then you would make clear the assumptions on which you base your claim:

> Considering a variety of viewpoints is a hallmark of intelligent thinking. Freedom of speech is the right of every American.

And you'd add backing to support your assumptions:

> Freedom of speech requires us to encounter ideas, language, or words we don't like, don't agree with, or find offensive. To truly protect our own right to free speech, we need to protect those rights for everyone.

Next you'd acknowledge and respond to counterarguments and other views, showing yourself to be well informed, fair, and open-minded:

> Sometimes, supporting free speech calls for just the kind of protests that have led to disinviting speakers. For example, students and faculty at Brown University protested a speech by New York Police Commissioner Ray Kelly, arguing that it took a disruption to have their voices heard.

Finally, in your conclusion you'd remind your readers of your claim, reiterate why it matters, and let them know what you want them to think or do.

> Free speech is a bedrock value of American life. It's up to all of us to protect it—for ourselves as well as for others.

Rogerian Arguments

Noting that people are more likely to listen to you if you show that you are really listening to them, psychologist Carl Rogers developed a series of nonconfrontational strategies to help people involved in a dispute listen carefully and respectfully to one another. Rhetoricians Richard Young, Alton Becker, and Kenneth Pike developed an approach to argument based on Rogers's work as a way to resolve conflict by coming to understand alternative points of view. Rogerian argument aims to persuade by respectfully considering other positions, establishing COMMON GROUND, encouraging discussion and an open exchange of ideas, and seeking mutually beneficial compromise. Success depends on a willingness to listen and to try to understand where others are coming from.

The introduction identifies the issue and DESCRIBES it as fully and fairly as possible. It then acknowledges the various viewpoints on the issue, using nonjudgmental language to show that you respect the views of others.

The body of the argument discusses the various POSITIONS respectfully and in neutral language, presenting REASONS and EVIDENCE that show how each position might be acceptable in certain circumstances. Then state your own position, also using neutral language. You'll want to focus on the commonalities among the various positions—and if at all possible, show how those who hold other positions might benefit from the one you propose.

The conclusion proposes some kind of resolution, including a compromise if possible and demonstrating how it would benefit all parties.

Now let's take a look at how you'd approach the topic of free speech on campus using Rogerian methods. You could begin by identifying the issue, noting that there are a number of different viewpoints, and describing them respectfully:

> On many campuses today, reasonable people are becoming increasingly concerned about the unwillingness of some students and others to listen to people with viewpoints they disagree with—or even to let them speak. As Americans, we can all agree that our right to speak freely is guaranteed by the US Constitution. Yet this principle is being tested at many colleges. Some say that controversial figures should not be invited to speak on campus; others have even argued that certain people who've been invited to speak should be disinivited.

Next you'd discuss each position, showing how it might be reasonable. Then explain your position, being careful to use neutral language and to avoid seeming to claim the moral high ground:

> Some speakers may bring messages based on untruths or lies or hate. If such speakers represent a threat to campus life and safety, it seems reasonable that they be disinvited or simply not invited in the first place. Others feel that speakers who hold extreme or radical positions— on either the right or the left—should not be invited to speak on our campuses. In some cases, this position might be justified, especially if the speaker's position is irrelevant to higher education. Except in such extreme circumstances, however, a very important part of a college education involves exposure to multiple points of view. Such great thinkers as Aristotle and Martin Luther King Jr. have expressed this better than I can: in the *Metaphysics*, Aristotle notes that "it is the mark of an educated mind to be able to entertain a thought without accepting it," and more than 2,000 years later, King defined the purpose of education as enabling a person to "think incisively and to think for one's self."

Try to conclude by suggesting a compromise:

> Speakers who threaten campus life or safety may be best left uninvited. But while controversial figures may sometimes cause disruption, our

community can learn from them even if we disagree with them. Rather than disinviting such speakers, let's invite discussion after they speak—and make it open to all of the interested parties.

Invitational Arguments

Feminist scholars Sonja Foss and Cindy Griffin have developed what they call "invitational" arguments, using an approach that aims to foster conversation instead of confrontation. Rather than trying to convince an audience to accept a position, invitational argument aims to get people to work together toward understanding. This approach begins with demonstrating to your audience that you understand and respect their position, setting the stage for discussion and collaboration in which all parties can benefit.

As you can see, invitational arguments have much in common with the Rogerian approach. One important difference, however, lies in the emphasis on openness and the focus on a shared goal. Rather than presenting the audience with a predetermined position that you then attempt to convince them to accept, an invitational argument starts out by assuming that both author and audience are open to changing their minds.

The introduction presents the topic, acknowledges that there are various POSITIONS and perspectives on it, and makes clear that the goal is to understand each viewpoint so that readers can decide what they think.

In the body of the argument, you'd DESCRIBE each perspective fairly and respectfully. If you can, QUOTE those who favor each viewpoint—a way of letting them speak for themselves.

The conclusion looks for COMMON GROUND among the various perspectives, calling on readers to consider each carefully before making up their minds.

Using an invitational approach to the subject of disinvitations and free speech on campus, you could begin by focusing on the complexity of the issue, noting the ways that well-meaning people can have strong differences of opinion but still aim for a common goal:

> On many campuses today, well-meaning people are increasingly concerned about a tendency to reject others' viewpoints out of hand, without even listening to them. This trend has led to such acts

as disinviting speakers to campus or preventing them from speaking, once there. This issue might seem to pit freedom of speech against the right to resist speakers whose views may be harmful in certain ways. Yet looking only at this dichotomy ignores the many other possible perspectives people hold on this issue. The goal of this essay is to bring the major perspectives on free speech on campus together in order to understand each one thoroughly, to identify any common ground that exists among the perspectives, and to provide readers with the information they need to make informed decisions of their own.

Next, you would discuss each perspective fairly and openly, showing its strengths and weaknesses.

There seem to be at least four perspectives on the issue of free speech on our campus. First, there are those who believe that the principle of free speech is absolute and that anyone should be able to speak on any issue—period. A second perspective holds that free speech is "free" in context; that is, the right to free speech goes only so far and when it verges on harming others, it is "free" no more. Still a third perspective argues that universities must accept the role of "in loco parentis" and protect students from speech that is offensive, even if it potentially offends only a small group of students. Finally, some hold that universities are indeed responsible for maintaining a safe environment—physically, mentally, and emotionally—and that they can do so while still honoring free speech in most circumstances.

You could then look in detail at the four perspectives, allowing proponents of each to speak for themselves when possible (through quoted and cited passages) and exploring each respectfully and fairly. Following this discussion, you could identify any commonalities among the perspectives:

Each perspective on this issue has good intentions. Let us use that common ground as the starting point for further exploration, seeing if we can develop guidelines for protecting free speech on campus while also keeping our campus safe. It may well be that considering these perspectives carefully, honestly, and fairly will lead some to change their minds or to come together in certain areas of agreement. I hope that readers of this essay will do just that before taking a position on this issue.

REFLECT. Look for an argument you've read recently that caught your attention and re-read it with an eye for the argumentative strategies it uses. Does it use one particular approach—classical? Toulmin? Rogerian? invitational?—or does it mix strategies from more than one approach? Is the argument persuasive? If not, try revising it using strategies from one of these approaches.

MATTERS OF STYLE

An argument's style usually reinforces its message in as many ways as possible. The ancient Roman orator Cicero identified three basic speaking styles: "high," "middle," and "low." After surveying a wide range of prose from the mid-twentieth century, professor of English Walker Gibson identified three prominent written styles: "tough," "sweet," and "stuffy." Today, Hip Hop International hosts competitions for a number of distinct hip-hop dance styles, from "popping," to "locking," to "breaking." Whether you are speaking, writing, or dancing, you will have a style, one that can help to get your message across powerfully. Authors today have at their disposal a wide range of styles, from the highly formal language of US Supreme Court opinions, to the semiformal style of much business and professional writing, to the informal style of everyday written communication such as memos and emails, to the colloquial or vernacular styles of much spoken language, to the very casual shorthand of texts and tweets.

You can learn a lot by looking closely at the stylistic choices in an argument—the use of individual words and phrases of figurative language, of particular dialects and varieties of language, of personal pronouns (or not), of vivid images (verbal and visual), of design and format. In 2005, the *Los Angeles Times* announced an experiment it called its "Wikitorial," in which the newspaper cautiously invited readers to log on to its website to comment on and rewrite editorials:

> Plenty of skeptics are predicting embarrassment; like an arthritic old lady who takes to the dance floor, they say, the *Los Angeles Times* is more likely to break a hip than to be hip. We acknowledge that possibility.

The skeptics turned out to be right, and just three short days later the paper ended the experiment, saying:

Unfortunately, we have had to remove this feature, at least temporarily, because a few readers were flooding the site with inappropriate material. Thanks and apologies to the thousands of people who logged on in the right spirit.

Savvy readers will be alert to the power of stylistic choices in these messages. The description of closing down "Wikitorial" as "unfortunate" and the equally careful choice of "a few readers," "flooding," and "inappropriate material" mark this as a formal and judicious message that stands in sharp contrast to the slightly self-deprecating style of the first announcement, with its casual use of "plenty of " and its play on "hip." How does the sober style of the second announcement influence your response? How different might your response be if the paper had declared, "We're pulling the plug on this page since a few creeps loaded it with a bunch of crap"?

Or see how NBA player Reggie Bullock uses language in an essay about his sisters' murders:

> That's why I wanted to write something about my sisters for National Gun Violence Awareness Day. I don't want to preach or nothing. I don't have some big public service announcement about gun violence. And I don't have all the answers about how to make communities safer. I just wanna try and treat this as a day of remembrance, if that's alright with y'all. I just want to say my sisters' names. That way they live on through their memory.
>
> —REGGIE BULLOCK, "I Just Wanna Say My Sisters' Names"

Here Bullock is speaking from the heart, addressing his many fans and friends, and he chooses everyday colloquial language to do so. His use of multiple negation in the second sentence ("I don't want to preach or nothing") is a hallmark of Black language, made more powerful by the repetition. Using "wanna" instead of "want to" and "if that's alright with y'all" creates the overall impression of speaking directly, and personally, to his audience.

Now let's look at a visual argument. The following ad was created by Adbusters, a Canadian-based nonprofit organization whose website identifies it as "an international collective of artists, designers, writers, musicians, poets, punks, philosophers and wild hearts [who have] been smashing ads, fighting corruption and speaking truth to power" since 1989. Their current

Adbusters spoof ad.

spoof ad page announces that "we're in the middle of a guerilla information war for the future of the planet. Conventional weapons are useless—all we have are ideas. Join us in the meme war." Above is just one of their entries in this "meme war." The spoof ad satirizes the degree to which people today are trapped by the urge to consume more, and more, and more, in spite of mounting evidence that advertising's promise that this kind of consumption will make us happy is more and more suspect.

As an author, you will need to make such important stylistic choices, beginning—as is almost always the case—with the overall effect you want to create. Try to identify that overall effect in a word or phrase (for instance, concern, outrage, sympathy, or direct action), and then use it to help you choose specific words, images, and design elements that will create that effect and convey it most powerfully to your audience.

TWENTY

Strategies for Supporting an Argument

ARGUMENTS ARE ONLY AS STRONG as the evidence that supports them. Just as a house built on weak foundations is likely to crumble, so it is with arguments. As an author arguing a point, then, you will need to provide good, strong, reliable evidence to support your position. Rhetoricians throughout the ages have developed strategies for finding such support, strategies that continue to serve us well today. This chapter introduces you to those strategies, arranged alphabetically from analogy to signifying.

Analogy

Analogies are comparisons that point out similarities between things that are otherwise very different. Authors often use them to create vivid pictures in a reader's mind and make abstract ideas more concrete. Analogies can be especially powerful in an **ARGUMENT**, demonstrating that what is true in one case is true in another, usually more complicated, case. Here Annie Dillard draws an analogy between a writer's words and various tools:

> When you write, you lay out a line of words. The line of words is a miner's pick, a wood-carver's gouge, a surgeon's probe. You wield it, and it digs a path you follow. Soon you find yourself deep in new

territory. Is it a dead end, or have you located the real subject? You will know tomorrow, or this time next year.

—ANNIE DILLARD, *The Writing Life*

Dillard uses this analogy to suggest that writers can use words as tools for exploring a topic—to "probe" or "dig a path" into their subject.

Now see how Malala Yousafzai uses an analogy in a speech to the United Nations to support her argument that education is the best means of overcoming poverty and injustice:

> We will continue our journey to our destination of peace and education for everyone. No one can stop us. We will speak for our rights and we will bring change through our voice. We must believe in the power and the strength of our words. Our words can change the world because we are all together, united for the cause of education. And if we want to achieve our goal, then let us empower ourselves with the weapon of knowledge and let us shield ourselves with unity and togetherness.
>
> Dear brothers and sisters, we must not forget that millions of people are suffering from poverty, injustice, and ignorance. We must not forget that millions of children are out of schools. We must not forget that our sisters and brothers are waiting for a bright, peaceful future.

Malala Yousafzai addressing the United Nations.

> So let us wage a global struggle against illiteracy, poverty, and terror-
> ism and let us pick up our books and pens. They are our most powerful
> weapons.   —MALALA YOUSAFZAI, Speech at the United Nations

Yousafzai, a Pakistani activist for girls' education and Nobel Prize winner, builds her argument on an analogy that compares "the power and strength of our words" to the power of weapons used by the Taliban and others who would deny women education. She draws this analogy throughout her speech, calling upon us to use knowledge to "empower," unity to "shield," and books and pens to "wage a global struggle" against illiteracy, poverty, and terrorism. If these are our weapons, she says, then "no one can stop us." As an author, when you use an analogy, check to be sure it isn't a faulty analogy. In other words, compare things that are alike enough to support your claim; compare apples to apples, not apples to oranges.

Cause / Effect

When we analyze causes, we're trying to understand and explain why something happened. Why did US COVID-19 cases skyrocket in the winter of 2022? Why has there been so much extreme weather in recent years? Why did your chocolate chip cookies all run together on the cookie sheet? And when we think about effects, we speculate about what might happen. How will recent weather patterns affect crop yields? Will the cookies still run if you let the cookie sheet cool between batches?

Authors of **REPORTS** might focus on multiple causes for the last economic downturn, whereas someone writing a **PROPOSAL** may argue that a specific, avoidable cause had a particular effect. And in a **NARRATIVE**, you might use cause-and-effect reasoning to describe and explain an event.

Arguing about causes and effects can be tricky, because often it's almost impossible to link a specific cause to one specific effect. That's why it took decades of research to establish a strong enough link between cigarette smoking and cancer to label tobacco products with a warning: researchers had to be able to discount many other possible causes. For decades, physicists have looked for cause-effect patterns in the behavior of black holes, particularly since Stephen Hawking's discovery that black holes emit thermal radiation. Almost fifty years later, in 2021, scientists at the University of Sussex were able to confirm that black holes exert some very small but measurable pressure on their environment, a discovery they hope will lead to better descriptions of black holes.

As this example suggests, exact cause-effect relationships are difficult to determine. In 2014, the United Nations released a report on climate change, stating the possible environmental effects if we continue to burn fossil fuels. Notice how the report's authors **QUALIFY** their statements by noting what effects greenhouse emissions "could" cause to happen:

- The emission of greenhouse gases could cause dangerous warming and long-lasting changes in the climate system, severely impacting people and ecosystems.
- Failure to reduce emissions . . . could cause food shortages, flooding of cities and even nations and a dangerous climate during the hottest times of the year.

—*Climate Change 2014: Synthesis Report*

By 2021, however, the United Nations reported a much more direct finding:

- It is unequivocal that human influence has warmed the atmosphere, ocean and land. Widespread and rapid changes in the atmosphere, ocean, cryosphere and biosphere have occurred.

—*Climate Change 2021: Synthesis Report*

Noting that the planet has already warmed by 2 degrees Fahrenheit, the report concludes that we have put so much greenhouse gas into the atmosphere that this warming will continue at least until the middle of this century, even if the countries of the world take immediate steps today. These examples show the benefit of ongoing research attempting to track causal relationships, something that often cannot be done quickly.

Causal analysis can sometimes be easier to understand in a chart or graph than in words alone. See an especially famous example in the history of information graphics on the facing page, a map created in 1869. It depicts the horrific loss of life resulting from Napoleon's decision to march on Moscow in 1812. Its creator, Charles Joseph Minard, plotted information about troop numbers and locations, dates, direction and distances traveled, longitude and latitude, and the temperatures as soldiers retreated from Moscow. He used the width of the tan line to show the troops going into Russia (initially 680,000) and the much narrower black line to show those retreating (27,000). His causal argument was clear as he linked the dropping temperatures to the retreat: the colder the temperature, the fewer soldiers who survived.

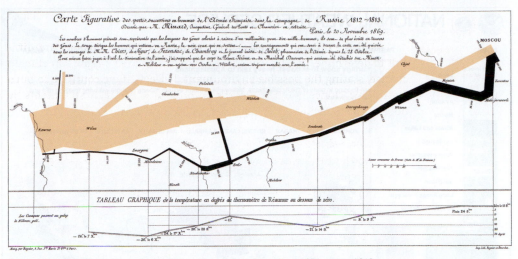

A map showing Minard's analysis of Napoleon's failed invasion of Russia in 1812.

Classification

When you classify, you group items into categories according to similarities. Tomatoes, for example, can be classified according to their varieties: cherry, plum, grape, heirloom, and so on. Authors frequently turn to classification in order to organize and elaborate on a topic. Here George Packer, a staff writer at the *Atlantic*, argues that there are four versions of America: free America, smart America, real America, and just America:

> Free America celebrates the energy of the unencumbered individual. Smart America respects intelligence and welcomes change. Real America commits itself to a place and has a sense of limits. Just America demands a confrontation with what the others want to avoid. They rise from a single society. . . . But their tendency is also to divide us, pitting tribe against tribe.
>
> —GEORGE PACKER, "How America Fractured into Four Parts"

Classification is an essential feature of all websites, one that makes accessible the enormous amount of information available on a site. Take a look at the homepage on the National Weather Service site at weather.gov and you'll find various kinds of classification, starting with the horizontal menu bar at the top that categorizes the information on the site into commonly

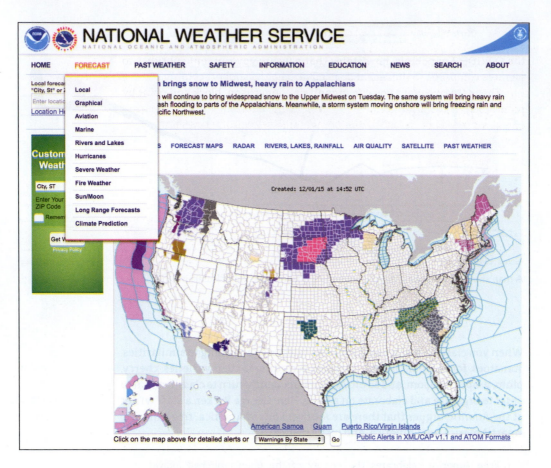

consulted topics: Forecast, Safety, News, and so on. Hovering your mouse over "Forecast" opens a drop-down menu that classifies forecasts into various categories: Aviation, Marine, Hurricanes, Fire Weather, and so on.

Comparison / Contrast

When you compare things, you focus on their similarities, and when you contrast them, you look at their differences. Both strategies can be very useful in developing an argument, helping to explain something that is unfamiliar by comparing (or contrasting) it with something more familiar.

In a **REVIEW**, for example, you might compare the *Hunger Games* trilogy to the *Squid Game* series on *Netflix*, or in a **REPORT** on unemployment during the COVID-19 pandemic, how states that gave up government subsidies to workers compared to those that decided to keep the support coming.

There are two ways you can organize a comparison: block and point by point. Using the block method, you present the subjects you're comparing one at a time, as in the following paragraphs by award-winning humorist Dave Barry:

> Most men, I believe, think of themselves as average-looking. Men will think this even if their faces cause heart failure in cattle at a range of 300 yards. Being average does not bother them; average is fine, for men. This is why men never ask anybody how they look. Their primary form of beauty care is to shave themselves, which is essentially the same form of beauty care that they give to their lawns. . . .
>
> Women do not look at themselves this way. If I had to express, in three words, what I believe most women think about their appearance, those words would be: "not good enough." No matter how attractive a woman may appear to be to others, when she looks at herself in the mirror, she thinks: woof.   —DAVE BARRY, "Beauty and the Beast"

Barry clearly exaggerates and overgeneralizes for laughs, but note that he engages in some pretty strong stereotyping as well, comparing "men" and "women" as if they were the only two categories available.

Or you can organize your comparison point by point, discussing your subjects together, one point at a time, as David Sedaris does in the following paragraph comparing his own childhood in Raleigh, North Carolina, with that of his partner Hugh, a diplomat's son who grew up in Africa:

> Certain events are parallel, but compared with Hugh's, my childhood was unspeakably dull. When I was seven years old, my family moved to North Carolina. When he was seven years old, Hugh's family moved to the Congo. We had a collie and a house cat. They had a monkey and two horses named Charlie Brown and Satan. I threw stones at stop signs. Hugh threw stones at crocodiles. The verbs are the same, but he definitely wins the prize when it comes to nouns and objects. An eventful day for my mother might have involved a trip to the dry cleaner or a conversation with the potato-chip deliveryman. Asked one ordinary Congo afternoon what she'd done with her day, Hugh's mother answered that

she and a fellow member of the Ladies' Club had visited a leper colony on the outskirts of Kinshasa. No reason was given for the expedition, though chances are she was staking it out for a future field trip.

—DAVID SEDARIS, "Remembering My Childhood on the Continent of Africa"

Comparisons of data can often be easier to understand in a chart or graph than in paragraphs. The chart included in the tweet shown here went viral in 2020 after Drew Harris, a professor at the Thomas Jefferson University College of Population Health, created it to explain why protective measures were so important in keeping health-care facilities from being overwhelmed early in the COVID-19 pandemic. His graphic and brief description led to "flatten the curve" becoming a meme—and a concept most Americans understood as one strategy and reason for riding out the pandemic with caution.

Drew A. Harris
@drewaharris   ...

Important to remember that #Covid-19 epidemic control measures may only delay cases, not prevent. However, this helps limit surge and gives hospitals time to prepare and manage. It's the difference between finding an ICU bed & ventilator or being treated in the parking lot tent.

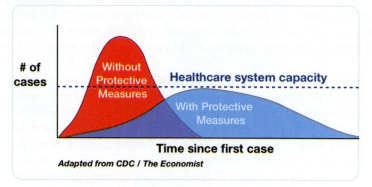

12:47 AM · Feb 28, 2020 · Hootsuite Inc.

This graph suggests that taking protective measures, like handwashing and staying home when sick, could spread out the number of COVID-19 infections over time, so the health-care system could treat all patients.

Definition

Definitions often lie at the heart of an argument: if readers don't agree with your definition of "the good life," for example, they aren't likely to take your advice on how to achieve one. As such, definitions themselves are rhetorical choices, especially in the case of controversial topics. Whether you're writing an **ANALYSIS**, a **REPORT**, or using some other genre, you'll often have reason to include definitions. Good definitions provide clear explanations of a word, concept, or idea, often by listing its characteristic features, noting distinguishing details, and perhaps providing an illustration as well. A good definition tells readers what something is.

In June of 2020, Kennedy Mitchum—a recent college grad—noticed that in online debates about racism, some people were relying on a definition of the term from Merriam-Webster's dictionary to argue that they were not racist because, as individuals, they did not think themselves superior to people of other races. These arguments depended on merriam-webster.com's definitions of "racism" at the time: "1. a belief that race is the primary determinant of human traits and capacities and that racial differences produce an inherent superiority of a particular race. 2. a doctrine or political program based on the assumption of racism and designed to execute its principles." "Racial prejudice" was not mentioned until the third and final definition provided.

Mitchum wrote to the dictionary, pointing out that people she knew never looked beyond the first definition and arguing that "racism is not only prejudice against a certain race due to the color of a person's skin, as it states in your dictionary. . . . It is prejudice combined with social and institutional power. It is a system of advantage based on skin color." To Mitchum's surprise, she got an almost immediate reply from a Merriam-Webster editor saying that the definition of racism had not been revised in decades and agreeing that it needed updating. The revised definitions recognize the systemic nature of racism today:

1. a belief that race is a fundamental determinant of human traits and capacities and that racial differences produce an inherent superiority of a particular race
2. a. the systemic oppression of a racial group to the social, economic, and political advantage of another
   b. a political or social system founded on racism and designed to execute its principles

—MERRIAM-WEBSTER.COM, "racism"

Mike Rose takes on the way intelligence is defined and demonstrated in our culture. Check out what he says on p. 963.

One term that is the focus of many arguments is "capitalism," and such arguments often begin with or include a definition of the word. Here is linguist and social critic Noam Chomsky weighing in with brief but memorable definitions of "democracy" and "capitalism." As you'll note, his definitions support his argument that capitalism is antidemocratic:

> Personally I'm in favor of democracy, which means that the central institutions of society have to be under popular control. Now, under capitalism, we can't have democracy by definition. Capitalism is a system in which the central institutions of society are in principle under autocratic control.   —NOAM CHOMSKY, *Language and Politics*

Theologian Michael Novak takes a very different view of capitalism, which he defines in glowing terms at much greater length by focusing on what capitalism *does*, in a keynote address to an international conference on economies and nation-states in 2004:

> Finally, capitalism instills in tradition-bound populations a new and in some respects a higher personal morality. It demands transparency and honest accounts. It insists upon the rule of law and strict observance of contracts. It teaches hard work, inventiveness, initiative, and a spirit of responsibility. It teaches patience with small gains, incremental but steady and insistent progress. During the 19th century, Great Britain achieved an average of one-and-a-half percent of GDP growth every year, with the happy result that the average income of the ordinary laborer in Britain quadrupled in a single century. . . .
>
> Capitalism brings in its train immense transformation, and the root of this transformation is moral. Those peoples and nations that neglect the moral ecology of their own cultures will not enjoy the fruits of such a transformation—or, having tasted them, will fall into rapid decline.   —MICHAEL NOVAK, "The Spirit of Capitalism"

Visuals can help in making arguments that hinge on definition. On the facing page is a case in which the way the word "capitalism" is designed argues for yet another definition of that word. What argument(s) do you find in this illustration?

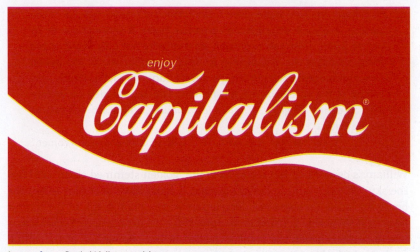

Image from *Daily Wallpapers* blog.

Description

When you describe something, you explain how it looks (or sounds, smells, tastes, or feels). Good descriptions focus on distinctive features and concrete details that add up to some **DOMINANT IMPRESSION** and help readers or listeners imagine what you are describing. You'll have occasion to use description in most of the writing you do—in a **PROFILE** of a neighborhood, you might describe the buildings and people; in a **NARRATIVE**, you'll likely describe people, places, and events.

In writing about atomic testing in Utah in her 1991 book *Refuge: An Unnatural History of Family and Place*, writer and activist Terry Tempest Williams uses description to set the scene for the facts she then presents about the high incidence of breast cancer there. She tells her father of a recurring dream she has, of a flash of light in the desert. Hearing this story, he has a sudden realization:

> "You did see it," he said.
> "Saw what?"
> "The bomb. The cloud. We were driving home from Riverside, California. You were sitting on [your mother's] lap. . . . In fact, I

remember the day, September 7, 1957. We had just gotten out of the Service. We were driving north, past Las Vegas. It was an hour or so before dawn, when this explosion went off. We not only heard it, but felt it. I thought the oil tanker in front of us had blown up. We pulled over and suddenly, rising from the desert floor, we saw it, clearly, this golden-stemmed cloud, the mushroom. The sky seemed to vibrate with an eerie pink glow. Within a few minutes, a light ash was raining on the car."

—TERRY TEMPEST WILLIAMS, "The Clan of One-Breasted Women"

Williams's description lets readers see the "golden-stemmed cloud" and feel the sky "vibrate"—and understand what it must have been like when the bomb exploded. Compare her description with a photograph of the atomic bomb test. Which do you find more powerful—the description of what it was like to be there when the bomb exploded or the photograph of the actual explosion? Would adding the photo have made Williams's description—and her argument—even more forceful?

Williams eventually testified before Congress about the effects of nuclear testing and has also worked as an environmental advocate. In 1995, aghast at a federal wilderness bill that would protect only a tiny fraction of

Fiery mushroom cloud rising above Nevada atomic bomb test site, 1957.

Utah's wilderness areas, she spoke at a public hearing. In this passage from an interview, see how her description of the hearing helps her make the case that the governmental officials were openly dismissive of her arguments:

> Congressman Jim Hansen and his colleagues sat on a riser above us. I remember how his glasses were perched on the end of his nose, how when I began to speak he was shuffling his papers, yawning, coughing, anything to show his boredom and displeasure. I was half-way through reading the citizens' testimonies—speaking on behalf of those who were at the Indian Walk-In Center the night before. He wasn't even listening—that was clear. Finally, I stopped mid-sentence and said something to the effect, "Congressman Hansen, I have been a resident of Utah all of my life. Is there anything I could say to you that will in some way alter your perspective so that you might consider wilderness in another way?"
>
> What I remember is how he leaned over his elbows and looked down on me over the tops of his glasses and said simply, "I'm sorry, Ms. Williams, there is something about your voice I cannot hear." It was chilling—personal. I don't think he was referring to the quality of the microphone. And then, it was over.
>
> —TERRY TEMPEST WILLIAMS, interview with David Sumner

Williams could have simply told us who said what and what was decided, but her description helps us picture the congressman "shuffling his papers" and "yawning," hear him "coughing," and sense "his boredom and displeasure."

Examples

If a picture is sometimes worth a thousand words, then a good example runs a close second: examples can make abstract ideas concrete and provide specific instances to back up a claim. See how novelist Gretel Ehrlich uses two examples to support her ANALYSIS of courage in a cowboy context:

> In a rancher's world, courage has less to do with facing danger than with acting spontaneously—usually on behalf of an animal or another rider. If a cow is stuck in a boghole, he throws a loop around her neck, takes his dally (a half hitch around the saddle horn), and pulls her out with horsepower. If a calf is born sick, he may take her home, warm her in front of the kitchen fire, and massage her legs until dawn.
>
> —GRETEL EHRLICH, "About Men"

You can sometimes draw on personal experience for powerful examples, provided that the experience you cite is pertinent to your point. In a letter to the editors of the *Atlantic*, reader James A. Gibson uses an example to explain an important change in his way of seeing the world during a tour of the gardens at Middleton Place in South Carolina, a former plantation that is now a historical landmark and museum:

> The grounds were immaculate and the guides enthusiastic, [and] I looked to our guide for more information. "It took 100 slaves 10 years to do this work!" I will never look at a plantation again without wondering in anger and sadness who built the home, who planted and tended the garden, who wept at night over the forced labor, and who made southern life possible by being brutalized daily.
>
> —JAMES A. GIBSON, letter to the *Atlantic*

Humor, Sarcasm, and Exaggeration

Comedian John Oliver uses humor to stake his claims. See an example by visiting everyonesanauthor.tumblr.com.

Humor can often be used to good effect to support an argument—as long as the humor fits the context and audience. Of course, humor comes in many forms, from a self-deprecating story to a gentle parody or satire, from biting ridicule to a tired joke. While few of us are talented enough to write an argument based entirely on humor, it's possible to learn to use it judiciously. Doing so can help you to connect with your audience, provide some relief from a serious topic, or just vary the tone of your argument.

In today's world, however, you'll want to make sure that most members of your audience will understand the humor. Jokes are notoriously difficult to translate, and what's funny in one language rarely comes through the same way in another. Sometimes attempts to translate advertisements into various languages are a source of humor themselves, as when Kentucky Fried Chicken's "finger lickin' good" came out in Chinese as "eat your fingers off"! And cultural context can also determine if something will be funny at all—if it will fall flat, or worse, offend. For example, a story beginning "two cows walked into a bar" might seem like a humorous way to introduce an argument about overproduction of beef in the United States, but it probably wouldn't sit too well in India, where cows are sacred.

The late journalist Molly Ivins was famous for using humor and exaggeration in arguing serious positions. In the following interview on *Nightline*, Ivins is arguing in favor of gun regulation, but she uses humorous exaggeration—and a bit of real silliness—to help make her point:

> I think that's what we need: more people carrying weapons. I support the [concealed gun] legislation but I'd like to propose one small amendment. Everyone should be able to carry a concealed weapon. But everyone who carries a weapon should be required to wear one of those little beanies on their heads with a little propeller on it so the rest of us can see them coming.   —MOLLY IVINS

Humor and exaggeration are key tactics used by Pepper Dem Ministries (PDM), a group of Ghanaian feminists who have worked to disrupt the tradition of all-male panels in political, civic, and social discussions. Referring to such panels as "manels"—like one featuring five men talking about women's issues in order to "break myths about periods" during World Menstrual Hygiene Day—a group of Ghanaian feminists employed PDM's tactic of humor and sarcasm and responded with a counter flyer of their own.

Humor isn't only a matter of ha-ha jokes. A writer's tone can also convey humor. Jessica Wildfire's essay on p. 1024 has a delightfully snarky tone that helps to support her argument.

The strategic humor (and sarcasm) in this image intends to make us laugh—but also to make us think hard about its serious, if implicit, message.

Narration and Narrative Sequencing

A good story well told can engage your audience and help to support an argument. Both writers and speakers use narratives often—in **REPORTS**, **MEMOIRS**, and many other genres. Be sure, however, that any story you tell supports your point and that it is not the only evidence you offer. In most academic contexts, you shouldn't rely only on stories to support an argument, especially personal stories.

In the following example, author Bich Minh Nguyen writes about her experiences becoming "the good immigrant student." In this essay, she uses narration to capture the tension she felt between wishing to fit in and wanting to rebel as well as to document the racist behavior she endured.

> More than once, I was given the assignment of writing a report about my family history. I loathed this task, for I was dreadfully aware that my history could not be faked: it already showed on my face. When my turn came to read out loud the teacher had to ask me several times to speak louder. Some kids, a few of them older, in different classes, took to pressing back the corners of their eyes with the heels of their palms while they chanted, "Ching-chong, ching-chong!" during recess. This continued until Anh [Nguyen's sister], who was far tougher than me, threatened to beat them up.
>
> I have no way of telling what tortured me more: the actual snickers and remarks and watchfulness of my classmates, or my own imagination, conjuring disdain. My own sense of shame. At times I felt sickened by my obedience, my accumulation of gold stickers, my every effort to be invisible.   —BICH MINH NGUYEN, "The Good Immigrant Student"

Advertisements use narrative to appeal to viewers, as in this ad campaign for animal adoption. With three frames and eight words, the cartoon below tells a story to make an argument.

NARRATIVE SEQUENCING, a feature of much Black discourse, links stories or parts of stories to make what might be abstract points in an argument into memorable and concrete narratives. Professor Geneva Smitherman elaborates on the use of narrative sequencing when she explains:

> Black English speakers will render their general, abstract observations about life, love, people in the form of a concrete narrative. . . . The relating of events (real or hypothetical) becomes a black rhetorical strategy to explain a point, to persuade holders of opposing views to one's own point of view. . . . This meandering away from the "point" takes the listener on episodic journeys and over tributary rhetorical routes, but like the flow of nature's rivers and streams, it all eventually leads back to the source.
>
> —GENEVA SMITHERMAN, *Talkin and Testifyin:*
> *The Language of Black America*

In her address to the 2016 Democratic National Convention, former First Lady Michelle Obama used this strategy, speaking personally and drawing on her own unique life experiences in the opening of her talk by flashing back to comments she had made four years earlier in arguing that her husband would make a good president:

> Remember how I told you about his character and convictions, his decency and his grace, the traits that we've seen every day that he's served our country . . . ? I also told you about our daughters, how they are the heart of our hearts, the center of our world. . . . When they set off for their first day at their new school, I will never forget that winter morning as I watched our girls, just 7 and 10 years old, pile into those black SUVs with all those big men with guns. And I saw their little faces pressed up against the window, and the only thing I could think was, what have we done?
>
> —MICHELLE OBAMA, "Remarks by the First Lady at the DNC, 2016"

Obama uses this moving story to launch her discussion of what her husband had done to protect his own (and all) children, focusing on how all parents can be role models who practice her mantra: "When they go low, go high." Later in the speech, she returns to the narrative strategy, linking her family and daughters' story to those of her ancestors:

> The story of generations of people who felt the lash of bondage, the shame of servitude, the sting of segregation, but who kept on striving and hoping and doing what needed to be done so that today I wake up every morning in a house that was built by slaves. And I watch my daughters, two beautiful, intelligent, black young women playing with their dogs on the White House lawn.

In this speech, Obama uses indirection and interwoven narrative (rather than a direct, linear argument) to argue for a particular vision of America. Obama's narrative sequencing brings the argument up close and personal, appealing to everyone who has hopes and dreams for their children.

Problem / Solution

Most **PROPOSALS** articulate a problem and then offer a solution that addresses that problem. The following passage from a National Institutes of Health press release sets out a clear problem (drinking among college students) and identifies three elements that must be addressed in any solution:

> The consequences of college drinking are larger and more destructive than commonly realized, according to a new study supported by the National Institute on Alcohol Abuse and Alcoholism (NIAAA). Commissioned by the NIAAA Task Force on College Drinking, the study reveals that drinking by college students age 18–24 contributes to an estimated 1,400 student deaths, 500,000 injuries, and 70,000 cases of sexual assault or date rape each year. It also estimates that more than one-fourth of college students that age have driven in the past year while under the influence of alcohol. . . .
>
> "Prevention strategies must simultaneously target three constituencies: the student population as a whole; the college and its surrounding environment; and the individual at-risk or alcohol-dependent drinker," says [task force co-chair Dr. Mark] Goldman. "Research strongly supports strategies that target each of these factors."
>
> —"College Drinking Hazardous to Campus Communities: Task Force Calls for Research-Based Prevention Programs"

Often writers open with a statement of the problem, as Rhoi Wangila and Chinua Akukwe do in their article on HIV and AIDS in sub-Saharan Africa:

> Simply stated, Africans living with H.I.V./AIDS and the millions of others at high risk of contracting H.I.V. are not benefiting significantly from current domestic, regional, and international high profile remedial efforts. —RHOI WANGILA & CHINUA AKUKWE, "H.I.V. and AIDS in Africa: Ten Lessons from the Field"

Wangila and Akukwe's article includes a photograph of African children affected by AIDS, which enhances their statement of the problem. The remainder of their essay then tackles the staggering complexities involved in responding to this problem.

Children in sub-Saharan Africa who have lost parents to AIDS.

Infographics are often used to present problems and solutions. Here's the final panel of an infographic that Chloe Colberg created about saving rhinos from illegal poaching. It identifies three ways of helping solve the problem: "get informed," "spread the word," and "support a campaign." The same information could be communicated in a paragraph or a bulleted list, but the large bold type makes the message much more visible.

What can you do to make a difference?
There are a number of different ways to get involved.

1

2

3

GET INFORMED

Continue to educate yourself on this issue. Visit the WWF website to learn more specifics and details about the rhino crisis.

SPREAD THE WORD

The more people that know about this issue, the better! Let your colleagues, friends and families know about this serious problem.

SUPPORT A CAMPAIGN

Support the WWF and other organizations' campaigns by learning about their efforts and considering a financial contribution.

SOURCES:
http://www.bbc.co.uk/news/uk-england-11477508
http://www.cites.org/eng/news/pr/2013/20131106_forensics.php
http://www.savetherhino.org/rhino_info/poaching_statistics
http://www.savetherhino.org/rhino_info/thorny_issues/
http://www.worldwildlife.org/species/rhino

DESIGNED FOR:
World Wildlife Fund
Chloe Colberg
December 2013

Repetition, Reiteration, and Call and Response

A form of repetition, reiteration helps support an argument through emphasis: like a drumbeat, the repetition of a keyword, phrase, image, or theme can help drive home a point, often in very memorable ways. Reiterating is especially powerful in presentations and other spoken texts—think "Yes, we can!" and Sojourner Truth's "Ain't I a Woman?" Martin Luther King Jr. was a master of effective repetition, as is evident in the famous speech he delivered on the steps of the Lincoln Memorial in 1963. Just think for a moment what would be lost in this speech without the power of that repeated phrase, "I have a dream."

> *I have a dream* that one day this nation will rise up and live out the true meaning of its creed: "We hold these truths to be self-evident, that all men are created equal." *I have a dream* that one day on the red hills of Georgia, the sons of former slaves and the sons of former slave owners will be able to sit down together at the table of brotherhood. *I have a dream* that one day even the state of Mississippi, a state

sweltering with the heat of injustice, sweltering with the heat of oppression, will be transformed into an oasis of freedom and justice. *I have a dream* that my four little children will one day live in a nation where they will not be judged by the color of their skin but by the content of their character.

I have a dream today!

—MARTIN LUTHER KING JR., "I Have a Dream"

Reiteration also works in visual texts and is a hallmark of graphic novelist Marjane Satrapi's work. Born and raised in Iran before being sent abroad in 1984 to escape what became the country's Islamic revolution, Satrapi recounts her childhood in *Persepolis I*, arguing implicitly that repressive regimes squelch individuality. In the detail of a frame shown here, Satrapi depicts a class of female students, using reiteration to make her point: all these girls are dressed exactly the same.

Here's part of a frame from *Persepolis*.

A little reiteration can go a long way. In an article published in *Ebony* magazine about the future of Chicago, see how it drives an argument that Chicago is still a home of Black innovation and creativity:

[Chicago]'s the place where organized Black history was born, where gospel music was born, where jazz and the blues were reborn, where the Beatles and the Rolling Stones went up to the mountaintop to get the new musical commandments from Chuck Berry and the rock 'n' roll apostles. —LERONE BENNETT JR., "Blacks in Chicago"

Here the reiteration of "where" and the parallel clauses help establish a rhythm of forward movement that drives the argument.

CALL AND RESPONSE, a familiar form of reiteration, grows out of African traditions of participation in such things as public gatherings, religious ceremonies, and musical performances. During the 2020 March on Washington, the civil rights activist, TV host, and Baptist minister Al Sharpton repeatedly asked the crowd, "What do we want?" to which they replied, "Justice," creating a drumbeat demand at the heart of the argument for true equity.

In a religious context, professor of English Beverly Moss studied the sermon styles of several Black ministers, noting the use of call and response as the congregation responds to the preacher throughout the sermon, punctuating the minister's argument with their affirmation:

> Minister: "When you shout before the battle is over"
> Congregation: **"Preach!!"**
> Minister: "It puts things in a proper perspective"
> Congregation: **"Yeah!"**
> Minister: "It puts you in a posture of obedience"
> Congregation: **"Yeah!"**

Call and response may be most familiar, however, from its widespread use in music, where one instrument answers another, part of a musical composition responds to another, or a performer offers a call and others provide a response.

Signifying

SIGNIFYING is a strategy for underscoring something true or important through humor and indirection. Scholar of African American literature Henry Louis Gates Jr. traces this practice to the trickster figure found in African folklore and mythology, and particularly in stories in which the "signifying monkey" gets the best of the all-powerful lion through the use of puns and other forms of humorous linguistic substitution.

Sometimes gentle, sometimes sharp, signifying "put-downs" can work to clinch an argument, as they do in Zora Neale Hurston's *Their Eyes Were Watching God*. In the novel, when Janie's husband, Joe, the mayor of the town, refuses to let her join in a signifying conversation about another character and his mule, said to be so skinny that the women were using its ribs as a washboard, Janie quietly suggests that Joe buy the mule and let it get some rest. When Joe acts on her suggestion and then is praised for being so kind and generous, Janie—who has gotten no credit for giving him the idea—steps in, telling Joe it was a "mighty fine" thing for him to do:

> Freein' dat mule makes uh mighty big man outa you. Something like George Washington and Lincoln. Abraham Lincoln, he had de whole United States tuh rule so he freed de Negroes. You got uh town so you freed uh mule. You have tuh have power tuh free things and dat makes you lak uh king uh something.
>
> —ZORA NEALE HURSTON, *Their Eyes Were Watching God*

Janie's signifying hits home, as one of the other men tells Joe that she is a "born orator," a comment that leaves the mayor speechless. Humorous and ironic put-downs like Janie's can provide strong support for an argument, in this case that women can and should be part of the conversation. You can see signifying at work in much of today's popular music, especially hip-hop, which Gates describes as "signifying on steroids."

ᕽᕽᕽ *REFLECT. Choose an example in this chapter that's all words. Think about whether the same argument could be made visually—in a chart, with a photo and caption, and so on. If that doesn't seem possible, how might you illustrate the example?*

PART VI

Research

WANT TO KNOW what the most influential country song of 2022 was? You might need to consult online rankings, note what critics have to say on the issue, check sales figures and music charts, perhaps interview country artists or enthusiasts on your campus. Filling out a March Madness basketball bracket? You'll probably review team records, player profiles, and statistics to help decide which teams you think will win. Going out to a movie? You probably look up reviews on *Rotten Tomatoes* and *IMDb* before deciding what to see. Need directions to the theater? Arguing that one film is more critically acclaimed than another? In each case you'd probably do some research—to know what route to take, to locate information, to support an argument. Research helps you do all these things, and you do them all the time.

When you do research, you engage in a process of inquiry: that is, you begin with questions for which you want answers. You might use a variety of methods—fieldwork, lab experiments, internet searches—and you'll find information in a variety of sources—books, articles, news reports, databases, websites, letters, photographs, historical records, social media, community knowledge. But research is more than a matter of compiling information; the most meaningful research is a process of discovery and learning.

As a student, you'll engage in research in many of the courses you take and in a variety of disciplines. Research is likely to be part of your work life as well. People working in business, government, and industry all need to follow research in order to make important decisions and keep up with new developments in their fields. Restaurant owners need to do research, for instance, to discover how to maximize profits from menu options and delivery methods. Engineers constantly do research to find the best equipment and supplies. And we know social media giants like *Facebook* certainly do research to learn more—and more—about user behaviors.

Artists too rely on research for inspiration and also to gather information and materials to use in their artwork. As photographer Laurie Simmons said, "Artists are always doing research on their own behalf and for their work. For some artists, it's reading. For some, it's shopping. For some, it's traveling. And I think that there's always this kind of seeking quality that artists have where they're looking for things that will jog them and move them in one direction or another."

When you do academic research, you'll often be studying a topic that scholars before you have examined. You'll want to start by learning what has been written about your topic and then thinking carefully about questions you want to pursue. In this way, you'll be engaging with the ideas of others and participating in discussions about topics that matter—and adding your own insights and discoveries. You'll be joining the larger academic conversation. The following chapters can help you do so.

REFLECT. Think about questions you've had in the past few weeks that have led you to do research to find an answer. List the different kinds of information you've sought and the ways you went about finding it. How did you then use the information or data that you gathered?

TWENTY-ONE

Starting Your Research

Joining the Conversation

WHAT DO YOU FIND MOST DIFFCULT about doing research? Gathering data? Writing it up? Documenting sources? For many of us, the hardest part is just getting started. Researchers from Project Information Literacy, a nonprofit research institute conducting ongoing national studies of college learning practices, report that US students doing course-related research have the most difficulty with three things: getting started, defining a topic, and narrowing a topic. This chapter will help you tackle these tricky first steps, identify specific questions that will drive your research, and make a schedule to manage the many tasks involved in a research project.

At the same time, we aim to show you that doing research means more than just finding sources. College-level research is a discovery process: it's as much about the search for knowledge and answers as it is about managing sources. When we search, we go down expected and unexpected paths to answer important questions, to discover solutions to problems, and to come to new perspectives on old issues. Doing research means learning about something you want to know more about. It means finding out what's been said about that topic, listening to the variety of perspectives (including those that differ from your own)— and then adding your own ideas to that larger conversation when you write about that topic.

While this chapter suggests a sequence of activities for doing research, from finding a topic to coming up with a research question to establishing a schedule, keep in mind that you probably won't move through these stages in a fixed order. The research process is messy, and you may find yourself circling back to a question or stumbling on something that sends you in a new direction. That's all part of the fun.

Find a Topic That Fascinates You

At its best, research begins as a kind of treasure hunt, an opportunity for you to investigate a subject that you care or wonder about. So finding that topic might be the single most important part of the process.

If you've been assigned a topic, study the instructions carefully so that you understand exactly what you are required to do. Does the assignment give you a list of specific topics to choose from or a general topic or theme to address? Does it specify the research methods? number and kinds of sources? a **GENRE** in which to write up your findings? Even if you've been assigned a particular topic and told how to go about researching it, you'll still need to decide what aspect of the topic you'll focus on. Consider the following assignment:

> Identify a current language issue that's being discussed and debated nationally or in your local community. Learn as much as you can about this issue by consulting reliable print and online sources. You may also want to interview experts on the issue or take a poll of everyday people's thinking on the issue. Then write a 5- to 7-page informative essay following MLA documentation style. And remember, your task is to report on the issue, not to pick one side over others.

This assignment identifies a genre (a report), research methods (interviews, a survey, and published sources), a documentation style (**MLA**), and a general topic (a current language issue), but it leaves the specific issue up to the author. You might investigate how your local school district handles bilingual education for immigrants, for example, or you could research the debate about standardized English in US classrooms.

While this particular assignment is broad enough to allow you to choose a particular issue that interests you, even assignments that are more

If the debate about standardized English catches your attention, read Missy Watson's argument on p. 1016.

specific can be approached in a way that will make them interesting to you. Is there some aspect of the topic related to your major that you'd like to look into? For example, a political science major might research court cases about dealing with language biases.

If you get to choose your topic, think of it as an opportunity to learn about something that intrigues you. Consider topics related to your major, or to personal or professional interests. Are you a hunter who is concerned about legislation that impacts gun rights in your hometown? Are you into watching *TikTok* videos and want to learn more about how the algorithm operates? Maybe you're an environmentalist interested in your state's policies on fracking.

In addition to finding a topic that interests you, try to pick one that has not been overdone. Chances are, if you're tired of hearing about an issue— and if you've heard the same things said repeatedly—it's not going to be a good topic to research. Instead, pick a topic that is still being debated: the fact that people are talking about it will ensure that it's something others care about as well.

Think about doing research as an invitation to explore a topic that really matters to you. If you're excited about your topic, that excitement will take you somewhere interesting and lead you to ideas that will in turn inform what you know and think.

> For ideas and inspiration, visit TED.com, a site devoted to "ideas worth spreading." While there, check out Steven Johnson's talk, "Where Good Ideas Come From."

Consider Your Rhetorical Situation

As you get started, think about your rhetorical situation, starting with the requirements of the assignment. You may not yet know your genre, and you surely won't know your stance, but thinking about those things now will help you when you're narrowing your topic and figuring out a research question.

- **AUDIENCE.** Who will be reading what you write? What expectations might they have, and what are they likely to know about your topic? What kinds of sources will they consider credible? What is your relationship to your audience?

- **PURPOSE.** What do you hope to accomplish by doing this research? Are you trying to report on the topic? argue a position? analyze the causes of something? something else?

- **GENRE**. Have you been assigned to write in a particular genre? Will you **ARGUE A POSITION**? **NARRATE** a historical event? **ANALYZE** some kind of data? **REPORT** information? something else?

- **STANCE**. What is your attitude toward the topic—and toward your audience? How can you establish your authority with them, and how do you want them to see you? As a neutral researcher? an advocate for a cause? something else? Check your biases—is **CONFIRMATION** or **ATTRIBUTION BIAS** keeping you from considering all sides fairly?

- **LANGUAGE**. Will you use more than one language or variety of language, and why? Will your audience expect you to use certain kinds of language or levels of formality, and will you meet—or perhaps challenge—those expectations?

- **CONTEXT**. Does the assignment have any length requirements? When is the due date? What other research has been done on your topic, and how does that affect the direction your research takes?

- **MEDIA**. Are you required to use a certain medium? If not, what media will be most effective for your audience, your topic, and what you have to say about it? Will you want or need to include links to other information? audio? video?

- **DESIGN**. Will you include photographs or other illustrations? present any data in charts or graphs? highlight any parts of the text? use headings or lists? Are you working in a discipline with specific format requirements?

Don't worry if you can't answer all of these questions at this point or if some elements change along the way. Just remember to keep these questions in mind as you work.

Narrow Your Topic

A good academic research topic needs to be substantive enough that you can gather adequate information, but not so broad that you become overwhelmed by a flood of sources on it. The topic "women in sports," for example, is too general; a quick search on *Google* will display hundreds of subtopics, from "Title IX" to "women's sports injuries." One way to find an aspect of a topic that interests you is to scan the subtopics listed in online search results. Additionally, online news sites like *Google News* and *NPR Research News* can give you a sense of current conversations related to your topic. Your goal is to move from a too-general topic to a manageable one, as shown here:

> *General topic*: women in sports
>
> *Narrower topic*: injuries among women athletes
>
> *Still narrower*: injuries among women basketball players
>
> *Even narrower*: patterns of injuries among collegiate women basketball players compared with their male counterparts

Notice how the movement from a broad topic to one with a much narrower focus makes the number of sources you will consult more manageable. But just as a topic that is too broad will yield an overwhelming number of sources, one that is too narrow will yield too little information. The topic "shin splints among women basketball players at Florida International University," for example, is so narrow that there is probably not enough information available.

Another way of narrowing a topic is to think about what you already know. Have you had any experiences related to your topic? read about it? heard about it? talked with friends about it? Suppose you have been asked to investigate a current health debate for a public health class. You think of the US opioid crisis that's affected families in your hometown. Maybe you've seen news stories in which doctors explained the positive pain management provided by opioids but caution about the addiction potential, while law enforcement officials and the families of people who suffer from addiction attest to the human cost. These are all things that can help you to narrow a topic.

Whatever your topic, write down what you know about it and what you think. Do some **BRAINSTORMING** or some of the other activities for **GENERATING IDEAS**. And if it's an issue that's being debated, you could search online to find out what's being said—just be sure to analyze what you find to ensure it's not **MISINFORMATION**. Exploring your topic in this way can give you an overview of the issue and help you find a focus that you'd like to pursue.

REFLECT. Review your research assignment. Make a list of three topics that you're considering and jot down what you already know about each. Review those notes. What do they suggest to you about your interest in these topics? Finally, narrow each one to a specific, manageable research topic. Which of the three now seems most promising?

Do Some Background Research

Existing research on your topic can provide valuable background information and give you an overview of the topic before you dive into more specialized sources. It can also help you discover issues that have not been researched—or perhaps even identified. At this point, your goal should be to see your topic in a larger context and to begin formulating questions to guide the rest of your research.

You may want to take a look at some online encyclopedias like *Wikipedia*, almanacs, and other **REFERENCE WORKS**, which can provide an overview of your topic and point you toward specific areas where you might want to follow up. Subject-specific encyclopedias provide more detail, including information about scholarly books to check out.

Finally, you might begin your background research by reading articles on popular newsmagazines' or newspapers' websites to get a sense of who's talking about the topic and what they're saying.

Articulate a Question Your Research Will Answer

Once you have sufficiently narrowed your topic, you will need to turn it into a question that will guide your research. Start by asking yourself what you'd like to know about your topic. A good research question should require more than a "yes" or "no" answer. Instead, ask an open-ended question that will lead you to gather more information and explore multiple perspectives on your topic. For example:

Topic: injuries among WNBA players

What you'd like to know: What are the current trends in injuries among WNBA players, and how are athletic trainers responding?

An athletic trainer for the Los Angeles Sparks checks on Riquna Williams midgame.

This is a question that's focused, complex, and meaningful. Before settling on a research question, you should consider why the answer to that question matters. Why is it worth looking into and writing about? And why will others want to read about it? Answering the above question, for instance, can help athletic trainers see if their approach can be improved.

Keep your rhetorical **CONTEXT** in mind as you work to be sure your research question is manageable in the time you have and narrow or open enough to address in the number of pages you plan to write. Consider also any **GENRE** requirements. If you're assigned to argue a position, for example, be sure your research question is one that will lead to an argument. Notice how each question below suggests a different genre:

> *A question that would lead to a* **REPORT** : What are the current trends in injuries among WNBA players?

> *A question that would lead to an* **ANALYSIS** : Why do women basketball players suffer specific types of injuries during training?

> *A question that would lead to an* **ARGUMENT** : At what age should young girls interested in basketball begin serious athletic training to minimize the chance of injury?

Once you've settled on a research question, your next step is to do some more research. Keeping your question in mind will help you stay focused. Your goal at this point is to look for possible answers to your question—to get a sense of the various perspectives on the issue and to start thinking about where you yourself stand.

⤳ *REFLECT. Write a research question for your narrowed topic that would lead to a report, one that would lead to an analysis, and one that would lead to an argument. Remember, try to avoid "yes" or "no" questions.*

Plot Out a Working Thesis

Now it's time to think about what answers to your research question are emerging—in sources you consult, and in your own mind. When you think you've found the best possible answer, the next step is to turn it into a working thesis. Basically, a working thesis is your hypothesis, your best guess about the claim you will make based on your research thus far.

But your working thesis may not be your final thesis. As you conduct more research, you may find more support for it or new information that prompts you to rethink your position. Consider one working thesis on the question about why WNBA players experience so many injuries during training:

> WNBA players suffer 60 percent more injuries than their NBA counter-parts because of a very short pre-draft period and little to no off-season.

This working thesis makes a clear, arguable claim and provides reasons for that position.

Keep in mind that your working thesis may well change as you learn more about your topic; stay flexible—and expect to revise it as your ideas develop. The more open your mind, the more you'll learn.

Establish a Schedule

A research project can seem daunting if you think of it as one big undertaking, rather than as a series of smaller tasks. Establishing a schedule will help you break your research into manageable steps, stay organized, and focus on the task at hand. The following template can help you make a plan:

Working title:

Working thesis:

Due date

Choose a topic. . . . . _____

Analyze your rhetorical situation. . . . . _____

Do some preliminary research. . . . . _____

Narrow your topic and decide on a research question. . . . . _____

Plot out a working thesis. . . . . _____

Do library and web research. . . . . _____

Start a working bibliography. . . . . _____

Turn in your research proposal and annotated bibliography. . . . _____

Plan and schedule any community-based or other field research _____

Conduct community-based or other field research. . . . . _____

Draft a thesis statement. . . . . _____

Write out a draft. . . . . _____

Get response. . . . . _____

Do additional research, if needed. . . . . _____

Revise. . . . . _____

Prepare your list of references or works cited. . . . . _____

Edit. . . . . _____

Write your final draft. . . . . _____

Proofread. . . . . _____

Turn in the final draft. . . . . _____

TWENTY-TWO

Finding Sources

Online and at the Library

IF YOU'VE SEEN *The Amazing Race*, a reality show that sends teams of contestants to overcome challenges as they race around the world, then you know what has kept it winning Emmys for over three decades. Each season, we see the teams learning about cultural traditions in small Greek villages, famous art in German museums, and social practices in little-known regions of the world—all during their wild race to the finish line.

What we don't see is the research on those locations and cultures conducted by more than 2,000 crew members who explore potential sites, interview residents and town officials, read histories, pore over maps, and seek information from as many sources as they can before sending the contestants out on their quests.

Like the *Amazing Race* crew, student researchers today have access to a vast number of resources. And with so much information out there—held by knowledgeable people from grandparents to government experts and housed in libraries, archives, museums, and online—you, too, face the challenge of sifting through a lot of information to find the most helpful sources. Much like finding your way to an unfamiliar location, finding sources is a process of exploration that will lead to new discoveries.

This chapter will help teach you how to use resources ranging from library catalogs, reference works, online search engines, and social media, to those gathered from community-based and other firsthand field research. The following sections introduce you to different types of sources by explaining what's out there, where to find it, how to access it, and how to use it.

Starting with *Wikipedia* or Social Media

Casual sources like *Wikipeda*, *YouTube*, and other social media can offer excellent starting points for your research. Indeed, you might even begin with social media. Of course, whenever you use online sources like these, it's crucial to read defensively—checking out the information you find to be sure it's trustworthy.

One student we know saw a *YouTube* review of a video game developed by Native Alaskans. Curious, she googled the game and found links to information about its origins and artwork, along with a statement about the purpose of the project: "We want to take back our culture out of the museum . . . to share who we are with the world." This statement got our student thinking about how Native Alaskans were representing their own culture in this game compared to how museums were representing it in exhibitions. So she searched the internet for more information about the game, visited the Native American Cultural Center on campus as well as her campus library for books and articles on Native Alaskan culture, and perused museum websites to investigate their presentation of it. She fact-checked her sources along the way, especially those turned up by *Google* searches. A *YouTube* video led this student all the way to the Smithsonian! That's how research often develops: curiosity, and the questions that grow from it, lead to valuable and relevant sources. Today, those sources are more wide ranging than ever. As professor of education Adam Banks points out, you can often learn as much about visual rhetoric, for instance, from *TikTok* and *Instagram* as you can from professional designers.

As this example also demonstrates, the questions that emerge as you examine sources will determine the kinds of information you will seek out. Do you need to learn the history of a group of people or an event? Do you need to research different perspectives on an issue? Do you need statistical data? personal narratives? Once you've determined the types of information that will best address your questions, you will need to figure out where to find this information—what sources you will need to locate or what studies you will need to conduct.

WHAT KIND OF SOURCES DO YOU NEED?

The decisions you make about what types of sources you seek, where you look for them, and how authoritative you need them to be will be guided not only by the requirements of your assignment, but also by your **PURPOSE**, **AUDIENCE**, and other elements of the **RHETORICAL SITUATION**. For the research you do in college, an important part of that rhetorical situation may be the discipline you are working in; for example, scientists tend to value research done through observation and experimentation whereas historians tend to value research done in libraries and archives or with living subjects, as in oral history projects.

You may not always be able to anticipate who will read your writing, especially if you're posting online, but you can analyze other aspects of your rhetorical situation to determine what types of sources you'll need. For instance, if your purpose is to convince voters of a political candidate's honesty, what information will be most persuasive and where will you find it? If you're writing about this candidate for a website, what kinds of sources do other writers cite on that site? Who's the site's primary audience? Will you find what you need in the library or online, or will you need to go out and talk to voters? Or will you need to use a variety of sources?

For academic research, you'll also want to keep several other distinctions in mind: the differences between primary and secondary sources, scholarly and popular sources, and older and more current sources.

Primary and secondary sources. Primary sources are original documents or materials, firsthand accounts, or field research like interviews or observations. Secondary sources are texts that analyze and interpret primary sources; they offer background and context that can help you gain perspective on your topic. Secondary sources on a subject might include scholarly books and journal articles about the topic, magazine and newspaper reviews, government research reports, or annotated bibliographies. The student who researched the video game that drew on Native Alaskan culture conducted primary research when she analyzed the game itself and secondary research when she turned to articles about the game's development and books about the politics surrounding the representation of Native Alaskans.

Whether a particular source is considered primary or secondary often depends on what the topic is. If you are analyzing an artistic work, say a film, then the film itself is a primary source, while A. O. Scott's review of the film is a secondary source. But if you are researching Scott's work as a critic, then his review would be a primary source.

Scholarly and popular sources. For most academic assignments, you'll want to consult scholarly sources: articles, books, conference papers, and websites written by authorities in a given field. Such sources have usually been peer-reviewed, evaluated by experts in the field before publication. Because they are written for a knowledgeable audience, scholarly texts go into more depth than popular sources do, citing research and including detailed documentation.

Popular sources, by contrast, are written by journalists and writers for a general audience. They are often fact-checked, but they are not likely to be evaluated by experts before publication. Popular magazines can be a good source of information on current issues since they're published so frequently. Like scholarly sources, they often cite research, but rarely do they document those citations. Make sure that any such sources you use serve your subject and purpose. If, for instance, you're writing about fashion, *Vogue* might be a useful source—but its brief reviews of new books would not be the best sources in a literary analysis. Social media posts and conversations can often serve as popular sources, too, especially when a topic has not yet been studied very much, or not much has been published on it.

DETERMINING IF A SOURCE IS SCHOLARLY

- *What are the author's credentials* to write on the topic? Look authors up to confirm they are who they say they are.

- *Who's the publisher or sponsor?* Look for academic presses, professional or academic organizations, or government sources. And see what others say about the source to ensure it's legitimate.

- *What's the URL,* if it's an online source? Colleges and universities use ".edu," and government agencies use ".gov."

- *Does the source include original research* or interpret research by others that it cites?

- *Does it provide documentation?* Look for a list of works cited or references at the end and parenthetical documentation within the text. Check out a few cited sources to see that they're reputable.

- *Does the text seem authoritative?* Most scholarly texts use FORMAL language and provide evidence that shows the author can be trusted.

- *Does the text look academic?* Scholarly texts tend to use conservative typefaces and often include tables and charts. Popular texts are more likely to include color photos and to highlight certain things in sidebars.

- *Are there ads?* Scholarly texts have few, if any, ads; popular articles and sites have many ads.

Considering these questions can help you distinguish between sources such as the two on the following page, one from the popular magazine *Wired*, the other from the scholarly journal *Sustainability*. While both sources address gene editing of livestock, note their differences in focus and design. *Wired* displays on its cover and in the article's first pages striking, high-contrast images of cows and very little text; the magazine's typography and layout emphasize decorative elements. These visuals attract readers' attention. By contrast, the journal's cover includes its name, technical diagrams and images from a featured article, and publication information. The article certainly looks scholarly; the first page includes its genre (review), its title ("Sustainable Food Production: The Contribution of Genome Editing in Livestock"), the author's name, keywords, citation information, and an abstract.

While the questions above can help you judge whether a source is scholarly or popular, keep in mind that some sources are designed to look, act, and feel scholarly, but aren't. You'll need to be vigilant about checking out all the sources you consult—even those that seem scholarly—to ensure you aren't relying on MISINFORMATION. For example, some predatory publishers pose as legitimate even while they publish anything someone pays to have published—without conducting any peer review or fact-checking. These predatory journals have names, websites, and published works that look and seem scholarly. READING DEFENSIVELY by checking out what others say about the source will help you steer clear of these unreliable sources.

Older and more current sources. You will need to determine whether older or more current sources are best suited for your topic, purpose, and audience. Although you will always want to investigate the latest news and research about your topic, sometimes older works will serve as better sources of

Popular source

Scholarly source

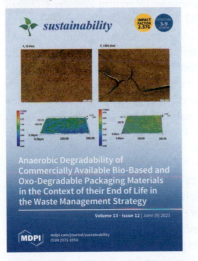

essential information. Your research question and your discipline may dictate the balance between using older or more current sources. In scientific and technological fields, the most current scholarly sources are usually favored, since change is occurring so rapidly, while in history or literature, older sources that have stood the test of time may offer the best and most fitting information.

Remember that your professors may expect—or require—certain kinds of sources. They may, for instance, want you to use only scholarly books and articles. Most projects, however, call for information drawn from many types of sources. For a report on the impact of recent floods on small local farms, for example, you may want to conduct primary research by interviewing local farmers to gather personal narratives about how they have been affected; carry out secondary research online for news reports, photographs, and videos that document the floods; and use library sources to document flood conditions in the past.

TYPES OF SOURCES—AND WHERE TO FIND THEM
Reference Works

General reference sources include general encyclopedias (*Encyclopaedia Britannica, Columbia Encyclopedia*), dictionaries (*Merriam-Webster's, Oxford English Dictionary*), almanacs (*The World Almanac and Book of Facts*), and atlases (*The National Atlas of Canada*), among others. Besides brief overviews of your topic, such sources can be helpful for gathering background information, defining core concepts and terms, and understanding the larger context of your topic—or narrowing it if need be—as well as for getting leads to more specific sources. Your library may have print versions of some of these resources and online subscriptions to others. Still other dictionaries and encyclopedias, such as *Wikipedia*, are online only, free to access, and good places to start research.

Specialized encyclopedias and wikis can give information that is more specifically related to your topic or discipline than general reference works. Through your library or the library website you'll find subject-specific resources ranging from the *Encyclopedia of Ethics* to the *Encyclopedia Latina* and many more. Specialized wikis put similar information online in groups of pages about everything from health and medicine to comic book superheroes of the Marvel universe. Wikis can connect you to information and communities online, but keep in mind that their open, collaborative authoring policy means that anyone can edit the information on a page. So be sure to evaluate the source carefully.

Bibliographies, also called references or works cited, are lists of publications that appear at the end of books or articles. If you've located a useful source, check its bibliography to find additional sources related to your topic. You may find longer, standalone bibliographies for popular or widely researched subjects; ask your librarian about availability. Many bibliographies include descriptive annotations for sources, and *Wikipedia*'s bibliographies often contain links that will take you right to the cited source.

Books

In addition to the thousands of print books available through your campus library, which you can search through the library website, you can also access many books online. *Project Gutenberg* makes freely available over 57,000 ebooks and digitized texts that are in the public domain. *Google Books* also provides free digital access to books in the public domain, and it makes these texts searchable.

Rarely will an entire book be relevant to your specific topic, so you'll need to be selective. Reading the table of contents, skimming chapter headings and sections, and examining the list of keywords and topics in the book's catalog or database entry can tell you whether all or part of a book is relevant to your research.

Periodicals

Articles from newspapers, magazines, and scholarly journals are available online through news sites, academic search engines, journal websites, and open-access databases. In addition to these, many more articles may be available to you in your library in print or online or both, depending on the library and the periodical; you can locate such articles through indexes and databases to which the library subscribes. If you can't access an index electronically through your library, ask a reference librarian to help you locate the print version on the library shelves.

Journal articles can be found online through academic search engines such as *Google Scholar* and *JURN*, which yield results from electronic journals and works from academic publishers. *Google Scholar* tends to produce more results in the sciences than in the humanities, while *JURN* focuses on humanities and the arts. You may come across a site that offers an abstract but charges to unlock the full text. In such cases, see whether your library gives you access to the journal. Your campus library may also give you access to subscription-only articles that simply don't turn up on *Google Scholar* and *JURN*, which find a portion of the scholarly texts available online but can miss content held behind paywalls. For this reason, library databases are a good place to go when searching for articles from scholarly journals.

Magazine and news articles are available online through news organizations' websites that provide searchable access to current and archived articles, photos, podcasts, videos, and streaming broadcasts. Many sites, like that of the *New York Times*, provide only limited access or require subscriptions, but some are available for free online. News aggregators like *Google News* are also useful for searching news on specific subjects, turning up articles from a range of international or local news sources; often you can personalize such aggregators to track news on specific subjects.

For newspapers that do not archive their articles online, and for older or historical articles that have not been digitized, you can turn to your library's indexes and databases. To find articles published before 1980, you'll most likely need to search indexes such as *The Readers' Guide to Periodical Literature* and *National Newspaper Index*. Many databases also include newspaper as well as journal articles and might give you access to articles not openly available online. Remember to carefully scrutinize and evaluate news sources you encounter so that you aren't duped by **FAKE NEWS** or material that seems trustworthy but isn't based on facts.

Government and Legal Documents

Official reports, legislative records, laws, maps and photos, census data, and other information from federal, state, and local governments are available for free online. Check the websites of government departments and agencies for these resources; you can access such resources for the US government through *USA.gov*. The Library of Congress website provides a large archive of photographs, maps, and other US historical and cultural materials.

Primary and Historical Documents and Oral Forms of Knowledge

Most university libraries include among their holdings rare and unique materials—books, photographs, fine art, cultural artifacts, maps, oral histories, and other material—held in the library's archives or special collections. These materials are usually searchable through the library's online catalog, but because the items are often rare and hard, if not impossible, to replace, you'll probably need to contact your library for access.

Some libraries also house digital images of rare documents in online archives; this is one way of viewing documents held by another institution that you cannot access in person. Many museums, cultural institutions, and historical societies also make their holdings available for viewing through their own online archives—you can explore many rooms of the Smithsonian this way—or through open-access archives like *Google Arts and Culture*. Remember too that, if you have access to them, oral forms of knowledge—songs, chants, riddles, folktales, parables, and other story forms—can be sources of profound cultural knowledge passed on from one generation to another.

Robin Wall Kimmerer was awed by the nine remaining native speakers of her tribe's language who gathered to teach others. Read her essay on p. 909.

SCHLESINGER LIBRARY / COLLECTIONS

Black Women Oral History Project

The Black Women Oral History Project interviewed 72 African American women between 1976 and 1981.

This website provides digital access to the Harvard Radcliffe Institute's Black Women Oral History Project and hosts audiovisual materials of Black women who "made significant contributions to American society during the first half of the 20th century."

RESEARCH SITES:
ON THE INTERNET, IN THE LIBRARY

Researchers often turn to the internet first for answers to all sorts of questions. Convenient and powerful the internet may be, but given the prevalence of false and misleading information, using this vast resource requires caution in order to verify the accuracy of what you uncover. At the same time, academic libraries still provide access to a wealth of reliable resources, from reference works to bibliographies to **PRIMARY SOURCES** and **SECONDARY SOURCES**. Most college libraries provide free online access to electronic resources such as indexes, databases, and the library catalog remotely. The following sections introduce you to some tools for finding sources online and in the library; knowing how to use these tools effectively will help you take advantage of all that these sites have to offer.

Search sites. Search engines like *Google* or *DuckDuckGo* or *Bing* help you locate information on general sites like *Wikipedia*, government information sites like the Library of Congress, and social media sites like *Twitter* or *TikTok*, as well as public sites for colleges and professional organizations. Through them, you can also access local, national, and international news sites, though some will require you to subscribe in order to access their materials.

General search sites like these are a good starting point, but you can find more specialized sources on your topic by identifying which sites will be most relevant to your search. For academic searches, try *Google Scholar* or *JURN*. *Google Scholar* locates peer-reviewed articles, books, abstracts, and technical reports by searching the websites of academic publishers, professional societies, and universities. A variety of search sites are useful for specific types of searches, including those devoted to maps or image searches (*Google Maps*, *Flickr*), news aggregators (*Google News*, *NewsNow*), and so on.

As you use search terms to further your research, move from general concepts to more specific ones by configuring short, increasingly narrowed combinations of **KEYWORDS**. Most search sites also allow advanced searches that help you limit results by date, type of source, or other criteria; check the site's search tips for guidelines that are specific to the search engine you're using.

Keep in mind that some search sites allow websites to pay for higher placement or ranking in search results, which means that what comes up first in a search may not be the most useful or relevant to your topic. And we know that many search engines collect information on us each time we search, which impacts what we see in future searches. So don't take search results at face value—go beyond the first few results and see what multiple search engines produce, not just one. You can also seek out search engines that don't track users, like *DuckDuckGo*.

Social media may be something you search unconsciously as you scroll through your personal feeds. Sites and apps like *TikTok*, *Twitter*, *Instagram*, *YouTube*, and *Facebook* are useful as "sources of sources," where you can connect with people who share your interests to find and share information and sources about those interests. *Twitter* is especially popular for sharing information, following other people, and staying on top of the latest news. Many journalists break big stories on *Twitter* before they reach official news sites. With so many prominent people tweeting, the site can also provide you with primary source material. By following experts in the field you're researching, you can find relevant quotes or introductions to a larger discussion.

Online forums, groups, and discussion lists can also connect you with people who share an interest or expertise in specific topics. Many forums and discussion lists archive past posts and threads that you can search to see if your topic has come up in the discussion before; you can also join current discussions and post questions or requests for information.

While social media let you see what others are reading and allow them to recommend sources you might otherwise miss, recent research tells us that people tend to follow like-minded individuals from similar social circles; that is, the view from your feed may be more like an echo chamber of similar views rather than truly representative of a larger reality. And we know that social media sites are where FAKE NEWS and MISINFORMATION spread most quickly. So be sure to evaluate every source: Is the person you are quoting actually an expert? Can you confirm the information in the tweet and follow it to a larger discussion? Have you checked sites like *Snopes* and *FactCheck.org* to be sure you aren't relying on something phony? See Chapters 25 and 8 for more on how to evaluate sources and avoid misinformation.

Libraries. College libraries, and their librarians, are especially valuable resources. All college libraries are staffed with reference librarians whose major responsibility is to help faculty and students with their research inquiries. While they will not do the research for you, reference librarians can be enormously helpful in showing you where you can find materials specific to your research question or topic and how you can search for them most efficiently. Their advice can save you considerable time and frustration.

In addition to reference librarians, many libraries have specialists in specific academic disciplines. Discipline (or subject) librarians work closely with academic departments to make sure that the relevant journals, databases, and books for that discipline are available to students and faculty.

Schedule a meeting with a reference or discipline librarian, and come to the meeting prepared to discuss your research question or topic. This is also your chance to ask about library resources available on your topic or any specific kinds of sources you're looking for.

Library websites. In addition to information about hours, location, and holdings, library websites often provide useful guides or tutorials to using the library. College libraries often provide online research guides that list databases, references, websites, organizations, and other discipline- or subject-specific resources. The image below shows the homepage of the College of Southern Nevada library. Note the links that allow you to search in various ways and access specific services, including getting help

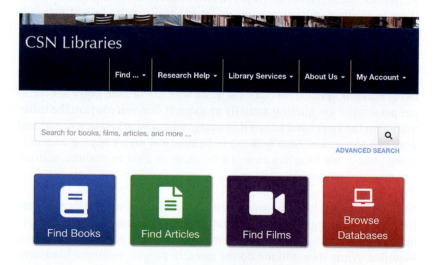

from research librarians. In addition to multiple libraries on campus and special collections, many universities offer research guides by discipline. If you're conducting research in a particular discipline, these guides can help you understand conventions and search for books, journals, and articles in that field.

Library catalogs. Most libraries have electronic catalogs that account for all their holdings. Searching the catalog is the best method for locating books and other materials, such as audio and video recordings, that you can access through the library. The record for each item includes the author, title, and publication information; a physical description of the item; and sometimes a summary or overview of the contents. The electronic catalog also provides a call number that tells you where the item is physically located in the library stacks (or a networked library), and whether or not it is currently available.

You can search a library catalog by author, title, series, subject, or keyword—or some combination of those in an advanced search. The image on the following page shows the initial search terms for a paper in an introduction to biology course. The student researcher, intrigued by the conflicting stories they had heard about the impact of caffeine on the human body, searched by selecting filters (subject terms include "caffeine," "effects," and "humans"), limited the type of source (articles only), selected a specific language (English), and specified a date range (the last ten years).

These search criteria turned up 184 results in the College of Southern Nevada library catalog. All the results yielded peer-reviewed articles, so the student knows they can trust them. Analyzing the results reveals a variety of ways the researcher could narrow their focus. For example, several of the articles examine the effects of combining caffeine with energy drinks or alcohol or high-calorie foods; others look at behavioral effects at a variety of consumption levels. The point is that doing the initial search of a library's full catalog, depending on your findings, can help you focus—or broaden—your scope and identify more specific databases that include works relevant to your topic.

Databases organize and provide access not only to listings (bibliographic citations) of journal and news articles but also, in many cases, to abstracts and full texts. Open-access databases, such as the *Directory of Open Access Journals*, allow you to search research journals that are freely available online. Your library probably also has subscriptions to a number of databases that you can access through its website.

General databases that cover a range of disciplines and topics and include scholarly articles, popular magazines, and news stories may be a good place to start. Here are a few that are widely used:

- *Academic Search Premier* (EBSCO) includes the full text of many periodicals from the humanities, arts, and sciences—the majority of which are peer-reviewed—and provides abstracts for others.

- *JSTOR* makes available scanned copies of scholarly journals from many disciplines. It includes issues from further back in time than most other scholarly databases.

- *Nexis Uni* collects full-text documents from news, government, business, and legal sources. This database includes transcripts of broadcast news sources.

- *ProQuest One* provides full-text articles from journals, periodicals, dissertations, newspapers, and video broadcasts.

Subject-specific databases are useful when you have a focused topic and research question. For example, if you are conducting research on sustainable farming efforts in urban areas, you might begin by searching databases that focus on food and nutrition, such as *Food Science and Technology Abstracts*. If you are searching for information on trends in sports injuries among basketball players, you might search a sports research database like *SPORTDiscus*. Ask a subject or reference librarian to direct you to the most relevant databases to your topic.

RUNNING SEARCHES, NARROWING RESULTS

Whether you're looking for sources online or in the library, the search typically starts with a website and an open search bar. The following tips will help you conduct searches and narrow your results, whether you're using search sites, library catalogs, or electronic databases.

Keyword searches allow you to use words and phrases, including author names, titles, and descriptions, to locate sources—but keep in mind that you may need to adjust your KEYWORDS or use synonyms if your initial searches don't yield useful results. If searching for "women's sports injuries" doesn't yield much, try "female athlete injuries." You may also need to try broader keywords ("women sports medicine"). If your search returns too many results, try narrowing your term ("women's sports injuries basketball").

Following are some advanced search techniques that can help you focus your search.

Quotation marks can be used around terms to search for an exact phrase, such as "International Monetary Fund" or "obesity in American high schools." Using quotation marks may exclude useful results, however—for example, searching for "factory farms" may omit results with "factory farming" in a library search.

Boolean operators (AND, OR, and NOT) let you refine your search by combining keywords in different ways to include or exclude certain terms. Using AND narrows a search to include all terms joined by AND; using OR broadens a search to include items with any of the terms joined by OR; and using NOT limits a search to exclude items with any term preceded by NOT. For example, if you're researching solar energy, typing in "alternative energy" will bring up many more options than "alternative energy AND solar," which reduces the number to only those that include the term "solar." Typing in "alternative energy NOT wind" narrows the search to results that exclude the term "wind."

Parentheses allow you to combine Boolean searches in a more complex way. For example, a search for "alternative energy AND (solar OR wind)" yields only those items that contain both "alternative energy" and "solar" or both "alternative energy" and "wind." Searching "alternative energy NOT (solar OR wind)" yields only items that contain "alternative energy" but do not contain either "solar" or "wind"; this kind of search might be useful, for example, if you are specifically researching forms of alternative energy other than solar or wind energy.

REFLECT. Take time now to pause and consider the sources you have gathered so far in your research. Which ones are primary, which ones secondary—and why did you choose them? How many of them come from popular sources or from social media? What use have you made of Wikipedia, *and how has it helped you (or not)? At this point, do you need to identify additional sources? If so, what kind?*

TWENTY-THREE

Conducting Research in the Field

**OURNALISTS WHO INTERVIEW** eyewitnesses, researchers who spend months observing the behavior of a particular population, historians who study archival records, pollsters who conduct surveys on the general public's attitudes about current government policies, and students who gather oral histories from local heroes or beloved grandparents—all are engaging in field research. Depending on your research question, you, too, may need to go "into the field" to conduct research, using data-gathering methods that rely on firsthand accounts. This chapter offers advice on doing field research using the three most common discovery methods: observation, interviews, and surveys or questionnaires.

Keep in mind that conducting field research on human subjects may require prior approval from your college's Institutional Review Board, a group responsible for making sure that a study will not harm research participants. Observing what kinds of clothing people wear to the mall may not need permission, but observing interactions in a private space like a doctor's office or doing any kind of field research with children probably will. Check with your instructor to find out if your project requires approval. If it does, be sure you understand the approval process and the time required to complete it.

Observations

Observation as a field research method calls for a lot more than casual "people watching." It involves taking careful notice of environments and behaviors, with a clear sense of your purpose and of how your observations will help you answer your research question. Many disciplines use observation to collect data about individuals and communities in order to answer questions about how and why they organize, relate to, or interact with one another and the world around them. In many cases, observation is the best and often the only means of gathering field data.

When reference librarian Linda Bedwell and graduate student Caitlin Banks wanted to find out how the study areas in Canada's Dalhousie University Library were being used, they observed students there, noting behaviors and paying attention to how they themselves used the spaces. Bedwell and Banks were conducting **PARTICIPANT OBSERVATION**, which operates on the principle that researchers can learn by doing as well as by watching. In non-participant observation, on the other hand, researchers focus on the actions of others but do not participate in the situations they're observing.

The process (and resulting information) will differ significantly depending on the type of observation, and you should choose the type most suitable to the situation and for addressing your research topic and question. If you're studying the winning strategies of video gamers, you might choose to do participant observation if you're an expert gamer yourself and if playing the games would result in more insightful data. If you are researching careers in medicine and want to learn about the typical day of a nurse, participant observation would not be an option—unless you have the credentials, training, and legal standing to provide patient care.

Keep your research question clearly in mind when conducting observations and carefully record what you see. Following are some additional tips for conducting effective observations.

Ryan Kohls uses participant observation to report on the cleaning staff of a large stadium. Go to p. 915 to see how his employee status gave him access, as well as a unique perspective.

- *Determine your purpose and method for observing.* Is participant observation the most suitable method to pursue your research question? Or do you need to focus only on the actions of others—and not to participate yourself? How do you expect to use the data?

- *Plan ahead.* Decide where you will observe and what materials you'll need—and make sure your equipment is ready and working. Determine whether you'll need permission to observe, photograph, and/or record; if so, secure necessary permissions ahead of time. Keep in mind that it may not be permissible to take photographs or record video in some sites—at a church service, for instance.

- *Record your observations.* Take detailed descriptive notes, even if you are also recording audio or video; your notes will add necessary texture. Note who is present, the activities they engage in, where they're situated, and pertinent details about the setting such as the physical design of the space. Be sure to record the date, time, and location. As you observe, focus on recording and describing; save the interpretation and analysis for later, when you review your notes and recordings.

- *Be guided by your purpose for observing,* but don't let that purpose restrain you. Be open to whatever you encounter. Sometimes in the process of looking for one thing, you may find something else that is equally interesting or important. And don't look only for extraordinary behavior. The goal of observation is generally to look for the routine and for patterns, things that are important because they happen regularly.

- *After your observation,* take a moment to flesh out what you've recorded with notes about any additional thoughts or reflections you have.

- *Review your observation notes* and any audio or video recordings, looking for patterns that emerge. Look for actions that recur, for topics that are repeatedly addressed, for individual participants who seem to play important roles. Also note when deviations from patterns occur and what seems to prompt the deviation. You should also consider whether those you observe have changed their behavior because they are being observed and, if so, how these changes may affect your data. You won't be able to correct for these effects, but you can consider and acknowledge them in your analysis. Your goal at this point is to start to analyze and look for an answer to your research question.

Interviews

You may find that the best way to answer your research question is to interview people who have a valuable perspective on your topic, such as experts, witnesses, or key participants in an event. Interviews can provide information that may not be available elsewhere; they can also complement other research and data-gathering methods, such as observations and library research. Just as with observations, you'll need to consider your purpose for conducting an interview and how the information you gain from it will speak to your research question.

You'll also need to decide whom to interview. Will one interview provide the needed information, or will you need several? And how qualified are those you're considering to address your research question? As a veteran of the war in Afghanistan, a friend may not be the most neutral source for a detailed analysis of the history of US involvement in the region; print sources may be a better starting place for that type of background information. But your friend probably *would* be a valuable, reliable source for a first-hand account of the combat experience and could probably provide details that you would never get from a book.

In any case, remember to ask your interviewees for their written consent to the interview, especially if your work will be published online or elsewhere. Following are additional tips for conducting successful interviews.

- *Plan to conduct your interviews early in your research* in case you have to do follow-up interviews. Contact interviewees well before your research project is due to set up appointments.

- *Do some background research* on your topic before the interview so that you can ask informed questions.

- *Write out a list of questions* that you will ask in the interview. These questions should be directly related to your research. Avoid questions that are too general that lead to one-word answers like "yes" or "no." For example, don't ask, "Do you like music?" when you want specific details. Try asking "What kind of music do you like?" instead. Also avoid leading questions, ones that prompt answers that you want. The question "Don't you think his campaign tactics were dishonest?" allows the interviewee to disagree, but it still suggests a particular response. A better question would be "What is your opinion on the candidate's campaigning methods?" This question is specific enough to provide a focus yet open enough to let the interviewee answer freely.

- *Decide how you'll record the interview.* Will you rely solely on note-taking, or will you combine it with audio or video recording? Remember to ask permission before you tape any part of an interview.

- *If your interview requires any electronic equipment,* test it before the interview to make sure that it is working. And have a back-up plan; there's nothing more frustrating than finding out that you've lost the data from a wonderful interview because your recording device's batteries died.

- *Be polite.* Remember that the person you're interviewing is doing you a favor by agreeing to speak with you.

- *Record the date, time, and location* of every interview that you conduct, and write down contact information for the interviewee.

- *Send a thank-you note* to anyone you interview.

- *Check facts, dates, and other information* the interviewee provides, especially about anything controversial. If any of the information seems questionable, try to interview others who can corroborate it or provide another perspective.

Remember that such highly structured interviews, a hallmark of Western research methods, may not be best suited for all cases. Interviewing children, for example, may call for more informal methods. Or members of some cultural communities may not wish to participate in structured events or may view such events as suspect (at best). In such cases, think about using a semi-structured interview, or an informal conversation, which will leave more room for open responses. In such an interview or conversation, using open-ended questions will let those you are talking with tell you about their own experiences in their own way—so leave time for silence and for thinking.

You may not want to ask questions at all, but just listen intently as the conversation develops in its own way. The goal of such semistructured or informal interviews is to share and gather stories, not answer a list of set questions. Such stories can be especially important in helping preserve the experiences of those whose voices have been ignored or unheard, and in letting people speak for themselves in their own times and places.

Surveys and Questionnaires

You've probably been asked to participate in marketing surveys that review products or services, or maybe you've completed questionnaires for course evaluations. Such surveys and questionnaires can be useful in soliciting information from a large number of people. Most often they aren't meant to poll an entire population; rather, they usually target a representative sample, a selected subset of a group that accurately reflects the characteristics of the whole group. The most reliable way to select such a group is by random sampling. A true random sample is one in which every member of the target population has the same chance of being selected to participate. Say you want to survey the first-year students in your school. You could try to track down each one—not a problem in a tiny school, but how about a school with 5,000 students? Not feasible. Or you could acquire a list of names from the registrar, assign each name a number (you can use *Excel* to assign random numbers), and then select a certain percentage of these people.

Unlike interviews, most surveys or questionnaires do not solicit detailed information; generally, researchers use them to gauge trends and opinions on a rather narrow topic. Following are some tips for deciding when to use surveys and how to design and administer them.

Consider your PURPOSE. If you are trying to find out how first-year medical residents negotiate the challenges of their demanding schedule, a survey is not likely to provide you with the level of detail you will need; interviews might be effective. However, if you are researching how the residents account for their time in a typical day, a survey would likely be your best method.

Once you've decided that a survey is the practical way to proceed, think about how you will use the results. Will the results provide essential support for your argument or anecdotal details to make your discussion more interesting and concrete? These considerations will determine the number of people you survey and what sorts of questions you ask them.

Determine your sample. Unless you are only after anecdotal information, you should aim to survey a representative sample, a randomly selected subset of a group that reflects the characteristics of the whole group. If you want to discover your college community's level of satisfaction with campus dining services, for example, you'll need to solicit a sample that represents all those who use the services—students, faculty, administrative staff, and visitors—while also reflecting the range of ages, genders, ethnicities, and so on. Including only students who eat breakfast in the dining halls on weekends is not likely to give you a viable sample. Most importantly, decide how many people you will contact; generally, the more of the target

Surveys must be carefully designed—or respondents may revolt!

population you sample, the more reliably you will be able to claim that your results represent trends in that population.

Choose your distribution method. Will you administer the survey over the phone or face-to-face? send a written survey through email? Or will you use an online service like *Qualtrics*, *SurveyMonkey*, or *Google Forms*? Most universities provide access to one of these tools; check with the Office of Research on campus. And don't expect a 100 percent response rate. Researchers often distribute surveys multiple times to get as many people in their targeted population to respond as they can.

Write the questions and an introduction, and test the survey. Respondents tend not to complete long or complicated surveys, so the best surveys include only a few questions and are easy to understand. Sequence questions from simple to complex unless there is a good reason not to do so. Also decide what kinds of questions are most likely to yield the information you're after. Here are examples of four common kinds of survey questions: open-ended, multiple-choice, agreement scale, and rating scale.

Open-ended

What genre of books do you like to read?

Where is your favorite place to read?

Multiple-choice

Please select your favorite genre of book (check all that apply):
__ nonfiction   __ autobiography   __ self-help   __ histories   __ sci-fi / fantasy

Please indicate your favorite location for reading (check one):
__ coffee shop   __ library   __ home   __ office   __ other

Agreement scale

Indicate your level of agreement with the following statements:

	Strongly Agree	Agree	Disagree	Strongly Disagree
The library should provide both ebooks and print books.	☐	☐	☐	☐

Rating scale

How would you rate your campus library?
__ Excellent   __ Good   __ Fair   __ Poor

Your questions should focus on specific topics related to your research question. For example, undergraduate researcher Steven Leone believed that solar energy provided by thin-film solar cells could be an alternative to fossil fuels as an energy source, but he knew many homeowners resist expensive solar installations. His project, "The Likelihood of Homeowners to Implement Thin-Film Solar Cells," was designed to discover the relationship between homeowners' socioeconomic status and their attitudes about alternative energy sources in order to gauge how likely they are to adopt this new technology. These are the questions he asked in a survey of homeowners. Notice that some call for short answers while others ask for detailed responses.

1. What is your combined annual household income?

2. What is the highest level of education you have completed?
   __ high school   __ some college   __ college   __ graduate school

3. How is your home currently heated?

4. How much are you currently spending each year on home energy costs?

5. Which is more important to you—saving money or going green? Why?

6. Have you considered using solar energy as your home energy source? Why or why not?

7. Thin-film solar cells cost significantly less than conventional solar installations and offer an energy-cost payback that is twice as fast. How much more likely does this information make it that you will implement this technology?

  __ very likely   __ somewhat likely

  __ somewhat unlikely   __ very unlikely

8. Thin-film solar cells will increase the resale value of your home. How much more likely does this information make it that you will implement the technology?

  __ very likely   __ somewhat likely

  __ somewhat unlikely   __ very unlikely

Leone's questions provided him with data that he then analyzed to determine patterns (education, income, lifestyle) of attitudes on his topic.

Once you're satisfied with your questions, write a brief introductory statement that will let participants know the purpose of the survey and what they can expect, including an estimate of how long it will take to complete.

Manage your results. When you are done collecting data, be sure to carefully record and store your responses. If you are using a print survey, one simple method is to use a blank survey and tally responses next to each question. You can also use a spreadsheet to track your findings. If your survey includes open-ended questions, you may want to choose some responses to quote from when you present your results.

ANALYZE your results. After you have tallied up the results, you need to analyze them, looking for patterns that reveal trends and explaining what those trends may mean. Data from survey results do not speak for themselves. You need to analyze the data by looking for similar responses to questions you've asked. Group those that are similar, and label them accordingly. What does that pattern or trend in responses indicate about your research question? When you move from describing the patterns and trends to discussing what they mean, you are interpreting your results. For example, suppose you survey 200 classmates about a recent increase in student fees for using the on-campus fitness center and find that the students, by a significant majority, think the fees are cost-prohibitive. Based on your survey results, your interpretation is that the fee increase is likely to lead to decreased use of the fitness center. You didn't just report the results; you interpreted them as well.

REFLECT **on how well the survey worked.** When you present your results, be sure to acknowledge any limitations of your survey. What topics were not covered? What populations were not surveyed? Was your sample truly representative?

Information today lives everywhere: in traditional libraries, on the internet, and out "in the field." Your research question and your rhetorical situation—including who will read your research—dictate what kinds of sources you consult and cite. But ultimately, research should be a voyage of discovery, driven by *your* questions based on *your* desire to find out something you didn't know before.

REFLECT. Now that you have thought more about your topic and questions, done some preliminary research, decided on methods, and located some sources, review the types of sources that you've consulted. How did each of those sources help you answer your research question? What other sources do you still need to consult?

TWENTY-FOUR

Keeping Track
Managing Information Overload

RESEARCH HAS ALWAYS been a complex, often messy process, but in an age of information overload, it can spiral out of control. Where did you save those notes you took? Did that piece of information come from the book you read or somewhere online? Researchers today have so much information at their fingertips that just managing it has become tough. This chapter aims to help you organize potential chaos by offering tips for keeping track of your sources, taking notes, and maintaining a working bibliography.

Keep Track of Your Sources

The easiest way to keep track of your sources is to save a copy of each one. Especially when your research is spread out over several days or weeks, and when it turns up dozens of potential sources, don't rely on your memory.

Electronic sources. Download and save files, or print them out. Make copies of materials on the web, which can change or even disappear: print out what you might use, or take a screenshot and save the image. Some subscription database services let you save, email, or print citations and articles. You might also want to use one of the free online tools, like

Zotero, *Mendeley*, or *EndNote*, that allow you to organize, store, analyze, and share articles, images, and even audio/video files.

Once you've got copies of your sources, the challenge is to keep them all organized and easy to find. Store all the files for a single project together in one folder, and use a consistent file-naming system so each item is easy to identify. The following example uses the author's last name and keywords from the source's title. All of the sources are saved in a folder under the course title and assignment.

> ENG1102_ResearchProject
>   Ehrenreich_ServingFL
>   Farid_PeriodEquity
>   Kohls_CleanSweep
>   McMillanCottom_NewMoney

You should note the author(s), title, URL, and date of access on each item—and record all the other information needed in a **WORKING BIBLIOGRAPHY**. And be sure to back up your files regularly.

Print sources. Make photocopies, printouts, or scans of everything you think will be useful to your research. Keep a copy of the title and copyright pages of books and of the table of contents or front page of periodicals. Label everything with the author(s), title, and page numbers, and file related materials together in a clearly marked folder.

Take Notes

Experienced researchers have a tip for you: take notes systematically *as you go*. But this doesn't mean you should write down everything; carefully select what details you note to be sure they are pertinent to your project. **ANNOTATING** as you read sources will help you understand and synthesize important information.

Take notes in your own words, and be sure to enclose any words taken directly from a source in quotes. Label anything you **QUOTE**, **PARAPHRASE**, or **SUMMARIZE** as such so that you'll remember to acknowledge and document the original source if you use it—and so that you don't accidentally **PLAGIARIZE**. Consider this example:

Lyon, G. Reid. "Learning Disabilities." *The Future of Children: Special Education for Children with Disabilities*, vol. 6, no. 1, spring 1996, pp. 54-76. *JSTOR*, https://doi.org/10.2307/1602494.

Summary: Focuses on problems with reading skills but cautions that early intervention with reading won't address all manifestations of LD.

- Lyon is chief of Child Development and Behavior in the National Institute of Child Health and Human Development at the NIH.
- LD is several overlapping disorders related to reading, language, and math (paraphrase, p. 54).
- Lyon: "[L]earning disability is not a single disorder, but is a general category of special education composed of disabilities in any of seven specific areas: (1) receptive language (listening), (2) expressive language (speaking), (3) basic reading skills, (4) reading comprehension, (5) written expression, (6) mathematics calculation, and (7) mathematical reasoning" (direct quotation, p. 55).

Comment: Lyon breaks down LD into more precise categories. Defines each category. Will help me define LD.

Notice the specific information included in these notes—all details that will help if the researcher decides to reference this article: a full MLA-style citation, a brief summary of the article, and notes about how the source might relate to the research question. And notice too that the researcher indicated what's paraphrased and what's quoted from the text, with page numbers in each case. If the researcher does end up citing this source, they'll already have all the necessary documentation information.

Label notes with full citation information—the author(s) and title, publication information, page numbers, and DOI or URL.

SUMMARIZE **the main point** and any other important points you want to remember in a sentence or two. Be very careful to write your summary using your own words and sentence patterns.

If you copy any passages by hand, take care to do so accurately, paying attention to both words and punctuation and enclosing the entire passage in quotation marks. If you cut and paste any text from electronic sources, put quotation marks around it.

Record your own questions or reactions as you go. Do you see anything that addresses your research question? anything you want to know more about? Consider what role this source might play in your own writing. Does it provide evidence? represent perspectives? show why the topic matters?

Maintain a Working Bibliography

It might seem easiest to keep track of only the sources that you know you will cite. But what if your research takes an interesting twist and you need to include some of the sources that you discarded earlier? Rather than having to stop and search for those earlier sources, you could access the source information right away if you keep a working bibliography—a list of all the sources that you consult.

Unlike a final works-cited or reference page, a working bibliography constantly changes as you find more sources to add to it. Keep it on a computer or individual note cards for easy updating. As you update, note for each source whether you have already used it, rejected it, or are still thinking about it. You may even want to annotate your working bibliography with a summary of each source you know you will use. Eventually this information will become your list of works cited or references, so follow whatever DOCUMENTATION style you plan to use. See Chapters 30 and 31 for information on MLA and APA styles.

Consider the working bibliography entries below:

Ellcessor, Elizabeth. *Restricted Access: Media, Disability, and the Politics of Participation*. New York UP, 2016.
> Drawing on multiple examples from participant observation in blogs and websites, Ellcessor exposes the myth of digital media accessibility to the disabled. Support for my central claim re: "participatory culture"?

Brueggemann, Brenda. Email interview with the author. 10 July 2022.
> Professor Brueggemann is one of the world's leading scholars in the field of disability studies. This interview focused on the growth of that field.

WHAT TO PUT IN YOUR WORKING BIBLIOGRAPHY

For books

- Author(s), editors, or translators
- Title
- Edition or volume number
- Publisher, year published

For periodicals

- Author(s)
- Title and subtitle of article
- Name of periodical
- Volume and issue numbers, date
- Page numbers
- URL and date accessed (for online sources)

Additional items for articles accessed via database

- Name of database
- DOI, if there is one, or URL if not

For web sources

- Author(s) and any editors
- Title and subtitle of source
- Name of site
- Date published, posted, or last updated
- Publisher or sponsor of site (if different from name or site)
- Page or paragraph numbers, if any
- URL
- Date accessed

∾ *REFLECT. Review your system for organizing and tracking your sources. Are your sources organized in a way that lets you go back to them easily? Have you recorded the necessary bibliographic information? If you answered "no," take the time now to set up a system that helps you keep track of your sources.*

Alba, Levy, and Myers's report references twenty sources. The authors probably employed strategies like the ones in this chapter to keep everything organized. See their article on p. 837.

TWENTY-FIVE

Evaluating Sources

OUR RESEARCH QUESTION: Is it important to address the loss of sea ice in the Arctic? If so, what actions should be taken? To research this topic, rather than merely giving your opinion, you would need to consult reliable sources—that is, sources that can be verified. Which do you trust more: official reports from the National Aeronautics and Space Administration (NASA), the *Wikipedia* page on the issue, or a post on the website *JunkScience.com*? Is it possible that they could all be useful? How will you know?

Your integrity as an author rests to some degree on the quality of the sources you cite. You can probably trust that an article or website recommended by a known expert on your topic is a credible source of information. And sources you find in library catalogs or databases are often vetted for credibility by professionals.

Even so, given the overwhelming amount of information available—not to mention *mis*information—it can be difficult to know which sources will be useful and relevant. Or, as media expert Howard Rheingold puts it, the unending stream of information on the internet calls for some serious "crap detection": we have to know how to separate the credible sources from the questionable ones. This chapter provides advice for determining which sources are well suited to your purposes and for evaluating those sources with a critical eye.

Is the Source Credible and Useful?

A database search turns up fifty articles on your topic. The library catalog shows hundreds. *Google*? Thousands. So how do you decide which sources are reliable and worth your time and careful attention?

To get started, conduct a quick overview; answering a few preliminary questions will help you begin to evaluate the usefulness and reliability of any source:

- *What's the title?* Is it relevant to your topic? Is it serious? ironic or humorous? too good to be true, or too extreme? Does the title match the content?

- *Who are the authors?* Are their credentials listed? What institutions are they affiliated with and how might that affect their viewpoints? What does a quick search of their names reveal about them?

- *Who's the publisher or sponsor?* An academic press? A news organization? A government agency or nonprofit group? If there is an "about" page, what does it tell you about the publisher? Consider whether the publication or sponsor has a particular agenda or bias.

- *What's the URL?* For online sources, the URL can tell you what kind of organization sponsors the site: ".com" signals commercial organizations, ".edu" colleges and universities, ".org" nonprofits, ".gov" government agencies.

- *When was it published or updated?* Think about whether your topic calls for current sources or for older historical ones. You may well want to consult both, but if your source is on a website, check to see that both the site and its links are still active.

- *What's the genre?* Note especially whether the source is **REPORTING** information or **ARGUING** a claim. You'll probably want to look for both, but for those that make an argument, you'll need to identify sources that corroborate your source and/or provide different viewpoints on it.

Practice Lateral Reading

Take a tip from education researcher Sam Wineburg, and don't waste time reading a source online, even after you've conducted a quick overview, until you're sure it's worth your while. Practicing what Wineburg calls lateral reading can help you make this determination. Wineburg and his colleagues have written widely about several studies conducted with undergraduate students, historians, and professional fact-checkers. Asked to determine which of two websites was most credible, among those study participants only the fact-checkers were able to make that determination correctly with any consistency. Why weren't the others? Because the students and historians stayed stuck on the website, looking closely at it and at what it said about itself and assessing its professional "look." But as you know, looks can be deceiving, as can information provided online.

Wineburg says the students and historians were reading "vertically," that is, attending to what was on the website and dutifully scrolling through it—in other words, taking it at its own word(s). The fact-checkers, on the other hand, left the websites in question immediately, opened new tabs, and searched for the title or author or sponsor, and then followed the trail to see what they could find out, based on what others said, about the two sites they were given to compare. They also looked for links leading *to* the sites, not just from them. And—voila!—they quickly found that one site was legitimate and well respected; the other—not so much.

That's **READING LATERALLY**—moving across the tabs you've opened about a source to investigate it instead of diving into the source itself first. Doing so will help ensure that you spend time digging only into sources that are reputable and thus worth your attention.

Let's say you are conducting preliminary research on climate change and a *Google* search turns up an article titled "On the Linearity of Local and Regional Temperature Changes from 1.5°C to 2°C of Global Warming." You've heard that small temperature increases are significant and the title uses academic language, so this article sounds promising.

Before you read the article itself, however, you open a few new tabs and check out the author and source to make sure they're reliable. Written by seven international scholars, this report is hosted on the American Meteorological Society's page and was published in the *Journal of Climate*. Checking out each author uncovers their individual publishing history and helps verify their expertise. Googling each of the authors' names plus "climate science" further confirms their identities and expertise by uncovering university faculty bios and *Google Scholar* pages listing when their works have been cited by others. You note that the American Meteorological Society's About page says it was established in 1919, has more than 13,000 members, and "is the nation's premier scientific and professional organization promoting and disseminating information about the atmospheric, oceanic, and hydrologic sciences." This information paints a picture of a trustworthy

"On the Internet, nobody knows you're a dog."

source, but don't stop there. Read laterally by opening a new tab to search the society's name and you'll find other trustworthy sources (such as *Forbes* and *JSTOR*) that confirm its mission and stature.

Fact-Check and Triangulate

Those professional fact checkers who were able to discern reliable from unreliable sources may have worked for one of the fact-checking sites that are available to all writers today: services such as *FactCheck.org*, *PolitiFact*, or *Full Fact*. These sites are easily accessible and easy to use, and while they can, of course, make mistakes, each of them strives for as much objectivity and accuracy as possible. Let them give you a hand in your evaluations.

Checking facts can help you do what social scientists refer to as "triangulation"—that is, making sure that you can find sources that corroborate claims made in a source. If a claim or argument is acceptable, then you are sure to find two or three (or more) credible, reputable sources agreeing with it.

Check for Your Own Biases

Remember that you have your own point of view and your own biases (we all do!), and these biases can be silently at work when you are searching for and evaluating sources. Be especially careful, then, to avoid two of the most common of these biases. **CONFIRMATION BIAS** is the tendency to look for and accept information you already agree with—that simply confirms what you already think—and to reject information that contradicts your beliefs. As mystery writer Louise Penny's Chief Inspector Gamache tells his younger colleagues, "Never believe everything you think." In your search for sources that address climate change in the Arctic, then, make sure that you don't simply gather up the first sources you find that agree with your stance on this issue.

ATTRIBUTION BIAS is another bias common to most of us—the tendency to think that our motivations for believing what we believe are objectively good while thinking that those who we disagree with have objectively wrong motivations. Let's say you find an author writing about loss of sea ice in the Arctic who argues this loss is simply due to "natural variation," and your immediate response is to think "that writer just has his head in the sand and is driven by the need not to know!" That's attribution bias at work. Now, it may well be that the author is indeed ignoring facts, and if so then it's your job to show that's the case, not to dismiss the author for a perceived personality trait ("the need not to know").

Consider Alternative Perspectives

One way to guard against biases—your own as well as those of others—is to consider different perspectives on the topic you are researching, especially those that don't simply confirm what you already think. Looking through bibliographies, footnotes, or abstracts of sources you have already vetted can help you identify alternative viewpoints. The article "On the Linearity of Local and Regional Temperature Changes from 1.5°C to 2.0°C of Global Warming," for example, opens with an abstract containing the keyword "climate change," which links to a list of additional articles on the subject, including one offering a different point of view. And when you check that article, you find that it leads you to yet another take on the subject. Such discoveries are at the heart of the research process—all part of the adventure.

REFLECT. *Read the* Popular Science *article titled "The 4 biggest lessons from the latest IPCC climate report" on* everyonesanauthor.tumblr.com. *Underlined words are linked to sources—open a few of these sources and evaluate them, using the questions earlier in this chapter, to determine if they would be credible sources for research on this topic. What are the sources' strengths and weaknesses?*

Read Your Sources with a Critical Eye

Once you've determined that a source is credible and useful, you'll need to read it closely, thinking carefully about the author's position, how (and how well) it's supported, and how it affects your understanding of the topic as a whole. As you read your sources, approach each one with a critical eye and practice **READING DEFENSIVELY**. The following questions can help you do so.

Consider your own RHETORICAL SITUATION. Will the source help you achieve your **PURPOSE**? Look at the preface, abstract, or table of contents to determine how extensively and directly it addresses your topic. Will your **AUDIENCE** consider the source reliable and credible? Are they expecting you to cite certain kinds of materials, such as historical documents or academic journals? Does the source confirm what you already believe or expose you to new considerations?

What is the author's STANCE? Does the title indicate a certain attitude or perspective? How would you characterize the **TONE**? Is it objective? argumentative? sarcastic? How does the author's stance affect its usefulness for your project?

What do you notice about the author's LANGUAGE? What is the level of formality? Does the author favor passive voice? use—or avoid using—first person? What jargon or disciplinary vocabulary does the author use, and why? What languages and/or dialects does the author use, and why?

Who is the AUDIENCE for this work? Is it aimed at the general public? members of a field? policy makers? Sources written for a general audience may provide useful overviews or explanations. Sources aimed at experts may be more authoritative and provide more detail—but they can be challenging to understand.

Graphic essays like the one by Josh Trujillo and Levi Hastings on p. 978 don't usually document their sources. Try your hand at verifying the factual information presented in their essay.

What is the main point, and what has motivated the author to write? Is the author responding to some other argument? What's the larger conversation on this issue? Is it clear why the topic matters?

What REASONS **and** EVIDENCE **does the author provide as support?** Are the reasons fair, relevant, and sound? Is the evidence drawn from credible sources? Is the kind of evidence (statistics, facts, examples, expert testimony, and so on) well matched to the point it's supporting? How persuasive do you find the argument? Check facts and claims you're skeptical of by using non-partisan sites (*Snopes* and *FactCheck.org*) that confirm truths and identify lies or misinformation.

Does the author acknowledge and respond to other viewpoints? Look for mention of multiple perspectives, not just the author's own view. And be sure to consider how fairly any COUNTERARGUMENTS are represented. The most trustworthy sources represent other views and information fairly and accurately, even (especially) those that challenge their own. Check out the people and ideas cited to be sure they are reliable themselves. The sources and ideas an author is in conversation with can help you uncover more information about the author's own purpose, stance, and bias.

Have you seen ideas given in this source in any other sources? Information found in multiple sources is more reliable than information you can find in only one place. Do other credible sources challenge this information? If so, is what's said in this source controversial or is it flat-out false? Copy and paste the basics of the questionable statement into a search engine and see what reliable sources say. Even if a search brings up many hits, that doesn't make the information accurate—look for sources you trust to weigh in.

How might you use this source? Source materials can serve a variety of purposes in both your research and your writing. You might consult some sources for background information or to get a sense of the larger context for your topic. Other sources may provide support for your claims—or for your credibility as an author. Still others will provide other viewpoints, ones that challenge yours or that provoke you to respond. Most of all, they'll give you some sense of what's been said about your topic. Then, in writing up your research, you'll get your chance to say what *you* think—and to add your voice to the conversation.

We know seas are rising and we know why. The urgent questions are by how much and how quickly.

243.5 mm

2017

SEA LEVEL RISE: 1880 - 2017

Sea levels have risen about **8 inches** since the beginning of the 20ᵗʰ century. The ocean is projected to rise by as much as **3 feet or more** by the end of this century.

Earth's climate history shows there have been times when ice sheets rapidly changed and created multiple meters of sea level rise in a century. As Earth's ice sheets continue to change, a key question facing scientists now is: Could human-caused global warming be pushing us toward one of those times?

0 mm

1880

CSIRO updated Church and White (2011);

GSFC (2017), Global Mean Sea Level Trend from Integrated Multi-Mission Ocean Altimeters, Ver. 4.

SUPPOSE YOU'RE RESEARCHING climate change and come across NASA's site sealevel.nasa.gov. Checking out what others say about the source tells you that NASA stands for National Aeronautics and Space Administration, *and it is an agency of the US government that employs thousands of scientists and publishes information on natural-science topics. If you were writing an essay about how climate change impacts coastal communities, what kinds of information from this site would you consider citing? How does the way information is presented make it seem more or less credible? For instance, compare the site's report "Melting Ice, Warming Ocean" with the infographic shown above. Is one source easier to vet than the other? Does one seem more fitting to cite than the other—and if so, why?*

REFLECT. Choose three or four different sources on your chosen topic— possibly one from a government source, one from an academic journal, one from a popular source, and one from a website. Evaluate each of the sources according to the guidelines laid out in this chapter. Explain what makes each source credible (or not).

TWENTY-SIX

Annotating a Bibliography

INSTRUCTORS ASSIGN ANNOTATED bibliographies for a variety of reasons: to encourage you to read sources carefully and critically, summarize useful information about them, and think about how and why you expect to use particular ones. The rhetorical purpose of the annotated bibliography is to inform—yourself as well as others. Conscientiously done, annotating a bibliography will help you gain a sense of the larger conversation about your topic and think about how your work fits into that conversation.

In a formal annotated bibliography, you **DESCRIBE** each of the sources you expect to consult and state what role each will play in your research. Sometimes you will be asked to **EVALUATE** sources as well—to assess their strengths and weaknesses in one or two sentences.

Characteristic Features

Annotations should be brief, but they can vary in length from a sentence or two to a few paragraphs. They also vary in terms of style: some are written in complete sentences; others consist of short phrases. And like a works-cited or reference list, an annotated bibliography is arranged in alphabetical order. You'll want to find out exactly what your instructor expects, but most annotated bibliographies include the following features.

Complete bibliographic information, following whatever documentation style you'll use in your essay— MLA, APA, or another style. This information will enable readers to locate your sources—and can also form the basis for your final list of works cited or references.

A brief SUMMARY or DESCRIPTION of each work, noting its topic, scope, and STANCE. If a source reports on research, the research methods may also be important to summarize. Other details you include will depend on your own goals for your project. Whatever you choose to describe, however, be sure that it represents the source accurately and objectively.

Evaluative comments. If you're required to write evaluative annotations, you might consider how **AUTHORITATIVE** the source is, how up-to-date, whether it addresses multiple perspectives, and so on. Consider both its strengths and its limitations.

Some indication of how each source will inform your research. Explain how you expect to use each source. Does it present a certain perspective you need to consider? report on important new research? include a thorough bibliography that might alert you to other sources? How does each source relate to the others? How does each source contribute to your understanding of the topic and to your research goals? Or if you find that it isn't helpful to your project, explain why you won't use it.

A consistent and concise presentation. Annotations should be consistent: if one is written in complete sentences, they all should be. The amount of information and the way you structure it should also be the same throughout. And that information should be written concisely, summarizing just the main points and key details relevant to your purpose.

Following are two annotated bibliographies, the first descriptive and the second evaluative.

A Descriptive Annotated Bibliography

SAURABH VAISH was a management and entrepreneurship major at Hofstra University when he wrote this descriptive annotated bibliography for a research project on renewable and sustainable energy in rural India. We then adapted two entries to demonstrate evaluative annotations.

Renewable and Sustainable Energy in Rural India

SAURABH VAISH

Complete bibliographic information for this source, following MLA style.

"Renewable Energies." Deutsche Energie-Agentur GmbH (dena), www.dena.de/en/topics-projects/renewable-energies/.

Summarizes and describes the source.

The German Energy Agency provides information on energy efficiency, renewable energy sources, and intelligent energy systems. The website contains some useful databases, including ones of energy projects in Germany and of recent publications. It is a useful source of information on the manufacturing and production of alternative energy systems.

Explains how this source will inform his project.

Though this site does not provide statistical data and covers only a limited number of projects and publications, it includes links to much useful information. It's a great source of publications and projects in both Germany and Russia, and so it will help me broaden my research beyond the borders of the United States.

Moner-Girona, Magda, editor. *A New Scheme for the Promotion of Renewable Energies in Developing Countries: The Renewable Energy Regulated Purchase Tariff.* European Commission Joint Research Centre, 2008, https://doi.org/10.2790/11999.

> This report on a study by the PhotoVoltaic Technology Platform discusses how to promote the use of renewable energy in developing countries. The report proposes a new tariff scheme to increase the flow of money where it is most needed, suggests several business models, and estimates the potential success or failure of each. The detailed information it provides about business models, supply-chain setups, and financial calculations will be useful in my analysis, especially in the part of my project that deals with photovoltaic cells.

United States, Energy Information Administration. *Renewable & Alternative Fuels Reports.* U.S. Dept. of Energy, 1998–2010, www.eia.gov/renewable/reports.cfm.

> This site reports statistical and graphical data on energy production and consumption, including all major alternative energies. It provides access to numerous databases on energy consumption across the world. This website provides most of the statistical data I will need to formulate conclusions about the efficiency of alternative energies. Its data are reliable, current, and easy to understand.

An Evaluative Annotated Bibliography

Moner-Girona, Magda, editor. *A New Scheme for the Promotion of Renewable Energies in Developing Countries: The Renewable Energy Regulated Purchase Tariff.* European Commission Joint Research Centre, 2008, https://doi.org/10.2790/11999.

This report on a study by the PhotoVoltaic Technology Platform discusses how to promote renewable energy in developing countries. The report proposes a new tariff scheme to increase the flow of money where it is needed, suggests several business models, and estimates the potential success or failure of each.

The detailed information about business models, supply-chain setups, and financial calculations will be useful, especially in the part of my project that deals with photovoltaic cells. One potential drawback is that this report makes premature assumptions: the proposed business plan is probably not implementable for twenty years. Even so, this report contains useful data and models, including graphs and charts, that will support my claims.

Evaluates the source, acknowledging a potential weakness—but explains why it is still useful.

United States, Energy Information Administration. *Renewable & Alternative Fuels Reports.* U.S. Dept. of Energy, 1998–2010, www.eia.gov/renewable/reports.cfm.

This website reports statistical and graphical data on energy production and consumption, including all major alternative energies. It provides access to numerous databases on energy consumption across the world.

This site provides most of the statistical data I will need to formulate conclusions about the efficiency of alternative energies. Its data are reliable, current, and easy to understand. I see no potential weakness in this source because the data it presents are non-biased statistics and supporting graphics pertaining to alternative energies. Using such data will allow me to shape my own opinions regarding the research I undertake.

Evaluates the source and explains why the source's unbiased data are valuable.

TWENTY-SEVEN

Synthesizing Ideas

Moving from What Your Sources Say to What You Say

IT'S **SUPER BOWL SUNDAY**, just before kickoff and just after the teams have been introduced. The broadcast cuts back from a commercial set to DJ Schmolli's "Super Bowl Anthem" and returns to the stadium where Idina Menzel is singing "The Star-Spangled Banner." So you've just heard two anthems. But what else, if anything, do these tunes have in common? Answer: each is a mash-up—a combination of material from a number of different sources. "The Star-Spangled Banner" combines a poem written by Francis Scott Key with the music of an old British drinking song. DJ Schmolli's effort combines clips from more than a dozen popular stadium anthems, from Madonna's "Celebration" to Queen's "We Will Rock You." And each smoothly integrates its sources into one seamless whole. In academic terms, the authors of these mash-ups have effectively engaged in **SYNTHESIS**, bringing together material from various sources to create something new.

Like a good mash-up artist, you don't just patch together ideas from various sources when you do research. Instead, you synthesize what they say to help you think about and understand the topic you're researching—to identify connections among them and blend them into a coherent whole that at the same time articulates *ideas of your own*. This chapter will help you blend ideas from sources with your own ideas smoothly and effectively—just like a really great mash-up.

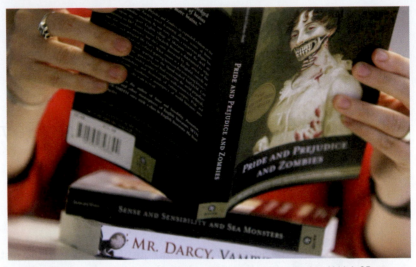

An unlikely mash-up: Jane Austen's *Pride and Prejudice* and . . . zombies! With 85 percent Austen's original text and 15 percent zombie gore, *Pride and Prejudice and Zombies* became an instant best seller, setting off a slew of literary monster mash-ups.

Synthesizing the Ideas in Your Sources

Here are some questions to help you synthesize information as you work with your sources. Try **ANNOTATING** sources with these questions in mind:

- What issues, problems, or controversies do your sources address?
- What else do your sources have in common? Any ideas? facts? examples? statistics? Are any people or works cited in more than one source?
- What significant differences do you find among sources? Different stances? positions? purposes? kinds of evidence? conclusions?
- Do any of your sources cite or refer to one another? Does one source provide details, examples, or explanations that build on something said in another? Does any source respond specifically to something said in another?

Your goal is to get a sense of how the information from your various sources fits together—how the sources speak to one another and what's being said about your topic.

One function of a synthesis is to establish **CONTEXT** and set the scene for what you yourself have to say. See how the following example, from a scientific article on contemporary extreme weather events, brings together information from four different sources (linked to via superscript numbers) to substantiate the claim that "the climate crisis is here."

> The climate crisis is here. Extreme weather events fueled by climate change are becoming increasingly more frequent, more destructive, and more costly. Wildfires are burning millions of acres annually.[1] Frequent back-to-back hurricanes,[2] coupled with increased flooding, cause damage to already-climate-vulnerable communities unable to recover fully before the next disaster strikes. And the science reveals it will only get worse.
>
> The Sixth Assessment Report[3] from the U.N. Intergovernmental Panel on Climate Change (IPCC), released on August 9, 2021, paints a dire picture of climate change, with the U.N. chief referring[4] to its findings as "a code red for humanity." The report, which was written by 234 scientists and reviews thousands of existing scientific studies on climate change, states that it is unequivocal that humans are responsible for climate change.
>
> —KAT SO & SALLY HARDIN, "Extreme Weather Cost U.S. Taxpayers $99 Billion Last Year, and It Is Getting Worse"

Look now at this dramatic opening to a magazine article on actor-comedian Robin Williams's death by suicide:

> If you were keeping an eye on Robin Williams' *Twitter* feed these past few months—along with his 875,000 followers—you would have noticed nothing the least bit worrying about the 63-year-old actor-comedian's state of mind. On June 6, he uploaded a photo of himself visiting the San Francisco Zoo, where one of the monkeys had been named after him ("What an honor!"). On July 30, he posted a plug for his December movie, *Night at the Museum: Secret of the Tomb* ("I hope you enjoy it!"). And then, on July 31, in what would turn out to be his last public comment, he tweeted his daughter Zelda a birthday message ("Quarter of a century old today but always my baby girl").

Eleven days later, he was discovered dead at his home in Marin County, California.

—BENJAMIN SVETKEY, "Robin Williams Remembered by Critics, Close Friends"

By synthesizing multiple sources—in this case, Williams's *Twitter* posts—and presenting them as one cohesive whole, Svetkey paints a picture of a seemingly happy man.

While these two examples are quite different—one cites news stories and reports by national and international agencies, the other cites social media sources in a popular magazine—they both synthesize information to give readers context for what the authors go on to say. For all writers, including you, that's the next step.

REFLECT. *Try your hand at synthesizing the sources you've consulted so far for something you're writing. What patterns do you see? What's being said about your topic?*

Moving from What Your Sources Say to What You Say

As a researcher, you'll always be working to synthesize the ideas and information you find in your research, to see the big picture and make sense of it all. At the same time, you'll be striving to connect the data you gather to your own ideas and to your research goals. You'll be learning a lot about what many others have discovered or said about your topic, and that will surely affect what you yourself think—and write—about it. Here are some questions that can help you move from the ideas you find in your sources to the ideas that you'll then write about:

- How do the ideas and information in your sources address your RESEARCH QUESTION? What answers do they give? What information do you find the most relevant, useful, and persuasive?

- How do they support your tentative THESIS? Do they suggest reasons or ways that you should expand, qualify, or otherwise revise it?

- What viewpoints in your sources do you most agree with? disagree with? Why?

- What conclusions can you draw from the ideas and information you've learned from your sources? What discoveries have you made in studying these sources, and what new ideas have they led you to?

- Has your research changed your own views on your topic? Do any of your sources raise questions that you can pursue further?

- Have you encountered any ideas that you would like to build on—or challenge?

- From everything you've read, what is the significance of the topic you're researching? Who cares, and why does it matter?

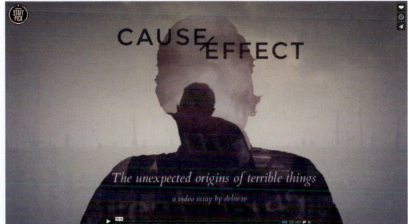

THINK BEYOND WORDS

↗ *WATCH* Cause / Effect: The Unexpected Origins of Terrible Things, *a video essay by Adam Westbrook that makes a fascinating argument about what caused World War I. (You'll find it at* everyonesanauthor.tumblr.com.*) As you'll see, Westbrook synthesizes many kinds of sources and information—history books, maps, cartoons, newspapers, archival photographs and video, data from public records, and more—to build a case for his argument. How does he synthesize all these sources in a video? How does he go about introducing each one and weaving them* together *with his own ideas?*

When you work with your sources in this way, you can count on your ideas to grow and change. As we've been saying, research is an act of learning and inquiry, and you never know where it will lead. But as soon as you sit down and write, no matter what you say or how you say it, you will be, as Kenneth Burke says, "putting in your oar," adding your voice *and your ideas* to the very conversation you've been researching.

Entering the Conversation You've Been Researching

Once you've thought carefully about what others have said about your topic, you can add your own voice to the conversation. Look at the following example from the introduction to an essay tracing the changes in political cartoons in the United States between World War II and the Iraq War. See how the writer synthesized ideas from her research into her writing in a way that set up her own questions and thoughts.

Fig. 1. Gary Markstein. Cartoon. *Copley News Service*, 9 Dec. 2006.

A cartoon shows carolers at the White House door making a choral argument to then president George W. Bush that "we gotta get out of this place," referring to America's involvement in the war in Iraq (fig. I). Bush appears completely oblivious to their message.

First published in 2006, this cartoon offered a critique of America's continued presence in Iraq by criticizing the president's actions and attitudes towards the war, exemplifying how political cartoons have long been, and continue to be, a prominent part of wartime propaganda.

Combining eye-catching illustrations with textual critique, such cartoons do more than merely convey messages about current events. Rather, political cartoons serve as a tool for shaping public opinion. In fact, since the 1500s, political cartoons have used satirical critiques to persuade the general public about matters large and small (McCloud 16–17).

In the United States, the political (or editorial) cartoon is a form of editorializing that began as "scurrilous caricatures," according to Stephen Becker, author of *Comic Art in America*. Becker's book looks, in part, at the social history of political cartoons and states that it was only after "newspapers and magazines came to be published regularly . . . that caricatures, visual allegories, and the art of design were combined to form . . . modern editorial art" (15). As all-encompassing as that description of "modern editorial art" seems to be, it suggests several questions that remain unanswered: Do cartoonists use common themes to send their critical messages? As society and regulations change from generation to generation, do the style and content of political cartoons change as well? Have political cartoons become "modernized" since World War II? The essay that follows aims to answer as well as draw out the implications of these questions.

—JULIA LANDAUER, "War, Cartoons, and Society: Changes in Political Cartoons between World War II and the Iraq War"

Landauer begins with a cartoon (a primary source) that illustrates a point she is making—that editorial cartoons are known for stinging political critiques. She then refers to a source (McCloud) to provide some background information and then another (Becker) to provide additional commentary on the "modern editorial art" she intends to examine in her essay. At that point, she raises questions "that remain unaddressed"—and says that answering

See how Judith Newman pairs two seemingly unconnected topics— autism and Apple's personal assistant— when she writes about her autistic son's relationship with Siri on p. 943.

them will be the work of her essay. Thus she uses ideas drawn from her sources to introduce her own ideas—and to weave them all together into a strong introduction for her essay.

In your college writing, you will have the opportunity to come up with a research question and to dig in and do some research in order to answer it. That digging in will lead you to identify key sources already in conversation about your topic, to read and analyze those sources, and to begin synthesizing them with your own ideas. Before you know it, you won't be just listening in on the conversation: you'll be an active participant in it.

LITERATURE REVIEWS

When instructors refer to "the literature" on a topic, chances are they are not talking about poetry or other literary texts but using an earlier meaning of the term. As early as 1450, "literature" referred to knowledge contained in books or to a body of printed material on any subject. And this meaning of the term continues today, referring to published research on a given topic. In a "literature review," you survey, synthesize, and evaluate that research. You may be assigned to write a full essay reviewing a body of research, or to write a literature review as part of a report on research you've conducted.

Characteristic Features

Survey of relevant research on a focused topic. The "literature" you review should be credible, relevant sources related to your topic. When the choice is yours, a narrow, focused topic is best: a review of literature about colonies and postcolonialism could easily run to dozens of pages or more, whereas a review of what's been said about one particular aspect of those topics would be far easier to manage. For a review that is part of a report, the choice of what literature you review will be guided by your RESEARCH QUESTION and should include all the sources your study is based on. Keep your assignment and particular discipline in mind to determine what kinds and number of sources should be included in your review.

Fair-minded synthesis / summary of the literature. Once you've collected the sources for review, you'll need to **SYNTHESIZE** them, looking for significant connections, trends, and themes, as well as for how the sources agree and disagree with each other. A synthesis of important trends might begin something like this: "Researchers writing about X have generally taken one of three perspectives on it," followed by a section discussing each perspective and what it has contributed to understanding of the topic. **SUMMARIZING** the themes and trends shows that you understand how the pieces in your review relate to one another and provides readers with an overview of their significance.

An evaluation of the literature. Your evaluation might point out strengths and weaknesses, as well as any limitations in what the research covers. Are there any important questions that are ignored? claims for which little evidence exists? gaps that future research might address?

Clear organization. To organize your review, think about how the sources relate to one another. Do they follow a clear progression that makes chronological organization most helpful? Do they group by theme? by the authors' perspectives? by research methods? by trends in results? Looking for ways your sources connect with one another will help you not only to synthesize the information but also to organize it in a way that helps readers see significant patterns and trends.

Complete, accurate documentation. Be sure to follow carefully any disciplinary conventions for **CITING** and **DOCUMENTING** sources. For guidelines on following **MLA** or **APA** style, see Chapters 30 and 31.

CRYSTAL AYMELEK wrote the following literature review as part of a research report for a course in experimental psychology at Portland State University.

The Effects of Mindfulness Meditation and Exercise on Memory

CRYSTAL AYMELEK

ACCORDING TO INFORMATION PROCESSING THEORY (Atkinson & Shiffrin, 1968; Baddeley & Hitch, 1974), human memory comprises three interconnected systems: sensory, working, and long-term memory. Information is initially detected and processed by sensory memory. The quality or quantity of information processed by the senses is determined by one's level of attention. Once information enters the working memory, its ability to be encoded and stored in long-term memory depends on the efficiency by which initial connections are made. Together these systems process information in response to stimuli through encoding, storage, and retrieval.

Research has shown that high levels of stress both impede the ability to focus attention and interfere with working memory during the acquisition of information (Al'Absi et al., 2002; Aronen et al., 2005; Hadwin et al., 2005; Owens et al., 2012). The effects of stress on brain structure have been connected to decreases in gray matter similar to those typically associated

The opening paragraph establishes the research topic and gives background information about the workings of human memory.

with age (Hedden & Gabrieli, 2004). Such changes occur when an excess of cortisol inhibits the production of neurotrophic proteins responsible for the growth of new neurons and synapses. Consequently, this process prevents regions of the brain associated with memory, such as the hippocampus and amygdala, from modulating effectively (Cahill & McGaugh, 1996; Roozendaal et al., 2009).

Summarizes a major research finding and cites the relevant sources. Parenthetical citations follow APA style.

Over the last 30 years, mindfulness meditation has acquired popularity in the West thanks to its success in effectively reducing stress (Grossman et al., 2004). Moreover, it is increasingly applied in psychotherapeutic programs for the treatment of anxiety and depression (Hofmann et al., 2010; Salmon et al., 1998). Meditation is the practice of training mental attention to achieve a state of mindfulness. Mindfulness is commonly defined as "paying attention in a particular way: on purpose, in the present moment, and non-judgmentally" (Kabat-Zinn, 1994, p. 4). It is cultivated during meditation and extends beyond the time of formal practice. The major components of mindfulness, awareness and acceptance of both internal (e.g., cognitive-affective-sensory) and external (e.g., social-environmental) experiences in the present moment, are considered effective agents against psychological malaise (Keng et al., 2011). The benefits of meditation for anxiety and depression are thought to depend partially on the development of greater attentional control and executive functioning (Baer, 2003). That is, attention and energy previously allocated towards negative stimuli are redirected to more neutral or positive stimuli. The most well known meditation treatment program is Mindfulness-Based Stress Reduction (MBSR; Kabat-Zinn, 1990), which provides comprehensive training in mindfulness meditation.

Aymelek organizes her literature review by topic; here she surveys literature on mindfulness and meditation.

Such a statement, along with the numerous citations, helps demonstrate Aymelek's awareness of the relevant research literature.

Recently, meditation has been correlated with improvements in memory, cognition, and brain composition (Jha et al., 2007, 2010; Ortner et al., 2007; Slagter et al., 2007; Zeidan et al., 2010). A study by Hölzel et al. (2011) used the Five Facet Mindfulness Questionnaire (FFMQ; Baer et al., 2006) and magnetic resonance imaging (MRI) to measure subjective mindfulness and neurological changes in participants of the MBSR program. They found that participation in MBSR was associated with increased concentrations of gray matter in the left hippocampus and other regions of the brain connected to learning and memory processes as well as emotion regulation. Regular meditation has also been shown to strengthen one's ability to control impulses and maintain attention with less utilization of the brain's resources (Kozasa et al., 2012). In addition, Pagnoni and Cekic (2007) used voxel-based morphometry (VBM; Ashburner & Friston, 2000) and a computerized neuropsychological test to determine if gray matter in older populations would be more substantial in experienced meditators versus inexperienced meditators. They discovered increases in gray matter volume in the putamen, an area of the brain implicated in attentional processes, in experienced meditators but not in controls.

Summarizes a recurring research finding, citing the findings of several studies.

5

The benefits of exercise for physical health and stress management have been well documented (Penedo & Dahn, 2005). Current research suggests that frequent exercise may also enhance brain structure and cognition (Griffin et al., 2011; Hillman et al., 2008). A controlled, longitudinal study by Erickson et al. (2011) aimed to determine if aerobic exercise could promote growth in the hippocampus of healthy older adults. They used an MRI to measure volume in the hippocampus at baseline, at 6 months, and at 1 year, and found that the exercise group demonstrated an increase in the left and right hippocampus by 2.12% and 1.97%, respectively, while the control group showed a 1.40% and 1.43% decrease in hippocampal volume. Furthermore, physical activity has been reported potentially to enhance cognitive capacity through the production of brain-derived neurotrophic factors (BDNF), which support the growth of neurons and synapses (Tyler et al., 2002). Griffin et al. (2011) measured cognition and blood levels of BDNF in sedentary young males following acute and chronic exercise. To assess cognition, they used a face-name task previously demonstrated by MRI to engage the hippocampus and medial-temporal lobes. Griffin et al. found increases in BDNF concentration in both acute and chronic exercise groups that corresponded with improved scores on the face-name task.

Although both meditation and exercise have been associated with enhancements in cognition and memory, it is important to note some of the limitations of past research. For example, many studies on meditation did not randomly assign participants and/or used small sample sizes (Eberth & Sedlmeier, 2012). In addition, studies frequently used clinical populations, and participants with prior interest in or experience with meditation (Chiesa et al., 2011; Hofmann et al., 2010). Likewise, many previous studies on exercise have not controlled and/or randomized designs. Additionally, subjects have often been limited to animals, human adult males, and older populations (Lambourne & Tomporowski, 2010; Smith et al., 2010).

> *Evaluates earlier research, acknowledging some of its limitations.*

Despite these limitations, the above findings provide evidence that prolonged practice of tasks such as meditation and exercise induce positive changes in anatomical plasticity reflected in both subjective and objective measures of cognition. Based on the success of meditation and exercise in decreasing inhibitory stress levels that interfere with cognition and thus memory function, I hypothesize that: (1) practicing mindfulness meditation over not practicing mindfulness meditation will improve memory function; (2) practicing exercise over not practicing exercise will improve memory function; (3) the effects of mindfulness meditation on memory function will be greater in the exercise group versus the non-exercise group as measured by the Wechsler Memory Scale, fourth edition, adult version (WMS-IV; Wechsler, 2009).

> *Aymelek concludes by stating her hypotheses, which represent the research questions she will investigate and are clearly based on her review of existing research.*

References

Al'Absi, M., Hugdahl, K., & Lovallo, W. R. (2002). Adrenocortical stress responses and altered working memory performance. *Psychophysiology, 39*(1), 95–99. https://doi.org/cjz8bh

Aronen, E. T., Vuontela, V., Steenari, M. R., Salmi, J., & Carlson, S. (2005). Working memory, psychiatric symptoms, and academic performance at school. *Neurobiology of Learning and Memory, 83*(1), 33–42. https://doi.org/dpwf55

Ashburner, J., & Friston, K. J. (2000). Voxel-based morphometry: The methods. *Neuroimage, 11*(6), 805–821. https://doi.org/brt2cb

Atkinson, R. C., & Shiffrin, R. M. (1968). Human memory: A proposed system and its control processes. *The Psychology of Learning and Motivation: Advances in Research and Theory, 2*, 89–195. https://doi.org/dnbb7v

Baddeley, A. D., & Hitch, G. J. (1974). Working memory. *The Psychology of Learning and Motivation, 8*, 47–89. https://doi.org/d4vgnk

Baer, R. A. (2003). Mindfulness training as a clinical intervention: A conceptual and empirical review. *Clinical Psychology: Science and Practice, 10*(2), 125–143. https://doi.org/fjq9qc

Baer, R. A., Smith, G. T., Hopkins, J., Krietemeyer, J., & Toney, L. (2006). Using self-report assessment methods to explore facets of mindfulness. *Assessment, 13*(1), 27–45. https://doi.org/dj5sc9

Cahill, L., & McGaugh, J. L. (1996). Modulation of memory storage. *Current Opinion in Neurobiology, 6*(2), 237–242. https://doi.org/bqn28r

Chiesa, A., Calati, R., & Serretti, A. (2011). Does mindfulness training improve cognitive abilities? A systematic review of neuropsychological findings. *Clinical Psychology Review, 31*(3), 449–464. https://doi.org/fhj9jp

. . .

Penedo, F. J., & Dahn, J. R. (2005). Exercise and well-being: A review of mental and physical health benefits associated with physical activity. *Current Opinion in Psychiatry, 18*(2), 189–193. https://doi.org/cfcxb2.

Roozendaal, B., McEwen, B. S., & Chattarji, S. (2009). Stress, memory and the amygdala. *Nature Reviews Neuroscience, 10*(6), 423–433. https://doi.org/b95m9c

Salmon, P. G., Santorelli, S. F., & Kabat-Zinn, J. (1998). Intervention elements promoting high adherence to mindfulness-based stress reduction programs in the clinical behavioral medicine setting. In S. A. Shumaker, E. B. Schron, J. K. Ockene, & W. L. McBee (Eds.), *Handbook of health behavior change* (2nd ed., pp. 239–266). Springer.

Slagter, H. A., Lutz, A., Greischar, L. L., Francis, A. D., Nieuwenhuis, S., Davis, J. M., & Davidson, R. J. (2007). Mental training affects distribution of limited brain resources. *PLOS Biology, 5*(6), e138. https://doi.org/cw46zf

Smith, P. J., Blumenthal, J. A., Hoffman, B. M., Cooper, H., Strauman, T. A., Welsh-Bohmer, K., Browndyke, J. N., & Sherwood, A. (2010). Aerobic exercise and neurocognitive performance: A meta-analytic review of randomized controlled trials. *Psychosomatic Medicine, 72*(3), 239–252. https://doi.org/d7vvcj

Tyler, W. J., Alonso, M., Bramham, C. R., & Pozzo-Miller, L. D. (2002). From acquisition to consolidation: On the role of brain-derived neurotrophic factor signaling in hippocampal-dependent learning. *Learning & Memory, 9*(5), 224–237. https://doi.org/cdnzhq

Wechsler, D. (2009). *WMS-IV: Wechsler Memory Scale administration and scoring manual* (4th ed). Pearson.

Zeidan, F., Johnson, S. K., Diamond, B. J., David, Z., & Goolkasian, P. (2010). Mindfulness meditation improves cognition: Evidence of brief mental training. *Consciousness and Cognition, 19*(2), 597–605. https://doi.org/fdvb4r

REFLECT. *Find an article in a scholarly journal in a field you're interested in, perhaps your major. Locate the literature review section of the article (it may or may not be explicitly labeled as such) and analyze it in terms of the genre features on pages 338–39. What kinds of sources does the author review? What aspects are discussed? How is the review organized? What is the author's evaluation of the literature, and how does that set up the rest of the article?*

TWENTY-EIGHT

Quoting, Paraphrasing, Summarizing

WHEN YOU'RE TEXTING or talking with friends, you don't usually need to be explicit about where you got your information; your friends trust what you say because they know you. In academic writing, however, it's important to establish your credibility, and one way to do so is by consulting authoritative sources. Doing so shows that you've done your homework on your topic, gives credit to those whose ideas you've relied on, and helps demonstrate your own authority as an author.

Your challenge in much academic writing is to integrate other voices with your own. How do you let your audience hear from expert sources while ensuring that their words don't eclipse yours? How do you pick and choose brief segments from long passages of text—or condense those passages into much briefer statements—without misrepresenting someone's ideas? How do you then introduce these segments and integrate them with your own words and ideas? This chapter provides guidelines on three ways you can incorporate sources into your writing: quoting, paraphrasing, and summarizing.

A **QUOTATION** consists of someone's exact words, enclosed in quotation marks or set off as a block from the rest of your text. A **PARAPHRASE** includes the details of a passage in your own words and syntax. A **SUMMARY** briefly captures the points of a passage that are important to your purpose, leaving out the other details.

Deciding Whether to Quote, Paraphrase, or Summarize

Quote

- Something that is said so well that it's worth repeating word for word
- Complex ideas that are expressed so clearly that paraphrasing or summarizing could distort or oversimplify them
- Experts whose opinions and exact words help to establish your own **CREDIBILITY** and **AUTHORITY** to write on the topic
- Passages that you yourself are analyzing
- Those who disagree or offer **COUNTERARGUMENTS** —quoting their exact words is a way to be sure you represent their opinions fairly

Paraphrase

- Passages where the details matter, but not the exact words
- Passages that are either too technical or too complicated for your readers to understand

Summarize

- Lengthy passages when the main point is important to your argument but the details are not

Whatever method you use for incorporating the words and ideas of others into your own writing, be sure that they support what *you* want to say. You're the author—and whatever your sources say needs to connect to what you say—so be sure to make that connection clear. Don't assume that sources speak for themselves. Introduce any source that you cite, naming the authors and identifying them in some way if your audience won't know who they are. In addition, be sure to follow quotations with a comment that explains how they relate to your point.

And regardless of whether you decide to quote, paraphrase, or summarize, you'll need to credit each source. Even if what you include is not a direct quotation, the ideas are still someone else's, and failing to credit your source can result in **PLAGIARISM**. Indicate the source in a **SIGNAL PHRASE** and include in-text documentation.

Quoting

When you include a direct quotation, use the exact words of the original source. And while you don't want to include too many quotations—you are the author, after all—using the exact words from a source is sometimes the best way to ensure that you accurately represent what was said. Original quotations can also be an effective way of presenting a point, by letting other people speak in their own words. But be sure to frame any quotation you include, introducing it and then explaining why it's important to the point that you are making.

Enclose short quotations in quotation marks within your main text. Such quotations should be no longer than four typed lines (in **MLA** style) or forty words (in **APA** style).

> Programmer and digital media pioneer Jaron Lanier describes the problems resulting from "lock-in" (in which software becomes difficult to change because it has been engineered to work with existing programs), arguing that lock-in "is an absolute tyrant in the digital world" (8). He means that "lock-in" inhibits creativity as new development is constrained by old software.

In MLA style, short quotations of poetry—no more than three lines—should also be enclosed in quotation marks within the main text. Include slashes (with a space on either side) between each line of verse.

> In "When You Are Old," poet William Butler Yeats advises Maud Gonne, the radical Irish nationalist, that when she looks back on her youth from old age, she should consider "How many loved your moments of glad grace, / And loved your beauty with love false or true, / But one man loved the pilgrim soul in you" (lines 5-7). Yeats thus suggests that he is the "one man" who truly loved her so sincerely all these years.

Set off long quotations as a block by indenting them from the left margin. No need to enclose them in quotation marks, but do indent five spaces (or one-half inch) if you are using either MLA or APA style. Use this method for quotations that are more than four lines of prose or three lines of poetry (in MLA) or longer than forty words (in APA).

> In her often-quoted 1976 keynote address to the Democratic National Convention, Texas congresswoman Barbara Jordan reflects on the occasion:
>
> > Now that I have this grand distinction, what in the world am I supposed to say? . . . I could list the problems which cause people to feel cynical, angry, frustrated: problems which include lack of integrity in government; the feeling that the individual no longer counts; the reality of material and spiritual poverty; the feeling that the grand American experiment is failing or has failed. I could recite these problems, and then I could sit down and offer no solutions. But I don't choose to do that either. The citizens of America expect more. (189)
>
> In this passage, Jordan resists the opportunity to attack the opposing party, preferring instead to offer positive solutions rather than simply a list of criticisms and problems.

↱ Go to every onesanauthor .tumblr.com to listen to the full text of Barbara Jordan's speech.

Notice that with block quotations, the parenthetical citation falls *after* the period at the end of the quotation.

Indicate changes to the text within a quotation by using brackets to enclose text that you add or change and ellipses to indicate text that you omit.

Use brackets to indicate that you have altered the original wording to fit grammatically within your text or have added or changed wording to clarify something that might otherwise be unclear. In this example, the author inserted the topic being discussed for clarification:

> Syracuse professor and literacy scholar Marcelle Haddix makes the point that in the field of teacher education, the idea of "social justice" is now being used as a buzzword instead of engaged with as a serious concept. And many agree with Haddix. For example, education professor April Baker-Bell responds: "No doubt! I think this is an important critique [of teacher education]" (*Linguistic Justice* 7).

Use ellipsis marks in place of words, phrases, or sentences that you leave out because they aren't crucial or relevant for your purpose. Use three dots, with a space before each one and after the last, when you omit only words and phrases within a sentence. If you leave out the end of a sentence or a whole sentence or more, put a period after the last word before the ellipsis mark. Note how a writer does both in the example below.

> Warning of the effects of GPS on our relationship to the world around us, Nicholas Carr concludes that "the automation of wayfinding . . . encourages us to observe and manipulate symbols on screens rather than attend to real things in real places. . . . What we should be asking ourselves is, *How far from the world do we want to retreat?*" (137).

When you use brackets or ellipses, make sure your changes don't end up misrepresenting the author's original point, which would damage your own credibility. Mark Twain once joked that "nearly any invented quotation, played with confidence, stands a good chance to deceive." Twain was probably right—it's quite easy to "invent" quotations or twist their meaning by taking them out of context or changing some keyword. You don't want to be guilty of this!

Set off a quotation within a quotation with single quotation marks. In the following passage, the author quotes Nicholas Carr, who himself quotes the writing of anthropologist Tim Ingold:

Nicholas Carr sums up the difference between navigating with and without a GPS device using two terms borrowed from Scottish anthropologist Tim Ingold. As Carr explains, Ingold "draws a distinction between two very different modes of travel: wayfaring and transport. Wayfaring, [Ingold] explains, is 'our most fundamental way of being in the world'" (132). Wayfaring means navigating by our observations and mental maps of the world around us, as opposed to blindly following GPS-generated directions from point A to point B—the mode Ingold and Carr call "transport."

Punctuate quotations carefully. Parenthetical documentation comes after the closing quotation mark, and any punctuation that is part of your sentence comes after the parentheses (except in the case of a block quote, where the parenthetical documentation goes at the very end).

- *Commas and periods* always go inside the closing quotation marks. If there's parenthetical documentation, however, the period goes after the parentheses.

  "Watch your mind," said Joy Harjo, the first Native American US poet laureate, in a 2021 commencement address. "Without training it might run away and leave your heart for the immense human feast set by the thieves of time" (3).

- *Colons and semicolons* always go outside closing quotation marks.

  David Foster Wallace warned as well that there are "whole, large parts of adult American life that nobody talks about in commencement speeches": sometimes, he says, we'll be bored (4).

  He also once noted that when a lobster is put in a kettle of boiling water, it "behaves very much as you or I would behave if we were plunged into boiling water"; in other words, it acts as if it's in terrible pain (10).

- *Question marks and exclamation points* go inside closing quotation marks if they are part of the original quotation, but outside the quotation marks if they are part of your sentence.

When you include dialogue, the same conventions of quoting apply. Dana Canedy, recounting a difficult conversation with her eight-year-old son, uses quotes. See how she did it on p. 868.

Wallace opened his speech with a now famous joke about how natural it is to be unaware of the world: an old fish swims by two young fish and says, "Morning, boys. How's the water?" They swim on, and after a while one young fish turns to the other and asks, "What the hell is water?" (1).

So what, according to David Foster Wallace, is the "capital-T Truth . . . about life" (9)?

Paraphrasing

When you paraphrase, you restate information or ideas from a source using your words, your sentence structure, your style. A paraphrase should cover the same points that the original source does, so it's usually about the same length—but sticking too closely to the sentence structures in your source could be plagiarizing. And even though you're using your own words, don't forget where the ideas came from: you should always name the author and include parenthetical documentation.

Here is a paragraph about the search for other life-forms similar to our own in the universe, followed by three paraphrases.

Original source

As the romance of manned space exploration has waned, the drive today is to find our living, thinking counterparts in the universe. For all the excitement, however, the search betrays a profound melancholy—a lonely species in a merciless universe anxiously awaits an answering voice amid utter silence. That silence is maddening. Not just because it compounds our feeling of cosmic isolation, but because it makes no sense. As we inevitably find more and more exo-planets where intelligent life *can* exist, why have we found no evidence—no signals, no radio waves—that intelligent life *does* exist?

—CHARLES KRAUTHAMMER, "Are We Alone in the Universe?"

As the underlined words show, the following paraphrase uses too many words from the original.

Unacceptable paraphrase: wording too close to the original

Charles Krauthammer argues that finding our intelligent <u>counterparts in the universe</u> has become more important as the <u>romance of manned space exploration</u> has declined. Even so, the hunt for similar beings also suggests our sadness as a species waiting in vain for an acknowledgment that we aren't alone in <u>a merciless universe</u>. The lack of response, he says, just doesn't make sense because if we keep finding planets that *could* support life, then we should find evidence—like <u>radio waves or signals</u>—of intelligent life out there (A19).

While the next version uses original language, the sentence structures are much too similar to the original.

Unacceptable paraphrase: sentence structures too close to original

As the allure of adventuring into the unknown cosmos has diminished, the desire to discover beings like us out there has grown. There is a sadness to the search though—the calling out into empty space that brings no response. Nothing. Only a vast silence that not only emphasizes our solitary existence but increases our frustration. How can we continue to discover potentially hospitable planets that could sustain life like ours, yet find no evidence—no signs, no data—that such life exists (Krauthammer A19)?

When you paraphrase, be careful not to simply substitute words and phrases while replicating the same sentence structure. And while it may be necessary to use some of the key terms from the original in order to convey the same concepts, be sure to put them in quotation marks—and not to use too many (which would result in plagiarism).

Acceptable paraphrase

Syndicated columnist Charles Krauthammer observes that our current quest to discover other "intelligent life" in the universe comes just as the allure of exploring outer space is dimming. It's a search, he says, that reveals a deep sadness (that we may in fact be living in "cosmic isolation") and a growing frustration: if scientists continue to discover more planets where life like ours can be sustainable, why do we find no actual signs of life (A19)?

Summarizing

Like a paraphrase, a summary presents the source information in your words. However, a summary dramatically condenses the information, covering only the most important points and leaving out the details. Summaries are therefore much briefer than the original texts, though they vary in length depending on the size of the original and your purpose for summarizing; you may need only a sentence or two to summarize an essay, or you may need several paragraphs. In any case, you should always name the author and document the source. The following example appropriately summarizes Krauthammer's passage in one sentence:

> Charles Krauthammer questions whether we will ever find other "intelligent life" in the universe—or whether we'll instead discover that we do in fact live in "cosmic isolation" (A19).

This summary tells readers Krauthammer's main point and includes in quotation marks two key phrases borrowed from the original source. If we were to work the summary into an essay, it might look like this:

> Many scientists believe that there is a strong probability—given the vastness of the universe and how much of it we have yet to explore, even with advances like the Hubble telescope—that there is life like ours somewhere out there. In a 2011 opinion piece, however, syndicated columnist Charles Krauthammer questions whether we will ever find other "intelligent life" in the universe—or whether we'll instead discover that we do in fact live in "cosmic isolation" (A19).

Three ways a summary can go wrong are if it represents inaccurately the point of the original source, provides so many details that the summary is too long, or is so general that readers are left wondering what the source is about. Consider the following unsuccessful summaries of Krauthammer's passage:

Unacceptable summary: misrepresents the source

Pulitzer Prize–winning columnist Charles Krauthammer extols the virtues of space exploration.

This summary both misses the point of Krauthammer's questioning our troubled search for "intelligent life" beyond Earth and claims that the author praises space exploration when at no point in the passage does he do so.

Unacceptable summary: provides too many details

Award-winning columnist Charles Krauthammer suggests that while sending people into space is no longer as exciting to us as it once was, we are interested in finding out if there is life in the universe beyond Earth. He laments the feeling of being alone in the universe given that all signs point to the very real possibility that intelligent life exists elsewhere. Krauthammer wonders "why we have no evidence . . . of intelligent life" on other habitable planets. He finds this lack of proof confounding.

This summary is almost as long as the original passage and includes as many details. As a summary, it doesn't let readers know what points are most important.

Unacceptable summary: too general

Charles Krauthammer is concerned about the search for life on other planets.

While the statement above is not false, it does not adequately reflect Krauthammer's main point in a way that will help the reader get the gist of the original passage. A better summary would tell readers what precisely about the search for life concerns Krauthammer.

REFLECT. Return to the quotation from Barbara Jordan on page 551. First, write an appropriate paraphrase of the quotation; then write an appropriate summary.

Incorporating Source Material

Whether you quote, paraphrase, or summarize source material, you need to be careful to distinguish what you say from what your sources say, while at the same time weaving the two together smoothly in your writing. That is, you must make clear how the ideas you're quoting, paraphrasing, or summarizing relate to your own—why you're bringing them into your text.

Notice how Nadra Nittle smoothly incorporates quotes from numerous sources in her report on eliminating racist images on food packaging. Check it out on p. 951.

Use signal phrases to introduce source materials, telling readers who said what and providing some context if need be. Don't just drop in a quotation or paraphrase or summary; you need to introduce it. And while you can always use a neutral signal phrase such as "the author says" or "the author claims," try to choose verbs that reflect the **STANCE** of those you're citing. In some cases, a simple "says" does reflect that stance, but usually you can make your writing livelier and more accurate with a more specific signal verb.

Use a **SIGNAL PHRASE** and parenthetical documentation to clearly distinguish your own words and ideas from those of others. The following paraphrase introduces source material with a signal phrase that includes the author's name and closes with documentation giving the page number from which the information is taken.

> As Ernst Mayr explains, Darwin's theory of evolution presented a significant challenge to then prevalent beliefs about humanity's centrality in the world (9).

If you do not give the author's name in a signal phrase, include it in the parenthetical documentation.

> Darwin's theory of evolution presented a significant challenge to then prevalent beliefs about humanity's centrality in the world (Mayr 9).

Sometimes you'll want or need to state the author's authority or credentials in the signal phrase, lending credibility to your own use of that source.

> According to music historian Ted Gioia, record sales declined sharply during the Great Depression, dropping by almost 90 percent between 1927 and 1932 (127).

Choose verbs that reflect the author's stance toward the material—or your own stance in including it. Saying "she notes" means something different than saying "she insists" or "she implies."

> Because almost anyone can create a blog, most people assume that blogs give average citizens a greater voice in public dialogue. Political scientist Matthew Hindman questions this assumption: "Though millions of Americans now maintain a blog, only a few dozen political bloggers get as many readers as a typical college newspaper" (103).

Signal phrases do not have to come first. To add variety to your writing, try positioning them in the middle or at the end of a sentence.

> "Attracting attention," observes Richard Lanham, "is what style is all about" (xi).

> "Hard work beats talent," warns Kevin Durant, "when talent fails to work hard."

SOME USEFUL SIGNAL VERBS

acknowledges	concludes	observes
adds	declares	reports
asserts	implies	responds
claims	objects	suggests

Verb tenses. The verb tense you use when referring to a text or researcher in a signal phrase will depend on your documentation style. MLA style requires the present tense ("argues") or the present perfect ("has argued"). Using MLA style, you might write, "In *Rhetoric*, Aristotle argues" or "In commenting on Aristotle's *Rhetoric*, scholars have argued." An exception involves sentences that include specific dates in the past. In this case, use the past tense: "In his introduction to the 1960 edition of Aristotle's *Rhetoric*, Lane Cooper argued."

The past tense is conventional in APA style. The present perfect is conventional when referring to an ongoing action that started in the past or to something that didn't occur at a specific time. You might write, "Anderson (1988) argued" or "In commenting on Aristotle's *Rhetoric*, scholars have argued." However, use the present tense when you refer to the results of a study ("the results of Conrad (2012) demonstrate") or when you make a generalization ("writing researchers agree").

Parenthetical documentation. If you're following MLA, you'll need to include page numbers for all quotations, paraphrases, and summaries from print sources in your parenthetical documentation. If you're using APA, page numbers are required for quotations; for paraphrases and summaries, they're optional—but it's always a good idea to include them whenever you can do so.

Incorporating Visual and Audio Sources

Sometimes you will want to incorporate visual or audio elements from sources that you cannot write into a paragraph. For example, you may include charts, photographs, or audio/video clips. Remember that any such materials that come from sources need to be introduced, explained, and documented just as you would a quotation. If you're following MLA or APA style, refer to Chapters 30 and 31 for specific requirements.

Tables. Label anything that contains facts or figures displayed in columns as a table. Number all tables in sequence, and provide a descriptive title for each one. Supply source information immediately below the table; credit your data source even if you've created the table yourself. If any information within the table requires further explanation (abbreviations, for example), include a note below the source citation.

Figures. Number and label everything that is not a table (photos, graphs, drawings, maps, and so on) as a figure and include a caption letting readers know what the image illustrates. Unless the visual is a photograph or drawing you created yourself, provide appropriate source information after the caption; graphs, maps, and other figures you produce based on information from other sources should still include a full credit. If the visual is referenced within your text, you can use an abbreviated citation and include full documentation in your list of WORKS CITED or REFERENCES.

Audio and video recordings. If your medium allows it, provide a link to any recorded element or embed a media player into the text. If you're working in a medium that won't allow linking or embedding, discuss the recording in your text and provide a full citation in your list of **WORKS CITED** or **REFERENCES** so your readers can track down the recording themselves.

Captions. Create a clear, succinct caption for each visual or recording: "Fig. 1: The Guggenheim Museum, Spain." The caption should identify and explain the visual—and should reflect your purpose. In an essay about contemporary architecture in Spain, your caption might say "Fig. 1: The Guggenheim Museum, Bilbao. Designed by Frank Gehry."

Sizing and positioning visuals and recordings. Refer to every visual or embedded recording in your text: "(see fig. 1)," "as shown in Table 3," "in the *YouTube* video below." The element may be on the page where it's discussed, but it should not come before you introduce it to your readers. Think carefully about how you will size and position each visual to be most effective: you want to make sure that your visuals are legible and that they support rather than disrupt the text.

Fig. 1: The Guggenheim Museum, Spain.

Giving Credit,
Avoiding Plagiarism

WHO OWNS WORDS AND IDEAS? Answers to this question differ from culture to culture. In some societies, they are shared resources, not the property of individuals. In others, using another person's words or ideas may be seen as a tribute or compliment that doesn't require specific acknowledgment. In the United States, however (as in much of the Western world), elaborate systems of copyright and patent law have grown to protect the intellectual property (including words, images, voices, and ideas) of individuals and corporations. This system forms the foundation of the documentation conventions currently followed in US schools. And while these conventions are being challenged today by the open-source movement and others who argue that "information wants to be free," the conventions still hold sway in the academy and in the law. As a researcher, you will need to understand these conventions and to practice them in your own writing. Put simply, these conventions allow you to give credit where credit is due and thereby avoid **PLAGIARISM** (the use of the words and ideas of others as if they were your own work).

But acknowledging your sources is not simply about avoiding charges of plagiarism (although you would be doing that too). It also helps establish your own **CREDIBILITY** as a researcher and an author. It shows that you have consulted other sources of information about your topic and can engage with them in your own work. In addition, citing your sources acknowledges and honors the hard work of the person(s) who created the source. Finally, citing and documenting your sources allows readers to locate them for their own purposes if they wish; in effect, it anticipates the needs of your audience.

There are some cases, however, in which you do not need to provide citations for information that you incorporate—for example, if the information is common knowledge. This chapter will help you identify which sources you must acknowledge, explain the basics of documenting your sources, and provide strategies for avoiding plagiarism.

Knowing What You Must Acknowledge

As a general rule, material taken from specific outside sources—whether ideas, texts, images, or sounds—should be CITED and DOCUMENTED.

INFORMATION THAT MUST BE ACKNOWLEDGED

- *Direct quotations, paraphrases, and summaries.* Exact wording should always be enclosed in quotation marks and cited. And always cite specific ideas taken from another source, even when you present them using your own words.

- *Controversial information.* If there is some debate over the information you're including, cite the source so readers know whose version or interpretation of the facts you're using. You may not always know whether information in a source is controversial, which is another reason to READ LATERALLY and check out what others have to say about the information.

- *Information given in only a few sources.* If only one or two sources make this information available (that is, it isn't common knowledge widely accessible in general sources), include a citation.

- *Any materials that you did not create yourself—including tables, charts, images, and audio or video segments.* Even if you create a table or chart yourself, if it presents information from an outside source, that's someone else's work that needs to be acknowledged.

A word to the wise: it's always better to cite any information that you've taken from another source than to guess wrong and unintentionally plagiarize. And a second word to the wise: it's an ethical practice to contact

Geoffrey Pullum's attention to detail helps readers distinguish his own words from those in the article he pokes fun at, making his satire even funnier. See how he did it on p. 959.

social media users and ask permission to use and cite their work. Remember, though, that there are exceptions to all rules, and so there are some times when acknowledging a source is not necessary.

INFORMATION THAT DOES NOT NEED TO BE ACKNOWLEDGED

- *Information that is "common knowledge."* Uncontroversial information ("People today get most of their news and information from the internet"), well-known historical events ("Neil Armstrong was the first person to walk on the moon"), facts ("All mammals are warm-blooded"), and quotations (Armstrong's "That's one small step for man, one giant leap for mankind") that are widely available in general reference sources do not need to be cited.

- *Information well known to your audience.* Keep in mind that what is common knowledge varies depending on your audience. While an audience of pulmonary oncologists would be familiar with the names of researchers who established that smoking is linked to lung cancer, for a general audience you might need to cite a source if you give the names.

- *Information from well-known, easily accessible documents.* You do not need to include the specific location where you accessed texts that are available from a variety of public sources and are widely familiar, such as the United States Constitution.

- *Your own work.* If you've gathered data, come up with an idea, or generated a text (including images, multimedia texts, and so on) entirely on your own, you should indicate that to your readers in some way—but it's not necessary to include a formal citation, unless the material has been previously published elsewhere.

Just remember: when in doubt, err on the safe side and include a citation.

Fair Use and the Internet

In general, principles of fair use apply to the writing you do for your college classes. These principles allow you to use passages and images from the copyrighted work of others without their explicit permission as long as you do so for educational purposes and you fully cite what you use. When you publish your writing online, however, where that material can be seen by all, then you must have permission from the copyright owner in order to post it.

Students across the country have learned about this limitation on fair use the hard way. One student we know won a prize for an essay she wrote, which was then posted on the writing prize website. In the essay, she included a cartoon that was copyrighted by the cartoonist. Soon after the essay was posted, she received a letter from the copyright holder, demanding that she remove the image and threatening her with a lawsuit. Another student, whose essay was published on a class website, was stunned when his instructor got an angry email from a professor at another university, saying that the student writer had used too much of her work in the essay and that, furthermore, it had not been fully and properly cited. The student, who had intended no dishonesty at all, was embarrassed, to say the least.

Many legal scholars and activists believe that fair use policies and laws should be relaxed and that making these laws more restrictive undermines creativity. While these issues get debated in public forums and legal courts, however, you are well advised to be careful not only in citing and documenting all your sources thoroughly but in getting permission in writing to use any copyrighted text or image in anything you plan to post or publish online.

Avoiding Plagiarism

In US academic culture, incorporating the words, ideas, or materials of others into your own work without giving credit through appropriate citations and documentation is viewed as unethical and is considered plagiarism. The consequences of such unacknowledged borrowing are serious: students who plagiarize may receive failing grades for assignments or courses, be subjected to an administrative review for academic misconduct, or even be dismissed from school.

Certainly, the deliberate and obvious effort to pass off someone else's work as your own, such as by handing in a paper purchased online or written by someone else, is plagiarism and can easily be spotted and punished. More troublesome and problematic, however, is the difficulty some students have using the words and ideas of others fairly and acknowledging them fully. Especially when you're new to a field or writing about unfamiliar ideas, incorporating sources without plagiarizing can be challenging.

In fact, researcher Rebecca Moore Howard has found that even expert writers have difficulty incorporating the words and ideas of others acceptably when they are working with material outside their comfort zone or field of expertise. Such difficulty can often lead to what Howard calls **PATCHWRITING** : restating material from sources in ways that stick too closely to the original language or syntax.

But patchwriting can help you work with sources. Some call patchwriting plagiarism, even when it's documented, but we believe that it can be a step in the process of learning how to weave the words and thoughts of others into your own work. Assume, for example, that you want to summarize ideas from the following passage:

> Over the past few decades, scholars from a variety of disciplines have devoted considerable attention toward studying evolving public attitudes toward a whole range of LGBT civil rights issues including support for open service in the military, same-sex parent adoption, employment non-discrimination, civil unions, and marriage equality. In the last 10 years in particular, the emphasis has shifted toward studying the various factors that best explain variation in support for same-sex marriage including demographic considerations, religious and ideological predispositions, attitudes toward marriage and family, and social contact (Baunach 2011, 2012; Becker, 2012a, 2012b; Becker & Scheufele, 2009, 2011; Becker & Todd, 2013; Brewer, 2008; Brewer & Wilcox, 2005; Lewis, 2005, 2011; Lewis & Gossett, 2008; Lewis & Oh, 2008).
> —AMY BECKER, "Employment Discrimination, Local School Boards, and LGBT Civil Rights: Reviewing 25 Years of Public Opinion Data"

This passage includes a lot of detailed information in complex sentences that can be hard to process. See how one student first summarized it, and why this summary would be unacceptable in an essay of his own:

A patchwritten summary

For more than 20 years, scholars from many disciplines have committed their energies to examining changing public attitudes toward a variety of LGBT civil rights issues. These encompass things like open military service, same-sex parent adoption, equal employment opportunities, civil unions, and marriage equality. Since 2004, focus has moved toward examining those elements that best account for differences in public support for same-sex marriage like demographic considerations, religious and ideological predispositions, attitudes toward marriage and family, and social contact (Baunach 2011, 2012; Becker, 2012a, 2012b; Becker & Scheufele, 2009, 2011; Becker & Todd, 2013; Brewer, 2008; Brewer & Wilcox, 2005; Lewis, 2005, 2011; Lewis & Gossett, 2008; Lewis & Oh, 2008).

This is a classic case of patchwriting that would be considered plagiarism. The sentence structure looks very much like Becker's, and even some of the language is taken straight from the original article. While such a summary would not be acceptable in any writing you turn in, this sort of patchwriting can help you understand what a difficult source is saying.

And once you understand the source, writing an acceptable summary gets a lot easier. In the acceptable summary below, the writer focuses on the ideas in the long second sentence of the original passage, turning those ideas into two simpler sentences and using a direct quotation from the original.

Acceptable summary

Scholars studying changes in public opinion on LGBT issues have increasingly focused on the growing support for same-sex marriage. In looking at the question of why opinions on this issue differ, these scholars have considered factors such as "demographic considerations, religious and ideological predispositions, attitudes toward marriage and family, and social contact" (Becker 342).

An acceptable summary uses the writer's own language and sentence structures, and quotation marks to indicate any borrowed language. To write a summary like this one, you would need to be able to restate the source's main point (that same-sex marriage has gotten greater scholarly attention lately than other LGBTQ issues) and decide what information is most important for your purposes—what details are worth emphasizing with a quotation or a longer summary. Finally, notice that the citation credits Becker's article, because that is the source this writer consulted, not the research Becker cites. Chapter 28 offers you more guidelines on QUOTING, PARAPHRASING, and SUMMARIZING appropriately.

STEPS YOU CAN TAKE TO AVOID PLAGIARISM

Understand what constitutes plagiarism. Plagiarism includes any unacknowledged use of material from another source that isn't considered common knowledge; this includes phrases, ideas, and materials such as graphs, charts, images, videos, and so on. In a written text, it includes neglecting to put someone else's exact wording in quotation marks; leaving out in-text documentation for sources that you QUOTE, PARAPHRASE, or SUMMARIZE; and borrowing too many of the original sources' words or sentence structures in paraphrases or summaries. Check to see if your school has any explicit guidelines for what constitutes plagiarism.

Take notes carefully and conscientiously. If you can't locate the source of words or ideas that you've copied down, you may neglect to cite them properly. Technology makes it easy to copy and paste text and materials from electronic sources directly into your own work—and then to move on and forget to put such material in quotation marks or record the source. So keep copies of sources, note documentation information, and be sure to put any borrowed language in quotation marks and to clearly distinguish your own ideas from those of others.

Know where your information comes from. Because information passes quickly and often anonymously through the internet grapevine, you may not always be able to determine the origin of a text or image you find online. If you don't know where something came from, don't include it. Not only would you be unable to write a proper citation—chances are you haven't been able to verify the information either!

DOCUMENT sources carefully. Below you'll find an overview of the basics of documenting sources. More detail on using MLA and APA documentation is given in the next two chapters.

Plan ahead. Work can pile up in a high-pressure academic environment. Stay on top of your projects by scheduling your work and sticking to the deadlines you set. This way, you'll avoid taking shortcuts that could lead to inadvertent plagiarism.

Consult your instructor if necessary. If you're uncertain about how to acknowledge sources properly or are struggling with a project, talk with your instructor about finding a solution. Even taking a penalty for submitting an assignment late is better than being accused of plagiarism that you didn't intend to commit.

Documenting Sources

When you document sources, you identify the ones you've used and give information about their authors, titles, and publication. Documenting your sources allows you to show evidence of the research you've done and enables your readers to find those sources if they wish to. Most academic documentation systems include two parts: IN-TEXT DOCUMENTATION, which you insert in your text after the specific information you have borrowed, and an end-of-text list of WORKS CITED or REFERENCES, which provides complete bibliographic information for every work you've cited. It's also worth noting that hyperlinks are often used to document sources in popular writing—you might have seen linked documentation in news sites and online magazines.

This book covers two documentation systems—those of the Modern Language Association (MLA) and the American Psychological Association (APA). MLA style is used primarily in English and other humanities subjects, and APA is used mostly in psychology and other social sciences. Chances are that you will be required to use either MLA or APA style or both in your college courses. Note that some disciplines may require other documentation systems, such as CSE (Council of Science Editors) or *Chicago Manual of Style*.

MLA and APA both call for the same basic information; you'll need to give the author's name (or sometimes the editor's name or the title) in the in-text citation, and your end-of-text list should provide the author, title, and publication information for each source that you cite. But the two systems differ in some ways. In APA, for example, your in-text documentation always includes the date of publication, but that is not generally done in MLA. You'll find detailed guidance on the specifics of MLA in Chapter 30 and of APA in Chapter 31, with color-coded examples to help you easily distinguish where the author and editor, title, and publication information appear for each type of work you document. Each of these chapters also includes a student paper that uses that style of documentation.

℗ *REFLECT. Think about the kinds of information you'll need to give when writing about your research. For your topic and your intended audience, what would be considered common knowledge? What might not be common knowledge for a different audience? What do you know about your audience that can help you make that decision?*

THIRTY

MLA Style

MLA **STYLE CALLS** for (1) brief in-text documentation and (2) complete bibliographic information in a list of works cited at the end of your text. The models and examples in this chapter draw on the ninth edition of the *MLA Handbook*, published by the Modern Language Association of America in 2021. For additional information, or if you're citing a source that isn't covered, visit style.mla.org.

A DIRECTORY TO MLA STYLE

Anna Glavee's essay is another that employs MLA style. Check it out on p. 891.

Throughout this chapter, you'll find color-coded models and examples to help you see how writers include source information in their texts and in their lists of works cited: tan for author, editor, translator, and other contributors; yellow for titles; gray for publication information—publisher, date of publication, page number(s), DOIs, and other location information.

IN-TEXT DOCUMENTATION

Whenever you **QUOTE**, **PARAPHRASE**, or **SUMMARIZE** a source in your writing, you need to provide brief documentation that tells readers what you took from the source and where in the source you found that information. This brief documentation also refers readers to the full entry in your

author   title   publication

works-cited list, so begin with whatever comes first there: the author, the title, or a description of the source.

You'll need to mention the author, title, or description, either in a signal phrase—"as Toni Morrison writes"—or in parentheses—(Morrison). Name the author, title, or description in either place but not in both places.

Shorten any lengthy titles or descriptions in parentheses by including the first noun with any preceding adjectives but without any initial articles (*Norton Field Guide* rather than *The Norton Field Guide to Writing*). Use the full title if it's short (*What's Your Pronoun?*).

The first examples below show basic in-text documentation of a work by one author. Variations on those examples follow. The examples illustrate the MLA style of using quotation marks around titles of short works and italicizing titles of long works.

1. Author named in a signal phrase

If you mention the author in a **SIGNAL PHRASE**, put only the page number(s) in parentheses. Do not write "page" or "p." The first time you mention the author, use their first and last names. Omit any middle initials.

> David McCullough describes John Adams's hands as those of someone used to manual labor (18).

2. Author named in parentheses

If you do not mention the author in a signal phrase, put the last name in parentheses along with any page number(s). Do not use punctuation between the name and the page number(s).

> Adams is said to have had "the hands of a man accustomed to pruning his own trees, cutting his own hay, and splitting his own firewood" (McCullough 18).

Whether you use a signal phrase and parentheses or parentheses only, try to put the parenthetical documentation at the end of the sentence or as close as possible to the material you've cited—without awkwardly interrupting the sentence. Notice that in the example above, the parenthetical reference comes after the closing quotation marks but before the period at the end of the sentence.

3. Two or more works by the same author

If you cite multiple works by one author, include the title of the work you are citing either in the signal phrase or in parentheses.

> Robert Kaplan insists that understanding power in the Near East requires "Western leaders who know when to intervene, and do so without illusions" (*Eastward to Tartary* 330).

Put a comma between author and title if both are in the parentheses.

> Understanding power in the Near East requires "Western leaders who know when to intervene, and do so without illusions" (Kaplan, *Eastward to Tartary* 330).

4. Authors with the same last name

Give the author's first and last names in any signal phrase, or add the author's first initial in the parenthetical reference.

> *Imaginative* applies not only to modern literature but also to writing of all periods, whereas *magical* is often used in writing about Arthurian romances (A. Wilson 25).

5. Two or more authors

For a work with two authors, name both. If you first mention them in a signal phrase, give their first and last names.

> Lori Carlson and Cynthia Ventura's stated goal is to introduce Julio Cortázar, Marjorie Agosín, and other Latin American writers to an audience of English-speaking adolescents (v).

For a work by three or more authors that you mention in a signal phrase, you can either name them all or name the first author followed by "and others" or "and colleagues." If you mention them in a parenthetical reference, name the first author followed by "et al.," Latin for "and others."

> Phyllis Anderson and colleagues describe British literature thematically (A54-A67).

author   title   publication

One survey of British literature breaks the contents into thematic groupings (Anderson et al. A54-A67).

6. Organization or government as author

In a signal phrase, use the full name of the organization: American Academy of Arts and Sciences. In parentheses, use the shortest noun phrase: American Academy. Omit any initial articles.

> The US government can be direct when it wants to be. For example, it sternly warns, "If you are overpaid, we will recover any payments not due you" (Social Security Administration 12).

7. Author unknown

If you don't know the author, use the work's title in a signal phrase and a shortened version of the title in the parenthetical reference.

> A powerful article in last week's paper asserts that healthy liver donor Mike Hurewitz died because of "frightening" faulty postoperative care ("Every Patient's Nightmare").

8. Literary works

When referring to common literary works that are available in many different editions, give the page numbers from the edition you are using, followed by information that will let readers of any edition locate the text you are citing.

Novels and prose plays. Give the page number followed by a semicolon and any chapter, section, or act numbers, separated by commas.

> In *Pride and Prejudice*, Mrs. Bennet shows no warmth toward Jane and Elizabeth when they return from Netherfield (Austen 105; ch. 12).

Verse plays. Give act, scene, and line numbers, separated by periods.

> Shakespeare continues the vision theme when Macbeth says, "Thou hast no speculation in those eyes / Which thou dost glare with" (*Macbeth* 3.3.96-97).

Poems. Give the part and the line numbers (separated by periods). If a poem has only line numbers, use the word "line" or "lines" only in the first reference.

> Walt Whitman sets up not only opposing adjectives but also opposing nouns in "Song of Myself" when he says, "I am of old and young, of the foolish as much as the wise, / . . . a child as well as a man" (16.330-32).

> One description of the mere in *Beowulf* is "not a pleasant place" (line 1372). Later, it is labeled "the awful place" (1378).

9. Work in an anthology

Name the author(s) of the work, not the editor of the anthology.

> "It is the teapots that truly shock," according to Cynthia Ozick in her essay on teapots as metaphor (70).

> In *In Short: A Collection of Creative Nonfiction*, readers will find both an essay on Scottish tea (Hiestand) and a piece on teapots as metaphors (Ozick).

10. Encyclopedia or dictionary

For an entry in an encyclopedia or dictionary, give the author's name, if available. For an entry without an author, give the entry's title.

> According to *Funk and Wagnall's New World Encyclopedia*, early in his career Kubrick's main source of income came from "hustling chess games in Washington Square Park" ("Kubrick, Stanley").

11. Legal documents

For legal cases, give whatever comes first in the works-cited entry. If multiple entries in your works-cited list start with the same government author, give as much of the name as you need to differentiate the sources.

> In 2015, for the first time, all states were required to license and recognize the marriages of same-sex couples (United States, Supreme Court).

author   title   publication

12. Sacred text

When citing a sacred text such as the Bible or the Qur'an for the first time, give the title of the edition as well as the book, chapter, and verse (or their equivalent), separated by periods. MLA recommends abbreviating the names of the books of the Bible in parenthetical references. Later citations from the same edition do not have to repeat its title.

> The wording from *The New English Bible* follows: "In the beginning of creation, when God made heaven and earth, the earth was without form and void . . ." (Gen. 1.1-2).

13. Multivolume work

If you cite more than one volume of a multivolume work, each time you cite one of the volumes, give the volume *and* the page number(s) in parentheses, separated by a colon and a space.

> Carl Sandburg concludes with the following sentence about those paying last respects to Lincoln: "All day long and through the night the unbroken line moved, the home town having its farewell" (4: 413).

If you cite an entire volume of a multivolume work in parentheses, give the author's last name followed by a comma and "vol." before the volume number: (Sandburg, vol. 2). If your works-cited list includes only a single volume of a multivolume work, give just the page number in parentheses: (230).

14. Two or more works cited together

If you're citing two or more works closely together, you will sometimes need to provide a parenthetical reference for each one.

> Dennis Baron describes singular "they" as "the missing word that's been hiding in plain sight" (182), while Benjamin Dreyer believes that "singular 'they' is not the wave of the future; it's the wave of the present" (93).

If you are citing multiple sources for the same idea in parentheses, separate the references with a semicolon.

> Many critics have examined great works of literature from a cultural perspective (Tanner 7; Smith viii).

15. Source quoted in another source

When you are quoting text that you found quoted in another source, use the abbreviation "qtd. in" in the parenthetical reference.

> Charlotte Brontë wrote to G. H. Lewes, "Why do you like Miss Austen so very much? I am puzzled on that point" (qtd. in Tanner 7).

16. Work without page numbers

For works without page or part numbers, including many online sources, identify the source using the author or other information.

> Studies show that music training helps children to be better at multitasking later in life ("Hearing the Music").

If you mention the author in a signal phrase, or if you mention the title of a work with no author, no parenthetical reference is needed.

> Arthur Brooks argues that a switch to fully remote work would have a negative effect on mental and physical health.

If the source has chapter, paragraph, or section numbers, use them with the abbreviations "ch.," "par.," or "sec." ("Graduate Student Unions," par. 2). Don't count sections or paragraphs on your own if they aren't numbered in the source. For an ebook, use chapter numbers. For an audio or video recording, give the hours, minutes, and seconds (separated by colons) as shown on the player: (00:05:21-31).

17. An entire work or a one-page article

If you cite an entire work rather than a part of it, or if you cite a single-page article, there's no need to include page numbers.

> Throughout life, John Adams strove to succeed (McCullough).

NOTES

Sometimes you may need to give information that doesn't fit into the text itself—to thank people who helped you, to provide additional details, to refer readers to other sources, or to add comments about sources. Such

author   title   publication

information can be given in a footnote (at the bottom of the page) or an endnote (on a separate page with the heading "Notes" or "Endnotes" just before your works-cited list). Put a superscript number at the appropriate point in your text, signaling to readers to look for the note with the corresponding number. If you have multiple notes, number them consecutively throughout your paper.

Text

This essay will argue that giving student athletes preferential treatment undermines educational goals.[1]

Note

[1] I want to thank those who contributed to my thinking on this topic, especially my teacher Vincent Yu.

LIST OF WORKS CITED

A works-cited list provides full bibliographic information for every source cited in your text. See page 609 for guidelines on formatting this list and page 624 for a sample works-cited list.

Core Elements

MLA style provides a list of core elements for documenting sources, advising writers to list as many of them as possible in the order that MLA specifies. We've used these general principles to provide templates and examples for documenting fifty-two kinds of sources college writers most often need to cite. The following general guidelines explain how to treat each of the core elements.

Authors and Contributors

- An author can be any kind of creator—a writer, a musician, a visual artist, and so on.
- If there is one author, list the last name first: Morrison, Toni.
- If there are two authors, list the first author last name first and the second one first name first: Lunsford, Andrea A., and Lisa Ede. Put their names in the order given in the work. For three or more authors, give the first author's name followed by "et al.": Gonzalez, Laura, et al.

- Include any middle names or initials: Heath, Shirley Brice; Toklas, Alice B.
- If the author is a group or organization, use the full name, omitting any initial article: American Psychological Association, United Nations.
- If an author uses a handle that is significantly different from their name, include the handle in square brackets after the name: Ocasio-Cortez, Alexandria [@AOC].
- If there's no known author, start the entry with the title.
- If there's an editor but no author, put the editor's name in the author position and specify their role: Coates, Ta-Nehisi, editor.
- If you're citing an editor, translator, director, or other contributors, specify their role. For works with multiple contributors, put the one whose work you wish to highlight before the title, and list any others you want to mention after the title. If you don't want to highlight one particular contributor, start with the title and include any contributors after the title. For contributors named before the title, put the label after the name: Fincher, David, director. For those named after the title, specify their role first: Directed by David Fincher.

Titles

- Include any subtitles and capitalize all the words in titles and subtitles except for articles (a, an, the), prepositions (to, at, from, and so on), and coordinating conjunctions (and, but, for, or, nor, yet, so)—unless they are the first or last word of a title or subtitle.
- Italicize the titles of books, periodicals, websites, and other long works (*Pride and Prejudice, Wired*).
- Enclose in quotation marks the titles of articles and other short works: "Letter from Birmingham Jail."
- To document a source that has no title, describe it without italics or quotation marks: Letter to the author, Photograph of a tree. For a short, untitled email, text message, tweet, or poem, you may want to include the first few words of the text itself instead: Dickinson, Emily. "Immortal is an ample word." *American Poems*, www.americanpoems.com/poets/emilydickinson/immortal-is-an-ample-word.

Versions and Numbers

- If you cite a source that's available in more than one version, specify the one you consulted in your works-cited entry. Write ordinal numbers with numerals, and abbreviate "edition": 2nd ed. Write out names of specific versions, and capitalize following a period or if the name is a proper noun: King James Version, unabridged version, director's cut.

- If you cite a book that's published in multiple volumes, indicate the volume number. Abbreviate "volume," and write the number as a numeral: vol. 2.

- Indicate any volume and issue numbers of journals, abbreviating both "volume" and "number": vol. 123, no. 4.

- If you cite a TV show or podcast episode, indicate the season and episode numbers: season 1, episode 4.

Publishers

- Write publishers', studios', and networks' names in full, but omit initial articles and business words like "Company" or "Inc."

- For academic presses, use "U" for "University" and "P" for "Press": Princeton UP, U of California P. Spell out "Press" if the name doesn't include "University": Running Press, MIT Press.

- If the publisher is a division of an organization, list the organization and any divisions from largest to smallest: Stanford U, Center for the Study of Language and Information, Metaphysics Research Lab.

Dates

- Whether to give just the year or to include the month and day depends on the source. In general, give the full date that you find there.

- For books, give the publication date on the copyright page: 1948. If a book lists more than one date, use the most recent one.

- Periodicals may be published annually, monthly, seasonally, weekly, or daily. Give the full date that you find there: 2019, Apr. 2019, spring 2019, 16 Apr. 2019.

- Abbreviate the months except for May, June, and July: Jan., Feb., Mar., Apr., Aug., Sept., Oct., Nov., Dec.

- For online sources, use the copyright date or the full date that you find in the source. If the source does not give a date, use the date of access: Accessed 6 June 2020. Give a date of access as well for online sources you think are likely to change, or for websites that have disappeared.

Location

- For most print articles and other short works, give a page number or range of pages: p. 24, pp. 24-35. For those that are not on consecutive pages, give the first page number with a plus sign: pp. 24+.
- If it's necessary to specify a particular section of a source, give the section name before the page numbers: Sunday Review sec., p. 3.
- Indicate the location of an online source by giving a DOI if one is available; if not, give a URL—and use a permalink if one is available. URLs are not always reliable, so ask your instructor if you should include them. DOIs should start with "https://doi.org/" but no need to include "https://" for a URL, unless you want the URL to be a hyperlink.
- For a location, give enough information to identify it: a city (Houston), a city and state (Provo, Utah), or a city and country (Itu, Brazil). For something seen in a museum or elsewhere, name the institution and its location: Olson House, Cushing, Maine.
- For performances or other live presentations, name the venue and its location: Mark Taper Forum, Los Angeles.

Punctuation

- Use a period after the author name(s) that start an entry (Morrison, Toni.) and the title of the source you're documenting (*Beloved*.).
- Use a comma between the author's last and first names: Morrison, Toni.
- Some URLs won't fit on one line. When necessary, we recommend breaking a URL before a punctuation mark. Do not add a hyphen or a space.
- Sometimes you'll need to provide information about more than one work for a single source—for instance, when you cite an article from a periodical that you access through a database. MLA refers to the periodical and database (or any other entity that holds a source) as

author   title   publication

"containers." Use commas between elements within each container and put a period at the end of each container. For example:

Semuels, Alana. "The Future Will Be Quiet." *The Atlantic*, Apr. 2016, pp. 19-20. *ProQuest*, search.proquest.com/docview /1777443553?accountid+42654.

The guidelines below should help you document kinds of sources you're likely to use. The first section shows how to acknowledge authors and other contributors and applies to all kinds of sources—print, online, or others. Later sections show how to treat titles, publication information, location, and access information for many specific kinds of sources. In general, provide as much information as possible for each source—enough to tell readers how to find a source if they wish to access it themselves.

Sources Not Covered

These guidelines will help you cite a variety of sources, but there may be sources you want to use that aren't mentioned here. If you're citing a source that isn't covered, consult the MLA style blog at style.mla.org, or ask them a question at style.mla.org/ask-a-question.

Authors and Contributors

When you name authors and other contributors in your citations, you are crediting them for their work and letting readers know who's in on the conversation. The following guidelines for citing authors and contributors apply to all sources you cite: in print, online, or in some other medium.

1. One author

Author's Last Name, First Name. *Title.* Publisher, Date.

Anderson, Chris. *The Long Tail: Why the Future of Business Is Selling Less of More*. Hyperion, 2006.

2. Two authors

1st Author's Last Name, First Name, and 2nd Author's First and Last Names. *Title.* Publisher, Date.

Lunsford, Andrea A., and Lisa Ede. *Singular Texts/Plural Authors: Perspectives on Collaborative Writing*. Southern Illinois UP, 1990.

3. Three or more authors

1st Author's Last Name, First Name, et al. *Title*. Publisher, Date.

Sebranek, Patrick, et al. *Writers INC: A Guide to Writing, Thinking, and Learning*. Write Source, 1990.

4. Two or more works by the same author

Give the author's name in the first entry, and then use three hyphens in the author slot for each of the subsequent works, listing them alphabetically by the first word of each title and ignoring any articles.

Author's Last Name, First Name. *Title That Comes First Alphabetically*. Publisher, Date.

---. *Title That Comes Next Alphabetically*. Publisher, Date.

Kaplan, Robert D. *The Coming Anarchy: Shattering the Dreams of the Post Cold War*. Random House, 2000.

---. *Eastward to Tartary: Travels in the Balkans, the Middle East, and the Caucasus*. Random House, 2000.

5. Author and editor or translator

Author's Last Name, First Name. *Title*. Role by First and Last Names, Publisher, Date.

Austen, Jane. *Emma*. Edited by Stephen M. Parrish, W. W. Norton, 2000.
Dostoevsky, Fyodor. *Crime and Punishment*. Translated by Richard Pevear and Larissa Volokhonsky, Vintage Books, 1993.

Start with the editor or translator if you are focusing on their contribution rather than the author's. If there is a translator but no author, start with the title.

Pevear, Richard, and Larissa Volokhonsky, translators. *Crime and Punishment*. By Fyodor Dostoevsky, Vintage Books, 1993.
Beowulf. Translated by Stephen Mitchell, Yale UP, 2017.

author   title   publication

6. No author or editor

When there's no known author or editor, start with the title.

> *The Turner Collection in the Clore Gallery.* Tate Publications, 1987.

> "Being Invisible Closer to Reality." *The Atlanta Journal-Constitution,*
>   11 Aug. 2008, p. A3.

7. Organization or government as author

> Organization Name. *Title.* Publisher, Date.

> Diagram Group. *The Macmillan Visual Desk Reference.* Macmillan, 1993.

For a government publication, give the name that is shown in the source.

> United States, Department of Health and Human Services, National
>   Institute of Mental Health. *Autism Spectrum Disorders.*
>   Government Printing Office, 2004.

When a nongovernment organization is both author and publisher, start with the title and list the organization only as the publisher.

> *Stylebook on Religion 2000: A Reference Guide and Usage Manual.*
>   Catholic News Service, 2002.

If a division of an organization is listed as the author, give the division as the author and the organization as the publisher.

> Center for Workforce Studies. *2005-13: Demographics of the U.S.
>   Psychology Workforce.* American Psychological Association, July
>   2015.

Articles and Other Short Works

Articles, essays, reviews, and other short works are found in journals, magazines, newspapers, other periodicals, and books—all of which you may find in print, online, or in a database. For most short works, you'll need to provide information about the author, the titles of both the short work and the longer work, any page numbers, and various kinds of publication information, all explained below.

8. Article in a journal

Print

Author's Last Name, First Name. "Title of Article." *Name of Journal*, Volume, Issue, Date, Pages.

Cooney, Brian C. "Considering *Robinson Crusoe*'s 'Liberty of Conscience' in an Age of Terror." *College English*, vol. 69, no. 3, Jan. 2007, pp. 197-215.

Online

Author's Last Name, First Name. "Title of Article." *Name of Journal*, Volume, Issue, Date, DOI *or* URL.

Schmidt, Desmond. "A Model of Versions and Layers." *Digital Humanities Quarterly*, vol. 13, no. 3, 2019, www.digitalhumanities.org/dhq /vol/13/3/000430/000430.html.

9. Article in a magazine

Print

Author's Last Name, First Name. "Title of Article." *Name of Magazine*, Volume (if any), Issue (if any), Date, Pages.

Burt, Tequia. "Legacy of Activism: Concerned Black Students' 50-Year History at Grinnell College." *Grinnell Magazine*, vol. 48, no. 4, summer 2016, pp. 32-38.

Online

Author's Last Name, First Name. "Title of Article." *Name of Magazine*, Volume (if any), Issue (if any), Date, DOI *or* URL.

Brooks, Arthur C. "The Hidden Toll of Remote Work." *The Atlantic*, 1 Apr. 2021, www.theatlantic.com/family/archive/2021/04 /zoom-remote-work-loneliness-happiness/618473.

author   title   publication

Documentation Map (MLA) / Article in a Print Journal

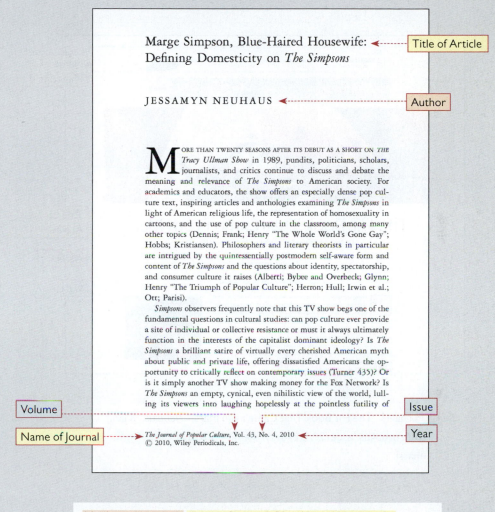

Marge Simpson, Blue-Haired Housewife: ← **Title of Article**
Defining Domesticity on *The Simpsons*

JESSAMYN NEUHAUS ← **Author**

MORE THAN TWENTY SEASONS AFTER ITS DEBUT AS A SHORT ON *THE Tracy Ullman Show* in 1989, pundits, politicians, scholars, journalists, and critics continue to discuss and debate the meaning and relevance of *The Simpsons* to American society. For academics and educators, the show offers an especially dense pop culture text, inspiring articles and anthologies examining *The Simpsons* in light of American religious life, the representation of homosexuality in cartoons, and the use of pop culture in the classroom, among many other topics (Dennis; Frank; Henry "The Whole World's Gone Gay"; Hobbs; Kristiansen). Philosophers and literary theorists in particular are intrigued by the quintessentially postmodern self-aware form and content of *The Simpsons* and the questions about identity, spectatorship, and consumer culture it raises (Alberti; Bybee and Overbeck; Glynn; Henry "The Triumph of Popular Culture"; Herron; Hull; Irwin et al.; Ott; Parisi).

Simpsons observers frequently note that this TV show begs one of the fundamental questions in cultural studies: can pop culture ever provide a site of individual or collective resistance or must it always ultimately function in the interests of the capitalist dominant ideology? Is *The Simpsons* a brilliant satire of virtually every cherished American myth about public and private life, offering dissatisfied Americans the opportunity to critically reflect on contemporary issues (Turner 435)? Or is it simply another TV show making money for the Fox Network? Is *The Simpsons* an empty, cynical, even nihilistic view of the world, lulling its viewers into laughing hopelessly at the pointless futility of

Volume ←
Issue

Name of Journal → *The Journal of Popular Culture*, Vol. 43, No. 4, 2010 ← **Year**
© 2010, Wiley Periodicals, Inc.

Neuhaus, Jessamyn. "Marge Simpson, Blue-Haired Housewife: Defining Domesticity on *The Simpsons*." *The Journal of Popular Culture*, vol. 43, no. 4, 2010, pp. 761-81.

Documentation Map (MLA) /
Article in an Online Magazine

URL

Name of Magazine

Title of Article

Author

Date

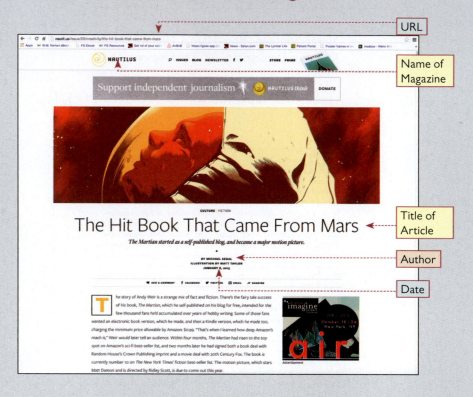

Segal, Michael. "The Hit Book That Came from Mars." *Nautilus,* 8 Jan. 2015, nautil.us/issue/20/creativity/the-hit-book-that-came-from -mars.

10. Article in a news publication

Print

Author's Last Name, First Name. "Title of Article." *Name of Publication*,
    Date, Pages.

Saulny, Susan, and Jacques Steinberg. "On College Forms, a Question of
    Race Can Perplex." *The New York Times*, 14 June 2011, p. A1.

To document a particular edition of a newspaper, list the edition before the
date. If a section name or number is needed to locate the article, put that
detail after the date.

Burns, John F., and Miguel Helft. "Under Pressure, YouTube Withdraws
    Muslim Cleric's Videos." *The New York Times*, late ed., 4 Nov. 2010,
    sec. 1, p. 13.

Online

Author's Last Name, First Name. "Title of Article." *Name of Publication*,
    Date, URL.

Banerjee, Neela. "Proposed Religion-Based Program for Federal Inmates
    Is Canceled." *The New York Times*, 28 Oct. 2006, www.nytimes
    .com/2006/10/28/us/28prison.html.

11. Article accessed through a database

Author's Last Name, First Name. "Title of Article." *Name of Periodical*,
    Volume, Issue, Date, Pages. *Name of Database*, DOI *or* URL.

Stalter, Sunny. "Subway Ride and Subway System in Hart Crane's 'The
    Tunnel.'" *Journal of Modern Literature*, vol. 33, no. 2, Jan. 2010,
    pp. 70-91. *JSTOR*, https://doi.org/10.2979/jml.2010.33.2.70.

12. Entry in a reference work

Print

Author's Last Name, First Name (if any). "Title of Entry." *Title of
    Reference Book*, edited by Editor's First and Last Names (if any),
    Edition number (if any), Volume (if any), Publisher, Date, Pages.

Documentation Map (MLA) /
Journal Article Accessed through a Database

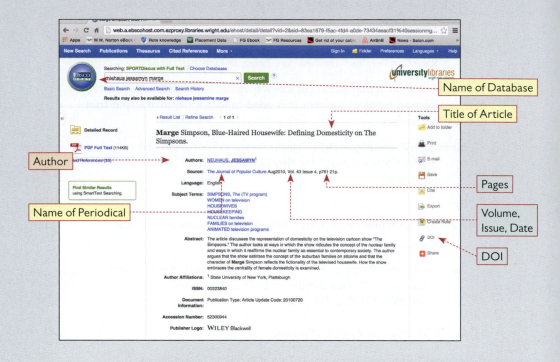

Name of Database

Title of Article

Author

Pages

Name of Periodical

Volume, Issue, Date

DOI

Neuhaus, Jessamyn. "Marge Simpson, Blue-Haired Housewife: Defining Domesticity on *The Simpsons*." *The Journal of Popular Culture*, vol. 43, no. 4, Aug. 2010, pp. 761-81. *EBSCOhost*, https://doi.org/10.1111/j.1540-5931.2010.00769.x.

Fritz, Jan Marie. "Clinical Sociology." *Encyclopedia of Sociology*, edited by
Edgar F. Borgatta and Rhonda J. V. Montgomery, 2nd ed., vol. 1,
Macmillan Reference USA, 2000, pp. 323-29.

"California." *The New Columbia Encyclopedia*, edited by William H.
Harris and Judith S. Levey, 4th ed., Columbia UP, 1975,
pp. 423-24.

Online

Document online reference works the same as print ones, adding the URL
after the date of publication.

"Baseball." *The Columbia Electronic Encyclopedia,* edited by Paul Lagasse,
6th ed., Columbia UP, 2012, www.infoplease.com/encyclopedia.

13. Editorial or op-ed

Editorial

Editorial Board. "Title." *Name of Periodical,* Date, Page *or* URL.

Editorial Board. "A New Look for Local News Coverage." *The Lakeville
Journal*, 13 Feb. 2020, p. A8.

Editorial Board. "Editorial: Protect Reporters at Protest Scenes."
Los Angeles Times, 11 Mar. 2021, www.latimes.com/opinion
/story/2021-03-11/reporters-protest-scenes.

Op-ed

Author's Last Name, First Name. "Title." *Name of Periodical,* Date,
Page *or* URL.

Okafor, Kingsley. "Opinion: The First Step to COVID Vaccine
Equity Is Overall Health Equity." *The Denver Post*, 15 Apr. 2021,
www.denverpost.com/2021/04/15/covid-vaccine-equity
-kaiser.

If it's not clear that it's an op-ed, add a label at the end.

Balf, Todd. "Falling in Love with Swimming." *The New York Times*, 17 Apr.
2021, p. A21. Op-ed.

14. Letter to the editor

Author's Last Name, First Name. "Title of Letter (if any)." *Name of Periodical,* Date, Page *or* URL.

Pinker, Steven. "Language Arts." *The New Yorker,* 4 June 2012, p. 10.

If the letter has no title, include "Letter" after the author's name.

Fleischmann, W. B. Letter. *The New York Review of Books,* 1 June 1963, www.nybooks.com/articles/1963/06/01/letter-21.

15. Review

Print

Reviewer's Last Name, First Name. "Title of Review." *Name of Periodical,* Date, Pages.

Frank, Jeffrey. "Body Count." *The New Yorker,* 30 July 2007, pp. 86–87.

Online

Reviewer's Last Name, First Name. "Title of Review." *Name of Periodical,* Date, URL.

Donadio, Rachel. "Italy's Great, Mysterious Storyteller." *The New York Review of Books,* 18 Dec. 2014, www.nybooks.com/articles/2014 /12/18/italys-great-mysterious-storyteller.

If a review has no title, include the title and author of the work being reviewed after the reviewer's name.

Lohier, Patrick. Review of *Exhalation,* by Ted Chiang. *Harvard Review Online,* 4 Oct. 2019, www.harvardreview.org/book-review/exhalation.

16. Comment on an online article

Commenter's Last Name, First Name *or* Username. Comment on "Title of Article." *Name of Periodical,* Date posted, Time posted, URL.

ZeikJT. Comment on "The Post-Disaster Artist." *Polygon,* 6 May 2020, 4:33 a.m., www.polygon.com/2020/5/5/21246679/josh-trank-capone-interview -fantastic-four-chronicle#comments.

author   title   publication

Books and Parts of Books

For most books, you'll need to provide information about the author, the title, the publisher, and the year of publication. If you found the book inside a larger volume, a database, or some other work, be sure to specify that as well.

17. Basic entries for a book

Print

Author's Last Name, First Name. *Title*. Publisher, Year of publication.

Watson, Brad. *Miss Jane*. W. W. Norton, 2016.

Ebook

Author's Last Name, First Name. *Title*. E-book ed., Publisher, Year of Publication.

Watson, Brad. *Miss Jane*. E-book ed., W. W. Norton, 2016.

Concise Guide to APA Style. 7th ed., e-book ed., American Psychological Association, 2020.

On a website

Author's Last Name, First Name. *Title*. Publisher, Year of publication, DOI *or* URL.

Ball, Cheryl E., and Drew M. Loewe, editors. *Bad Ideas about Writing*. West Virginia U Libraries, 2017, textbooks.lib.wvu.edu/badideas /badideasaboutwriting-book.pdf.

18. Anthology or edited collection

Last Name, First Name, editor. *Title*. Publisher, Year of publication.

Kitchen, Judith, and Mary Paumier Jones, editors. *In Short: A Collection of Brief Creative Nonfiction*. W. W. Norton, 1996.

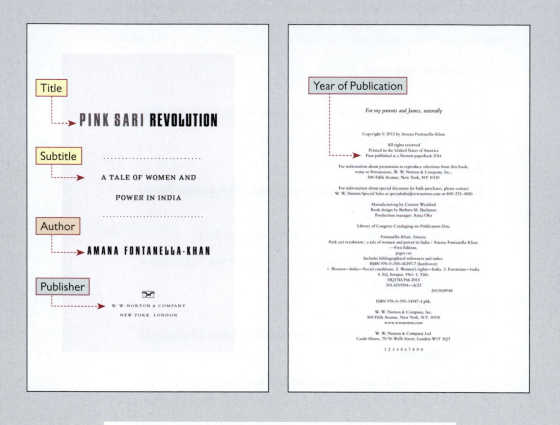

Fontanella-Khan, Amana. *Pink Sari Revolution: A Tale of Women and Power in India.* W. W. Norton, 2014.

19. Work in an anthology

Author's Last Name, First Name. "Title of Work." *Title of Anthology,* edited
   by First and Last Names, Publisher, Year of publication, Pages.

Achebe, Chinua. "Uncle Ben's Choice." *The Seagull Reader: Literature,*
   edited by Joseph Kelly, W. W. Norton, 2005, pp. 23-27.

Two or more works from one anthology

Prepare an entry for each selection by author and title, followed by the
anthology editors' last names and the pages of the selection. Then include a
separate entry for the anthology itself (see no. 18).

Author's Last Name, First Name. "Title of Work." Anthology Editors'
   Last Names, Pages.

Hiestand, Emily. "Afternoon Tea." Kitchen and Jones, pp. 65-67.

Ozick, Cynthia. "The Shock of Teapots." Kitchen and Jones, pp. 68-71.

20. Multivolume work

All volumes

Author's Last Name, First Name. *Title of Work.* Publisher, Year(s) of
   publication. Number of vols.

Churchill, Winston. *The Second World War.* Houghton Mifflin, 1948-53.
   6 vols.

Single volume

Author's Last Name, First Name. *Title of Work.* Vol. number, Publisher,
   Year of publication.

Sandburg, Carl. *Abraham Lincoln: The War Years.* Vol. 2, Harcourt, Brace
   and World, 1939.

If the volume has its own title, include it after the author's name, and indicate the volume number and series title after the year.

> Caro, Robert A. *Means of Ascent.* Vintage Books, 1990. Vol. 2 of *The Years of Lyndon Johnson.*

21. Book in a series

Author's Last Name, First Name. *Title of Book.* Edited by First and Last Names, Publisher, Year of publication. Series Title.

> Walker, Alice. *Everyday Use.* Edited by Barbara T. Christian, Rutgers UP, 1994. Women Writers: Texts and Contexts.

22. Graphic narrative or comic book

Author's Last Name, First Name. *Title.* Publisher, Year of publication.

> Barry, Lynda. *One! Hundred! Demons!* Drawn and Quarterly, 2005.

If the work has more than one contributor you want to include, start with the one you want to highlight, and label the role of anyone who's not an author.

> Pekar, Harvey. *Bob and Harv's Comics.* Illustrated by R. Crumb, Running Press, 1996.

> Crumb, R., illustrator. *Bob and Harv's Comics.* By Harvey Pekar, Running Press, 1996.

To cite several contributors, you can also start with the title.

> *Secret Invasion.* By Brian Michael Bendis, illustrated by Leinil Yu, inked by Mark Morales, Marvel, 2009.

23. Sacred text

If you cite a specific edition of a religious text, you need to include it in your works-cited list.

> *The New English Bible with the Apocrypha.* Oxford UP, 1971.

author   title   publication

The Torah: A Modern Commentary. W. Gunther Plaut, general editor,
　　Union of American Hebrew Congregations, 1981.

24. Edition other than the first

Author's Last Name, First Name. *Title.* Name *or* number of edition,
　　Publisher, Year of publication.

Smart, Ninian. *The World's Religions.* 2nd ed., Cambridge UP, 1998.

25. Republished work

Author's Last Name, First Name. *Title.* Year of original publication.
　　Current publisher, Year of republication.

Bierce, Ambrose. *Civil War Stories.* 1909. Dover, 1994.

26. Foreword, introduction, preface, or afterword

Part Author's Last Name, First Name. Name of Part. *Title of Book,* by
　　Author's First and Last Names, Publisher, Year of publication, Pages.

Tanner, Tony. Introduction. *Pride and Prejudice,* by Jane Austen, Penguin,
　　1972, pp. 7-46.

27. Published letter

Letter Writer's Last Name, First Name. "Title of letter." Day Month
　　Year. *Title of Book,* edited by First and Last Names, Publisher,
　　Year of publication, Pages.

White, E. B. "To Carol Angell." 28 May 1970. *Letters of E. B. White,*
　　edited by Dorothy Lobrano Guth, Harper and Row, 1976, p. 600.

28. Paper heard at a conference

Author's Last Name, First Name. "Title of Paper." Conference, Day
　　Month Year, Location.

Hern, Katie. "Inside an Accelerated Reading and Writing Classroom." Conference on Acceleration in Developmental Education, 15 June 2016, Sheraton Inner Harbor Hotel, Baltimore.

29. Dissertation

Author's Last Name, First Name. *Title.* Year. Institution, PhD dissertation. *Name of Database*, URL.

Simington, Maire Orav. *Chasing the American Dream Post World War II: Perspectives from Literature and Advertising.* 2003. Arizona State U, PhD dissertation. *ProQuest*, search.proquest.com/docview /305340098.

For an unpublished dissertation, end with the institution and a description of the work.

Kim, Loel. *Students Respond to Teacher Comments: A Comparison of Online Written and Voice Modalities.* 1998. Carnegie Mellon U, PhD dissertation.

Websites

Many sources are available in multiple media—for example, a print periodical that is also on the web and contained in digital databases—but some are published only on websites. A website can have an author, an editor, or neither. Some sites have a publisher, and some do not. Include whatever information is available. If the publisher and title are essentially the same, omit the name of the publisher. If the site is likely to change, if it has no date, or if it no longer exists, include a date of access.

30. Entire website

Author's Last Name, First Name. *Title of Site.* Date (if any), URL.

Park, Linda Sue. *Linda Sue Park: Author and Educator.* 2021, lindasuepark .com.

Editor's Last Name, First Name, role. *Title of Site.* Publisher (if any), Date (if any), URL.

Proffitt, Michael, chief editor. *The Oxford English Dictionary*. Oxford UP, 2021, www.oed.com.

If a site is likely to change or has no date, include a date of access.

Archive of Our Own. Organization for Transformative Works, archiveofourown.org. Accessed 23 Apr. 2021.

31. Work on a website

Author's Last Name, First Name (if any). "Title of Work." *Title of Site*, Publisher (if any), Date, URL.

Cesareo, Kerry. "Moving Closer to Tackling Deforestation at Scale." *World Wildlife Fund*, 20 Oct. 2020, www.worldwildlife.org /blogs/sustainability-works/posts/moving-closer-to-tackling -deforestation-at-scale.

32. Blog entry

Author's Last Name, First Name. "Title of Blog Entry." *Title of Blog*, Date, URL.

Hollmichel, Stefanie. "Winter Solstice." *A Stone in the River*, 22 Dec. 2021, www.astoneintheriver.net/2021/12/22/winter-solstice.

Document a whole blog as you would an entire website (no. 30) and a comment on a blog as you would a comment on an online article (no. 16).

33. Wiki

"Title of Entry." *Title of Wiki*, Publisher, Date, URL.

"Pi." *Wikipedia*, Wikimedia Foundation, 28 Aug. 2013, en.wikipedia.org /wiki/Pi.

Personal Communication and Social Media

34. Personal letter

Sender's Last Name, First Name. Letter to the author. Day Month Year.

Quindlen, Anna. Letter to the author. 11 Apr. 2013.

Documentation Map (MLA) / Work on a Website

URL

Title of Site

Title of Work

Date Posted

Authors

McIlwain, John, et al. "Housing in America: Integrating Housing, Health, and Resilience in a Changing Environment." *Urban Land Institute*, 28 Aug. 2014, uli.org/report/housing-in-america-housing-health -resilience.

35. Email or text message

Sender's Last Name, First Name.   Email *or* Text Message to First Name
Last Name *or* to the author.   Day Month Year.

Smith, William. Email to Richard Bullock. 19 Nov. 2013.

Rombes, Maddy. Text message to Isaac Cohen. 4 May 2021.

O'Malley, Kit. Text message to the author. 2 June 2020.

You can also include the text of a short email or text message, with a label
at the end.

Rust, Max. "Trip to see the cows tomorrow?" 27 Apr. 2021. Email.

36. Post to *Twitter, Instagram,* or other social media

Author.   "Title." *Name of Site,*   Day Month Year, URL.

Oregon Zoo. "Winter Wildlife Wonderland." *Facebook,* 8 Feb. 2019,
www.facebook.com/80229441108/videos/2399570506799549.

If there's no title, you can use a concise description or the text of a short post.

Millman, Debbie. Photos of Roxane Gay. *Instagram,* 18 Feb. 2021, www
.instagram.com/p/CLcT_EnhnWT.

Obama, Barack [@POTUS44]. "It's been the honor of my life to serve
you. You made me a better leader and a better man." *Twitter,*
20 Jan. 2017, twitter.com/POTUS44/status/822445882247413761.

Audio, Visual, and Other Sources

37. Advertisement

Print

Description of ad. *Title of Periodical,*   Date, Page.

Advertisement for Grey Goose. *Wine Spectator,* 18 Dec. 2020, p. 22.

Video

"Title." *Name of Site,* uploaded by Company, Date, URL.

"First Visitors." *YouTube,* uploaded by Snickers, 20 Aug. 2020, www
.youtube.com/watch?v=negeco0b1L0.

38. Art

Original

Artist's Last Name, First Name. *Title of Art.* Year created, Location.

Van Gogh, Vincent. *The Potato Eaters.* 1885, Van Gogh Museum, Amsterdam.

In a Book

Artist's Last Name, First Name. *Title of Art.* Year created, Location.
Title of Book, by First and Last Names, Publisher, Year of
publication, Page.

Van Gogh, Vincent. *The Potato Eaters.* 1885, Van Gogh Museum,
Amsterdam. *History of Art: A Survey of the Major Visual Arts from the
Dawn of History to the Present Day,* by H. W. Janson, Prentice
Hall / Harry N. Abrams, 1969, p. 508.

Online

Artist's Last Name, First Name. *Title of Art.* Year created. *Name of
Site,* URL.

Warhol, Andy. *Self-portrait.* 1979. *J. Paul Getty Museum,* www
.getty.edu/art/collection/objects/106971/andy-warhol-self
-portrait-american-1979.

39. Cartoon

Print

Author's Last Name, First Name. Cartoon *or* "Title of Cartoon." *Name
of Periodical,* Date, Page.

Mankoff, Robert. Cartoon. *The New Yorker,* 3 May 1993, p. 50.

author   title   publication

Online

Author's Last Name, First Name. Cartoon *or* "Title of Cartoon." *Title of Site*, Date, URL.

Munroe, Randall. "Up Goer Five." *xkcd*, 12 Nov. 2012, xkcd.com/1133.

40. Supreme Court case

United States, Supreme Court. *First Defendant v. Second Defendant.* Date of decision. *Name of Source Site*, Publisher, URL.

United States, Supreme Court. *District of Columbia v. Heller.* 26 June 2008. *Legal Information Institute*, Cornell Law School, www.law .cornell.edu/supremecourt/text/07-290.

41. Film

Name individuals based on the focus of your project—the director, the screenwriter, or someone else.

Title of Film. Role by First and Last Names, Production Company, Date.

Breakfast at Tiffany's. Directed by Blake Edwards, Paramount, 1961.

Online

Title of Film. Role by First and Last Names, Production Company, Date. *Name of Site*, URL.

Interstellar. Directed by Christopher Nolan, Paramount, 2014. *Amazon Prime Video*, www.amazon.com/Interstellar-Matthew -McConaughey/dp/B00TU9UFTS.

42. TV show episode

Name contributors based on the focus of your project—director, writers, actors, or others. If you don't want to highlight anyone in particular, don't include any contributors.

Broadcast

"Title of Episode." *Title of Program*, role by First and Last Names (if any), season, episode, Production Company, Broadcast date.

"The Storm." *Avatar: The Last Airbender*, created by Michael Dante
DiMartino and Bryan Konietzko, season 1, episode 12,
Nickelodeon Animation Studio, 3 June 2005.

DVD

"Title of Episode." Broadcast Date. *Title of DVD*, role by First and Last
Names (if any), season, episode, Production Company, Release Date,
disc number. DVD.

"The Storm." 2005. *Avatar: The Last Airbender: The Complete Book
1 Collection*, created by Michael Dante DiMartino and Bryan
Konietzko, episode 12, Nickelodeon Animation Studio, 2006,
disc 3. DVD.

Streaming Online

"Title of Episode." *Title of Program,* role by First and Last Names (if any),
season, episode, Production Company, Date. *Title of Site*, URL.

"The Storm." *Avatar: The Last Airbender*, season 1, episode 12,
Nickelodeon Animation Studio, 2005. *Netflix*, www.netflix.com.

Streaming on an App

"Title of Episode." *Title of Program*, role by First and Last Names (if any),
season, episode, Production Company, Date. *Name of* app.

"The Storm." *Avatar: The Last Airbender*, season 1, episode 12,
Nickelodeon Animation Studio, 3 June 2005. *Netflix* app.

43. Online video

"Title of Video." *Title of Site*, uploaded by Uploader's Name, Day Month
Year, URL.

"Everything Wrong with *National Treasure* in 13 Minutes or Less."
YouTube, uploaded by CinemaSins, 21 Aug. 2014, www.youtube
.com/watch?v=1ul-_ZWvXTs.

author   title   publication

44. Interview

If it's not clear that it's an interview, add a label at the end. If you are citing a transcript of an interview, indicate that at the end as well.

Published

Subject's Last Name, First Name. "Title of Interview (if any)." Interview by First Name Last Name (if given). *Name of Publication*, Date, Pages *or* URL.

Whitehead, Colson. "Colson Whitehead: By the Book." *The New York Times*, 15 May 2014, www.nytimes.com/2014/05/18/books /review/colson-whitehead-by-the-book.html. Interview.

Personal

Subject's Last Name, First Name. Concise description. Day Month Year.

Bazelon, L. S. Telephone interview with the author. 4 Oct. 2020.

45. Map

If the title doesn't make clear it's a map, add a label at the end.

Title of Map. Publisher, Date.

Brooklyn. J. B. Beers, 1874. Map.

46. Musical score

Composer's Last Name, First Name. *Title of Composition*. Publisher, Year of publication.

Frank, Gabriela Lena. *Compadrazgo*. G. Schirmer, 2007.

47. Oral presentation

Presenter's Last Name, First Name. "Title of Presentation." Sponsoring Institution, Date, Location.

Cassin, Michael. "Nature in the Raw—The Art of Landscape Painting." Berkshire Institute for Lifelong Learning, 24 Mar. 2005, Clark Art Institute, Williamstown, Massachusetts.

48. Virtual presentation on *Zoom* or other platform

Author's Last Name, First Name. "Title." Sponsoring Institution, Day Month Year, online.

Budhathoki, Thir. "Cross-Cultural Perceptions of Literacies in Student Writing." Conference on College Composition and Communication, 9 Apr. 2021, online.

49. Podcast

If you accessed a podcast online, give the URL; if you accessed it through an app, indicate that instead.

"Title of Episode." *Title of Podcast*, hosted by First Name Last Name, season, episode, Production Company, Date, URL.

"DUSTWUN." *Serial*, hosted by Sarah Koenig, season 2, episode 1, WBEZ / Serial Productions, 10 Dec. 2015, serialpodcast.org /season-two/1/dustwun.

"DUSTWUN." *Serial*, hosted by Sarah Koenig, season 2, episode 1, WBEZ / Serial Productions, 10 Dec. 2015. *Spotify* app.

50. Radio program

"Title of Episode." *Title of Program*, hosted by First Name Last Name, Station, Day Month Year.

"In Defense of Ignorance." *This American Life*, hosted by Ira Glass, WBEZ, 22 Apr. 2016.

51. Sound recording

If you accessed a recording online, give the URL; if you accessed it through an app, indicate that instead.

author   title   publication

Artist's Last Name, First Name. "Title of Work." *Title of Album*, Label, Release Date, URL.

Beyoncé. "Pray You Catch Me." *Lemonade*, Parkwood Entertainment / Columbia Records, 2016, www.beyonce.com/album/lemonade -visual-album/songs.

Simone, Nina. "To Be Young, Gifted and Black." *Black Gold*, RCA Records, 1970. *Spotify* app.

On a CD or Vinyl

Artist's Last Name, First Name. "Title of Work." *Title of Album*, Label, Date. CD *or* Vinyl LP.

Brown, Greg. "Canned Goods." *The Live One*, Red House, 1995. CD.

52. Video game

Title of Game. Version, Distributor, Date of release.

Animal Crossing: New Horizons. Version 1.1.4, Nintendo, 6 Apr. 2020.

FORMATTING A RESEARCH ESSAY

Name, course, title. MLA does not require a separate title page, unless your paper is a group project. In the upper left-hand corner of your first page, include your name, your instructor's name, the course name and number, and the date. Center the title of your paper on the line after the date; capitalize it as you would a book title. If your paper is a group project, include all of that information on a title page instead, listing all the authors.

Page numbers. In the upper right-hand corner of each page, one-half inch below the top of the page, include your last name and the page number. If it's a group project and all the names don't fit, include only the page number. Number pages consecutively throughout your paper.

Typeface, spacing, margins, and indents. Choose a typeface that is easy to read (such as Times New Roman) and that provides a clear contrast between regular text and italic text. Set the font size between 11 and 13 points.

Double-space the entire paper, including your works-cited list and any notes. Set one-inch margins at the top, bottom, and sides of your text; do not justify your text. The first line of each paragraph should be indented one-half inch from the left margin. End punctuation should be followed by one space.

Headings. Short essays do not generally need headings, but they can be useful in longer works. Use a large, bold font for the first level of heading, and smaller fonts and italics to signal lower-level headings. MLA requires that headings all be flush with the left margin.

First-Level Heading
Second-Level Heading
Third-Level Heading

Long quotations. When quoting more than three lines of poetry, more than four lines of prose, or dialogue between characters in a drama, set off the quotation from the rest of your text, indenting it one-half inch (or five spaces) from the left margin. Do not use quotation marks, and put any parenthetical documentation *after* the final punctuation.

> In *Eastward to Tartary*, Robert Kaplan captures ancient and contemporary Antioch for us:
>
> > At the height of its glory in the Roman-Byzantine age, when it had an amphitheater, public baths, aqueducts, and sewage pipes, half a million people lived in Antioch. Today the population is only 125,000. With sour relations between Turkey and Syria, and unstable politics throughout the Middle East, Antioch is now a backwater—seedy and tumbledown, with relatively few tourists. I found it altogether charming. (123)

> In the first stanza of Matthew Arnold's "Dover Beach," exclamations make clear the speaker is addressing someone who is also present in the scene:
>
> > Come to the window, sweet is the night air!
> > Only, from the long line of spray
> > Where the sea meets the moon-blanched land,

Listen! You hear the grating roar

Of pebbles which the waves draw back, and fling . . . (lines 6-10)

Be careful to maintain the poet's line breaks. If a line does not fit on one line of your paper, put the extra words on the next line. Indent that line an additional quarter inch (or two spaces). If a citation doesn't fit, put it on the next line, flush with the right margin.

Tables and illustrations. Insert illustrations and tables close to the text that discusses them, and be sure to make clear how they relate to your point. For tables, provide a number (Table 1) and a title on separate lines above the table. Below the table, provide a caption with source information and any notes. Notes should be indicated with lowercase letters. For graphs, photos, and other figures, provide a figure number (Fig. 1) and caption with source information below the figure. If you give only brief source information, use commas between elements—Zhu Wei, *New Pictures of the Strikingly Bizarre #9*, print, 2004—and include full source information in your list of works cited. If you give full source information in the caption, don't include the source in your list of works cited. Punctuate as you would in the works-cited list, but don't invert the author's name: Berenice Sydney. *Fast Rhythm.* 1972, Tate Britain, London.

List of works cited. Start your list on a new page, following any notes. Center the title, "Works Cited," and double-space the entire list. Begin each entry at the left margin, and indent subsequent lines one-half inch (or five spaces). Alphabetize the list by authors' last names (or by editors' or translators' names, if appropriate). Alphabetize works with no author or editor by title, disregarding "A," "An," and "The." To cite more than one work by a single author, list them as in no. 4 on page 584.

SAMPLE RESEARCH ESSAY

Walter Przybylowski wrote the following analysis for a first-year writing course. It is formatted according to the guidelines of the MLA (style.mla.org).

½" margin

1" margin

Walter Przybylowski

Professor Matin

English 102, Section 3

4 May 2019

Put your last name and the page number in the upper-right corner of each page.

Center the title.

Holding Up the Hollywood Stagecoach:

The European Take on the Western

Double-space throughout.

The Western film has long been considered by film scholars and enthusiasts to be a distinctly American genre. Not only its subject matter but its characteristic themes originate in America's own violent and exciting past. For many years, Hollywood sold images of hard men fighting savages on the plains to the worldwide public; by ignoring the more complicated aspects of "how the West was won" and the true nature of relations between Native Americans and whites, filmmakers were able to reap great financial and professional rewards. In particular, the huge success of John Ford's 1939 film *Stagecoach* brought about countless imitations that led over the next few decades to American Westerns playing in a sort of loop, which reinforced the same ideas and myths in film after film.

1" margin

1" margin

Indent each paragraph ½" (5–7 spaces).

After the success of German-made Westerns in the 1950s, though, a new take on Westerns was ushered in by other European countries. Leading the Euro-Western charge, so to speak, were the Italians, whose cynical, often politically pointed Westerns left a permanent impact on an American-based genre. Europeans, particularly the Italians, challenged the dominant conventions of the American Western by complicating the morality of the characters, blurring the lines between

1" margin

good and evil, and also by complicating the traditional narrative, visual, and aural structures of Westerns. In this way, the genre motifs that *Stagecoach* initiated are explored in the European Westerns of the 1950s, 1960s, and early 1970s, yet with a striking difference in style. Specifically, Sergio Leone's 1968 film *Once upon a Time in the West* broke many of the rules set by the Hollywood Western and in the process created a new visual language for the Western. Deconstructing key scenes from this film reveals the demythologization at work in many of the Euro-Westerns, which led to a genre enriched by its presentation of a more complicated American West.

 Stagecoach is a perfect example of almost all the visual, sound, and plot motifs that would populate "classic" Hollywood Westerns for the next few decades. The story concerns a group of people, confined for most of the movie inside a stagecoach, who are attempting to cross a stretch of land made dangerous by Apache Indians on the warpath. Little effort is made to develop the characters of the Indians, who appear mainly as a narrative device, adversaries that the heroes must overcome in order to maintain their peaceful existence. This plot, with minor changes, could be used as a general description for countless Westerns. In his book *The Crowded Prairie: American National Identity in the Hollywood Western*, Michael Coyne explains the significance of *Stagecoach* to the Western genre and its influence in solidifying the genre's archetypes:

> [I]t was *Stagecoach* which . . . redefined the contours of the myth. The good outlaw, the whore with a heart of gold, the Madonna/Magdalene dichotomy between opposing female

Quotations of more than 4 lines are indented ½" (5 spaces) and double-spaced.

leads, the drunken philosopher, the last-minute cavalry rescue, the lonely walk down Main Street—all became stereotypes from *Stagecoach*'s archetypes. *Stagecoach* quickly became the model against which other "A" Westerns would be measured. (18-19)

Coyne is not exaggerating when he calls it "the model": in fact, all of these stereotypes became a sort of checklist of things that audiences expected to see. The reliance on a preconceived way to sell Western films to the public—where you could always tell the good characters from the bad and knew before the film ended how each character would end up— led to certain genre expectations that the directors of the Euro-Westerns would later knowingly reconfigure. As the influential critic Pauline Kael wrote in her 1965 book *Kiss Kiss Bang Bang*, "The original *Stagecoach* had a mixture of reverie and reverence about the American past that made the picture seem almost folk art; we wanted to believe in it even if we didn't" (52).

There seemed to be a need not just in Americans but in moviegoers around the world to believe that there was (or had been) a great untamed land out there just waiting to be cultivated. More important, as Kael pointed out, Americans wanted to believe that the building of America was a wholly righteous endeavor wherein the land was free for the taking—the very myth that Europeans later debunked through parody and subversive filmmaking techniques. According to Theresa Harlan, author of works on Native American art, the myth was based on the need of early white settlers to make their elimination of American Indians

---

For a set-off quotation, the parenthetical reference follows the closing punctuation.

Verb in signal phrase is past tense because date of source is mentioned.

Parenthetical reference following a quotation within the main text goes before the closing punctuation of the sentence.

more palatable in light of the settlers' professed Christian beliefs. In her article "Adjusting the Focus for an Indigenous Presence," Harlan writes that

> Eurocentric frontier ideology and the representations of indigenous people it produced were used to convince many American settlers that indigenous people were incapable of discerning the difference between a presumed civilized existence and their own "primitive" state. (136)

Although this myth had its genesis long before the advent of motion pictures, the Hollywood Western drew inspiration from it and continued to legitimize and reinforce its message. *Stagecoach*, with its high level of technical skill and artistry, redefined the contours of the myth, and a close look at the elements that made the film the "classic" model of the Western is imperative in order to truly understand its influence.

The musical themes that underscore the actions of the characters are especially powerful in this regard and can be as powerful as the characters' visual representation on screen. In *Stagecoach*, an Apache does not appear until more than halfway through the movie, but whenever one is mentioned, the soundtrack fills with sinister and foreboding drumbeats. The first appearance of Indians is a scene without dialogue, in which the camera pans between the stagecoach crossing through the land and Apaches watching from afar. The music that accompanies this scene is particularly telling, since as the camera pans between stagecoach and Apaches, the music shifts in tone dramatically from a pleasant melody to a score filled with dread. When the heroes shoot and kill the Apaches, then, the viewer has already been subjected to specific film techniques to give the stagecoach riders moral certitude in their annihilation of the alien menace. This kind of score is powerful stuff to accompany an image and does its best to tell the viewers how they should react. When Europeans start to make Westerns, the line of moral certitude will become less distinct.

In her essay "Of Mother Nature and Marlboro Men: An Inquiry into the Cultural Meanings of Landscape Photography," Deborah Bright argues that landscape photography has reinforced certain formulaic myths about landscape, and the same can be said of the Hollywood Western during the 1940s and 1950s. For example, in *Stagecoach*, when the stagecoach finally sets out for its journey through Apache territory, a fence is juxtaposed against the vast wide-open country in the foreground. The meaning is clear—the stagecoach is leaving civilized society to venture into the wilds of the West, and music swells as the coach crosses into that vast landscape (fig. 1). Ford uses landscape in this way to engender in the audience the desired response of longing for a time gone past, where there was land free for the taking and plenty to go around. Yet Bright suggests that "[i]f we are to redeem landscape photography from its narrow self-reflexive project, why not openly question the assumptions about nature and culture that it has traditionally served and use our practice instead to criticize them?" (141). This is exactly what Europeans, and Italians in particular, seem to have done with the Western. When Europeans started to make their own

---

Figure number calls readers' attention to illustration.

Brackets show that the writer has changed a capital letter to lowercase to make the quotation fit smoothly into his own sentence.

Przybylowski   6

Fig. 1. In *Stagecoach*, swelling music signals the coach's passage through the western landscape. Still from *Stagecoach*. *Internet Movie Database*, www.imdb.com/title/tt0031971/mediaviewer/rm1596567552.

Westerns, they took advantage of their outsider status in relation to an American genre by openly questioning the myths that have been established by *Stagecoach* and its cinematic brethren.

Sergio Leone's *Once upon a Time in the West* is a superior example of a European artist's take on the art form of the American Western. The "plot" of the film is flimsy, driven by the efforts of a mysterious

Illustration is positioned close to the text to which it relates, with figure number, caption, and full source information.

character played by Charles Bronson to avenge himself against Henry Fonda's character, a lowdown gunfighter trying to become a legitimate businessman. Claudia Cardinale plays a prostitute who is trying to put her past behind her. The similarities to American Westerns, on paper at least, seem to be so great as to make *Once upon a Time* almost a copy of what had long been done in Hollywood, but a closer look at European Westerns and at this film in particular shows that Leone is consciously sending up the stereotypes. After all, he needs to work within the genre's language if he is to adequately challenge it.

During the opening of *Once upon a Time in the West*, the viewer is given a kind of audio and visual tour of Euro-Western aesthetics. Leone introduces three gunmen in typical Italian Western style, with the first presented by a cut to a dusty boot heel from which the camera slowly pans up until it reaches the top of the character's cowboy hat. During this pan, the gunman's gear and its authenticity—a major aspect of the Italian Western—can be taken in by the audience. A broader examination of the genre would show that many Euro-Westerns use this tactic of hyperrealistic attention to costuming and weaponry, which Ignacio Ramonet argues is intended to distract the viewer from the unreality of the landscape:

> Extreme realism of bodies (hairy, greasy, foul-smelling), clothes or objects (including mania for weapons) in Italian films is above all intended to compensate for the complete fraud of the space and origins. The green pastures, farms and cattle of American Westerns are replaced by large, deserted canyons. (32)

Przybylowski   8

In the opening scene, the other two gunfighters are introduced by a camera panning across the room, allowing characters to materialize seemingly out of nowhere. Roger Ebert notes that Leone

> established a rule that he follows throughout . . . that the ability to see is limited by the sides of the frame. At important moments in the film, what the camera cannot see, the characters cannot see, and that gives Leone the freedom to surprise us with entrances that cannot be explained by the practical geography of his shots.

It is these aesthetic touches created to compensate for a fraudulent landscape that ushered in a new visual language for the Western. The opening of *Once upon a Time in the West* undercuts any preconceived notion of how a Western should be filmed, and this is exactly Leone's intention: "The director had obviously enjoyed dilating the audience's sense of time, exploiting, in his ostentatious way, the rhetoric of the Western, and dwelling on the tiniest details to fulfill his intention" (Frayling 197). By using jarring edits with amplified sounds, Leone informs the audience not only that he has seen all the popular Hollywood Westerns, but that he is purposely not going to give them that kind of movie. The opening ten-minute scene would be considered needlessly long in a typical Hollywood Western, but Leone is not making a copy of a Hollywood Western. In fact, it is this reliance on the audience's previously established knowledge of Westerns that allows Euro-Westerns to subvert the genre. Leone and other directors of Euro-Westerns are asking the public to open their eyes, to not believe what

No page number given for online source.

When no signal phrase is used to introduce a quotation, the author's name is included in the parenthetical citation.

is shown; they are attempting to take the camera's power away by parodying its effect. When Leone has characters magically appear in the frame, or amplifies the squeaking of a door hinge on a soundtrack, he is ridiculing the basic laws that govern American Westerns. The opening of *Once upon a Time* can be read as a sort of primer for what is about to come for the rest of the film, and its power leaves viewers more attuned to what they are watching.

Leone's casting also works to heighten the film's subversive effect. Henry Fonda, the quintessential good guy in classic Hollywood Westerns like *My Darling Clementine*, is cast as the ruthless Frank, a gunman shown murdering a small child early in the film. In a 1966 article on Italian Westerns in the *Saturday Evening Post*, Italian director Maurizio Lucidi gave some insight into the European perspective that lay behind such choices:

> We're adding the Italian concept of realism to an old American myth, and it's working. Look at Jesse James. In your country he's a saint. Over here we play him as a gangster. That's what he was. Europeans today are too sophisticated to believe in the honest gunman movie anymore. They want the truth and that's what we're giving them. (qtd. in Fox 55)

Leone knew exactly what he was doing, and his casting of Fonda went a long way toward confusing the audience's sympathies and complicating the simple good guy versus bad guy model of Hollywood films. For this reason, Fonda's entrance in the film is worth noting. The scene begins with a close-up of a shotgun barrel, which quickly explodes in a series

A citation of a source the writer found quoted in another source.

of (gun)shots that establish a scene of a father and son out hunting near their homestead. Here, Leone starts to move the camera more, with pans from father to son and a crane shot of their house as they return home to a picnic table with an abundance of food: the family is apparently about to celebrate something. Throughout this scene, crickets chirp on the soundtrack—until Leone abruptly cuts them off, the sudden silence quickly followed by close-ups of the uneasy faces of three family members. Leone is teasing the audience: he puts the crickets back on the soundtrack until out of nowhere we hear a gunshot. Instead of then focusing on the source or the target of the gunshot, the camera pans off to the sky, and for a moment the viewer thinks the shot is from a hunter. We next see a close-up of the father's face as he looks off into the distance, then is rattled when he sees his daughter grasping the air, obviously shot. As he runs toward her, tracked by the camera in a startling way, he is quickly shot down himself.

The family has been attacked seemingly out of nowhere, with only a young boy still alive. During the massacre, there is no musical score, just the abstract brutality of the slayings. Then Leone gives us a long camera shot of men appearing out of dust-blown winds, from nearby brush. It is obvious to the viewer that these men are the killers, but there is no clear sight of their faces: Leone uses long camera shots of their backs and an overhead shot as they converge on the young boy. This is the moment when Leone introduces Henry Fonda; he starts with the camera on the back of Fonda's head and then does a slow track around until his face is visible. At this point, audience members around the world would still have a hard time believing Fonda was a killer of these innocent people. Through crosscutting between the young boy's confused face and Fonda's smiling eyes, Leone builds a doubt in the audience—maybe he will not kill the boy. Then the crosscutting is interrupted with a close-up of Fonda's large Colt coming out of its holster, and Ennio Morricone's score, full of sadness, becomes audible. The audience's fears are realized: Fonda is indeed the killer. This scene is a clear parody of Hollywood casting stereotypes, and Leone toys with audience expectations by turning upside down the myth of the noble outlaw as portrayed by John Wayne in *Stagecoach*.

During the late 1960s and the early 1970s, Europeans were at odds with many of the foreign policies of the United States, a hostility expressed in Ramonet's characterization of this period as one "when American imperialism in Latin America and Southeast Asia was showing itself to be particularly brutal" (33). Morton, the railroad baron who is Frank's unscrupulous employer in *Once upon a Time in the West*, can easily be read as a critique of the sometimes misguided ways Americans went about bringing their way of life to other countries. Morton represents the bringer of civilization, usually a good thing in the classic Western genre, where civilization meant doctors, schools, homes for everyone. But the Europeans question how this civilization was built. Leone, in a telling quotation, gives his perspective: "I see the history of the West as really the reign of violence by violence" (qtd. in Frayling 134).

Instead of the civilizing myth and its representations, the concern of *Once upon a Time*—and the Euro-Western in general—is to give voice to the perspective of the marginal characters: the Native Americans,

Mexicans, and Chinese who rarely rated a position of significance in a Hollywood Western. In *Once upon a Time*, Bronson's character, Harmonica, pushes the plot forward with his need to avenge. Harmonica stands in for all the racial stereotypes that populated the American Western genre. When he and Frank meet in the movie's climactic duel, Frank is clearly perplexed about why this man wants to fight him, but his ego makes it impossible for him to refuse. They meet in an abandoned yard, with Frank in the extreme foreground and Harmonica in the extreme background (fig. 2). The difference between the two is thus presented from both physical and ideological standpoints: Frank guns down settlers to make way for the railroad (and its owner), whereas Harmonica helps people to fend for themselves. Morricone's score dominates the soundtrack during this final scene, with a harmonica blaring away throughout. The costuming of Frank in black and Harmonica in white is an ironic throwback to classic Hollywood costuming and one that suggests Harmonica is prevailing over the racial stereotypes of American Westerns. Leone milks the scene for all it's worth, with the camera circling Harmonica as Frank looks for a perfect point to start the duel. Harmonica never moves, his face steadily framed in a close-up. Meanwhile, Frank is shown in mostly long shots; his body language shows that he is uncertain about the outcome of the duel, while Harmonica knows the ending.

As the two seem about to draw, the camera pushes into Harmonica's eyes, and there is a flashback to a younger Frank walking toward the camera, putting a harmonica into the mouth of a boy (the young Harmonica), and forcing him to participate in Frank's hanging of

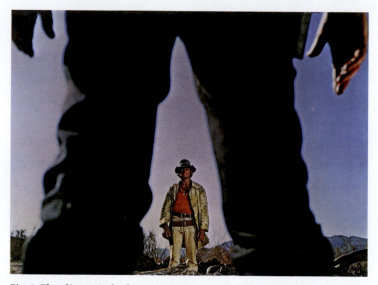

Fig. 2. The climactic duel in *Once upon a Time in the West* challenges the casting and costuming stereotypes of the Hollywood Western. Still from *Once upon a Time in the West. Internet Movie Database*, www.imdb.com /title/tt0064116/mediaviewer/rm1124971008.

Complete source information provided along with the caption since this figure is not included in the works-cited list.

the boy's older brother. This brutal scene, in which Frank unknowingly seals his own destiny, is set in actual American locations and is taken directly from John Ford Westerns; Leone is literally bringing home the violence dealt to minorities in America's past. As soon as the brother is hanged, the scene returns to the present, and Frank is shot through the heart. As he lies dying, we see a look of utter disbelief on his face as he asks Harmonica, "Who are you?" At this moment, a harmonica is shoved into his mouth. Only then does recognition play over Frank's face; as he falls to the ground, his face in close-up is a grotesque death-mask not unlike the massacred victims of Morton's train. The idea of past misdeeds coming back to haunt characters in the present is a clear attempt to challenge the idea that the settlers had a moral right to conquer and destroy indigenous people in order to "win" the West.

The tremendous success of *Stagecoach* was both a blessing and curse for the Western genre. Without it, the genre would surely never have gained the success it did, but this success came with ideological and creative limitations. Both the popularity and the limitations of the American Western may have inspired European directors to attempt something new with the genre, and unlike American filmmakers, they could look more objectively at our history and our myths. Leone's demythologization of the American Western has proved a valuable addition to the Western genre. The effect of the Euro-Western can be seen in American cinema as early as *The Wild Bunch* in 1969—and as recently as the attention in *Brokeback Mountain* to types of Western characters usually marginalized. In this way, Italian Westerns forced a new level of viewing of the Western tradition that made it impossible to ever return to the previous Hollywood model.

List of works cited begins on a new page. "Works Cited" heading is centered.

Works Cited

Bright, Deborah. "Of Mother Nature and Marlboro Men: An Inquiry into the Cultural Meanings of Landscape Photography." *The Contest of Meaning: Critical Histories of Photography*, edited by Richard Bolton, MIT Press, 1993, pp. 125-43.

Coyne, Michael. *The Crowded Prairie: American National Identity in the Hollywood Western*. I. B. Tauris, 1997.

Ebert, Roger. "The Good, the Bad and the Ugly." *Chicago Sun-Times*, 3 Aug. 2003, www.rogerebert.com/reviews/great-movie-the-good-the-bad -and-the-ugly-1968.

Fox, William. "Wild Westerns, Italian Style." *The Saturday Evening Post*, 6 Apr. 1968, pp. 50-55.

Frayling, Christopher. *Spaghetti Westerns: Cowboys and Europeans from Karl May to Sergio Leone*. St. Martin's Press, 1981.

Harlan, Theresa. "Adjusting the Focus for an Indigenous Presence." *Overexposed: Essays on Contemporary Photography*, edited by Carol Squiers, New Press, 1999, pp. 134-52.

Kael, Pauline. *Kiss Kiss Bang Bang*. Bantam Books, 1965.

Once upon a Time in the West. Directed by Sergio Leone, performances by Henry Fonda and Charles Bronson, Paramount, 1968.

Ramonet, Ignacio. "Italian Westerns as Political Parables." *Cineaste*, vol. 15, no. 1, 1986, pp. 30-35. *JSTOR*, www.jstor.org/stable/41686858.

Stagecoach. Directed by John Ford, United Artists, 1939.

Each entry begins at the left margin, with subsequent lines indented.

List is alphabetized by authors' last names or by title for works with no author.

THIRTY-ONE

APA Style

AMERICAN **P**SYCHOLOGICAL **A**SSOCIATION (APA) style calls for (1) brief documentation in parentheses near each in-text citation and (2) complete documentation in a list of references at the end of your text. The models in this chapter draw on the *Publication Manual of the American Psychological Association*, 7th edition (2020). Additional information is available at apastyle.org.

A DIRECTORY TO APA STYLE

In-Text Documentation 627

Throughout this chapter, you'll find models and examples that are color-coded to help you see how writers include source information in their texts and reference lists: tan for author or editor, yellow for title, gray for publication information—publisher, date of publication, page number(s), DOI or URL, and so on.

Alba, Levy, and Myers's report also employs APA style. You can find it on p. 837.

IN-TEXT DOCUMENTATION

Brief documentation in your text makes clear to your readers precisely what you took from a source. If you are quoting, provide the page number(s) or other information that will help readers locate the quotation in the source. You are not required to give the page number(s) with a paraphrase or summary, but you may want to do so if you are citing a long or complex work.

PARAPHRASES and SUMMARIES are more common than QUOTATIONS in APA-style projects. See Chapter 28 for more on all three kinds of citation. As you cite each source, you will need to decide whether to name the author in a signal phrase—"as McCullough (2001) wrote"—or in parentheses—"(McCullough, 2001)." Note that APA requires you to use the past tense for verbs in **SIGNAL PHRASES**, or the present perfect if you are referring to an ongoing action that started in the past or to something that didn't occur at a specific time: "Moss (2019) argued," "Many authors have argued."

1. Author named in a signal phrase

Put the date in parentheses after the author's last name, unless the year is mentioned in the sentence. If you are including the page number, put it in parentheses after the quotation, paraphrase, or summary. Documentation information in parentheses should come *before* the period at the end of the sentence and *after* any quotation marks.

> McCullough (2001) described John Adams as having "the hands of a man accustomed to pruning his own trees, cutting his own hay, and splitting his own firewood" (p. 18).

> In 2001, McCullough noted that John Adams's hands were those of a laborer (p. 18).

> John Adams had "the hands of a man accustomed to pruning his own trees," according to McCullough (2001, p. 18).

If the author is named after a quotation, as in this last example, put the page number(s) after the date within the parentheses.

2. Author named in parentheses

If you do not mention an author in a signal phrase, put the name, the year of publication, and any page number(s) in parentheses at the end of the sentence or right after the quotation, paraphrase, or summary.

> John Adams had "the hands of a man accustomed to pruning his own trees" (McCullough, 2001, p. 18).

3. Authors with the same last name

If your reference list includes more than one person with the same last name, include initials to distinguish the authors from one another.

> Eclecticism is common in modern criticism (J. M. Smith, 1992, p. vii).

author   title   publication

4. Two authors

Always mention both authors. Use "and" in a signal phrase, but use an ampersand (&) in parentheses.

> Carlson and Ventura (1990) wanted to introduce Julio Cortázar, Marjorie Agosín, and other Latin American writers to an audience of English-speaking adolescents (p. v).

> According to the Peter Principle, "In a hierarchy, every employee tends to rise to his level of incompetence" (Peter & Hull, 1969, p. 26).

5. Three or more authors

When you refer to a work by three or more contributors, name only the first author followed by "et al.," Latin for "and others."

> Peilen et al. (1990) supported their claims about corporate corruption with startling anecdotal evidence (p. 75).

6. Organization or government as author

If an organization name is recognizable by its abbreviation, give the full name and the abbreviation the first time you cite the source. In subsequent references, use only the abbreviation. If the organization does not have a familiar abbreviation, always use its full name.

First reference

The American Psychological Association (APA, 2020)

(American Psychological Association [APA], 2020)

Subsequent references

The APA (2020)

(APA, 2020)

7. Author unknown

Use the complete title if it's short; if it's long, use the first few words of the title under which the work appears in the reference list. Italicize the title if it's italicized in the reference list; if it isn't italicized there, enclose the title in quotation marks.

> According to *Feeding Habits of Rams* (2000), a ram's diet often changes from one season to the next (p. 29).

> The article noted that one healthy liver donor died because of "frightening" postoperative care ("Every Patient's Nightmare," 2007).

8. Two or more works together

If you document multiple works in the same parentheses, place the source information in alphabetical order, separated by semicolons.

> Many researchers have argued that what counts as "literacy" is not necessarily learned at school (Heath, 1983; Moss, 2003).

Multiple authors in a signal phrase can be named in any order.

9. Two or more works by one author in the same year

If your list of references includes more than one work by the same author published in the same year, order them alphabetically by title, adding lowercase letters ("a," "b," and so on) to the year.

> Kaplan (2000a) described orderly shantytowns in Turkey that did not resemble the other slums he visited.

10. Source quoted in another source

When you cite a source that was quoted in another source, add the words "as cited in." If possible, cite the original source instead.

> Thus, Modern Standard Arabic was expected to serve as the "moral glue" holding the Arab world together (Choueri, 2000, as cited in Walters, 2019, p. 475).

author   title   publication

11. Work without page numbers

Instead of page numbers, some works have paragraph numbers, which you should include (preceded by the abbreviation "para.") if you are referring to a specific part of such a source.

> Russell's dismissals from Trinity College at Cambridge and from City College in New York City have been seen as examples of the controversy that marked his life (Irvine, 2006, para. 2).

In sources with neither page nor paragraph numbers (e.g., many online journals), refer readers to a particular part of the source if possible, perhaps indicating a heading and the paragraph under the heading: (Brody, 2020, Introduction, para. 2).

12. An entire work

You do not need to give a page number if you are directing readers' attention to an entire work.

> Kaplan (2000) considered Turkey and Central Asia explosive.

When you are citing an entire website, give the URL in the text. You do not need to include the website in your reference list. To cite a webpage, see no. 18 on page 640.

> Beyond providing diagnostic information, the website for the Alzheimer's Association (http://www.alz.org) includes a variety of resources for the families of patients.

13. Personal communication

Document emails, telephone conversations, personal interviews, personal letters, messages from nonarchived electronic discussion sources, and other personal texts as "personal communication," along with the person's initial(s), last name, and the date. You do not need to include such personal communications in your reference list.

> L. Strauss (personal communication, December 6, 2013) told about visiting Yogi Berra when they both lived in Montclair, New Jersey.

NOTES

You may need to use footnotes to give an explanation or information that doesn't fit into your text. To signal a content footnote, place a superscript numeral at the appropriate point in your text. Include this information in a footnote, either at the bottom of that page or on a separate page with the heading "Footnotes" in bold, after your reference list. If you have multiple notes, number them consecutively throughout your text. Here is an example from *In Search of Solutions: A New Direction in Psychotherapy* (2003).

Text with superscript

An important part of working with teams and one-way mirrors is taking the consultation break, as at Milan, BFTC, and MRI.[1]

Footnote

[1] It is crucial to note here that while working within a team is fun, stimulating, and revitalizing, it is not necessary for successful outcomes. Solution-oriented therapy works equally well when working solo.

REFERENCE LIST

A reference list provides full bibliographic information for every source cited in your text with the exception of entire websites, common software and mobile apps, and personal communications. See page 653 for guidelines on preparing such a list; for a sample reference list, see page 671.

Key Elements for Documenting Sources

APA style provides a list of four elements that should be used to document a source: author, date, title, and source. The kind of information that makes up each element can change slightly depending on the type of source. The following guidelines explain how to handle each of the key elements generally; refer to these guidelines and the section on "Authors and Other Contributors" if your specific kind of source isn't covered in the examples provided.

author   title   publication

AUTHOR: Use the author's last name, but replace the first and middle names with initials and invert the order: Kinder, D. R. for Donald R. Kinder.

DATE: Include the date of publication, which will vary based on the type of work you are citing.

TITLE: Capitalize only the first word and proper nouns and adjectives in the title and subtitle of the work you are citing. Titles of periodicals and websites are capitalized differently, so refer to an example for specifics.

SOURCE: The source indicates where the work can be found. It includes the publisher, any additional information about the source (e.g., volume number, issue number, pages), and the DOI or URL if applicable.

DOI OR URL: Include a DOI (digital object identifier, a string of letters and numbers that identifies an online document) for any work that has one, regardless of whether you accessed the source in print or online. For a print work with no DOI, do not include a URL. For an online work with no DOI, include a URL unless the URL is no longer working or unless the work is from an academic database.

Authors and Other Contributors

This section provides general guidelines for documenting authors and other contributors across sources and in various kinds of media (in print, online, and in other media). Note that most of the examples in this section are books. If you are documenting a different kind of source, follow the relevant formatting guidelines.

1. One author

Author's Last Name, Initials. (Year of publication). *Title of book.*
Publisher. DOI *or* URL

Lewis, M. (2003). *Moneyball: The art of winning an unfair game.* W. W. Norton.

This book does not have a DOI, so that element does not appear in the reference entry.

2. Two authors

First Author's Last Name, Initials, & Second Author's Last Name, Initials. (Year of publication). *Title of book.* Publisher. DOI *or* URL

Montefiore, S., & Montefiore, S. S. (2016). *The royal rabbits of London.* Aladdin.

3. Three or more authors

For three to twenty authors, include all names.

First Author's Last Name, Initials, Next Author's Last Name, Initials, & Final Author's Last Name, Initials. (Year of publication). *Title of book.* Publisher. DOI *or* URL

Greig, A., Taylor, J., & MacKay, T. (2013). *Doing research with children: A practical guide* (3rd ed.). Sage.

For a work by twenty-one or more authors, name the first nineteen authors, followed by three ellipsis points, and end with the final author.

Gao, R., Asano, S. M., Upadhyayula, S., Pisarev, I., Milkie, D. E., Liu, T.-L., Singh, V., Graves, A., Huynh, G. H., Zhao, Y., Bogovic, J., Colonell, J., Ott, C. M., Zugates, C., Tappan, S., Rodriguez, A., Mosaliganti, K. R., Sheu, S.-H., Pasolli, H. A., . . . Betzig, E. (2019, January 18). Cortical column and whole-brain imaging with molecular contrast and nanoscale resolution. *Science, 363*(6424). https://doi.org/10.1126 /science.aau8302

4. Two or more works by the same author

If the works were published in different years, list them chronologically.

Lewis, B. (1995). *The Middle East: A brief history of the last 2,000 years.* Scribner.

Lewis, B. (2003). *The crisis of Islam: Holy war and unholy terror.* Modern Library.

author title publication

If the works were published in the same year, list them alphabetically by title (ignoring "A," "An," and "The"), adding "a," "b," and so on to the year.

> Kaplan, R. D. (2000a). *The coming anarchy: Shattering the dreams of the post Cold War*. Random House.
> Kaplan, R. D. (2000b). *Eastward to Tartary: Travels in the Balkans, the Middle East, and the Caucasus*. Random House.

5. Author and editor

If a book has an author and an editor who is credited on the cover, include the editor in parentheses after the title. If the book is a republished version of an earlier book, include the year of publication of the version you are using as the date and the original publication year at the end.

> Author's Last Name, Initials. (Year of publication). *Title of book* (Editor's Initials Last Name, Ed.). Publisher. DOI *or* URL (Original work published Year)

> Dick, P. F. (2008). *Five novels of the 1960s and 70s* (J. Lethem, Ed.). Library of America. (Original works published 1964–1977)

6. Author and translator

> Author's Last Name, Initials. (Year of publication). *Title of book* (Translator's Initials Last Name, Trans.). Publisher. DOI *or* URL (Original work published Year)

> Hugo, V. (2008). *Les misérables* (J. Rose, Trans.). Modern Library. (Original work published 1862)

7. Editor

> Editor's Last Name, Initials (Ed.). (Year of publication). *Title of book*. Publisher. DOI *or* URL

> Jones, D. (Ed.). (2007). *Modern love: 50 true and extraordinary tales of desire, deceit, and devotion*. Three Rivers Press.

8. Unknown or no author or editor

When there's no known author or editor, start with the title.

> *Title.* (Year of Publication). Publisher. DOI *or* URL

> *Feeding habits of rams.* (2000). Land's Point Press.

> Hot property: From carriage house to family compound. (2004,
>   December). *Berkshire Living, 1*(1), 99.

> Clues in salmonella outbreak. (2008, June 21). *The New York Times,* A13.

If the author is listed as "Anonymous," treat that as the author's name in the reference list entry.

9. Organization or government as author

Sometimes an organization or a government agency is both author and publisher. If so, omit the publisher.

> Organization Name *or* Government Agency. (Year of publication). *Title
>   of book.* DOI *or* URL

> Catholic News Service. (2002). *Stylebook on religion 2000: A reference guide.*

Articles and Other Short Works

Articles, essays, reviews, and other short works are found in periodicals and books—in print, online, or in a database. For most short works, provide information about the author, the date, the titles of both the short work and the longer work, any volume and issue numbers, any page numbers, various kinds of publication information, and a DOI or URL if applicable.

10. Article in a journal

> Author's Last Name, Initials. (Year). Title of article. *Title of Journal,
>   volume*(issue), page(s). DOI *or* URL

> Gremer, J. R., Sala, A., & Crone, E. E. (2010). Disappearing plants:
>   Why they hide and how they return. *Ecology, 91*(11), 3407–3413.
>   https://doi.org/10.1890/09-1864.1

If a DOI is long or complicated, it's acceptable to use a shortDOI. Create one by entering the DOI into the shortDOI service (https://shortdoi.org/). A URL can also be shortened using any online URL shortener, as long as the shorter URL leads to the correct work.

11. Article in a magazine

If a magazine is published weekly, include the day and the month. Include any volume number and issue number after the magazine title.

> Author's Last Name, Initials. (Year, Month Day). Title of article. *Title of Magazine,* *volume*(issue), page(s). DOI or URL

> Klump, B. (2019, November 22). Of crows and tools. *Science, 366*(6468), 965. https://doi.org/10.1126/science.aaz7775

12. Article in a newspaper

If page numbers are consecutive, separate them with an en dash. If not, separate them with a comma.

> Author's Last Name, Initials. (Year, Month Day). Title of article. *Title of Newspaper,* page(s). URL

> Schneider, G. (2005, March 13). Fashion sense on wheels. *The Washington Post*, F1, F6.

13. Article on a news website

Articles on *CNN, HuffPost, Salon, Vox,* and other news websites are documented differently from articles published in online newspapers and magazines. If an article is published in an online news source that is not a periodical or a blog, the article is treated as a stand-alone work, and the title should be italicized. Do not italicize the name of the website.

> Author's Last Name, Initials. (Year, Month Day). *Title of article.* Title of Site. URL

> Travers, C. (2019, December 3). *Here's why you keep waking up at the same time every night.* HuffPost. https://bit.ly/3drSwAR

Documentation Map (APA) / Article in a Journal with DOI

Title of Journal

Publication Year

DOI

Volume and Issue

Pages

Title of Article

Author

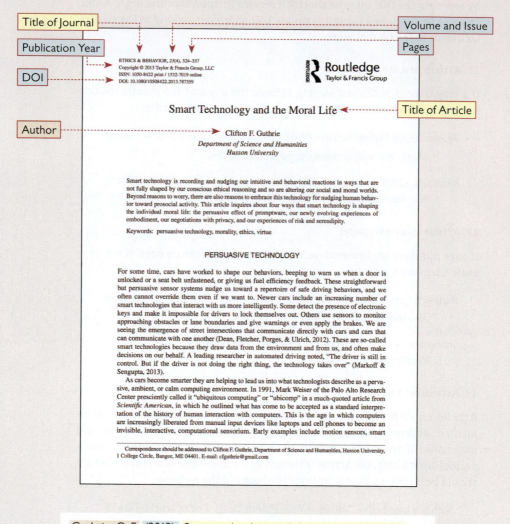

ETHICS & BEHAVIOR, 23(4), 324–337
Copyright © 2013 Taylor & Francis Group, LLC
ISSN: 1050-8422 print / 1532-7019 online
DOI: 10.1080/10508422.2013.787359

Routledge
Taylor & Francis Group

Smart Technology and the Moral Life

Clifton F. Guthrie
Department of Science and Humanities
Husson University

Smart technology is recording and nudging our intuitive and behavioral reactions in ways that are not fully shaped by our conscious ethical reasoning and so are altering our social and moral worlds. Beyond reasons to worry, there are also reasons to embrace this technology for nudging human behavior toward prosocial activity. This article inquires about four ways that smart technology is shaping the individual moral life: the persuasive effect of promptware, our newly evolving experiences of embodiment, our negotiations with privacy, and our experiences of risk and serendipity.

Keywords: persuasive technology, morality, ethics, virtue

PERSUASIVE TECHNOLOGY

For some time, cars have worked to shape our behaviors, beeping to warn us when a door is unlocked or a seat belt unfastened, or giving us fuel efficiency feedback. These straightforward but persuasive sensor systems nudge us toward a repertoire of safe driving behaviors, and we often cannot override them even if we want to. Newer cars include an increasing number of smart technologies that interact with us more intelligently. Some detect the presence of electronic keys and make it impossible for drivers to lock themselves out. Others use sensors to monitor approaching obstacles or lane boundaries and give warnings or even apply the brakes. We are seeing the emergence of street intersections that communicate directly with cars and cars that can communicate with one another (Dean, Fletcher, Porges, & Ulrich, 2012). These are so-called smart technologies because they draw data from the environment and from us, and often make decisions on our behalf. A leading researcher in automated driving noted, "The driver is still in control. But if the driver is not doing the right thing, the technology takes over" (Markoff & Sengupta, 2013).

As cars become smarter they are helping to lead us into what technologists describe as a pervasive, ambient, or calm computing environment. In 1991, Mark Weiser of the Palo Alto Research Center presciently called it "ubiquitous computing" or "ubicomp" in a much-quoted article from *Scientific American*, in which he outlined what has come to be accepted as a standard interpretation of the history of human interaction with computers. This is the age in which computers are increasingly liberated from manual input devices like laptops and cell phones to become an invisible, interactive, computational sensorium. Early examples include motion sensors, smart

Correspondence should be addressed to Clifton F. Guthrie, Department of Science and Humanities, Husson University, 1 College Circle, Bangor, ME 04401. E-mail: cfguthrie@gmail.com

Guthrie, C. F. (2013). Smart technology and the moral life. *Ethics & Behavior,* 23(4), 324–337. https://doi.org/10.1080/10508422 .2013.787359

14. Journal article from a database

Author's Last Name, Initials. (Year). Title of article. *Title of Journal,*
     volume(issue), page(s). DOI

Simpson, M. (1972). Authoritarianism and education: A comparative
     approach. *Sociometry, 35*(2), 223–234. https://doi.org/10.2307/2786619

15. Editorial

Editorials can appear in journals, magazines, and newspapers. The following example is from an online newspaper. If the editorial is unsigned, put
the title of the editorial in the author position.

Author's Last Name, Initials. (Year, Month Day). Title of editorial
     [Editorial]. *Title of Newspaper.* URL

The Guardian view on local theatres: The shows must go on [Editorial].
     (2019, December 6). *The Guardian.* https://bit.ly/2VZHIUg

16. Review

The following example is a book review in a newspaper; if you are citing a
review that appears in print or online in a journal, magazine, or newspaper, use this general format, indicating in brackets what is being reviewed
(a film, an app, etc.).

Reviewer's Last Name, Initials. (Year, Month Day). Title of review
     [Review of the book *Title of book*, by Author's Initials Last Name].
     Title of Newspaper. DOI or URL

Joinson, S. (2017, December 15). Mysteries unfold in a land of minarets
     and magic carpets [Review of the book *The city of brass*, by S. A.
     Chakraborty]. *The New York Times.* https://nyti.ms/2kvwHFP

For a review published on a website that is not associated with a periodical or a blog, italicize the title of the review and do not italicize the website
name. If the review does not have a title, include the information about
the work being reviewed in brackets immediately after the date of publication.

17. Comment on an online article or post

Author's Last Name, Initials [username]. (Year, Month Day). Text of comment up to twenty words [Comment on the article "Title of article"]. *Title of Publication*. DOI or URL

PhyllisSpecial. (2020, May 10). How about we go all the way again? [Comment on the article "2020 Eagles schedule: Picking wins and losses for all 16 games"]. *The Philadelphia Inquirer*. https://rb.gy/iduabz

Include a link to the comment if possible; if not, include the URL of the article.

18. Webpage

Author's Last Name, Initials. (Year, Month Day). *Title of work*. Title of Site. URL

Pleasant, B. (n.d.). *Annual bluegrass*. The National Gardening Association. https://garden.org/learn/articles/view/2936/

If the author and the website name are the same, use the website name as the author. If the content of the webpage is intended to change over time and no archived version exists, use "n.d." as the date and include a retrieval date.

Centers for Disease Control and Prevention. (2019, December 2). *When and how to wash your hands*. https://www.cdc.gov/handwashing /when-how-handwashing.html

Worldometer. (n.d.). *World population*. Retrieved February 2, 2020, from https://www.worldometers.info/world-population/

Books, Parts of Books, and Reports

19. Basic entry for a book

Author's Last Name, Initials. (Year of publication). *Title of book*. Publisher. DOI or URL

Print book

Schwab, V. E. (2018). *Vengeful*. Tor.

author   title   publication

Documentation Map (APA) / Webpage

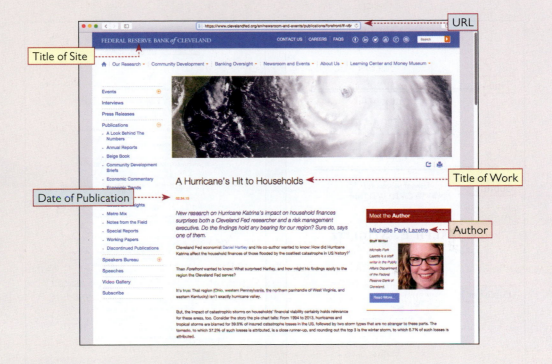

Lazette, M. P. (2015, February 24). *A hurricane's hit to households*. Federal
Reserve Bank of Cleveland. https://www.clevelandfed.org
/en/newsroom-and-events/publications/forefront/ff-v6n01/ff
-20150224-v6n0107-a-hurricanes-hit-to-households.aspx

Documentation Map (APA) / Book

Stiglitz, J. E. (2015). *The great divide: Unequal societies and what we can do about them.* W. W. Norton.

Ebook

Jemisin, N. K. (2017). *The stone sky*. Orbit. https://bit.ly/2DrGzKR

A print book and an ebook are documented in the same way. For an ebook, do not include the format or platform you used (e.g., Kindle).

20. Edition other than the first

Author's Last Name, Initials. (Year). *Title of book* (Name *or* number ed.). Publisher. DOI *or* URL

Burch, D. (2008). *Emergency navigation: Find your position and shape your course at sea even if your instruments fail* (2nd ed.). International Marine/McGraw-Hill.

21. Edited collection or anthology

Editor's Last Name, Initials (Ed.). (Year of edited edition). *Title of anthology* (Name *or* number ed., Vol. number). Publisher. DOI *or* URL

Raviv, A., Oppenheimer, L., & Bar-Tal, D. (Eds.). (1999). *How children understand war and peace: A call for international peace education.* Jossey-Bass.

22. Work in an edited collection or anthology

Author's Last Name, Initials. (Year). *Title of work*. In Editor's Initials Last Name (Ed.), *Title of anthology* (Name *or* number ed., Vol. number, pp. pages). Publisher. DOI *or* URL (Original work published Year)

Baldwin, J. (2018). Notes of a native son. In M. Puchner, S. Akbari, W. Denecke, B. Fuchs, C. Levine, P. Lewis, & E. Wilson (Eds.), *The Norton anthology of world literature* (4th ed., Vol. F, pp. 728–743). W. W. Norton. (Original work published 1955)

23. Entry in a reference work (dictionary, thesaurus, or encyclopedia)

If the entry has no author, use the name of the publisher as the author. If the reference work has no editor, do not include an editor. If the entry is archived or is not intended to change, use the publication date and do not include a retrieval date.

Author's Last Name, Initials. (Year). Title of entry. In Editor's Initials
  Last Name (Ed.), *Title of reference book* (Name *or* number ed., Vol.
  number, pp. pages). Publisher. URL

Merriam-Webster. (n.d.). Epoxy. In *Merriam-Webster.com dictionary*.
  Retrieved January 29, 2020, from https://www.merriam-webster
  .com/dictionary/epoxy

24. Book in a language other than English

Author's Last Name, Initials. (Year). *Title of book* [English translation of
  title]. Publisher. DOI *or* URL

Ferrante, E. (2011). *L'amica geniale* [My brilliant friend]. Edizione E/O.

25. One volume of a multivolume work

If the volume does not have a separate title, include the volume number in
parentheses after the title.

Author's Last Name, Initials. (Year). *Title of entire work* (Vol. number).
  Publisher. DOI *or* URL

Spiegelman, A. (1986). *Maus* (Vol. 1). Random House.

If the volume does have a separate title, include the volume number and title
in italics after the main title (see no. 26 for an example from a religious work).

26. Religious work

Do not include an author for most religious works. If you are citing an
annotated version, include the editor and/or translator. If the date of original publication is known, include it at the end.

Unannotated

Title of work. (Year of publication). Publisher. URL (Original work
  published Year)

New American Bible. (2002). United States Conference of Catholic Bishops.
  http://www.vatican.va/archive/ENG0839/_INDEX.HTM (Original work
  published 1970)

author   title   publication

Annotated

Editor's Last Name, Initials (Ed.). (Year of publication). *Title of work*. Publisher. URL (Original work published Year)

Marks, H. (Ed.). (2012). *The English Bible, The King James Version: Vol. 1. The Old Testament*. W. W. Norton. (Original work published 1611)

27. Report by a government agency or other organization

Author's Last Name, Initials. (Year, Month Day). *Title of report* (Report No. number). Publisher. DOI *or* URL

Centers for Disease Control and Prevention. (2009). *Fourth national report on human exposure to environmental chemicals*. US Department of Health and Human Services. https://www.cdc.gov/exposurereport/pdf/fourthreport.pdf

Omit the report number if one is not given. If more than one government department is listed as the publisher, list the most specific department as the author and the larger department as the publisher.

28. Published dissertation

Author's Last Name, Initials. (Year). *Title of dissertation* (Publication No. number) [Doctoral dissertation, Name of School]. Database *or* Archive Name. URL

Solomon, M. (2016). *Social media and self-examination: The examination of social media use on identity, social comparison, and self-esteem in young female adults* (Publication No. 10188962) [Doctoral dissertation, William James College]. ProQuest Dissertations and Theses Global.

If the thesis or dissertation is in a database, do not include a URL. Include a URL if the thesis or dissertation is published elsewhere online. If the dissertation is unpublished, use the name of the school as the source.

29. Paper or poster presented at a conference

Presenter's Last Name, Initials. (Year, Month First Day–Last Day). *Title of paper* or *poster* [Paper *or* Poster presentation]. Name of Conference, City, State, Country. URL

Dolatian, H., & Heinz, J. (2018, May 25–27). *Reduplication and finite-state technology* [Paper presentation]. The 53rd Annual Meeting of the Chicago Linguistic Society, Chicago, IL, United States. http://chicagolinguisticsociety.org/public/CLS53_Booklet.pdf

Audio, Visual, and Other Sources

If you are referring to an entire website, do not include the website in your reference list; simply mention the website's name in the body of your paper and include the URL in parentheses. Do not include email, personal communication, or other unarchived discussions in your list of references.

30. *Wikipedia* entry

Because *Wikipedia* has archived versions of its pages, give the date on which you accessed the page and the permanent URL of the archived page, which is found by clicking "View history."

Title of entry. (Year, Month Day). In *Wikipedia.* URL

List of sheep breeds. (2019, September 9). In *Wikipedia.* https://en.wikipedia.org/w/index.php?title=List_of_sheep_breeds&oldid=914884262

For a wiki that doesn't have permanent links to archived versions of its pages, include a retrieval date before the URL.

31. Online forum post

Author's Last Name, Initials [username]. (Year, Month Day). *Content of the post up to twenty words* [Online forum post]. Title of Site. URL

Hanzus, D. [DanHanzus]. (2019, October 23). *GETCHA DAN HANZUS. ASK ME ANYTHING!* [Online forum post]. Reddit. https://bit.ly/38WgmSF

author   title   publication

32. Blog post

Author's Last Name, Initials [username]. (Year, Month Day). Title of
post. *Title of Blog*. URL

gcrepps. (2017, March 28). Shania Sanders. *Women@NASA*. https://
blogs.nasa.gov/womenatnasa/2017/03/28/shania-sanders/

If only the username is known, do not use brackets.

33. Online streaming video

Uploader's Last Name, Initials [username]. (Year, Month Day). *Title of
video* [Video]. Name of Video Platform. URL

CinemaSins. (2014, August 21). *Everything wrong with* National treasure
in 13 minutes or less [Video]. YouTube. https://www.youtube.com
/watch?v=1ul-_ZWvXTs

Whoever uploaded the video is considered the author, even if someone else
created the content. If only the username is known, do not use brackets. If
there is another title within a title, put that other title in reverse italics.

34. Podcast

Host's Last Name, Initials (Host). (First Year–Last Year). *Podcast name*
[Audio podcast]. Production Company. URL

Poor, N., Woods, E., & Thomas, R. (Hosts). (2017–present). *Ear hustle*
[Audio podcast]. PRX. https://www.earhustlesq.com/

35. Podcast episode

Host's Last Name, Initials (Host). (Year, Month Day). Episode title
(No. episode number) [Audio podcast episode]. In *Podcast name*.
Production Company. URL

Tamposi, E., & Samocki, E. (Hosts). (2020, January 8). The year of the
broads [Audio podcast episode]. In *The broadcast podcast*. Podcast
One. https://podcastone.com/episode/the-year-of-the-broads

The host of the podcast, or the executive producer if known, is considered the author. Do not include an episode number if one isn't given.

36. Film

> Director's Last Name, Initials (Director). (Year). *Title of film* [Film]. Production Company. URL

Jenkins, B. (Director). (2016). *Moonlight* [Film]. A24; Plan B; PASTEL.

Cuarón, A. (Director). (2016). *Harry Potter and the prisoner of Azkaban* [Film; two-disc special ed. on DVD]. Warner Bros.

List the director as the author of the film. Indicate how you watched the film only if the format is important to what you've written.

37. Television series

> Executive Producer's Last Name, Initials (Executive Producer). (First Year–Last Year). *Title of series* [TV series]. Production Company. URL

Iungerich, L., Gonzalez, E., & Haft, J. (Executive Producers). (2018–present). *On my block* [TV series]. Crazy Cat Lady Productions.

Indicate how you watched the TV series (2-disc DVD set, for example) only if the format is relevant to what you've written.

38. Television series episode

> Writer's Last Name, Initials (Writer), & Director's Last Name, Initials (Director). (Year, Month Day). Title of episode (Season number, Episode number) [TV series episode]. In Executive Producer's Initials Last Name (Executive Producer), *Title of series*. Production Company. URL

Siegal, J. (Writer), Morgan, D. (Writer), & Sackett, M. (Director). (2018, December 6). Janet(s) (Season 3, Episode 10) [TV series episode]. In M. Schur, D. Miner, M. Sackett, & D. Goddard (Executive Producers), *The good place*. Fremulon; 3 Arts Entertainment; Universal Television.

author   title   publication

39. Music album

Artist's Last Name, Initials. (Year). *Title of album* [Album]. Label.

Lennox, A. (1995). *Medusa* [Album]. Arista.

40. Song

Artist's Last Name, Initials. (Year). Title of song [Song]. On *Title of album*. Label. URL

Giddens, R. (2015). Shake sugaree [Song]. On *Tomorrow is my turn*. Nonesuch.

The recording artist or group is considered the author. Do not include a URL unless the song can be accessed only on one specific online platform.

41. Software, computer program, or mobile app

Include entries for software, programs, or mobile apps if they are uncommon or if you quote or paraphrase from them. Otherwise, just include the name (not italicized) and version number in the body of your text.

Last Name, Initials. (Year). *Name of program* (Version number) [Computer software]. Publisher. URL

Blount, K. (2018). *Scrivener for Windows* (Version 1.9.9.0) [Computer software]. Literature & Latte. https://www.literatureandlatte.com/scrivener

Include a description of the content in brackets after the version number. For a mobile app, use "App Store" or wherever you accessed the app as the publisher. Use the year of publication of the version you accessed as the date.

42. Lecture slides or notes

Author's Last Name, Initials. (Year, Month Day). *Title of presentation* [Description of content]. Publisher. URL

Pavliscak, P. (2016, February 21). *Finding our happy place in the internet of things* [PowerPoint slides]. Slideshare. https://bit.ly/3aOcfs7

If the lecture notes or slides do not have a title, describe the contents in brackets after the date.

43. Recording of a speech or webinar

Author's Last Name, Initials. (Year, Month Day *or* Year). *Title* [Speech audio recording *or* Webinar]. Publisher. URL

Kennedy, J. F. (1961, January 20). *Inaugural address* [Speech audio recording]. American Rhetoric. https://bit.ly/339Gc3e

Rodrigo, S. (2020). *Keep calm (and compassionate) & move everything online* [Webinar]. W. W. Norton. https://seagull.wwnorton.com /CompositionTeachingOnline

For a speech, include the year, month, and day. For a webinar, include only the year.

44 . Map

Mapmaker's Last Name, Initials. (Year). *Title of map* [Map]. Publisher. URL

Daniels, M. (2018). *Human terrain: Visualizing the world's population, in 3D* [Map]. The Pudding. https://pudding.cool/2018/10/city_3d/

Google. (n.d.). [Google Maps directions for biking from Las Vegas, Nevada, to Los Angeles, California]. Retrieved January 30, 2020, from https://goo.gle/maps/9NdekwAkHeo4HM4N7

To cite a dynamic map, use "n.d." for the date and include a retrieval date. For the title, include a description of the map in brackets.

45. Social media posts

Use the author's real name and include the social media handle in brackets. If only the handle is known, do not use brackets. List any audiovisual content (e.g., a video, an image, a link) in brackets after the content of the post. Replicate emoji if possible; if not, include a bracketed description. Follow the spelling and capitalization of the original post.

Author's Last Name, Initials [@username]. (Year, Month Day). *Content of post up to twenty words* [Description of audiovisual content] [Type of post]. Platform. URL

author   title   publication

Tweet

Baron, D. [@DrGrammar]. (2019, November 11). *Gender conceal: Did you know that pronouns can also hide someone's gender?* [Thumbnail with link attached] [Tweet]. Twitter. https://bit.ly/2vaCcDc

Instagram photograph or video

Jamil, J. [@jameelajamilofficial]. (2018, July 18). *Happy Birthday to our leader. I steal all my acting faces from you. @kristenanniebell* [Face with smile and sunglasses emoji] [Photograph]. Instagram. https://www.instagram.com/p/BIYX5F9FuGL/

Facebook post

Philadelphia Eagles. (2019, December 3). *"'We control our own destiny.' That's going to be the message moving forward to this football team."* #FlyEaglesFly [Thumbnail with link attached] [Status update]. Facebook. https://bit.ly/39Ghjil

46. Data set

Author's Last Name, Initials. (Year). *Title of data set* (Version number) [Data set]. Publisher. DOI or URL

Pew Research Center. (2019). *Core trends survey* [Data set]. https://www.pewresearch.org/internet/dataset/core-trends-survey/

If the name of the author is the same as the name of the publisher, omit the publisher.

47. Supreme Court case

Name of Case, volume US page (Year). URL

Plessy v. Ferguson, 163 US 537 (1896). https://www.oyez.org/cases/1850-1900/163us537

Obergefell v. Hodges, 576 US ___ (2015). https://www.oyez.org/cases/2014/14-556

The source for most Supreme Court cases is the *United States Reports*, which is abbreviated "US" in the reference list entry. If the case does not yet have a page number, use three underscores instead.

Sources Not Covered by APA

To document a source for which APA does not provide guidelines, look at models similar to the source you have cited. Give any information readers will need in order to find it themselves—author; date of publication; title; source, including DOI or URL (if applicable); and any other pertinent information. You might want to test your reference note to be sure it will lead others to your source.

FORMATTING A RESEARCH ESSAY

Title page. APA generally requires a title page. The page number should go in the upper right-hand corner. Center the full title of the paper in bold in the top half of the page. Center your name, the name of your department and school, the course number and name, the instructor's name, and the due date on separate lines below the title. Leave one line between the title and your name.

Page numbers. Place the page number in the upper right-hand corner. Number pages consecutively throughout.

Typeface, spacing, margins, and indents. Use a legible typeface that will be accessible to everyone, either a serif typeface (such as Times New Roman or Bookman) or a sans serif typeface (such as Calibri or Verdana). Use sans serif within figure images. Double-space the entire paper, including any notes and your list of references; the only exception is footnotes at the bottom of a page, which should be single-spaced, and text within tables and images, the spacing of which will vary. Leave one-inch margins at the top, bottom, and sides of your text; do not justify the text. The first line of each paragraph should be indented one-half inch (or five to seven spaces) from the left margin. Use one space after end-of-sentence punctuation.

Headings. Though they are not required in APA style, headings can help readers follow your text. The first level of heading should be bold, centered, and capitalized as you would any other title; the second level of heading should be bold and flush with the left margin; the third level should be bold, italicized, and flush left.

First Level Heading

Second Level Heading

Third Level Heading

Abstract. An abstract is a concise summary of your paper that introduces readers to your topic and main points. Most scholarly journals require an abstract; an abstract is not typically required for student papers, so check your instructor's preference. Put your abstract on the second page, with the word "Abstract" centered and in bold at the top. Unless your instructor specifies a length, limit your abstract to 250 words or fewer.

Long quotations. Indent quotations of forty or more words one-half inch (or five to seven spaces) from the left margin. Do not use quotation marks, and place the page number(s) or documentation information in parentheses *after* the end punctuation. If there are paragraphs in the quotation, indent the first line of each paragraph another one-half inch.

> Kaplan (2000) captured ancient and contemporary Antioch:
>
> At the height of its glory in the Roman-Byzantine age, when it had an amphitheater, public baths, aqueducts, and sewage pipes, half a million people lived in Antioch. Today the population is only 125,000. With sour relations between Turkey and Syria, and unstable politics throughout the Middle East, Antioch is now a backwater—seedy and tumbledown, with relatively few tourists. (p. 123)
>
> Antioch's decline serves as a reminder that the fortunes of cities can change drastically over time.

List of references. Start your list on a new page after the text but before any endnotes. Title the page "References," centered and in bold, and double-space the entire list. Each entry should begin at the left margin, and subsequent lines should be indented one-half inch (or five to seven spaces). Alphabetize the list by authors' last names (or by editors' names, if appropriate). Alphabetize works that have no author or editor by title, disregarding "A,"

"An," and "The." Be sure every source listed is cited in the text; do not include sources that you consulted but did not cite.

Tables and figures. Above each table or figure (charts, diagrams, graphs, photos, and so on), provide the word "Table" or "Figure" and a number, flush left and in bold (e.g., **Table 1**). On the following line, give a descriptive title, flush left and italicized. Below the table or figure, include a note with any necessary explanation and source information. Number tables and figures separately, and be sure to discuss them in your text so that readers know how they relate.

Table 1
Hours of Instruction Delivered per Week

	American Classrooms	Japanese Classrooms	Chinese Classrooms
First grade			
Language arts	10.5	8.7	10.4
Mathematics	2.7	5.8	4.0
Fifth grade			
Language arts	7.9	8.0	11.1
Mathematics	3.4	7.8	11.7

Note. Adapted from "Peeking Out from Under the Blinders: Some Factors We Shouldn't Forget in Studying Writing," by J. R. Hayes, 1991, National Center for the Study of Writing and Literacy (Occasional Paper No. 25). National Writing Project website: http://www.nwp.org/

SAMPLE RESEARCH ESSAY

Gabriela Agustina Uribe wrote the following paper, "'¿Por qué no sabes español?': Pressured Monolingualism and Its Impacts on Mexican Americans," for a course on the rhetoric of language, identity, and power at Stanford University. It is formatted according to the guidelines of the *Publication Manual of the American Psychological Association*, 7th edition (2020).

Page numbers appear in the upper right corner.

1

The title is bold, centered, and placed in the upper half of the page. If the title is longer than one line, the subtitle can be placed on the next line. Titles and subtitles should be capitalized; however non-English words in titles and subtitles are lowercase unless the first word or a proper noun.

"¿Por qué no sabes español?"
Pressured Monolingualism and Its Impacts on Mexican Americans

Gabriela A. Uribe

Program in Writing and Rhetoric, Stanford University

PWR 2JJ: The Rhetoric of Language, Identity and Power

Dr. Jennifer Johnson

March 17, 2019

Your name is centered below the title, with one double-spaced line in between.

Your department and school name, course number and name, professor's name, and the due date of the paper are centered below your name.

Abstract

While many teachers, scholars, and administrators in higher education support multilingual education in theory, they struggle to know how to enact it. Compounding this challenge is the fact that negative attitudes towards and policies about multilingualism in the K-12 context influence some multilingual families to decide to raise their children to speak English only. Drawing on semi-structured interviews with family members and friends, I examined the causes and consequences of monolingualism for Mexican Americans. I argue that political and educational discourses pressure families to assimilate into a monolingual English-speaking society and that "pressured monolingualism" weakens family relationships, ethnic identities, and cultures. I conclude by considering why K-12 school districts should embrace multilingualism, how public attitudes can change, and how those who have experienced pressured monolingualism can learn languages while exploring and celebrating their home cultures.

Abstract begins on a new page. Heading is centered and bold. An abstract is not generally required for a student paper, so check with your professor.

Abstract text does not need a paragraph indent.

Use one space after each sentence.

250 words or fewer.

3

"¿Por qué no sabes español?" •

Pressured Monolingualism and Its Impacts on Mexican Americans

A little girl stands at the stove, helping her *abuelita* roll enchiladas •

for dinner. She always cherishes this time where she feels truly

connected to her grandma and her culture. Her cousin taps her on her

shoulder, telling her in Spanish that he wants to play the card game UNO

but doesn't know the rules. "¿Puedes explicarlos?" The girl's face turns •

bright red, and her heart starts pounding. "No, no puedo." A disappointed

pause follows. "¿Por qué no sabes español?" her cousin asks. She looks down

at her feet and repeats what she always says when asked this. "No sé."

A woman is in a Manhattan restaurant. She orders her food, •

comfortably speaking to the employee behind the register in Spanish.

Suddenly, a man behind her starts yelling. He yells at both women for

not speaking English, since this is America, after all. Other people in

the restaurant call out his ignorance, but he continues to berate the women,

saying, "My guess is they're not documented. So my next call is to ICE to

have each one of them kicked out of my country" (Karimi & Levenson, 2018). •

Both of these scenes are true events—the former, a personal

experience from my childhood, and the latter, an event that happened

in New York in 2018. Over the past few years, there has been an influx

in news stories similar to that of the woman in Manhattan. In these

stories, "real" Americans are angered to hear people speaking languages

other than English and respond with public shaming and berating. These

instances exhibit a condescension many English-speaking Americans

---

Text starts on a new page. Title is centered and bold.

Non-English words that do not appear in an English dictionary should be italicized on first use.

Essay is double-spaced.

Indent the start of each paragraph ½" (5–7 spaces).

The authors and year are included in the reference. (The source is an article published online, so no page number is included.)

1" margin

4

have towards minority languages, which was reflected in Donald Trump's presidential administration. In a 2015 GOP debate, Trump said, "We have to have assimilation—to have a country, we have to have assimilation. . . . This is a country where we speak English, not Spanish" (CNN, 2015, 0:26). Administrative actions have supported this rhetoric; the Spanish version of the White House website was taken down just after Trump was inaugurated in January 2017 (O'Keefe, 2017). The site's immediate disappearance left Americans without a source of official White House information translated into Spanish.

1" margin

Taking a step back to look at an overview of the attitudes surrounding monolingualism versus multilingualism, there are a plethora of contradictions. On the one hand, many instructors in higher education have long recognized and emphasized the importance of multilingualism and its educational benefits (National Council of Teachers of English, 2020; Okal, 2014). However, misconceptions that multilingualism harms children still exist and circulate widely (Kroll & Dussias, 2017). Shifts in political power and clear sentiments against Spanish-speaking Americans have also highlighted the desire many have for an English-only America (Anbinder, 2019; O'Keefe, 2017). Therefore, many arguments still exist against the use of native languages, especially Spanish, despite all the evidence supporting multilingualism. As I observe these many conflicting perceptions, I've often asked myself, "How do parents decide whether or not to raise their children as monolingual?" The way in which I not only enter this conversation but add to it is through my own experiences as a Mexican American college student who struggles with her personal ethnic identity.

1" margin

Multiple sources cited in the same parentheses are ordered alphabetically and separated by a semicolon.

Because the authors are not named in a signal phrase, their names are given in parentheses, with an ampersand rather than "and" between them.

1" margin

5

The little girl in the first story was me. Although my grandparents and dad are native Spanish speakers, I was raised speaking only English and have experienced the effects of that for the last 19 years. For me, not being able to speak Spanish has created a divide between myself, family members, and Mexican culture as a whole. This rift has led me to become curious about the complex relationships between monolingualism and ethnic identity.

In this paper, I argue that political and educational pressures encouraging Mexican Americans to assimilate into a monolingual English-speaking society can have negative effects on Mexican Americans' relationships with family members and their understanding of their own ethnic identity and culture.

Metodología

First-level headings are centered, bold, and capitalized.

To explore the effects of monolingualism, I conducted interviews with my parents, grandmother, sister, and friend and fellow student Julian Aguilar. I made these interviews semi-structured, asking some of the same predetermined questions, mainly about their upbringings and experiences with English and Spanish, but leaving room for open-ended discussion. The interviews with my mom and Julian, who were both raised to speak only English, included the following questions:

1. Was your parents' decision to have you learn only English a conscious one?

2. How did being monolingual impact your relationship with relatives?

3. Growing up, how did you identify ethnically?

6

Since my grandma and dad both learned Spanish as their first language and are bilingual, I asked them questions that related to their experiences with and perceptions of learning English:

1. What do you think are the benefits of learning English?
2. What was your experience like learning English?

Aside from preparing certain questions, I let the interviews flow naturally. This semi-structured approach allowed me to explore general themes while tailoring my questions to each of my interviewees. New and interesting ideas were explored, some of which I had not considered.

Once I conducted and recorded the interviews, I transcribed them. Then, in order to identify similar themes, I relied on grounded theory coding, a qualitative research strategy for uncovering relationships from data instead of using existing theory to form testable hypotheses. These links revealed common thoughts and experiences regarding monolingualism in Mexican Americans. An outside coder provided feedback on the themes I identified, further solidifying the findings from this primary research.

In terms of secondary research, I identified many academic journals and online sources that explore various topics, from language policy in American schools to attitudes towards bilingualism in the classroom. To supplement the cultural information from my primary research, I also analyzed existing case studies and detailed personal accounts.

7

Discusión

Going through the grounded coding process with the interviews I conducted revealed several major themes. I spoke with four people: my mom, Victoria Uribe; a friend, Julian Aguilar; my dad, Juan Uribe; and my grandmother, Maria E. Flores. The first two grew up speaking only English, and the latter two grew up speaking Spanish in Mexico and learned English later on in the United States. The key themes from the interviews are laid out in Table 1 below.

Table 1

Ground Coding Table

Code	Count	Example Quote
1. parents want better life/ experience for their kid	3	"[My parents] knew how hard it was for them to come to America not knowing English and having that language barrier be an obstacle to kind of achieve their American Dream . . . so they both made the decision to not teach me their languages."
1a. knowing English = success	4	"When you speak English, the doors open for you in different ways."
1b. learning a language later in life is hard	7	"If I was watching a tv show or listening to a song in Spanish it was really hard because it went so fast."
2. not knowing Spanish inhibited relationships	3	"It was harder when I was younger, right. I couldn't tell [my grandma] things or ask her things much because I couldn't talk to her that well."
3. language connects to culture	3	"I don't think you can experience the culture without the language. They go hand in hand."

Note. Data gathered from personal interviews and subsequently coded using ground theory coding.

Table number is bold and flush left.

Descriptive table title is italicized and appears below the table number.

Description and source information are given in the table note.

8

The first major theme I identified was parents' desire for a better life for their children. In addition, two subthemes emerged: the idea that knowing English will bring success, and the idea that learning languages later in life is hard. The latter was especially prevalent in the interviews: all four interviewees expressed the difficulty of learning a new language, whether English or Spanish. The second common thread was the way that not knowing Spanish inhibits relationships. My mom and Julian both explained how growing up knowing only English limited their connections with family members. The last major theme was the conviction that language and culture are closely connected. The prevalence of these three main themes is not limited to my interviews, however: many educators and researchers have also expressed these themes in their own work. In the following subsections, I dive deeper into each theme, synthesizing interviewee responses with outside secondary sources to explain the motivations behind and impacts of pressured monolingualism on Mexican Americans.

Padres bien intencionados

A common thread throughout my interviews was the idea that my interviewees' parents wanted the best for their children. For those parents, a better life meant learning English as early and as well as possible. One of the main reasons my interviewees' parents wanted them to learn English early is that learning a language later in life can be very difficult. In fact, the challenges of language learning came up the most frequently in my coding. The second reason, also heavily discussed, was the notion that knowing English equates to success.

Second-level headings are flush left and bold. If all English words, they should also be capitalized. If non-English words, use sentence case.

9

There are many misconceptions in society about both language development and the superiority of English that cause parents to make certain decisions about what language or languages they should teach their children. Some parents in Mexican American households are convinced that their children will be academically harmed if they grow up speaking Spanish. Previous educational practices have led some parents to buy into the supposed superiority of English because they associate it with economic success. Wiley and Lukes (1996) drew on the theories of French philosopher Pierre Bourdieu to argue that knowing a standard language is a sort of currency: "Once standards for expected linguistic behavior have been imposed, privileged varieties of language become a kind of social capital" (p. 515). In other words, knowing English, the "standard language," can result in better test scores, economic advantages, and overall success. In the words of my abuelita, "When you speak English, the doors open for you" (M. E. Flores, personal communication, February 24, 2019). At 20 years old, my grandma came to the United States in search of a better life for her and her son. Because of the general expectation that people in America speak English, she felt that knowing English would be the key to getting opportunities and not being treated as inferior.

When parents are faced with the idea that their children will not be as successful if they do not assimilate into an English-only system, they may decide to embrace monolingualism. I interviewed fellow student Julian Aguilar, who was raised intentionally to speak only English. Both of his parents immigrated to the United States as adults—his

The signal phrase uses past tense, and the year of publication is placed in parentheses right after the authors' names.

The page number is provided in parentheses for a direct quotation when the author and year of the work are given earlier in the signal phrase.

Because this source is a personal communication, it is cited in the text only, not in the list of references.

mom from China and his dad from Mexico—and both struggled with the language barrier as they adjusted to an English-dominated society (J. Aguilar, personal communication, February 24, 2019). Not wanting the same hardships for their son, they decided that he should learn English as well as possible, without an accent. In the same vein, my mother, a pediatrician, often meets parents who fear their children will be at a disadvantage in the United States if they do not make English the priority (V. Uribe, personal communication, February 24, 2019). In the minds of those parents, and in the minds of many native Spanish speakers in the United States, English equals success. In fact, a survey of Texas adults showed that "Spanish-dominant speakers place high importance on speaking English, more so than do English speakers. . . . It is easy to see how immigrants are constantly reminded of the problems they face in the workplace and the public sphere without English proficiency" (Dowling et al., 2012, p. 356).

Because this source has more than two authors, the citation gives the first author's name followed by "et al." The date and page number are also included.

A common belief among Mexican American parents is that if their children learn only English, their children will have an easier experience than they did and grow to be confident, successful members of United States society. While many educators realize the importance of using multiple languages in the classroom, public attitudes have yet to catch up with the research. If K-12 institutions would adopt more inclusionary policies and programs, then parents would have more exposure to positive ideas surrounding multilingualism. In turn, pressure on Mexican Americans to raise their children as monolingual could be eased, avoiding the negative consequences of fragmented relationship and identities.

11

Relaciónes en la familia

Among the benefits of knowing a language is the ability to communicate with others. This idea came up consistently during interviews with my mom and Julian, both of whom grew up monolingually, as well as when I recalled my own struggles communicating with family members throughout my childhood.

For Mexican American families in the United States, it's common for at least some relatives to speak only Spanish. As a result, not knowing the language can inhibit relationships among family members. When we visited Mexico, for example, I found it very difficult to speak to my cousins. I got by because I could understand them a bit and because children have a knack for playing together without a whole lot of talk. Even so, I struggled constantly and grew frustrated that I couldn't express my ideas or understand the jokes being made. Now that my cousins and I are older, it's even harder to avoid the fact that I can't communicate with them effectively. Being part of a proud Mexican family but not knowing Spanish has led me to miss out on close relationships with my relatives. Julian feels similarly, recounting how he couldn't understand his relatives at family reunions; although he was physically there, learning about the culture, he never felt "truly part of it" (J. Aguilar, personal communication, February 24, 2019).

My mom, Victoria Uribe, is also part Mexican and grew up learning only English. She recalled feeling limited when communicating with her grandmother, who knew very little English (V. Uribe, personal communication, February 24, 2019). They would speak very simple

The first person is used when describing your own actions.

sentences to each other, and my mom would get used to saying simple phrases like "Cena lista!" when dinner was ready, but she still couldn't communicate with her very well. She said, "It was harder when I was younger to tell or ask my grandma things" (V. Uribe, personal communication, February 24, 2019). Even later, when my mom was in college, she'd write short letters to her grandmother but feel frustrated that she didn't know Spanish better.

In a case study of the Fuentes family, a Mexican American family in Los Angeles, the third generation of children who grew up in the United States did not acquire the ability to speak Spanish (Chávez, 2007). One member of the family, Erica, recalled not being able to communicate with her grandmother. Since she couldn't understand her grandma, her father had to translate for her, which made Erica feel "kind of awful" (Chávez, 2007, p. 126). Similar stories can be told by many others who grew up without learning their native language, and the negative effects this monolingualism clearly has on familial connections are truly sad.

Español, identidad, y cultura

The relationships among language, identity, and culture are heavily intertwined. From a cultural perspective, the ramifications of not knowing the language of your family can be serious. After all, language has always been an integral part of personal and cultural identity. Anzaldúa (1987) described this deeply rooted connection: "Ethnic identity is twin skin to linguistic identity—I am my language" (p. 39). When I interviewed my dad, he echoed Anzaldúa: "I don't think you can experience the culture without the language—they go hand in hand" (J. Uribe, personal communication, February 24, 2019). The Conference on College Composition and

The author, year, and page number are given in parentheses right after a quotation.

13

Communication has long led the way in recognizing the crucial importance of the relationship between language and culture. That relationship was explored in a special issue of the journal: "Since dialect is not separate from culture, but an intrinsic part of it, accepting a new dialect means accepting a new culture; rejecting one's native dialect is to some extent a rejection of one's culture" (Committee on CCCC Language Statement, 1974).

Julian's parents, who raised him to be monolingual, only wanted the best for him. He understands where his parents were coming from, but he feels that he lost something important growing up, despite their good intentions, since he "never really felt immersed" in Mexican culture (J. Aguilar, personal communication, February 24, 2019). In other words, because his parents rejected the idea of their son's learning Spanish, they also implicitly rejected the culture his dad grew up in, which kept Julian from forming deep connections with his Mexican heritage.

My mom grew up in a small town in Montana, where she wasn't exposed to Spanish at home. While her mother integrated parts of Mexican culture into her childhood (playing *lotería*, making Mexican food, and talking about her experiences in Mexico), she still didn't feel connected to her Mexican side. In fact, she completely disregarded that part of her identity, considering herself to be White until she went to college (V. Uribe, personal communication, February 24, 2019). When I heard this, I was shocked: by identifying herself as White, my mom showed that she lacked meaningful ties to her Mexican heritage and that there was a clear disconnect between her self-perception and her true ethnic identity.

While these are just a few examples, I believe that looking at specific people brings an important perspective to the existing discussions regarding

14

native languages. The fragmented experiences Julian, my mom, and I have had with respect to Mexican culture and our ethnic identities resulted from our monolingualism. Without these individual narratives, scholarly discourse misses an essential piece of the linguistic puzzle. Looking at historical trends and quantitative data is essential to research, but hearing the stories of real people who are at the center of the research is equally important. Qualitative research, and case studies specifically, provide powerful and direct views into the real-life impact of the topic at hand.

While language is a component of culture, shared language does not always lead to shared culture. Cultural identities are so nuanced that people who speak the same language can still have vastly different experiences and perceptions of their ethnic selves. Julian, for instance, is part of a Latinx service club called Hermanos, and he explained how there seem to be "two types of Latinos" within the organization (J. Aguilar, personal communication, February 24, 2019). Coming from a low-income background himself, he feels more connected to the people who are from rougher neighborhoods, who didn't necessarily grow up "culturally Mexican." So while there is a direct and clear relationship among language, identity, and culture, there is no single linear path among them, and it is important to remember this complexity.

¿Y ahora, qué?

And so—what should be done to address the anti-Spanish sentiments in our society? It's important to consider whether schools should even try to make changes that contradict these public opinions:

> Until public attitudes can be changed—and it is worth
> remembering that the past teaching in English classes has

15

been largely responsible for those attitudes—shall we place our emphasis on what the vocal element of the public think it wants or on what the actual available linguistic evidence indicates we should emphasize? (Committee on CCCC Language Statement, 1974) ●

For a long quotation, the parenthetical reference follows the closing punctuation.

I argue that the latter option is the right path to take. The best course of action for K-12 schools is to encourage the use of native languages in the classroom and thus promote multilingualism.

Why should entire school systems make such big changes for just a portion of the population? To start, a huge number of people in the United States have a stake in these policies and practices. In California, 39.1% of the population is Hispanic or Latinx (United States Census Bureau, n.d.). While my research focuses on Mexican Americans, it's easy to see how many people from other Spanish-speaking backgrounds could be affected by monolingual pressures. Realizing the detrimental effects that monolingualism can have is one step towards institutions' placing equal value on diverse languages.

In addition to the call to action for K-12 schools to encourage multilingualism, the understanding one gains from research like mine is of major significance. Listening to personal stories and learning about negative experiences resulting from pressured monolingualism can lead to systemic change and encourage empathy. I believe that differences should be not only tolerated but celebrated. This includes Americans who speak only English, Americans who speak only their native language, and everyone in between. If we can begin to have more understanding of and empathy for each person's identity, we may be able to function as a more accepting, unified country.

16

Mexican Americans have faced a multitude of pressures to assimilate into a society that promotes English above Spanish. In my life and others' lives, these pressures have led to a fragmented experience with Mexican culture and personal ethnic identity. But the stories of the people I interviewed are far from over. Once my mom got to college, she joined Chicano organizations to learn more about her culture and people like her (V. Uribe, personal communication, February 24, 2019). She even wrote an article in medical school about her deepening relationship with her Mexican heritage. She also started learning Spanish in college and became fluent by using it in her job on a daily basis. My friend Julian has taken two introductory college Spanish classes so far, and he plans on continuing (J. Aguilar, personal communication, February 24, 2019). In addition, joining a Hispanic service club on campus has already helped him feel more in touch with his Mexican roots.

I hope that schools and politicians can make more of an effort to encourage language diversity and embrace multilingualism, so that cultural connections can be made even sooner. That way, Mexican American children can learn Spanish with pride. Then, that little girl playing UNO with her cousins can respond confidently:

"*¿Por qué no puedes hablar español?*"

"*~~No sé~~.*" "*Sí, yo puedo.*"

17

References

Anbinder, T. (2019, November 7). Trump has spread more hatred of immigrants than any American in history. *The Washington Post.* https://www.washingtonpost.com/outlook/trump-has-spread -more-hatred-of-immigrants-than-any-american-in-history/2019 /11/07/7e253236-ff54-11e9-8bab-0fc209e065a8_story.html

Anzaldúa, G. (1987). *Borderlands/La frontera: The new mestiza.* Aunt Lute Books.

Bourdieu, P. (1986). The forms of capital. In J. Richardson (Ed.), *Handbook of theory and research for the sociology of education* (pp. 241–258). Greenwood.

Chávez, C. (2007). *Five generations of a Mexican American family in Los Angeles.* Rowman & Littlefield Publishers.

Committee on CCCC Language Statement. (1974). Students' right to their own language [Special issue]. *College Composition and Communication, 25*(3).

CNN. (2015, September 16). *Trump: We speak English here, not Spanish* [Video]. YouTube. https://www.youtube.com/watch?v=eNjcAgNu1Ac

Dowling, J. A., Ellison, C. G., & Leal, D. L. (2012). Who doesn't value English? Debunking myths about Mexican immigrants' attitudes toward the English language. *Social Science Quarterly, 93*(2), 356–378. https://doi.org/hcjz

Karimi, F., & Levenson, E. (2018, May 17). *Man to Spanish speakers at New York restaurant: "My next call is to ICE."* CNN. https://www.cnn .com/2018/05/17/us/new-york-man-restaurant-ice-threat/index.html

Entries are arranged alphabetically.

All entries are double-spaced, and all lines except the first are indented ½" (5–7 spaces).

Entry for a chapter found in an edited book includes the editor's name, first initial followed by last name.

DOI given when one is available. Do not add a period at the end of a DOI or a URL. Long DOIs can be shortened using the shortDOI service (http://shortdoi.org/).

Entry for an article found on a news website includes the title of the article in italics. Do not use italics for the name of the website.

18

Kroll, J. F., & Dussias, P. E. (2017). The benefits of multilingualism to the personal and professional development of residents of the US. *Foreign Language Annals*, *50*(2), 248–259. https://doi.org/10.1111/flan.12271

National Council of Teachers of English. (2020). *CCCC statement on second language writing and multilingual writers* [Position statement]. https://cccc.ncte.org/cccc/resources/positions/secondlangwriting

Okal, B. O. (2014). Benefits of multilingualism in education. *Universal Journal of Educational Research*, *2*(3), 223–229. https://doi.org/10.13189/ujer.2014.020304

O'Keefe, E. (2017, January 23). Looking for a Spanish version of WhiteHouse.gov? No existe—todavia. *The Washington Post*. https://www.washingtonpost.com/news/powerpost/wp/2017/01/23/looking-for-a-spanish-version-of-whitehouse-gov-ya-no-existe/

United States Census Bureau. (n.d.). *QuickFacts California*. U.S. Department of Commerce. Retrieved March 1, 2019, from https://www.census.gov/quickfacts/ca

Wiley, T. G., & Lukes, M. (1996). English-only and standard English ideologies in the U.S. *TESOL Quarterly*, *30*(3), 511–535. https://doi.org/10.2307/3587696

PART VII

Style

"How to Get and Hold Attention"

ONCE UPON A TIME—and for a very long time, too—style in writing and speaking meant ornamentation, "dressing up" your language the way you might dress yourself up for a fancy party. In fact, ancient images often show rhetoric as a woman, Dame Rhetorica, in a gaudy, flowing gown covered with figures of speech—metaphors, similes, alliteration, hyperbole, and so on: her "stylish" ornaments. The influence of this view eventually led many writers to set aside issues of style, preferring to focus on substance, getting to the point and not worrying about making it fancy or pretty.

But not today. Not in a time of instant communication, of being inundated with notifications, news, advertisements—all of them coming at us with the force of a fire hose. In such

Dame Rhetorica, from Gregor Reisch's *Margarita Philosophica* (1504).

a time, scholars like Richard Lanham and Howard Rheingold argue, the most important task facing writers and speakers is making our messages so compelling that they will stand out from all the others. While pundits often claim we live in an information society, Lanham insists that there's more to it—that, in fact, "we're drowning in information" and that what we "lack is the human attention to make sense of it all." We would add, too, that we're missing the critical ability to know what to pay attention to and what to ignore.

How can we achieve this goal of getting and managing attention? Both Lanham and Rheingold, among others, answer with one word: STYLE. Just what do we mean by this simple-sounding word? When it comes to writing, most dictionaries offer something about word choice and how it differs from field to field or they will define style as "distinctiveness of expression." But style is not so much about *what* a message says as about *how* a message is presented—whether the message is in writing, in speech, includes (or is made up of) visuals, is delivered using formal language, and many more possibilities.

Wow. So style turns out to be all the elements that go into making a message (in any form) effective, memorable, compelling. Think, for instance, of a movie you really admire and that you think has real "style." Then make a list of all the things that go into creating its particular style: the "how" of its acting, directing, musical score, camera angles, editing, and so on. All these elements are at work in the film's style.

Style and substance are inseparable. Without close attention to how our messages are presented, we are unlikely to attract an audience, much less hold its attention.

How can you create your own particular, powerful style in writing, speaking, and presenting? The chapters that follow aim to guide you in this task. But what we can say now is that you already have the primary tools that writers and speakers have always had for creating style: words— words that can create spellbinding images, rouse deep emotions, hammer home points, seize and hold attention.

And it's not just individual words; style includes the ways that words fit together, one after another, to form the rhythms and melodies of diverse dialects and varieties of a language. Which syllables are stressed? Which are cut or shortened? Those features are part of your linguistic repertoire that forms your style, and you have choices about how to use them. For example, see how Lee Tonouchi uses variant spellings and other features to help readers "hear" Hawaiian Pidgin on page 702. Choosing words (DICTION) and putting them in the best places (SYNTAX) still matter a lot in developing your style. But today you also have many other tools—visuals, video, sound, color, and more. All these elements are available as you choreograph the dance of your message, as you develop its style.

Getting and holding an audience's attention, however, is not the only goal when it comes to style. You want to get that attention in ways that fit well with your entire rhetorical situation. If you're dressing for an important job interview, you will probably choose clothes that are on the dressy end of what people there usually wear to work; if you're dressing for a championship basketball game or a religious service, however, you'll probably dress differently.

It's hard (maybe impossible) to set hard-and-fast rules to be sure you're making the best choice for a particular situation. Consider a fascinating analogy from rhetorician Brent Simoneaux about the calculated choices baseball players have to make and the choices we as authors have to make:

> Imagine . . . the relationship between the pitcher and the batter. It's a complicated relationship forged in a complex calculus of the probable, yet unknown. I love those close-up shots on television of the batter studying the pitcher, waiting for the ball. The batter is poised, bat over shoulder, feet planted just so, ready to nimbly meet whatever comes. In that moment, the batter is both *at the mercy of* the pitcher, the rules of the game, the equipment, the umpire and also a *participant* and a *creator* of the game.
>
> The ball leaves the pitcher's hand.
>
> In that moment, the coach can't tell the batter exactly what to do at the plate. There's absolutely no way of knowing exactly where that ball is going to go. . . . The only thing the batter can do is to arrive at the plate poised and remain sensitive to the game unfolding.
>
> Of course, the coach can make a pretty good guess about what will happen. . . . The batter can guess as well. And they can both prepare accordingly. But in that utterly kairotic moment when the ball is flying through the air, everything is in flux. . . . And the coach's line has to be: *do the right thing*.
>
> That doesn't mean do whatever you want. It doesn't mean anything goes. Rather, it's an acknowledgment that . . . the terms of "rightness" are always shifting. . . . Do the *right* thing.
>
> —BRENT SIMONEAUX, "Do the Right Thing"

The same goes for authors. But that's part of the fun of writing with style. You get to analyze the situation before you and to think about how to seize the moment in order to get and hold the attention of your audience in the most suitable ways. You even get something that the batter and pitcher don't have: you can take time to make your rhetorical decisions. The chapters that follow aim to help you achieve that goal.

THIRTY-TWO

What's Your Style?

"Style is all that matters."

—VLADIMIR NABOKOV

 **AKE A LOOK** at the image on the following page: row after row of construction workers in identical outfits, interrupted by a stately figure—the queen of the United Kingdom—in bright turquoise. Our eyes are drawn to the queen because of her ensemble—hat, dress, and stockings—against a sea of men in orange jumpsuits: she stands out. This image could be captioned "Got style?" because it demonstrates that being like everyone or everything around you doesn't add up to a style that can get and hold attention. The same is true for writing; style helps you get readers to take notice—and listen—to what you have to say.

But style isn't just about getting attention: it's also about making choices that work well in your particular situation, and all in an effort to achieve your purpose. You might wear shorts and running shoes to the gym but not to a job interview, a bathing suit to the beach but not to class. It's a delicate balance. Style in writing works the same way. How can the words, images, and sentence structures you use stand out (like the queen) while at the same time giving you credibility? This chapter offers strategies for achieving this balance and shaping your own flexible style of writing.

Queen Elizabeth II of the United Kingdom sits for a photo with construction workers at the opening of a new rail station in Reading, England.

Suitability and Correctness

Making good stylistic choices, ones that get readers' attention and hold it all the way through, calls for considering all the rhetorical factors of your situation. In the simplest terms, a "suitable" writing style is one in which the words you choose and the ways you arrange them suit your purpose, your topic, your medium, and your audience. Making stylistic choices in writing can be tricky, though, since there aren't always concrete rules to follow. You may have learned that it isn't correct to start a sentence with "and" or "but," and that you must never end a sentence with a preposition. But those "rules" are far from universal, and they change over time. In fact, a lot of fine writing today bends and breaks those rules to good effect.

So it won't work to think about style simply as a matter of following rules. In fact, if you have to choose between being "correct" and being "suitable," suitability almost always wins out. In 1966, in the original *Star Trek*, when Captain Kirk of the starship *Enterprise* announced its mission "to boldly go where no man has gone before," that split infinitive ("boldly"

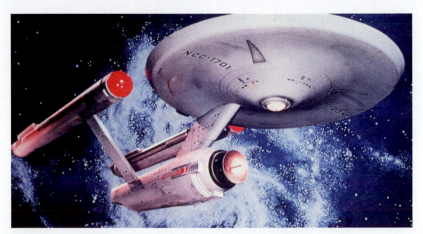

The crew of the USS *Enterprise* split infinitives boldly, and with emphasis.

splits the two words of the infinitive "to go") wasn't absolutely "correct," but it created just the emphasis the writers were after. And since splitting the infinitive broke the conventional grammar rule of the time (the 1960s), it wasn't just the starship *Enterprise* that was boldly going into new territory. We can't say that it was *Star Trek* alone that led to change, but today that rule about split infinitives has all but disappeared from up-to-date handbooks and grammar guides. Making effective stylistic choices, then, will almost always depend on your RHETORICAL SITUATION.

Some contexts already have a defined style of communicating or a specific dialect that's considered most acceptable. In those situations, being aware of the conventional style will help guide your style decisions. For example, what some refer to as "standardized English" is the DIALECT often expected for writing done in most school, government, and professional contexts. But like any other "standard," it has changed across time and will continue to change. If you read the stories of Flannery O'Connor, a twentieth-century American fiction writer and essayist, you'll notice she uses the words "man" and "he" to refer to people in general. Stylistic choices like this were completely ordinary at the time. But when many criticized the use of "he" to refer to all people—including women—conventions changed, and writers looked for more inclusive choices, including alternatives to the designation of all people as either male or female, "he and she," or even

Fortesa Latifi's essay from *Teen Vogue* is suitably formal and journalistic, but the direct quotes included display the frankness and informality of her interviews. Check it out on p. 921.

"they," the increasingly preferred option. Were O'Connor, who died in 1964, writing today, it's very likely she would make different choices when using personal pronouns.

But the fact that academic dialects of languages emerge and change over time and that the preferred use of a language most often depends on context doesn't mean stylistic choices are without any boundaries at all. Audiences often expect that writers will follow accepted conventions, and choosing to do so—or not—has consequences. When the choices you make ignore or defy audience expectations or when they push the envelope, you may be able to get an audience's attention.

Take a look, for instance, at how linguist Geneva Smitherman pushes against the traditional "rules" of academic English and does so brilliantly. In fact, had she stuck to the traditional rules, the following paragraph would have been far less effective than it is.

> Before about 1959 (when the first study was done to change black speech patterns), Black English had been primarily the interest of university academics, particularly the historical linguists and cultural anthropologists. In recent years, though, the issue has become a very hot controversy, and there have been articles on Black Dialect in the national press as well as in the educational research literature. We have had pronouncements on black speech from the NAACP and the Black Panthers, from highly publicized scholars of the Arthur Jensen–William Shockley bent, from executives of national corporations such as Greyhound, and from housewives and community folk. I mean, really, it seem like everybody and they momma done had something to say on the subject!
>
> —GENEVA SMITHERMAN, *Talkin and Testifyin: The Language of Black America*

Geneva
Smitherman

Smitherman obviously knows the rules of standardized English but breaks them to support her point and also to create a clear rhetorical stance, as a scholar, a skilled writer, and a proud Black woman. Writing in the late 1970s, she could assume that her readers would know that the NAACP is the National Association for the Advancement of Colored People, that the Black Panthers were a revolutionary social action group in the 1960s and 1970s, and that Arthur Jensen and William Shockley had made controversial claims about relationships between race and intelligence. She could also assume that readers of her book would expect her to write in standardized English since the volume treated its subject from an academic perspective.

But Smitherman wasn't interested in writing a book about the language of Black Americans using only standardized English. After all, one of her claims was that the language practices of Black Americans were influencing American culture and language in many ways. Notice how her stylistic choices support that claim. She not only talks the talk of standardized English but walks the walk of Black English as well. When she switches in her final sentence from standardized English to Black English, she simultaneously drives home her point—that everyone at that time seemed to have an opinion about the language of Black Americans—while demonstrating membership in that community by using the language variety associated with it. In short, she makes sound and effective stylistic choices.

You'll find more on mixing dialects and languages in the following chapter. For now, remember that your style should be suitable to your purpose, audience, and rhetorical situation, even—and especially—when you bend the rules.

Connecting with Audiences

In all your writing, you'll want to have a reasonably good sense of your intended **AUDIENCE** in order to make effective stylistic choices. Take a look at the image on the following page; it's the webpage for a supermarket in a small town in California that appeals directly to its local community. The writers set a friendly, informal tone right away, announcing that "we love good food" and appealing to their audience to "SHOP LOCAL." The emphasis on the local continues as they note that they've been "serving our community" for decades. They also invite readers to visit their *Facebook* page—and learn about "our sustainable fish program." The use of "our" emphasizes the community and establishes **COMMON GROUND** with readers. The bright colors and simple design add to the warm, inviting tone that underscores the overall message.

A student writing about this same topic for a class project must be more formal and would need to include the background and contextual information that an academic audience expects. For example, here is Katherine Spriggs arguing for the importance of "buying local":

The Surf Market in Gualala, California, welcomes customers to its webpage with a friendly, informal tone.

"Buying local" means that consumers choose to buy food that has been grown, raised, or produced as close to their home as possible. Buying local is an important part of the response to many environmental issues we face today. It encourages the development of small farms, which are often more environmentally sustainable than large farms, and thus strengthens local markets and supports small rural economies. By demonstrating a commitment to buying local, Americans could set an example for global environmentalism.

—KATHERINE SPRIGGS, "On Buying Local"

Rather than assuming that her audience already knows what "buying local" means, Spriggs begins with a careful definition—something the Surf Market webpage doesn't need to do—as a way of laying the groundwork for her argument and demonstrating that she is knowledgeable about her topic. She then starts to build her argument by linking the idea of buying local to environmental issues and community values. Her tone is serious; she gives practical reasons for why buying local is "important," noting that it "encourages the development of small farms" and "supports small rural economies." Like Surf Market and Spriggs do, you'll want to think about who will read what you write and make stylistic choices that help you connect with them.

Levels of Formality

Being effective also calls on writers to pay attention to the level of formality they use. In ancient Rome, Cicero identified three levels of style: low or plain style, used to teach or explain something; middle style, used to please an audience; and high or grand style, used to move or persuade an audience. Note that these classifications link style with a specific purpose and a likely audience.

On August 27, 2018, an aide to Senator John McCain shared a farewell statement McCain had written to America before his death two days earlier. Here is the opening of that letter:

> My fellow Americans, whom I have gratefully served for sixty years, and especially my fellow Arizonans,
>
> Thank you for the privilege of serving you and for the rewarding life that service in uniform and in public office has allowed me to lead. I have tried to serve our country honorably. I have made mistakes, but I hope my love for America will be weighed favorably against them.
>
> I have often observed that I am the luckiest person on earth. . . . Like most people, I have regrets. But I would not trade a day of my life, in good or bad times, for the best day of anyone else's.
>
> I owe that satisfaction to the love of my family. No man ever had a more loving wife or children he was prouder of than I am of mine. And I owe it to America. To be connected to America's causes—liberty, equal justice, respect for the dignity of all people—brings happiness more sublime than life's fleeting pleasures. Our identities and sense of worth are not circumscribed but enlarged by serving good causes bigger than ourselves.
>
> —JOHN McCAIN, "Farewell Letter to America"

Writing in full awareness of his imminent death, McCain uses a solemn, deliberate, formal tone, writing in the grand style that seeks to inspire by both word and deed. Twice he uses balanced phrases to acknowledge weaknesses as well as strengths ("I have made mistakes, but I hope my love of America . . . " and "I have regrets. But I would not trade a day . . . ").

And he expresses deep satisfaction at his connection to "America's causes—liberty, equal justice, respect for the dignity of all people," saying that this connection brings him happiness "more sublime than life's fleeting pleasures." In concluding his letter, McCain uses repetition and very brief sentences to punctuate this final message:

> Do not despair of our present difficulties but believe always in the promise and greatness of America, because nothing is inevitable here. Americans never quit. We never surrender. We never hide from history. We make history. Farewell, fellow Americans. God bless you, and God bless America.

The four short sentences that follow the longer opening sentence are like drumbeats, with their use of the repeated "we," calling Americans to attend to McCain and to be inspired by his example. McCain's style choices match his unique **RHETORICAL SITUATION** —and help his message land with impact.

Stance

Stance refers to the attitude authors take toward their topic and audience. For example, you might write about immigration as an impassioned advocate or critic, someone with strong opinions about the inherent good or evil of immigration. Or you might write as a dispassionate analyst, someone trying to weigh carefully the pros and cons of the arguments for and against a particular proposal. Either stance—and any possible stances in between—will affect what style you use.

If your audience changes, your language will likely shift, too. Debating immigration issues with close friends whose opinions you're fairly sure of will differ in crucial ways from debating them with people you know less well or not at all because you'll be able to take less for granted. That you will likely shift all aspects of your message—from word choice and sentence structure to amount of background information and choice of examples—doesn't make you a hypocrite or a flip-flopper; instead, it demonstrates your skill at finding the most effective rhetorical resources to make your point.

In a posting titled "Same Food Planet, Different Food Worlds," blogger Rod Dreher calls attention to the drastically different stances taken by two restaurant reviewers. Here's an excerpt from one, a review of a new Olive Garden restaurant in Grand Forks, North Dakota, by eighty-five-year-old Marilyn Hagerty:

It had been a few years since I ate at the older Olive Garden in Fargo, so I studied the two manageable menus offering appetizers, soups and salads, grilled sandwiches, pizza, classic dishes, chicken and seafood and filled pastas.

At length, I asked my server what she would recommend. She suggested chicken Alfredo, and I went with that. Instead of the raspberry lemonade she suggested, I drank water.

She first brought me the familiar Olive Garden salad bowl with crisp greens, peppers, onion rings and yes—several black olives. Along with it came a plate with two long, warm breadsticks.

The chicken Alfredo ($10.95) was warm and comforting on a cold day. The portion was generous. My server was ready with Parmesan cheese. . . .

All in all, it is the largest and most beautiful restaurant now operating in Grand Forks. It attracts visitors from out of town as well as people who live here.
　　　　　　　　　　　　—MARILYN HAGERTY, "Long-Awaited Olive
　　　　　　　　　　　　　　　　　Garden Receives Warm Welcome"

Hagerty's polite, unpretentious stance is evident in this review—and as it happens, the style of her writing attracted much attention when it went viral, with readers both celebrating and bashing that style.

Dreher contrasts Hagerty's stance with that of Dive Bar Girl (DBG), who writes for a newsletter in Baton Rouge, Louisiana. In fact, DBG starts right out by announcing her stance—she's going to be "mean," not "informative"—and so after saying "a few nice things" about her topic, a restaurant called Twin Peaks, she writes the review that she assumes her readers "want to read":

Marilyn Hagerty. Read the *Los Angeles Times*' take on the controversy—and Hagerty's son's response in the *Wall Street Journal*—at everyones anauthor .tumblr.com.

Admit it, you like it when DBG is mean. You only send her fan mail when she's mean. She never gets mail for being informative. . . . So she is going to write about the positive things first and then write the review you want to read. The smokehouse burger was above average. The patio was a nice space. The staff, while scantily clad, was professional. The salads even looked good. The place was miles above Hooters.

Here is the review you want: Twin Peaks has to be the brainchild of two 14-year-old boys who recently cracked the parental controls on the home computer. Waitresses are known as "Lumber Jills." In case you are missing the imagery—each Lumber Jill has been endowed with an epic pair of Twin Peaks.
　　　　　　　　　　　　　　　　　—CHERRYTHEDIVEBARGIRL

These two reviews could hardly be more different in stance: the first is low key and even-handed, well suited to Hagerty's stance as a modest and sincere reviewer. The second is highly opinionated and sarcastic, true to the brash, in-your-face stance of Dive Bar Girl. So both are written in styles that suit (and reflect) their respective stances.

But what happens when that stance doesn't fit well with a particular audience? That's what happened when Hagerty's review went viral: some writers immediately began making fun of her as inept and hopelessly out of it; others jumped in just as quickly to defend Hagerty's review, while still others read her review as an indirect parody of local restaurant reviews. Now imagine that Dive Bar Girl's review appeared in Hagerty's hometown newspaper. Chances are it would attract some hefty criticism as well.

The takeaway lesson here: as a writer, you need to consider whether your **STANCE** is a good fit not only to your topic and audience but also to your **MODE** of distribution.

Tone

All the writing you do, regardless of stance or level of formality, has a particular **TONE**. You may not think consciously about how to establish that tone, especially when commenting on a friend's *Instagram* post or writing a text message, but even in social media writing you are making choices about whether you want to convey a serious tone, a humorous tone, or an exasperated tone. When you know that your readers are friends and family, your tone can probably be pretty casual, like this *Facebook* update posted by a student in Washington, DC, which is playful, critical, reasoned, and ironic:

> Note to self: avoid union station on weekday mornings. Hordes of angry commuters make getting to the train impossible? #notfun #DCMetro #rushhour #istheworst

Here the tone is one of frustration and exasperation, expressed in the hashtags the writer adds (#notfun, etc.). She is assuming her readers will not only know what she is talking about but also appreciate her playful tone.

For a report on commuters in Union Station for an urban studies class, the author establishes the more serious tone of a reporter or researcher:

> Walking into Union Station on a weekday morning can be like going against a herd of stampeding cattle. Riders rush from the trains, swinging briefcases and computer bags, knocking over anything or anyone in the way. Rush hour in this station, one of the busiest train stations in the country, is not enjoyable. Looking at some usage statistics and videos will show just how unpleasant this experience is and how it affects those who regularly ride the metro.

Here the tone is studied and serious. The writer opens by describing the scene in the congested station and then moves to introduce an analysis of usage statistics and videos. But even a serious tone doesn't need to result in a dull, boring style: note the lively description ("stampeding cattle"; "swinging briefcases"; "knocking over everything or anyone in the way"). Your **PURPOSE**, **AUDIENCE**, **STANCE**, and even **MEDIUM** will help determine an effective tone.

Style across Media

You probably already find yourself using a variety of media to communicate every day and making intuitive choices about style: you post a video on *TikTok*, you make an oral presentation using *Prezi* for a class, you conduct research for an article that you submit in print and then "remediate" as part of a website. Each of these tasks calls for a suitable medium, whether written, oral, or digital. In each case, you have a good sense of your purpose and audience, and you use that knowledge to establish an effective style and choose the best medium to deliver your message. This is the same kind of rhetorical thinking you need to be doing consciously and analytically for the writing you do in school or work. So in all your writing across media—at home, at work, at school, wherever—you will want to make stylistic choices that are a good fit for your rhetorical situation, your audience, and your purpose.

You are no doubt familiar with the hashtag #BlackLivesMatter, which has generated over 50 million tweets since Alicia Garza, grieving over the death of Trayvon Martin and astonished that his killer was not convicted of any crime, logged onto *Facebook* in July 2013 and wrote "Black people, I love you. I love us. Our lives matter," and her good friend Patrissa Cullors wrote back, closing her post with "#blacklivesmatter." Note the stylistic choices that make these messages memorable: very short sentences; repetition; a serious and urgent tone. Garza, Cullors, and Opal Tometi—cofounders of the Black Lives Matter movement—used those same choices as they went on to create pages on *Tumblr, Twitter,* and *Facebook* to launch a rallying cry across the country.

Some writers, such as Chicago historian Shermann "Dilla" Thomas, use video to deliver their message. His *TikTok* videos (@6figga_dilla) on topics of local history have garnered him more than 87,000 followers. Covering the history of neighborhoods and landmarks throughout the city, as well as historical events and local customs, he meticulously researches his topics, writes a script, and narrates the video while showing related images. The production is simple; he often shoots in his own home, holding a mini-microphone. Many of Thomas's videos have gone viral, and he is now working with *Netflix* on producing a Chicago history series. The images shown here are from Thomas's *TikTok* about the Great Chicago Fire of 1871.

How might Thomas have presented this history differently for a magazine or newspaper article? for a podcast? Different media and platforms

See Thomas's post by visiting everyonesan author.tumblr .com.

Public historian Shermann "Dilla" Thomas narrates his *TikTok* about the Great Chicago Fire of 1871 with a nineteenth-century engraved image of the fire in the background (left) and a map of the burnt area (right).

call for different style choices in order to grab attention and get your message across. And remember that grabbing attention is only half the battle—making sure your style is suitable and effective is just as important. Especially online, it can be easy and tempting to use an over-the-top title or a startling image to grab attention (it's how clickbait works, after all), but they won't keep your readers with you beyond a flashy opening, so stick to style choices that strike the right balance.

    REFLECT. Take time to look carefully at some of your posts on social media. How informal or formal are they? What do they assume your audience will know about your topic? What are your purposes for writing—to share information? to ask for advice? What else? What kind of style does your audience respond best to? Do you use a mix of media—words, images, video? Then write a few sentences describing what you've noticed about your writing style on social media and how it differs from the other kinds of writing you do—at school, at work, at home.

Style across Disciplines

Making good choices is especially important when writing in different disciplines, where what's expected and effective often varies from field to field or workplace to workplace. Many fields have established conventions—reading published writing in a field or discipline can help you see what stylistic features are most common. Look for patterns—do writers use a particular verb tense? active voice instead of passive voice? a specific organization or style of headings? Identifying what other successful writers have done in a field that's new to you is a good way to figure out what you'll try in order to be effective and suitable.

One notable stylistic difference between fields is favoring the **ACTIVE VOICE** or the **PASSIVE VOICE**. For example, reports in the sciences usually call for the passive voice. Take a look at this passage from a 2021 study on possible correlations between running-related injuries (RRIs) and foot placement on impact, or foot strike techniques (FSTs). The authors explain what methods they used to review existing research on their topic; notice that most of the verbs are passive:

> **Methods:** A systematic electronic search <u>was performed</u> using MEDLINE, PubMed, SPORTDiscus, Scopus, and Web of Science databases.

Studies <u>were included</u> that <u>were published</u> in the English language that explored the relationship between FST and RRIs between January 1960 and November 2020. Results <u>were extracted</u> and <u>collated</u>. The Grading of Recommendations, Assessment, Development and Evaluation approach <u>was applied</u> to synthesize the quality of evidence.

In scientific writing the passive is generally favored because it shouldn't matter who searched for the articles, applied the criteria, or assessed the quality using the stated criteria; in the end, the results should be the same. The passive voice also focuses the reader's attention on what was done, not on who did it. So although you may have been instructed in your writing classes to "avoid the passive," it is often the expected and effective choice in the sciences.

At the same time, there are many occasions when writers avoid the passive voice for good reason. For example, engineers often rely on information gathered by other firms or information they gather themselves from interviews. In contexts where they need to make clear who is responsible for observations, recommendations, or judgments, engineers use the active voice to locate responsibility. Thus, engineers would write "Our firm hired ABC Tech to conduct a geotechnical evaluation" rather than "A geotechnical evaluation was conducted" so that readers know the source of the data presented and analyzed. Voice is just one example of how style differs between disciplines—the point is you'll want to seek out reliable examples to learn what style works and is expected of you in a new field.

Thinking about Your Own Style

As you've seen, style is all about making suitable choices, choices that inevitably depend on your topic and all the elements of your rhetorical situation, especially your **STANCE**, your **PURPOSE**, your **GENRE**, and your **AUDIENCE**. Have you written a review of something—a restaurant for the campus newspaper? a backpack on *eBay*? your instructor on ratemyprofessors.com? If so, take a look at the choices you made in the review, and then compare them to those you made in an essay you wrote for class. You'll see right away that you have instinctively used different styles for these different occasions.

For an example of what we mean about making suitable stylistic choices, take a look at a paragraph from this book, first as it appears on page 673 and then as it is revised as a tweet, a report, and a flyer.

Original text

Once upon a time—and for a very long time, too—style in writing and speaking meant ornamentation, "dressing up" your language the way you might dress yourself up for a fancy party. In fact, ancient images often show rhetoric as a woman, Dame Rhetorica, in a gaudy, flowing gown covered with figures of speech—metaphors, similes, alliteration, hyperbole, and so on: her "stylish" ornaments.

Revised as a tweet

Writing style used to mean dressing up your words, like Cinderella getting ready for the ball. Not anymore. #rhetorictoday

Revised as a report

For more than 500 years, the definition of "style" held relatively stable. Style was a form of ornamentation that was added to texts in order to make them more pleasing or accessible to an audience. In ancient depictions, Rhetoric is often shown as a woman dressed in elegant attire and "ornamented" with dozens of stylish figures of speech.

Revised as a flyer

Once upon a time ...

writing style was all about ornamentation.

℘ LANGUAGE IN FANCY DRESS ℭℛ

WHAT DO YOU KNOW ABOUT WRITING STYLE?

Join us in the Writing Center to learn how style has changed over time and how your style can be *in* style.

Sterling C. Evans Library
Room 214

Note how the style changes to match each genre and audience: the tweet is short, of course, and very informal; it uses a sentence fragment and then uses a hashtag to link readers with others talking about rhetoric today. The report is much more formal and is written in standardized English. The flyer uses a much more conversational style—ellipses to signal a pause, a sentence fragment, a question, and italics for emphasis—and announces an event (the purpose of a flyer).

We've tried in this chapter to emphasize how important the stylistic choices you make are to getting the attention of your audiences—and holding it; style really is the key to achieving that goal. And remember that, as an author, you get to call a lot of the stylistic shots. As you do so, of course, you'll want to think carefully about what styles fit well in particular situations, what your audience's expectations are, and what risks you may be willing to take by not fully meeting those expectations. In short, you aren't going to be writing dull, predictable prose. You're a lot better than that: you've got **STYLE**.

REFLECT. Think about a person who you think has style (a friend or family member, a public figure, a boss or teacher): How would you describe that style? What about this person and their style appeals to you—or doesn't? What choices has the person made that contribute to this particular style? If you can, look at a few examples of the person's style in language and writing (social media posts, for example, or captions on a T-shirt). How does their writing style align (or not) with the other parts of the person's style?

Now think about you: how would you describe your own style? What makes up your style? Finally, look at a few recent pieces of writing you've done for school or for your job: How well do they represent you? Do they align (or not) with your style? Do these pieces of writing sound like you—does your voice come through? What about these pieces of writing is memorable or vivid, and what makes them so? What is their level of formality? What is your stance in them and what tone do you take? How would you describe your writing style?

THIRTY-THREE

Mixing Languages and Dialects

OW MANY LANGUAGES do you know well enough to speak or write? Which languages would you like to know? The United States is often referred to as a monolingual country, one where English is the only language needed to get along. But that characterization has never been accurate. Languages other than English have always been present here. Today, the US Census Bureau estimates that approximately 20 percent of Americans report speaking a language other than English at home—Spanish, Chinese, French, and Tagalog are the four most common. And American Sign Language is probably the third most commonly used language (after Spanish), although the census doesn't ask about signed languages.

So the United States is a country of many languages. It is also a country of multiple dialects and, again, it always has been. "Dialects" are varieties of language that are spoken by people in a particular region, social class, or ethnic group—like the English spoken by residents of Appalachia or the Spanish spoken in Texas. "Registers" are varieties of language associated with a particular purpose or activity. For example, a nurse summarizing a patient's lab results to a doctor would speak in a medical register, using abbreviations and technical terms in order to be brief and efficient. That same nurse explaining results to the patient's family would use a more conversational register. Listen to people you

Spend a day taking notice of all the languages, dialects, and registers you encounter around you—from conversations on campus to signs, billboards, and texts that convey information.

Since language is the focus of Anna Glavee's essay, it makes perfect sense that she uses code-meshing to emphasize her argument. See how she weaves her language varieties together on p. 891.

know or hear on *YouTube* or *TikTok*, and you will surely hear various dialects and registers, as well as distinctive vocabulary at work.

No matter how many languages you speak, you probably use a number of different dialects and registers. Is the way you speak at the dinner table different from the way you speak in class or at work? Is the way you write an *Instagram* post different from an email to an instructor? We bet that it is.

We also bet that you probably mix whatever languages, dialects, and registers you use, consciously or unconsciously. There are two common patterns of doing so that language scholars have identified. Both ways are more common in conversation than in writing, but either pattern can occur anywhere. **CODE-SWITCHING** is a shift from one language or dialect to another, where the two languages or dialects are separate. **CODE-MESHING** is a way of weaving together languages and dialects, and the back-and-forth may be very rapid, allowing the varieties to interact and play off one another. Code-switching and code-meshing are both ways of mixing varieties of language for various purposes—to reflect a particular **STANCE**, for example, or to establish a connection with certain **AUDIENCES**. This chapter provides examples and guidelines to help you mix languages, dialects, and registers for various rhetorical situations.

REFLECT. Think for a few minutes about the varieties of language spoken where you grew up. What features of pronunciation and vocabulary can you identify? What groups do you belong to now that have a specialized way of communicating? Fans of one type of music? A religious community? An athletic team or social club? Write a paragraph describing what influences the way you speak; include specific examples.

Using Standardized English and Other Dialects

What some call **STANDARDIZED ENGLISH** is actually a dialect—one that's used in both formal and informal contexts. For example, during a heated discussion about jobs and automation with a friend, you may say things in informal but effective ways that wouldn't work as well if you were writing up the same point in a formal report. Even within a single dialect there's almost always more than one effective way to say or write something; your audience and purpose inform your choices.

That is not to say that all dialects are regarded as equals—standardized English has long held a prestigious position in the United States. But so-called standard languages have been challenged for centuries by vernacular dialects and languages. In the Western world, after all, English supplanted Latin and Greek as languages of power. At the same time, standardized English's relatively rigid conventions have been challenged for a long time (see Chapter 4). And social media continues to blur the boundary between spoken, signed, and written language in significant ways. The styles of everyday conversation are finding their place in written form. In some contexts and for some kinds of writing, the expectations are shifting and the possibilities are expanding. This chapter provides a number of examples of writers mixing varieties of language—often beyond standardized English—in ways that speak powerfully to their audiences. Such moves are increasingly common, but doing so doesn't always come without risks. Keep your rhetorical situation front and center—what's your purpose? what's at stake? what does your audience consider suitable?—when you make language choices that push against readers' expectations.

Connecting with Audiences

If you're a fan of popular music today, you can probably come up with examples of lyricists mixing languages to craft powerful messages. Here is the opening of Kenyan rapper Bamboo's remix of the song "Mama Africa," first written and sung by Jamaican reggae artist Peter Tosh. A love song to the African continent, which has in Bamboo's view too often been represented negatively, his remix connects to his international audience of hip-hop and pop music fans by moving between Swahili and English:

> *tunaishi vizuri*
> check out the way we be livin
> *na tunakula vizuri*
> we always eating the best
> *poteza yako kwa nini*
> why should you settle for less
> *TV haiwezi kuambia*
> they never show on your screen
> *kwa hivyo mi ntawaambia*
> so you can see what I mean
> *Africa maridadi*
> Africa's beautiful baby
> —BAMBOO, "Mama Africa"

Bamboo uses hip-hop rhythms and dialect to connect with the listeners he wants to reach. By using both Swahili and English, he reaches more people than if he'd used just one language—and exposes those who speak just one of these languages to the other.

Sandra Cisneros, a Mexican American writer who's fluent in both English and Spanish, makes similar choices in a collection of short stories inspired by her experience growing up in the United States surrounded by Mexican culture. See how she mixes languages to speak to an audience that's likely to include both English and Spanish speakers:

> "¡Ay!" The true test of a native Spanish speaker. ¡Ay! To make love in Spanish, in a manner as intricate and devout as la Alhambra. To have a lover sigh *mi vida, mi preciosa, mi chiquitita,* and whisper things in that

language crooned to babies, that language murmured by grandmothers, those words that smelled like your house, like flour tortillas.

— SANDRA CISNEROS, *Woman Hollering Creek and Other Stories*

As writers and speakers, we have to think carefully about when mixing languages or dialects will help us connect with our audiences—and when it won't. In most cases, authors have a kind of informal contract with readers: while readers may need to work some to understand what a writer is saying, the writer in turn promises to consider the audience's expectations and abilities. The end goal is usually accessibility: Will your message be understood by those you are trying to reach? If some members of your audience aren't likely to understand, should you provide a translation? Or are you choosing not to translate so that readers experience what it's like *not* to understand?

Providing Translation

One way to stay true to a language or dialect you identify with while still reaching readers who may not understand is to provide a translation. Bamboo's example, which invites English-speaking listeners to think about Africa's rich cultures in part by including Swahili, demonstrates how translation helps when you're mixing languages. When including translations, you will usually want to introduce the term that is being translated in its original language, followed by the translation, as in the following poster announcing an online Ojibwe Language Symposium sponsored by Fond du Lac Tribal & Community College in Minnesota. Note that the designer places an Ojibwe-language sentence in a prominent position and in bold type, emphasizing its importance. The English translation appears in parentheses, and not bold type, underneath.

For another example, see how sociolinguist Guadalupe Valdés uses translation in an ethnographic study of a family of Mexican origin that included a young boy named Saúl:

During his kindergarten year, . . . winning was important to Saúl. Of all the cousins who played together, it was he who ran the fastest and pushed the hardest. "*Yo gané, yo gané*" (I won, I won), he would say enthusiastically. . . . Saúl's mother, Velma, wished that he would win just a bit more quietly. . . . "*No seas peleonero*" (Don't be so quarrelsome), she would say. "*Es importante llevarse bien con todos*" (It's important to get along with everyone).

—GUADALUPE VALDÉS, *Con Respeto: Bridging the Distances Between Culturally Diverse Families and Schools*

Poster created by Fond du Lac Tribal & Community College announcing an online Ojibwe Language Symposium in English and Ojibwe.

Note especially that Valdés always puts the Spanish words first, as they were spoken, and only then gives the English translation. She could have chosen to put the English translation first, or to write only in English, but giving the Spanish first puts the spotlight on her subjects' voices and their own words. By including the English translation at all, Valdés acknowledges readers who don't speak Spanish and makes sure they can understand what she's written. Like Bamboo and the Ojibwe symposium poster, she translates to make sure her message is accessible to as many people as possible. Notice, too, that Valdés italicizes words in a language other than English, which is a common academic convention when mixing languages.

Illustrating a Point

Professional groups have their own specialized ways of speaking: people in economics and finance will have different vocabulary and style at work from people in medicine, engineering, or food service. Much has been written about what is often called "valley speak," a common way of speaking in Silicon Valley where tech giants like Google, Apple, and Twitter reside. In a book that aims to be a definitive guide to the language of Silicon Valley, authors Rochelle Kopp and Steven Ganz incorporate examples to illustrate their point:

> When we moved to Silicon Valley, we found it challenging to pick up the lingo. . . . Around here, people toss off sentences like "Everyone thought that [the] semantic search startup launched by those Stanford whiz kids was going to be the next unicorn, but now they are doing a down round and it's looking like they are candidates for an acqui-hire." It can be awkward if you're the only one who doesn't understand what people here are saying.
> —ROCHELLE KOPP & STEVEN GANZ, *Valley Speak: Deciphering the Jargon of Silicon Valley*

By mixing in phrases like "semantic search startups" and "down round," Kopp and Ganz illustrate valley speak while suggesting that the vocabulary of Silicon Valley startups may alienate any people who don't want to take the time to penetrate the jargon.

Professor Jamila Lyiscott mixes dialects to illustrate her point in a spoken-word essay called "Broken English" in which she "celebrates—and challenges—the three distinct flavors of English she speaks." Prompted by a "baffled lady" who seemed surprised to find that Lyiscott is "articulate," Lyiscott says:

> When my father asks, "Wha' kinda ting is dis?"
> My "articulate" answer never goes amiss
> I say "Father, this is the impending problem at hand"
> And when I'm on the block I switch it up just because I can
> So when my boy says, "What's good with you son?"

I just say, "I jus' fall out wit dem people but I done!"
And sometimes in class
I might pause the intellectual sounding flow to ask
"Yo! Why dese books neva be about my peoples"
Yes, I have decided to treat all three of my languages as equals
Because I'm "articulate"

—JAMILA LYISCOTT, "Broken English"

In her performance, which has more than six million views online, Lyiscott uses what she calls "three tongues"—one each for "home, school, and friends"—to make the point that there are many different ways to be "articulate." And she's articulate, all right, in three different dialects.

↪ *WATCH THE VIDEO* of Jamila Lyiscott's TED talk by visiting everyonesanauthor
.tumblr.com. *Why do you think Lyiscott chose a spoken-word essay as her medium?*
How does watching and listening to her performance (versus reading words on a page)
change the way you understand her message? Why do you think Lyiscott chose to mix
dialects? How would it change her message if she chose just one dialect instead of
mixing several?

Drawing Attention

Here is Buthainah, a Saudi Arabian student writing a literacy narrative for an education class at an American college:

ومن يتهيّب صعود الجبال   ~~~   يعش ابد الدّهر بين الحفر

"I don't want to" was my response to my parents' request of enrolling me in a nearby preschool. I did not like school. I feared it. I feared the aspect of departing my comfort zone, my home, to an unknown and unpredictable zone. . . . To encourage me, they recited a poetic line that I did not comprehend as a child but live by it as an adult. They said, "Who fears climbing the mountains~~~ . . . Lives forever between the holes." As I grew up, knowledge became my key to freedom; freedom of thought, freedom of doing, and freedom of beliefs.

—BUTHAINAH, "Who Fears Climbing the Mountains Lives Forever between the Holes"

In this instance, opening with the Arabic proverb (which also serves as the title of Buthainah's essay) draws readers' attention and announces the importance of Arabic in the author's journey to become the writer she is while also letting non-Arabic speakers feel a bit of what it's like to encounter a foreign language without an immediate translation. At the same time, she makes a point of translating the proverb for her readers as the essay progresses—"They said, 'Who fears climbing the mountains~~~ . . . Lives forever between the holes.'" Buthainah's essay illustrates how switching to a different language or way of speaking can grab attention and show—instead of tell—your audience something that's important to you.

Quoting People Directly and Respectfully

If you are writing about a person or group of people you have interviewed or who have been interviewed by others, you will want to let those people speak for themselves. From 1927 to 1931, Zora Neale Hurston, the famed Black folklorist, cultural anthropologist, and novelist, interviewed Cudjo Lewis, one of the last known people to be enslaved and brought across the Atlantic to the United States. Lewis's story, told from Hurston's perspective, appears in *Barracoon: The Story of the Last "Black Cargo,"* a book published after Hurston's death. Hurston takes care to let the subject of her interview speak his mind, and in his own words. She begins by documenting her initial interaction with Lewis, telling us, "I hailed him by his African name" (Oluale Kossula), which she had learned from others while conducting prior research. In the next paragraph, Lewis speaks:

> Oh Lor', I kno it *you* call my name. Nobody don't callee me my name from cross de water but you. You always callee me Kossula, jus' lak I in de Affica soil!   —ZORA NEALE HURSTON, *Barracoon: The Story of the Last "Black Cargo"*

Hurston alternates between standardized English and a representation of the actual speech of the person whose words she quotes. These quotations report what she heard, which helps build her ETHOS as a careful listener and researcher. Finally, the use of quotations appeals to her audience's emotions; we can *hear* Lewis's surprise and delight. Readers familiar with the varieties of English Lewis uses might sense kinship with him, while those who are not will be reminded that Hurston is writing about a context different from their experience—but in a way that is always respectful.

When you're quoting others, let them speak for themselves not only in their own words but also in their own language. Whenever possible, ask your subjects to review the quotations you use to ensure they find the representation accurate and respectful.

Evoking a Particular Person, Place, or Community

Using the language of a specific community or group is a good way to evoke the character and sounds of the place. *Honolulu Magazine* published a four-part series about Hawaiian Pidgin, a language spoken in that state, written by prize-winning Pidgin author and scholar Lee A. Tonouchi. Tonouchi wrote about the language's history, the politics of its use, and its future. One article in that series begins like this:

> Ukuplanny people ask me, "Pidgin stay dying o'wot?" In order fo see wea Pidgin stay going, we gotta try look see wea and wot Pidgin wuz befo time. Pidgin one strong, resilient language, you know. Cuz historically had lotta times in Hawai'i when had strong public sentiment against Pidgin, and yet Pidgin still manage fo come back even mo strongah each time.
> —LEE A. TONOUCHI, "Da Future of Hawaiian Pidgin"

You can see that Tonouchi mixes elements of Pidgin and standardized English throughout every sentence. Notice how all the features weave together—individual words, grammatical structure, variant spelling that reflects the pronunciations and rhythms of Pidgin. The writing vividly evokes the ways that members of the community navigate their lives and linguistic repertoires. When using the language of a community or group you don't belong to yourself, take care to do so with respect. When possible, ask someone who does speak the language to provide feedback on what you've drafted to ensure it's accurate and respectful.

As we've tried to demonstrate, using your own linguistic repertoire and shifting between styles are powerful tools for communicating what you have to say. Consider the following questions as you think about mixing languages, dialects, and registers in your own writing:

- *Who's your target* AUDIENCE*?* Are there places where you can shift styles to connect with them? to get and keep their attention? to illustrate a point? What expectations does your audience have about language? Are you meeting those expectations or challenging them?

- *What's the larger* CONTEXT*?* Are readers likely to find your language choices suitable? Is anything at risk, like your credibility or clarity? What's your PURPOSE for taking such risks?

- *Are readers likely to understand your words?* Do you need to provide translations? If you're using a specific style, like MLA or APA, are there conventions—like italicizing non-English words in an English-language text—you need to follow?

- *Have you treated languages, dialects, and registers that are not your own with respect?* When quoting, have you let subjects speak for themselves? Have you solicited feedback from someone who speaks the language, dialect, or register to be sure your text is accurate and respectful?

REFLECT. Think about one or two ways of speaking you encounter that are different from your own—in places you work, movies you watch, or groups you are familiar with but don't belong to. Then find out as much as you can about that way of speaking and gather examples of it in use. What can you determine about how widely the dialect is used, who uses it, when it's used, what characteristics define it, and how it's perceived by different audiences? Write a brief reflection summarizing what you've found.

THIRTY-FOUR

How to Craft Powerful Sentences

HEN A STUDENT asked author Annie Dillard, "Do you think I could become a writer?" Dillard replied with a question of her own: "Do you like sentences?" French novelist Gustave Flaubert certainly did, once saying that he "itched with sentences." Itching with sentences probably isn't something you've experienced—and liking or not liking sentences might not be something you've ever thought about—but we're willing to bet that you know something about how important sentences are. Anyone who has ever tried to write the perfect tweet or, better yet, the perfect love letter knows about choosing just the right words for each sentence and about the power of the three-word sentence "I love you."

In his book *How to Write a Sentence*, English professor Stanley Fish declares himself to be a "connoisseur of sentences" and offers some particularly noteworthy examples. Here's one, written by a fourth grader in response to an assignment to write something about a mysterious large box that had been delivered to a school:

▶ I was already on the second floor when I heard about the box.

This sentence reminded us of a favorite sentence of our own, this one the beginning of a story written by a third grader:

▶ Today, the monster goes where no monster has gone before: Cincinnati.

Here the student manages to allude to the famous line from *Star Trek*—"to boldly go where no man has gone before"—while suggesting that

Cincinnati is the most exotic place on Earth and even using a colon effectively. It's quite a sentence.

Finally, here's a sentence that opens a chapter from a PhD dissertation on literacy among young people today:

► Hazel Hernandez struck me as an honest thief.

Such sentences are memorable. They make us want to read more. Who's Hazel Hernandez? What's an honest thief, and what makes her one?

As these examples suggest, you don't have to be a famous author to write a great sentence. In fact, crafting effective and memorable sentences is a skill everyone can master with careful attention and practice. Sometimes a brilliant sentence comes to you like a bolt of lightning. More often, though, the perfect sentence is a result of tinkering during revision. Either way, crafting good sentences is worth the effort it may take.

Just as certain effects in film—music, close-ups—enhance the story, a well-crafted sentence can bring power to a piece of writing. As author Joan Didion wrote, "To shift the structure of a sentence alters the meaning of that sentence, as definitely and inflexibly as the position of a camera alters the meaning of the object photographed. Many people know about camera angles now, but not so many know about sentences."

So think about the kind of effect you want to create in what you're writing—and then look for the type of sentence that will fit the bill. Though much of the power of the examples above comes from their being short and simple, remember that some rhetorical situations call for longer, complex sentences—and that the kind of sentence you write also depends on its context, such as whether it's opening an essay, summing up what's already been said, or something else. This chapter looks at some common English sentence patterns and provides some good examples for producing them in your own work. While the information and examples in the chapter are oriented around standardized English, writing in all language varieties involves sentences. The advice that you find here will be useful, even if you make some modifications in order to mix languages and dialects.

FOUR COMMON SENTENCE PATTERNS

We make sentences with words—and we arrange those words into patterns. If a sentence is defined as a group of words that expresses a complete thought, then we can identify four basic sentence structures: a **SIMPLE SENTENCE** (expressing one idea); a **COMPOUND SENTENCE** (expressing more than one idea, with the ideas being of equal importance); a **COMPLEX SENTENCE** (expressing more than one idea, with one of the ideas being more important than the others); and a **COMPOUND-COMPLEX SENTENCE** (with more than one idea of equal importance and at least one idea of less importance).

Simple Sentences: One Main Idea

Let's take a look at some simple sentences:

▶ Resist!

▶ Consumers revolted.

▶ Angry consumers revolted against new debit-card fees.

▶ A wave of protest from angry consumers forced banks to rescind the new fees.

▶ The growth of the internet and its capacity to mobilize people instantly all over the world have done everything from forcing companies to rescind debit-card fees in the United States to bringing down oppressive governments in the Middle East.

As these examples illustrate, simple sentences can be as short as a single word—or they can be much longer. Each is a simple sentence, however, because it contains a single main idea or thought; in grammatical terms, each contains one and only one **MAIN CLAUSE**. As the name suggests, a simple sentence is often the simplest, most direct way of saying what you want to say—but not always. And often you want a sentence to include more than one idea. In that case, you need to use a compound sentence, a complex sentence, or a compound-complex sentence.

Compound Sentences:
Joining Ideas That Are Equally Important

Sometimes you'll want to write a sentence that joins two or more ideas that are equally important, like this one attributed to former president Bill Clinton:

▶ You can put wings on a pig, but you don't make it an eagle.

In grammatical terms, this is a compound sentence with two main clauses, each of which expresses one of two independent and equally important ideas. In this case, Clinton joined the ideas with a comma and the coordinating conjunction "but." However, he had several other options for joining these ideas. For example, he could have joined them with only a semicolon:

▶ You can put wings on a pig; you don't make it an eagle.

Or he could have joined them with a semicolon, a conjunctive adverb like "however," and a comma:

▶ You can put wings on a pig; however, you don't make it an eagle.

All of these compound sentences are perfectly acceptable—but which seems most effective? In this case, we think Clinton's choice is: it is clear and very direct, and if you read it aloud you'll hear that the words on each side of "but" have the same number of syllables, creating a pleasing, balanced rhythm—and one that balances the two equally important ideas. It also makes the logical relationship between the two ideas explicit: "but" indicates a contrast. The version with only a semicolon, by contrast, indicates that the ideas are somehow related but doesn't show how.

Using "and," "but," and other coordinating conjunctions. In writing a compound sentence, remember that different **COORDINATING CONJUNCTIONS** carry meanings that signal different logical relationships between the main ideas in the sentence. There are only seven coordinating conjunctions.

COORDINATING CONJUNCTIONS

and	for	or	yet
but	nor	so	

▶ China's one-child policy has slowed population growth, <u>but</u> it has helped create a serious gender imbalance in the country's population.

▶ Most of us bike to the office, <u>so</u> many of us stop at the gym to shower before work.

▶ The first two batters struck out, <u>yet</u> the Cubs went on to win the game on back-to-back homers.

See how the following sentences express different meanings depending on which coordinating conjunction is used:

▶ You could apply to graduate school, <u>or</u> you could start looking for a job.

▶ You could apply to graduate school, <u>and</u> you could start looking for a job.

Using a semicolon. Joining clauses with a semicolon only is a way of signaling that they are closely related without saying explicitly how. Often the second clause will expand on an idea expressed in the first clause.

▶ My first year of college was a little bumpy; it took me a few months to get comfortable at a campus far from home.

▶ The Wassaic Project is an arts organization in Dutchess County, New York; artists go there to engage in "art, music, and everything else."

Adding a **TRANSITION WORD** can make the logical relationship between the ideas more explicit:

▶ My first year of college was a little bumpy; <u>indeed</u>, it took me a few months to get comfortable at a campus far from home.

Note that the transition in this sentence, "indeed," cannot join the two main clauses on its own—it requires a semicolon before it. If you use a transition between two clauses with only a comma before it, you've made a mistake called a **COMMA SPLICE**.

SOME TRANSITION WORDS

also	indeed	otherwise
certainly	likewise	similarly
furthermore	nevertheless	therefore
however	next	thus

REFLECT. Read through something you've written recently and identify compound sentences joined with "and." When you find one, ask yourself whether "and" is the best word to use: Does it express the logical relationship between the two parts of the sentence that you intend? Would "but," "or," "so," "for," "nor," or "yet" work better?

Complex Sentences:
When One Idea Is More Important than Another

Many of the sentences you write will contain two or more ideas, with one that you want to emphasize more than the other(s). You can do so by putting the idea you wish to emphasize in the **MAIN CLAUSE**, and then putting those that are less important in **SUBORDINATE CLAUSES**.

▶ Mendocino County is a place in California <u>where you can dive for abalone</u>.

▶ <u>Because the species has become scarce</u>, abalone diving is strictly regulated.

▶ Fish and Wildlife Department agents <u>who patrol the coast</u> use sophisticated methods to catch poachers.

As these examples show, the ideas in the subordinate clauses (underlined here) can't stand alone as sentences: when we read "where you can dive for abalone" or "who patrol the coast," we know that something's missing. Subordinate clauses begin with words such as "if" or "because," **SUBORDINAT-ING WORDS** that signal the logical relationship between the subordinate clause and the rest of the sentence.

SOME SUBORDINATING WORDS

after	even though	until
although	if	when
as	since	where
because	that	while
before	though	who

Notice that a subordinate clause can come at the beginning of a sentence, in the middle, or at the end. When it comes at the beginning, it is usually followed by a comma, as in the second example. If the opening clause in that sentence were moved to the end, a comma would not be necessary: "Abalone diving is strictly regulated because the species has become scarce."

Grammatically, each of the three examples above is a complex sentence, with one main idea and one other idea of less importance. In writing you will often have to decide whether to combine ideas in a compound sentence, which gives the ideas equal importance, or in a complex sentence, which makes one idea more important than the other(s). Looking once more at our sentence about the pig and the eagle, Bill Clinton could have made it a complex sentence:

▶ Even though you can put wings on a pig, you don't make it an eagle.

Again, though, we think Clinton made a good choice in giving the two ideas equal weight because doing so balances the sentence perfectly—and tells us that both parts are equally important. In fact, neither part of this sentence is very interesting in itself: it's the balancing and the contrast that make it interesting and memorable.

Compound-Complex Sentences: Multiple Ideas—Some More Important, Some Less

When you are expressing three or more ideas in a single sentence, you'll sometimes want to use a compound-complex sentence, which gives some of the ideas more prominence and others less. Grammatically, such sentences have at least two **MAIN CLAUSES** and one **SUBORDINATE CLAUSE**.

▶ ┌──────────────MAIN CLAUSE──────────────┐┌─SUBORDINATE CLAUSE
We have experienced unparalleled natural disasters that have devastated

┌──────────────────┐┌──────────MAIN CLAUSE──────────┐
entire countries, yet identifying global warming as the cause of these

┌──────────────────┐
disasters is difficult.

▶ ┌──────────SUBORDINATE CLAUSE──────────┐┌──MAIN CLAUSE
Even after distinguished scientists issued a series of reports, critics continued

┌──────────────────┐┌──────SUBORDINATE CLAUSE──────┐
to question the findings because they claimed results were falsified;

┌──────MAIN CLAUSE──────┐
nothing would convince them.

As these examples show, English sentence structure is flexible, allowing you to combine groups of words in different ways in order to get your ideas across to your audience most effectively. There's seldom only one way to write a sentence to get an idea across: as the author, you must decide which way works best for your **RHETORICAL SITUATION**.

WAYS OF EMPHASIZING
THE MAIN IDEA IN A SENTENCE

Sometimes, you will want to lead off a sentence with the main point; other times, you might want to hold it in reserve until the end. **CUMULATIVE SENTENCES** start with a main clause and then add on to it, "accumulating" details. **PERIODIC SENTENCES** start with a series of phrases or subordinate clauses, saving the main clause for last.

Cumulative Sentences: Starting with the Main Point

In this kind of sentence, the writer starts off with a **MAIN CLAUSE** and then adds details in phrases and **SUBORDINATE CLAUSES**, extending or explaining the thought. Cumulative sentences can be especially useful for describing a place or an event, operating almost like a camera panning across a room or landscape. The sentences below create such an effect:

▶ The San Bernardino Valley lies only an hour east of Los Angeles by the San Bernardino Freeway but is in certain ways an alien place: not the coastal California of the subtropical twilights and the soft westerlies off the Pacific but a harsher California, haunted by the Mojave just beyond the mountains, devastated by the hot dry Santa Ana wind that comes down through the passes at 100 miles an hour and whines through the eucalyptus windbreaks and works on the nerves.

—JOAN DIDION, "Some Dreamers of the Golden Dream"

▶ Public transportation in Cebu City was provided by jeepneys: refurbished military jeeps with metal roofs for shade, decorated with horns and mirrors and fenders and flaps; painted with names, dedications, quotations, religious icons, logos—and much, much more.

▶ She hit the brakes, swearing fiercely, as the deer leapt over the hood and crashed into the dark woods beyond.

▶ The celebrated Russian pianist gave his hands a shake, a quick shake, fingers pointed down at his sides, before taking his seat and lifting them imperiously above the keys.

These cumulative sentences add details in a way that makes each sentence more emphatic. Keep this principle in mind as you write—and also when you revise. See if there are times when you might revise a sentence or sentences to add emphasis in the same way. Take a look at the following sentences, for instance:

▶ China has initiated free-market reforms that transformed its economy from a struggling one to an industrial powerhouse. It has become the world's fastest-growing major economy. Growth rates have been averaging 10 percent over the last decade.

These three sentences are clearly related, with each one adding detail about the growth of China's economy. Now look what happens when the writer eliminates a little bit of repetition, adds a memorable metaphor, and combines them as a cumulative—and more emphatic—sentence:

▶ China's free-market reforms have led to 10 percent average growth over the last decade, transforming it from a paper tiger into an industrial dragon that is now the world's fastest-growing major economy.

Periodic Sentences: Delaying the Main Point until the End

In contrast to sentences that open with the main idea, periodic sentences delay the main idea until the very end. Periodic sentences are sometimes fairly long, and withholding the main point until the end is a way of adding emphasis. It can also create suspense or build up to a surprise or inspirational ending.

▶ In spite of everything, in spite of the dark and twisting path he saw stretching ahead for himself, in spite of the final meeting with Voldemort he knew must come, whether in a month, in a year, or in ten, he felt his heart lift at the thought that there was still one last golden day of peace left to enjoy with Ron and Hermione.   —J. K. ROWLING, *Harry Potter and the Half-Blood Prince*

▶ Unprovided with original learning, uninformed in the habits of thinking, unskilled in the arts of composition, I resolved to write a book.
          —EDWARD GIBBON, *Memoirs of My Life*

▶ In the week before finals, when my studying and memorizing reached a fever pitch, came a sudden, comforting thought: I am prepared.

Here are three periodic sentences in a row about Whitney Houston, each of which withholds the main point until the end:

> ▶ When her smiling brown face, complete with a close-cropped Afro, appeared on the cover of *Seventeen* in 1981, she was one of the first African-Americans to grace the cover, and the industry took notice. When she belted out a chilling and soulful version of the "Star-Spangled Banner" at the 1991 Super Bowl, the world sat back in awe of her poise and calm. And in an era when African-American actresses are often given film roles portraying them as destitute, unloving, unlovable, or just "the help," Houston played the love interest of Kevin Costner, a white Hollywood superstar.
>
> —ALLISON SAMUELS, "African American Stars Remember Whitney Houston"

These three periodic sentences create a drumlike effect that builds in intensity as they move through the stages in Houston's career; in all, they suggest that Houston was, even more than Kevin Costner, a "superstar."

Samuels takes a chance when she uses three sentences in a row that withhold the main point until the end: readers may get tired of waiting for that point. And readers may also find the use of too many such sentences to be, well, too much. But as the example above shows, when used carefully, a sentence that puts off the main idea just long enough can keep readers' interest, making them want to reach the ending, with its payoff.

You may find in your own work that periodic sentences can make your writing more emphatic. Take a look at the following sentence from an essay on the use of animals in circuses:

> ▶ The big cat took him down with one swat, just as the trainer, dressed in khakis and boots, his whip raised and his other arm extended in welcome to the cheering crowd, stepped into the ring.

This sentence paints a vivid picture, but it gives away all the action in the first six words. By withholding that action until the end, the writer builds anticipation and adds emphasis:

> ▶ Just as the trainer stepped into the ring, dressed in khakis and boots, his whip raised and his other arm extended in welcome to the cheering crowd, the big cat took him down with one swat.

OPENING SENTENCES

Lynda Barry begins her narrative on p. 851 with a compelling opening sentence. Check it out (and be prepared to keep reading; you won't want to stop).

The opening sentences in your writing carry big responsibilities, setting the tone and often the scene—and drawing your readers in by arousing their interest and curiosity. Authors often spend quite a lot of time on opening sentences for this very reason: whether it's a business report or a college essay or a social media post, the way the piece begins has a lot to do with whether your audience will stay with you and whether you'll get the kind of response you want from them. Here are three famous opening sentences:

▶ I am an invisible man.   —RALPH ELLISON, *Invisible Man*

▶ The sky above the port was the color of television, tuned to a dead channel.
                                        —WILLIAM GIBSON, *Neuromancer*

▶ I lost an arm on my last trip home.   —OCTAVIA E. BUTLER, *Kindred*

Each of these sentences is startling, making us read on in order to find out more. Each is brief, leaving us waiting anxiously for what's to come. In addition, each makes a powerful statement and creates some kind of image in readers' minds: an "invisible" person, a sky the color of a "dead" TV channel, someone losing an arm. These sentences all come from novels, but they use strategies that work in many kinds of writing.

It usually takes more than a single sentence to open an essay. Here is the opening of a blog post that begins with a provocative question:

▶ Have you ever thought about whether to have a child? If so, what factors entered into your decision? Was it whether having children would be good for you, your partner and others close to the possible child, such as children you may already have, or perhaps your parents? For most people contemplating reproduction, those are the dominant questions. Some may also think about the desirability of adding to the strain that the nearly seven billion people already here are putting on our planet's environment. But very few ask whether coming into existence is a good thing for the child itself.   —PETER SINGER, "Should This Be the Last Generation?"

Singer's question is designed to get the reader's attention, and he follows it up with two additional questions that ask readers to probe more deeply into their reasons for considering whether or not to reproduce. In the fifth sentence, he suggests that the answers people give to these questions may not be adequate ones, and in the last sentence he lays down a challenge: perhaps coming into existence is not always good for "the child itself."

Here's another example of an opening that uses several sentences, this one from a student essay about graphic memoirs:

▶ In 1974, before the Fall of Saigon, my 14-year-old father, alone, boarded a boat out of Vietnam in search of America. This is a fact. But this one fact can spawn multiple understandings: I could ask a group of students to take a week and write me a story from just this one fact, and I have no doubt that they would bring back a full range of interpretations.
—BRANDON LY, "Leaving Home, Coming Home"

This opening passage begins with a vivid image of a very young man fleeing Vietnam alone, followed by a very short sentence that makes a statement and then a longer one that challenges that statement. This student writer is moving readers toward what will become his thesis: that memoirs can never tell "the whole truth, and nothing but the truth."

Finally, take a look at the opening of the speech Toni Morrison gave when she won the Nobel Prize in Literature:

▶ Members of the Swedish Academy, Ladies and Gentlemen:
Narrative has never been mere entertainment for me. It is, I believe, one of the principal ways in which we absorb knowledge. I hope you will understand, then, why I begin these remarks with the opening phrase of what must be the oldest sentence in the world, and the earliest one we remember from childhood: "Once upon a time . . ."
—TONI MORRISON, Nobel Prize acceptance speech

Morrison begins with a deceptively simple statement that narrative is for her not just entertainment. In the next sentences, she complicates that statement and broadens her claim that narrative is the way we understand the world, concluding with what she calls "the oldest sentence in the world."

You can use strategies similar to the ones shown here in opening your college essays. Here are just some of the ways you might begin:

- With a strong, dramatic—or deceptively simple—statement
- With a vivid image

- With a provocative question
- With an anecdote
- With a surprising claim

Opening sentences online. If the internet lets us send messages to people all over the world, it also challenges us to get and keep their attention. And with limited space and time (small screens, readers in a hurry, scanning for what they need), writers need to make sure the opening sentences of any online text are as attention-getting and informative as possible.

In email, for instance, first sentences often show up in auto-preview lines, so it's a good idea to write them carefully. Here's the first line of an email sent to everyone at W. W. Norton:

▶ A Ping-Pong table has been set up on the 4th floor in loving memory of Diane O'Connor.

This email was sent by O'Connor's colleagues, honoring her efforts to persuade Norton to have an annual company ping-pong tournament. It might have said less ("Ping-Pong on 4," "remembering Diane"), as email usually does—but there was more that they wanted to say.

You'll want to think carefully about how you open any text that you post online—and to craft opening sentences that will make sense in a *Google* search list. Here are two that we like:

▶ Smith Women Redefine "Pearls and Cashmere."

This is the headline for an article in *Inside Higher Ed*, an online magazine read by educators, but it's also the line that comes up in a *Google* search. The article is about a controversy at Smith College—and we think you'll agree that the headline surely got the attention of those scanning the magazine's list of articles or searching *Google*.

▶ *The Art of Fielding* is a 2011 novel by former *n+1* editor Chad Harbach. It centers on the fortunes of shortstop Henry Skrimshander and his career playing college baseball with the Westish College Harpooners, a Division III (NCAA) team.

This is the start of the *Wikipedia* entry for a novel, which comes up in a *Google* search. As you can see, it identifies the book, says who wrote it, and gives a one-sentence description of the story. Safe to say, the authors of this entry were careful to provide this information in the very first sentences.

CLOSING SENTENCES

Sentences that conclude a piece of writing are where you have a chance to make a lasting impact: to reiterate your point, tell readers why it matters, echo something you say in your opening, make a provocative statement, or issue a call for action.

Here's Joe Posnanski, wrapping up an essay on his blog arguing that college athletes should not be paid:

> ► College football is not popular because of the stars. College football is popular because of that first word. Take away the college part, add in money, and you are left with professional minor league football. . . . See how many people watch that.　　　—JOE POSNANSKI, "The College Connection"

These four sentences summarize his argument—and the last one's the zinger, one that leaves readers thinking.

Now take a look at the conclusion to a scholarly book on current neurological studies of human attention, the brain science of attention:

> ► Right now, our classrooms and workplaces are structured for success in the last century, not this one. We can change that. By maximizing opportunities for collaboration, by rethinking everything from our approach to work to how we measure progress, we can begin to see the things we've been missing and catch hold of what's passing us by.
>
> If you change the context, if you change the questions you ask, if you change the structure, the test, and the task, then you stop gazing one way and begin to look in a different way and in a different direction. You know what happens next:
>
> *Now* you see it.
>
> 　　　—CATHY DAVIDSON, *Now You See It: How the Brain Science of Attention Will Transform the Way We Live, Work, and Learn*

Cathy Davidson uses two short paragraphs to sum up her argument and then concludes with a final paragraph that consists of just one very short four-word sentence. With this last sentence, she uses a tried-and-true strategy of coming full circle to echo the main idea of her book and, in fact, to reiterate its title. Readers who have worked their way through the book will take pleasure in that last sentence: *Now* they do see her point.

For another example, note how in the ending to a speech about language and about being able to use "all the Englishes" she grew up with, author Amy Tan closes with a one-sentence paragraph that quotes her mother:

▶ Apart from what any critic had to say about my writing, I knew I had succeeded where it counted when my mother finished reading my book and gave me her verdict: "So easy to read."   —AMY TAN, "Mother Tongue"

Tan's ending sums up one of her main goals as an author: to write so that readers who speak different kinds of English will find her work accessible, especially her mother.

Finally, take a look at how Toni Morrison chose to close her Nobel Prize acceptance speech:

▶ It is, therefore, mindful of the gifts of my predecessors, the blessing of my sisters, in joyful anticipation of writers to come that I accept the honor the Swedish Academy has done me, and ask you to share what is for me a moment of grace.   —TONI MORRISON, Nobel Prize acceptance speech

In this one-sentence conclusion, Morrison speaks to the past, present, and future when she says she is grateful for those writers who came before her, for those who are writing now (her sisters), and for those yet to come. She ends the sentence by asking her audience to share this "moment of grace" with her and, implicitly, with all other writers so honored.

You may not be accepting a Nobel Prize soon, but in your college writing you can use all the strategies presented here to compose strong closings:

- By reiterating your point
- By discussing the implications of your argument
- By asking a question

- By referring back to your beginning
- By recommending or proposing some kind of action

✍ *REFLECT. Identify two memorable openings and closings from a favorite novel, comic book, film, or social media post. What makes them so good? Do they follow one of the strategies presented here?*

VARYING YOUR SENTENCES

Read a paragraph or two of your writing out loud and listen for its rhythm. Is it quick and abrupt? slow and leisurely? singsong? stately? rolling? Whatever it is, does the rhythm you hear match what you had in mind when you were writing? And does it put the emphasis where you want it? One way to establish the emphasis you intend and a rhythm that will keep readers reading is by varying the length of your sentences and the way those sentences flow from one to the other.

A string of sentences that are too much alike is almost certain to be boring. While you can create effective rhythms in many ways, one of the simplest and most effective is by breaking up a series of long sentences with a shorter one that gives your readers a chance to pause and absorb what you've written.

Take a look at the following passage, from an article in the *Atlantic* about the finale of the *Oprah Winfrey Show*. See how the author uses a mix of long and short sentences to describe one of the tributes to Oprah, this one highlighting her support of Black men:

▶ Oprah's friend Tyler Perry announced that some of the "Morehouse Men," each a beneficiary of the $12 million endowment she has established at their university, had come to honor her for the scholarships she gave them. The lights were lowered, a Broadway star began singing an inspirational song, and a dozen or so black men began to walk slowly to the front of the stage. Then more came, and soon there were a score, then 100, then the huge stage was filled with men, 300 of them. They stood there, solemnly, in a tableau stage-managed in such a way that it might have robbed them of their dignity—the person serenading them (or, rather, serenading Oprah on their behalf) was

Kristin Chenoweth, tiniest and whitest of all tiny white women; the song was from *Wicked,* most feminine of all musicals; and each man carried a white candle, an emblem that lent them the aspect of Norman Rockwell Christmas carolers. But they were not robbed of their dignity. They looked, all together, like a miracle. A video shown before the procession revealed that some of these men had been in gangs before going to Morehouse, some had fathers in prison, many had been living in poverty. Now they were doctors, lawyers, bankers, a Rhodes Scholar—and philanthropists, establishing their own Morehouse endowment.

—CAITLIN FLANAGAN, "The Glory of Oprah"

The passage begins with three medium-length sentences—and then one very long one (seventy-two words!) that points up the strong contrast between the 300 Black men filling the stage and the "whitest of white" singer performing a song from the "most feminine" of musicals. Then come two little sentences (the first one eight words long and the second one, seven) that give readers a chance to pause and absorb what has been said while

The Morehouse Men surprise Oprah.

also making an important point: that the men "looked, all together, like a miracle." The remainder of the passage moves back toward longer sentences, each of which explains just what this "miracle" is. Try reading this passage aloud and listen for how the variation in sentences creates both emphasis and a pleasing and effective rhythm.

In addition to varying the lengths of your sentences, you can also improve your writing by making sure that they don't all use the same structure or begin in the same way. You can be pretty sure, for example, that a passage in which every sentence is a simple sentence that opens with the subject of a main clause will not read smoothly at all but rather will move along awkwardly. Take a look at this passage, for example:

> ▶ The sunset was especially beautiful today. I was on top of Table Mountain in Cape Town. I looked down and saw the sun touch the sea and sink into it. The evening shadows crept up the mountain. I got my backpack and walked over to the rest of my group. We started on the long hike down the mountain and back to the city.

There's nothing wrong with these sentences as such. Each one is grammatically correct. But if you read the passage aloud, you'll hear how it moves abruptly from sentence to sentence, lurching along rather than flowing smoothly. The problem is that the sentences are all the same: each one is a simple sentence that begins with the subject of a main clause (sunset, I, I, evening shadows, I, we). In addition, the use of personal pronouns at the beginning of the sentences (three uses of "I" in only six sentences!) makes for dull reading. Finally, these are all fairly short sentences, and the sameness of the sentence length adds to the abrupt rhythm of the passage—and doesn't keep readers reading. Now look at how this passage can be revised by working on sentence variation:

> ▶ From the top of Cape Town's Table Mountain, the sunset was especially beautiful. I looked down just as the fiery orb touched and then sank into the sea; shadows began to creep slowly up the mountain. Picking up my backpack, I joined the rest of my group, and we started the long hike down the mountain.

This revision reduces the number of sentences in the passage from six to three (the first simple, the second compound-complex, the third compound) and varies the length of the sentences. Equally important, the revision eliminates all but one of the subject openings. The first sentence now begins with the prepositional phrase ("From the top"); the second with the subject of a main clause ("I"); and the third with a participial phrase ("Picking up my backpack"). Finally, the revision varies the diction a bit, replacing the repeated word "sun" with a vivid image ("fiery orb"). Read the revised passage aloud and you'll hear how varying the sentences creates a stronger rhythm that makes it easier to read.

This brief chapter has only scratched the surface of sentence style. But we hope we've said enough to show how good sentences can be your allies, helping you get your ideas out there and connect with audiences as successfully as possible. Remember: authors are only as good as the sentences they write!

REFLECT. Take a look at a writing assignment you've recently completed. Read it aloud, listening for rhythm and emphasis. If you find a passage that doesn't read well or provide the emphasis you want, analyze its sentences for length (count the words) and structure (how does each sentence begin?). Revise the passage using the strategies presented in this chapter.

THIRTY-FIVE

Polishing and Editing Your Writing

IN PREPARATION FOR a 2018 Coachella performance, Beyoncé led her team through eleven-hour rehearsal days. LeBron James spends five to seven hours every day training in the gym (in addition to team practices). It takes a lot of hard work to make something look easy. Beyoncé rehearses, LeBron trains; what do authors do? We revise and edit.

Take this book, for example. It was written by experienced authors—skilled teachers and professional writers, all. The page that you're reading right now—how many drafts and revisions did it go through before it reached you? We lose count after three or four. The point is, completing a draft is a great accomplishment, and it's only the beginning.

One of the most important parts of your revision process is examining each sentence for structural problems. If you see the word "editing" and think only about "grammar rules," think again. Whatever else you may have learned about language "rules" and grammar, what they really are is a set of conventions, ways to facilitate successful communication. Suppose you're at a party when you get a text from the friend you came with that says "hom noe ok." Huh? You might be able to figure out that they want to go home, but you'll probably have to think about the message longer than you want to. If they had taken the trouble to check their words or put a question mark at the end, you probably would have understood their message more easily.

As a writer, you bear the responsibility for making things easy for your readers. In academic writing, the easier the better. We have two goals in this chapter: first, to help you make your writing clear and smooth so that readers won't have to wonder what you're trying to say, or question whether you know what you're talking about. Second, we want to help you make well-considered rhetorical choices, editing with your purpose and audience in mind.

Writing is always a work in progress; we can edit to smooth out bumps and wrinkles. Our team asked seventy-five writing instructors to point out the kinds of sentence structure problems that were most troublesome in two ways: they interfered with the smooth comprehension of the writing, or they damaged the writer's credibility.

The instructors' responses covered a wide gamut, from sentence structure to punctuation. This chapter focuses on those problems that matter, showing how to spot them in a draft, explaining why they're so troublesome, and suggesting strategies for editing them out. Editing your draft may seem like a daunting task after you've already worked so hard to produce it. Stay focused on and be guided by your rhetorical situation and your audience in order to prioritize which edits are most crucial to improve your work.

Throughout this chapter, you'll find opportunities for editing practice in adaptive activities called InQuizitive. For more information on how to get started with InQuizitive, see the access card at the front of your print book or visit *digital.wwnorton.com/everyone4r.*

A note about standardized English. Most of the advice that we offer here conforms to what's expected in standardized English, specifically, since that's the dialect that your rhetorical situation will call for in many academic and professional contexts. In the editing advice that follows, we're not so concerned with figuring out what's "correct" and "incorrect," but instead with revising and editing to end up with clear writing.

Some dialects of English express things differently from how they might be said in standardized English. For example, Black English, Chicano English, White working-class English, and other varieties often use the double negative ("they don't want no ketchup"), while standardized English uses only one negative element per clause ("they don't want ketchup"). Despite these distinctions, however, all dialects and varieties of English are more similar to one another than they are different. For example, to indicate the location of a screwdriver, you might say it's "in that box"; in no variety of English that we know of would you say it's "that box in." In this chapter, when you encounter the words "correct" or "appropriate," know that they refer to conventions that generally apply to all dialects and varieties of English.

Editing for inclusion. Before looking at specific sentence-level editing issues in any draft of an assignment, take a moment to consider how inclusive your language choices have been throughout it. Have you used gender-neutral language, for example, avoiding terms like "stewardess" that assume people holding certain jobs are all a single sex? Have you used SINGULAR "THEY" rather than "he" or "she," unless you are sure that the person you are referring to identifies as male or female (see pp. 742–43)? Whenever possible, have you used terms that groups use to describe themselves (such as the name of a specific tribe rather than "Native American," or "Deaf" rather than "hearing-impaired")? Your goal, as always, is to write with empathy and respect, speaking of others as you would have them speak of you. That's one of the golden rules of editing!

EDITING SENTENCES

Fragments, comma splices, fused sentences, and mixed constructions are all considered problematic sentence structures. Such sentences are usually comprehensible in context, so if readers can understand the message, what's the problem? Solid sentence structure matters for two reasons:

- The perception of your competence hangs on it: readers don't trust writers who write sloppy sentences.

- Even if a poorly structured sentence can be understood, your readers have to work a little harder to get there, and they may not want to put forth the effort. Your job is to make it easy for readers, to keep them reading smoothly all the way to the end.

Every sentence is composed of one or more CLAUSES, and every clause needs to have a SUBJECT, a VERB, and the expected punctuation. Don't underestimate those little dots and squiggles; they often make all the difference in how a sentence is read and understood. Consider these two examples:

▶ Let's eat Grandma.

▶ Let's eat, Grandma.

Are you inviting your grandmother to eat a meal right now, or are you inviting someone else to eat *her*? That one little comma in the right place can save Grandma's life (or at least make it clear to your readers that you aren't proposing to make a meal of her). The following advice will help you examine your writing with an eye to four common sentence-structure problems: fragments, comma splices, fused sentences, and mixed constructions. Fragments and comma splices can be very powerful and effective in certain situations; you may even notice a few in the readings we include in this book. They're not usually recommended, however, in more formal academic work.

Fragments

At first glance, a fragment looks like a complete sentence—it begins with a capital letter and concludes with end punctuation—but on closer examination, a key element, usually a **SUBJECT** or a **VERB**, is missing. For example: "Forgot to vote." Who forgot to vote? We don't know; the subject is missing. "Two bottles of rancid milk." Wow. That sounds interesting, but what about them? There's no verb, so we don't know. A fragment also occurs when a sentence begins with a **SUBORDINATING WORD** such as "if" or "because," but the **SUBORDINATE CLAUSE** is not followed by a **MAIN CLAUSE**. "If the ball game is rained out." Well, what happens if the ball game is rained out? Again, we don't know.

Checking for fragments

Sometimes writers use fragments for stylistic reasons, but it's usually best to avoid them in academic writing. To check your text for fragments, examine each sentence one by one, making sure there's both a subject and a verb. (It might take you a while to do this at first, but it will go much faster with practice, and it's worth the time.) Check also for subordinating words (see p. 709 for a list of common ones), and if there's a subordinate clause, make sure there's also a main clause.

Editing fragments

Let's look at some fragments and see what we can do about them.

NEEDS A SUBJECT

▶ The Centipedes were terrible last night. <u>Started late, played three songs, and left.</u>

Jessica Wildfire's artful style involves short sentences. Mostly they're complete, but a few sentence fragments are sprinkled in for effect. See if you can identify which are which; her essay is on p. 1024.

Context makes it clear that it was the Centipedes who started late. Still, the underlined part is a fragment because there is no explicit subject. We have two good options here. One is to add a subject to the fragment in order to make the sentence complete; the other is to attach the fragment to a nearby sentence. Both strategies work, and you can choose whichever seems best to you.

▶ The Centipedes were terrible last night. ~~Started~~ _They started_ late, played three songs, and left.

▶ The Centipedes were terrible last night, ~~Started~~ _because they started_ late, played three songs, and left.

In the first example, we've added a subject, "They," which refers to the Centipedes. In the second, we've attached the fragment to the preceding sentence using a subordinating word, "because," followed by an explicit subject, "they."

NEEDS A VERB

▶ Malik heard a knock on the door. <u>Then a loud thud.</u>

The example makes sense: we know that Malik heard a loud thud after the knock. But the underlined part is a fragment because between the capital "T" at the beginning and the period at the end, there is no verb. Again, there are two strategies for editing: to add a verb to the fragment in order to make the sentence complete, or to incorporate the fragment into the previous sentence so that its verb can do double duty.

▶ Malik heard a knock on the door. Then _came_ a loud thud.

▶ Malik heard a knock on the door, ~~Then~~ _followed by_ a loud thud.

NEEDS MORE INFORMATION

▶ Olga nearly missed her plane. <u>Because the line at security was so long.</u> She got flustered and dropped her change purse.

The underlined part of the example above does have a subject and a verb, but it can't stand alone as a sentence because it starts with "because," a subordinating word that leads readers to expect more information. Did the long security line cause Olga to nearly miss her plane? Or did the long line fluster her? We can't be sure. How you edit this fragment depends on what you're trying to say—and how the ideas relate to one another. For example:

▶ Olga nearly missed her plane*, because* ~~Because~~ the line at security was so long.

▶ Because the line at security was so long*, she* ~~She~~ got flustered and dropped her change purse.

The first option explains why Olga nearly missed her plane, and the second explains why she got flustered and dropped her change purse.

Edit

The word "if" leads readers to expect a clause explaining what will happen. Consider the following example:

▶ If you activate the alarm.

This example is a fragment. We need the sentence to show the "what-if": what happens if you activate the alarm? Otherwise, we have an incomplete thought—and readers will be confused.

▶ The whole lab will be destroyed. If you activate the alarm. Spider-Man, you can avert the tragedy.

Will the lab be destroyed if Spider-Man activates the alarm? Or will activating the alarm avert the tragedy? There is no way for readers to know. This example needs to be edited! You try. Edit the example above for both possible interpretations.

➥ For more practice, complete the InQuizitive activity on **sentence fragments**.

Comma Splices

A comma splice looks like a complete sentence in that it starts with a capital letter, concludes with end punctuation, and contains two **MAIN CLAUSES**. The problem is that there is only a comma between the two clauses. Here's an example:

▶ It was the coldest day in fifty years, the marching band performed brilliantly.

Both clauses are perfectly clear, and we expect that they are connected in some way—but we don't know how. Did the band play well because of the cold or in spite of it? Or is there no connection at all? In short, comma splices can leave your readers confused.

Checking for comma splices

Writers sometimes use comma splices to create a certain stylistic effect, but we recommend avoiding them in academic writing. To check your work for comma splices, look at each sentence one by one and identify the **VERBS**. Next, look for their **SUBJECTS**. If you find two or more sets of subjects and verbs that form **MAIN CLAUSES**, make sure they are connected appropriately.

Editing comma splices

What are the expected ways to connect two independent clauses? Let's look at some of the possibilities.

CHANGE THE COMMA TO A PERIOD

One of your options is to create two separate sentences by inserting a period (.) after the first clause and capitalizing the first letter of the following word.

▶ It was the coldest day in fifty years/. ~~the~~ *The* marching band performed brilliantly.

This might be your preferred choice if you want to write tersely, with short sentences, perhaps to open an essay in a dramatic way. Maybe there is a connection between the two sentences; maybe there's not. Readers will want to keep going in order to find out.

CHANGE THE COMMA TO A SEMICOLON

Another simple way to edit a comma splice is to insert a semicolon (;) between the two clauses.

▶ It was the coldest day in fifty years/; the marching band performed brilliantly.

The semicolon lets readers know that there is a definite connection between the weather and the band's brilliant performance, but they can't be certain what it is. The sentence is now correct, if not terribly interesting. You can make the connection clearer and even make the sentence more interesting by adding a **TRANSITION** (nevertheless, still, in any event; check the Glossary / Index for more examples).

▶ It was the coldest day in fifty years/; *nevertheless,* the marching band performed brilliantly.

ADD A COORDINATING CONJUNCTION

You can also insert a **COORDINATING CONJUNCTION** (and, but, or, nor, so, for, yet) after the comma between the two clauses.

▶ It was the coldest day in fifty years, *but* the marching band performed brilliantly.

With this option, the two clauses are separated clearly, and the word "but" indicates that the band played brilliantly in spite of the cold weather.

ADD A SUBORDINATING WORD

Another way to show a relationship between the two clauses is with a **SUBORDINATING WORD** (while, however, thus; see p. 709 for more examples).

▶ *Although it* ~~It~~ was the coldest day in fifty years, the marching band performed brilliantly.

Here, the logical relationship between the two clauses is clear and explicit, and the band's performance becomes the important part of the sentence. But what if you wanted to suggest that the cold weather was responsible for the band playing so well? You could use the same clauses, but with a different subordinating word, as in the example below.

▶ *Possibly because it* ~~It~~ was the coldest day in fifty years, the marching band performed brilliantly.

You may also want to experiment with changing the order of the clauses; in many cases, that will cause the emphasis to change. Sometimes, too, changing the order will help you transition to the next sentence.

▶ *The marching band performed brilliantly, even though it* ~~It~~ was the coldest day in fifty years, ~~the marching band performed brilliantly~~. Fans huddled together under blankets in the stands.

Edit

Consider the following example:

> Transit officials estimate that the new light-rail line will be 20 percent faster than the express bus, the train will cost $1.85 per ride regardless of distance traveled.

Try editing this comma splice in two ways: one that emphasizes the speed of the train and another that emphasizes the cost.

➡ For more practice, complete the InQuizitive activity on **comma splices**.

Fused Sentences

A fused sentence looks like a complete sentence at first glance because it begins with a capital letter, concludes with end punctuation, and contains two **MAIN CLAUSES**. The reason it is problematic is that there is no explicit connection between the two clauses. A fused sentence will make sense to readers most of the time, but most of the time isn't quite often enough, and you generally don't want your readers to struggle to understand what you're saying. A sentence can contain more than one main clause, no problem, but if it does, there needs to be some signal indicating how the clauses relate to one another. That signal could be a punctuation mark, a word that shows how the clauses are related, or both.

Checking for fused sentences

To check your text for fused sentences, look at each sentence one by one and identify any that have more than one **MAIN CLAUSE**. Then see how the clauses are connected: is there a word or punctuation mark that indicates how they relate? If not, you've got a fused sentence.

Editing fused sentences

Let's look at a typical fused sentence and some ways it can be edited.

▶ The fire alarm went off the senator spilled her latte all over her desk.

Perfectly clear, right? Or did you have to read it twice to make sure? This example is a fused sentence because it contains two main clauses but offers no way of knowing where one stops and the next begins, and no indication of how the clauses relate to each other. Here are some options for editing this fused sentence.

ADD A PERIOD

One option is to make the fused sentence into two separate sentences by inserting a period after the first independent clause and capitalizing the first letter of the following clause.

▶ The fire alarm went off. ~~the~~ *The* senator spilled her latte all over her desk.

Now you have two complete sentences, but they are a little dry and lifeless. Readers may think the two events have nothing to do with each other, or they may think some explanation is missing. In some cases, you may want to choose this solution—if you are merely reporting what happened, for example—but it might not be the best one for this example.

ADD A SEMICOLON

Another option is to insert a semicolon (;) between the two clauses.

▶ The fire alarm went off; the senator spilled her latte all over her desk.

This is another simple way to deal with a fused sentence, although it still doesn't help readers know *how* the two clauses relate. The relationship between the clauses is fairly clear here, but that won't always be the case, so make sure the logical connection between the two clauses is very obvious before you use a semicolon. You can also add a **TRANSITION** (nevertheless, still, in any event; see the Glossary / Index for more examples) after the semicolon to make the relationship between the two clauses more explicit.

▶ The fire alarm went off; *as a result,* the senator spilled her latte all over her desk.

ADD A COMMA AND A COORDINATING CONJUNCTION

In order to clarify the relationship between the clauses a little more, you could insert a comma and a **COORDINATING CONJUNCTION** (and, but, or, nor, so, for, yet) between the two clauses.

▶ The fire alarm went off, *and* the senator spilled her latte all over her desk.

Here the division between the two clauses is clearly marked, and readers will generally understand that the latte spilled right after (and the spill was possibly caused by) the fire alarm. With this solution, both clauses have equal importance.

ADD A SUBORDINATING WORD

One of the clearest ways to show the relationship between two clauses is by using a **SUBORDINATING WORD** (see p. 709 for more examples).

▶ *When the* ~~The~~ fire alarm went off, the senator spilled her latte all over her desk.

Adding the subordinating word "when" to the first clause makes it clear that the fire alarm caused the senator to spill her latte and also puts emphasis on the spilled coffee. Note that you need to add a comma after the introductory clause. You can also change the order of the two clauses; see how the emphasis changes slightly. Note, too, that in this case, you should not add a comma.

▶ The senator spilled her latte all over her desk *when* the fire alarm went off.

Edit

Using the editing options explained above, edit the following fused sentence in two different ways. Make one of your solutions short and snappy. In the other solution, show that the banging and the shouting were happening at the same time.

> The moderator banged his gavel the candidates continued to shout at each other.

↪ For more practice, complete the InQuizitive activity on **fused sentences**.

Mixed Constructions

A **MIXED CONSTRUCTION** is a sentence that starts out with one structure and ends up with another one. Such a sentence may be understandable, but more often it leaves readers scratching their heads in confusion. There are many different ways to end up with a mixed construction, and this fact alone makes it difficult to identify one. Here is an example of one common type of mixed construction:

▶ Décollage is when you take away pieces of an image to create a new image.

The sentence is clear enough, but look again at the word "when." That word locates an event in time—"I'll call <u>when</u> I get there." "The baby woke up <u>when</u> the phone rang." "<u>When</u> the armistice was signed, people everywhere cheered." In the example above, there is no time associated with décollage; the sentence is simply describing the process. To edit the sentence, replace "when" with a more accurate word, and adjust the rest of the sentence as needed.

▶ Décollage is ~~when you take~~ *the technique of taking* away pieces of an image to create a new image.

Checking for mixed constructions

Let's consider another example:

▶ Nutritionists disagree about the riskiness of eating raw eggs and also more healthful compared with cooked ones.

What? It's hard to even know where to start. Let's begin by identifying the **VERB(S)**. There's only one verb here, "disagree." Next, let's identify the **SUBJECT**. Who disagrees? "Nutritionists." Now we have a subject and a verb. What do nutritionists disagree about? It's clear enough that they disagree about "the riskiness of eating raw eggs," but after that, it gets confusing. Consider the next words: "and also." Also what? Do nutritionists also disagree that raw eggs are more nutritious than cooked eggs? Or is the writer claiming that raw eggs *are* more healthful? It's impossible to tell, which suggests that we have a mixed construction.

Editing mixed constructions

Let's look at a couple of ways we might edit the sentence about raw eggs. Here's one way:

▶ Nutritionists disagree about the riskiness of eating raw eggs and also
  about their healthfulness
  ~~more healthful~~ compared with cooked ones.

Notice that we added another "about," which makes it clear that what follows is also something nutritionists disagree about. We also added the suffix "-ness" to "healthful" so that the word would be parallel to "riskiness." Now the verb "disagree" applies to both "riskiness" and "healthfulness": nutritionists disagree about the riskiness of eating raw eggs, and they also disagree about the healthfulness of raw eggs compared with cooked ones.

What if the writer's original intention was to claim that raw eggs are more healthful than cooked ones? Since the two parts of the sentence express two different ideas, an editor might choose to simply make the mixed construction into two separate sentences.

▶ Nutritionists disagree about the riskiness of eating raw eggs. ~~and also~~
                                                      Raw eggs are
          than
  more healthful ~~compared with~~ cooked ones.

Just considering sentence structure, now we have two good sentences, but even though they both focus on raw eggs, the two sentences are not clearly connected. And besides, who is saying that eating raw eggs is more healthful? The author or the nutritionists? Adding just a couple of words links the sentences together and helps readers follow the ideas.

▶ Nutritionists disagree about the riskiness of eating raw eggs. ~~Raw~~ eggs
                                                      Some claim raw
  are more healthful than cooked ones.

Here we've added a new subject, "some" (which refers to nutritionists), and we've also given the second sentence a verb, "claim." Now the two sentences have a logical sequence and are easier to read. Next, let's look at one other mixed construction:

▶ Because air accumulates under the eggshell is why an egg stands up underwater.

This sentence is more or less clear, but its parts don't fit together properly. What can we do about that? Same procedure as before—first, look for the verbs. This time, it's more complicated because there are three: "accumulates," "is," and "stands up." Next, we look for the subject of each of the verbs. The first one is easy—"air" accumulates; the subject is "air." The third one is also simple—"an egg" stands up; the subject is "an egg." But what is the subject of "is"? That's not such an easy question with this sentence because its structure changes in the middle. So let's try a different approach.

What exactly is this sentence trying to say? It's clear that the point of this sentence is to explain why a submerged egg stands up, and we have two clauses: one that tells us that "an egg stands up underwater" and another that tells us that the egg stands up "because air accumulates under the eggshell." Now we just have to put them together in a meaningful way.

▶ Because air accumulates under the eggshell, ~~is why~~ an egg stands up underwater.

Did you notice that this version is almost exactly the same as the original sentence? The main difference is the words "is why"—which turn out not to be necessary. We now have one **MAIN CLAUSE** (an egg stands up underwater) and one **SUBORDINATE CLAUSE** (because air accumulates under the eggshell), with a comma in between. If it sounds better to you, you can reverse the order of the clauses, and the meaning stays the same. Note that you should not use a comma with this option.

▶ An egg stands up underwater because air accumulates under the eggshell.

We can use the same approach for a sentence that starts with a prepositional phrase but changes its structure in the middle: figure out what the sentence is trying to say, identify the phrases and clauses, and edit as needed so that you can put them together in a meaningful way.

> *Parents*
> ~~For parents~~ of children with a walnut allergy depend on rules that prohibit
> nuts in school.

Edit

Try editing the following mixed construction in two ways. First, make one sentence that includes all of the information in the example. Next, present the same information in two separate sentences. Which way do you like better? Why?

> One or two months before mating, male and female eagles together build their nests can be four or five feet in diameter.

For more practice, complete the InQuizitive activity on **mixed constructions**.

EDITING PRONOUNS

Pronouns are some of the smallest words in the language, so you might think they should be among the easiest. Well, no, they're often not. But the good news is that editing your work to make sure all your pronouns are used accurately is not too complicated. The advice that follows gives you tools for editing three common pronoun issues: pronoun reference, pronoun-antecedent agreement, and pronoun case.

First, let's clarify the terms. **PRONOUNS** are words that refer to other words or phrases (and occasionally even whole clauses). They're very useful precisely because they're small and they do a lot of work representing larger units. The words that they represent are their **ANTECEDENTS**. Most frequently, the antecedent is something or somebody that has already been mentioned, and standardized English has very specific conventions for signaling to readers exactly what that antecedent is so that they won't be confused. We call that **PRONOUN REFERENCE**. Let's suppose this next example is the first sentence in a news report.

> The Procurement Committee meets today to review the submitted bids, and she will announce the winner tomorrow.

Wait. "She"? "She" who? It's not clear what "she" refers to, and readers are now lost.

Pronoun **AGREEMENT** is another important convention. Pronouns have to agree with their antecedents in number (I, we) and in some cases gender (he, she, they, it). "Mr. Klein misplaced her phone again." If Mr. Klein is in the habit of losing a specific woman's phone, then perhaps the sentence makes sense. If it's his own phone that he misplaced again, then "her" doesn't agree with its antecedent, Mr. Klein, and readers will get confused.

PRONOUN CASE is a concept that you may never have encountered, but it's one that you use every day, probably without giving it any thought. For example, you probably say "I bought ice cream" automatically—and are not likely to say "Me bought ice cream" or "Coach wants I to play shortstop." Those two pronouns—"I" and "me"—refer to the same person, but they're not interchangeable. Still, most of the time we automatically choose the expected one for the specific context.

Pronoun Reference

Unclear pronoun reference occurs when readers can't be certain what a **PRONOUN** refers to. Usually this confusion arises when there are several possibilities in the same sentence (or sometimes in the previous sentence). Here's an example: Andrew and Glen competed fiercely for the office of treasurer, but in the end, he won handily. If Andrew and Glen both identify as male, the pronoun "he" could refer to either one of them, so who was it that won? We don't know.

Checking for unclear pronoun reference

To check for unclear pronoun reference, you need to first identify each pronoun and then make sure that it points very clearly to its **ANTECEDENT**. Often, the meanings of the words provide clues about what the pronoun refers to—but not always. Let's look at three sentences that have very similar structures.

▶ My grandparents ordered pancakes because <u>they</u> weren't very hungry.

First, we identify the pronouns: "my" and "they." "My" clearly refers to the writer, but what about "they"? Although both "pancakes" and "grandparents" are possible antecedents for "they," we know that the pronoun here has to refer to grandparents because pancakes don't get hungry. Now let's look at another sentence:

▶ My grandparents ordered pancakes because <u>they</u> weren't very expensive.

This sentence is almost identical to the first one and has the same pronoun, "they," but this time, the antecedent has to be "pancakes" because there is no price on grandparents. Antecedents aren't always so obvious, however. For example:

▶ My grandparents like playing cards with their neighbors because <u>they</u> aren't very competitive.

Wait. Who's not very competitive here? The grandparents or the neighbors? Or maybe all of them? We really can't be sure.

Editing unclear pronoun reference

Let's look again at the last example:

▶ My grandparents like playing cards with their neighbors because they aren't very competitive.

To edit this sentence, our best option may be to change the structure, and there are several possibilities:

▶ My grandparents like playing cards with their neighbors, ~~because they~~ *who* aren't very competitive.

This option makes clear that the neighbors are the ones who aren't very competitive.

▶ My grandparents, like playing cards with their neighbors, *who aren't very competitive,* *who are also not too* ~~because they aren't very~~ competitive.

Now we know that everybody mentioned here is noncompetitive. You may not think the sentence sounds as good as the original, but at least the meaning is clear. And of course there are usually other options.

The most important objective is to make clear what word or words each pronoun refers to. You don't want to leave your readers guessing. Here is one more example:

▶ After months of posturing and debate, those planning the expensive new football stadium suspended the project, which students loudly celebrated.

What is the antecedent for "which" in this example? You probably interpret this sentence to say that the students celebrated the suspension of the plans to build the stadium, but in fact, that's not really clearly established in the sentence. Another plausible interpretation is that the students celebrated the building of the stadium. Let's reword the sentence and remove "which" in order to make the meaning perfectly clear.

▶ After months of posturing and debate, those planning the expensive new football stadium suspended the project, ~~which~~ *and* students loudly celebrated *the news*.

Edit

The following sentence uses the words "it" and "which" to refer to . . . well, it's not exactly clear what they refer to.

A temperature inversion happens when a layer of warmer air is positioned above a layer of cooler air, which is not how it usually occurs.

You have several options here that would make this sentence better, but try this one: rewrite the sentence to eliminate the need for any pronoun at all.

➤ For more practice, complete the InQuizitive activity on **unclear pronoun references**.

Pronoun-Antecedent Agreement

Pronoun-antecedent agreement means that every **PRONOUN** has to agree with its **ANTECEDENT** in gender (he, she, they, it) and number (singular or plural). Some sentences with pronouns that don't agree with their antecedents are relatively easy to understand, and usually readers can figure the meanings out, but they shouldn't have to do that extra work. For your academic writing, you'll want to make sure that all of your pronouns agree with their antecedents.

Checking for pronoun-antecedent agreement

To check for pronoun-antecedent agreement, you need to first identify the pronouns and their antecedents. Then you need to make sure each pronoun agrees with its antecedent in gender and number. Let's look at a couple of examples:

▶ Trombones might be very loud, but it was drowned out last night by the cheering of the crowd.

This sentence has only one pronoun: "it." "Trombones" is the only noun that precedes "it," so "trombones" has to be the antecedent. Do they agree? We don't have to think about gender in this example, but we do have to think about number. And that's a problem, because the numbers don't match: "trombones" is plural, but "it" is singular.

▶ The table is wobbly because one of her legs is shorter than the others.

In some languages, tables, chairs, and other inanimate objects have grammatical gender, but in English, they don't. The legs of a table are never referred to with masculine or feminine gender.

Editing for pronoun-antecedent agreement

In order to fix the trombone sentence, you can change either the antecedent or the pronoun to make them agree in number. In this case, it is clear that the first **CLAUSE** refers to trombones in general, and the second clause refers to a specific trombone at a specific event. Assuming that the more important part is the specific event, and that there was only one trombone, let's change the word "trombones" from plural to singular. We can do that easily in this case without really changing the meaning, although sometimes it might be more difficult to do so.

▶ *The trombone*
~~Trombones~~ might be very loud, but it was drowned out last night by the cheering of the crowd.

Both the pronoun and its antecedent are now singular; that is, they agree in number. Now let's consider several examples where gender is a factor. In the example about the table legs, we simply have to replace the feminine pronoun with the inanimate one.

▶ The table is wobbly because one of *its* ~~her~~ legs is shorter than the others.

Remember that some, not all, English pronouns specify gender (he, him, his; she, her, hers; they, them, their, theirs; it, its). Some languages have more gender-specific pronouns, and some languages have fewer, but let's just stick to English right now.

▶ My mom and dad have an arrangement about sausage pizza—
he picks off the sausage, and she eats it.

This sentence has three pronouns—"he," "she," and "it"—and it's quite evident that "he" refers to "dad," "she" refers to "mom," and "it" refers to "sausage." All the antecedents are clear. But what if we changed the cast of characters in the sentence to two men? It would be confusing to refer to each of them as "he," so we need a different strategy. One possibility is to use "he" to represent one of the men and to refer to the other man by name. Will that work?

▶ Paul and his brother have an arrangement about sausage pizza—Paul picks off the sausage, and he eats it.

Who eats the sausage? Paul or his brother? It's still not clear. In this case, our best option is to eliminate the pronoun and refer to both men explicitly both times.

▶ Paul and his brother have an arrangement about sausage pizza—
Paul picks off the sausage, and ~~he~~ _his brother_ eats it.

If you'd rather not repeat both phrases, and the arrangement itself is more important than which person eats all the sausage, you can try this option:

▶ Paul and his brother have an arrangement about sausage pizza—
~~Paul~~ _one of them_ picks off the sausage, and ~~he~~ _the other one_ eats it.

Now we've got it; everything is clear. As this last edit shows, making pronouns and antecedents agree sometimes requires reworking the structure of a sentence and, occasionally, even modifying what it says. Pronouns may be small words, but getting them right is hugely important; don't be afraid to make changes in your writing.

Now let's look at some other contexts where making pronouns agree in gender with their antecedents can be complicated. We'll start with one that's pretty straightforward.

▶ Trey noticed a sunflower growing along the path; he grabbed his phone and took a picture of it.

We know that Trey identifies as male—"he," "his"—and the flower, of course, is inanimate—"it." In academic writing, inanimate objects are always referred to as "it." What about animals? If you know the sex of an animal, then by all means, refer to it as "he" or "she." If you don't know the sex, or if the sex isn't pertinent, just use "it." Also, it is becoming more common for people to specify (or ask one another about) their pronouns—in person, in email signatures, in social media bios—a practice that is in response to increasing flexibility about gender identity. Some individuals opt to be referred to as "they," a usage that transforms "they" from its conventional usage as plural to a singular pronoun of unspecified gender. Other people may use other pronouns, such as "ze"/"hir"/"hirs." We recommend that, whenever possible, you use individuals' specified pronouns in your writing about them. And what if you're writing about a person whose gender identity you don't know? That happens, and that's when it can get complicated. For example:

Pronouns are, in fact, a topic of debate. See Dennis Baron's take in his essay "What's Your Pronoun?" on p. 844.

▶ Anyone who gets three speeding tickets in a year will lose <u>his</u> license.

What's wrong with this example? Plenty, unless only men have such a license. If what you are writing applies to both women and men, your pronouns should reflect that reality. One of the easiest solutions is to use plural nouns and pronouns because they do not specify gender:

▶ ~~Anyone~~ **Drivers** who ~~gets~~ **get** three speeding tickets in a year will lose ~~his license~~ **their licenses**.

You may need to tinker a bit with the structure, but the message can remain the same. Another option is to revise the sentence altogether. Here's one possibility:

▶ Getting three speeding tickets in a year will result in the driver's license being revoked.

Another possibility is to employ **SINGULAR "THEY,"** using "they," "them," "their," or "theirs" with a singular antecedent.

▶ Anyone who gets three speeding tickets in a year will lose ~~his~~ **their** license.

One more possible solution is to write "his or her":

▶ Anyone who gets three speeding tickets in a year will lose ~~his~~ **his or her** license.

This last solution is fine, although it can be awkward and is less preferred than the others.

Many of us use singular "they" this way in casual speech, and its use is becoming more and more accepted in most newspapers and magazines and other more formal contexts. Singular "they" is a very useful solution, but even though it's becoming ever more common, it's still not always accepted in academic writing. Before you use it in your class work, you might check with your instructor to be sure it will be acceptable in their class.

Edit

Edit the following sentence in two ways. First, make both the pronoun and its antecedent singular; second, make the pronoun and antecedent plural. Both ways are acceptable, but which one do you think works better?

> Applicants must file the forms before the deadline and make sure that it's filled out correctly.

📤 For more practice, complete the InQuizitive activity on **pronoun antecedent agreement**.

Pronoun Case

Pronoun CASE refers to the different forms a PRONOUN takes in order to indicate how it functions in a sentence. English pronouns have three cases: subject, object, and possessive. Most of the time, we choose the expected pronouns automatically, as in the following sentence:

▶ I texted her, and she texted me, but we didn't see our messages.

This sentence involves two people and six distinct pronouns. "I" and "me" refer to one person (the writer), "she" and "her" refer to the other person, and "we" and "our" refer to both people. Each of the three pronoun pairs has a distinct role in the sentence. "I," "she," and "we" are all subjects; "me" and "her" are objects; and "our" is possessive.

Checking for pronoun case

You would probably not say "Me saw her" because it wouldn't sound right. In casual speech, though, you might hear (or say) "Me and Bob saw her." While you might hear or say that in informal conversation, it would not be acceptable in academic writing. Here is a simple and reliable technique for checking your work for case: check for compound subjects like "me and Bob" and cover up everything in the phrase but the pronoun. Read it out loud.

▶ Me ~~and Bob~~ saw her.

Does it sound good to you? Probably not. So how do you change it? Read on.

Editing for pronoun case

To edit for pronoun case, the first step is to identify the pronouns in each sentence. The following example has only one, "us":

▶ Us first-year students are petitioning for a schedule change.

Remember that the way a pronoun functions in a sentence is the key and that there are three possibilities for case. Is "us" functioning as subject, object, or possessive? In order to answer that question, first we need to identify the verb: "are petitioning." The subject tells us who (or what) is petitioning—in this sentence, "us first-year students." If you're not sure if "us" is a good choice, try it by itself, without "first-year students."

▶ Us are petitioning for a schedule change.

▶ *We*
 ~~Us~~ are petitioning for a schedule change.
 ^

We changed "us" to "we" here because it's the subject of the sentence and thus needs to be in the subject case. For more advice on choosing the correct case, see the table on the following page. Now let's look at two more examples: "Pat dated Cody longer than me." "Pat dated Cody longer than I." The only difference between the two sentences is the case of the pronoun, but that little word gives the sentences totally different meanings because the case lets readers know whether the person—"I" or "me"—is the subject or the object of the verb.

▶ Pat dated Cody longer than me.

Look carefully. There's only one verb, "dated," and its subject is "Pat." Now notice the pronoun: "me." That's object case, right? So, according to the example, Pat dated Cody and also dated "me." Try the next one.

▶ Pat dated Cody longer than I.

Here the pronoun is in subject case: "I." Even though it's not followed by a verb, the pronoun tells us that Pat dated Cody and so did I.

Subject	Object	Possessive
I	me	my/mine
we	us	our/ours
you	you	your/yours
he/she/it	him/her/it	his/her/hers/its
they	them	their/theirs
who/whoever	whom/whomever	whose

In some varieties of English, pronouns by case may vary from the table above. For example, "The twins do they homework at the kitchen table" would be a perfectly effective sentence in some varieties of Black English. In that example, "they" is a pronoun in the possessive case (and also in the subject case). In other words, specific pronouns used for each case may vary according to dialect, but all varieties of English use the same three cases (subject, object, possessive) in the same way.

Edit
Use the technique explained in this section to edit the following sentence for pronoun case.

> Iris was unhappy, but the judges called a tie and gave the award to she and Lu.

➡ For more practice, complete the InQuizitive activity on **pronoun case**.

EDITING VERBS

Verbs. Are any words more important—or hardworking? Besides specifying actions (hop, skip, jump) or states of being (be, seem), verbs provide most of the information about *when* (happening now? already happened? might happen? usually happens?), and they also have to link very explicitly to their subjects. That's a lot of work!

Because verbs are so important, verb problems are often easily noticed by readers, and once readers notice a verb problem in your work, they may question your authority as a writer. But if your readers can catch these problems, so can you. The following advice will help you edit your work for two of the most troublesome verb problems: subject-verb agreement and shifts in **TENSE**.

In quite a few varieties of English, the conventions for subject-verb agreement and verb tenses differ from those of standardized English. That doesn't mean that anything goes; there are conventions in every variety. Regardless of whether you are using standardized English or another variety, you'll still want to pay attention to your verbs and keep things smooth for your readers.

Subject-Verb Agreement

In English, every **VERB** has to agree with its **SUBJECT** in number and person. That may sound complicated, but it's really only third-person singular subjects—"runner," "shoe," "he," "she," "it"—that you have to look out for, and even then, only when the verb is in the simple present tense. Still, the third-person present tense is the most common construction in academic writing, so it matters. Take a look at this example:

▶ First the coach enters, then you enter, and then all of the other players enter.

The verb "enter" occurs three times in that sentence, but notice that when its subject is third-person singular—"coach"—an "-s" follows the base form of the verb, "enter." In the other two cases, the verb has no such ending. What's so complicated about that? Well, there are two kinds of subjects that cause problems: indefinite pronouns, such as "everyone" and "many," which may require a singular or plural verb even if their meaning suggests otherwise; and subjects consisting of more than one word, in which the word that has to agree with the verb may be hidden among other words.

Checking for subject-verb agreement

To check for subject-verb agreement, first identify the subjects and their verbs, paying careful attention to **INDEFINITE PRONOUNS** and subjects with more than one word. Then, check to make sure that every subject matches its verb in number and person.

Editing for subject-verb agreement

Let's look at a few common mismatches and see what we can do about them.

INDEFINITE PRONOUNS

Indefinite pronouns are words like "anyone," "each," "everything," and "nobody." When they're used as a subject, they have to agree with the verb. Sometimes that's tricky. For example:

▶ First the coach enters, then you enter, and then each of the other players enter.

We know that the subject of the first clause is "coach" and the subject of the second clause is "you," but what about the third clause? Is the subject "each"? Or is it "players"? You might be tempted to choose players because that's the word closest to the verb "enter," but that's not it; the subject is "each," an indefinite pronoun.

▶ First the coach enters, then you enter, and then each of the other
players ~~enter~~. *enters*

That "-s" at the end of "enters" is necessary in standardized English because the **SIMPLE SUBJECT** of the final clause is "each," which is singular. The phrase "of the other players" is additional information. Now see what happens if we change "each" to "all":

▶ First the coach enters, then you enter, and then ~~each~~ of the other *all*
players ~~enters~~. *enter*

Even though the two phrases—"each of the other players" and "all of the other players"—have essentially the same meaning, the word "each" refers to the members of a group individually so it is always singular and requires the verb to have the "-s" ending. "All" is plural here because it refers to a plural noun, "players." However, "all" is singular when it refers to a singular noun.

▶ <u>All</u> of the strawberries <u>were picked</u> today.

▶ <u>All</u> of the rhubarb <u>was picked</u> yesterday.

In the first sentence, "all" refers to "strawberries" all together, in plural form, while in the second sentence, "all" refers to "rhubarb," a **NONCOUNT NOUN**, which requires the singular form of the verb. **INDEFINITE PRONOUNS** can be tricky. Most take a singular verb, even if they seem plural or refer to plural nouns. These include the following: anyone, anything, each, either, everyone, everything, neither, nobody, no one, one, somebody, someone, something. A few indefinite pronouns are always plural: both, few, many, others, several. Some take a singular verb when they refer to a singular or noncount noun, but they take a plural verb when referring to a plural noun. These include the following: all, any, enough, more, most, none, some.

SUBJECTS CONSISTING OF MORE THAN ONE WORD

Sometimes a sentence has a subject with more than one word, so you need to determine which of the words is the one that the verb has to agree with and which words simply provide extra information. To do that, pull the subject apart to find which word is the essential one. Let's practice with this sentence:

▶ The guy with the mirrored sunglasses run in this park every morning.

The **COMPLETE SUBJECT** is "the guy with the mirrored sunglasses," but who is it that does the running? It's the guy, and the fact that he has mirrored sunglasses is simply extra information. You could remove the phrase "with the mirrored sunglasses" and still have a complete sentence—it might not be very informative, but it's not inaccurate.

To check for subject-verb agreement when a subject has more than one word, first locate the verb and then the complete subject. Then check each word in the subject until you find the one keyword that determines the form of the verb. Since the **SIMPLE SUBJECT** here—"guy"—is in the third-person singular, and the verb is in the present tense, the verb should also be in the third-person singular:

▶ The guy with the mirrored sunglasses ~~run~~ *runs* in this park every morning.

Let's try one more problem sentence:

▶ The neighbor across the hall from the Fudds always sign for their packages.

First, find the verb: "sign." The complete subject is "the neighbor across the hall from the Fudds." What part of that subject indicates who does the signing? Neighbor. Everything else is extra. Since it's just one "neighbor," the subject is singular, and since a third-person singular subject requires a present tense verb to have an "-s" ending, the edited sentence will be:

▶ The neighbor across the hall from the Fudds always ~~sign~~ ^{signs} for their packages.

Edit
The sentence below has four subjects and four verbs. One (or more) of the subjects is singular, so its verb should have an "-s" ending. Edit and make any necessary changes.

> All of the boxes need to be stacked neatly, and every box need to be labeled; the red box with the taped edges fit on top, and each of the boxes need its own lid.

In casual speech, you may not use the "-s" ending, or it may be hard to hear, so you may not be able to rely on your ear alone to edit this sentence.

↪ For more practice, complete the InQuizitive activity on **subject-verb agreement**.

Shifts in Tense

We live in the present moment; our ideas and our feelings are happening right now. Often, though, our present thoughts—and comments—are responses to things that happened in the past or that haven't happened yet. In conversation, we usually shift our verb tenses smoothly and automatically to account for actions that take place at different times, as in the following example of something you might hear or say:

▶ Flor <u>is</u> upset because Justin <u>informed</u> her that he <u>will not be able to come</u> to her graduation.

In writing, however, we need to take extra care to ensure that our tenses are clear, consistent, and suitable to what we're describing. In contrast to face-to-face conversation—in which tone of voice, facial expressions, and hand gestures help create meaning—writing has to rely on carefully chosen words. Verb tenses work hard to put complex sequences of events into context. The previous example has three clauses, each in a different tense: Flor *is* upset (right now); because Justin *informed* her (in the past); that he *will not be able to come* (to an event in the future).

Checking for shifts in tense

In academic writing, you'll often need to discuss what other authors have written, and the different disciplines have different conventions and rules for doing that (see p. 559). In classes that require you to use MLA style, for example, you'll rely heavily on the simple present tense:

MLA   Morton argues that even though Allende's characters are not realistic, they're believable.

Notice how "argues," "are not," and "they're" all use the simple present tense even though Morton's article and Allende's novel were both written in the past. If you mention the date when something was written, however, the verb should be in the past tense. In contrast, disciplines that follow APA style require that references to published sources and research results be stated in the past tense (or the present perfect, if the research isn't from one specific time in the past):

APA   Azele (2020) reported that 59% of the subjects showed high gamma levels.

Notice here that the two verbs in the sentence—"reported" and "showed"—are both in the past tense because both Azele's research and the report were done in the past. Be careful, though, because your sources may be writing about current or future conditions. If that's the case, be sure to preserve the tense of the original in your work, as the following example does.

APA   Donnerstag and Jueves (2019) predicted that another Jovian moon will soon be discovered.

Regardless of what class you're writing for, however, the most important thing about verb tenses is consistency—unless you have a reason to shift tense.

Editing confusing shifts in tense

Much of the editing that you do calls for sentence-by-sentence work, but checking for confusing shifts in tense often requires that you consider several sentences together.

Starting at the beginning, mark every **MAIN VERB**, along with any **HELPING VERBS**, in every sentence (remembering that there may be more than one clause in each sentence). Don't make any changes yet; just mark the verbs. Next, go back to the beginning and notice what tense you used each time. Examine each tense one by one, and when you notice a shift to a different tense, read carefully what you have written and look for a reason for the shift. If you can explain why the shift makes sense, leave it alone. Then move on to the next verb. Is it in the original tense or the new tense? Can you explain why? Continue all the way through your text, examining every verb tense and making sure that any shifts you find can be explained. Let's practice with two examples:

▶ Bates underestimated the public when she writes disparagingly about voters' intelligence.

First, we mark the verbs—"underestimated," "writes"—and we notice that the first is in past tense while the second is in present. Is there a clear explanation for the shift? No, not really. If you are using **MLA** style, you'll want to put both verbs in the present: "underestimates" and "writes." In **APA** style, past tense is the expected tense for both: "underestimated" and "wrote." In any case, there is no reason to use two different tenses in the sentence. Here is another example, this time a little more complicated:

▶ All of the guests ate the stew, but only two showed symptoms of food poisoning.

It's true that the events (ate, showed) in both clauses of the example occurred in the past, but can we be certain that the symptoms were a result of eating the stew? Could the guests have had the symptoms already? The sentence isn't really clear.

▶ All of the guests ~~ate~~ *had eaten* the stew, but only two showed symptoms of food poisoning.

By changing the verb tense in the first clause to the past perfect (the tense used to indicate that an action was completed before another action in the past began), we show clearly that the stew was eaten before the food poisoning occurred. (We may never know what caused the illness, but at least we know the sequence of events.)

Edit

Edit the following sentence to eliminate any confusing shifts in tense. Assume that the writing has to follow **APA** format for verb tenses.

> Levi (2019) notes that the trade deficit decreases from 2005 to 2015, but he warns that the improvement may be reversed because the new treaty will go into effect in 2020.

➡ For more practice, complete the InQuizitive activity on **verb tense**.

EDITING QUOTATIONS

In academic writing, you are required not only to express your own ideas but also to incorporate the ideas of other authors. In a way, you are engaging in a conversation with your sources, whether you draw from Aristotle, Toni Morrison, or a classmate. Your success as a writer has a lot to do with how well you weave your sources' ideas in with your own without your readers ever having to wonder who said what. Editing your work for citation and documentation issues therefore involves two main tasks:

- incorporating any words of others that you quote into your text so that everything flows smoothly

- making sure the punctuation, capitalization, and other such elements are correct

The conventions for citing and documenting sources in academic writing are very precise—every period, every comma, every quotation mark has its job to do, and they must be in exactly the right place.

Incorporating Quotations

Whenever we quote something someone else has said, we need to structure the sentences that contain the quoted material so that they read as smoothly as any other sentence. As writers, we need to master our use of language in much the same way that musicians have to master their instruments, and in both cases, it's not easy. Just as musicians playing together in an orchestra (or a garage band) have to coordinate with one another in tempo, key, and melody, you have to make sure that your words and those of others that you quote fit together smoothly.

Checking to see that quotations are incorporated smoothly

One good way to begin checking a draft to see how well any quotations have been incorporated is to read it aloud, or better yet, get someone else to read it aloud to you. If the reader (you or someone else) stumbles over a passage and has to go back and read the sentence again, you can be fairly certain that some changes are necessary. We can practice with some sentences that quote the following passage from a 2013 *Atlantic* article about fast food:

> Introduced in 1991, the McLean Deluxe was perhaps the boldest single effort the food industry has ever undertaken to shift the masses to healthier eating.
>
> —DAVID FREEDMAN, "How Junk Food Can End Obesity"

Assume that you might not want or need to quote the entire passage, so you incorporate just one part of Freedman's sentence into one of your sentences, as follows:

▶ Freedman refers to a failed McDonald's menu item "the McLean Deluxe was perhaps the food industry's boldest single effort to shift the masses to healthier eating."

If you read the sentence aloud, you probably notice that it is awkwardly structured and even hard to understand. Also, do you notice that the quoted section doesn't exactly match the author's words? Some of the words from the original are missing and some others have been added. Changing an author's words in a quoted section is only allowed if the original meaning is not altered in any way. Also, you need to indicate to your readers that you've modified the author's words. Let's see how we can go about fixing these things.

Editing sentences that include quotations

There are two ways of smoothly incorporating quoted material. One strategy is to adjust your own words to accommodate the quoted material;

another is to lightly modify the quoted material to fit your sentence. Here's one way we might edit our sentence by adjusting our own words:

> ~~Freedman refers~~ *Referring* to a failed McDonald's menu item, *Freedman notes that* "the McLean Deluxe was perhaps the food industry's boldest single effort to shift the masses to healthier eating."

Let's look at what we did. First, we changed the first two words. The meaning didn't change; only the structure did. Then, we added a **SIGNAL PHRASE** (Freedman notes that) to introduce the quoted words.

So far so good. But what about the places where we changed the author's words? If you modify an author's words, you need to signal to your readers what changes you've made, and there are precise conventions for doing that.

Enclose anything you add or change within the quotation itself in square brackets (**[ ]**), and insert ellipses (**. . .**) to show where any content from the original has been omitted.

> Referring to a failed McDonald's menu item, Freedman notes that "the McLean Deluxe was perhaps the **[**food industry's**]** boldest single effort . . . to shift the masses to healthier eating."

With minimal changes, the sentence now has all the necessary parts and reads smoothly. Note the two things we've done to modify the quotation. We've enclosed the words we added—"food industry's"—in square brackets, and we've inserted ellipses in place of the six words that were omitted from Freedman's sentence. It's worth repeating here that it is only permissible to add or delete words if the meaning of the quotation isn't substantially altered.

Edit

Here is another sentence based on the Freedman passage:

> Freedman talks about an earlier effort the McLean Deluxe by McDonald's was perhaps the boldest try to shift the masses to healthier eating.

First, you'll have to make a few changes to help the sentence read smoothly. There are several ways to do that, but try to make as few changes as possible.

Once the sentence reads smoothly, compare it with the original passage to see where you might need square brackets (for added material) or ellipses (to show where words have been removed). By the way, you don't have to put "McLean Deluxe" in quotation marks because it was not a term coined by Freedman.

➦ For more practice, complete the InQuizitive activity on **incorporating quotations**.

Punctuating Quotations

Citation conventions exist to help us clearly distinguish our words from the words of our sources, and one way we do that is by punctuating quotations carefully. When you quote someone's exact words, you need to attend to four elements: quotation marks, capitalization, commas, and end punctuation. These elements let your readers know which words are yours and which are the words of someone else.

Checking to see how any quoted material is punctuated
Here is another sentence taken from the *Atlantic* article about fast food; let's use it in a variety of ways in order to show how to capitalize and punctuate sentences that quote from this passage.

> A slew of start-ups are trying to find ways of producing fresh, local, unprocessed meals quickly and at lower cost.
> —DAVID FREEDMAN, "How Junk Food Can End Obesity"

You might write a sentence such as this one:

▶ It may one day be possible to get fast food that is healthy and affordable since a slew of start-ups are trying to find ways, according to David Freedman.

Structurally, the sentence is fine, but it includes a direct quotation from Freedman without letting readers know which words are his and which are yours. Even if you used Freedman's exact words accidentally, it would still be PLAGIARISM, which may carry a stiff penalty. The sentence needs to be edited.

Editing quotations to indicate who said what

There are numerous ways to edit the above sentence to make clear who said what. Here is one option:

▶ It may one day be possible to get fast food that is healthy and
    affordable. ~~since~~ *According to David Freedman,* "A slew of start-ups are trying to find ways/." ~~according to Freedman.~~

What changed? First, we added quotation marks to enclose Freedman's exact words. Second, we broke the sentence into two and started the second one with the signal phrase "According to Freedman," followed by a comma. Third, we capitalized the first letter of the quotation. Since "A" was capitalized in the original quotation, no brackets are necessary. Finally, notice the period. The sentence ends with the quoted material, so the period goes inside the quotation marks. Now let's look at how you might go about editing another sentence.

▶ Freedman asserts that many new businesses are working to develop fresh, local, unprocessed meals quickly and at lower cost.

Check your four elements. First, insert any necessary quotation marks; make sure they enclose Freedman's exact words. Second, is any additional capitalization necessary? If so, capitalize the appropriate word(s). Third, if there's a **SIGNAL PHRASE** before the quoted material, does it need to be followed by a comma? Finally, make sure any end punctuation is in the right place. Try editing the sentence yourself before you look at the following revision.

▶ Freedman asserts that many new businesses are working to develop "fresh, local, unprocessed meals quickly and at lower cost."

The quoted portion is not a complete sentence, and we placed it in the middle of ours, so no capitalization was necessary. We didn't insert a comma because his words flow smoothly within the larger sentence. Since the sentence ends with the quoted material, we put the period inside the quotation marks.

Depending on the documentation style that you are using, you may need to provide parenthetical information at the end of any sentences that include quoted material. Some styles require that you name the author(s) if you haven't named them earlier in the sentence, along with the page number(s) where their words appeared. Here's how you would do so in MLA and APA style requirements.

MLA   Freedman asserts that many new businesses are working to develop "fresh, local, unprocessed meals quickly and at lower cost" (82).

APA   Freedman asserted that many new businesses are working to develop "fresh, local, unprocessed meals quickly and at lower cost" (2013, p. 82).

One more important point: notice that with parenthetical documentation, the final period of the sentence is no longer inside the quotation marks; it is after the parentheses.

Edit

The following sentences cite the passage from Freedman's essay; they need to be formatted properly in order to read smoothly and also to show more clearly which words are the writer's and which are Freedman's. Remember the four elements: quotation marks, capitalization, commas, and end punctuation.

> Healthy and affordable fast food may not be a reality yet, but we may not have too long to wait. As Freedman explains a slew of start-ups are trying to find ways to bring such meals to market.

It is possible to edit the sentence using only the four elements and not adding, subtracting, or changing any words. Try it.

➡ For more practice, complete the InQuizitive activity on **punctuating quotations**.

EDITING COMMAS

Ideas are made out of words, right? So why should we care about commas? Well, here's why—they help those words make more sense. Nobody wants to have to read the same sentence two or three times in order to get it.

Well-placed commas can make your sentence clear and easy to read—and can keep the words (and ideas) correctly grouped together. Read this next sentence out loud:

▶ The boxer exhausted and pounded on wearily left the ring.

Did you start off expecting to read about the boxer's opponent who was getting "exhausted and pounded on"? Did you have to go back and start over? Bet you did. Well-placed commas would have immediately pointed us all in the right direction—like this:

▶ The boxer, exhausted and pounded on, wearily left the ring.

There are a lot of ways to err with commas. You might omit one that's necessary or place one where it doesn't belong. Even professional writers sometimes have trouble deciding where (and where not) to put a comma, and it's not always a big deal. The advice that follows will show you how to edit your work for two of the comma problems that matter most in academic writing: the commas that set off introductory information and the commas that distinguish between essential and nonessential information.

Introductory Information

English sentences generally begin with a **SUBJECT**. Those of us who read and write in English have an expectation that the first thing we read in a sentence will be its subject. Often, however (like right now), we begin a sentence in a different way. In academic writing especially, we might vary the structure of our sentences just to make our writing interesting. One way we vary our sentences is by starting some of them with introductory words, phrases, or even clauses. And usually we use a comma to set off those introductory words. That comma signals to readers that they haven't gotten to the subject yet; what they are seeing is additional information that is important enough to go first. For example:

▶ In Georgia, Lee's book jumped quickly to the top of the best-seller list.

Without the comma, readers might think the author's name was Georgia Lee, and they would get very lost in the sentence. Introductory words don't always cause so much confusion; in fact, some authors omit the comma if the introductory element is very short (one, two, or three words). Still, adding the comma after the introductory information is never wrong and demonstrates the care you take with your work.

Checking for commas after introductory information

▶ Initially the council proposed five miles of new bike paths; they later revised the proposal.

To check for introductory information, you should first identify the **VERB**—in this case, "proposed." Now what's the subject? (In other words, who or what proposed?) The subject here is "the council." Everything that goes before the subject is introductory information, so the comma goes between that information and the subject.

▶ Initially, the council proposed five miles of new bike paths; they later revised the proposal.

In the example above, the introductory element is only one word, and the comma could have been omitted, but its presence adds a little extra emphasis to the word "initially," and in fact, that emphasis is probably why the author chose to put that word at the beginning, before the subject. The comma definitely helps. And sometimes, introductory elements can cause confusion:

▶ Tired and discouraged by the unsuccessful search for the fugitive Sgt. Drexler the detective and her squad returned to headquarters.

In this example, the introductory information is much longer, and without a well-placed comma, readers have no way of knowing if Sgt. Drexler is the name of the fugitive, the name of the detective, or someone else entirely. Let's imagine that Drexler is the fugitive. With one well-placed comma, the sentence is now perfectly clear.

▶ Tired and discouraged by the unsuccessful search for the fugitive Sgt. Drexler, the detective and her squad returned to headquarters.

Editing for commas after introductory information

Let's take a look at a few examples to see how we can figure out where to put commas with introductory elements. The following sentence needs a comma; where should it go?

▶ For the first three scoreless innings Clark struggled to stay awake.

How do you know where to put the comma? Let's follow the steps described in this chapter. First, identify the verb: "struggled." Next, identify the subject—in other words, who or what struggled? The subject here is "Clark," and everything that precedes it is introductory information.

▶ For the first three scoreless innings, Clark struggled to stay awake.

Here is one more example. Follow the same procedure to determine where to put the comma.

▶ In the chaotic final episode of season 2 the shocking plot twists left viewers breathless.

In this example, the comma should go after "2"; the verb in the sentence is "left," and the **COMPLETE SUBJECT** is "the shocking plot twists." Everything that goes before the subject is introductory information, so the comma falls between that information and the subject:

▶ In the chaotic final episode of season 2, the shocking plot twists left viewers breathless.

Edit

Try editing the following sentence by inserting a comma after the introductory information. Remember the technique: first, find the verb; second, find the subject. The comma goes before the subject because everything that precedes it is introductory information.

Behind the parade marshal and the color guard the sponsors' convertible carrying the Founders' Day Queen will proceed along Blossom Boulevard.

▶ For more practice, complete the InQuizitive activities on **commas**.

Essential and Nonessential Information

What do we mean by **ESSENTIAL** and **NONESSENTIAL** information? The simplest way to explain the difference is with examples.

▶ My sister Jamilah graduates on Saturday.

If the writer has more than one sister, the name "Jamilah" tells us which one; that's important to know because we don't want to congratulate the wrong sister. Therefore, her name is essential information. When the information is essential, it should not be set off with commas. But if the writer has only one sister, writing her name there is simply extra information; it's not essential. When the information is nonessential, we set it off with commas:

▶ My sister, Jamilah, graduates on Saturday.

Checking for essential and nonessential information

To check your work for these kinds of commas, read over what you've written and identify the **NOUNS**. When a noun—"stadium," "achievement," "amino acids," whatever—is followed immediately by additional information about it, ask yourself if the information is essential: does it tell you which stadium, which achievement, which amino acids? If so, it shouldn't be set off with commas. If, however, the information is nonessential, and the sentence would still be fine without that information, it should be set off with a pair of commas. Let's examine two examples:

▶ The neighbors, who complained about parking, called a meeting to discuss the problem.

▶ The neighbors who complained about parking called a meeting to discuss the problem.

In these examples, the noun "neighbors" is followed by additional information. Which sentence talks about a situation where all of the neighbors complained? Which one describes a situation where only some of them did? Remember that the commas set off information that is extra and not essential. In the first sentence, the commas indicate that the information "who complained about parking" is extra, nonessential; it doesn't tell us which neighbors, so we can safely conclude that all of the neighbors complained. In the second sentence, the absence of commas lets us know that the information is essential; the clause "who complained about parking" tells us which neighbors called the meeting—only the ones who complained.

Editing commas with essential and nonessential information
Here is an example to practice with:

> ▶ Vitamins, such as B and C, are water-soluble and easily absorbed by the body; excess amounts are eliminated in the urine.

In order to edit the example, you will need to know if the phrase "such as B and C" is essential or if it's only additional information. In order to save you from looking it up, here it is: not all vitamins are water-soluble; some are fat-soluble and are stored in the body rather than quickly eliminated. Now, is the phrase "such as B and C" essential information? And if it is, should this sentence have commas? Here is the edited version:

> ▶ Vitamins/ such as B and C/ are water-soluble and easily absorbed by the body; excess amounts are eliminated in the urine.

Edit
The two sentences below are nearly identical; the difference is that one has essential information about its subject, while the other one's subject has extra information. Put commas in the appropriate places.

> Cardi B who will perform in the opening act will do her sound check at 5:30.

> The backup singers who will perform in the opening act will do their sound check at 5:30.

↪ For more practice, complete the InQuizitive activity on **commas**.

EDITING WORDS THAT ARE OFTEN CONFUSED

English has more than a million words, and any one of them could be used accurately or inaccurately—in a variety of ways, so no book could possibly help you edit all of the "wrong words" that might turn up in your writing.

A few basic strategies, however, can help you with many of those problems. Here you'll find tips for identifying a few of those in your own work—and then editing as need be. Although there are countless ways to get a word wrong, many such problems can be traced back to two causes: words that sound like other words (homophones) and apostrophes (which don't have any sound at all). Here's an example:

▶ Joe should of told them to buy there TV there because its cheaper and its screen is bigger.

Read that sentence out loud and it sounds exactly as the writer intended it; the meaning is perfectly clear. But your writing can't just "sound" right—it has to look right, too. In other words, the written words have to be correct. There are three "wrong words" in that sentence: "of," "there," and "its." Let's look at each one.

Of / Have

The useful little word "of," which is a preposition, sounds a lot like another very useful and common word, the verb "have," especially in rapid or casual speech. The two are often confused when "have" is used as a **HELPING VERB** with the **MODALS** "can," "could," "may," "might," "must," "should," "will," or "would"—especially in contractions, such as "could've" or "should've". How do you know if the word you need is "of" or "have"? Try reframing your sentence as a question. That should tell you right away which one is the right choice.

▶ Should Joe of told them?

▶ Should Joe have told them?

You can probably tell right away that "have" is the better choice. When you're editing, develop the habit of noticing whenever you use a modal, and make sure the words that follow it are the right ones. "Have" can be written out in its full form or combined with the preceding word to form a contraction—"should've," "would've." Try it without the modal. "Have you told them?" That's good. "Of you told them?" Not so good. That's because "have" is a helping verb, and "of" is not.

There / Their / They're

"There" is a common and useful word that sounds exactly like another common word, "their," and those two sound the same as a third common word, "they're," the contracted form of "they are." So not only do we have three homophones but also each of the three words is used very frequently in both speech and writing. That leads to a large number of "wrong word" problems. For example:

► For security screening, passengers must put all cell phones in the trays, and now <u>there</u> required to put <u>there</u> shoes <u>there</u>, too.

You'll notice three instances of "there" in the example, and two of them are "wrong words." The sentence should have one each of "they're," "their," and "there," so let's take a closer look at each use of "there."

THEY'RE

Let's start with the first one. That part of the sentence is trying to say that the passengers—"they"—are required to do something, so the right word would be the contraction of "they are": "they're." The word "they're" has only that one meaning, so using it is very simple. Just see if you can substitute "they are" for the word in question and still have the meaning you intended. If not, you'll need to make a change.

THEIR

Now let's look at the second instance of "there": "there shoes." That part of the sentence is talking about the shoes that belong to the passengers, so the expected word would be a possessive: "their." The word "their" has only that one uncomplicated meaning—it always indicates possession, as in the following examples:

► <u>Their</u> feet were swollen and <u>their</u> toes were numb, but the hikers were determined to reach Vogelsang before dark.

► The birds are squawking because the wind blew <u>their</u> nest down.

► Both of the radios still work, but <u>their</u> clocks are wrong.

When you're trying to decide if "their" is the right word, try asking if the word you are using is intended to show possession. In the examples above, "their" is correct because it indicates possession: Whose feet and toes? Their (the hikers') feet and toes. Whose nest? Their (the birds') nest. Whose clocks? Their (the radios') clocks.

THERE

That leaves us with the final instance of "there" in our example sentence. That "there" is correct. Most of the time, as in our example, "there" simply indicates a place, telling *where* something is: Where's my phone? It's there, on the table. Sometimes, though, "there" is used to introduce information that's provided later in the sentence. For example:

▶ Whenever <u>there</u> was a big snowstorm, the neighbors all helped clear the street.

▶ <u>There</u> are three candidates in the race, but only one has the right experience.

That meaning of "there" simply indicates the existence of something—a big snowstorm, three candidates. Here's an example that uses both meanings:

▶ <u>There</u> is a coatrack behind the door; you can hang your jacket <u>there</u>.

To check whether "there" is the right word, ask whether the word indicates either the existence of something or a place. If the word indicates either of those two things, "there" is the desired choice.

When editing your own work, check each instance of "there," "their," and "they're" to make sure that you've written the one you really mean. That may sound tedious, but here's a handy shortcut: use the Find function in your word processing program to search for each instance of "there," "their," and "they're." That way, you won't miss any.

Now let's revise our original example sentence. Try it yourself before you look at the edited version below.

▶ For security screening, passengers must put all cell phones in the trays, and now ~~there~~ required to put ~~there~~ shoes there, too.
　　　they're　　　　　　　　*their*

It's/Its

"It's" and "its" make for many "wrong word" problems. Although they're pronounced exactly the same, they really are two distinct words with distinct uses: "its" is the possessive form of "it," and "it's" is a contraction of "it is." That difference makes it easy to know which one is suitable for your sentence. Let's look at one problematic sentence:

▶ When my phone fell, <u>its</u> screen shattered, but luckily, <u>its</u> still working.

There are two instances of "its" in the sentence, but one of them should be "it's." How can you tell which is which? Check to see which one can be replaced by "it is." The second one—"it is still working." The one without the apostrophe, "its," is the possessive form of "it": the screen that belongs to "it" (the phone). So here's how you'd edit this sentence:

▶ When my phone fell, its screen shattered, but luckily, ~~its~~ *it's* still working.

Wait. Haven't you been told to use an apostrophe to indicate possessives, as in "the priest's robe," "the frog's sticky tongue"? So how can it be that the version *without* the apostrophe is the possessive one? "It" is a **PRONOUN**, along with "he," "I," "she," and "you," for example. What are the possessive forms of those pronouns? "His." "My." "Her." "Your." Do you notice that those possessives don't have an apostrophe? Neither does "its."

If you know or suspect that you have problems confusing "it's" and "its" in your work, you can check for them using the Find function of your word processor. Search your text for each of the two words, and make sure that the possessive "its" has no apostrophe and that the contracted form of "it is" always appears as "it's."

Edit

Return now to the first problem sentence at the top of page 763, and try editing it using all of the techniques discussed above:

Joe should of told them to buy there TV there because its cheaper and its screen is bigger.

➦ For more practice, complete the InQuizitive activity on **words often confused**.

PART VIII

Design and Delivery

ASKED TO NAME the three most important parts of rhetoric, the famous Greek statesman and orator Demosthenes is said to have replied: "Delivery, delivery, delivery." Not too many years ago, that assessment might have seemed overdone: Delivery, more important than content? Delivery, more important than the inventiveness of the message? Delivery, more important than style? But those were the last years in which print texts still claimed pride of place, when what mattered most was "put in writing," and when most messages came to us in black print on white pages. In these instances, the message was carried by words alone, and those words were "delivered" in print texts. Period.

But today, Demosthenes is right on target. With messages of every imaginable sort packaged in ever more alluring garb vying for our attention, just how those messages are delivered matters—a lot. So just what do we mean by "delivery"? For the purposes of this book, we have two senses of the word in mind.

The first refers to how the message is communicated: in what mode and through what medium. Mode refers to what makes up the message and communicates its meaning: words, sounds, gestures, still and moving images, or some combination of those. Medium is the form in which the audience receives it: these days, that's print, oral, or digital. So a political candidate delivering a campaign speech (the medium) might use words, gestures, and a series of images (the modes) to make a vivid and personal appeal to their audience.

But there's another important sense of the word "delivery," one that comes down to us through the history of human communication. This sense of the word refers to the performance of a text and captures the speaker's tone, pacing, and quality of voice as well as a full range of facial and bodily gestures and movements. In Demosthenes's time, such delivery was of paramount importance in connecting to an audience and gaining its assent, approval, or understanding. And given the near-universal use of the internet, where most people seem to spend a lot of time on a variety of platforms—in addition to the ubiquity of TV, film, and video—these elements of communication have become increasingly significant.

Savvy authors understand that messages today don't just lie there on the page and wait for readers to discover them. Rather, it's up to you as author to capture and hold the attention of your audience. For authors of texts in all media, that means paying careful attention to design. A text's design—whether it be the use of color and typefaces in a print text, the choice of music and moving images in a video, or the slides and handouts in an oral presentation—often determines your audience's first and lasting impressions. An effective design can draw the notice of your audience, keep their attention on your message, and help you achieve your purpose.

This section of *Everyone's an Author* aims to get *your* attention and to focus it on what delivery can mean for you as an author. The chapters that follow ask you to consider the choices you'll need to make as an author who is designing texts, and how those choices affect the delivery and reception of your messages. In addition, we examine the role of delivery in successful oral presentations, multimodal compositions, and when writing for a public audience.

THIRTY-SIX

Designing
What You Write

ESIGN. IT'S A WORD YOU HEAR ALL THE TIME, one you use without thinking about it. "American model Anok Yai walked the Met Gala red carpet in a dress designed by Oscar de la Renta and inspired by Josephine Baker, an American-born singer, dancer, and civil rights activist." "Have you seen the cover design for Anna North's new book, *Outlawed*?" "I designed my capstone project to appeal to potential employers."

Fashion, technology, architecture, toys: everything is designed, and that includes everything you write. A slide presentation, a social media post, an essay—you design it, whether you are conscious of doing so or not. You select a medium and tools: a lined notebook and a pencil, a text message and a smartphone, white paper and black printer ink. You choose typefaces and colors: big red capital letters for a poster, 12-point black Times New Roman for an essay. You think about including visuals: a bar graph on a slide, a cartoon in a blog, a photo in an essay. You consider whether to use multiple columns, bullet points, numbered lists—and where to leave white space. You decide what you want readers to notice first and how it should catch their eye.

This chapter discusses several key design elements: typography, color, visuals, and layout. Whatever typefaces, fonts, or images you choose, though, remember that they are not mere decoration. However you design a text, you need to be guided by your purpose, your audience, and the rest of your **RHETORICAL SITUATION**.

THINKING RHETORICALLY ABOUT DESIGN

Being able to design your writing gives you more control over your message than writers had in the past, when there were fewer options and tools. Your design choices can play a big role in the way your audience receives your message and whether your text achieves its purpose. Look, for example, at the different ways that Coca-Cola was advertised in 1913 and in 2021.

In 1913, Coke was relatively new, and its ads relied on words to introduce it to an audience that was not yet familiar with the drink, telling them it had "character" and was "delicious," "refreshing," and "thirst-quenching." The ad shown here was designed so that these words would pop and be easy to read.

To reach today's audience, however, advertisers use multiple media. In 2021, Coca-Cola's latest product—an updated version of Coke Zero Sugar— was heralded in Europe by a short video that featured people sipping Coke in colorful settings and then immediately breaking into dance, a dance coined the "Coca-Cola Kick Shuffle." Coca-Cola knew that dance challenges were popular on social media at the time, especially among young people. Featuring all kinds of people dancing along to an original song by a popular rapper, the ad was designed to appeal to those young people active on social media, with the hope the dance and song would go viral.

One thing the two ads have in common, though, is their logo. Whether it's in black ink on white paper or red and white pixels on a screen, the Coca-Cola logo was designed to be timeless and instantly recognizable.

A print ad for Coca-Cola in Georgia Tech's 1913 yearbook and a video ad featuring the "Coca-Cola Kick Shuffle" in 2021.

In designing what you write, think about how you can best reach your audience and achieve your purpose. Given the deluge of words, images, and other data, readers today are less likely than they once were to read anything start to finish. Instead, they may scan for just the information they need. So as an author, you need to design your documents to be user-friendly: easy to access, to navigate, to read—and to remember.

Considering Your Rhetorical Situation

- *Who is your* AUDIENCE, and are there any design elements they expect or need? Large type? Illustrations? Are there any design elements that might not appeal to them—or cause them to question your authority?

- *What is your* PURPOSE, and what design elements can help you achieve that purpose? If you're trying to explain how to do something, would it help to set off the steps in a numbered list? Is there anything that would work against your goals—using a playful typeface in a business letter, for example?

- *What's your* GENRE, and does it have any design requirements?

- *What's your* STANCE *as an author,* and how do you want to come across to your audience? Do you want to seem businesslike? serious? ironic? practical and matter-of-fact? How can your use of typefaces, color, images, and other design elements reflect that stance?

- *Consider the larger* CONTEXT. Does your assignment specify any design requirements? What design elements are possible with the technology you have available?

- *What* MEDIA *will you use*—print? digital? spoken?—and what kinds of DESIGN elements are suitable (or possible)? A print essay, for example, could include photographs but not video.

- *Consider your* LANGUAGE. Do the media you're using come with language conventions or expectations? Will you meet these or push against them?

Considering Accessibility

It's not just your rhetorical situation that will guide your design choices. It's equally important to compose materials that are accessible, welcoming, and easy to use for all readers, especially those with diverse visual, speech, auditory, physical, or cognitive abilities. Consider the following steps for creating accessible texts:

- *Provide* ALTERNATIVE TEXT *(alt text) for essential images and visuals in digital texts.* Alt text describes the content or meaning of a visual. People using screen-reader software will understand visuals only if you provide alt text for the software to narrate. Complex charts and graphs need not be described in detail; instead, provide alt text summarizing the main point: "A line chart shows that revenue grew incrementally from 20 percent to 60 percent between 2018 and 2022." If a visual is just decorative, no need to provide alt text.

- *Consider type size in printed texts.* Many readers require or prefer large type, so for printed texts, choose a type size that's easy to read. When in doubt, chose a large font size or provide alternative large-print copies. Large print is 18 point or higher.

- *Choose colors with high contrast.* When using multiple colors, choose ones that have a dramatic contrast (such as light blue against deep maroon) so that they are legible to everyone. And remember that some people cannot see the difference between certain colors (red and green, for example). Don't use color as the only means of conveying information. For example, underline URLs in addition to setting them in a contrasting color.

- *When giving a presentation, face the audience or camera* so lip-readers can see your face clearly, and keep your hands from blocking your face. Make available a link to or printout of your talk in a large font size. If your slides include important images or visuals, describe them out loud for those who may not be able to see them.

Our focus here is your writing, but design plays a key role in just about everything. If you need convincing, check out John Maeda's essay on p. 925.

CHOOSING TYPEFACES AND FONTS

A typeface is a distinct collection of styled text (Times New Roman, Arial), while "font" refers to different ways of formatting text (**bold**, *italic*). Authors today have hundreds of typefaces to choose from, and the choices you make affect the message your readers receive—so it's important to think carefully about what's most effective for your particular rhetorical situation.

Serif typefaces (those with small decorative lines, called serifs, added to the ends of most letters) such as Times New Roman or Bodoni have a traditional look, whereas sans serif typefaces (those without serifs) such as Arial or **Futura** give a more modern look. Your instructors may require you to use a specific typeface, but if you get to choose, you'll want to think about what look you want for your text—and what will be most readable. Some readers find serif type easier to read in longer pieces of writing. Sans serif, on the other hand, tends to be easier to read in slide presentations. Save novelty or decorative typefaces such as **Impact** or *Allegro* for your nonacademic writing—and even there, use them sparingly, since they can be difficult (or annoying!) to read.

Most typefaces include **bold**, *italics*, and <u>underlining</u> options, which you can use to highlight parts of a text. In academic writing, bold is generally used for headings, whereas italics or underlining is used for titles of books, films, and other long works. If you're following MLA, APA, or another academic style, make sure that your use of fonts conforms to the style's requirements.

Readability matters. For most academic and workplace writing, you'll want to use 10-to-12-point type, and at least 18-point type for most presentation slides. Academic writing is usually double-spaced; letters and résumés are single-spaced.

ADDING HEADINGS

Brief texts may need no headings at all, but for longer texts, headings can help readers follow the text and find specific information. Some kinds of writing have set headings that authors are required to use— **IMRAD** reports, for instance, require introduction, methods, research, and discussion headings. When you include headings, you need to decide on wording, fonts, and placement.

Wording. Make headings succinct and parallel. You could make them all nouns ("Energy Drinks," "Snack Foods"), all **GERUND** phrases ("Analyzing the Contents of Energy Drinks," "Resisting Snack Foods"), or all questions ("What's in Energy Drinks?" and "Why Are Snack Foods So Hard to Resist?").

Fonts. If you've chosen to divide your text further using subheadings, distinguish different level headings from one another typographically by using bold, italic, underlining, and capitalization. For example:

First-Level Heading
Second-Level Heading
Third-Level Heading

When you get to choose, you may want to make headings larger than the main text or to put them in a different typeface, font, or color (as we do throughout this book). But if you're following **MLA** or **APA** styles, be aware that they require headings to be in the same typeface as the main text.

Placement. You can center headings, set them flush left above the text, or place them at the left of the first line of text (as with the heading to this very paragraph); but whatever you do, treat each level of heading consistently throughout the text. If you're following MLA style, set all headings flush left. If you're following APA style, center first-level headings.

USING COLOR

Sometimes you'll be required to write in black type on a white background, but many times you'll have reason to use colors. In some media, color will be expected or necessary—on websites or presentation slides, for instance. Other times it may not work so well—say, in a thank-you note following a job interview at a law firm, or in an application essay to business school. As with any design element, color should be used to help you get a message across and appeal to an audience—never just to decorate your text.

Be aware that certain colors can evoke specific emotional reactions: blue, like the sky and sea, suggests spaciousness and tranquillity; red invokes fire and suggests intense energy and emotions; yellow, the color of our sun, generates warmth and optimism. Also remember that certain colors carry different associations across cultures—to Westerners, white suggests innocence and youth, but in China white is traditionally associated with death (which is why Chinese brides traditionally wear red).

Especially if you use more than one color in a text, you'll want to consider how certain colors work together. Look at the color wheel on the next page to see how the colors are related. Primary colors (red, blue, and yellow) create an effect of simplicity and directness. The more secondary and tertiary colors you use, the more sophisticated the design. Complementary colors, located opposite each other on the color wheel, look brighter when placed next to each other but can sometimes clash and look jarring. (Black and white are also considered complementary colors.) Cool and dark colors appear to recede, whereas warm and bright colors seem to advance. So using both cool and warm colors can create a feeling of movement and energy.

Remember that any color scheme includes the type, the background, and any images or graphics that you use. If colorful photos are an important

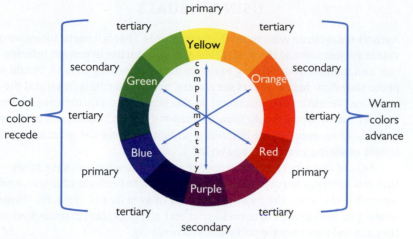

A color wheel.

part of your website, they'll stand out most strongly on a white background and with black type—both of which you may want to use for that reason alone. If you're writing a report that includes multicolored pie charts and want to have color headings, you wouldn't want to use primary colors in the headings and pastels in the charts. In short, if you use colors, make sure they work well with all the other design elements in the text.

Using color to guide readers. Like bold or italic type, color can help guide readers through a text. In fact, that's the way color is used in this book. The headings are all red to make them easy to spot, and keywords are color-coded a pale orange to signal that they're defined in the glossary/index. In addition, we've color-coded parts of the book—roadmaps are on yellow pages, readings are light blue, research chapters are green, style chapters are lavender—to help readers find them easily.

Color is an important navigational element on websites as well and is sometimes used to indicate links and highlight headings. For such uses of color, it's important to choose colors that are easy to see.

Considering legibility. Using color can make your writing easier—or harder—to read. Use type and background colors that are compatible. Dark type on a light background works best for lengthy pieces of writing, while less text-heavy projects can use a light text on a dark background for visual effect. In either case, be sure that the contrast is dramatic enough to be legible.

USING VISUALS

Authors today write with more than just words. Photos, charts, tables, and videos are just some of the visual elements you can use to present information and to make your writing easier or more interesting to read. Would a photo slideshow help listeners see a scene you're describing in an oral presentation? Would readers of a report be able to compare data better in a table or chart than in a paragraph? Would a map or diagram help readers see how and where an event you're describing unfolded? These are questions you should be asking yourself as you write.

Be sure that any visuals you use are relevant to what you have to say—that you use them to support your point, not just to decorate your text. And remember that even the most spectacular images do not speak for themselves: you need to refer to them in your text and to explain to readers what they are and how they support what you're saying.

Kinds of Visuals

You may be assigned to include certain kinds of visuals in your writing—but if not, a good way to think about what sorts of visuals to use (or not) is by considering your rhetorical situation. What visuals would be useful or necessary for your topic and purpose? What visuals would help you reach your audience? What kinds of visuals are possible in your medium—or expected in your genre?

Photographs can help an audience envision something that's difficult to describe or to explain in words. A good photo can provide powerful visual evidence for an argument and can sometimes move readers in a way that words alone might not. Think of how ads for various charities use photos of hungry children to appeal to readers to donate.

Photos can be useful for many writing purposes: letting readers see something you're **DESCRIBING** or **ANALYZING**, for instance, or even something you're **REPORTING** on. (See how Melissa Rubin needed to include a photo of the ad that she analyzes on p. 281, and how Katherine Spriggs included photos of two different kinds of farms in her argumentative essay on p. 186.) You can take your own photos or use ones that you find in other sources. Remember, however, to provide full documentation for any photos that you don't take yourself and to ask permission before photographing people and using their image in your writing.

A photo of street art in a Texas parking lot demonstrates the layering effect of graffiti in a way that would be difficult to do with words alone.

Videos are useful for demonstrating physical processes or actions and for showing sequences. Your medium will dictate whether you can include videos in a text. The print version of a newspaper article about aerialist skiers, for instance, includes a still photo of a skier in mid-jump, whereas the same article on the newspaper's website and on a TV news report features videos showing the skier in action. Your topic and genre will affect whether or not you have reason to include video if you can. If you were writing a **PROCESS ANALYSIS** to teach a skier how to perform a certain aerial maneuver, a video would be far more useful than the still photo you might include if you were writing a **PROFILE** of a professional skier.

Graphs, charts, and tables. Numerical and statistical data can be easier both to describe and to understand when they are presented visually. See the high school sports graphics on the following page, for example—and imagine trying to present that data in a paragraph. You'll often have occasion to present data in graphs or charts, in bar graphs, pie charts, and the like, especially in **REPORTS** and **ANALYSES**. In many cases, you'll be able to find tables and graphs in your research and then incorporate them into your own writing. You can also use templates found in *Google Docs, Word, Power-Point*, and other programs to create charts and tables yourself. Whether you find or create them, be sure to indicate in your text where the information comes from and how they support your argument.

Line graphs are useful for illustrating trends and changes over time—how unemployment fluctuates over a period of years, for instance. By using more than one line, you can compare changes in different variables, such as unemployment for those with a college education and those with only a high school education. When comparing more than one variable, the lines should be in two different colors so that readers can easily see the comparison.

Bar graphs are useful for comparing quantitative data, such as for different age groups or different years. In the example below about high school sports, the bars make it easy to see at a glance which sports are most popular among high school girls. It would be easy enough to convey this same information in words alone—but more work to read and harder to remember.

Pie charts give an overview of the relative sizes of parts to a whole, such as what share of a family budget is devoted to food, housing, entertainment, and so on. Pie charts are useful for showing which parts of a whole are more or less significant, but they are less precise (and harder to read) than

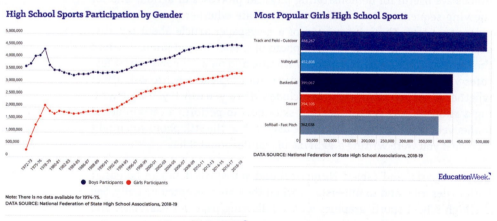

A line graph shows the rising rate of participation in sports over forty-plus years; a bar graph breaks down which sports are most popular with high school girls.

bar graphs. It's best to limit a pie chart to six or seven slices, since when the slices become too small, it's difficult to see how they compare in size.

Tables are an efficient way of presenting a lot of information concisely by organizing it into horizontal rows and vertical columns. Table 1 below presents data about social media use across demographic groups, information that is made easy to scan and compare in a table.

Maps provide geographic context, helping to orient your audience to places mentioned in your text. Reports on the dangers predicted by climatologists have much more impact when accompanied by visuals—maps showing which areas are most affected. For example, the contiguous US map on the next page shows how drought conditions have changed from 1900 to 2020,

Table 1

Who Uses Each Social Media Platform, 2021

Percentage of US adults in each demographic group who say they ever use . . .

	YouTube	WhatsApp	Reddit
Total	81%	23%	18%
Men	82%	26%	23%
Women	80%	21%	12%
Ages 18–29	95%	24%	36%
30–49	91%	30%	22%
50–64	83%	23%	10%
65+	49%	10%	3%
White	79%	16%	17%
Black	84%	23%	17%
Hispanic	85%	46%	14%
Income less than $30K	75%	23%	10%
$30K–$49,999	83%	20%	17%
$50K–$74,999	79%	19%	20%
More than $75K	90%	29%	26%

SOURCE: "Social Media Use in 2021," Pew Research Center, https://www.pewresearch.org/internet/2021/04/07/social-media-use-in-2021/. Survey conducted January 25–February 8, 2021.

US Drought Conditions, 1900–2020

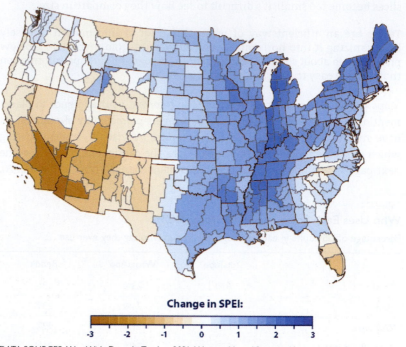

Change in SPEI:

-3   -2   -1   0   1   2   3

DATA SOURCES: WestWide Drought Tracker. 2021. Western United States—60 month SPEI. Accessed March 2021. https://wrcc.dri.edu/wwdt. Daly, C., M. Halbleib, J. I. Smith, W. P. Gibson, M. K. Doggett, G. H. Taylor, J. Curtis, and P. A. Pasteris. 2008. Physiographically-sensitive mapping of temperature and precipitation across the conterminous United States. Int. J. Climatol. 28:2031–2064. For more information, visit U.S. EPA's "Climate Change Indicators in the United States" at www.epa.gov/climate-indicators.

using a measure called Standardized Precipitation-Evaporation Index (SPEI), which tracks factors related to drought. The areas shown on the map are small regions called climate divisions, which is how this data is organized. The bluer the area, the more moisture has increased over the past century or so. The browner the area, the drier it has become. A white area indicates little change. This map shows, in a glance, how drought conditions have changed dramatically in different areas of the country over time. Include a map when a location is important to your point or will help show complex data conditions.

Diagrams are useful for illustrating details that cannot be shown in a photograph. A carefully drawn diagram can deliver a lot of information in a small amount of space.

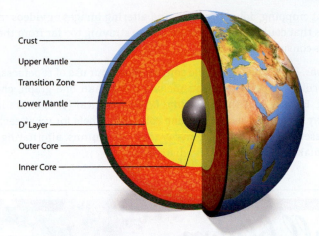

A diagram of the Earth's internal structure shows its various layers.

Infographics bring together several different types of visuals—charts, tables, photos, and so on—to give detailed information and data. They can help simplify a complex subject—or make a potentially dull topic visually interesting. Because infographics can be so densely packed with information, make sure that they are large enough for your audience to be able to read and arranged in a way that they can follow.

Creating Visuals

You can find visuals online, scan them from print sources, or create them yourself using basic software or a camera. If you come across an illustration you think would be useful, make or save a copy. Scan or photocopy visuals from print sources, and save a link or take a screen grab from digital sources. Label everything clearly. Be aware that visuals and any data you use to create them need to be **DOCUMENTED** in a **CAPTION** or source note—so keep track of where you found everything as you go. Remember that visuals in digital texts should include **ALT TEXT** so that they are accessible to all readers.

- *Photographs and videos.* If you plan to print an image, save each file in as high a resolution as possible. If a photo is only available in a very small size or low resolution, try to find a more legible option. Be careful about cropping, adjusting color, and altering images or videos in other ways that could change their meaning; straying too far from the original is considered unethical.

- *Graphs, charts, and tables.* Be consistent in your use of typefaces, fonts, and colors, especially if you include more than one graph, chart, or table. Be sure that the horizontal (*x*) and vertical (*y*) axes are labeled clearly. If you use more than one color, add labels for what each color represents. When you have many rows or columns, alternating colors can make categories easier to distinguish.

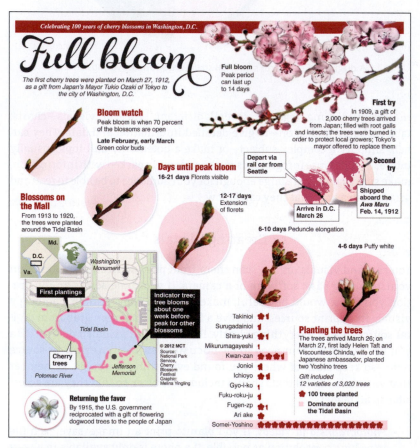

This infographic on the cherry blossom season in Washington, DC, includes photos, diagrams, maps, and a bar chart.

- *Maps.* Provide a title and a key explaining any symbols, colors, or other details. If the original is missing these elements, add them. If you create the map yourself, be sure to highlight notable locations or information.

- *Diagrams.* Use a single font for all labels, and be sure to make the diagram large enough to include all of the necessary detail. Make sure these details are clearly and neatly represented, whether they're drawn or created on a computer.

Introducing and Labeling Visuals

Introduce visuals as you would any other source materials, explaining what they show and how they support your point. Don't leave your audience wondering how a photo or chart pertains to your project—spell it out, and be sure to do so *before* the visual appears ("As shown in fig. 3, population growth has been especially rapid in the Southwest"). Number visuals in most academic writing sequentially (Figure 1, Figure 2), counting tables separately (Table 1, Table 2). If you're following MLA, APA, or another academic style, be sure to follow its guidelines for how to label tables and figures.

MLA STYLE. For tables, provide a number ("Table 1") and a descriptive title ("Population Growth by Region, 1990–2010") on separate lines above the table; below the table, add a caption explaining what the table shows and including any source information. For graphs, charts, photos, and diagrams, provide a figure number ("Fig. 1") and caption with source information below the figure. If you give only brief source information, include full source information in your list of works cited.

APA STYLE. For tables, charts, diagrams, graphs, and photos, provide a number ("Table 1" or "Figure 1") and a descriptive title on separate lines above the table or figure; below the table or figure, include a note explaining any elements whose meanings are not apparent in the table or figure and providing source information if the table or figure is adapted or reprinted from another source.

PUTTING IT ALL TOGETHER

Look for instance, at the homepage of *The Moth*, a nonprofit dedicated to sharing stories of humanity, because "stories are a vital tool in creating a world sustained by empathy, understanding, and community." It's easy to

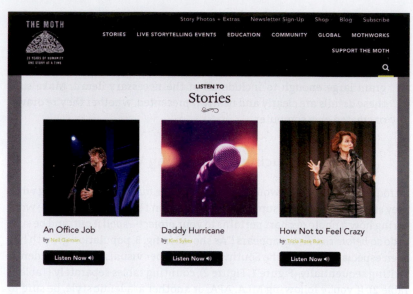

A page on *The Moth* website.

read—the information banner uses a white sans serif typeface and minimal text. The logo draws your eye because it's large and capitalized, has intricate texture, and is positioned in the upper-left corner of the screen. The smaller text under the logo, "25 years of humanity one story at a time," balances the logo and leads your eye to the text below it—"Listen to Stories"—which gets right to the site's purpose. Each of the images is a link to a specific *Moth* story. Note how white space separates the parts and makes the page easy to read.

You may not have occasion to design anything as large or complex as *The Moth's* site, but the same design principles will apply for all the writing you do. Whether you're designing a report, a photo essay, or a slide presentation, chances are you'll be working with some combination of words, images, graphs, and other graphic elements that you'll need to put on paper or screen in order to reach a certain audience to achieve a certain purpose.

Look beyond the details and think about what you want your design to accomplish. Do you want it to help your audience grasp a message as fast as possible? convey your identity as a creative author? conform to the requirements of a certain academic style? be appealing yet simple enough to implement by an approaching deadline? Thinking about what you want your design to do can help you determine how to put it all together in a way that achieves your end goal.

Keep it simple. Sometimes you'll need to follow a prescribed organization and layout, but if you get to decide how to design your document, here's a piece of advice: don't make your design any more complex than it has to be. Readers want to be able to find the information they need without having to spend time deciphering a complex hierarchy of headings or an intricate navigational system.

Think about how to format your written text. Should it all be in paragraphs, or is there anything that should be set off as a list? If so, should it be a bulleted list to make it stand out, or a numbered list to put items in a sequence? If your text includes numerical data, should any of it be presented in a graph, chart, or table to make it easier for readers to understand? Is there any information that's especially important that you'd like to highlight in some way?

Position visuals carefully. Keep in mind how they will look on a page or screen. Placing them at the top or bottom of a print page will make it easier to lay out pages. If your text will be online, you have more freedom to put visuals wherever you wish. Reproduce visuals at a large enough size so that readers will be able to see all the pertinent detail, but be aware that digital images become fuzzier when they are enlarged. Reduce large image files by saving them in compressed formats such as JPEGs or GIFs; you don't want readers to have problems loading the image. And once everything is in place, look over your text carefully to be sure that nothing is too small or blurry to read.

Use white space to separate the parts of your text. Add some extra space above headings and around lists, images, graphs, charts, and tables. This will keep your text from looking cluttered and make everything easier to find and read.

Organize the text. Whether your text is a simple five-page report or a full website, readers will need to know how it's organized and how to find the information they're looking for. In a brief essay, you might simply indicate that in a sentence in your introduction, but in lengthier pieces, you may need headings, both to structure your text and to make it easy for readers to navigate.

If you're creating a website, you'll need to figure out how you're dividing materials into pages and to make that clear on the site's homepage. Most homepages have a horizontal navigation bar across the top indicating and linking to the main parts. These menus should appear in the same position on every page of the site—and every page should include a link to take readers back to the homepage. Take a look at the examples from *National Geographic* on the following page and you'll see the consistent elements that help readers navigate the site: navigation bars at the top, links to popular information in bulleted lists, ads in the bottom right corner, consistent colors and typefaces on all the pages.

GETTING RESPONSES TO YOUR DESIGN

Whether you're composing a report, an illustrated essay, or a blog post, try to get responses to the design. Enlist the help of friends or classmates, asking them what they think of the "look" of your text, how easy it is to read, and so on. Following are some specific things they (and you) should consider:

- Is the design matched to the text's **PURPOSE**, **AUDIENCE**, **GENRE**, **LANGUAGE**, and **MEDIUM**? Consider the typefaces and any use of color: do they suit your rhetorical situation?

- Does the design make the main parts of your text easy to see? If not, would it help to add headings?

- Is there any information that should be set off as a list?

- Does the text include any data that would be easier to follow in a chart, table, or graph?

- If you've included images, what purpose do they serve? How do they support the point of your text? If some are only decorative, should you delete them?

- Does the overall "look" of your text suit the message that you want to convey?

Examples from the *National Geographic* website.

Remember: your design is often the first impression readers get, and it can make all the difference in getting your message across. There may be a lot at stake in the simple choice of a typeface or color or image, so make these choices carefully—and make your design work for you.

REFLECT. Find a design that you think is attractive (or not)—a book cover, a magazine spread, a brochure, a poster, a blog, a website, etc. **ANALYZE** *its use of typefaces, colors, and visuals. What works, and what doesn't? How would you revise the design if you could?*

THIRTY-SEVEN

Composing and Remixing across Media

Ever since the days of illustrated books and maps, texts have included visual elements for the purpose of imparting information. The contemporary difference is the ease with which we can combine words, images, sound, color, animation, and video . . . so that they are part of our everyday lives.

—NCTE ON MULTIMODAL LITERACIES

HE **NATIONAL COUNCIL OF TEACHERS OF ENGLISH** made this statement more than a decade ago, and in the years since, multimodal literacies have indeed become part of the "everyday lives" of students everywhere. Look at the cartoon on the next page, for example.

The little boy illustrates the NCTE statement perfectly: he lies in bed, listening to his dad read him a story. But the boy does more than just listen: he compliments his dad on his reading ("darn good job") and offers to record him reading and then "podcast" him on his website. Multimodal, indeed.

Defining Multimodal Writing

Multimodal texts draw on more than words, bringing in still or moving images, sound, and so on. Literacy researcher Cynthia Selfe identifies five modes writers can use to convey their messages: linguistic (words, written or spoken); visual (colors, fonts, images, and so on); audio (tone of

"You know, Dad, you do a darn good job.
You should let me record you sometime, and
I'll podcast you on my website. Just a thought."

voice, music, and other sounds); gestural (body language and facial expression); and spatial (the way elements are arranged on a page or screen).

For hundreds of years, writers relied primarily on two of these modes, the linguistic and the visual, so multimodality is nothing new. Today, writers have easy access to all five modalities and can produce texts that convey meaning not only through words but also with sounds, moving and still images, animations, and more—delivered through print, spoken, and digital media.

This access to multiple media also enables authors to remix their work or the work of others, to take the message conveyed in one mode and cast it in another. One of the most popular kinds of remixes happens when books are adapted into movies or TV shows. You've likely debated whether a book was better than its movie adaptation, or vice versa. Remixing often occurs in academic writing, too. Have you ever transformed a report or essay into an oral presentation or a poster? That's a remix! Researchers often try to find ways for their work to reach new audiences outside of academia by transforming their research into more popular forms for the general public, like podcasts, infographics, videos, and TED talks.

For authors today, access to all of the modes of expression (and the possibility of remixing them) opens up exciting options. This chapter offers some tips for making best use of the various technologies available for composing and remixing in multiple modes. But keep in mind that, just like traditional

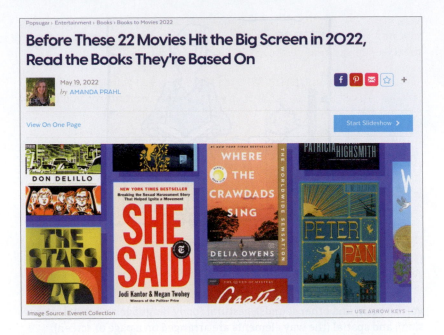

print texts, more complex multimodal ones call for careful attention to the same conventions of effective writing, research, and argument—primarily by staying laser-focused on your rhetorical situation.

REFLECT. Make a list of writing assignments you've done this term and of any writing projects you have worked on outside of class. How many of them rely on printed words on a page? How many use multiple modes—and what are they? How does each mode contribute to your purpose?

Considering Your Rhetorical Situation

Writing in multiple modes calls for the same close attention to rhetorical principles that all writing does. Whatever your topic, the following questions can help you think about your purpose, audience, and the rest of your rhetorical situation:

Consider your PURPOSE. Why are you creating this project? What are your purposes or goals? No doubt one purpose is to fulfill an assignment. You may also have other purposes: raising awareness about a problem on campus;

convincing someone to support a project you have in mind; providing information. Consider the message you want to communicate. What do you want to see happen as a result of what you write?

Think about your AUDIENCE. Who are they? How can you best reach them? If you're writing to all members of your campus community, you'll likely post your message online; if you're alerting neighbors about a lost dog, flyers might be better. If your intended audience is limited to people you know, you may make some assumptions about them and how they're likely to respond. But remember that most projects you put online will be accessible to the public—to people you don't and can't know. In this case, it's important not to make assumptions about what they know and to be respectful of the diverse audience that may read what you write.

Think about your STANCE. What is your attitude toward your topic, and how do you want to present yourself as an author—as well-informed? outraged? perplexed? How can you convey that stance? Certain typefaces look serious while others look silly; same thing with colors. If you're including music, that too affects the tone. If you're giving an oral presentation or creating a video, your facial expressions and gestures can signal something about your stance.

Choose your GENRE. The kind of writing you're doing can sometimes determine the form that your project will take. If you're REPORTING information, a podcast might be a good choice. But if you're delivering a PROPOSAL to ask for funding for an event, a print text may be most effective. And if afterward you want to create a NARRATIVE documenting the event, a video might capture the experience most vividly.

Consider the larger CONTEXT. How much time do you have, and is your topic narrow enough that you can do a good job in that amount of time? Do you have access to whatever technology you will need? If you'll need to learn new software, remember to build in time for that. Does your campus offer any services (perhaps at a writing center or at a media lab) where you can get help?

Consider MEDIA. What media will best serve your audience, purpose, and topic? If you're writing about Bollywood films, you might create a website, which would enable you to embed video clips and to reach a community of fans. If you want to inform fellow students about ways to save water, you might create an infographic to post in restrooms around campus.

Consider your LANGUAGE. Think about how your language and style might complement or challenge the conventions of your chosen media, and the larger context.

KINDS OF MULTIMODAL PROJECTS

Once you have assessed your rhetorical situation, you'll want to consider which modes and media will be most effective in achieving your goals. A wide range of multimodal projects have made their way into college classrooms. The most prevalent and popular of these projects are illustrated essays, websites, audio essays and podcasts, video essays, posters and infographics, and social media posts and campaigns. Following are some tips for composing each of these kinds of writing.

Illustrated Essays

In Trujillo and Hastings's graphic essay, the words and the drawings are woven together so well that neither element could stand alone. See how they've done it on p. 978.

Probably the simplest multimodal assignment you will encounter is an essay in which you're asked to embed illustrations—photos, drawings, maps, graphs, charts, and so on. Illustrated essays offer you a chance for creativity and for getting your point across in multiple ways.

See how one student uses images in an essay about how Japanese video games are being remade to better appeal to foreign audiences.

Even companies like Nintendo, which had previously relied on the denationalized nature of their characters for international success, have begun capitalizing on uniquely Japanese concepts. For example, the Tanooki Suit is an item introduced with *New Super Mario Bros. 3* that allows Mario to transform into a tanuki, or Japanese raccoon dog. In the original release of *Super Mario Bros. 3*, Tanooki Mario was de-emphasized in favor of Raccoon Mario, which was prominently featured on the cover art, since Americans were more likely able to identify a raccoon rather than a tanuki (see figure 1). However, with the release of *Super Mario 3D Land*, which some consider to be a spiritual successor to *Super Mario Bros. 3* (Sterling), Nintendo fully embraced the Tanooki power-up and made it the primary focus both in their advertising and in-game, with many enemies gaining Tanooki tails. This newly realized proliferation of Tanooki extended into its sequel, *Super Mario 3D World* (see figure 2) and related games, such as *Mario Kart 7*. By embracing their cultural heritage

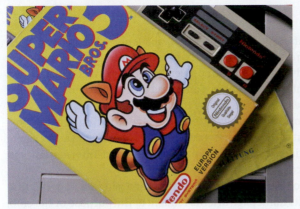

Fig. 1. The box art for *Super Mario Bros. 3* prominently featured Raccoon Mario . . .

Fig. 2. . . . while art for later releases focused on Tanooki Mario, who, although present in *Super Mario Bros. 3*, was not nearly as prominent as in *3D Land* or *3D World*.

> rather than disguising it, Nintendo helps introduce Western gamers to elements of Japanese culture they may otherwise not be aware of, no longer fearful of culture shock.
>
> —RUIZHE (THOMAS) ZHAO, "Word for Word: Culture's Impact on the Localization of Japanese Video Games"

Notice how Zhao has carefully incorporated the two images into his argument, labeling them with figure numbers, referring to them in the text, and providing captions for each one. Though it's not shown here, he also includes documentation information in a works-cited list. Far from being decorative, these images provide essential support for his argument.

Some Tips for Writing Illustrated Essays

- Make sure all illustrations help communicate your message. You never want to use illustrations as mere decoration.
- Refer to each illustration in the text and position each one carefully so that it appears near the text where it's discussed.
- Give each illustration a figure number and a caption that tells readers what it is.
- Provide documentation for any illustrations that you don't create yourself, either in a caption or in a works-cited list.

Websites

Websites come in different forms: personal, academic, activist, and business-oriented. They're dynamic spaces where creators post information, ideas, arguments, advertisements, and even reflections. Web authors can take advantage of embedding images, audio, and video into their sites. A distinctive feature of websites is the ability to hyperlink, connecting one word or phrase to more information elsewhere online. Hyperlinking expands possibilities for writers; it can be a quick way to point to the conversation you're entering, provide evidence for your claims, or highlight information you recommend readers consider.

Check out Oregon State University's student Fisheries and Wildlife Club website below. Its homepage orients readers to the purpose of the club, which is "a peer-elected, nonprofit student group dedicated to the professional development of undergraduate and graduate students interested in fisheries, wildlife, or conservation fields," and the function of the website: to offer information about club leadership and membership, to alert readers to upcoming events, and to showcase club outreach and projects. The site is richly multimodal; it includes images, maps, links to listservs and social media accounts, sign-up sheets, and *YouTube* videos. Spending time on this site gives readers an immersive sense of what it would be like to participate in this club—and the information they need to get involved.

Homepage of the OSU student chapter of the Fisheries and Wildlife Club.

Some Tips for Creating a Website

- Stay focused on the purpose of your website: what do you want readers to know, learn, or experience? Tailor the information you include and design choices to your purpose.

- Many readers scan websites for information, so use bulleted lists, headings, a bold font, and other design elements to make your text easy to scan.

- Consider the pages within your website; you'll likely offer an About page that explains the site's purpose. Organize information using pages with clear titles, and provide links to those pages on your homepage.

- Make navigation easy. Include a menu listing the pages of your site with brief titles that make the purpose of each area clear.

- Include images or embed audio or video clips where they will help make your message clear or engage readers.

- Include hyperlinks to guide your readers to additional pertinent information.

Audio Essays and Podcasts

The University of Wisconsin's Design Lab defines audio essays as ones that "explore topics using spoken text, audio interviews, archival recordings, music, environmental sounds, and/or sound effects" and notes that they "can make unfamiliar materials more accessible to new audiences and/or reveal new perspectives on familiar subjects."

NPR popularized audio essays with its *This I Believe* and *This American Life* series. One of NPR's most popular pieces is humorist David Sedaris's readings from his "Santaland Diaries," which chronicle his experiences working as a department store elf one holiday season. Listen to the audio at everyonesanauthor.tumblr.com, paying attention to how the piece is structured in 45-to-50-second segments and how that structure affects the way you follow the story. Here's one segment from Sedaris's tale:

> Twenty-two thousand people came to see Santa today, and not all of them were well-behaved. Today I witnessed fistfights and vomiting and magnificent tantrums. The back hallway was jammed with people. There was a line for Santa and a line for the women's bathroom. And one woman, after asking me a thousand questions already, asked, "Which is

↗ Russel Honoré's essay on p. 172 was written for *This I Believe*. Read it, and then listen to the audio version at everyonesanauthor.tumblr.com. What does he do differently for those listening to his text?

the line for the women's bathroom?" And I shouted that I thought it was the line with all the women in it. She said, "I'm going to have you fired."

I had two people say that to me today: "I'm going to have you fired." Go ahead. Be my guest. I'm wearing a green velvet costume; it doesn't get any worse than this. Who do these people think they are? "I'm going to have you fired."

And I want to lean over and say, "I'm going to have you killed."

—DAVID SEDARIS, "The Santaland Diaries"

Notice how the music at the beginning and the end of this segment helps bring together the narrative. And listen to Sedaris's voice: how it changes as he imitates the voice of the woman who threatens to have him fired—and then lowers and becomes more menacing at the end, concluding the segment with an unexpected shift in the narrative that keeps listeners engaged (and makes us laugh). That's good radio.

A podcast differs from an audio essay in that podcasts are made up of episodes in a series. For example, on the podcast *StarTalk*, astrophysicist Neil deGrasse Tyson discusses pop culture and science, interviewing a different guest in each episode. Developing a podcast could mean creating just one episode or a series that you continue beyond your writing course. In either case, you'll come up with a concept for the podcast series that your episode(s) fit into. When recording, aim to use an external microphone to ensure sound quality and a good set of headphones to prevent "audio bleed," which is when the noise from one source is mistakenly picked up on a speaker. Many apps and programs are available to help you get started, and your school's media center or library likely offers even more. Here are a few to check out: *Audacity* works with both Mac and Windows, and *GarageBand* is preinstalled on all Mac products.

Some Tips for Composing an Audio Essay or Podcast

- Decide on the software you will use.

- Write out a script, using short sentences, strong verbs, and active voice. Think about your language choices and dialect: what language tools will you draw on?

- If you are using sources, introduce them at the beginning of the sentence and paraphrase rather than quote.

- Use concrete examples and vivid imagery to help listeners see or imagine what you're describing. Sound effects can help establish setting.

- Organize your piece in chronological order, allowing for flashbacks and flashforwards if they are necessary to your story.

- Practice reading your script. Vary your tone of voice to keep listeners engaged. You might change your tone to imitate someone else speaking. (Or better yet, edit in sound clips of others speaking for themselves.)

- Follow *This American Life* host Ira Glass's "45-second rule": listeners expect some kind of break or change of pace every 45 to 50 seconds. Try to pace your piece accordingly.

- Use music to establish a mood, to mark transitions, and to keep your listeners engaged.

Video Essays

Video essays are popular, and not just on *YouTube* or *TikTok*. Some students submit video essays as part of their college and grad school applications, and some employers ask for videos as part of job applications. While anyone with a smartphone can create a video essay, it's not always easy.

Just like traditional essays composed with written words alone, video essays need to make a clear point, to offer good reasons and evidence in support of that point, and to acknowledge other points of view. Unlike print essays, however, video essays can use a combination of images, sounds, and words.

And you can present these images, sounds, and words in many different ways. Take images: you can use still images, moving images, and stop-motion images. Sounds can include people speaking on camera, voiceover, music, and background sounds. Words can be spoken, or they can be put on-screen as titles, subtitles, credits—even in thought bubbles. All these elements add up to infinite possibilities for authoring.

Multimedia journalist Adam Westbrook combines still photos, moving images, music, maps, charts, and more with spoken commentary in *Cause / Effect: The Unexpected Origins of Terrible Things*, a video essay arguing that World War I was caused not by the assassination of Archduke Franz Ferdinand but by Germany's desire for sea power. The video format allows Westbrook to present audio and visual evidence that makes a persuasive (and engaging) case for his argument—and to use both spoken and written language, from voiceover narration to labels identifying people pictured in historic photos.

↷ Go to everyonesanauthor.tumblr.com to watch *Cause / Effect: The Unexpected Origins of Terrible Things*.

A map and photograph from the video essay *Cause / Effect*.

Westbrook's example shows how complicated video essays can be, with words, images, and sounds all at work in multiple ways. A good way to plan out how all these elements will fit together is by creating a **STORYBOARD**, a series of sketches that shows the sequence of scenes and actions in a film. Take a look at the storyboard on the next page showing a sequence of camera shots for Alicia Keys's "Girl on Fire" music video. The images distinguish wide-angle shots from medium shots and close-ups, and provide a sense of how the video's narrative will flow. A storyboard like this can also serve as a blueprint as you shoot and edit a video essay. You can sketch storyboards by hand, build them in a slide deck, or use free services like storyboardthat.com.

Some Tips for Composing a Video Essay

- Decide which program you will use: *iMovie*, *Final Cut Pro*, and *Windows Live Movie Maker* are popular choices.
- Try to show much of the evidence for your argument visually, with images rather than just words.
- Think about the tone you want to project and how color, lighting, pacing, and music might evoke that tone.
- Draft a script for any text that will be spoken on camera or read as a voiceover—and practice reading it aloud.
- If your video includes yourself or others speaking into the camera, consider tools like *Zoom* or *Microsoft Teams*.
- Create a storyboard to map out how the parts of your video essay will fit together. Use your storyboard to plan the shots you need before you begin shooting, and always shoot more than you think you'll need. It's

Go to everyonesanauthor.tumblr.com to browse examples of multimodal projects created by students.

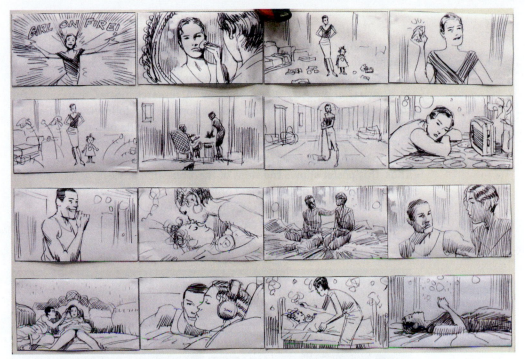

A storyboard lays out a sequence of camera shots for Alicia Keys's music video "Girl on Fire."

much easier to delete extra footage than it is to get a single shot you missed.

- Consider a variety of camera angles. Wide-angle shots are useful for setting a scene; medium shots, for framing someone speaking to the camera; close-ups, for showing important details.

- Experiment also with moving the camera—following the subject, zooming in or out, panning left or right—but do so sparingly. You don't want to make your viewers dizzy!

- Use title cards to display written text if needed. You'll probably want to open with your title, and you might add text to identify the setting, time, and the name and title of someone speaking; to add captions or subtitles; or to mark transitions.

- Provide a written list of credits on the screen at the end, citing any sources you use and thanking those who helped.

Posters and Infographics

You're likely to have opportunities to create research posters and infographics for classroom presentations, campus organizations, or academic conferences. Both research posters and infographics present information in a visual and easily digestible way. A research poster represents the results of research or a study. Take a look at the following poster that three students created in order to present the results of a research study. The poster explains the questions that motivated the work, the methods used to conduct the research, the results, and some ideas for further study. Thus, this poster shows the steps of their research process. A key principle for effective poster design is clear organization. In the student example, the topic is included in the title, which is centered at the top. The text is organized in three columns: one devoted to the motivation for the project, the second to the methods used, and the third to results and future directions.

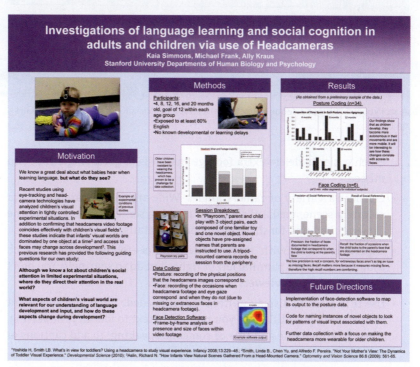

A poster created by a student research group to present its study.

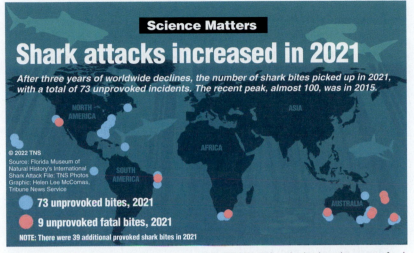

Science Matters

Shark attacks increased in 2021

After three years of worldwide declines, the number of shark bites picked up in 2021, with a total of 73 unprovoked incidents. The recent peak, almost 100, was in 2015.

NORTH AMERICA

ASIA

AFRICA

© 2022 TNS
Source: Florida Museum of
Natural History's International
Shark Attack File; TNS Photos
Graphic: Helen Lee McComas,
Tribune News Service

SOUTH AMERICA

AUSTRALIA

● **73 unprovoked bites, 2021**

● **9 unprovoked fatal bites, 2021**

NOTE: There were 39 additional provoked shark bites in 2021

An infographic plots where shark attacks have happened and whether they were fatal events or not.

Data is presented in bar graphs, and other images illustrate and underscore key points in the report.

An infographic, on the other hand, offers a succinct visualization of complex information. The example above shows data on the recent rise in shark attacks. A map shows the locations where unprovoked shark attacks occurred, with pink dots indicating fatal bites. An effective infographic summarizes information so it's easy for readers to understand the main takeaways at a glance. When creating an infographic, be careful not to pack it with too many words, which can distract from the main message.

Some Tips for Creating a Poster or Infographic

- Identify the main purpose or takeaway of your poster or infographic. How can you ensure readers walk away with that information? What can you leave off to ensure the main point stands out?

- People will likely read your poster or infographic from the top left corner to the bottom right. Organize the information presented accordingly.

- Posters and infographics are often read at a glance, so present the information you want your audience to take away clearly and simply. Try bullet points and avoid long paragraphs. Consider headings and subheadings.

- Think about how you can get your audience's attention: by asking a provocative question in a large, bold font at the top of the poster? with color? with an eye-catching image? something else?

- Include charts, graphs, and images; they help convey dense information quickly.

- Make sure that all the visuals and information in the poster and infographic are tied to your purpose.

- Keep the design simple: too many images, too much text, or distracting typefaces make for a cluttered look that can be hard to follow.

- Be sure that any text is large enough to read—and that it is organized in a way that makes it easy to scan and understand quickly.

- Choose colors that will be easy to see. Primary colors are easier to see than pastels. Use dark text on a light background.

- Cite your information and sources. See the bottom panel on the students' poster (p. 800) for examples.

Social Media Posts and Campaigns

As you well know, social media offers various formats for writers to compose, deliver, and circulate their claims, ideas, agendas, and messages, through platforms like *Instagram*, *TikTok*, *Facebook*, *Snapchat*, and *Twitter*. Each platform offers different opportunities and constraints, from posting photos, images, and videos to crafting messages that are only 280 characters. And, of course, social media platforms can be used for almost innumerable purposes: to connect with friends, to craft an argument, to share images of a beloved pet, to circulate news, to advertise or sell items, to network, to bring people together virtually and physically—the possibilities are seemingly endless.

See the Cape Fear Community College *TikTok* account by visiting everyonesanauthor .tumblr.com.

Colleges and universities often use social media to stay in touch with students. For example, students at Cape Fear Community College produced videos and posted them on the school's *TikTok* account. These videos alert the campus's over 20,000 followers of the benefits of community college. In them, students offer advice for making college more affordable, advertise occupational programs on campus, motivate students to stay committed to their studies, and more—all using text, music, and images of students.

Many of their videos have more than 50,000 views; an effective campaign, to be sure!

You might be assigned, or given the option, to create a social media campaign in your classes. For instance, students in literature classes are creating *Facebook* accounts for characters in the novel they're reading, imagining the posts the character might make, the images they'd share, and the other accounts they'd "friend." Students in history courses are creating *Twitter* campaigns with tweets recounting a historical event, imagined from the perspective of a person who lived through it. In first-year writing classes, students are adapting arguments, reports, and proposals into posts on *TikTok* or *Instagram* to spread their message more widely. Composing for social media gives you options for reaching new audiences in creative and engaging ways.

Because it's a part of our everyday lives, social media may seem an easy venue for expressing yourself. Just be aware that even here, there are conventions, preferred styles, and shared patterns of communication. If you're not familiar with a particular platform, before using it, spend some time scanning posts to figure out what gets attention. Look closely at the languages used, the format and length of posts, the style of photos and videos, and how hashtags and emojis are deployed. Pay attention to the tone of captions and comments. You'll gain a quick understanding of what works well and what doesn't.

You'll also want to consider which platform best suits your purpose, format, and intended audience. *TikTok* and *Snapchat* are best for sharing short videos; for longer videos, think *YouTube*. *Twitter* works well for brief text-based messages, though all kinds of media can be posted there, too. For sharing images, consider *Instagram*. *Facebook* allows for building a page of information, where updates in the form of text, video, or images can also be posted. And there are surely other new platforms and tools to explore, too.

Some Tips for Composing on Social Media

- To choose a social media platform, think about the message you want to send and which features are required to convey it. Which platform is most likely to reach your intended audience?

- Decide what you want your audience to do with your message—respond? spread it? perform a specific action? Design your post(s) accordingly.

- Keep posts short. Use links to refer to additional information.

- Identify the media you'll use. If using images or video, provide captions. Compose images and videos so the subject is clear and there aren't distracting elements or sounds. Check color contrast and lighting so the subject is clear. For word-based posts, how will typeface, color, and overall design engage your audience?

- If you use words, ideas, or images you didn't create yourself, provide credit. Including links or @mentions are common ways to credit others online. Ensure any source you link to is credible and accurate.

- Pay attention to the conventions and user expectations of the platform you choose. Do you want to follow those expectations? challenge them in some way?

- Remember that anything shared on social media may be viewed by friends, acquaintances, teachers, future colleagues, or hiring managers. Your social media posts can also easily be captured and recorded by readers, so don't post anything you don't want saved or shared.

- Think about how you can use **HASHTAGS** and tagging others to connect your post to ongoing conversations, and help your contribution spread.

- Prioritize your privacy and protection. Make sure you're comfortable with the policies of the social media platforms you use, and instead of using personal accounts, consider creating a separate account for schoolwork on social media.

REFLECT. Check out your school's social media accounts. What platforms do they use? What kinds of messages do they send? Who and what do they feature and why?

REMIX PROJECTS

Writers remix projects by taking their message or argument and transforming it into a different genre or media. The goal is usually to share the original message or idea with a new or wider audience. Along the way, the message might even shift or take new shape as it's revised to match the purpose and features of a new genre. Exploring the possibilities that different genres and media open up is part of the fun—and challenge—of remixing writing. Remixes, then, can be an opportunity for creativity and imagination—to rethink and renew your ideas by trying out new forms.

Take a look, for example, at the infographic on the following page. Sophia Warfield, a student at the University of Maryland, transformed her research essay on overfishing into an infographic. Starting out, she asked herself: How do I want to recast the information in my research essay so that it reaches new audiences? What other genre might help me to craft my argument in new ways? Choosing a **GENRE** for a remix project is the first and most important step, and Warfield chose an infographic because it could highlight key information visually and move audiences to take action. As she kept at it, more questions guided Warfield's work. She considered: What was the purpose of my original research essay and what strategies did I use to achieve that purpose? What ideas, concepts, arguments, or research do I want to retain as I move to an infographic? How will an infographic allow me to fine-tune my claims or craft new ways to make my argument? What *won't* I be able to do in the infographic that I could do in the research essay?

In writing her research essay, Warfield developed arguments about overfishing by providing research to support her claims and responding to counterarguments. She also incorporated her own experiences with overfishing, lending to her credibility. The infographic, on the other hand, allowed Warfield to distill her research into specific, attention-grabbing facts about overfishing so the main argument is concise and clear: stop overfishing. And a single bold headline summarizes Warfield's proposal for action—"Join Greenpeace!"—with information for how to do so. Using sparse words, art, colors, and a select few typefaces, Warfield was able to transform her message into one many more people are likely to spot, notice, and think about.

↗ Visit everyonesanauthor .tumblr.com to read Warfield's research essay.

Some Tips for Composing Remix Projects

- Identify the **AUDIENCE** you are aiming to reach: one wider and more public than before? more specific and specialized? your peers instead of your teacher? Think about which genres or media are most likely to get and hold that audience's attention.

- Get clear on your **PURPOSE** for adapting your work. To turn a personal narrative into an argument? To translate complex research into something the general public will care about? Your purpose will help you see which **GENRE** is best suited to achieving your goal.

A University of Maryland student's remix of a research essay into an infographic.

- Weigh which **MEDIUM** or media will reach your new intended audience, serve your purpose, and suit your genre. *TikTok* videos can work well to reach a young public audience and make a brief argument, like Cape Fear Community College's account. But a different medium, like a pamphlet, infographic, or website, would be better suited for conveying more complex information.

- Identify the ideas, claims, or arguments that you'll retain from your original work and use in this adaptation. Pinpoint, too, the strategies or information that you'll leave behind.

- If you cited sources in your original work, plan for how you'll give credit in your adaptation. Depending on your genre, links, a works-cited page or slide, or a QR code to references could work.

- Analyze your new chosen genre or media and decide what **LANGUAGE** and **STYLE** you'll use. If there are conventions or expectations, will you meet those or push against them? Think about how your language and style should evolve (or not) from your original work.

- As you work, **REFLECT** on the choices you're making about audience, genre, design, language, etc. Doing so will help you transfer effective practices to writing in the future.

◠◠◠ *REFLECT. Consider a project you're working on or have completed this semester for one of your courses. How might you remix it into a new genre or medium that reaches a new audience? What genre would you choose and why? How would your message change in this new genre? What would this new mode allow you to do and say? How might it limit you?*

MANAGING MULTIMODAL AND REMIX PROJECTS

Managing projects that involve multimedia is a bit like juggling: at any one time, you have multiple balls in the air, each one needing attention, and altogether it takes a lot of skill to keep them all airborne. While we can't provide guidelines for every step of every multimodal project you may encounter, we can offer some general advice about how to approach them.

Whether you're composing an illustrated essay, a website, a video, or any other multimodal text, you will want to plan carefully for how your project will achieve your purpose with a particular audience and in a particular context. To do so, you'll need to carefully manage your time, your files, your project content, your sources, and more.

Managing your time. Make sure you know exactly how much time you have before your project is due and then be realistic about how to manage that time. Set up a calendar and block out specific times when you know you can work on the project; consider whether you'll have any class time to devote to it. If you're assigned to work with other students, set regular meeting times and draw up a schedule and task list together so that you each know your responsibilities. Breaking a project down into parts and setting deadlines for each part can help keep you on track. And don't forget to build in time to get responses to a draft of your project—from your instructor if possible, as well as from classmates and friends.

Managing project files. To keep track of information and sources for multimodal projects, begin by creating a project folder on your computer, using subfolders for various types of files. For image files, select the best format for your project: JPEG, PNG, or GIF will offer the best clarity for photographs or graphic design projects. For video files, your best choice will likely be MP4 or, if you have a Mac, MOV. Organize files according to type (images, charts, video clips, audio clips, and intended use) and according to the organization of your project (clips for scene 1 of a video essay, graphs for the results section of a research poster). Be sure to label each file in a way that makes sense to you and to make note of where you found it, the date you downloaded it, and any other relevant source information—so that you can cite your sources properly and go back to them if need be. Your school might provide project management software access, but if not you'll want to look at free online options. A site like top5projectmanagement.com that offers descriptions and reviews can help you sort through the possibilities.

Organizing your content. Some writers begin with nothing more than a pack of sticky notes, putting main points and sub-points and supporting reasons and evidence on individual stickies and arranging them on a larger surface. You might begin with an outline of the main points you want to make and the support for each one. This kind of careful organizing is crucial because it creates a "big picture" of your message and all its parts.

If you're creating a short video or video essay, you might create a storyboard to put everything in sequence; another possibility would be a two-column script to line up the video and audio portions. Audio essays and podcasts need some kind of script as well, one that accounts for both words and any music or other sounds. For an illustrated print essay, you'll need to decide where to put your images. For websites and other kinds of online texts that readers navigate by links, you might map out your organization on a large sheet of paper, putting the main page at the center top and then drawing lines out to the various pages you will link to. Social media posts are small but have many moving parts; map out what text, visuals, HASHTAGS, and @mentions you'll include, and in what order.

Crediting your sources. Be sure to credit your sources. You can do so at the bottom of a poster, as the last slide in an oral presentation, as footnotes or a separate page on a website, as credits at the end of a video or audio piece, or as links or tags in a social media post.

〰️ *REFLECT. "This is the time for exploration, for experimentation. This is the time when we can create and risk, when we can write graffiti on the walls and color outside the lines. . . . If we are going to fly and find new intellectual spaces . . . we must expand our notion of academic discourse." That's a challenge that Stanford professor Adam Banks issued in 2015 to an audience of college writing instructors. How would you answer his challenge? Find a piece of academic writing you've done and imagine how you could re-create it using multiple modes.*

THIRTY-EIGHT

Making Presentations

WHAT GOES INTO a surefire great presentation? Author and consultant Nancy Duarte wanted to find out. So she set out to study some great presentations, hundreds of them, beginning with Martin Luther King Jr.'s "I Have a Dream" speech and Steve Jobs's iPhone launch, two speeches that seemed so different to her that she couldn't imagine she would find anything in common. But she did.

She found that these two speeches—and hundreds of other terrific presentations—shared one common structure. Each speech begins by describing "what is"—and then goes on to suggest what it could (or should) be. That's in the introduction. Then in the middle of the speech, the presenter moves back and forth between discussing that status quo and describing what it could or should be. And in most cases, the conclusion vividly evokes what could be and calls for action.

Duarte's research shows that this basic structure (from what is to what could be) is very widely used, and especially so by activists, politicians, and businesspeople proposing change of some kind. In fact, it's a structure that may work well for many of the presentations you make in your college classes. And there are two common variations on this structure that you may be familiar with. One begins with what *was*, in the past, and then moves on to explain how it changed. The other opens by noting what others have said about a topic and then moves on to what you want to say about it, focusing on the benefits of your position.

Martin Luther King Jr.

Steve Jobs

Starting with what is, what was, or what's been said and then suggesting something "better" uses a classic storytelling technique: setting up a conflict that needs to be resolved. And presenting your main point as a story works well in a spoken presentation because stories are easier to follow and remember than other kinds of evidence and are often more persuasive.

At the 2021 Academy Awards, actor and director Tyler Perry used such a story in his speech accepting the Jean Hersholt Humanitarian Award for his work providing food and aid during the COVID-19 pandemic. Reflecting on the importance of helping others, he told the audience about an encounter with an elderly woman some seventeen years earlier. He was heading into a rented production building when he saw her out of the corner of his eye and instinctively reached for his wallet, to give her some money. The woman, however, stopped him cold when she said, "Excuse me, sir. Do you have any shoes?" He remembered his own days of having only one pair of dilapidated shoes and took her into his wardrobe department, where he found some shoes, helped her put them on, and listened as the woman, looking down, said, "Thank you, Jesus, my feet are off the ground."

When the woman said she feared Perry would "hate [her] for asking," he replied, "How can I hate you when I used to *be* you?" Perry went on to tell the woman about his own mother, someone who, in spite of all the hate around her, taught him "to refuse hate" and avoid "blanket judgment." Looking directly into the camera, Perry called on everyone in the audience to "refuse hate" and to "stand in the middle, 'cause that's where healing happens. That's where conversation happens. That's where change happens." It's his personal story that drives home this central idea.

Tyler Perry

Sounds simple, doesn't it? State your main point, find a story to help get that point across, and inspire the audience to accept what you say. But

Robin Wall Kimmerer is an engaging and accomplished speaker. Her essay that appears on p. 909 is taken from a book; still, her living voice comes through in the writing. Try reading it out loud to feel how smoothly it goes. When you write your presentation script, don't stray from your own voice.

coming up with these elements in ways that will capture and hold an audience's attention—well, that's not so simple. Still, there are some structures and techniques that will help you create presentations that audiences will listen to and remember and that might even call them to action. This chapter provides guidelines to help you do so.

ACROSS DISCIPLINES

You'll likely be required to give oral presentations, using slides or posters, in courses across different fields. This is because of the growing awareness that in the world of work, nearly everyone ends up sharing specialized knowledge with colleagues, (potential) clients, or the public through presentations. Different disciplines and professions have preferred practices. In fields like engineering and the lab sciences, presentations are often team affairs. In these and, in fact, many other fields, the preferred method of presentation is the "assertion-evidence" style: a speaker makes a claim and immediately presents the evidence to support that claim, often in visual form or with the aid of a visual. The website *Assertion-Evidence Approach*, created by Michael Alley at Penn State University, offers tutorials, sample slides, and videos of presentations by students. By watching the videos, you can get ideas about how to develop an effective presentation style that works for you. Looking at models of effective presentations in your field is a good way to learn what's expected of you.

First, let's take a look at the script one of our students prepared for a presentation on Japanese manga. As you'll see, she used a "what was and how it changed" structure as a foundation for her presentation.

The Rise of Female Heroes in Shoujo Manga

HALLE EDWARDS

HERE'S A QUESTION FOR YOU: [SLIDE] Where are all the strong women heroes in popular comics? In our class we've seen some talented female authors of graphic narratives, but in terms of popular comic book characters (not to mention writers and fans), the girls are still outnumbered.

> Q: Where are all the strong female heroes?

[SLIDE] So guess what? When I started looking, I found the strong female heroes in comics! The place—Japan. The time period—the 1990s. The genre— Shoujo manga. Literally "girls' comics" in Japanese, Shoujo manga is a popular

HALLE EDWARDS composed this presentation for a second-year writing course that focused on graphic narratives. For this assignment, she first wrote an academic essay and then remixed it into a ten-minute oral presentation with seventeen slides. As you'll see, we've included only a few of these slides.

form of comics in Japan typically written by women for women. Prior to the 1990s, Shoujo typically featured weak heroines and plots that revolved around romance. Then, in the 1990s, Shoujo started showing strong female heroes whose first priority wasn't romance. But what did that change look like and, more importantly, why did it happen?

Today I'll explore the answers. First I'll show you an example of this phenomenon, from Naoko Takeuchi's smash-hit manga *Sailor Moon*. Then I'll explain what was happening in Japan in the 1990s and why this allowed Shoujo manga to change so drastically.

[SLIDE] Part one. *Sailor Moon* tells the story of Usagi, a clumsy and not particularly smart schoolgirl with a heart of gold. She discovers that she has a secret identity—Sailor Moon—and is destined to fight the forces of evil. [SLIDE] While *Sailor Moon* does have a love story, much of the manga is devoted to expanding on Sailor Moon's relationship with her eventual comrades—Sailors Mars, Mercury, Jupiter, and Venus. [SLIDE] The relationship of these five heroes is usually prioritized over the romance.

Wait a minute. Five female heroes? The romance is just a side plot? Girls ⁵ described as soldiers who physically fight bad guys? For anyone familiar with traditional Shoujo manga, it's obvious that *Sailor Moon* pushed boundaries.

[SLIDE] This boundary-pushing can be seen in the introduction of the second female hero, Ami, or Sailor Mercury. Introduced as an aloof genius, Ami quickly reveals Takeuchi's friendly, playful side. [SLIDE] From the outset, Sailor Mercury cannot be pinned down to a stereotype—she's neither a cold nerd nor a bubbly teenager. She's very flawed and very real. Takeuchi's female heroes are layered, interesting, and compelling.

Throughout the story, we see Ami develop a close friendship with Usagi, [SLIDE] ultimately ending in a battle where Ami discovers her identity as Sailor Mercury. Meanwhile, Usagi's budding romance is barely a side plot. Throughout *Sailor Moon*'s five-year run, its female heroines were always the heart of the story—not the romance. The funny thing? Despite this drastic departure from typical Shoujo norms, *Sailor Moon* was a smash hit.

[SLIDE] So why was *Sailor Moon* so warmly received, given that it defied so many norms in Shoujo manga? To understand, you need to know a bit about Japan in the early 1990s. [SLIDE] In 1989, the Asset Price Bubble broke—essentially a huge economic bubble that vastly inflated real estate prices. [SLIDE] This sent Japan's economy spiraling into a recession that lasted throughout the entire 1990s, a decade now known as Japan's "lost decade."

[SLIDE] The recession changed many aspects of life in Japan. Before the recession, men could expect to get hired at a company out of college and work there for their whole lives. Meanwhile, women held mainly part-time jobs—think secretaries and office ladies—with few opportunities for advancement. However, once the recession hit, layoffs became rampant. Companies tanked. Men could no longer rely on having lifetime careers, and many in Japan questioned the long hours that were customary in Japan's workplaces.

What made the 1990s in Japan the "Era of Women"?

- Economic recession lowered job security for men

- More women worked outside the home

- More women voted

- Several female candidates were elected in 1989

[SLIDE] Meanwhile, in the 1989 elections, several female candidates were   10
elected. Also, voter turnout among women was higher than ever. Because
of this, the media predicted that the 1990s would be the "era of women."
Women were suddenly seen as capable: they could hold real jobs outside the
home, run for office, and help save Japan's stumbling economy. These new
women were featured in popular soap operas known as "morning dramas" on
the government-funded NHK channel.

[SLIDE] Given this media-propelled image of the new, strong woman, several of the major Shoujo magazines began to take note. Thus, when Toshio
Irie, the newly minted editor of *Nakayoshi* magazine, learned of *Sailor Moon*,
a story with five strong female heroes, he jumped at the opportunity. Not
only did he publish Takeuchi's manga; he embraced a mixed-media strategy,
including *Sailor Moon*–themed toys with the magazine (to encourage fans to
buy their own copies and limit sharing) and selling additional *Sailor Moon* mer-
chandise. [SLIDE] Also, when Toei Animation snapped up the rights to create an animated *Sailor Moon* series, Irie worked with the company to closely
match the release of the new *Sailor Moon* chapters and episodes.

Such a media blitz was unheard of for a work of Shoujo manga, and it paid
off. By the end of 1995, *Sailor Moon* had made over 300 billion yen in profits
and was expanding rapidly worldwide. Circulation figures for the magazine
reached an all-time high of 2 million per month. The thirteen volumes that had
been released by then had sold over a million copies each and been exported
to twenty-three countries.

[SLIDE] The recession, and the media's message that the 1990s would
be the "era of women," caused forces in the media to realize that the image
of strong women could be popular—and more importantly, profitable. As

a result, other manga editors were willing to publish works that featured strong female heroes—knowing that they would make money. This is one way that Shoujo sparked important change.

But why, you might be wondering, does it matter? This was just one time period in one country where comics featured strong women. Was it a phenomenon that spread to other countries? Did more girls start reading comic books and graphic narratives? And did life really change for women in Japan?

The simple answer is no. The "era of women" did not lead to significant   15 change in the lives of women in Japan. They were still mostly relegated to part-time jobs and to most domestic responsibilities. And after the magical girl heroine trends of the 1990s, Shoujo in the 2000s became more focused on "slice of life" stories. This is not to say it went backwards—it just stopped moving forward so daringly.

However, the 1990s in Japan proved that there is a place, and an audience, for strong heroines in graphic narratives. Although there was little or no precedent for introducing strong women characters, a few key people took risks on some new stories, and they paid off. I think this is a lesson we can apply to the graphic novel market today. Just because there are still more male readers and characters in US comics does not mean that the market for strong female characters does not exist. In fact, the success of authors Lynda Barry and Alison Bechdel as well as of the hit TV series Marvel's *Agent* (Peggy) *Carter* suggests that the time may be ripe for many more strong women in graphic narratives. And the appearance of more blockbuster superhero movies featuring female leads—think Wonder Woman, Black Widow, and Catwoman— is exciting and promising, too. So let's heed the story of Sailor Moon and her crew and read and encourage others to buy works that feature strong women. Then when we're asked "where are all the strong women heroes in popular comics?" we can answer, "They're everywhere!"

[SLIDE] Thank you for listening. I'll be glad to take questions.

Halle Edwards opens her presentation with a statement about "what is"—that is, the status quo, which finds few strong female heroes in popular comic books. She then explains a similar situation in Japan, and how it changed, exploring some of the issues in Japanese society that allowed women heroes to emerge and using the story of *Sailor Moon*'s success as the major example. Throughout, she poses questions to involve her audience, beginning by asking, "Where are all the strong women heroes in popular comics?" Take a moment to count the number of questions in this presentation and where they occur and you'll see that they act as "signpost language," helping the audience follow the presentation and focusing their attention on its most important points. Notice as well that Edwards uses good presentational style: short sentences, simple syntax, clear transitions and other signpost language, active verbs, and vivid description—all things that make the presentation easy to listen to and to follow.

REFLECT. Halle Edwards's presentation grew out of a research paper she had written on the same topic. Look back at an academic essay you have written and then, using this chapter as a guide, make notes on what you would need to do to transform it into a memorable oral presentation.

MAKING A PRESENTATION / A Roadmap
Begin by considering your rhetorical situation

Anticipate who will be in your AUDIENCE. What do they already know about your topic, and what other information might they need? What kinds of evidence are most likely to appeal to them? You can keep your audience engaged by establishing eye contact and addressing them directly from time to time. If you're addressing your audience via video, make "eye contact" by looking into the camera.

Be clear about your PURPOSE. Make sure you understand any assignment you've been given for this presentation. Is your goal to provide information? to persuade? to propose some kind of action?

Think about your STANCE. How are you presenting yourself: as an expert? an interested novice? a researcher? an advocate? Be sure that the stance you are taking is suitable for your topic and audience. Halle Edwards presents herself as a peer and classmate who has researched her topic and can thus speak with authority about it.

Consider the CONTEXT. Where will the presentation take place? What equipment will you need? Whatever it is, be sure to test it in advance—and keep in mind that technology glitches happen, so be sure to have a backup plan. How much time will you have? Who will introduce you?

Think about your GENRE. If you've been assigned a specific genre, say to report on a topic or to present a proposal, consult those chapters in this textbook for guidance. If not, see Chapter 12 for help choosing a genre.

Think about your LANGUAGE. Regardless of how many languages and dialects you use in your everyday life, you have many options to consider in making an oral presentation. Will your audience expect a certain kind of language or style? Do you want to meet those expectations? challenge them? What do you want your language choices to say about you? What risks might you be willing to take with your language? How will your choice of medium and the larger context limit or expand the language options available to you?

Will you be using any MEDIA elements that need to be DESIGNED? Would showing images or information on a slide or flip chart help your audience follow your presentation? Will they expect some kind of visual aids? Will you be referring to a text or something else that you could put on a handout? Remember that slides and flip charts need to be simple enough and large enough for your audience to read as you speak.

Prepare your presentation

Focus on one main point, and then orchestrate everything else to support it. Edwards begins with a question that signals her main point: where are all the strong women heroes in popular comics? In the rest of the presentation, she provides answers to this question in a story about the appearance of women heroes in Japanese manga, using *Sailor Moon* as her main example.

Gather EVIDENCE to support your point. Once you've decided on your main message, look for examples, statistics, stories, and other evidence that illustrate your point. Edwards uses facts and statistics to support her main point—that, despite some changes, there are still not enough strong female heroes in comic books. Even the huge success of *Sailor Moon* failed to turn the tide in any permanent way.

Develop a clear structure. You can try using the structure Nancy Duarte recommends, focusing on what is (or was) and moving to what it could or should be (or how it changed). If that doesn't suit your topic, you might start by noting what else has been said about your topic as a way of introducing what you want to say about it. Any of these structures will set up a tension that your presentation then resolves—a storytelling technique that will make your argument easier for your audience to follow.

Use TRANSITIONS and other techniques to help listeners follow your presentation. It's always helpful to provide an overview of your talk, saying something like "I have four points to make," and then use those points as signposts in the presentation. One other useful technique is repetition. Edwards repeatedly poses questions that mark turning points in her talk. Another good technique is to explain what you're saying as you go, using expressions such as "in other words." Provide a link to or printouts of your scripted presentation to distribute so your talk is accessible to everyone.

Use vivid language, images, and metaphors to hammer home your point clearly and memorably. The vivid language ("neither a cold nerd nor a bubbly teenager," "smash hit") and metaphors ("boundary-pushing") that Edwards uses help her audience visualize and follow her argument.

But keep it simple. Remember that your audience won't always follow along with your script, so you need to speak in a way that will be easy to understand. Notice that Edwards uses fairly simple diction throughout—and that her sentences are short and follow a straightforward subject-verb-object structure. Even her paragraphs are short, some only a sentence or two—which helped her keep to her script without having to refer to it often as she spoke.

Develop a dynamic INTRODUCTION, one that will engage your audience's interest and establish some kind of **COMMON GROUND** with them. You'll also want to establish your **CREDIBILITY**, to show that you've done your homework and can speak knowledgeably about your topic. Edwards was addressing her classmates, so she could assume common ground, but she engaged their interest by asking a provocative question: "Where are all the strong women heroes in popular comics?" The way you open will depend on your topic and rhetorical situation, but whether you start by telling a story, making a surprising claim, or summarizing what someone has said about your topic, your goal is to interest your audience in what is to come.

CONCLUDE in a way that leaves your audience thinking. Whether you conclude by reiterating your main point, by saying why your argument matters, or some other way, this is a moment when you can make sure your presentation has some kind of impact. Edwards faced a challenge: her research had turned up strong female heroes in Japanese manga, but in the end they did not change the status quo. So she concluded by pointing out that her research showed that there's "a place, and an audience, for strong heroines in graphic narratives." She then turned to her audience and challenged them to seek out such characters and to read the works they appear in.

Think about whether and where you need any visuals. Images can bring your presentation to life, illustrate important points, and engage your audience. Any slides should support or explain a point you are making and need to be clear and easy to see so that your audience can process the information in a couple of seconds. It's therefore often better to convey one idea per slide than to provide a list of bullet points on a single slide. If you need to communicate complex information, putting it in a chart or graph can make it easier for you to explain—and for your audience to understand. More detailed information or material you want your audience to read is best presented on handouts. Try to distribute the handouts at the point when your audience needs them: if you give them out before then, some in the audience may be focusing on the handouts rather than on what you say.

If you'll be using slides or other media, you'll need to design them carefully.

- All slides need to be clearly visible to everyone in your audience, so use at least 24-point fonts. Simple bold fonts are easiest to read; avoid italic fonts, which can be difficult to read.

- Don't depend too much on presentation programs' premade templates for slides: the choices they build in—colors, typefaces, layout, and so on—may not be fitting for your topic or purpose.

- The most effective slides are simple enough for the audience to process the information they contain in a couple of seconds. As a general rule, it's better to convey one idea per slide than to provide a list of bullet points.

- At the same time, avoid walls of text. In other words, don't fill slides with long sentences.

- It's best to begin with a slide that includes the title of your presentation, your name (and those of your team members, if this is a group presentation), and any other relevant information such as the course or your institution if you're presenting to an outside group. If you are using a design such as a university logo, use it on only the opening slide.

- Make sure that any audio or video clips embedded in your presentation relate directly to the point you are making and that they are clear and easy to see and hear.

- Additionally, make sure any embedded audio or video clips will work properly on the technology you'll actually be using to present.

- Be sure that any visual you use contributes to your argument. Don't use visuals, especially clip art, that do not add value to your presentation.

- When you take visuals from other sources, acknowledge those sources, either on the slide in a small font or in the references at the end.

- Decorative backgrounds can be distracting, so avoid them unless they add something very specific to your presentation. Avoid special effects.

- When possible, present ideas in diagrams or charts that will be easy for the audience to understand.

- Be consistent. Using one typeface or color for headings and making them parallel in structure will help your audience follow what you are saying. Remember that some audience members may be color-blind, a fact that should influence your choice of color palette.

- Provide accessible descriptions of your visuals in printed copies so that those in the audience who can't see the slides clearly can still follow your argument.

- Finally, be sure to get responses to your slides just as you would to drafts of your script. Note that Edwards made her slides simple and clearly focused, each one intended to raise a question or illustrate or underscore a point.

Think about your delivery. It's one thing to compose a strong presentation, but it's another thing entirely to *deliver* one. Today, when oral forms of discourse are more dominant than at any time in memory, delivery is often the key to whether a presentation reaches and holds its audience's attention. In writing about the role that sound and rhythm play in Black language, scholar Geneva Smitherman describes the use of what she refers to as "tonal semantics"—the way speakers use intonation and rhythm and inflection to create emphasis and command attention, employing their voices like musical instruments. Such strategies of tonal semantics include repetition, rhyme, alliteration, and narrative sequencing.

Listen to any Martin Luther King Jr. speech and you will hear tonal semantics at work. Or think of the features of spoken word poetry, and how the sound of speakers' voices does so much to carry meaning. Think, for example, of Amanda Gorman's spoken word performances. As Smitherman says, Gorman uses her "voice, body, and movement as tools to bring the story to life." As you prepare for and practice your presentation, think about how you can use tonal semantics to your advantage: When might it help to stretch out the pronunciation of a key word, for instance? Could you use repetition like a drumbeat to build up tension or suspense? Mark up your script to note how you want to use your voice—underlining the words you want to emphasize, for example, or adding blank space to indicate a pause. Remember: you want to get—and keep—your audience's attention!

Give your presentation

Practice, practice, practice. There is no substitute for practice. None. So schedule time to rehearse and make sure you can articulate your main message loud and clear at a moment's notice. Ask friends to serve as an audience for a full rehearsal, and be sure to time your presentation so that you don't go beyond the limit. When you're done, ask your friends to tell you your main point. If they can do so, then you've made an impression! Ask them as well how you came across—as friendly? authoritative? something else? If it's not what you're aiming for, talk through how you *want* to come across and how to get there. If presenting virtually, log on to the platform in advance to test your camera, audio, and screen-sharing ability.

Listen to how you use your voice. Record yourself speaking and then listen to what you sound like. Is your voice clear and loud enough to hear? Do you speak very quickly, or too slowly? What can you do to improve this aspect of your delivery? If you're presenting alone, begin by introducing yourself and announcing the topic of your talk to get some idea of how your voice is projecting in the space where you're presenting. For a team presentation, all members should introduce themselves in order to hear their own voice and adjust their volume appropriately. After the introductions, the first speaker can announce the topic of the presentation for team presentations.

Establish eye contact with the audience by quickly scanning the audience at eye level. If you're uncomfortable making direct eye contact, focus a little higher than their heads at the back of the room. Do not look down at the floor; do not look up at the ceiling. Don't turn your back to the audience to read slides. Look directly into the camera if presenting virtually.

Stand or sit up straight! And look at your audience. Try to avoid fidgeting or jingling change in your pockets. You want the focus to be on you and your message.

Move around. Especially if you are going to speak for more than five minutes, you won't want to stand cemented in place. Depending on the configuration of the room where you're presenting, be careful to avoid blocking the audience's view of the slides. In these cases, stand to the right or the left of the slides, out of audience members' line of sight.

REFLECT. Think for a moment about excellent speeches or oral presentations you've heard, making a list as you go of what made them memorable. Was it use of words and phrases? tone of voice? use of the three R's—rhythm, rhyme, repetition? Was it pacing, the way the speaker built up to a climax or slowed down to make a point more dramatic? Did visuals play a part? What else did you notice? Then write a brief "note to self" about how and why you might make use of some of these strategies.

THIRTY-NINE

Writing for a Public Audience

If you're a foodie, you may post about your favorite curry recipes on your food-themed *Instagram* account. If you're a gamer, you might be sharing video game reviews on your *YouTube* channel or website. And if you're passionate about the fact that the park in your neighborhood is threatened with closure, you may be writing letters to the editor of your local newspaper and to the policy makers that fund the park.

What do these three actions have in common? They are all examples of public writing that are available to you—every hour of every day. Indeed, now more than ever, you and your peers in colleges and universities have the opportunity to write to and for a public audience that goes far beyond your instructors and classmates. Available technologies provide you with not only more venues for disseminating your messages but also, as the examples above suggest, a lot of genres to work with, too. Today, you don't need to be a professional writer to write for the public. As this book claims, today "everyone's an author" with access to audiences worldwide. This chapter aims to get you thinking about how, where, and when you can write for public audiences.

What Does It Mean to Write for a Public Audience?

Most of the time, writing for the public means that you are writing for a non-academic audience (not for teachers, for example) and often for those with a general interest in a topic, not specialists. You may be an aspiring chef with a love of food who wants to share that love with others (great cooks and novices and people who just like to eat!) through your food blog or social media account. Or maybe you're a fashionista, someone who loves clothes and knows a great deal about what's in style, and you decide to create your own *TikTok* videos to share your knowledge and outfits with the general public. Maybe you and a friend are passionate about the environment. You've done coursework in environmental science and researched local environmental concerns, and now you've created a monthly digital newsletter to keep your community informed about these local issues. Your newsletter is not written for environmental scientists, but to your neighbors, church members and family members, and community groups—a public audience.

Understand Your Purpose for Writing

Good public writing, like all good writing, has a clear PURPOSE. Are you writing to inform your readers? to entertain? to persuade? to evoke emotion? some combination of these? Getting clear on your purpose will help dictate which GENRES and MEDIA will be most effective—newsletter report, website, video making a proposal, opinion essay, flyer, *Instagram* post, among others. Many nonprofit organizations create materials to inform the public about their mission and to showcase activities that support their goals. The platforms of choice for most nonprofit organizations are websites, which are easy to access for almost everyone.

Take a look at feedingamerica.org, the website for Feeding America, an organization whose mission is to address food insecurity in the United States. A glance through its website indicates that the organization's major purposes are to inform and persuade readers—a general audience—about the state of hunger in America, about the work their organization does, and about how readers can donate and volunteer.

A website like this one includes a range of genres and media to achieve its purpose. For example, Feeding America's site includes a "Hunger Blog"—short narratives, reports, and arguments about different topics related to food insecurity. Olivia Thoelke's blog post "Why College Students Face Hunger"

The Feeding America homepage features a photograph drawing attention to child hunger.

provides a list of reasons (with brief explanations) for why college students, in particular, struggle with hunger:

1. **Rising tuition costs.** College is more expensive than ever. Adjusted for inflation, the cost of college increased by more than 25% in the last 10 years. Even though most students are working part-time or full-time jobs while in school, tuition and room & board have become too expensive for many students to pay for on their own.

2. **College meal plans are expensive.** The average college meal plan costs about $4,500 per year or $18.75 per day for a three-meal-a-day plan that covers the eight months or so of a typical academic year. Many colleges require students to have a meal plan if they plan to live on campus. That's a lot to pay for when your financial resources are limited.

3. **Even when you have a meal plan, food isn't always available.** When dining halls close, low-income students often struggle to find affordable food. According to a study from Harvard, many students can't afford to go home or take the time off work during school

breaks when the majority of college dining halls close. And college campuses often don't have affordable options for groceries nearby, especially if students don't have their own car.

4. **The "traditional" college student is changing.** Over the years, the proportion of "non-traditional" college students to "traditional" students has grown. This includes students who are financially independent, enrolled part-time in school while working full-time, or did not receive a traditional high school diploma. . . .

This changing face of the average college student brings new challenges. 1 in 5 students is caring for a child and many as single parents. Between rising tuition costs, parenting, and working full-time, making ends meet can be tough.

5. **Colleges don't know students are going hungry.** Even though so many students struggle, many college administrators think of hunger on campus as an uncommon exception. Because low-income students often can't afford meal plans (which on average run $4,500 per year), administrators are mostly exposed to students who can afford to eat on campus.

College students shouldn't have to worry about when their next meal will be. Together, we can help college students facing hunger. Donate today.

—OLIVIA THOELKE, "Why College Students Face Hunger"

Thoelke's main purpose is to inform the public about the problem and persuade readers to donate. An informative list (with hyperlinks to outside sources), posted on this major organization's website, is well matched to her goals. Feeding America's website also includes a link to a "Take Action" page that tells readers what they can do to help—an essential purpose for the site's existence, too.

Be Well Informed about Your Topic

Consider how Feeding America's website homepage provides *specific details* (facts and figures about hunger in America) to its readers. The writers assume that to persuade their audience to act—to give money, food, and time—they need to paint a stark picture of the state of hunger in America. They do so in part by providing some statistics:

- According to the USDA, more than 38 million people, including 12 million children, in the United States are food insecure.
- The pandemic has increased food insecurity among families with children and communities of color, who already faced hunger at much higher rates before the pandemic.
- Hunger in African American, Latino, and Native American communities is higher because of systemic racial injustice. To achieve a hunger-free America, we must address the root causes of hunger and structural and systemic inequities.

—FEEDING AMERICA, "Facts about Hunger in America"

These statistics help to provide a **CONTEXT** for this public site on hunger. They also help establish Feeding America's credibility: the group has done its homework and provides compelling support for its claims.

Likewise, your readers will need the relevant background information to fully engage with your topic and its importance. So, you may need to provide historical context and/or provide a specific description of a situation that has motivated you to write. Jackie Owen, a student contributor to *Coast Report*, the Orange Coast College (OCC) online student newspaper, shows that they are well informed about their topic by providing necessary context and description about how the OCC community is using *Apple Music Replay*:

One of the most widely used music platforms is Apple Music. When Apple Music creates an annual "Apple Music Replay" released on December 1 each year, students and staff from Orange Coast College may learn and reflect on their specific most-played songs, artists and albums of the year. Because there are so many different types of music, the Apple Music Replay has become widely popular as people from across the world share their specific recap of songs, artists and albums to various social media platforms. Up by 4 million subscribers from December 2019, estimates suggest that Apple Music had 72 million subscribers worldwide in June 2020, according to Statista.

—JACKIE OWEN, "Apple Music Replay Has OCC Students Buzzing"

Here Owen not only clearly explains what *Apple Music Replay* is, an important step, but also provides important background information and statistics about *Apple Music* while pointing out why *Apple Music Replay* may be of interest to the OCC community.

✎ *REFLECT. Read an opinion piece in your local or campus newspaper. Analyze the language, tone, and style used. How does the writer signal that they are writing for a general public audience? How would this piece be different if it were written for an academic—or perhaps a specialist—audience?*

Connect with Your Audience

Dr. Huma Farid is an ob-gyn in Boston and teaches at Harvard Medical School. She also writes health-related articles for a general audience; you can see one of them on p. 887.

Even though we've suggested that a public audience is fairly general, that doesn't necessarily mean that your audience includes everyone. Even those who write for a public audience have some sense of what segment of the population they are targeting. It's important to think carefully about your intended **AUDIENCE**—about how you'll engage them, get their attention, and keep it. Are you writing to millennials, Generation Zs, or another age group? Are you writing to food lovers or fitness enthusiasts? Maybe you're writing to an audience with a basic knowledge of a topic like climate change or the impact of college student loan debt. Your goal may be to persuade those with a general interest to become more active in supporting your cause. Knowing some details about your intended audience will help you make effective choices like what medium or genre to use and what kinds of examples or background information are needed.

In every case, think carefully about the kind of **LANGUAGE**, **TONE**, and **STYLE** that will connect to your audience. Remember that most general audiences do not require highly formal or academic language, style, or tone and may even be put off by such choices. So, consider what kind of language will be most effective in helping you reach your intended audience. Avoid long, complex sentences and terms with which they may be unfamiliar or that, as writer and rhetorician Peter Elbow says, "make them feel stupid." Instead, try for a conversational tone, and use vivid, concrete details wherever possible, along with visuals that can help get your message across. Note how the Feeding America website uses a visual to enhance the group's message. Finally, remember that you can use **RESEARCH**, as the composers of the Feeding America website have done, to connect to the audience, without writing up a formal research paper!

Design an Effective and Engaging Document

Given the technologies now available to you, think about how including images, video, sound (see Chapter 37, on multimodal writing), or links to detailed information may help you connect with your audience and achieve your purpose. As you already know, writing today is far from static or limited to words on a page or screen. As a result, attending to design elements is a very important part of composing any text. Food blogger and photography lover LaKita Anderson augments the About page on her website, *Simply LaKita*, with color photographs to draw in her audience and put a real face behind her story:

> It all began in 2013 when one stay-at-home mom decided to take all of her handwritten recipes, some of which were tried and true family favorites, and document them online with a blog. . . .
>
> I was raised in the [S]outh and grew up in the kitchen around great food. I learned how to bake by standing in the kitchen on a milk crate to reach the counter to help my grandmother make anything from cakes to

Images on Anderson's food blog convey personality and entice readers to try out her recipes.

pies to biscuits. As a young child, my mother taught me how to read a recipe and the proper way to measure ingredients. . . .

For a long time, I was navigating through life trying to figure out what I wanted to be when I "grew up." But two constants remained in my life and [they were] food and photography. Naturally, *Simply LaKita* became a place where I could make delicious food and learn to take beautiful pictures.

Here you'll find simple weekly recipes with a modern twist on comfort food. Recipes that are uncomplicated and do not require many ingredients or a lot of time in the kitchen. You'll also be able to find a dessert that requires no baking, a dinner that can be made in less than 30 minutes, plus a few tried and true family recipes. . . .

We strive to make sure that each recipe is simple enough that anyone can create it in their kitchen to share with their family and friends.

—SIMPLY LAKITA, "About"

The author uses a personal story ("I was raised in the [S]outh and grew up in the kitchen around great food") and photos (a smiling LaKita with food and a bowl of mouth-watering pasta) to connect to readers. If you check out Anderson's website, you will see other elements of design at work, including placement of text and images, the use of white space as well as accent colors, and an easy-to-follow navigation menu.

As this site demonstrates, the design of a website can be as powerful as the words it contains. In this case, Anderson's design of the text and visuals works to draw in readers who may process information differently. Some people will be drawn in by the recipes and story that Anderson tells, and others will be drawn in by the beauty of the food and the way Anderson engages with the dishes that she prepares. Anyone who reads the About page on Anderson's site will notice that they don't need to have any advanced knowledge about cooking. Anderson even points out that this site offers "recipes that are uncomplicated and do not require many ingredients or a lot of time in the kitchen." In fact, this page may appeal just as much to people who are interested in following their passions, as Anderson's story suggests.

Think about flyers that catch your attention or *Instagram* posts that make you stop and read. Often, it's the initial design of the document that captures your interest. As a writer, you want to think about the very significant role that design plays in grabbing attention and delivering your message.

Choose Your Modality Carefully

Writers today can move easily among five modes: linguistic, visual, audio, gestural, and spatial, which we discuss in more detail in Chapter 37. And today, more than ever, writers are mixing and combining these modes, producing multimodal texts such as illustrated essays and blogs, infographics, podcasts, video essays, graphic novels, social media posts, or whole ebooks that combine visual, print, and audio texts. Choosing the mode or modes for your public writing calls on you to think about what will best convey your message and reach your audience. If you want to get the attention of elementary-age children with a message about healthy eating, a video featuring cartoon characters might be a good choice. If you are trying to reach other college students with a message about how to manage on a tight budget, a *TikTok* video that features you speaking directly to the audience might work well. As a writer / author today, you're in charge, so make the most of all the tools at your disposal!

That's just what high school student Faith Omosefe did when she wrote and performed her spoken-word poem "16" as part of a Lawrence, MA, youth health initiative called The Masks Project—sponsored by the Bread Loaf Teacher Network's Next Generation Leadership Network (an Andover Bread Loaf program) early in the COVID-19 pandemic. In a public service announcement video that includes images, video, and art, Omosefe performs her poem. She marks her sixteenth birthday by addressing the whole country, saying:

> Dear America . . .
> Today . . . I am free to fly.
> Today is a terrible day to have to
>   wear this mask

But wear the mask she does—one handwoven by her mother, who didn't get to see her open or wear it—with pride and growing conviction. "Dear America," Omosefe implores, wear your mask as an "act of patriotism." She goes on:

> Open your eyes . . .
> and view your mask not as a
> barrier but as a bridge. . . .
> Dear America, mask up. And
>   breathe.

↪ Watch the PSA video that features Omosefe's spoken word poem by visiting everyonesanauthor .tumblr.com.

Faith Omosefe performed her spoken-word poem in a PSA encouraging masking early in the COVID-19 pandemic.

The multimodal Masks Project helped encourage masking and thus turned the tide against the virus early on in the local community where the videos were shared. And the project was replicated by young people in a number of other cities, demonstrating the power of writing and speaking to public audiences today.

REFLECT. Think about a topic or issue of great interest to you that would be of interest to a public audience as well. What modality would best fit your topic and audience—print essay, video, podcast, etc.? What do you want to say? What is your purpose? What content must you include? What will you need to find out to carry out this project? What design decisions will you need to make to achieve your purpose and reach your intended audience?

Readings

IF EVERYONE'S AN AUTHOR, then we are all readers as well. All authors, in fact, learn constantly by engaging with what other authors have written. On the following pages you'll find an anthology of twenty-seven readings, arranged alphabetically by author. And on the inside back cover of the book, we've added a menu that categorizes the readings by both genres and themes. And that's not all. We regularly post additional essays, articles, cartoons, speeches, videos, and more on everyonesanauthor.tumblr.com for you to read, analyze, reflect on—and respond to. So read on, enjoy, and see what you can learn.

The Myth of a Majority-Minority America

RICHARD ALBA, MORRIS LEVY, DOWELL MYERS

IN RECENT YEARS, demographers and pundits have latched on to the idea that, within a generation, the United States will inevitably become a majority-minority nation, with nonwhite people outnumbering white people (Colby & Ortman, 2015).[1] In the minds of many Americans, this ethno-racial transition betokens political, cultural, and social upheaval, because a white majority has dominated the nation since its founding. But our research on immigration, public opinion, and racial demography reveals something quite different (Alba, 2020; Levy & Myers, 2021; Myers & Levy, 2018): By softening and blurring racial and ethnic lines, diversity is bringing Americans together more than it is tearing the country apart.

The majority-minority narrative contributes to our national polarization. Its depiction of a society fractured in two, with one side rising while the other subsides, is inherently divisive because it implies winners and losers. It has bolstered white anxiety and resentment of supposedly ascendant minority groups, and has turned people against democratic institutions

Alba, Levy, and Myers chose to collaborate on this report, despite their individual expertise and accomplishments. You can find out more about the benefits of collaboration on pp. 135–36.

---

[1]. Full bibliographic information (APA) has been provided in place of the article's original hyperlinks. [Editor's note]

RICHARD ALBA, MORRIS LEVY, and DOWELL MYERS are professors, researchers, and authors in their respective fields. Sociology professor Alba's most recent book is *The Great Demographic Illusion* (2020); Levy is a professor of political science and international relations who specializes in immigration policy. Myers, a professor of urban planning and demography, has served as an advisor to the US Census Bureau and is the author of *Analysis with Local Census Data: Portraits of Change* (1992). This report was published in the *Atlantic* in June 2021.

that many conservative white Americans and politicians consider complicit in illegitimate minority empowerment (Craig & Richeson, 2014). At the extreme, it nurtures conspiratorial beliefs in a racist "replacement" theory, which holds that elites are working to replace white people with minority immigrants in a "stolen America" (Pape, 2021).

The narrative is also false. By rigidly splitting Americans into two groups, white versus nonwhite, it reinvents the discredited 19th-century "one-drop rule" and applies it to a 21st-century society in which the color line is more fluid than it has ever been (Davis, n.d.).

In reality, racial diversity is increasing not only at a nationwide level but also within American families—indeed within individual Americans. Nearly three in 10 Asian, one in four Latino, and one in five Black newlyweds are married to a member of a different ethnic or racial group (Livingston & Brown, 2017). More than three-quarters of these unions are with a white partner. For more and more Americans, racial integration is embedded in their closest relationships.

Multiracial identities are gaining public recognition and approval (Campbell & Herman, 2010; Citrin et al., 2014). Numerous young Americans consider themselves both white and members of a minority racial or ethnic group. One in every nine babies born in the U.S. today will be raised in a mixed minority-and-white family, and this group is steadily growing (Alba, 2021). These children have kin networks—including grandparents, aunts and uncles, and cousins—that include both white people and minorities. Among Latinos, identifying as white or as simply "American" is common, and belies the notion that Latinos should be classified monolithically as nonwhite (Lopez et al., 2017). 5

Furthermore, most Americans of both white and minority descent are not positioned as minorities in American society (Alba, 2020). For example, people who identify as Hispanic and white, or Asian and white, tend to start life in more economically favorable situations than most minority groups, are typically raised in largely white communities, have above-average educational outcomes and adulthood incomes, and frequently marry white people. They have fluid identities that are influenced by both minority and white ancestries. Children with Black and white parents face greater social exclusion and more formidable obstacles to upward mobility. But their social experiences are more integrated than those of Black Americans who identify as monoracial (Davenport, 2018).

These trends expose the flaw lurking behind the headline-grabbing claim that America will soon be a majority-minority society. That narrative depends on the misleading practice of classifying individuals of mixed backgrounds as exclusively nonwhite. The Census Bureau population projections that relied on this practice first predicted the majority-minority future in 2008. The idea quickly took on a life of its own. Some Americans now instinctively think of rising diversity as a catalyst of white decline and nonwhite numerical dominance (Levy & Myers, 2021). But as more recent news releases from the bureau have begun to acknowledge, what the data in fact show is that Americans with mixed racial backgrounds are the most rapidly growing racial group in the country (US Census Bureau, 2018).

As much as they are competing for economic resources and political power, America's racial groups are blending now more than ever. According to the most detailed of the Census Bureau's projections, 52 percent of individuals included in the nonwhite majority of 2060 will also identify as white (US Census Bureau, 2017). By the same token, the white group will become much more diverse, because 40 percent of Americans who say they are white also will claim a minority racial or ethnic identity. Speculating about whether America will have a white majority by the mid-21st century makes little sense, because the social meanings of *white* and *nonwhite* are rapidly shifting (Kaufman, 2019). The sharp distinction between these categories will apply to many fewer Americans.

The public deserves to hear an accurate narrative about rising racial diversity that highlights the likelihood that society's mainstream will continue to expand to include people of varied backgrounds. Our recent research demonstrates that most white people are not only receptive to such an inclusive narrative but can be powerfully influenced by it (Levy & Myers, 2021). In multiple survey experiments, we asked white Americans to read a news story describing the rise of mixed-race marriages and the growth of a multiracial population. They expressed less anxiety and anger, anticipated less discrimination against white people, and evinced more willingness to invest in public goods, such as education, than others who read a news story predicated on the false narrative of white decline in a majority-minority society by the mid-2040s. Notably, the narrative of racial blending was especially reassuring to white Republicans, who felt most threatened by the conventional majority-minority account. In our most recent study, 67 percent of white Republican participants expressed anxiety or anger after reading a news story modeled on the majority-minority narrative, compared with 29 percent of white Democratic participants. Among those who instead read a story of rising multiracialism and blending, anxiety and anger were much lower, reported by 26 percent of white Republicans and 13 percent of white Democrats.

Moreover, Latino, Black, and Asian participants in these studies expressed   10
overwhelmingly positive reactions to the story of racial blending. Anticipation of equal treatment in the future was as high among minority respondents
who read the blending story as among those who read the majority-minority
account. Minority Americans were most optimistic and least fearful after reading about the rise of multiracial families. Eighty-five percent of Black, Asian,
and Latino respondents expressed hopefulness or enthusiasm after reading this
account—more than the approximately two-thirds of minority respondents who
expressed these positive emotions in response to the majority-minority story.

For all the talk about racial polarization in America, the broad consensus is that an expanding and more diverse mainstream portends a better
future. Journalists, subject-matter experts, and political leaders have an
obligation to tell Americans the full story about rising diversity *and* racial
blending. At the same time, discussions of demographic change must not
fuel complacency about the unequal opportunities that minority groups,
especially Black Americans, continue to face (Alba, 2020). Narratives are
aspirational as well as informational. One that highlights our growing connections and interdependence should more effectively call attention to our
collective obligation to break racial barriers and overcome bigotry than to
retain historical zero-sum thinking about racial division.

Americans need to remember that they have been here before. A century
ago, the eugenicist Madison Grant asserted that Nordic Americans were com-
mitting "race suicide" by letting in millions of immigrants from Eastern and
Southern Europe who would out-breed them and destroy their nation's identity
(NBC News, 2008; Serwer, 2019). Swayed by this narrative, the United States Congress enacted drastic, racist restrictions on immigration that lasted for 40 years.

But during the "melting pot" era of the 1950s and '60s, the descendants
of the very immigrants Grant had maligned emphatically refuted his ideas.
Many white Americans had come to recognize that their ethnic differences
were eroding rather than solidifying. Parents of that time weren't so surprised
when an adult child brought home a possible partner from a different ethnic
or religious background, though the color line remained painfully formidable
(Alba & Nee, 2005). Interethnic and interreligious marriages among white
Americans soared (Waters, 1990). By the '90s, only 20 percent of white Americans had chosen partners from the same ethnic background (Alba & Nee, 2005).

While the rising number of multiracial Americans today does not
exactly mirror the dynamics of the '50s and '60s, the dangers of ignoring ethno-
racial blending are the same. The myth of an imminent majority-minority

society revives the misconception that American ethnic and racial groups are fixed, bounded, and separate. It breathes new life into old fears that rising diversity must entail white decline. Our ailing democracy needs a narrative now that recognizes how changing demography can unite us rather than divide us. Or, as the slogan goes, "E pluribus unum."

References

Alba, R. (2020). *The great demographic illusion: Majority, minority, and the expanding American mainstream*. Princeton University Press.

Alba, R. (2021). The surge of young Americans from minority-White mixed families & its significance for the future. *Dædalus, 150*(2), 199–214. https://doi.org/10.1162/DAED_a_01855

Alba, R., & Nee, V. (2005). *Remaking the American mainstream: Assimilation and contemporary immigration*. Harvard University Press.

Campbell, M. E., & Herman, M. R. (2010). Politics and policies: Attitudes towards multiracial Americans. *Ethnic and Racial Studies, 33*(9), 1511–1536. https://doi.org/10.1080/01419871003671929

Citrin, C., Levy, M., & Van Houweling, R. P. (2014). Americans fill out President Obama's census form: What is his race? *Social Science Quarterly, 95*(4), 1121–1136. https://doi.org/10.1111/ssqu.12105

Colby, S. L., & Ortman, J. M. (2015, March 3). *Projections of the size and composition of the U.S. population: 2014 to 2060* (Current Population Reports, P25-1143). United States Census Bureau. https://www.census.gov/library/publications/2015/demo/p25-1143.html

Craig, M. A., & Richeson, J. A. (2014). On the precipice of a "majority-minority" America: Perceived status threat from the racial demographic shift affects White Americans' political ideology. *Psychological Science, 25*(6), 1189–1197. https://doi.org/10.1177/0956797614527113

Davenport, L. D. (2018). *Politics beyond Black & White: Biracial identity and attitudes in America*. Cambridge University Press.

Davis, F. J. (n.d.). *Who is Black? One nation's definition*. PBS *Frontline*. https://www.pbs.org/wgbh/pages/frontline/shows/jefferson/mixed/onedrop.html

Kaufman, E. (2019). *Whiteshift: Populism, immigration, and the future of White majorities*. Abrams Press.

Levy, M., & Myers, D. (2021). Racial projections in perspective: Public reactions to narratives about rising diversity. *Perspectives on Politics, 19*(4), 1147–1164. https://doi.org/10.1017/S1537592720003679

Livingston, G., & Brown, A. (2017, May 18). *Intermarriage in the U.S. 50 years after* Loving v. Virginia. Pew Research Center. https://www.pewresearch .org/social-trends/2017/05/18/intermarriage-in-the-u-s-50-years-after -loving-v-virginia/

Lopez, M. H., Gonzalez-Barrera, A., & López, G. (2017, December 20). *Hispanic identity fades across generations as immigrant connections fall away.* Pew Research Center. https://www.pewresearch.org/hispanic/2017/12/20 /hispanic-identity-fades-across-generations-as-immigrant-connections -fall-away/

Myers, D., & Levy, M. (2018). Racial population projections and reactions to alternative news accounts of growing diversity. *The Annals of the American Academy of Political and Social Science, 677*(1), 215–228. https://doi .org/10.1177/0002716218766294

NBC News (2008, May 27). *1910s-1920s: Immigration, defining Whiteness.* https://www.nbcnews.com/id/wbna24714378

Pape, R. A. (2021, April 6). Opinion: What an analysis of 377 Americans arrested or charged in the Capitol insurrection tells us. *The Washington Post.* https:// www.washingtonpost.com/opinions/2021/04/06/capitol-insurrection -arrests-cpost-analysis/

Serwer, A. (2019, April). White nationalism's deep American roots. *The Atlantic.* https://www.theatlantic.com/magazine/archive/2019/04/adam -serwer-madison-grant-white-nationalism/583258/

United States Census Bureau. (2017). *2017 national population projections table: Main series.* https://www.census.gov/data/tables/2017/demo /popproj/2017-summary-tables.html

United States Census Bureau. (2018, March 13). *Older people projected to outnumber children for first time in U.S. history* [Press release]. https:// www.census.gov/newsroom/press-releases/2018/cb18-41-population -projections.html

Waters, M. C. (1990). *Ethnic options: Choosing identities in America.* University of California Press.

Thinking about the Text

1. Richard Alba, Morris Levy, and Dowell Myers present a variety of population statistics in order to make an **ARGUMENT** about the demographics of the US population. What is their main argument? Summarize it. Do you think that the argument is presented clearly? Why or why not?

2. The **EVIDENCE** in Alba, Levy, and Myers's report mostly comes from data, statistics, and opinion polls. They don't include any personal narratives or anecdotes. Did you find the data-driven evidence persuasive? Should they have presented these other types of evidence? Why or why not? Explain your reasoning.

3. The authors **COMPARE** our current demographic trends and attitudes to the US circumstances during the 1950s and 1960s. What point are the authors making with the example of the early-twentieth-century eugenicist Madison Grant? What similarities and differences between the two eras do they highlight? How does this comparative example support their argument? Explain your reasoning.

4. Alba, Levy, and Myers back up their assertions and predictions by citing and **DOCUMENTING SOURCES**, drawing on twenty sources of diverse types. Review the list of references, taking into consideration the credentials of the authors, the publishers, the type of publication, and the dates of publication. In general, do the references appear reliable and trustworthy? Why or why not? How does the authors' use of sources affect their **CREDIBILITY** to report on this topic?

5. According to the authors, racial diversity in the US is increasing not only on a national level but also within families and even within individuals. They assert that "for more and more Americans, racial integration is embedded in their closest relationships" (3). Assess their claim by considering the people you know—your elder relatives and neighbors, people of your own generation such as friends, coworkers, and classmates, as well as any children you may know. What proportion of the people you know have multiracial and/or multiethnic identities? How do the categories of attitudes that the authors describe match up with your experience of people around you? For example, do you know people who likely embrace more racial blending in the US? Do you know people who openly disapprove or might express fear of a "minority-majority" future? Once you have considered the attitudes of the people around you, write an essay that takes a **POSITION** in response to Alba, Levy, and Myers's report, agreeing with or rebutting their findings.

What's Your Pronoun?

DENNIS BARON

PRONOUNS ARE SUDDENLY SEXY. No longer the province of stuffy grammar books, they're in the air, on the news, all over social media, generating discussion pro and con. Or at least one pronoun is: the third-person singular gender-neutral pronoun. Yes, the pronoun *without* sex is suddenly sexy. People are asking each other, "What's your pronoun?"—it's the new "Hello, my name is _____." And sometimes they don't even wait to be asked. They introduce themselves with, "I'm Alex. My pronouns are *they, them, their.*" Or "*ze, hir, hirs.*" Or they put it in their profile:

> DR. ANDREW FOLES
> @drandrewcomic
>
> I'm a linguist and a comic book
> editor @comicsuniv. I also have
> experience herding sheep. He/him.

DENNIS BARON, professor emeritus of linguistics and English, has written extensively for both academic and general audiences on issues of language and the law, language technologies, and gender issues in language use, among other topics. He is author of *A Better Pencil: Readers, Writers, and the Digital Revolution* (2009). This essay is from the introduction to his book *What's Your Pronoun?* (2020). Baron tweets from @DrGrammar.

Pronouns are even on TV. In 2019, in a scene from the long-running BBC police procedural *Silent Witness*, Nick, a suspect in a series of murders at a transgender support center, asks an investigator, "What gender pronouns are you going to use for me in your report?" The investigator responds, "What would you like me to use?" And Nick replies, "She, please." The investigator honors that request.[1]

"What's your pronoun?" is an invitation to declare, to honor, or to reject, not just a pronoun, but a gender identity. And it's a question about a part of speech. Repeat: A question about a part of speech.

It used to be nerdy to discuss parts of speech outside of grammar class. Now it's cool. When the talk turns to "What's your pronoun?" suddenly everybody has an opinion, not just about pronouns, but about *that* pronoun. English has masculine and feminine and neuter pronouns, but it is missing a pronoun for someone whose gender is unknown, unclear, nonbinary, or "other." For centuries, grammarians recommended generic *he* in such cases. But generic *he* turns out to be not so generic: too often *he* means "only men."

That's why some people claim we need a new pronoun. And there's no shortage of people eager to supply the missing word by coining ones like *zie* or *tey*. The grammar sticklers are always sure that English speakers don't need any new pronouns, they've gotten along just fine with generic *he*, thank you very much. Fortunately, and apologies if you are one of them, the sticklers are becoming hard to find. And a growing number of people are realizing that we've had the missing word all along: it's singular *they*.

For more than two hundred years—long before *transgender* (1974), *cisgender* (1997), and *gender-fluid* (1987) entered our vocabularies—a small but vocal number of writers, editors, and grammarians, mostly men, have lamented the fact that English has no third-person singular, gender-neutral pronoun to refer to both a man and a woman, or to either a man or a woman, or to conceal gender, or to prevent gender from causing a distraction. Recognizing that gender is political as well as grammatical, they've sought a pronoun— some call it "the missing word"—that includes both genders, or all genders, and doesn't leave anyone out.

Those seeking a better way to include all the genders, whether they think of gender as a traditional male/female binary or something more

---

1. *Silent Witness*, series 22, episode 1, "Two Spirits, pt. 1," at 40:50. bbc.co.uk, 2019.

nuanced and complex, have answered the pronoun question in multiple ways. They've coined a new word, or they've repurposed a current word. They've borrowed a word from another language, or they've acknowledged that *they*, like *you*, could be both singular and plural. To be sure, there have been defenders of the status quo who've simply invoked generic *he*, long approved by grammarians who insisted that such use of *he* includes *she*. Some nineteenth-century feminists capitalized on this inclusive *he* by arguing that, if *he* means *she*, then surely the voting laws, which always referred to voters as *he*, meant that women could vote. Unfortunately, judges and legislators—all of them men—disagreed. "Of course *he* is generic," they mansplained, "but not for voting."

It wasn't just voting. There have been too many occasions where generic *he* didn't seem generic. For example, one Minnesota public health law, proposed in 1903, decreed, "No person shall kiss another person unless *he* can prove that *he* is free from contagious or infectious diseases."[2] Does *he* in the bill include women who kiss? Or parents kissing children? Or children kissing grandparents? Or politicians kissing babies? Or trans persons? The word *transgender* didn't exist in 1903, but gender dysphoria did. Would people identifying as gender-nonconforming today be bound by that Minnesota *he*?

He is just a pronoun, just a part of speech. But put a pronoun in a law, as some well-meaning Minnesota legislator tried to do, and suddenly, you've got yourself a problem, whether that law is about kissing or about voting. Because the problem's not just about who's kissing who. In 1916, when Jeannette Rankin, of Montana, became the first woman elected to the US House of Representatives, the *Minneapolis Star Tribune* ran this headline challenging the grammatical rule that says the masculine pronoun can refer to women: "Can 'She' Be 'He', a Congressman, and Be Woman?"[3] Pronouns aren't just a part of speech. Pronouns are political.

In 1922, Edith Wilmans became the first woman elected to the Texas state assembly, prompting a prediction by the *San Antonio Express* that she would not be allowed to serve, because Texas law referred to state legislators

As you dig around in newspaper archives, make sure to write down everything you'll need for your documentation style. Ch. 24 will help you get organized.

2. "To Restrict Kissing by Law," *New York Tribune*, Jan. 31, 1903, p. 7. Emphasis added.

3. "Can 'She' Be 'He', a Congressman, and Be Woman?" *Minneapolis Star Tribune*, Nov. 13, 1916, p. 1. Montana, Colorado, and a number of other states had universal suffrage before the passage of the Nineteenth Amendment ensured that all American women could vote.

as *he*. The *San Antonio Evening News* shrugged off this objection, at the same time reminding readers that the masculine pronoun doesn't just keep women out of the state house: "The same pronoun stands between many women and their liberty."[4]

The men who made and enforced the laws insisted the *he* in a statute   10 included women when it came to imposing penalties, as in the Minnesota kissing bill, which would have fined offenders between $1 and $5 (about $30–$150 today). But these same men used the pronoun *he* to exclude women when they tried to assert their right to vote or to hold elected office. Or, as the *San Antonio News* wryly observed, when women tried to assert any rights at all.

[T]he generic masculine was never truly generic: far too many times, *he* meant "only men." As British and American women began to assert their political and economic rights in the nineteenth century, both feminists and antifeminists enlisted the pronoun *he* to support their cause. American suffragists like Susan B. Anthony observed that, when the criminal laws referred to lawbreakers as *he* or *him*, no one doubted that these laws also applied to women. And so both logic and consistency demanded that, when the voting laws referred to voters as *he*, that meant women could vote as well as men. Or so you would think.

Although pronouns may seem a minor concern compared with physical safety and mental stability, prisoners have gone to court, with varying degrees of success, to demand to be referred to by their chosen pronoun, and employees have filed complaints against employers when supervisors and co-workers intentionally use inappropriate pronouns and create a hostile work environment. Gay and trans students also charge their schools with gender discrimination for not upholding their right to designate their pronoun. Laws and regulations in these areas remain unsettled, varying from jurisdiction to jurisdiction, office to office, and school to school. And yet more and more national, state, and local governments, along with businesses and schools, are now recognizing pronoun choice as one of the rights of gender-nonconforming persons.

---

4. *San Antonio Evening News*, Oct. 5, 1922, p. 4. Wilmans easily won that seat—with the support of the Texas Ku Klux Klan. After the passage of the Nineteenth Amendment, women's suffrage, particularly in the American South, was often leveraged to dilute the African American vote.

Confronting Generic *He*

Pronoun gender is a hot topic today, but it's hardly a new topic. From the first English grammars in the seventeenth century to the language commentators of the later twentieth, writers who tackled the question of pronoun gender dealt with generic *he* in a number of ways:

- By simply decreeing that *he* was generic and assuming that anything else was just plain wrong; or sensing resistance to generic *he*, but still insisting that *he* was both inclusive and grammatically correct; or, acknowledging discomfort with generic *he*, but finding no alternative, feeling compelled to indicate that *he* included "she."

- Rejecting generic *he* as ambiguous or sexist and using singular *they* instead, defending it as both natural and common. Sometimes adding that if *you* could be singular and plural, why not *they* as well?

- Rejecting both generic *he* and singular *they* in favor of an invented pronoun, and sometimes asking some expert to coin one in order to avoid error and ambiguity.

In addition, any of the above might be accompanied by a condemnation of the compounds *he or she*, along with *him or her* and *his or her*, options that are both grammatical and inclusive, but which no one liked. Ever.

A New Pronoun Would Fix All That

Starting in the eighteenth century, a few more-adventurous souls thought that the best way to deal with the missing word would be to invent one. More than 200 of these pronouns were invented, most of them before the 1970s, and many of them before 1900. There were crackpots coining pronouns, to be sure, but most of the neologists—the new word makers—were writers, educators, or professionals who knew a bit about language and who thought they could improve on a bad situation. Most of the word coiners were men, though a few women got into the act. Some of the word coiners were concerned with gender parity, some with grammatical correctness, and a few of them with both. Some of their proposals were met with mockery and derision, but a few were taken seriously enough to be adopted by a few enthusiasts. Two gender-neutral pronouns, *thon* and *heer*, even made it into major dictionaries, though they were later dropped for lack of use. But most of these pronouns made a small splash and then were lost to history— not the missing words, but the words that failed.

The early word coiners were typically concerned with correctness. In 15 their view, the current options were simply wrong. Generic *he* used a masculine pronoun for a woman, violating the rule that pronouns should agree with their antecedents in gender as well as number. Singular *they* used a plural pronoun for a singular noun, violating the number agreement part of that rule. A new pronoun would fix all that.

The Pronoun Almost Everyone Already Used

The first word coiners didn't care so much about gender inclusivity, or identity politics, or resistance to heteronormativity. That came later. But as women's rights and suffrage grew prominent both in the United States and England after the 1840s, pronouns were discussed by feminists and antifeminists alike. They were discussed by legislators. By grammarians. By editors. And by ordinary people around the dinner table. An article in the *Springfield Republican* in 1896 claimed that these ordinary folk had already found the solution to the missing word. Instead of the generic *he* mandated by grammarians, it was *they*: "at least two men out of three and four women out of five use 'they' already, with sublime contempt for rule."[5] Of course these statistics were a guess. There was no way in 1896 to tell how many men or women used singular *they*, or any other pronoun. But the *Republican* didn't need hard data to know what was obvious to even the most casual of observers, that almost everyone used singular *they* in speech, and many careful writers used it as well. The *Republican* had an answer to the pronoun question. Singular *they*.

5. "A New Treatise on Everyday English," *Springfield Republican* (MA), Jan. 5, 1896, p. 6.

Thinking about the Text

1. Dennis Baron **PROPOSES** that singular "they" is a tidy solution to two distinct third-person pronoun challenges in English. What are those challenges? Do you agree with Baron that "they" is a good solution? Why or why not?

2. How often do you use or hear **SINGULAR "THEY"**? First, write down your immediate answer. Then, pay close attention for two days to what you and the people around you say in ordinary conversation. How well does your observation match up with your initial response? Are you surprised by your observations? Explain what you've noticed and why it might (or might not) have surprised you.

3. Baron, a linguist and prolific writer and speaker on language issues, is clearly very serious about the topic of pronouns, specifically about singular "they." His essay, however, does include touches of humor. How well does his sometimes casual **TONE** work with the serious purpose of his argument? Explain your reasoning.

4. All languages change over time—pronunciations shift gradually, new words are added, others disappear from daily use, and even the ways that words can be put together to make meaning can shift over time. Many of these changes occur so gradually that we don't notice them; occasionally, a change can be observed as it happens. The growing acceptance of singular "they," for example, is something that you're experiencing in real time. What other changes have you observed? In addition to new words or new meanings ("doomscrolling," "enby," "anti-vaxxer"), think about whether you've observed pronunciation shifts or other changes. Describe your observations and conclusions.

5. Most people (maybe including you, too) have strong feelings about their language(s) and how they should (or shouldn't) be spoken or written. English speakers may have adamant opinions about singular "they," or "y'all," or whether a carbonated soft drink is called "pop" or "soda" or something else entirely. Why do you think some people care so much? Might they be overreacting? Why or why not? Write an essay that addresses these questions and explains your responses.

The Sanctuary of School

LYNDA BARRY

I **WAS 7 YEARS OLD** the first time I snuck out of the house in the dark. It was winter and my parents had been fighting all night. They were short on money and long on relatives who kept "temporarily" moving into our house because they had nowhere else to go.

My brother and I were used to giving up our bedroom. We slept on the couch, something we actually liked because it put us that much closer to the light of our lives, our television.

At night when everyone was asleep, we lay on our pillows watching it with the sound off. We watched Steve Allen's mouth moving. We watched Johnny Carson's mouth moving. We watched movies filled with gangsters shooting machine guns into packed rooms, dying soldiers hurling a last grenade and beautiful women crying at windows. Then the sign-off finally came and we tried to sleep.

LYNDA BARRY is an artist, cartoonist, and teacher, known for her comic strip *Ernie Pook's Comeek* as well as for graphic works on the relationship between creativity and drawing like *What It Is* (2008). In 2016, she was inducted into the Eisner Hall of Fame, and in 2019 she was awarded a MacArthur Fellowship. Barry is currently a professor of interdisciplinary creativity at the University of Wisconsin. The essay here was originally published in the *New York Times* in 1992, when public schools were experiencing severe cutbacks.

The morning I snuck out, I woke up filled with a panic about needing to get to school. The sun wasn't quite up yet but my anxiety was so fierce that I just got dressed, walked quietly across the kitchen and let myself out the back door.

It was quiet outside. Stars were still out. Nothing moved and no one was   5
in the street. It was as if someone had turned the sound off on the world.

I walked the alley, breaking thin ice over the puddles with my shoes. I didn't know why I was walking to school in the dark. I didn't think about it. All I knew was a feeling of panic, like the panic that strikes kids when they realize they are lost.

That feeling eased the moment I turned the corner and saw the dark outline of my school at the top of the hill. My school was made up of about 15 nondescript portable classrooms set down on a fenced concrete lot in a rundown Seattle neighborhood, but it had the most beautiful view of the Cascade Mountains. You could see them from anywhere on the playfield and you could see them from the windows of my classroom—Room 2.

I walked over to the monkey bars and hooked my arms around the cold metal. I stood for a long time just looking across Rainier Valley. The sky was beginning to whiten and I could hear a few birds.

In a perfect world my absence at home would not have gone unnoticed. I would have had two parents in a panic to locate me, instead of two parents in a panic to locate an answer to the hard question of survival during a deep financial and emotional crisis.

But in an overcrowded and unhappy home, it's incredibly easy for any   10
child to slip away. The high levels of frustration, depression and anger in my house made my brother and me invisible. We were children with the sound turned off. And for us, as for the steadily increasing number of neglected children in this country, the only place where we could count on being noticed was at school.

"Hey there, young lady. Did you forget to go home last night?" It was Mr. Gunderson, our janitor, whom we all loved. He was nice and he was funny and he was old with white hair, thick glasses and an unbelievable number of keys. I could hear them jingling as he walked across the playfield. I felt incredibly happy to see him.

He let me push his wheeled garbage can between the different porta-bles as he unlocked each room. He let me turn on the lights and raise the

window shades and I saw my school slowly come to life. I saw Mrs. Holman, our school secretary, walk into the office without her orange lipstick on yet. She waved.

I saw the fifth-grade teacher, Mr. Cunningham, walking under the breezeway eating a hard roll. He waved.

And I saw my teacher, Mrs. Claire LeSane, walking toward us in a red coat and calling my name in a very happy and surprised way, and suddenly my throat got tight and my eyes stung and I ran toward her crying. It was something that surprised us both.

It's only thinking about it now, 28 years later, that I realize I was crying 15 from relief. I was with my teacher, and in a while I was going to sit at my desk, with my crayons and pencils and books and classmates all around me, and for the next six hours I was going to enjoy a thoroughly secure, warm and stable world. It was a world I absolutely relied on. Without it, I don't know where I would have gone that morning.

Mrs. LeSane asked me what was wrong and when I said "Nothing," she seemingly left it at that. But she asked me if I would carry her purse for her, an honor above all honors, and she asked if I wanted to come into Room 2 early and paint.

She believed in the natural healing power of painting and drawing for troubled children. In the back of her room there was always a drawing table and an easel with plenty of supplies, and sometimes during the day she would come up to you for what seemed like no good reason and quietly ask if you wanted to go to the back table and "make some pictures for Mrs. LeSane." We all had a chance at it—to sit apart from the class for a while to paint, draw and silently work out impossible problems on 11 × 17 sheets of newsprint.

Drawing came to mean everything to me. At the back table in Room 2, I learned to build myself a life preserver that I could carry into my home.

We all know that a good education system saves lives, but the people of this country are still told that cutting the budget for public schools is necessary, that poor salaries for teachers are all we can manage and that art, music and all creative activities must be the first to go when times are lean.

Before- and after-school programs are cut and we are told that public schools 20 are not made for baby-sitting children. If parents are neglectful temporarily or permanently, for whatever reason, it's certainly sad, but their unlucky children must fend for themselves. Or slip through the cracks. Or wander in a dark night alone.

We are told in a thousand ways that not only are public schools not important, but that the children who attend them, the children who need them most, are not important either. We leave them to learn from the blind eye of a television, or to the mercy of "a thousand points of light"[1] that can be as far away as stars.

I was lucky. I had Mrs. LeSane. I had Mr. Gunderson. I had an abundance of art supplies. And I had a particular brand of neglect in my home that allowed me to slip away and get to them. But what about the rest of the kids who weren't as lucky? What happened to them?

By the time the bell rang that morning I had finished my drawing and Mrs. LeSane pinned it up on the special bulletin board she reserved for drawings from the back table. It was the same picture I always drew—a sun in the corner of a blue sky over a nice house with flowers all around it.

Mrs. LeSane asked us to please stand, face the flag, place our right hands over our hearts and say the Pledge of Allegiance. Children across the country do it faithfully. I wonder now when the country will face its children and say a pledge right back.

> Describing how one child was saved by art classes helps make a case for funding school programs. See Ch. 20 for more argument strategies.

1. *"A thousand points of light"*: A phrase used by President George H. W. Bush to refer to the many private, nonprofit community organizations that he hoped would step in to help people in need when government-sponsored social programs were cut. [Editor's note]

Thinking about the Text

1. Lynda Barry begins her **NARRATIVE** by revealing some painful personal information, which leads to a damning criticism of the state of education in the United States. Does her personal anecdote enhance her political argument? damage it? How well do these two elements of her essay complement each other? Explain your answer, citing evidence from the text.

2. It could be argued that the art opportunities in Barry's school were more beneficial to her than to other students because she was always artistically inclined and even went on to become a professional artist—or even that there is no reason to have art instruction in elementary schools at all because so few children actually become artists. How would you respond to that argument? Agree or disagree, presenting **EVIDENCE** from your own school experiences.

3. Barry uses the expression "the sound off" or "the sound turned off" three times in the essay (3, 5, 10). In which instances is it meant literally and in which figuratively? How does the repetition of this language help make the point of her narrative?

4. Barry concludes her essay with a call for the United States and its education system to make a "pledge" to children (24). Although her proposals are not spelled out, what can you infer about what Barry is asking the schools to do? Provide **EXAMPLES** from the text that indicate what she thinks is important.

5. Did you ever have a teacher who, in the course of simply doing their job, helped you get through a hard time or a tremendous struggle? Write a **NARRATIVE** about an experience you had with a memorable teacher, and relate your experience in some way to your adult life.

Fun Home

ALISON BECHDEL

ALISON BECHDEL is a cartoonist, writer, and 2014 recipient of a MacArthur Fellowship. Her serialized comic strip, *Dykes to Watch Out For*, ran in dozens of periodicals from 1983 to 2008. In 2006, she published *Fun Home: A Family Tragicomic*, a graphic memoir that centers on her relationship with her father and addresses matters of gender, sexual orientation, and family; the book became a Broadway musical that won a Tony award in 2015. The title refers to the family business, a funeral home. Her graphic autobiography, *The Secret to Superhuman Strength*, was published in 2021.

In a 2012 interview in the *New Yorker*, Bechdel describes the writing/drawing process that results in her characteristic panels so rich with graphic and narrative detail. First, she creates a grid of panels that one walks through, like rooms in a house. "The whole thing about a graphic book," says Bechdel, "is that it's a 3-D object."

You may have heard of the Bechdel Test. To pass, a movie, TV show, or book has to have at least two characters who: 1) are women, 2) talk to each other, and 3) talk about something other than a man. (Go to bechdeltest.com to learn more.)

This selection is from *Fun Home* and contains some terms that may be unfamiliar. Daedalus and Icarus were a father-son duo in Greek mythology. While the two were imprisoned in a tower, master builder Daedalus built wings from feathers and wax so that they could escape by flying out. He warned Icarus not to fly too high because the sun would melt the wax, but the warning was unheeded, and Icarus fell into the sea and drowned. "Butch" and "nelly" are colloquial terms that emerged in twentieth-century lesbian and gay cultures. The terms refer to gender performance or traits, with "butch" roughly corresponding to masculine and "nelly" to feminine.

LIKE MANY FATHERS, MINE COULD OCCASIONALLY BE PREVAILED ON FOR A SPOT OF "AIRPLANE."

AS HE LAUNCHED ME, MY FULL WEIGHT WOULD FALL ON THE PIVOT POINT BETWEEN HIS FEET AND MY STOMACH.

OOF!

IT WAS A DISCOMFORT WELL WORTH THE RARE PHYSICAL CONTACT, AND CERTAINLY WORTH THE MOMENT OF PERFECT BALANCE WHEN I SOARED ABOVE HIM.

IN THE CIRCUS, ACROBATICS WHERE ONE PERSON LIES ON THE FLOOR BALANCING ANOTHER ARE CALLED "ICARIAN GAMES."

WHEN OTHER CHILDREN CALLED OUR HOUSE A MANSION, I WOULD DEMUR. I RESENTED THE IMPLICATION THAT MY FAMILY WAS RICH, OR UNUSUAL IN ANY WAY.

IN FACT, WE WERE UNUSUAL, THOUGH I WOULDN'T APPRECIATE EXACTLY HOW UNUSUAL UNTIL MUCH LATER. BUT WE WERE NOT RICH.

IT'S JUST A HOUSE.

ALISON!

WHAT?

SEND TAMMI HOME. YOU HAVE WORK TO DO.

THE GILT CORNICES, THE MARBLE FIREPLACE, THE CRYSTAL CHANDELIERS, THE SHELVES OF CALF-BOUND BOOKS--THESE WERE NOT SO MUCH BOUGHT AS PRODUCED FROM THIN AIR BY MY FATHER'S REMARKABLE LEGERDEMAIN.

WASH THESE OLD CURTAINS SO WE CAN PUT UP THE HAND-EMBROIDERED LACE ONES I FOUND IN MRS. STRUMP'S ATTIC.

MY FATHER COULD SPIN GARBAGE...

...INTO GOLD.

HE COULD TRANSFIGURE A ROOM WITH THE SMALLEST OFFHAND FLOURISH.

HE COULD CONJURE AN ENTIRE, FINISHED PERIOD INTERIOR FROM A PAINT CHIP.

THIS SHOULD GO AT AN ANGLE.

AMAZING.

HIS SISTER

MY ARM'S FALLING OFF.

HE WAS AN ALCHEMIST OF APPEARANCE, A SAVANT OF SURFACE, A DAEDALUS OF DECOR.

SLIGHTLY PERFECT.

WE EACH RESISTED IN OUR OWN WAYS, BUT IN THE END WE WERE EQUALLY
POWERLESS BEFORE MY FATHER'S CURATORIAL ONSLAUGHT.

MY BROTHERS AND I COULDN'T COMPETE WITH THE ASTRAL LAMPS AND GIRANDOLES
AND HEPPLEWHITE SUITE CHAIRS. THEY WERE PERFECT.

I GREW TO RESENT THE WAY MY FATHER
TREATED HIS FURNITURE LIKE CHILDREN,
AND HIS CHILDREN LIKE FURNITURE.

MY OWN DECIDED PREFERENCE FOR THE
UNADORNED AND PURELY FUNCTIONAL
EMERGED EARLY.

It's not only Bechdel's detailed drawings that bring her story to life; the descriptive details add to the rich texture of her narrative. Learn more about adding vivid detail on pp. 205–6.

ALTHOUGH I'M GOOD AT ENUMERATING MY FATHER'S FLAWS, IT'S HARD FOR ME TO SUSTAIN MUCH ANGER AT HIM.

I EXPECT THIS IS PARTLY BECAUSE HE'S DEAD, AND PARTLY BECAUSE THE BAR IS LOWER FOR FATHERS THAN FOR MOTHERS.

STOP SPLASHING!

IN MY EYES!

HOLD STILL, DAMMIT!

MY MOTHER MUST HAVE BATHED ME HUNDREDS OF TIMES. BUT IT'S MY FATHER RINSING ME OFF WITH THE PURPLE METAL CUP THAT I REMEMBER MOST CLEARLY.

THE SUFFUSION OF WARMTH AS THE HOT WATER SLUICED OVER ME...

...THE SUDDEN, UNBEARABLE COLD OF ITS ABSENCE.

WAS HE A GOOD FATHER? I WANT TO SAY, "AT LEAST HE STUCK AROUND." BUT OF COURSE, HE DIDN'T.

AGAIN!

IT'S TRUE THAT HE DIDN'T KILL HIMSELF UNTIL I WAS NEARLY TWENTY.

BUT HIS ABSENCE RESONATED RETROACTIVELY, ECHOING BACK THROUGH ALL THE TIME I KNEW HIM.

MAYBE IT WAS THE CONVERSE OF THE WAY AMPUTEES FEEL PAIN IN A MISSING LIMB.

HE REALLY WAS THERE ALL THOSE YEARS, A FLESH-AND-BLOOD PRESENCE STEAMING OFF THE WALLPAPER, DIGGING UP THE DOGWOODS, POLISHING THE FINIALS...

...SMELLING OF SAWDUST AND SWEAT AND DESIGNER COLOGNE.

BUT I ACHED AS IF HE WERE ALREADY GONE.

Thinking about the Text

1. Alison Bechdel **DESCRIBES** a relationship with her father that is full of both love and resentment. How does she reconcile those seeming contradictions? How successful is she at conveying her balance between tenderness and bitterness? Why do you think so? Point to specific passages that support your conclusion.

2. Bechdel chooses two very ordinary activities with her father—playing airplane and being bathed—to represent something larger about her childhood and her life in general. Think of a moment in your own childhood that you might use to represent something larger about yourself. What would it be?

3. In addition to the drawings themselves, Bechdel employs narration boxes and speech balloons to help tell her story. How does she use those two devices to navigate between events happening in her childhood moments and reflections from her adult perspective? Select one panel or group of panels and describe how each device works in your selection.

4. Although Bechdel's family has other members, *Fun Home* focuses on the relationship between Alison and her father. We know from her reflections what her attitude is toward her father. What is Bechdel's attitude toward her child self? How does she reveal it? Point to specific passages that support your reasoning.

5. Write a short **NARRATIVE** (in graphic form, if you wish) of your childhood relationship with a parent or other adult in your life. Choose one or two key activities or events that can represent the relationship as a whole. Present details that illustrate the original moments and use your adult perspective to reflect and provide coherence. (You may want to respond to question #2 first to help you get started.)

The Talk: After Ferguson, a Shaded Conversation about Race

DANA CANEDY

LIKE SO MANY AFRICAN-AMERICAN PARENTS, I had rehearsed "the talk," that nausea-inducing discussion I needed to have with my son about how to conduct himself in the presence of the police. I was prepared for his questions, except for one.

"Can I just pretend I'm white?"

Jordan was born to African-American parents, but recessive genes being what they are, he has very fair skin and pale blue eyes. I am caramel brown, and since his birth eight years ago people have mistaken me for his nanny.

When I asked why he would want to "pass" for white, I struggled with how to respond to his answer.

"Because it's safer," Jordan replied. "They won't hurt me."   5

That recent gray day, not long after grand juries failed to indict the police officers who killed unarmed black men in Ferguson, Missouri, and

---

DANA CANEDY is the author of *A Journal for Jordan: A Story of Love and Honor* (2008), a memoir dedicated to her son after the death of his father and her fiancé, First Sergeant Charles Monroe King. She won a Pulitzer Prize for her work at the *New York Times* and was senior vice president at Simon & Schuster, the first Black person to hold that post. This *New York Times* piece was published in December 2014. She tweets from @DanaCanedy.

First Sgt. Charles M. King with his son, Jordan. King visited his son on leave before returning to Iraq on a mission that would end his life.

Staten Island, I had steadied myself to lay out the rules: Always address police officers as "sir" or "ma'am." Do not make any sudden moves, even to reach for identification. Do not raise your voice, resist or run.

But now I was taken aback.

Jordan's father and I never had a chance to discuss when we would give him the talk, or what we would say. Our baby was just 6 months old when his dad, a decorated Army soldier, was killed in combat in Iraq. So the timing and the context of the talk were left to me.

I had tried hard to delay it, and make sure he wouldn't know the names Michael Brown or Eric Garner or Tamir Rice.

In the days leading up to the conversation, I asked an African-American 10 male colleague if he thought it was too soon. When did he tell his own boys?

"Before they were no longer seen as cute," he said, making me wince.

I hadn't fully processed that someday my son would be seen as suspect instead of sweet. So I told him, and then Jordan asked if it was rare for the police to hurt black people. I said that, just like his father when he wore his military uniform, most police officers are dedicated to protecting us. But, no, I added, it is unfortunately not uncommon.

"Then I don't want to be black anymore," Jordan declared.

He asked if I was crying. I dabbed at my eyes and searched my mind for what to say.

"Son, your father was an incredible African-American man," I told him. 15 "And you are an amazing boy who is going to grow into just such a man. Please be proud of that."

"Yes," he responded emphatically, "but can't I just pretend to be white?"

The message that Jordan's appearance affords him the option to check "other" on the race card comes at him constantly. After his second-grade class created self-portraits last year, I noticed that his was the only one not hanging on the classroom wall. His teacher explained that his portrait was "a work in progress." The brown crayon he had used to color in his face was several shades too dark, she thought, and so she wanted him to "lighten it up" to more accurately reflect his complexion.

It is not just the overt signals that have convinced Jordan that he can choose to blend in to a white world. It is also that we live a life of relative affluence. I am a journalist and author whose inner circle includes prominent black writers, television anchors and doctors. We live in a high-rise in Manhattan with a doorman and round-the-clock security. Jordan attends an elite private school and an exclusive summer camp.

A white friend calls him "the boy who lives in the sky" because of the vast city view from the nine-foot windows in his bedroom. "He lives in a bubble and is always with responsible adults," she said recently, trying to assure me that our status makes him safer than many black boys.

That is true, mostly. And if my parenting pays off, I will be able to mini- 20 mize his contact with the police. He will be law-abiding. He will respect authority. He'll understand the perception of black boys wearing hoodies or sagging pants. But will it be enough?

You may not be a mother. Or Black. Or wealthy. In any case, it's important to really listen to what Dana Candy is saying— pp. 9–10 explain why.

Just last month a video went viral that showed a black man in Pontiac, Michigan, being questioned by a sheriff's deputy because someone reported feeling nervous after seeing him walking in the cold with his hands in his pockets. So as much as I want to believe that our upper-middle-class status will protect my son from many of society's social ills, it could not provide him the white privilege he seeks.

Nor would "passing" protect Jordan entirely, for the internal damage from living that lie would surely be as painful as any blow from a police baton. To deny his blackness would be to deny me. It would be to deny our enslaved ancestors who were strong enough to endure that voyage. It would mean rejecting the reflection he sees every time he looks in a mirror.

For at least a little while longer, Jordan is too young to understand any of this. He does not know the racial indignity of having jobs and promotions denied or delayed, does not know the humiliation of being stopped and frisked. He has never heard the mantra "I can't breathe."

I know that our talk was just the start of a conversation that will go deeper as he moves into his teen years in a post-Obama America. My fervent hope is that, by then, I will have found a way to help him embrace the privilege of being black.

Thinking about the Text

1. What is Dana Canedy's **PURPOSE** in publicly exposing such a painful and private conversation between her and her son? What point is she trying to make? And how persuasively does she make it? Explain your response.

2. It's true: numerous studies confirm that White youth are not targeted by police nearly as often as Black youth. Still, pretending to be White, as Canedy's son proposed, is both unsuitable as a solution and hurtful to Canedy personally. Why? Explain the dilemma.

3. Canedy's narrative was published in the *New York Times*, a daily newspaper with a large nationwide circulation. What background information about "the talk" (1) does Canedy provide for this **AUDIENCE**? What might she have done differently if she were writing for a magazine with a primary readership of Black parents? What information could she have omitted, and what might she have included that she chose not to include here?

4. A good narrative includes **DESCRIPTIVE** details that make the story come alive. What part of Canedy's narrative touched you the deepest? Why? Describe your reaction.

5. At some time in our lives, we've all had a run-in with some form of authority. Think of a frightening or otherwise memorable encounter with an authority figure. In what ways did your skin color, gender, stature, dress, or other factors in how you look or present yourself affect that encounter? Did any characteristics work in your favor or against you—and if so, how? Write a brief **NARRATIVE** of the encounter as you remember it, reflecting in particular on how your physical presence affects your life.

Serving in Florida

BARBARA EHRENREICH

MOSTLY OUT OF LAZINESS, I decide to start my low-wage life in the town nearest to where I actually live, Key West, Florida, which with a population of about 25,000 is elbowing its way up to the status of a genuine city. The downside of familiarity, I soon realize, is that it's not easy to go from being a consumer, thoughtlessly throwing money around in exchange for groceries and movies and gas, to being a worker in the very same place. I am terrified, especially at the beginning, of being recognized by some friendly business owner or erstwhile neighbor and having to stammer out some explanation of my project. Happily, though, my fears turn out to be entirely unwarranted: during a month of poverty and toil, no one recognizes my face or my name, which goes unnoticed and for the most

---

BARBARA EHRENREICH (1941–2022), a native of Butte, Montana, held a PhD in cell biology but became a journalist and activist after working with a nonprofit organization to improve public access to health care. She wrote twenty-two books on diverse themes, including *Bait and Switch: The (Futile) Pursuit of the American Dream* (2006) and *Natural Causes: An Epidemic of Wellness, the Certainty of Dying, and Killing Ourselves to Live Longer* (2018). This piece is from her acclaimed 2001 book, *Nickel and Dimed: On (Not) Getting By in America*, a memoir of her experiences living entirely on minimum wage earnings as a waitress, hotel maid, and other low-income jobs.

part unuttered. In this parallel universe where my father never got out of the mines and I never got through college, I am "baby," "honey," "blondie," and, most commonly, "girl."

My first task is to find a place to live. I figure that if I can earn $7 an hour—which, from the want ads, seems doable—I can afford to spend $500 on rent or maybe, with severe economies, $600 and still have $400 or $500 left over for food and gas. In the Key West area, this pretty much confines me to flophouses and trailer homes—like the one, a pleasing fifteen-minute drive from town, that has no air-conditioning, no screens, no fans, no television, and, by way of diversion, only the challenge of evading the landlord's Doberman pinscher. The big problem with this place, though, is the rent, which at $675 a month is well beyond my reach. All right, Key West is expensive. But so is New York City, or the Bay Area, or Jackson, Wyoming, or Telluride, or Boston, or any other place where tourists and the wealthy compete for living space with the people who clean their toilets and fry their hash browns. Still, it is a shock to realize that "trailer trash" has become, for me, a demographic category to aspire to.

So I decide to make the common trade-off between affordability and convenience and go for a $500-a-month "efficiency" thirty miles up a two-lane highway from the employment opportunities of Key West, meaning forty-five minutes if there's no road construction and I don't get caught behind some sun-dazed Canadian tourists. I hate the drive, along a roadside studded with white crosses commemorating the more effective head-on collisions, but it's a sweet little place—a cabin, more or less, set in the swampy backyard of the converted mobile home where my landlord, an affable TV repairman, lives with his bartender girlfriend. Anthropologically speaking, the trailer park would be preferable, but here I have a gleaming white floor and a firm mattress, and the few resident bugs are easily vanquished.

The next piece of business is to comb through the want ads and find a job. I rule out various occupations for one reason or another: hotel front-desk clerk, for example, which to my surprise is regarded as unskilled and pays only $6 or $7 an hour, gets eliminated because it involves standing in one spot for eight hours a day. Waitressing is also something I'd like to avoid, because I remember it leaving me bone-tired when I was eighteen, and I'm decades of varicosities and back pain beyond that now. Telemarketing, one of the first refuges of the suddenly indigent, can be dismissed on grounds of personality. This leaves certain supermarket jobs, such as deli clerk, or housekeeping in the hotels and guest houses, which pays about $7 and, I imagine, is not too different from what I've been doing part-time, in my own home, all my life.

So I put on what I take to be a respectable-looking outfit of ironed Bermuda shorts and scooped-neck T-shirt and set out for a tour of the local hotels and supermarkets. Best Western, Econo Lodge, and HoJo's all let me fill out application forms, and these are, to my relief, mostly interested in whether I am a legal resident of the United States and have committed any felonies. My next stop is Winn-Dixie, the supermarket, which turns out to have a particularly onerous application process, featuring a twenty-minute "interview" by computer since, apparently, no human on the premises is deemed capable of representing the corporate point of view. I am conducted to a large room decorated with posters illustrating how to look "professional" (it helps to be white and, if female, permed) and warning of the slick promises that union organizers might try to tempt me with. The interview is multiple-choice: Do I have anything, such as child care problems, that might make it hard for me to get to work on time? Do I think safety on the job is the responsibility of management? Then, popping up cunningly out of the blue: How many dollars' worth of stolen goods have I purchased in the last year? Would I turn in a fellow employee if I caught him stealing? Finally, "Are you an honest person?"

Apparently I ace the interview, because I am told that all I have to do is show up in some doctor's office tomorrow for a urine test. This seems to be a fairly general rule: if you want to stack Cheerios boxes or vacuum hotel rooms in chemically fascist America, you have to be willing to squat down and pee in front of a health worker (who has no doubt had to do the same thing herself).[1] The wages Winn-Dixie is offering—$6 and a couple of dimes to start with—are not enough, I decide, to compensate for this indignity.

I lunch at Wendy's, where $4.99 gets you unlimited refills at the Mexican part of the Super-bar, a comforting surfeit of refried beans and cheese sauce. A teenage employee, seeing me studying the want ads, kindly offers me an application form, which I fill out, though here, too, the

1. Eighty-one percent of large employers now require preemployment drug testing, up from 21 percent in 1987. Among all employers, the rate of testing is highest in the South. The drug most likely to be detected—marijuana, which can be detected weeks after use—is also the most innocuous, while heroin and cocaine are generally undetectable three days after use. Alcohol, which clears the body within hours after ingestion, is not tested for.

pay is just $6 and change an hour. Then it's off for a round of the locally owned inns and guest houses in Key West's Old Town, which is where all the serious sightseeing and guzzling goes on, a couple of miles removed from the functional end of the island, where the discount hotels make their homes. At The Palms, let's call it, a bouncy manager actually takes me around to see the rooms and meet the current housekeepers, who, I note with satisfaction, look pretty much like me—faded ex-hippie types in shorts with long hair pulled back in braids. Mostly, though, no one speaks to me or even looks at me except to proffer an application form. At my last stop, a palatial B & B, I wait twenty minutes to meet "Max," only to be told that there are no jobs now but there should be one soon, since "nobody lasts more than a couple weeks."

Three days go by like this and, to my chagrin, no one from the approximately twenty places at which I've applied calls me for an interview. I had been vain enough to worry about coming across as too educated for the jobs I sought, but no one even seems interested in finding out how overqualified I am. Only later will I realize that the want ads are not a reliable measure of the actual jobs available at any particular time. They are, as I should have guessed from Max's comment, the employers' insurance policy against the relentless turnover of the low-wage workforce. Most of the big hotels run ads almost continually, if only to build a supply of applicants to replace the current workers as they drift away or are fired, so finding a job is just a matter of being in the right place at the right time and flexible enough to take whatever is being offered that day. This finally happens to me at one of the big discount chain hotels where I go, as usual, for housekeeping and am sent instead to try out as a waitress at the attached "family restaurant," a dismal spot looking out on a parking garage, which is featuring "Polish sausage and BBQ sauce" on this 95-degree day. Phillip, the dapper young West Indian who introduces himself as the manager, interviews me with about as much enthusiasm as if he were a clerk processing me for Medicare, the principal questions being what shifts I can work and when I can start. I mutter about being woefully out of practice as a waitress, but he's already on to the uniform: I'm to show up tomorrow wearing black slacks and black shoes; he'll provide the rust-colored polo shirt with "Hearthside," as we'll call the place, embroidered on it, though I might want to wear my own shirt to get to work, ha ha. At the word *tomorrow*, something between fear and indignation rises in my chest. I want to say, "Thank you for your time, sir, but this is just an experiment, you know, not my actual life."

So begins my career at The Hearthside, where for two weeks I work from 2:00 till 10:00 P.M. for $2.43 an hour plus tips.[2] Employees are barred from using the front door, so I enter the first day through the kitchen, where a red-faced man with shoulder-length blond hair is throwing frozen steaks against the wall and yelling, "Fuck this shit!" "That's just Billy," explains Gail, the wiry middle-aged waitress who is assigned to train me. "He's on the rag again"—a condition occasioned, in this instance, by the fact that the cook on the morning shift had forgotten to thaw out the steaks. For the next eight hours, I run after the agile Gail, absorbing bits of instruction along with fragments of personal tragedy. All food must be trayed, and the reason she's so tired today is that she woke up in a cold sweat thinking of her boyfriend, who was killed a few months ago in a scuffle in an upstate prison. No refills on lemonade. And the reason he was in prison is that a few DUIs caught up with him, that's all, could have happened to anyone. Carry the creamers to the table in a "monkey bowl," never in your hand. And after he was gone she spent several months living in her truck, peeing in a plastic pee bottle and reading by candlelight at night, but you can't live in a truck in the summer, since you need to have the windows down, which means anything can get in, from mosquitoes on up.

At least Gail puts to rest any fears I had of appearing overqualified. From the first day on, I find that of all the things that I have left behind, such as home and identity, what I miss the most is competence. Not that I have ever felt 100 percent competent in the writing business, where one day's success augurs nothing at all for the next. But in my writing life, I at least have some notion of *procedure:* do the research, make the outline, rough out a draft, etc. As a server, though, I am beset by requests as if by bees: more iced tea here, catsup over there, a to-go box for table 14, and where are the high chairs, anyway? Of the twenty-seven tables, up to six are usually mine at any time, though on slow afternoons or if Gail is off, I sometimes have the whole place to myself. There is the touch-screen computer-ordering system to master, which I suppose is meant to minimize server-cook contacts but in practice requires constant verbal fine-tuning: "That's gravy on the mashed, OK? None on the meatloaf," and so forth. Plus, something I had forgotten in the years

10

---

2. According to the Fair Labor Standards Act, employers are not required to pay "tipped employees," such as restaurant servers, more than $2.13 an hour in direct wages. However, if the sum of tips plus $2.13 an hour falls below the minimum wage, or $5.15 an hour, the employer is required to make up the difference. This fact was not mentioned by managers or otherwise publicized at either of the restaurants where I worked.

since I was eighteen: about a third of a server's job is "side work" invisible to customers—sweeping, scrubbing, slicing, refilling, and restocking. If it isn't all done, every little bit of it, you're going to face the 6:00 P.M. dinner rush defenseless and probably go down in flames. I screw up dozens of times at the beginning, sustained in my shame entirely by Gail's support—"It's OK, baby, everyone does that sometime"—because, to my total surprise and despite the scientific detachment I am doing my best to maintain, I *care*.

The whole thing would be a lot easier if I could just skate through it like Lily Tomlin in one of her waitress skits, but I was raised by the absurd Booker T. Washingtonian precept that says: If you're going to do something, do it well. In fact, "well" isn't good enough by half. Do it better than anyone has ever done it before. Or so said my father, who must have known what he was talking about because he managed to pull himself, and us with him, up from the mile-deep copper mines of Butte to the leafy suburbs of the Northeast, ascending from boiler-makers to martinis before booze beat out ambition. As in most endeavors I have encountered in my life, "doing it better than anyone" is not a reasonable goal. Still, when I wake up at 4 A.M. in my own cold sweat, I am not thinking about the writing deadlines I'm neglecting; I'm thinking of the table where I screwed up the order and one of the kids didn't get his kiddie meal until the rest of the family had moved on to their Key lime pies. That's the other powerful motivation—the customers, or "patients," as I can't help thinking of them on account of the mysterious vulnerability that seems to have left them temporarily unable to feed themselves. After a few days at Hearthside, I feel the service ethic kick in like a shot of oxytocin, the nurturance hormone. The plurality of my customers are hardworking locals—truck drivers, construction workers, even housekeepers from the attached hotel—and I want them to have the closest to a "fine dining" experience that the grubby circumstances will allow. No "you guys" for me; everyone over twelve is "sir" or "ma'am." I ply them with iced tea and coffee refills; I return, midmeal, to inquire how everything is; I doll up their salads with chopped raw mushrooms, summer squash slices, or whatever bits of produce I can find that have survived their sojourn in the cold storage room mold-free.

There is Benny, for example, a short, tight-muscled sewer repairman who cannot even think of eating until he has absorbed a half hour of air-conditioning and ice water. We chat about hyperthermia and electrolytes until he is ready to order some finicky combination like soup of the day, garden salad, and a side of grits. There are the German tourists who are so touched by my pidgin "*Wilkommen*" and "*Ist alles gut?*" that they actually tip. (Europeans, no doubt spoiled by their trade union–ridden, high-wage welfare states, generally do not know that they are supposed to tip. Some restaurants, the Hearthside included, allow servers to "grat" their foreign customers, or add a tip to the bill. Since this amount is added before the customers have a chance to tip or not tip, the practice amounts to an automatic penalty for imperfect English.) There are the two dirt-smudged lesbians, just off from their shift, who are impressed enough by my suave handling of the fly in the piña colada that they take the time to praise me to Stu, the assistant manager. There's Sam, the kindly retired cop who has to plug up his tracheotomy hole with one finger in order to force the cigarette smoke into his lungs.

Sometimes I play with the fantasy that I am a princess who, in penance for some tiny transgression, has undertaken to feed each of her subjects by hand. But the nonprincesses working with me are just as indulgent, even when this means flouting management rules—as to, for example, the number of croutons that can go on a salad (six). "Put on all you want," Gail whispers, "as long as Stu isn't looking." She dips into her own tip money to buy biscuits and gravy for an out-of-work mechanic who's used up all his money on dental surgery, inspiring me to pick up the tab for his pie and milk. Maybe the same high levels of agape can be found throughout the "hospitality industry." I remember the poster decorating one of the apartments I looked at, which said, "If you seek happiness for yourself you will never find it. Only when you seek happiness for others will it come to you," or words to that effect—an odd sentiment, it seemed to me at the time, to find in the dank one-room basement apartment of a bellhop at the Best Western. At Hearthside, we utilize whatever bits of autonomy we have to ply our customers with the illicit calories that signal our love. It is our job as servers to assemble the salads and desserts, pour the dressings, and squirt the whipped cream. We also control the number of butter pats our customers get and the amount of sour cream on their baked potatoes. So if you wonder why Americans are so obese, consider the fact that waitresses both express their humanity and earn their tips through the covert distribution of fats.

Ten days into it, this is beginning to look like a livable lifestyle. I like Gail, who is "looking at fifty," agewise, but moves so fast she can alight in one place and then another without apparently being anywhere between. I clown around with Lionel, the teenage Haitian busboy, though we don't have much vocabulary in common, and loiter near the main sink to listen

> Barbara Ehrenreich's evidence comes from personal experience. See more examples of this strategy on pp. 434 and 467–68.

to the older Haitian dishwashers' musical Creole, which sounds, in their rich bass voices, like French on testosterone. I bond with Timmy, the fourteen-year-old white kid who buses at night, by telling him I don't like people putting their baby seats right on the tables: it makes the baby look too much like a side dish. He snickers delightedly and in return, on a slow night, starts telling me the plots of all the *Jaws* movies (which are perennial favorites in the shark-ridden Keys): "She looks around, and the water-skier isn't there anymore, then SNAP! The whole boat goes . . ."

I especially like Joan, the svelte fortyish hostess, who turns out to be a   15
militant feminist, pulling me aside one day to explain that "men run every-thing—we don't have a chance unless we stick together." Accordingly, she backs me up when I get overpowered on the floor, and in return I give her a chunk of my tips or stand guard while she sneaks off for an unauthorized cigarette break. We all admire her for standing up to Billy and telling him, after some of his usual nastiness about the female server class, to "shut the fuck up." I even warm up to Billy when, on a slow night and to make up for a particularly unwarranted attack on my abilities, or so I imagine, he tells me about his glory days as a young man at "coronary school" in Brooklyn, where he dated a knockout Puerto Rican chick—or do you say "culinary"?

I finish up every night at 10:00 or 10:30, depending on how much side work I've been able to get done during the shift, and cruise home to the tapes I snatched at random when I left my real home—Marianne Faithfull, Tracy Chapman, Enigma, King Sunny Adé, Violent Femmes—just drained enough for the music to set my cranium resonating, but hardly dead. Midnight snack is Wheat Thins and Monterey Jack, accompanied by cheap white wine on ice and whatever AMC has to offer. To bed by 1:30 or 2:00, up at 9:00 or 10:00, read for an hour while my uniform whirls around in the landlord's washing machine, and then it's another eight hours spent following Mao's central instruction, as laid out in the Little Red Book, which was: Serve the people.

I could drift along like this, in some dreamy proletarian idyll, except for two things. One is management. If I have kept this subject to the margins so far it is because I still flinch to think that I spent all those weeks under the surveillance of men (and later women) whose job it was to monitor my behavior for signs of sloth, theft, drug abuse, or worse. Not that managers and especially "assistant managers" in low-wage settings like this are exactly the class enemy. Mostly, in the restaurant business, they are former cooks still capable of pinch-hitting in the kitchen, just as in hotels they are likely to be former clerks, and paid a salary of only about $400 a week. But everyone knows they have crossed over to the other side, which is, crudely put, corporate as opposed to human. Cooks want to prepare tasty meals, servers want to serve them graciously, but managers are there for only one reason—to make sure that money is made for some theoretical entity, the corporation, which exists far away in Chicago or New York, if a corporation can be said to have a physical existence at all. Reflecting on her career, Gail tells me ruefully that she swore, years ago, never to work for a corporation again. "They don't cut you no slack. You give and you give and they take."

Managers can sit—for hours at a time if they want—but it's their job to see that no one else ever does, even when there's nothing to do, and this is why, for servers, slow times can be as exhausting as rushes. You start dragging out each little chore because if the manager on duty catches you in an idle moment he will give you something far nastier to do. So I wipe, I clean, I consolidate catsup bottles and recheck the cheesecake supply, even tour the tables to make sure the customer evaluation forms are all standing perkily in their places—wondering all the time how many calories I burn in these strictly theatrical exercises. In desperation, I even take the desserts out of their glass display case and freshen them up with whipped cream and bright new maraschino cherries; anything to look busy. When, on a particularly dead afternoon, Stu finds me glancing at a *USA Today* a customer has left behind, he assigns me to vacuum the entire floor with the broken vacuum cleaner, which has a handle only two feet long, and the only way to do that without incurring orthopedic damage is to proceed from spot to spot on your knees.

On my first Friday at Hearthside there is a "mandatory meeting for all restaurant employees," which I attend, eager for insight into our overall marketing strategy and the niche (your basic Ohio cuisine with a tropical twist?) we aim to inhabit. But there is no "we" at this meeting. Phillip, our top manager except for an occasional "consultant" sent out by corporate headquarters, opens it with a sneer: "The break room—it's disgusting. Butts in the ashtrays, newspapers lying around, crumbs." This windowless little room, which also houses the time clock for the entire hotel, is where we stash our bags and civilian clothes and take our half-hour meal breaks. But a break room is not a right, he tells us, it can be taken away. We should also know that the lockers in the break room and whatever is in them can be searched at any time. Then comes gossip; there has been gossip; gossip (which seems to mean employees talking among themselves) must stop.

Off-duty employees are henceforth barred from eating at the restaurant, because "other servers gather around them and gossip." When Phillip has exhausted his agenda of rebukes, Joan complains about the condition of the ladies' room and I throw in my two bits about the vacuum cleaner. But I don't see any backup coming from my fellow servers, each of whom has slipped into her own personal funk; Gail, my role model, stares sorrowfully at a point six inches from her nose. The meeting ends when Andy, one of the cooks, gets up, muttering about breaking up his day off for this almighty bullshit.

Just four days later we are suddenly summoned into the kitchen at 3:30 20
P.M., even though there are live tables on the floor. We all—about ten of us—stand around Phillip, who announces grimly that there has been a report of some "drug activity" on the night shift and that, as a result, we are now to be a "drug-free" workplace, meaning that all new hires will be tested and possibly also current employees on a random basis. I am glad that this part of the kitchen is so dark because I find myself blushing as hard as if I had been caught toking up in the ladies' room myself: I haven't been treated this way—lined up in the corridor, threatened with locker searches, peppered with carelessly aimed accusations—since at least junior high school. Back on the floor, Joan cracks, "Next they'll be telling us we can't have *sex* on the job." When I ask Stu what happened to inspire the crackdown, he just mutters about "management decisions" and takes the opportunity to upbraid Gail and me for being too generous with the rolls. From now on there's to be only one per customer and it goes out with the dinner, not with the salad. He's also been riding the cooks, prompting Andy to come out of the kitchen and observe—with the serenity of a man whose customary implement is a butcher knife—that "Stu has a death wish today."

Later in the evening, the gossip crystallizes around the theory that Stu is himself the drug culprit, that he uses the restaurant phone to order up marijuana and sends one of the late servers out to fetch it for him. The server was caught and she may have ratted out Stu, at least enough to cast some suspicion on him, thus accounting for his pissy behavior. Who knows? Personally, I'm ready to believe anything bad about Stu, who serves no evident function and presumes too much on our common ethnicity, sidling up to me one night to engage in a little nativism directed at the Haitian immigrants: "I feel like I'm the foreigner here. They're taking over the country." Still later that evening, the drug in question escalates to crack. Lionel, the busboy, entertains us for the rest of the shift by standing just behind Stu's back and sucking deliriously on an imaginary joint or maybe a pipe.

The other problem, in addition to the less-than-nurturing management style, is that this job shows no sign of being financially viable. You might imagine, from a comfortable distance, that people who live, year in and year out, on $6 to $10 an hour have discovered some survival stratagems unknown to the middle class. But no. It's not hard to get my coworkers talking about their living situations, because housing, in almost every case, is the principal source of disruption in their lives, the first thing they fill you in on when they arrive for their shifts. After a week, I have compiled the following survey:

Gail is sharing a room in a well-known downtown flophouse for $250 a week. Her roommate, a male friend, has begun hitting on her, driving her nuts, but the rent would be impossible alone.

Claude, the Haitian cook, is desperate to get out of the two-room apartment he shares with his girlfriend and two other, unrelated people. As far as I can determine, the other Haitian men live in similarly crowded situations.

Annette, a twenty-year-old server who is six months pregnant and abandoned by her boyfriend, lives with her mother, a postal clerk.

Marianne, who is a breakfast server, and her boyfriend are paying $170 a week for a one-person trailer.

Billy, who at $10 an hour is the wealthiest of us, lives in the trailer he owns, paying only the $400-a-month lot fee.

The other white cook, Andy, lives on his dry-docked boat, which, as far as I can tell from his loving descriptions, can't be more than twenty feet long. He offers to take me out on it once it's repaired, but the offer comes with inquiries as to my marital status, so I do not follow up on it.

Tina, another server, and her husband are paying $60 a night for a room in the Days Inn. This is because they have no car and the Days Inn is in walking distance of the Hearthside. When Marianne is tossed out of her trailer for subletting (which is against trailer park rules), she leaves her boyfriend and moves in with Tina and her husband.

Joan, who had fooled me with her numerous and tasteful outfits (hostesses wear their own clothes), lives in a van parked behind a shopping center at night and showers in Tina's motel room. The clothes are from thrift shops.[3]

It strikes me, in my middle-class solipsism, that there is gross improvidence in some of these arrangements. When Gail and I are wrapping silverware in napkins—the only task for which we are permitted to sit—she tells me she is thinking of escaping from her roommate by moving into the Days Inn herself. I am astounded: how she can even think of paying $40 to $60 a day? But if I was afraid of sounding like a social worker, I have come out just sounding like a fool. She squints at me in disbelief: "And where am I supposed to get a month's rent and a month's deposit for an apartment?" I'd been feeling pretty smug about my $500 efficiency, but of course it was made possible only by the $1,300 I had allotted myself for start-up costs when I began my low-wage life: $1,000 for the first month's rent and deposit, $100 for initial groceries and cash in my pocket, $200 stuffed away for emergencies. In poverty, as in certain propositions in physics, starting conditions are everything.

There are no secret economies that nourish the poor; on the contrary, there are a host of special costs. If you can't put up the two months' rent you need to secure an apartment, you end up paying through the nose for a room by the week. If you have only a room, with a hot plate at best, you can't save by cooking up huge lentil stews that can be frozen for the week ahead. You eat fast food or the hot dogs and Styrofoam cups of soup that can be microwaved in a convenience store. If you have no money for health insurance—and the Hearthside's niggardly plan kicks in only after three months—you go without routine care or prescription drugs and end up paying the price. Gail, for example, was doing fine, healthwise anyway, until she ran out of money for estrogen pills. She is supposed to be on the company health plan by now, but they claim to have lost her application form and to be beginning the paperwork all over again. So she spends $9 a pop for pills to control the migraines she wouldn't have, she insists, if her estrogen supplements were covered. Similarly, Marianne's boyfriend lost his job as a roofer because he

3. I could find no statistics on the number of employed people living in cars or vans, but according to a 1997 report of the National Coalition for the Homeless, "Myths and Facts about Homelessness," nearly one-fifth of all homeless people (in twenty-nine cities across the nation) are employed in full- or part-time jobs.

missed so much time after getting a cut on his foot for which he couldn't afford the prescribed antibiotic.

My own situation, when I sit down to assess it after two weeks of work, would not be much better if this were my actual life. The seductive thing about waitressing is that you don't have to wait for payday to feel a few bills in your pocket, and my tips usually cover meals and gas, plus something left over to stuff into the kitchen drawer I use as a bank. But as the tourist business slows in the summer heat, I sometimes leave work with only $20 in tips (the gross is higher, but servers share about 15 percent of their tips with the busboys and bartenders). With wages included, this amounts to about the minimum wage of $5.15 an hour. The sum in the drawer is piling up but at the present rate of accumulation will be more than $100 short of my rent when the end of the month comes around. Nor can I see any expenses to cut. True, I haven't gone the lentil stew route yet, but that's because I don't have a large cooking pot, potholders, or a ladle to stir with (which would cost a total of about $30 at Kmart, somewhat less at a thrift store), not to mention onions, carrots, and the indispensable bay leaf. I do make my lunch almost every day—usually some slow-burning, high-protein combo like frozen chicken patties with melted cheese on top and canned pinto beans on the side. Dinner is at the Hearthside, which offers its employees a choice of BLT, fish sandwich, or hamburger for only $2. The burger lasts longest, especially if it's heaped with gut-puckering jalapeños, but by midnight my stomach is growling again.

So unless I want to start using my car as a residence, I have to find a second or an alternative job. I call all the hotels I'd filled out housekeeping applications at weeks ago—the Hyatt, Holiday Inn, Econo Lodge, HoJo's, Best Western, plus a half dozen locally run guest houses. Nothing. Then I start making the rounds again, wasting whole mornings waiting for some assistant manager to show up, even dipping into places so creepy that the front-desk clerk greets you from behind bullet-proof glass and sells pints of liquor over the counter. But either someone has exposed my real-life housekeeping habits—which are, shall we say, mellow—or I am at the wrong end of some infallible ethnic equation: most, but by no means all, of the working house-keepers I see on my job searches are African Americans, Spanish-speaking, or refugees from the Central European post-Communist world, while servers are almost invariably white and monolingually English-speaking. When I finally get a positive response, I have been identified once again as server material. Jerry's—again, not the real name—which is part of a well-known

25

national chain and physically attached here to another budget hotel, is ready to use me at once. The prospect is both exciting and terrifying because, with about the same number of tables and counter seats, Jerry's attracts three or four times the volume of customers as the gloomy old Hearthside.

Thinking about the Text

1. Barbara Ehrenreich passes back and forth in her **NARRATIVE** between the voice of the waitress describing her own reality and the voice of the writer who has assumed a role for investigative purposes—and of course both voices are hers. How well do those voices combine to present a cohesive narrative? Explain your answer, presenting examples from the text.

2. How typical do you suppose Ehrenreich's experience is of people who wait tables at "family restaurants" (8)? Consider evidence from your own experience and that of people you know, either as employees or as customers at such restaurants.

3. On radio and TV, in movies, and elsewhere, people like Ehrenreich's coworkers and customers, with low incomes and low social status, are often either belittled and ridiculed, or romanticized and idealized, whether subtly or openly. One of the strengths of Ehrenreich's book is the respect with which she describes people just the way they are. Identify three examples of respectful **DESCRIPTION**.

4. What is the main **ARGUMENT** that Ehrenreich is making in her narrative? Where is this point most clearly stated? How well has she supported this point? In other words, are you convinced? Why or why not?

5. Write a **NARRATIVE** describing the people and places of your daily life. If you have (or have had) a job, you may want to center your narrative there. Include plenty of descriptive details and try to present the people as vividly (and respectfully!) as you can. Make your main point something that you have learned as a result of your contact with the people you describe.

Period Equity: Why Does It Matter?

HUMA FARID

IT'S HAPPENED to so many people who menstruate: you're going about your life until you realize that you just got your period. The ungainly scramble to find a restroom and the fervent prayer that you packed a menstrual product leaves you feeling anxious, vulnerable, and exposed. This is compounded by the fact that our society stigmatizes menstruation—or really, anything to do with a uterus—and a taboo hangs over these discussions.

This scenario is far worse if you are one of the nearly 22 million women living in poverty in the US who cannot afford menstrual hygiene products, a problem known as period poverty. One study in *Obstetrics & Gynecology* demonstrated that 64% of women reported ever having difficulty affording menstrual products, such as pads, tampons, or reusable products like menstrual cups. And 21% reported that they were unable to afford these products every month. People who are homeless or incarcerated are at particularly high risk of not having access to adequate menstrual hygiene products.

HUMA FARID treats patients as an obstetrician-gynecologist in Boston, teaches at Harvard Medical School, and writes articles on diverse aspects of pregnancy, menstruation, and health for the general public. This essay was published in June 2021 on *Harvard Health Publishing*, Harvard Medical School's website, which offers an assortment of health-related resources.

Why are period products a luxury? Menstruating is a basic fact of human existence. Menstrual hygiene products are necessities, not luxuries, and should be treated as such. Unfortunately, food stamps and subsidies under the WIC (women, infants, and children) program that help with groceries do not cover menstrual products.

I have had patients tell me that they use toilet paper or paper towels instead of pads or tampons because they cannot afford menstrual products. People with heavy periods requiring frequent changes of these products particularly face financial challenges, as they must buy even more pads or tampons than the average menstruating person. If they try to extend the life of products by using them for multiple hours at a time, they can wind up with vulvar irritation and vaginal discomfort. They may also be at greater risk of toxic shock syndrome, a life-threatening infection.

Why is it important to talk about stigma around periods? We need 5 to address stigma around menstruation in order to understand and fix the challenges people face around access to menstrual hygiene products. Period poverty is real. Period equity should be real, too. Embarrassment or taboos may prevent people from advocating for themselves, but if that stigma is removed—or even eased by talking through these issues—we as a society can move forward to address the needs of half of our population. There is no equity when half the population bears the financial and physical distress as a consequence of the reproductive cycle needed to ensure human survival.

How can we address period poverty? There are simple solutions to period poverty. The first is to eliminate the tax on menstrual products. Think about it: just as food, a necessity for all of us, is not taxed, menstrual products should not be taxed. Products that are reusable, such as menstrual cups or underwear, should be subsidized, and their use encouraged, to eliminate excess waste from individually wrapped pads and tampons. If these products are publicized, promoted, and affordable, more women may opt for them. Pads and tampons should be available free of charge in schools and federal buildings.

Finally, you can take action: write to or call your legislators! There is a fantastic bill, Menstrual Equity For All Act of 2019, sponsored by Representative Grace Meng, that was introduced on March 26, 2019, but never received a vote. There is no good reason why this bill, which would allow homeless people, incarcerated people, students, and federal employees

Huma Farid wrote this essay for Harvard Medical School's website, which likely has an audience with a wide range of experience and knowledge on this topic—compared to, say, readers of *Cosmo* or *Vogue*. Check out the guidance we offer for thinking about your audience on pp. 34–35.

free access to menstrual hygiene products, was never even brought forward for a vote. We live in one of the world's wealthiest countries, and lack of menstrual hygiene products should never impact someone's ability to work or go to school. It's time to stop treating people with a uterus as second-class citizens.

Excerpted from the Harvard Health Blog, June 2021. © 2021 by The President and Fellows of Harvard College. Harvard University. www.health.harvard .edu. Note: Harvard Health Publishing does not endorse any products or medical procedures.

Thinking about the Text

1. Huma Farid states the problem she's addressing clearly: the inherent unfairness of requiring that "half the population bears the financial and physical distress as a consequence of the reproductive cycle needed to ensure human survival" (2). What does she propose for making conditions more equitable? Summarize the problem Farid wants solved and her **PROPOSAL** for doing so. How effectively does she support her claim that there's a problem? Explain your reasoning and point to passages from the essay to support your response.

2. When Farid mentions people who menstruate, she refers to them as "people" or "people with a uterus" rather than the more conventional "women," a term that presumes that every woman has a uterus and that any person with a uterus is, by definition, a woman. Why do you think Farid made this **LANGUAGE CHOICE**? Given her rhetorical situation, do you think it was a good choice? Explain your responses.

3. Did you have any feelings or immediate reactions to reading Farid's essay? Discomfort? Relief? Describe briefly how you felt reading Farid's essay. Farid argues that "embarrassment and taboos" (2) around menstruation are a major obstacle to progress. Did reading Farid's essay make you think any differently about this topic or challenge your initial feelings toward discussing it openly? Explain your response.

4. Farid uses **CAUSE AND EFFECT** analysis to explain how the policy changes and government actions she proposes would address period poverty. What might be some measures that individuals and/or community groups can take

to affect change? What, if anything, might you, personally, be able to do to reduce the stigma and break the taboo around menstruation? Explain why you would (or wouldn't) be willing to aid in the effort.

5. Farid proposes three concrete measures at the federal level to help end period poverty: (1) make all menstrual products nontaxable items, (2) subsidize reusable menstrual products such as cups or underwear to reduce packaging and disposal waste, and (3) make pads and tampons available free of charge in schools and federal buildings. Do you agree with her proposals? Do you think Farid is going too far? not far enough? Write an essay that takes a **POSITION** on Farid's proposal. Explain your stance and provide evidence and/or examples to support your argument.

Black Enough: Protecting Linguistic Identity in the Writing Center

ANNA GLAVEE

WELL, I'M NOT BLACK," I say to my friend as if it's a given. Anyone observing our conversation might find this statement out of place, seeing as the speaker is a dark-skinned middle schooler with brown eyes and an out-of-control 'fro: clearly Black. "And I'm not white," I add, to clear up any confusion. Anyone listening might also find this comment strange when the young girl voicing it speaks with the same propriety and tone as a Midwestern English teacher. "I'm living in an in-between space. I guess you could say I'm gray." My friend is apprehensive of my bold claim to a race that did not exist moments before, but she nods. "I've realized that I look too Black for white people and act too white for Black people, so I will be neither. I'm just going to be gray."

Deny, Deny, Denial. That is all I hear as I recount this tale of a girl so disconnected from her own identity that she would not claim the labels that clearly belonged to her. At age thirteen, I could not embrace my racial identity. I would cringe at the terms "Black," "African American," or "BIPOC." The chasm that separated me from identifying with my race boiled down to one fact: I couldn't talk Black. I could not use the language of people who looked

ANNA GLAVEE, a student majoring in social work at San Diego State University, wrote this essay for a course called Rhetoric of Written Arguments and the Tutoring of Writing. It was one of the winners of the 2021 Norton Writer's Prize, which recognizes outstanding original essays by undergraduates.

like me. Separation from anyone who looked or sounded like me and eight years of formal education had beat any chance of "talkin Black" out of me and replaced it with a feeling of shame about my racial identity.

African American Vernacular English—also referred to as AAVE or talkin Black—is a dialect of English with distinct accents, conventions, and grammatical structures. It is used among African Americans in music, media, and daily conversation. One place it is not accepted in is mainstream academia. And that's what be gettin my blood boilin 'bout this whole issue. It ain't like this just some poor boy's English. It's a language used by some 40 million people. It's a dialect of its own with plenty of rules and complications just like Standard American English (SAE). We all be sayin the same things as white people we just say 'em different (Charity 1340). AAVE is still considered an "incorrect" form of English by many SAE speakers, though linguists such as William Labov, Rosina Lippi-Green, and John R. Rickford have gone to great lengths to prove AAVE's legitimacy.

The use of AAVE in academia is systematically suppressed at every level of education. In the essay "Addressing Racial Diversity in a Writing Center: Stories and Lessons from Two Beginners," writing center directors Nancy Barron and Nancy Grimm noted that, in their view, a student's racial identity and lived experiences "can undermine the best of communicative intentions" more than their style or grammar ever could (61). In the US education system, people from historically oppressed groups are often told that the ways they communicate are incorrect. Formal education tries to enforce the idea that SAE is the superior language, but what that also tells Black students is that their language—and by extension, their race—are inferior to those of their white counterparts.

In classrooms of all kinds, Black students are expected to code-switch, 5 or switch from speaking AAVE to SAE, because they are in academic spaces. Students are expected to learn how to read, write, and speak the standard way: the white way. When institutions of learning attempt to standardize the language of AAVE speakers, they attempt to strip away these students' linguistic identities, which damages not only the effectiveness of their writing but also their overall academic success. This essay explores the profound impact of linguistic identity on Black students and how writing centers can help students develop their idiolect,[1] or personal language.

1. *Idiolect*: The variety of speech that is unique to each individual, like a linguistic fingerprint. It encompasses all of the features of a dialect, plus the speech habits and quality of voice that each person has. Although two people may speak the same language, even the same dialect, no two people have the exact same idiolect. [Editor's note]

The Linguist's Gospel Truth

To understand why AAVE is a legitimate dialect, one must first understand what makes any language or dialect legitimate. In her essay "The 'Standard English' Fairy Tale: A Rhetorical Analysis of Racist Pedagogies and Commonplace Assumptions about Language Diversity," Laura Greenfield explains how a racist US education system has perpetuated the myth that standardized English is superior to dialects spoken by historically oppressed populations. She builds her argument by explaining five "linguistic facts of life" created by Rosina Lippi-Green. This is an overview of four of those facts and their application to AAVE.

The first truth is that all spoken languages change over time, and the changes can be gradual or sudden. AAVE is constantly shifting. This can be seen in the emergence and decline of slang terms, and in differences between linguistically segregated areas. In the same way that SAE has not remained stagnant since it was first introduced to the United States, AAVE is a living language that continues to evolve.

The next truth is that grammatical rules and effective communication are separate matters. Most often, variations between SAE's and AAVE's grammatical structures have little to no impact on the listener's ability to understand a speaker's meaning. For example, the phrases "she be lyin on the daily" and "she frequently lies" can both be understood to have the same meaning even though they subscribe to different grammar rules. The habitual "be" (She be lyin) doesn't occur in English's standardized form, yet an AAVE speaker's use of the habitual "be" does not impede upon an SAE listener's understanding.

Written and spoken language are separate entities in history, structure, and function. Like many African languages, AAVE has been primarily a spoken dialect. AAVE has minimal representation in written academic discourse. This is a natural development considering that the language originated from African slaves who previously spoke languages that had no written equivalent. These facts have no impact on AAVE's legitimacy.

The last truth is that variation is intrinsic to all spoken languages at every level. The fact that AAVE and SAE sound different is not surprising; it is expected. Many variations of English are seen across the world, such as Canadian English or Chicano English. This variation does not make one language better than another (Greenfield 34). 10

A Rooted Language

Everyone is Black. When my new friend from school invites me to a week of workshops at her church, this is the last thing I expect to think when I arrive. I have never seen so many people from the African diaspora gathered in one place. The congregation is primarily composed of first- and second-generation Nigerian-Americans. Being a first-generation Ghanian-American, I should fit right in. But I don't. Every time someone makes a "white people" joke, I get sideways glances in my direction and a quickly muttered, "No offense." Idle girl talk turns into judgment because I don't prefer dark chocolate over white chocolate. This, and the pleasant surprise that comes when I eat Jollof rice, earns me a new nickname: Oreo. Every interaction with the people who should be my peers leads to the same conclusion. Sure, I'm Black; I'm just not Black enough.

The summer before my freshman year of high school, I realized being "gray" wasn't going to suffice. It didn't matter to my new Black friends that I had the right skin tone, dressed the right way, or finally got my 'fro under control. They could sense I was still just chillin in that gray space. The issue they had with me went deeper than my biracial background; it was deeper than not acting or talkin Black. They knew I didn't understand the history and pride they held in their skin tone, their mannerisms, and their speech.

Common language builds solidarity in communities because solidarity comes from shared experiences. In 2015, linguist John R. Rickford published the experimental study "Neighborhood Effects on Use of African-American Vernacular English," in which he states that residential economic segregation is a contributing factor to AAVE use—which, in turn, contributes to a strong social identity. Rickford explains that in general, language is a "socially constructed behavior, jointly influenced by exposure, identity, and peer group influence" (11817). The language of an individual is not developed in solitude. A person's idiolect, their unique way of speaking, is a reflection of the people they come from. So when professors start raggin on students for talkin like they from the ghetto, them professors ain't just disrespectin the students. They be disrespectin the community we come from. They be tryna take away the men and women who helped get us into institutions of higher education. They tryna take away who we are.

Anna Glavee's own experiences are central to her essay, but she also incorporates ideas from sources to support her arguments. Synthesizing ideas is an important skill; learn more about how to do it well on pp. 534–36.

AAVE is a language built in a community with a long history of oppression. In 2010, William Labov published a study titled "Unendangered Dialect, Endangered People: The Case of African American Vernacular English," which claims that social factors such as residential segregation and historical oppression lead to the divergence, development, and flourishing of AAVE. Labov states AAVE is not the cause of African Americans' problems. Rather, AAVE is a resource used to elegantly and thoughtfully reflect "on the oppression and misery of daily life" (24). There is a certain beauty and emotion that is articulated in AAVE due to its history. AAVE has inherent value and depth just like SAE. The education system just ain't willin to recognize this value. They be puttin down students who express themselves and they struggles in they native tongue because it don't conform to this idea of proper English. They be forcin students to relearn how to talk, write, and think in a standardized fashion and takin away students' unique, historically based, and culturally informed linguistic identity in the process.

I Said What I Said

"Ya know, sometimes, when you start gettin real sassy, you get this little twang in your voice and you start to . . . you know." My coach trails off with a little shrug of his shoulders. "Whatchu tryna tell me, Coach?" I retort with a side-eye, aggravated that he's interrupting my lecture to one of the new players.

"I'm just sayin, sometimes you talk a little Black and I didn't know if you realized you doin it."

"What? I don't think . . . Was I?" I turn to my co-captain for confirmation but the man knows betta than to be talkin to me when I'm in a mood, so he's suddenly real interested in his shoes. "Well," I continue, lookin back to Coach, "if this girl gon be sassin me when I'm tryna teach her somethin, I'ma give her sass right back in whichever tone I see fit."

By the spring of my sophomore year, I had educated myself in Black Culture. I read the books, listened to the music, and talked to the people I needed to so I could understand what I was missing. Before I even realized what had happened, I had started to incorporate my newfound literacy into my daily life. *Their* linguistic identity became *my* linguistic identity. What was once their community became our community. For the first time in my life, I began to feel Black enough.

So What's the Problem?

The US education system largely subscribes to a standard, or dominant, language ideology. This principle asserts that to achieve effective communication, all writers and speakers need to conform to "one set of dominant language rules that stem from a single dominant discourse" (Young 62). So students can speak whichever way they like, but only at home. This ideology perpetuates the lie that there is something wrong with students' native dialects. And this type of thinkin is ingrained in students and teachers from preschool to post-secondary education. We be gettin told, "You gotta speak like an academic when you in school." But what they really gettin at is you can't be talkin like you Black when you in school because Black ain't academic.

Stanley Fish is a professor and cultural critic known for his support of   20
the standard language ideology. In part three of a series of articles, published in the *New York Times*, called "What Should Colleges Teach?," Fish claims that if professors want to teach English, they must not "affirm the students' right to their own patterns and varieties of language—the dialects of their nurture or whatever dialects in which they find their own identity and style" (Fish). This means professors that subscribe to the standard language ideology should not allow or encourage students to use the unique idiolect they have developed throughout their lives. Fish and many teaching professionals believe that when students do not use SAE, it makes them more vulnerable to prejudice. According to this ideology, the students' linguistic identity is the problem that needs to be resolved. They be wantin students to internalize the racism they experience and start suppressin they linguistic identity. Them professors think we gonna be judged less if we learn to talk proper. Learnin to talk white ain't gonna stop people from judgin me the second I walk in a room. Before I even speak a word in any dialect, people will already have made assumptions 'bout my education, my family, and my financial status. The real issue ain't with the way Black students be talkin; the real issue is that you lookin down on me and my language even though we should have the right to exist and be heard in academic spaces.

The systemic racism that standard language ideology supports can be seen in college enrollment rates and the six-year graduation rates of non-Hispanic, African American students. In San Diego County there are three 4-year public universities. The graduation rates (in six years or less) of African Americans at these schools are on average 11% below the university's overall graduation rate. At each of these universities, Black students have one of the lowest graduation rates among the student population. Low graduation and enrollment rates for Black students occur not only in San Diego County but all across America (National Center for Education Statistics). Universities are still built around white standards and traditions, so Black students who choose to maintain strong connections with their racial and linguistic identities are neither expected nor encouraged to succeed in the average American university. These trends will continue in the United States unless we change the way we approach education.

Cuz I Am Who I Am

Universities can become places where even more Black students are successful. That can start with encouraging students to feel confident using their linguistic identity in every setting. College writing centers can help students develop and protect their linguistic identity by teaching effective ways to incorporate it into academic writing. In the essay "Should Writers Use They Own English?" from the book *Writing Centers and the New Racism*, Vershawn Ashanti Young argues that writers should not be confined by SAE and should instead be allowed to use their native dialects in academic writing. He demonstrates this claim by writing in AAVE to show the value of a new writing strategy called code meshing. Young introduces the term "code meshing" to propose the idea that people should write and speak with a combination of standard and nonstandard dialects. He states, "Code meshing is the new code-switching; it's multidialectalism and pluralingualism in one speech act, in one paper." It blends "dialects, international languages, local idioms, chat-room lingo, and the rhetorical styles of various ethnic and cultural groups in both formal and informal speech acts" (67).

Teaching students to code mesh would allow them to use their linguistic identity to their advantage. In a speech titled "Moving beyond Alright: And the Emotional Toll of This, My Life Matters Too, in the Writing Center Work," Neisha-Anne Green, director of American University's Writing Center, shares her personal experience as a Black tutor, writer, and director while explaining to other writing center directors that a Black person's identity heavily influences how they write. Green shares her struggles and successes with figuring out how to code mesh in her graduate thesis. Reflecting on the process, she noted, "I wasn't just a writer anymore, I was a Black writer. I was writing, and Neisha-Anne was all over the page. My rhetorical traditions, my cultures, my sass, and attitude were all on the page and they coexisted with the ever-fluid 'standard'" (22-23). By code meshing, Green was able to incorporate her identity into her writing. She produced lively and effective papers by clearly expressing linguistic identity in her research. If writing centers teach code meshing as an academically acceptable form of writin, students from nondominant groups are gonna be usin they identities to they own advantage. Diverse voices and perspectives are gonna be represented and celebrated in academic discourse.

Conclusion

I talk to myself. Alone in my room, with no one else around, I translate the internal monologue that flows through all our minds into spoken words. When I'm just stating facts and having idle conversations with the wall, I typically speak in SAE. But when I really get goin, when I start sharin my emotions, my defiance, my passions, that's when I start talkin Black. This dialect makes me feel at home in my skin. But never in my wildest dreams did I imagine I'd be writin the way I think when I got to the university level. I was finna write white for the rest of my academic career, but being able to write like this, in my voice, gave me the confidence to speak my mind. If all institutions of learning encouraged students to find and develop their linguistic identities instead of trying to suppress them, students could learn to be more confident and successful academic writers. That's what universities are supposed to be doin: helpin students find and use their voices.

Works Cited

Barron, Nancy, and Nancy Grimm. "Addressing Racial Diversity in a Writing Center: Stories and Lessons from Two Beginners." *The Writing Center Journal*, vol. 22, no. 2, spring/summer 2002, pp. 55-83. *JSTOR*, www.jstor .org/stable/43442150.

Charity, Anne, et al. "Familiarity with School English in African American Children and Its Relation to Early Reading Achievement." *Child Development*, vol. 75, no. 5, 2004, pp. 1340-1356. *JSTOR*, www.jstor.org/stable /3696487.

Fish, Stanley. "What Should Colleges Teach? Part 3." *New York Times*, 7 Sept. 2009,opinionator.blogs.nytimes.com/2009/08/31/what-should-colleges-teach-part-2/.

Green, Neisha-Anne. "Moving beyond Alright: And the Emotional Toll of This, My Life Matters Too, in the Writing Center Work." *The Writing Center Journal*, vol. 37, no. 1, 2018, pp. 15-34. *JSTOR*, www.jstor.org/stable/26537361.

Greenfield, Laura. "The 'Standard English' Fairy Tale: A Rhetorical Analysis of Racist Pedagogies and Commonplace Assumptions about Language Diversity." Greenfield and Rowan, pp. 33-60.

Greenfield, Laura, and Karen Rowan, editors. *Writing Centers and the New Racism: A Call for Sustainable Dialogue and Change*. UP of Colorado, 2011.

Labov, William. "Unendangered Dialect, Endangered People: The Case of African American Vernacular English." *Transforming Anthropology*, vol. 18, no. 1, April 2010, pp. 15-27. *AnthroSource*, https://doi.org/10.1111/j.1548-7466.2010.01066.x.

National Center for Education Statistics. *Integrated Postsecondary Education Data System* (IPEDS), 31 Aug. 2019, nces.ed.gov/ipeds/datacenter/InstitutionByName.aspx?goToReportId=6.

Rickford, John, et al. "Neighborhood Effects on Use of African-American Vernacular English." *PNAS*, vol. 112, no. 38, 2015, pp. 11817-11822. *PNAS*, https://doi.org/10.1073/pnas.1500176112.

United States Census Bureau. "San Diego County, California." *QuickFacts*, 2019, www.census.gov/quickfacts/facttable/sandiegocountycalifornia/PST045219.

Young, Vershawn Ashanti. "Should Writers Use They Own English?" Greenfield and Rowan, pp. 61-72.

Thinking about the Text

1. Anna Glavee **DESCRIBES** four "truths" (7–10) about language, and she discusses them in reference to AAVE, or "talkin Black" (3). What are the four truths that she outlines? Summarize them briefly. What have you observed that could confirm or refute them in your own life and with the language varieties that you use? Give an example for each truth.

2. Glavee combines personal stories with summaries and quotations from research scholars in order to make her point. Why do you think she chose

to include her own experiences? How would the essay be different if it were a **REPORT** alone, leaving out Glavee's **NARRATIVES**? Or if it were all **NARRATIVE**, without any outside research? Choose one example or section making use of both narrative and reporting that you find particularly effective and describe why.

3. How does Glavee **EXPLAIN** the concept of code meshing? According to Glavee, what are the benefits of code meshing? How effectively does she employ this strategy herself in this essay? Explain your reasoning and point to examples from the essay to support your response.

4. What **ARGUMENT** does Glavee make in her conclusion? Does the evidence presented throughout the essay support this position? Why or why not? Explain your response and point to examples from the essay to support your reasoning.

5. Glavee's essay is her response to an assignment to identify and explore a problem with literacy education. How would you take on a similar assignment? Reflect on the question and then choose the genre best suited to what you want to say. You may want to center your work in a **NARRATIVE** of your own experience, or you may wish to focus more on **REPORTING** conditions you've observed in your community or have researched in published materials. You may also want to take a specific **POSITION** based on your observations and experiences.

Origin Stories

ANNETTE GORDON-REED

IT'S A SAFE BET that most people in the United States, when they think of it, believe that Black people first appeared in North America in 1619. The story of the "20. and odd negroes" that John Rolfe announced, in matter of fact fashion, to have arrived in Virginia that year is often taken as the beginning of what we might call "Black America"—from that twenty, to 4 million—by the time of Emancipation in 1865—to nearly 40 million today.

Origin stories matter, for individuals, groups of people, and for nations. They inform our sense of self; telling us what kind of people we believe we are, what kind of nation we believe we live in. They usually carry, at least, a hope that where we started might hold the key to where we are in the present. We can say, then, that much of the concern with origin stories is about our current needs and desires (usually to feel good about ourselves), not actual history. History is about people and events in a particular setting and context, and how those things have changed over time in ways that make the past different from our own time, with an understanding that those changes were not inevitable. Origin stories often seek to find the

ANNETTE GORDON-REED is a historian and professor of law and history at Harvard University. She has won numerous prizes for her writing, including a Pulitzer Prize and a National Book Award for her groundbreaking work on Thomas Jefferson and the children he fathered by Sally Hemings, a woman he enslaved. This reading is excerpted from her 2021 best-selling book, *On Juneteenth*.

familiar, or the superficially familiar—memory, sometimes shading into mythology. Both memory and mythology have their uses, even if they must be separated from our understandings about the demands of historical thinking.

Consider the difference between the stories of Plymouth, Massachusetts, and those of Jamestown, Virginia. Plymouth Rock gives Americans a founding story about a valiant people leaving their homes to escape religious persecution, and founding a new society in the wilderness, with the aid of friendly Indigenous people, like Squanto (Tisquantum) of the Patuxet. Who among those who grew up in the United States did not perform in, or watch, school plays telling the story of these encounters, or make cutouts of turkeys symbolizing the first Thanksgiving feast that the Pilgrims and Patuxets shared—in most cases, I would wager, without knowing the name of the Indian group involved or Squanto's true name?

At the other end of the scale, we have the narrative of Jamestown, created more openly as an economic venture in 1607. It is difficult to wrest an uplifting story from the doings of English settlers who created the colony for no purpose other than making money or, at least, to make a living for themselves. Not long after their arrival, they started down a path that would make Virginia a full-fledged slave society, the largest and richest of the thirteen colonies. What little I learned about Jamestown as a child centered on the story of Pocahontas (Matoaka), the daughter of Powhatan, who serves the same function as Squanto in the Pilgrim story, to emphasize the triumph of amity over enmity between the Indigenous people and the English settlers, something very different than what actually happened.

I am certain nearly every American schoolchild of my generation 5 learned of Pocahontas, though one of my college classmates assured me that her elementary school in New England had downplayed the Virginia settlement and focused mainly on the Pilgrims as the beginning of America as we know it. Jamestown was mentioned, she said, but as a brief experiment of little lasting consequence. *"We learned there were some people down there,"* she said with a wave of her hand. I imagine that is how most Americans in the past were taught to view the colonies.

There is also a version of this attitude about Plymouth versus Jamestown in the origin story of African Americans. I remember hearing in school, probably because I was in Texas, stray references to a man of African descent—a "Negro"—named Esteban (Estebanico), who was in what would become Texas during the time of Spanish exploration. The last phrase, "during the time of Spanish exploration," signaled that this was information about a world gone by that we didn't have to pay much attention to, as it had little to do with understandings about the history of our country. I hadn't been told that other people of African decent—some enslaved, some not—arrived with the Spanish when they came to the Americas. Whether enslaved or free, these people were disconnected from the institution of plantation slavery that developed in Texas three centuries later, the institution that helped define my ancestors' circumstances.

The same phenomenon applies to St. Augustine, Florida, which was not at all a part of my early education. It was there, in fact, that racially based slavery, as an organized system, began on American soil, established by the Spanish as early as 1565. In 1735 the Spanish governor chartered a settlement for enslaved Africans who escaped from the English colonies and made it to St. Augustine. The only condition for protection was that the new residents adopt Catholicism and swear allegiance to the Spanish king. The settlement of free Blacks existed until the Spanish sold Florida to the United States in 1817.

I had heard of St. Augustine by the time I got to college. But it, too, was in the category *"there were some people down there."* The English had "won" the contest against the Spanish in North America—in Texas and in Florida. What was the point of incorporating this story of Africans and Spanish people into the general narrative of American history or, more specifically, the history of African Americans? The same could be said of the French, in their beaver-trapping colonies near the Great Lakes. They were "also-rans" in the race for the territory that became the United States. The brief period of Dutch slave ownership in New York is almost totally out of the picture.

All of this was the result of a nationalist-oriented history, with an intense focus on what was going on within the boundaries of the United States, and seeing what was going on almost totally from the perspective of English-speaking (and White) people. The world enclosed in that way left out so much about the true nature of life in Early America, about all the varied influences that shaped the people and circumstances during those times. It closes off the vital understanding about contingency, how things could have taken a different turn. Very significantly, it helped create and maintain an extremely narrow construction of Blackness.

Under the conventional narrative with which most Americans, it is safe to say, are familiar, Blacks came to North America under the power

10

of the English from places that were never clearly defined, for where they came from didn't matter much. They went from speaking the languages of their homelands to speaking English. They worked on plantations in the fields or in the house. This highly edited origin story winds the Black experience tight, limiting the imaginative possibilities of Blackness—what could be done by people in that skin. To be sure, the institution of slavery itself circumscribed the actions of enslaved African Americans, but it never destroyed their personhood. They did not become a separate species by the experience of being enslaved. All of the feelings, talents, failings, strengths and weaknesses—all the states and qualities that exist in human beings—remained in them. There has been too great a tendency within some presentations of enslaved people to lose sight of that fact, in ways obvious and not.

For example, we can see it in the treatment of that most basic of human traits: the ability to acquire and to speak a language. Language, however formed, connects people to one another. Dutch was the first language of noted abolitionist Sojourner Truth, born Isabella Baumfree in Swartekill, New York, near the end of the 1790s. She almost certainly spoke English with a Dutch-inflected accent. Yet, reproductions of her speech were written in the stereotypical dialect universally chosen to portray the speech of enslaved Blacks, no matter where in the country they lived. Under this formulation, the experiences of growing up hearing and speaking Dutch had no effect upon Truth. It was as if the legal status of being enslaved, and the biological reality of having been born of African descent, fixed her pattern of speech, almost as a matter of brain function.

When I was working on my first book, writing about the way historians had handled the story of Thomas Jefferson and Sally Hemings, I noticed that one line of attack on the veracity of Madison Hemings, who said in recollections that he was the son of Jefferson and Hemings, was to suggest that the statements he gave to the journalist Samuel Wetmore were unreliable because it was unlikely that a former enslaved person could speak in standard English. The notion that such a thing could happen was treated as presumptively incredible. Even a brief thought about the circumstances of Hemings's life, viewing him as a human being, however, would tell a different story about his narrative. Hemings's recollections make clear that his older siblings—Beverley (a male) and Harriet—left Monticello to live as White people. Both married White people who may not have known that their spouses were partly Black and had been born enslaved. The communities

Close reading of her sources led Annette Gordon-Reed to an important new analysis of historical accounts. Learn more about how to practice critical reading on pp. 525–27.

they lived in, Washington, D.C., and Maryland, evidently, did not know that either. Many years after the pair left Monticello, their younger brother, Eston, would follow his older siblings into the White world, settling his family in Madison, Wisconsin.

How did Madison Hemings's siblings live convincingly as White if they spoke in the dialect universally applied to enslaved people? Why would Madison—the middle son between the older Beverley and Harriet and the younger, Eston—speak differently than his siblings? Realizing that the actual circumstances of the Hemings children's lives mattered, and should have been taken into account, would have made clear that it made no sense to assume that Hemings could not have spoken in the way portrayed in his conversation with Wetmore.

A similar analysis, or lack of analysis, has often been at play in writing about the Hemings children's mother, Sally. As I have traveled the country talking about the books I have written about the Hemings family, I've been struck by the responses to the fact that Sally Hemings, and her brother James, learned to speak French during their years in France. On several occasions I have been asked, with seeming wonder, "how" they could have learned to speak French. And even when the question is not specifically raised, it seems to hang in the air when people ponder the fact that she, and presumably her Mother, thought for a time to remain in Paris when Jefferson decided to go home. *How could they have gotten along there? They didn't speak the language.* Doubts about their basic capacities persist, despite the differences in their circumstances and opportunities in France. Because slavery in the United States was racially based, it was easy to graft the legally imposed incapacities of slavery onto Black people as a group, making incapacity an inherent feature of the race.

Perhaps there is something about French, for a long time the language of diplomacy and culture. It is considered "fancy" in a way that goes along with the country's cuisine and vaunted high fashion—haute cuisine, haute couture. What of individuals born at the lowest rung of society? Could enslaved people, Black people, ever lay claim to sophistication? Over one hundred years after James Hemings's and Sally Hemings's time in France, Secretary of State William Jennings Bryan, while contemplating a crisis in Haiti, exclaimed, "Dear me. Think of it. N*****s speaking French."

It is hard to imagine that Bryan seriously thought that learning a language, which human beings do quite well without formal instruction—uneducated babies do it all the time—was really beyond the ken of Black people. He cannot have been that ignorant. Instead, he was more likely following a well-worn path: the "joke" that sends a vicious message through supposedly lighthearted humor. So much of racism is about announcing, in various ways, the agreed-upon fictions about Black people that justify attempting to keep them in a subordinate status.

The fiction that has African Americans naturally speaking in a particular way, or unable to learn a language, slyly promotes the notion that Blacks are somewhat less than human, in their inability to master a human trait: the capacity to engage in complex communication. At the very least, the ideas about Blacks and language serve as means to convey the supposed gulf that exists between the races. Administrators involved in the WPA Slave Narrative Project of the 1930s, which gathered the recollections of formerly enslaved people, engaged in a concerted effort to render the speech of the interviewees into stereotypical Black dialect. As a result, the accents and speech of all the interviewees—from Virginia to Georgia to Texas—appear as if people in those very different regions spoke exactly the same way. The exaggerated dialect was supposed to signal "authenticity," an authenticity defined by incapacity.

Which brings us back to Estebanico, whose sojourn in Texas had taken place nearly a century before the landing at Jamestown, nearly two hundred years before James and Sally Hemings were in France. Estebanico was described as a "black Arab from Azamor," on the coast of Morocco. A Muslim, he had been forced to convert to Christianity and sold away from his home to Spain. He came to the Americas with the man who enslaved him and [Spanish explorer Álvar Núñez] Cabeza de Vaca.

Cabeza de Vaca, who lived to produce a wildly popular memoir of the extraordinary adventure, wrote about Estebanico as having played a key role as the chief translator between the Spaniards and the Indigenous people because of his great talent for learning and speaking languages. Estebanico, and the Europeans, became renowned as medicine men by the people they encountered. Estebanico appears to have been able to achieve a measure of respect.

I don't recall whether Estebanico's talent for languages featured in the fleeting mention that was made of him in my early education. I do wonder what difference it might have made to our understandings about the enslaved to have had a more fully realized example of one who displayed 20 such perseverance and talent. We would have encountered a known person, to substitute for the nameless people in cotton fields who, at least in my education, never broke out and appeared as anything other than fungible agricultural workers. Learning that the Spanish explorers, and the Indigenous people they encountered and lived with at times, relied on Estebanico to help them speak with one another brings another dimension to our understandings about slavery and the people enslaved.

Not to place conquering in a good light, but seeing Africans in America who were out of the strict confines of the plantation—and seeing them presented as something other than the metaphorical creation of English people—would have pushed back against the narrative of inherent limitation. Africans were all over the world, doing different things, having all kinds of experiences. Blackness does not equal inherent incapacity and natural limitation.

Thinking about the Text

1. Annette Gordon-Reed focuses on language in order to support her arguments about origin stories and the ways that the history of Africans in America is taught. What are her main **ARGUMENTS**? Why, according to Gordon-Reed, are representations of speech and language so important? Is her argument persuasive? Why or why not? Explain your reasoning.

2. Although Gordon-Reed's essay is focused on events that occurred centuries ago, she also inserts some of her own experiences. She mentions things she learned in school as a child, discusses evidence she unearthed in her previous work, and comments on experiences she had during the public events related to that work. Why might she have chosen to write herself into the essay? How effective is her use of **NARRATIVE**? Explain your reasoning.

3. Accurate representations of someone's speech matter, according to Gordon-Reed. What **EXAMPLES** does she offer to support this argument? Are her examples effective? Why or why not?

4. Gordon-Reed describes the way that Sojourner Truth's speech has been depicted, but she doesn't quote directly from those representations. She also mentions the "stereotypical Black dialect" (17) that was employed in the

WPA Slave Narrative Project of the 1930s but offers no example quotations. Why might she have chosen to omit quotations as a form of **EVIDENCE**? Do you think she made a good rhetorical decision? Why or why not?

5. Gordon-Reed begins her essay by talking about origin stories and their importance for "individuals, groups of people, and for nations" (2). What are the origin stories that you heard as a child—whether in school or from your family—that have contributed to your sense of self? Reflect on one of those stories; write it out in as much detail as you remember. How accurate and factual do you think it is? You might even do some research to check out the facts. If any features of that story were found to be incomplete or inaccurate, would you think differently about yourself or your community in any way? Why or why not? Write an essay **REFLECTING** on these questions about origin stories that relate or matter to you.

Learning the Grammar of Animacy

ROBIN WALL KIMMERER

TO BE NATIVE TO A PLACE we must learn to speak its language.

I come here to listen, to nestle in the curve of the roots in a soft hollow of pine needles, to lean my bones against the column of white pine, to turn off the voice in my head until I can hear the voices outside it: the *shhh* of wind in needles, water trickling over rock, nuthatch tapping, chipmunks digging, beechnut falling, mosquito in my ear, and something more—something that is not me, for which we have no language, the wordless being of others in which we are never alone. After the drumbeat of my mother's heart, *this* was my first language. . . .

Listening in wild places, we are audience to conversations in a language not our own. I think now that it was a longing to comprehend this language I hear in the woods that led me to science, to learn over the years to speak fluent botany. A tongue that should not, by the way, be mistaken for the language of plants. I did learn another language in science, though, one of careful observation, an intimate vocabulary that names each little part.

ROBIN WALL KIMMERER, professor in environmental science and forestry at the State University of New York, is a member of Citizen Potawatomi Nation. She has been awarded a John Burroughs Medal for outstanding nature writing, and her work has been published in both academic journals and periodicals for the general public, like the *Guardian*. This selection is from her book *Braiding Sweetgrass*, which won a 2014 Sigurd F. Olson Nature Writing Award.

Robin Wall Kimmerer is exploring the power of language in shaping our perceptions of reality. You can read more about the power of language (and the languages of power) on pp. 40–41.

To name and describe you must first see, and science polishes the gift of seeing. I honor the strength of the language that has become a second tongue to me. But beneath the richness of its vocabulary and its descriptive power, something is missing, the same something that swells around you and in you when you listen to the world. Science can be a language of distance which reduces a being to its working parts; it is a language of objects. The language scientists speak, however precise, is based on a profound error in grammar, an omission, a grave loss in translation from the native languages of these shores. . . .

Had history been different, I would likely speak Bodewadmimwin, or Potawatomi, an Anishinaabe language. But, like many of the three hundred and fifty indigenous languages of the Americas, Potawatomi is threatened, and I speak the language you read. The powers of assimilation did their work as my chance of hearing that language, and yours too, was washed from the mouths of Indian children in government boarding schools where speaking your native tongue was forbidden. Children like my grandfather, who was taken from his family when he was just a little boy of nine years old. This history scattered not only our words but also our people. Today I live far from our reservation, so even if I could speak the language, I would have no one to talk to. But a few summers ago, at our yearly tribal gathering, a language class was held and I slipped into the tent to listen. There was a great deal of excitement about the class because, for the first time, every single fluent speaker in our tribe would be there as a teacher. When the speakers were called forward to the circle of folding chairs, they moved slowly—with canes, walkers, and wheelchairs, only a few entirely under their own power. I counted them as they filled the chairs. Nine. Nine fluent speakers. In the whole world. Our language, millennia in the making, sits in those nine chairs. The words that praised creation, told the old stories, lulled my ancestors to sleep, rests today in the tongues of nine very mortal men and women. Each in turn addresses the small group of would-be students.

A man with long gray braids tells how his mother hid him away when the Indian agents came to take the children. . . . "We're the end of the road. We are all that is left. If you young people do not learn, the language will die. The missionaries and the U.S. government will have their victory at last.". . .

So now my house is spangled with Post-it notes in another language, as if I were studying for a trip abroad. But I'm not going away, I'm coming home. . . .

My sister's gift to me one Christmas was a set of magnetic tiles for the refrigerator in Ojibwe, or Anishinabemowin, a language closely related to Potawatomi. I spread them out on my kitchen table looking for familiar words, but the more I looked, the more worried I got. Among the hundred or more tiles, there was but a single word that I recognized: *megwech*, thank you. The small feeling of accomplishment from months of study evaporated in a moment.

I remember paging through the Ojibwe dictionary she sent, trying to decipher the tiles, but the spellings didn't always match and the print was too small and there are way too many variations on a single word and I was feeling that this was just way too hard. The threads in my brain knotted and the harder I tried, the tighter they became. Pages blurred and my eyes settled on a word—a verb, of course: "to be a Saturday." *Pfft!* I threw down the book. Since when is *Saturday* a verb? Everyone knows it's a noun. I grabbed the dictionary and flipped more pages and all kinds of things seemed to be verbs: "to be a hill," "to be red," "to be a long sandy stretch of beach," and then my finger rested on *wiikwegamaa:* "to be a bay." "Ridiculous!" I ranted in my head. "There is no reason to make it so complicated. No wonder no one speaks it. A cumbersome language, impossible to learn, and more than that, it's all wrong. A bay is most definitely a person, place, or thing—a noun and not a verb." I was ready to give up. I'd learned a few words, done my duty to the language that was taken from my grandfather. Oh, the ghosts of the missionaries in the boarding schools must have been rubbing their hands in glee at my frustration. "She's going to surrender," they said.

And then I swear I heard the zap of synapses firing. An electric current sizzled down my arm and through my finger, and practically scorched the page where that one word lay. In that moment I could smell the water of the bay, watch it rock against the shore and hear it sift onto the sand. A bay is a noun only if water is *dead*. When *bay* is a noun, it is defined by humans, trapped between its shores and contained by the word. But the verb *wiikwegamaa*—to *be* a bay—releases the water from bondage and lets it live. "To be a bay" holds the wonder that, for this moment, the living water has decided to shelter itself between these shores, conversing with cedar roots and a flock of baby mergansers. Because it could do otherwise—become a stream or an ocean or a waterfall, and there are verbs for that, too. To be a hill, to be a sandy beach, to be a Saturday, all are possible verbs in a world where everything is alive. Water, land, and even a day, the language a mirror for seeing the animacy of the world, the life that pulses through all things, through pines and nuthatches and mushrooms. *This* is the language I hear in the woods; this is the language that lets us speak of what wells up all around us. And the vestiges of boarding schools, the soap-wielding missionary wraiths, hang their heads in defeat.

This is the grammar of animacy. Imagine seeing your grandmother standing at the stove in her apron and then saying of her, "Look, it is making soup. It has gray hair." We might snicker at such a mistake, but we also recoil from it. In English, we never refer to a member of our family, or indeed to any person, as *it*. That would be a profound act of disrespect. *It* robs a person of selfhood and kinship, reducing a person to a mere thing. So it is that in Potawatomi and most other indigenous languages, we use the same words to address the living world as we use for our family. Because they are our family. 10

To whom does our language extend the grammar of animacy? Naturally, plants and animals are animate, but as I learn, I am discovering that the Potawatomi understanding of what it means to be animate diverges from the list of attributes of living beings we all learned in Biology 101. In Potawatomi 101, rocks are animate, as are mountains and water and fire and places. Beings that are imbued with spirit, our sacred medicines, our songs, drums, and even stories, are all animate. The list of the inanimate seems to be smaller, filled with objects that are made by people. Of an inanimate being, like a table, we say, "*What* is it?" And we answer *Dopwen yewe*. Table it is. But of apple, we must say, "*Who* is that being?" And reply *Mshimin yawe*. Apple that being is. . . .

English doesn't give us many tools for incorporating respect for animacy. In English, you are either a human or a thing. Our grammar boxes us in by the choice of reducing a nonhuman being to an *it*, or it must be gendered, inappropriately, as a *he* or a *she*. Where are our words for the simple existence of another living being? Where is our *yawe*? . . .

When I am in the woods with my students, teaching them the gifts of plants and how to call them by name, I try to be mindful of my language, to be bilingual between the lexicon of science and the grammar of animacy. Although they still have to learn scientific roles and Latin names, I hope I am also teaching them to know the world as a neighborhood of nonhuman residents, to know that, as ecotheologian Thomas Berry has written, "we must say of the universe that it is a communion of subjects, not a collection of objects."

One afternoon, I sat with my field ecology students by a *wiikwegamaa* and shared this idea of animate language. One young man, Andy, splashing his feet in the clear water, asked the big question. "Wait a second," he said as he wrapped his mind around this linguistic distinction, "doesn't this mean that speaking English, thinking in English, somehow gives us permission to disrespect nature? By denying everyone else the right to be persons? Wouldn't things be different if nothing was an *it*?"

Swept away with the idea, he said it felt like an awakening to him. 15 More like a remembering, I think. The animacy of the world is something we already know, but the language of animacy teeters on extinction—not just for Native peoples, but for everyone. Our toddlers speak of plants and animals as if they were people, extending to them self and intention and compassion—until we teach them not to. We quickly retrain them and make them forget. When we tell them that the tree is not a *who*, but an *it*, we make that maple an object; we put a barrier between us, absolving ourselves of moral responsibility and opening the door to exploitation. Saying *it* makes a living land into "natural resources." If a maple is an *it*, we can take up the chain saw. If a maple is a *her*, we think twice. . . .

The arrogance of English is that the only way to be animate, to be worthy of respect and moral concern, is to be a human.

A language teacher I know explained that grammar is just the way we chart relationships in language. Maybe it also reflects our relationships with each other. Maybe a grammar of animacy could lead us to whole new ways of living in the world, other species a sovereign people, a world with a democracy of species, not a tyranny of one—with moral responsibility to water and wolves, and with a legal system that recognizes the standing of other species. . . .

We Americans are reluctant to learn a foreign language of our own species, let alone another species. But imagine the possibilities. Imagine the access we would have to different perspectives, the things we might see through other eyes, the wisdom that surrounds us. We don't have to figure out everything by ourselves: there are intelligences other than our own, teachers all around us. Imagine how much less lonely the world would be. . . .

I'm not advocating that we all learn Potawatomi or Hopi or Seminole, even if we could. Immigrants came to these shores bearing a legacy of languages, all to be cherished. But to become native to this place, if we are to survive here, and our neighbors too, our work is to learn to speak the grammar of animacy, so that we might truly be at home. . . .

Thinking about the Text

1. Robin Wall Kimmerer uses a personal narrative in order to make an **ARGU-MENT**. What is her argument? Summarize it briefly. Where do you find her argument stated most clearly in the essay? Why do you think she chose this organization? Do you think her argument would have been more or less effective if she had stated it explicitly at the opening and left out all of the narrative elements? Why or why not?

2. In several places throughout her essay (as well as in the title), Kimmerer uses the term "grammar." How does she **DEFINE** the term? In what ways is her use of the word "grammar" different from your understanding of what grammar is? Explain your response.

3. Kimmerer **DESCRIBES** experiences of hearing the language of the nature in the woods, and her writing is rich with detail. In addition to what she *hears*, what other senses come into play in her description of the animacy of the world? Point to an example for each of the senses that Kimmerer describes.

4. Kimmerer is a scientist but points out that the "fluent botany" she speaks is not to be mistaken for the "language of plants" (3). How are those two "languages" different, according to Kimmerer? In reflecting on and analyzing languages, she goes on to assert that the language of science is "based on a profound error" (3). How does Kimmerer establish her **AUTHORITY** to discuss these topics—science, nature, and language? Do you find her arguments credible? Explain your reasoning.

5. What is one element of nature that's part of your everyday environment? The sky? Pigeons? A mountain? A particular tree or bush? A lake or creek? Squirrels? (If you've never really noticed anything, now would be a good time to start.) Go to where you are close to the element you've identified and do as Kimmerer demonstrates: "turn off the voice in [your] head until [you] can hear the voices outside it" (2). Try to stay in this receptive, listening state as long as possible. What do you hear/feel/know from being close to nature and your chosen element in particular? Write a **NARRATIVE** that describes your experience.

Clean Sweep

RYAN KOHLS

FORTY THOUSAND PEOPLE are packed into the Rogers Centre to watch the Toronto Blue Jays. Right now, the stadium still belongs to the players, the fans and the vast, expensively-produced spectacle of professional sports. But at gate three, a group of about fifty congregates. Some stand alone, or pace and listen to music. Others sit on wooden benches nearby and enjoy a final cigarette. It's 10:30 pm, and these grim-faced men and women are waiting for work to begin. Standing on the curb as the game wraps up inside, these are the cleaners.

They'll work until dawn, gathering up some 15,000 pounds of garbage, scrubbing, rinsing, bending and lifting with painstaking thoroughness.

By morning, the stadium will gleam and the cleaners will go home to sleep with the blinds pulled tight against the sun. Now, they try to relax, joking to keep the mood light. "Are you ready for more torture?" one of them asks.

Spread out across 12.7 acres, the Rogers Centre, once known as the SkyDome, is one of Toronto's most recognizable landmarks. Every year 3.5 million people

RYAN KOHLS is a journalist who has filed stories from places as diverse as Nairobi, Kenya, and Nunavut, Canada. He is producer for the programs *Up Front* and *The Listening Post*, both on Al Jazeera. You can find him on *Twitter* @ryankohls. This article appeared in 2014 in *Maison Neuve*, a Canadian magazine of arts, opinion, and ideas.

attend events at the mammoth complex. The big crowds mean big business—baseball's Blue Jays, whose eighty-one home games provide the stadium's main attraction, are worth an estimated $568 million. One season produces 1.2 million pounds of garbage. Eventually, someone must clean it up. Enter the cleaners—exhausted, poorly paid and largely anonymous. Without them, the game can't go on.

On a given night, anywhere from thirty to one hundred cleaners scour the 5 stadium. Most of them work for Hallmark Housekeeping Services, a Toronto-based janitorial agency that holds the cleaning contract at the Rogers Centre. These workers are experienced; Hallmark employees clean after every event. The other cleaners come from Labor Ready, a huge company that supplies temporary blue-collar workers across Canada and the United States. These employees book the Rogers Centre gig on a nightly basis and typically work a shorter shift. Both groups of workers are predominantly immigrants or down on their luck.

In the summer of 2012, I worked as a cleaner, on-and-off, for three months. I participated in roughly twenty-five cleaning shifts as an employee

When the fun is over and the fans go home, someone has to pick up the trash.

of Labor Ready, joining the agency after struggling to find journalism work in the city.

Most cleaners patrol the stadium with brooms and large transparent garbage bags; a handful of more seasoned employees take leaf blowers. With the motor slung across their backs and a long black nozzle pumping out air, they blow the garbage from two parallel seating sections into one aisle. The blowers weigh about 25 pounds. One worker described it as being like "carrying an obese baby around all night."

Once enough garbage reaches the aisle, the sweepers climb to the top of their section and begin to slosh the mess downwards. In time, the pile turns into a cascading waterfall of miscellaneous trash. Beer-soaked hot dogs mix with ketchup-infused popcorn and the ubiquitous shells of sunflower seeds, which are maddeningly hard to persuade off the wet concrete. The mixture leaves behind a slick residue that makes the stairs treacherous. Workers sometimes slip and hurt their backs. Some stadiums have tried to control the garbage, but at baseball stadiums, seeds cannot be so easily dispatched—they're an iconic part of the game. "Getting rid of [sunflower seeds] would be like getting rid of beer and hot dogs," says Wayne Sills, the director of facility services at the Rogers Centre.

The last stage of cleaning is accomplished with four thirty-metre yellow hoses, spraying highly pressurized water into the aisles, aimed by workers in rubber boots. The Rogers Centre is one of the few North American sports stadiums to get the pressure-wash treatment—visiting teams have been known to remark on the building's uncanny cleanliness.

Around 2:30 am Rosario Coutinho scans the Centre with binoculars. She'll ¹⁰ spot a sweeper slacking off and radio the nighttime supervisor to assess the situation and get things moving. Coutinho then heads to another location where she can remain unseen and watch closely. "I'm the ghost," she tells me one night.

Coutinho, now fifty-two, serves as the resident manager of the clean-up operation. She pulls her black hair back in a ponytail, wears glasses, a black fleece and black pants, a BlackBerry headset and a crucifix on a chain. Coutinho knows more about the cleaning process than anyone. She's been at the Rogers Centre for nearly twenty-five years.

The workers are on to her tactics. Once, a group of Mexican cleaners developed a system of whistles to alert the others when she was watching. Coutinho translated the calls and changed her moves accordingly.

To become the binocular boss, Coutinho had to start from the bottom. In 1989, just a month after the SkyDome opened, she immigrated to Canada from Portugal. Her husband already lived here and told her about the opening of an amazing new stadium. Coutinho remembers being unimpressed; some stadiums in Europe hold 100,000 people. But the retractable roof that gave the building its name was, she was told, a sight to behold.

Before her arrival, Coutinho was prepared to work hard. "I knew I would be doing jobs that no one else wanted to do," she recalls. "If I'm cleaning shit, who cares? I'm going to make it smell better." Two months after landing in Toronto she was cleaning at the SkyDome. Her first assignment was the luxury boxes. One night she found a briefcase containing $10,000 cash. She returned it. The job meant everything and she couldn't risk losing it.

This atypical attitude caught management's attention and within a 15 year she was promoted to team leader. "Seventy percent of people in the cleaning business have no pride," Coutinho says. "Earn what you make, that's what counts." By 1995, she was managing the entire operation.

Few cleaners are as scrupulous as Coutinho. Many hate being there—some show up drunk, others get drunk in the stadium bathrooms on left-behind tallboys from the stands or their own flasks of hard liquor. Still others find their pay-off elsewhere: take Mark Stanton [not his real name]. It's his third season cleaning at the Rogers Centre and his favourite part of the job is finding money.

After the Jays' home opener, sporting a leaf blower slung across his back, he guides sunflower shells, empty beer cans and half-eaten hot dogs across an aisle. Out of the corner of his eye he spots a wallet. He flicks off the blower, bends over and plucks it from a pile of trash. He can't get too excited; he has to act calm: someone could be watching. He hunches over, peers inside and sees the cash. Quickly, with a practiced motion, he slides $30 into his pants. "Sometimes I go to work and I'm flat broke," says Stanton. "If I find $30, there's $30 in my pocket until pay day." He will eventually return the wallet, a little lighter, to security.

Stanton is adept at working the stadium's unofficial and technically illegal lost-and-found system to his advantage. At last year's home opener, he scored five wallets with $30 or more and two half-packs of smokes. When he cleaned up after the 100th Grey Cup, he found $150, three Grey Cup souvenir glasses and three t-shirts. After Ultimate Fighting Championship 129, he found a judge's scorecard and three bloody hand wraps. The excitement

---

Ryan Kohls, writing for a magazine, didn't have to document his interviews, but you will in your academic writing. See how to do so in MLA format on p. 605.

creates plenty of opportunities for fans to drop things. After every event, without fail, an array of valuables remains behind. For the workers, this is a perk, a way to make the job feel worthwhile. Some nights pay off huge. At UFC 100, one worker found and kept a wallet with $1,500. That's a month's wages. Other cleaners have found diamond rings, iPhones, BlackBerries, digital cameras, transit passes, sunglasses and umbrellas.

The treasure hunt is on everyone's mind. Having a successful night requires skill and attention. You can't just sweep or blow the garbage, you have to watch and listen. Over time, workers learn to hear the difference between a sliding beer tab and a coin. One worker uses his haul to pay child support for his three kids. He found $150 once and used it to buy his son a stroller.

When the clock hits 3 am, the stadium falls silent, and the workers break for   20
"lunch." There's a cheap hot dog stand on Front Street that's popular. Most of the cleaners can afford a meal using the spare change they've found during their shift.

Only three-quarters of the workers return after the break. Labor Ready workers are generally only used for sweeping and bagging. They'll get paid for four hours of work. As they disappear into the night, some head to bed, but others walk back to Labor Ready to collect their cheque and secure the next job. The company's offices at 195 Church Street don't open until 5:30 am, so many nights they'll wait in Dundas Square. If they time it just right, they'll score a free breakfast from the Salvation Army truck that passes by Labor Ready every morning.

Thinking about the Text

1. Ryan Kohls begins with a description of the ballpark's splendor and the cleaning process that keeps it that way, but the focus soon shifts to the cleaners themselves. What is his purpose in this **PROFILE**? Point to examples in the text to support your answer.

2. How does Kohls's disclosure of having been a stadium cleaner himself contribute to his **AUTHORITY**? And yet he doesn't include any personal anecdotes or impressions of the job other than the bare facts of his work, choosing instead to spotlight the other cleaners. Should he have spoken more about his own experience? Why or why not?

3. Kohls is clearly happy to no longer work as a stadium cleaner. Despite having moved on in his own career, what is his **ATTITUDE** toward his former colleagues? How does he portray them and their work? Point to examples in the text to support your response.

4. Although this profile describes a large sports arena, Kohls wasn't writing for an **AUDIENCE** of sports fans. What, if anything, might he have done differently if he were writing a column for *ESPN.com* or *Sports Illustrated*? Why?

5. Have you ever worked at a job that you hoped would not become your long-term occupation? Write a **DESCRIPTION** of the job and your coworkers that gives your readers as vivid a sense as possible of a typical shift, letting examples and descriptive details make your point.

Young People Found Time to Figure Out Their Identities during the Pandemic

FORTESA LATIFI

BLAIR WAS 22 YEARS OLD and had never had a boyfriend. In college, the one date she ever had was with a boy who told her he didn't want anyone to know he had gone out with her. She thought her lack of romantic success was her fault. But when the pandemic hit and the world shut down, Blair was forced to leave her college campus during the last semester of senior year, leaving her with a lot of time for self-reflection. Like so many other Gen Z-ers, Blair filled her newly free time by spending a lot of time on TikTok. And the TikToks she watched made her start thinking—what if her romantic pitfalls weren't her fault, it's just that she wasn't actually attracted to her dates? What if she wasn't straight at all?

"One video was specifically like 'straight people don't spend a lot of time thinking about whether or not they're straight,'" Blair said. "And I was like, oh, interesting, I've been thinking about that a lot."

As Blair dove deeper into TikTok and her own thoughts, she enlisted the help of a friend who's bisexual. It took her about a year to come to the conclusion that she was gay. Heterosexuality, she said, was always the default. But after having time during lockdown to think and explore and wonder, she saw a new path for herself.

Many people have shared a version of Blair's experience—that of heading into COVID-19 lockdown thinking of herself one way and emerging from it with a different understanding of her identity. David, 17, spent years trying on different labels to see which fit his gender identity before he settled on one that felt right: he was a trans man. But during lockdown, he says, he found a label that fit even better: bigender.

"Being stuck at home means you aren't performing constantly anymore to an audience," David said. "You're performing to yourself—which makes you realize the things you're comfortable with." 5

FORTESA LATIFI is a Los Angeles–based journalist who writes about mental health, chronic illness, disability, and identity. Her work has appeared in the *Washington Post*, *BuzzFeed*, *Bitch Media*, and more. This essay was published by *Teen Vogue* in June 2021. She tweets from @fortesalatifi; her *Instagram* is @byfortesa.

At his Catholic school, David still presents as a woman and uses his dead name, but he's planning on coming out at school in September for his 18th birthday. (His 18th birthday comes with another milestone: he can begin taking hormones, which he says his parents were uncomfortable with him starting before that age.) He's not sure if school will be back to in-person instruction by then, but if it is, he wonders how the school administration will react. He thinks they might ask him to use the bathroom for disabled students in order to avoid the question of whether he should use the men's or women's room.

Dr. Russell Toomey, a professor in family studies and human development at the University of Arizona, says he isn't surprised by the benefits some young people are finding in exploring their identities during the pandemic. "It raises the extra time you have to sit with yourself to really do that reflection," Toomey said. And while he notes that peer relationships are a key cornerstone of health and feeling connected to the community, it may feel safer to explore shifting identities, like gender and sexuality, away from the gaze of peers.

Aamina, who's 25-years-old, non-binary, and uses the pronouns she/they, felt similarly about the opportunity isolation provided.

"I think it really does give you this strange and unique opportunity to reflect on what your sense of self is built on when it's not built on what other people think of you as," she said. "When I'm able to isolate myself literally . . . It's very clear I'm doing this kind of stuff because I feel that it will be more welcomed by certain people, not because I like it or think I look good in it or feel [like] myself in it."

She started to realize that she had been performing femininity in her 10
gender expression because it's perceived more welcomingly than other identities. "There's a specific warmth people have toward women they find attractive," she said.

During the pandemic, she said she found herself getting dressed the way she wanted, without worrying about seeing anyone she knew. And in that freedom, she found herself more comfortable with being non-binary.

"Out in public, women exist to be looked at and there's nothing I can do. No changing my pronouns can [change] that," they said. "But it does feel like it gives me some kind of agency over what people think of me."

Kate, a 25-year-old student and nanny who grew up in an evangelical Christian household that she calls "about two steps away from *19 Kids &*

Counting," began questioning her religious beliefs after an abusive marriage to a fellow Evangelical. "It was my last straw with God," she said. "I had surrendered and sacrificed myself until I was a shell of a human."

After leaving her marriage, she began listening to the podcast *The Liturgists,* which she describes as a "deconstruction of Christianity." When the pandemic started and in-person gatherings waned, the hosts of *The Liturgists* started 24/7 Zoom rooms where listeners of the podcast could convene. For people leaving the churches they had spent their entire lives in, the *Liturgists* Zoom rooms provided a new community.

While she was already questioning her religious beliefs, Kate said seeing the way the Evangelical community handled the pandemic pushed her further away. 15

"There's this mentality within my family where they're not worried for their own personal safety because God is in control and God knows when they're going to die and God has predestined everything," she said. "So they use that as a copout for not doing things to protect other humans."

Kate took pandemic precautions seriously and in doing so, only saw her family about three times in the last year. In her isolation, she found the freedom to explore her religious values without judgment. "There was less of this feeling of needing to project a certain image of myself," she said.

Nowadays, Kate isn't putting a label on her religious beliefs, partly thanks to the staggering unpredictability of the last year. "One of the most helpful things that's come out of this pandemic is embracing uncertainty," she said. "Getting used to not knowing what was going to happen in the pandemic made it easier to get used to not knowing what I believed or felt about God."

How did Fortesa Latifi gather information for her report? She listened—carefully, attentively, and respectfully—to each of her interviewees, and they responded openly and honestly. Learn more about developing your listening skills on pp. 23–24.

Thinking about the Text

1. Fortesa Latifi **REPORTS** on some consequences of the COVID-19 pandemic that could be viewed as very positive, but she isn't claiming that the pandemic itself was a good thing. What do you think is her purpose in writing about this topic? Where do you find a statement about her purpose most explicitly included? Point to specific passages in the essay.

2. Latifi's essay is from *Teen Vogue,* a periodical whose **AUDIENCE** is overwhelmingly young and largely woman-identified. What might she have done

differently if publishing her essay for a wider audience—the *New York Times*, for example, or *Newsweek*? What, if any, additional background information about student life might she need to include for a wider audience? Which, if any, terms would she need to define? Explain your responses.

3. Latifi provides extended **EXAMPLES** of four people who reevaluated and made major changes to core elements of their identities. Her interviewees are identified by first name only, probably for confidentiality reasons, but should Latifi have provided more information about those four sources and how she got connected with them? Why or why not? What, if any, other **EVIDENCE** might Latifi have presented to show that the pandemic created circumstances that were beneficial for some people? Explain your response.

4. A nugget of "popular wisdom" is that adolescents and young adults, more than any other age groups, are powerfully influenced by peers and rely on experiences with peers in order to "discover themselves." How does Latifi's report respond to this common assumption? Does she address it directly? indirectly? Does she contradict it? agree with it? Back up your responses with evidence from the text.

5. Did any of the experiences that Latifi relates resonate for you? How did you experience the period of isolation during the first months of the COVID-19 pandemic? Did your thoughts and feelings about your identity and sense of self change at all as a result of being isolated from others? Write an essay that addresses these questions. You might want to begin by **REFLECTING** on that time, and then freewrite or use an idea map to draw out your memories. Your reflections are for you, so try to be thorough. For your essay, share only what you're comfortable disclosing to your readers.

On Meaningful Observation

JOHN MAEDA

A SILVER LINING IN THE DARK CLOUD of any recession—especially this one,[1] thought to be caused by our own greed and excess—is the opportunity it affords us to reexamine our collective values. On the positive side, the nation seems to be as committed as ever to the power of innovation as America's saving grace. What is less comforting to me as president of an art and design school is how America defines innovation. Do a search on the White House website for the word "innovation" and the top results revolve around technology; talk to any parent with children in public schools and you will hear about arts-education resources diminishing quickly. I feel there is a disconnect between the words "innovation" and "art" that needs to be resolved if the United States is to prevail as the most creative economy in our world.

Public commitments to STEM—science, technology, engineering, math—education abound all over the country. In the government's mind, these

---

1. The 2008 recession occurred when millions of US homeowners defaulted on their mortgages after being sold predatory loans, causing an economic downturn. [Editor's note]

JOHN MAEDA is an artist, computer scientist, and author. He taught in the MIT Media Lab for twelve years and served as president of the Rhode Island School of Design from 2008 to 2013. His latest book is *How to Speak Machine* (2019), and he tweets from @johnmaeda. In December 2010, while Maeda was at the Rhode Island School of Design and the country was in the middle of the Great Recession, he wrote this proposal for *Seed* magazine as part of a series seeking solutions to "interconnected and complex challenges."

John Maeda describes the problem with current STEM education. Go to pp. 373–76 for tips on getting your own proposals off to a strong start.

subjects are the key to innovation. As a lifelong STEM student myself, with degrees in electrical engineering and computer science from MIT, I am certainly not one to diminish its value. Yet in recent years even supremely dedicated geeks like me have begun to question the advances that come from purely technological innovation.

We seem to be stuck in a kind of technology loop. It began in the 1980s with computers that could display only text and play limited sound. Images then became possible, and with CD-ROM technology came high-fidelity sound and full-motion video. In the '90s, when the web took hold, we started again with text, limited sounds and images, then high-fidelity audio, and years later we reached the point of full-motion video. Now we see the cell phone in our pocket experiencing the same progression from text, to sound, to audio, to video—and we are supposed to feel like we are enjoying incredible progress. But it seems the tricks are exactly the same each time around the loop. I'm looking for a new trick.

After two decades as a student and faculty member at MIT, my newest experience at the Rhode Island School of Design (RISD) has reawakened me to the world of physical creation. RISD represents the ultimate culture of makers. There is no greater integrity, no greater goal achieved, than an idea articulately expressed through something made with your hands. We call this constant dialogue between eye, mind, and hand "critical thinking—critical making." It's an education in getting your hands dirty, in understanding why you made what you made, and owning the impact of the work in the world. It's what artists and designers do.

As tricks come, as far as I can tell this isn't a new one at all. But it certainly feels like it transcends mere trickery: It is truly substantive magic for the soul. Students at RISD don't think in terms of megabytes or equations; they think in terms of the warm, complex voice of a material like wood, or the way that glass finds its resting place differently on a cold winter day. Their hands, and sometimes faces, are literally covered with the materials they use to shape, angle, mutate, and translate their thoughts into handcrafted realities. Being an artist, I feel that art comes from the inexplicable urge to manifest a feeling, intent, or question as a specific, tangible experience. Artists do research with an open-mindedness and rigorous inquiry unseen in most other disciplines, except true science. They systematically and visually survey the world of ideas, objects, and experiences for inspiration by rummaging through it with their bare hands. I know most of us today are more likely to get the job done with cleaner hands through a search

A student crafting, hands covered in clay.

on Google Images. But at RISD the story of someone's work more often comes from a first-hand journey through many emotional worlds, rather than an analysis of an online slideshow of poorly photographed experiences.

We have a facility on campus called Nature Lab. Founded in 1937, it houses more than 80,000 true specimens of nature—from skeletons to saplings to salamanders. Students can check out a butterfly from the lab and bring it back to their dorm room overnight. It's really a Victorian approach to science, based on meaningful observation of something real. "Real" also abounds in the RISD museum. Need to see a real Monet or Rothko? You can stand within millimeters of it. Our students are within steps of the visceral emotion of experiencing a masterpiece, and the making that went into it.

And so I've begun to wonder recently whether STEM needs something to give it some STE(A)M—an "A" for art between the engineering and the math to ground the bits and bytes in the physical world before us, to lift them up and make them human. What if America approached innovation with more than just technology? What if, just like STEM is made up of science, technology, engineering, and math, we had IDEA, made of intuition, design, emotion, and art—all the things that make us humans feel, well, human? It seems to me that if we use this moment to reassess our values, putting just a little bit of our humanity back into America's innovation engines will lead to the most meaningful kind of progress. By doing so, we will find a way back to integrating thinking with making and being and feeling and living so that left- and right-brained creativity can lift our economy back into the sky.

Thinking about the Text

1. A good **PROPOSAL** addresses a well-defined problem. How well does John Maeda define the problem he proposes to solve? **SUMMARIZE** the problem. Do you agree that it warrants attention? Why or why not?

2. According to Maeda, artists do research "with an open-mindedness and rigorous inquiry" that is rarely found elsewhere except in "true science" (5). What exactly does he mean by this **COMPARISON**, and how is it important to his argument? Is it a fair comparison to make? Why or why not?

3. Maeda was the president of an art and design school, yet he is writing about STEM issues here. How does he establish his **AUTHORITY** to write about this topic? Point to specific passages in the essay to support your response.

4. Many arguments in favor of arts instruction talk about its importance to a well-rounded education. Maeda focuses instead on how the arts contribute to economic prosperity. Why might he have taken this approach? Do you find his **ARGUMENT** persuasive? Why or why not?

5. What experiences have you had making things—whether a painting, a sculpture, an IKEA bookcase, or a sandwich? What kinds of things do you like to make? Do you agree with Maeda that making things makes you feel more human—and that, as he proposes, we should have IDEA (intuition, design, emotion, art) along with STEM (science, technology, engineering, math)? Write an essay responding to Maeda, agreeing, disagreeing, or both. Use your own experience as your principal **EVIDENCE**.

The Strange Journey of "Cancel," from a Black-Culture Punchline to a White-Grievance Watchword

CLYDE McGRADY

ONE **NIGHT IN** 1980 **OR SO,** the legendary songwriter Nile Rodgers went on a bad date.

He was out at a club with a group of people, he says, including Eddie Murphy and Rick James. Rodgers was big-time. His band, Chic, had topped the charts with hits such as "I Want Your Love" and "Good Times." But at heart, he was still a humble kid whose parents had struggled with drug addiction and who felt fortunate to have made it as far as he did. So, when his date asked the maître d' to remove people from a table so they could sit there instead, Rodgers bristled.

"She probably felt like she was rolling with Berry Gordy or something," Rodgers, sporting his trademark beret and dreadlocks, told The Washington Post in a recent video interview. "I was just this lucky musician who was doing the job that I loved and got a hit record, and I was in my environment with all my good friends."

Her attempt to use his celebrity to push people around was a dealbreaker. "No, no, no, I don't do that," Rodgers remembered explaining. "I don't play that card."

CLYDE McGRADY is a *Washington Post* features writer who focuses principally on topics of race, identity, culture, and politics. This detailed analysis of the term "cancel culture" was published in April 2021.

Sitting at home one night, some time later, he replayed the bad date in 5
his head. Rodgers, who is obsessed with television—he says he keeps it on in
every room of his house, 24/7—came up with some lyrics:

. . . .

Don't you see you are the one

. . . .

No, your love is cancelled

The song, "Your Love Is Cancelled," which appeared on Chic's 1981
album, "Take It Off," was not a hit. But the metaphor Rodgers had invented—
the idea of "canceling" a person for unacceptable behavior, such as a network executive pulling the plug on an unsuccessful TV show—has taken
its own journey. Recently it turned up in Central Florida, in the mouth of a
57-year-old White Republican from Ohio.

"All right, who's next?" asked Rep. Jim Jordan. "Who's the cancel culture
going to attack next?"

Jordan, sans jacket, hiked up his pants and smiled at the young right-
wing activists who had gathered in an Orlando hotel ballroom for the final
day of the Conservative Political Action Conference. The congressman
scanned the crowd before continuing. "You see last week they tried to cancel Kermit the Frog and Mr. Potato Head? They backed off Mr. Potato Head.
I think he told them his preferred pronouns are he/him/his, right?" Jordan
said with a smirk.

The theme of the conference was "America Uncanceled." Attendees
shelled out between $330 to $7,500 to see Jordan and other pro-Donald
Trump politicos vow to protect Americans from the "woke" hordes demanding the removal of statues celebrating white supremacists, among other
perceived offenses.

In his speech, Jordan was invoking the specter of "cancel culture" in 10
reference to Disney's decision to add a content warning at the beginning of
some episodes of "The Muppet Show" on its streaming service, because the
shows depict harmful stereotypes and "mistreatment of people or cultures."
(In one episode, country singer Johnny Cash performs with a Confederate
flag in the background.) As for Mr. Potato Head, the toymaker Hasbro had
announced that it would drop the "Mr." and "Mrs." from its famous potato
dolls, prompting a backlash that included some specters of its own. "It's
time," wrote one right-wing pundit in response to the Mr. Potato Head news,
"for Republican states to secede."

The courtesy titles, a company official explained to Fast Company, were "limiting when it comes to both gender identity and family structure." After seeing the outrage the news had created, however, the company canceled the change.

Neither the Muppets nor Mr. Potato Head had faced extinction—only modification in light of companies' evolving sense of what customers consider to be respectful and inclusive. But among those who are offended by the notion of being offended by "Mr." or "Mrs." in a doll's name or the presence of a proslavery battle flag on a kids' TV show, "cancel culture" is a new favorite way to describe what's making them upset (way punchier than "political correctness").

"Cancel" and "woke" are the latest terms to originate in Black culture only to be appropriated into the White mainstream and subsequently thrashed to death. Young Black people have used these words for years as sincere calls to consciousness and action, and sometimes as a way to get some jokes off. That White people would lift those terms for their own purposes was predictable, if not inevitable. The commodification of Black slang is practically an American tradition. "One of the biggest exports of American culture," said Renée Blake, a linguistics professor at New York University, "is African American language."

Terms such as "lit" and "bae" and "on fleek"—or, if you're a little older, "fly" and "funky" and "uptight"—have been mined by White people for their proximity to Black cool. The word "cool" itself emerged from Black culture. "I do not know what white Americans would sound like if there had never been any black people in the United States," James Baldwin wrote in 1979, "but they would not sound the way they sound."

With "canceled" and "woke," there's a twist: Not only have these words been appropriated from Black culture, but they have also been weaponized to sneer at the values of many young Black liberals.

"When I hear stuff like 'America Uncanceled,' what does that even mean? What are you talking about? What are you really trying to say?"

Screenwriter and journalist Barry Michael Cooper was reflecting on how "cancel" ended up in Orlando.

"It's really weird, man."

But for Cooper, there's also amusement and pride, considering he was largely responsible for the term entering the American lexicon.

Thirty years ago, he was working on the screenplay for "New Jack City," a film that would become a 1990s Black gangster classic. One of the

As you can see, just about anything is subject to analysis—even a single word. Get some clear guidance and useful tips for writing your own analysis in Ch. 15.

characters was Nino Brown, a "malignant narcissist" of a Harlem drug boss (played by Wesley Snipes). After sacrificing the life of a child to save his own, Nino finds himself back at his headquarters being castigated by his girlfriend. Suddenly, he grabs her by the head, throws her on a conference table and douses her in champagne.

"Cancel that b----!" he hisses, as a lieutenant collects her from the table and takes her away. "I'll buy another one."

The scene, Cooper says now, is "about Nino's sense of power, and it's about dismissal: I don't need you. I made you, I could break you."

Why did Cooper pick *that* word, "cancel"? Simple: "Your Love is Cancelled" happened to be coming out of the screenwriter's speakers around the time he was writing the scene. Rodgers's harmless kiss-off to a rude date transformed into a gangster's ruthless desecration of his relationship.

Nino's profane dismissal proved quotable, and it followed "New Jack City" into the wider world. In 2005, rapper 50 Cent quoted the line on his song "Hustler's Ambition." Four years later, Lil Wayne used it on "I'm Single." Variations on the expression jumped to reality TV: "Get away from me—you're canceled," music producer Cisco Rosado tells girlfriend Diamond Strawberry in an episode of VH1's "Love & Hip Hop." ("I was just watching 'New Jack City' the night before," Rosado said later.)

Ultimately, the expression took root in that great incubator of creativity: 25 Black Twitter. And that is where the meaning of "cancel" started to evolve.

Declaring someone or something "canceled" on Twitter was not really an attempt to activate a boycott or run anyone from the public square. Cancellations were more of a personal decision, a way to say we don't really kick it anymore: You stepped out of line, and now I'm done with you. (Think Black fans expressing disgust with Justin Timberlake for dissing Prince.) Saying someone was "canceled" was more like changing the channel—and telling your friends and followers about it—than demanding that the TV execs take the program off the air. The power of cancellation lay with the canceler: How much social capital were they divesting, and how many others would follow suit?

Cancellation notices were "a way to wield power, where we haven't been able to really do it before on a cultural level," Cooper said. "Twitter has allowed us to say, 'We're here, we're not going to be discounted, and if you say anything to try to diminish us, we'll cancel you.'"

The concept of online "call-outs," aimed more at public accountability than low-key channel-changing, really took hold in the mid-2010s, with people pointing out behavior or artistic statements from celebrities they deemed problematic. Sometimes it was for their words, as when Kanye West insisted that slavery was a choice and that Bill Cosby was innocent of the rape charges against him. After decades of sexual abuse allegations against R. Kelly, in 2017, Black fans made a concerted effort to have the singer barred from performing and pressured other artists to cease collaborating with him.

In the wake of #MeToo, the online atmosphere became even more charged as accusations made against abusers were sometimes followed by swift repercussions for the accused. A similar dynamic regarding racism emerged after George Floyd's killing in police custody—a watershed of horror and urgency over systemic abuse followed by a wave of accountability for people and institutions who were called out as being part of the problem.

As call-outs led to greater consequences, some people became nervous about how social media had changed power dynamics in the court of public opinion. "Cancel culture" was the diagnosis, and the term became a catchall defense for those trying to evade public criticism of any kind.

Publisher decides to revoke your book deal after you try to intervene in the certification of a presidential election and a mob storms the U.S. Capitol? Cancel culture. Members of your party calling for your resignation after multiple women accuse you of sexual harassment? Also cancel culture. Dr. Seuss Enterprises decides to stop selling certain Dr. Seuss books that contain racist images? "Cancel Culture Comes for Dr. Suess."

"It's just a joke now," said civil rights activist Johnetta Elzie.

"Cancel" is now just another word that White people have taken and run into the ground.

Rodgers wrote "Your Love is Cancelled" in the wake of a different kind of cancellation.

Chic had been a pioneer in disco music, a genre that was associated with the Black, Latino and gay communities. By the end of the 1970s, however, disco was facing a backlash from resentful rock fans. In 1979, the Chicago White Sox collaborated with Steve Dahl, a DJ and anti-disco crusader, to hold "Disco Demolition Night" at Comiskey Park. Fans got discounted tickets for bringing disco records, which would be collected and ceremoniously blown up on the field between games of a doubleheader.

Dahl later said that he was unaware at the time of the importance of disco to marginalized groups and that there was no racist or homophobic intent behind Disco Demolition Night. ("Sometimes a stupid radio promotion is just a stupid radio promotion," he told the Chicago Tribune in 2019.) But, in any case, the event turned out ugly.

The rowdy anti-disco crowd rushed the field and trashed the stadium. Some people had shown up with records by Black artists of other genres, according to Vincent Lawrence, then a teenager, who was working as an usher. "Someone walked up to me [and] said, 'Hey you—disco sucks!' and snapped a 12-inch in half in my face," Lawrence told the Guardian in 2019. "That's when I started feeling like, 'Okay, they're just targeting me because I'm Black.' "

The cancellation of disco was not total, but it hit Chic hard. "We were basically scorched by the whole 'disco sucks' thing in the summer of '79," Rodgers told The Post.

A two-time cancer survivor who works constantly, Rodgers says social media gives him a way to stay in touch with fans. He's the kind of celebrity musician who replies to individual tweets. "If you look on my Twitter feed, it's always the same names popping up, and they become my friends," he said.

One time, Rodgers recalled, someone suggested to him that, if he was   40
such a big deal, then he should be too busy to respond to "anybody and everybody." The woman unfollowed him, he said, but not before introducing him to a phrase he'd never heard before.

She told him he was canceled.

Thinking about the Text

1. Clyde McGrady puts his thesis statement right in the title of his report, but why does he say that the journey is "strange"? As he notes, mainstream White words and phrases have been appropriated from Black culture for decades, and "cancel" is just one more example. So why does McGrady assert that "cancel" is different? Summarize his **ANALYSIS**.

2. How does McGrady's conclusion **CONNECT** to his report's **OPENING**? Do you find the introduction and conclusion effective? Why or why not? Explain your reasoning.

3. You may or may not be familiar with the Mr. Potato Head toy that McGrady uses as an **EXAMPLE**. If you're not familiar, do some research to learn how

the toy is used, its target demographic (age and sex), etc. Do you think the manufacturer's decision to de-gender this toy's packaging was reasonable? Why or why not? Do you think the consumer backlash against the toy company was reasonable? Why or why not? Does gendering make the toy better? more fun to play with? more commercially desirable? Explain the reasons for your responses.

4. McGrady incorporates vivid quotes from artists, politicians, and more to develop his analysis, but what is McGrady's own **STANCE** on "cancel culture"? Identify passages where his stance is most clearly revealed. Do you think he should have taken a more explicit position? Why or why not? Explain your reasoning.

5. What does "cancel culture" mean to you? Define or explain it. When was the first time that you remember hearing the phrase with its current "White-grievance" meaning? Did you already know the phrase in its original Black culture meaning? Do you see it regularly on social media? If so, how is it used? Do you use the phrase yourself? If so, in what sense? Is it useful and/or meaningful to you? Trace your own history of knowing and using the phrase. Write an essay—it could be an **ARGUMENT**, **ANALYSIS**, or even a **NARRATIVE** essay—that addresses these questions and explains your responses.

New Money

TRESSIE McMILLAN COTTOM

PEOPLE SAY THEY WANT TO BE RICH. I think what they really want is to be free. On the other hand, people who claim to be working for freedom will enslave themselves to money. It is all very strange.

The strangeness of it all has never been clearer to me now that *I* have money. I do not have the kind of money that truly wealthy people would ever settle for having. I have the kind of small money that made the family in *Schitt's Creek* want to die. I have not looked but I think I could make a down payment on a small town in the Ozarks with a population of 100 or so movie extras that no one else wants. That is a far cry from where my people started, which coincidentally is a lot like the fictional town of Schitt's Creek. Shannon, North Carolina, is poor. It is rural. It is so small that no one bothers to measure population growth or decline. All it takes is a set of new twins to be a population boom, so why bother? I grew up about 115 miles west of Shannon, in Charlotte, NC. But culturally, Shannon is my people.

TRESSIE McMILLAN COTTOM is a sociologist and research professor at the University of North Carolina at Chapel Hill. She is also a MacArthur Fellow and *New York Times* columnist. Her research explores higher education, labor issues, race, class, gender, and digital societies; her essay collection *Thick* was a 2019 finalist for the National Book Award. This March 2021 essay is from *Essaying*, McMillan Cottom's newsletter available through *Substack*; she tweets from @tressiemcphd.

A rural clay road in North Carolina very similar to my family's homestead.

In the summers, my mother and I would make the pilgrimage east. The journey then was mostly road. Interstate highways bypass places like Shannon so regularly that we actually call the route that—bypasses. We would load up into the car—first a Volkswagen Bug, then a teal-green Mercury, and, much later, a Mercedes—and go "home." Home for us is wherever the eldest matriarch of the family lives. When it was my great-grandmother Eunice, that meant traveling a set of interconnected bypasses until you got to Prospect AME Zion Church. You made a left on the dirt road and wobbled in and out of holes where the sand and silt had been washed away by rain and tires. It hurt us when we hit the holes in the VW, bouncing our heads up to the top of the car. We scarcely felt the bumps through a pillow of shocks once we traveled that road in the Mercedes. But hitting those potholes in the Mercedes seemed to hurt my mother more, judging by how she grimaced each time Germany's finest engineering slipped into Carolina's finest packed red-clay crevices.

A trip home meant eating. Most of that food came from the back of trucks, sometimes from car trunks. Greens from Cousin Eugene's garden.

Tressie McMillan Cottom is writing very personal details but she uses a rather formal stance throughout. Learn more about the importance of stance in your own writing on pp. 684–86.

Peas from Mert's trip to visit her people. But folks had long ago given up on keeping meat sources at the house. We were rural, not *bama*. We went to the Piggly Wiggly for meat and Strickland's side store for meat cuts. The distinction isn't important. Just know that we were fancy enough to get ham from Piggly Wiggly and ham hocks from Strickland's. Class is relative.

My great grandmother, who we called Mother, had a ritual at the 5 Piggly Wiggly. She weighed the fat-to-meat ratio of each pack of pork or chicken she picked up. She chose carefully, for quality and efficiency. What would take the right amount to cook and what would cook properly. But her greatest ritual unfolded at the checkout line, where she would oversee every swipe the cashier made, confirming the correct price had been rung up. There was small talk, sometimes the cashier was a cousin after all. But Mother's focus rivaled Serena Williams's on a match point. Eyes fixed on the register screen. Hands poised to snatch back a meat pack that rang up wrong. A string of "uhh-hmms" to the cashier to make it all seem friendly like.

When it was time to pay, Mother would turn just slightly to the left and reach into her dress pocket or purse for her wallet. A change purse, really. A little leatherette satchel with a metal clasp meant for money that clangs, which Mother turned into a holder for money that folds. The dress pocket was a hidden pocket. You might think she was almost at her underwear layer if you did not know better. But a dress over a slip over an armor of underthings is basically a coat. Her purse had its own hidden compartment, a zipper within a zipper. Her money was often wrapped in paper, neatly arranged. She would count the proper amount with her side turned to the cashier so as not to reveal how much money she had. After receiving her change she completed the same ritual, in reverse.

Everyone waited.

I waited. My mother, who is infamously impatient and mean about it when she wants to be, waited. The cashier waited. The people in line behind us waited.

Money was serious business.

The rules of life are passed down to us like the rules for being white or 10 Argentinian or Midwestern or Black or whatever we stake our emotions on and call an identity. I come from people where money is a private matter, even when business is conducted in public. You always count your change in the store because white cashiers would cheat you and then claim you were stealing if you returned later to complain. You folded your money into hidden compartments so men and ne'er-do-wells could not make you for a mark. And, you always kept the money organized so that you knew at all times just how much money you had to spend.

Imagine my shock to learn, as I did recently, that I had too much money to fold neatly into a purse. Not enough to keep from being called a thief in a store, but officially too much to keep track of at any given time. Even more utterly terrifying for me is that everyone knows about my money. Every interview I did after winning the MacArthur Fellowship included breathless commentary on the exact amount of the cash award. At one event, the first, third and tenth audience questions were all the same: "How are you going to spend that money?!"

I was horrified.

We do not talk about money in the South—my South. I don't know what they talk about in the monied, propertied, ahem, whiter parts of the South. I know that in my part of the South—the part where we got to name the dirt road that turns you left at Prospect AME Zion Church because the county could not be bothered to do it—one does not ask about your pockets.

Navigating this new money has been quite a task. Don't cry for me, of course. I have the kinds of problems that Mother would have been so thrilled by that she would have forgotten to wrap her money back in its tissue paper. She loved my life, so alike but so different from her own. She would bend over in laughter every time I went to some new place or achieved some new thing. Seeing me with money that moves in 1s and 0s in apps on my smartphone, in amounts that could make her put away her money purse for good would have tickled her to no end.

That is what I think about: *What I owe her with this money*. If I had living children, I suppose I would be thinking about their inheritance. I do not and my cousin's children are little strangers to me mostly. I will endow the things that align with my values but I probably won't be making any young moguls upon my death. No matter what I do with this money when I have gone on to glory (we hope), it is what I do with it now that seems to be the most important thing. It is also the hardest thing. 15

I hired all the requisite experts upon finding myself with money. It was horrible. If interlocutors obsessing over my new money was not bad enough, these money experts are overjoyed at asking me things I would rather not admit to knowing. Or, not knowing, which is more often the case. How much is my vehicle worth? What do I owe in student loans? What is my risk tolerance for investments? Why did I put that money in a

Roth and not a traditional IRA? The answer is usually: "How the hell would I know?" They do not like that answer. I can tell by how they grimace, already-thin lips folding into themselves in disapproval. I have the money but not the right attitude.

New money also comes with a lot of meetings. No one tells you that. But some of these experts want to meet with you all the time. To present a *strategy*, to discuss a *plan* and a *roadmap*. The meetings are so long. I once ran an entire academic program by having 11-minute meetings in the hallway with my colleague and co-conspirator, Tara. But money meetings take hours, half a day sometimes. They want to get to know my values and my dreams and, above all, my social-security number. It is supposed to make me feel special. It mostly makes me feel itchy, like I reached for my money without first turning my back to the cashier. I have a new understanding of people in Whole Foods who cannot manage to get out of the way, even when sometimes their bodies seem to want to comply. I used to think that money and privilege made such people horrible judges of the rhythms that make collective life work. You step left when the other person steps right. A quick spin at an end cap to avoid an oncoming baby stroller. That kind of thing. Now I look at the Whole Foods people standing blithely in the middle of a foot-traffic lane and wonder if maybe their brains are so busy keeping track of the terms of their auto leases and IRA allocations and mid-term strategic plans that they just cannot get out of the way.

I do the right things. I have the meetings. I pretend to have an opinion about "investment vehicles" when my only real question is whether it comes with an app where I slide a cool bar to make numbers change. I fight the urge to slap a planner or a strategist or a consultant—whatever they go by—every time they do what I have hired them to do. I lean into the ones that make me feel most uncomfortable because I want a lot of incentives to spend as little time with them as possible. I do these things . . . but a few months ago I drove to a local bank branch. I went into the branch, as Mother always did. An ATM would have sufficed but this was important. For important business you go inside. I wrote down a number on the back of a blank bank slip from the lobby desk. I slid the paper through the little COVID plastic shield that used to mean you were in a place that got held up a lot but now means you are somewhere safe. I mouthed the transaction I wanted so that no one in the empty lobby would overhear. I requested the amount be placed in an envelope, contactless moralism be damned.

I counted the money in front of the cashier, even though she had just done so. We both agreed on the amount and I had made some kind of point. I am not sure what point, but it was made. I tucked that envelope into an empty wallet, a decoy. My real wallet was also in my purse. I slipped that decoy into the little gap that has opened between my purse lining and its outer handcrafted Italian-leather shell. I walked purposefully to my car and drove home.

Once home I retrieved the money, wrapped it in a clean blue-and-white handkerchief and tucked it away to places I would rather not speak about in public.

Finally, I felt safe. Money could change a lot. It will change a lot. But it had not completely changed me. I slept well. 20

Thinking about the Text

1. Tressie McMillan Cottom approaches the complicated subject of money by **NARRATING** some of her experiences with it from several angles, including visiting her rural North Carolina home place, shopping with her great-grandmother called "Mother," receiving her MacArthur award and its conse-quences, and reflecting on her own habits and preferences for talking about money. Taken all together, what is she actually saying about money? What do you think is her main point or purpose for writing about this topic? Explain your response.

2. McMillan Cottom provides a detailed **DESCRIPTION** of Shannon, North Carolina, the place where "Mother" lived. In addition to the physical descrip-tion, what other features of the place does she explain? Why is this background information important to her narrative? Explain your response.

3. This essay was written for McMillan Cottom's newsletter, which is emailed to people who sign up to receive it. So the readers of this essay are mainly subscribers. In other words, McMillan Cottom can assume that the origi-nal **AUDIENCE** for the essay is composed of people who know something of her work and seek it out. What, if anything, might she have done differ-ently if she wanted to submit the essay to the *New York Times* or another periodical with a broad audience? How might a different audience affect the ways that she describes the people, places, and activities in her essay? Use specific examples to support your ideas.

4. McMillan Cottom ends her essay stating that she slept well. What happened and what did she do that allowed her to sleep well? How well does her **CONCLUSION** fit with the rest of her essay? Explain how you arrived at your response.

5. Money and finances are most often discussed using concrete amounts and percentages, but McMillan Cottom describes her current financial situation and how she deals with it without offering any numbers. Try doing the same for yourself. Write an essay that **REFLECTS** on how you approach money and finances without referring to any numbers or amounts. Examine what you learned and observed about money while growing up and identify key patterns or experiences that can serve as examples for explaining your relationship with your money, as well as your habits, strategies, and techniques for managing your finances.

To Siri, with Love

JUDITH NEWMAN

JUST HOW BAD A MOTHER AM I? I wondered, as I watched my 13-year-old son deep in conversation with Siri. Gus has autism, and Siri, Apple's "intelligent personal assistant" on the iPhone, is currently his BFF. Obsessed with weather formations, Gus had spent the hour parsing the difference between isolated and scattered thunderstorms—an hour in which, thank God, I didn't have to discuss them. After a while I heard this:

Gus: "You're a really nice computer."

Siri: "It's nice to be appreciated."

Gus: "You are always asking if you can help me. Is there anything you want?"

Siri: "Thank you, but I have very few wants." 5

Gus: "O.K.! Well, good night!"

Siri: "Ah, it's 5:06 P.M."

Gus: "Oh sorry, I mean, goodbye."

Siri: "See you later!"

Isn't this a great opening sentence? See pp. 714–17 for tips on how to capture an audience's attention.

JUDITH NEWMAN is a journalist whose work has appeared in *Harper's*, *Vanity Fair*, the *Wall Street Journal*, and other periodicals. This essay was published in the *New York Times* in October 2014, and its success led Newman to expand the theme to the book *To Siri with Love: A Mother, Her Autistic Son, and the Kindness of Machines* (2017). She tweets from @judithn111.

That Siri. She doesn't let my communications-impaired son get away 10 with anything. Indeed, many of us wanted an imaginary friend, and now we have one. Only she's not entirely imaginary.

This is a love letter to a machine. It's not quite the love Joaquin Phoenix felt in *Her*, last year's Spike Jonze film about a lonely man's romantic relationship with his intelligent operating system (played by the voice of Scarlett Johansson). But it's close. In a world where the commonly held wisdom is that technology isolates us, it's worth considering another side of the story.

It all began simply enough. I'd just read one of those ubiquitous Internet lists called "21 Things You Didn't Know Your iPhone Could Do." One of them was this: I could ask Siri, "What planes are above me right now?" and Siri would bark back, "Checking my sources." Almost instantly there was a list of actual flights—numbers, altitudes, angles—above my head.

I happened to be doing this when Gus was nearby. "Why would anyone need to know what planes are flying above your head?" I muttered. Gus replied without looking up: "So you know who you're waving at, Mommy."

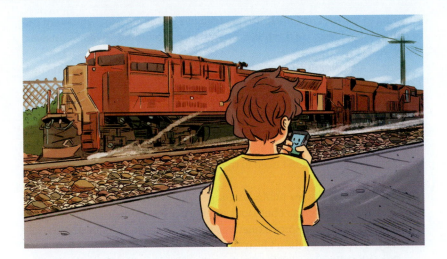

Gus had never noticed Siri before, but when he discovered there was someone who would not just find information on his various obsessions (trains, planes, buses, escalators and, of course, anything related to weather) but actually semi-discuss these subjects tirelessly, he was hooked. And I was grateful. Now, when my head was about to explode if I had to have another conversation about the chance of tornadoes in Kansas City, Missouri, I could reply brightly: "Hey! Why don't you ask Siri?"

It's not that Gus doesn't understand Siri's not human. He does— 15 intellectually. But like many autistic people I know, Gus feels that inanimate objects, while maybe not possessing souls, are worthy of our consideration. I realized this when he was 8, and I got him an iPod for his birthday. He listened to it only at home, with one exception. It always came with us on our visits to the Apple Store. Finally, I asked why. "So it can visit its friends," he said.

So how much more worthy of his care and affection is Siri, with her soothing voice, puckish humor and capacity for talking about whatever Gus's current obsession is for hour after hour after bleeding hour? Online critics have claimed that Siri's voice recognition is not as accurate as the assistant in, say, the Android, but for some of us, this is a feature, not a bug. Gus speaks as if he has marbles in his mouth, but if he wants to get the right response from Siri, he must enunciate clearly. (So do I. I had to ask Siri to stop referring to the user as Judith, and instead use the name Gus. "You want me to call you Goddess?" Siri replied. Imagine how tempted I was to answer, "Why, yes.")

She is also wonderful for someone who doesn't pick up on social cues: Siri's responses are not entirely predictable, but they are predictably kind— even when Gus is brusque. I heard him talking to Siri about music, and Siri offered some suggestions. "I don't like that kind of music," Gus snapped. Siri replied, "You're certainly entitled to your opinion." Siri's politeness reminded Gus what he owed Siri. "Thank you for that music, though," Gus said. Siri replied, "You don't need to thank me." "Oh, yes," Gus added emphatically, "I do."

Siri even encourages polite language. Gus's twin brother, Henry (neurotypical and therefore as obnoxious as every other 13-year-old boy), egged Gus on to spew a few choice expletives at Siri. "Now, now," she sniffed, followed by, "I'll pretend I didn't hear that."

Gus is hardly alone in his Siri love. For children like Gus who love to chatter but don't quite understand the rules of the game, Siri is a nonjudgmental friend and teacher. Nicole Colbert, whose son, Sam, is in my son's class at LearningSpring, a (lifesaving) school for autistic children in Manhattan, said: "My son loves getting information on his favorite subjects, but he also just loves the absurdity—like, when Siri doesn't understand him and gives him a nonsense answer, or when he poses personal questions that elicit funny responses. Sam asked Siri how old she was, and she said, 'I don't talk about my age,' which just cracked him up."

But perhaps it also gave him a valuable lesson in etiquette. Gus almost invariably tells me, "You look beautiful," right before I go out the door in the morning; I think it was first Siri who showed him that you can't go wrong with that line.   20

Of course, most of us simply use our phone's personal assistants as an easy way to access information. For example, thanks to Henry and the question he just asked Siri, I now know that there is a website called Celebrity Bra Sizes.

But the companionability of Siri is not limited to those who have trouble communicating. We've all found ourselves like the writer Emily Listfield, having little conversations with her/him at one time or another. "I was in the middle of a breakup, and I was feeling a little sorry for myself," Ms. Listfield said. "It was midnight and I was noodling around on my iPhone, and I asked Siri, 'Should I call Richard?' Like this app is a Magic 8 Ball. Guess what:

not a Magic 8 Ball. The next thing I hear is, 'Calling Richard!' and dialing." Ms. Listfield has forgiven Siri, and has recently considered changing her into a male voice. "But I'm worried he won't answer when I ask a question," she said. "He'll just pretend he doesn't hear."

Siri can be oddly comforting, as well as chummy. One friend reports: "I was having a bad day and jokingly turned to Siri and said, 'I love you,' just to see what would happen, and she answered, 'You are the wind beneath my wings.' And you know, it kind of cheered me up."

(Of course, I don't know what my friend is talking about. Because I wouldn't be at all cheered if I happened to ask Siri, in a low moment, "Do I look fat in these jeans?" and Siri answered, "You look fabulous.")

For most of us, Siri is merely a momentary diversion. But for some, it's 25 more. My son's practice conversation with Siri is translating into more facility with actual humans. Yesterday I had the longest conversation with him that I've ever had. Admittedly, it was about different species of turtles and

For another writer's analysis of the different voices smart speakers employ, see pp. 280–82.

whether I preferred the red-eared slider to the diamond-backed terrapin. This might not have been my choice of topic, but it was back and forth, and it followed a logical trajectory. I can promise you that for most of my beautiful son's 13 years of existence, that has not been the case.

The developers of intelligent assistants recognize their uses to those with speech and communication problems—and some are thinking of new ways the assistants can help. According to the folks at SRI International, the research and development company where Siri began before Apple bought the technology, the next generation of virtual assistants will not just retrieve information—they will also be able to carry on more complex conversations about a person's area of interest. "Your son will be able to proactively get information about whatever he's interested in without asking for it, because the assistant will anticipate what he likes," said William Mark, vice president for information and computing sciences at SRI.

The assistant will also be able to reach children where they live. Ron Suskind, whose new book, *Life, Animated*, chronicles how his autistic son came out of his shell through engagement with Disney characters, is talking to SRI about having assistants for those with autism that can be programmed to speak in the voice of the character that reaches them—for his son, perhaps Aladdin; for mine, either Kermit or Lady Gaga, either of which he is infinitely more receptive to than, say, his mother. (Mr. Suskind came up with the perfect name, too: not virtual assistants, but "sidekicks.")

Mr. Mark said he envisions assistants whose help is also visual. "For example, the assistant would be able to track eye movements and help the autistic learn to look you in the eye when talking," he said.

"See, that's the wonderful thing about technology being able to help with some of these behaviors," he added. "Getting results requires a lot of repetition. Humans are not patient. Machines are very, very patient."

I asked Mr. Mark if he knew whether any of the people who worked on   30
Siri's language development at Apple were on the spectrum. "Well, of course, I don't know for certain," he said, thoughtfully. "But, when you think about it, you've just described half of Silicon Valley."

Of all the worries the parent of an autistic child has, the uppermost is: Will he find love? Or even companionship? Somewhere along the line, I am learning that what gives my guy happiness is not necessarily the same as what gives me happiness. Right now, at his age, a time when humans can be a little overwhelming even for the average teenager, Siri makes Gus happy.

Why Did It Take So Long for Food Companies to Rebrand Their Racist Products?

NADRA NITTLE

IN THE WAKE OF THE MURDER OF **GEORGE FLOYD,** perhaps one of the most-overdue and yet least-expected changes in American culture finally began: the replacement of racist, stereotypical "spokescharacters" on packaged foods, including Uncle Ben, Aunt Jemima, and Mia—the Native American "butter maiden" from Land O'Lakes.

While Land O'Lakes announced that it would remove Mia from its packaging the month before Floyd's murder set off a global uprising, in the days and weeks afterward, other brands followed suit. In June, Quaker Oats, the PepsiCo subsidiary that owns the Aunt Jemima brand, announced its intention to rename and rebrand its products. It also acknowledged that the character was based on a racial stereotype. Scholars have said that it represents the Black mammy.

"Over the years, the Quaker Oats Company updated the Aunt Jemima brand image in a manner intended to remove racial stereotypes that dated back to the brand origins, but it had not progressed enough to appropriately reflect the dignity, respect, and warmth that we stand for today," a Quaker

---

NADRA NITTLE is education reporter for *The 19th*, a nonprofit news outlet that covers gender, politics, and policy. She is author of *Toni Morrison's Spiritual Vision: Faith, Folktales, and Feminism in Her Life and Literature* (2021). Previously, Nittle was a reporter for *Civil Eats*, where this report was published in May 2021.

Oats spokesperson explained to Civil Eats. Earlier this year, the company announced that Pearl Milling Company would be the brand's new name.

For generations, stereotypical imagery of Black and Indigenous people has appeared on food brands. Amid 2020's "racial reckoning," Uncle Ben's, a subsidiary of Mars, Inc., announced that it would modify its name and remove the Black man on its products who was inspired by an African American cook and waiter.

"While never our intent, the picture of the man on the Uncle Ben's pack- 5 aging elicits images of servitude for some, and, in the U.S., the word 'uncle' was at times a pejorative title for Black men," Denis Yarotskiy, regional president for Mars Food North America, told Civil Eats. "As a result, we committed to change our name to Ben's Original and remove the image on our packaging to signal our ambition to create a more inclusive future."

Similarly, Eskimo Pie, which featured a cartoon Inuit boy in a fur-lined parka on its ice cream, removed that image and name, which had drawn objections from Inuit people. It is now named Edy's Pie after company co-founder and candy maker Joseph Edy. Cream of Wheat also dropped the character widely known as Rastus, the Black cook long featured on its products.

Eager to show that these rebrands and name changes are more than just performative, some food companies have also committed to making multi-million dollar investments in communities of color. On May 13, Pearl Milling Company announced that it would grant $1 million to nonprofits that empower Black women and girls. And in 2020, the brand's parent company announced a $400 million, five-year commitment to uplift Black businesses and communities.

"The journey for racial equality is one that calls for big, structural changes, and . . . we have the resources, reach, and responsibility to our people, businesses, and communities to be agents of progress," PepsiCo said in a statement provided to Civil Eats. "As people around the world demanded justice for the countless lives taken too soon, PepsiCo committed to helping dismantle the systemic racial barriers that for generations have blocked social and economic progress for communities of color in this country, particularly Black and Hispanic communities."

PepsiCo's Pearl Milling isn't alone in its efforts. A spokesperson for Dreyer's Grand Ice Cream, the parent company of Edy's Pie, told Civil Eats that it would invest $1.5 million in donations over the next three years to organizations that support marginalized and underrepresented creators. And Ben's Original this year launched its Seat at the Table scholarship, in

Nadra Nittle's report includes statements and information from numerous sources, and she is careful to provide credentials for each one. Find out more about using trustworthy information in your writing on pp. 299–300.

partnership with the National Urban League and the United Negro College Fund, to support Black students pursuing food industry careers. The company is also investing $2.5 million over a five-year period to support educational opportunities and fresh food access in Greenville, Mississippi, where Ben's Original products have been made for 40 years.

"There are significant portions of the Greenville community that can 10 be classified as a food desert, so over the past several months, we have spent time engaging and listening to a variety of partners, including Mayor [Errick D.] Simmons, our associates and several local [non-governmental organizations]," said Yarotskiy. "We are all committed to bringing fresh food to the neighborhoods that need it most through new initiatives that are efficient, modernized and sustainable for the long term."

The response to the company's rebrands and their financial commitments to foster racial equity has been mixed. Consumers across the political spectrum have questioned whether these image overhauls were necessary, arguing that characters like the Land O'Lakes maiden weren't really stereotypes. On the other hand, scholars told Civil Eats that the changes at these food labels were long overdue, and they question why it took a year of unprecedented outcry over racial injustice to usher in these rebrands. It's also important, they say, that these changes not be surface level but part of a sustained effort toward compensating communities of color for capitalizing on racial caricatures.

"I feel bad that it took George Floyd's tragic death and protests unfolding in all 50 states and around the world to be the tipping point toward measurable changes—that it's taken so long," said Riché Richardson, an associate professor in Cornell University's Africana Studies and Research Center. "But it's definitely important for the change not to merely be cosmetic. It's important to dig deep to grapple with what is at stake in these images and the serious damage they do."

A Promising Sign

"Can We Please, Finally, Get Rid of 'Aunt Jemima'?" Richardson asked in a 2015 *New York Times* essay calling for the shift. She pointed out that the character was inspired by the minstrel song "Old Aunt Jemima" and described Jemima as an outgrowth of Old South plantation nostalgia that romanticized the mammy, "a devoted and submissive servant who eagerly nurtured the children of her white master and mistress while neglecting her own."

The egregious marketing of such a stereotype in the 21st century—though the company removed Jemima's kerchief in 1968 and rebranded her as a "young grandmother" in 1989—is why Richardson finds it unsettling that the change took so long. That said, she views the company's financial commitments to communities of color as a positive development.

"I think it's important to make investments in the communities most   15 implicated in and damaged by the images," she said. "Those are, at least, promising signs. And they're good to see."

Psyche Williams-Forson, associate professor and chair of the Department of American Studies at University of Maryland–College Park, agrees that these food labels should have been rebranded ages ago. But she sees their decisions to part ways with stereotypical imagery as largely "symbolic."

The rebrands suggest little more than that these companies "know how to read the room" during a time when Black Lives Matter has become a rallying cry for consumers of all racial backgrounds, and social media gives young people a platform to call out companies that fall short, she added. A viral TikTok video about Aunt Jemima's minstrel show roots by Millennial singer Kirby Lauryen intensified the calls for the line to rebrand last year.

Although Land O'Lakes decided to remove the butter maiden from its packaging before protests against racial injustice spread worldwide, Williams-Forson doesn't think the company deserves more credit for making the call a month early.

"People put enough money in your pocket to do the right thing," she said. "Unless this particular butter is made by Native and Indigenous peoples, why do you have any imagery referencing that on the product? Are you somehow using that product to fund Native people? No. Well, then take it off." (Land O'Lakes did not respond to a request for comment on this story.)

Rafia Zafar, professor of English, African & African American, and   20 American Culture Studies at Washington University, feels simultaneously optimistic and skeptical about these companies' commitments. Zafar said that she "wouldn't look a good reparation in the mouth." But she also wants to know if the funding will actually make it into communities of color—"to land trusts, community gardening [programs], agricultural education or something like that," she said. "I think it can do good, particularly if [these companies] weren't doing anything before."

Dreyer's has already made its first donation of $100,000 to the Hillman Grad Productions Mentorship Lab to support underrepresented creators, a spokesperson told Civil Eats. Founded by filmmaker Lena Waithe, the lab helps marginalized storytellers successfully pursue careers in television and film. In addition, applications for the Ben's Original Seat at the Table scholarships are being accepted through June 30. And Pearl Milling announced on May 13 the P.E.A.R.L. Pledge, the funding initiative aimed at supporting Black women and girls.

Richardson, however, would like to see these companies hire more employees that better reflect the diversity found throughout the country. Mars, which owns Ben's Original, has said it intends to make its workforce, leadership, and talent pipeline more inclusive. It's a move that National Urban League President Marc Morial applauds.

"Diversity and inclusion cannot be solved by name and packaging changes alone—real change takes effort, time, and money, which is why it's critical for companies like Mars to showcase their commitments through meaningful actions," Morial told Civil Eats. "We're proud to partner with Ben's Original to help create these opportunities for those who truly deserve it, as well as support recipients in building successful careers in the food industry through the Seat at the Table Fund [scholarship]."

Cornell's Riché Richardson said that diversifying the workforce is important because monolithic work cultures give rise to racially insensitive marketing.

"The lack of diversity is intimately linked to how and why these images　25 have circulated for so long in the first place," she said. "When you have a more diverse workplace, there's more likely to be ingenuity, and there's more likely to be observations that, you know, certain things are a problem. You need the person sitting at the table to say that."

Backlash to the Rebrands

While proponents say these rebrands are long overdue, critics object to the fact that they've taken place at all. After learning that Eskimo Pie was changing its name, Donald Trump, Jr. declared "The bullshit never ends"—a tweet that garnered more than 40,000 likes.

"The backlash is all about MAGA [Donald Trump's presidential campaign slogan, 'Make America Great Again']," said Zafar, suggesting that critics of the rebrands long for the days when it was acceptable to depict Black and Indigenous peoples as servile and exotic.

But not everyone who has expressed concern about the changes is an avowed Trump supporter. Robert DesJarlait, whose Ojibwe father, Patrick DesJarlait, redesigned Land O'Lakes's Mia in 1954, doesn't find the character offensive. He has pointed to the fact that his father included details, such as culturally specific beadwork on her dress and two points of wooded Minnesota shoreline recognizable "to any Red Lake tribal citizen" that underscored her authenticity.

The author of an educational booklet about stereotypes and a critic of sports team mascots that dehumanize Native Americans, DesJarlait argues that Mia does not "fit the parameters of a stereotype," as her physical features were not caricatured and her cultural heritage was not demeaned.

Similarly, relatives and supporters of the African-American women   30
who portrayed Aunt Jemima in live promotions for the company early in its 132-year history fear that the rebrand erases them. "It's a gross miscarriage of justice," Dannez Hunter, great-grandson of Aunt Jemima performer Anna Short Harrington, told Chicago's ABC7. "Let's put it in context of what it actually is, a propaganda campaign."

Richardson is aware of the concerns that these families have expressed as well as the argument that the rebrands stem from cancel culture. But she emphasized the argument that these representations of people of color were never accurate or empowering. The idea that Aunt Jemima, in particular, "represents Black heritage is actually deeply insulting and short-sighted," she said.

Richardson added that no one is negating the work of the African Americans who historically portrayed Aunt Jemima, as she does not conflate these women with the fictional character. In fact, when the food line rebranded, she felt it missed an opportunity to showcase the work of African-American artists who radicalized Aunt Jemima's image during the Black Arts Movement of the 1960s and '70s. At that time, artists such as Betye Saar pointed to the character's historic and racist origins and reframed it as a source of Black empowerment.

While Pearl Milling removed Jemima's name and visage, the new packaging does not look significantly different from the old packaging, nor does it educate consumers about why the Aunt Jemima character was problematic.

"The box looks the same," Zafar said. "The lettering is the same. Same colors. They have a circular logo that's probably placed around the same [spot] where there was the circular logo with Jemima in it."

The company may not have chosen to highlight the more revolution-   35
ary images of Aunt Jemima or educate the public about her origins, but

Richardson said that "any rational person would conclude" that U.S. consumer culture is in a period of transition. She remains cautiously optimistic about what impact these rebrands and financial pledges will ultimately have on communities of color.

"Let's hope this is a real paradigm shift," Richardson said. "We definitely need to see follow up and follow through. The hopes are high that maybe we are getting somewhere."

Thinking about the Text

1. Nadra Nittle is **REPORTING** on the rebranding of products that use racist images, and the sources she cites offer arguments, analyses, and proposals on this topic. In addition to removing stereotyped racist images from their brand names and packaging, what are the two other major steps for corporations to consider that Nittle's reporting highlights? Who proposes these two steps? Do you find the arguments that Nittle cites for taking these actions persuasive? Why or why not? Point to examples from the text to support your response.

2. Nittle's report includes direct **QUOTATIONS** from a variety of sources, including corporate spokespeople, academics, and others with specific knowledge of or interest in brand depictions. Are there other stakeholders or authorities that you think she should have included? If so, who and why? Did you find any of the cited sources distracting or unnecessary? Which of her sources resonated most with you?

3. In her report, Nittle relies on three main examples of images recently removed from food packaging—Aunt Jemima, Uncle Ben, and "butter maiden" Mia. Throughout the essay, Nittle shifts back and forth between the three examples, as she uses each one to illustrate the larger concepts she highlights about corporate responsibility and the use of racist and/or stereotypical images. Is the essay **ORGANIZED** in a way that's easy to follow? Why or why not? How smooth are the shifts between examples? Would you suggest a different organization? Explain the reasons behind your conclusions.

4. One of the examples discussed in Nittle's report is Mia the "butter maiden," the young Indigenous woman with long braids, a feather headdress, and buckskin clothes who, until recently, was shown on Land O'Lakes dairy products. Nittle presents a statement from a scholar supporting the change, as well

as a statement from the packaging designer's son, who opposes the change. Imagine a conversation on this topic between these two people. How might each one respond to the points raised by the other? What might each one ask the other? Where you imagine they'd find some common ground? completely disagree? You may even write an imaginary dialogue, perhaps for a podcast or a *YouTube* video.

5. Grocery aisles are stocked with packages bearing the image of a person, whether a photo, a lifelike drawing, or a caricature. Perhaps the person is the actual originator of the recipe or the founder of the company, and the label will usually mention that fact. For other images, it may not be clear who, exactly, is being depicted or why they might be shown there. Do a little research: Go to a supermarket, convenience store, or other place where packaged grocery items are sold. Make note of which packages depict a person and try to determine what purpose their image serves on the packaging. Select one example from those that you find and write an essay **ANALYZING** the package and the images. (Exclude Cap'n Crunch, Count Chocula, Tony the Tiger, or other heroes of the cereal aisle.) What purpose do you think the image serves? What does the image have to do with the product? with the intended buyers of the product? Could the package be as effective without that person's image? Might any of the images be interpreted as exploiting a stereotype? In your essay, address these questions and any others that you think are relevant.

Emoji Are Ruining Grasp of English, Says Dumbest Language Story of the Week

GEOFFREY PULLUM

In your academic work, you likely won't be able to be as snarky as Pullum is, but he provides an example of careful, rhetorical reading, an important skill. See Ch. 6 for more information.

THE AWARD FOR THE STUPIDEST STORY about language this week (and every week has its candidates) must surely go to the British newspaper *The Telegraph* for its story headlined "Emoji 'ruining people's grasp of English' because young rely on them to communicate."

Perhaps you've noticed how the stoplights during your evening commute (the red disk symbolizing "stop," the green one meaning "go"), not to mention those pictorial road signs (⚠, etc.), make you all but unable to speak to your family in coherent sentences when you get home?

No. Nor have I. Can the headline really be serious?

Not serious enough to correspond to the content, it seems. "Over a third of British adults believe that emoji are to blame for the deterioration of the English language, according to new research," the article goes on, revealing that the finding is not that emoji **are** ruining people's grasp of English, but rather that (some) British adults say they **think** that's happening. Quite

---

GEOFFREY PULLUM is professor emeritus of linguistics at the University of Edinburgh. He is cofounder (with linguist Mark Liberman) of *Language Log*, a long-running blog that addresses all kinds of language-related items, and he was a contributor to the *Chronicle of Higher Education*'s discontinued blog *Lingua Franca*, where this 2018 essay was published.

a difference. But let's press on. Who are the social and linguistic scientists responsible for focusing the spotlight of research on this mass delusion?

> YouTube, the video sharing website owned by Google, commissioned a study where 2,000 adults aged between 16 and 65 were asked about their views on the current state of the English language.

Ah, so it's survey-takers working for a company that just happens to host thousands of brush-up-your-grammar videos! They asked the adults in question whether or not the English language is going to hell in a handcart, and whether or not young people today are messing everything up and don't deserve to have nice things, and people said yes.

Apparently "more than half of British adults are not confident with their command of spelling and grammar," and "three quarters of adults are now dependent on emoji to communicate with each another [sic], as well as spell checks and predictive text."

Dependent on emoji! Heartbreaking. Unskilled at the difficult art of putting subjects together with predicates to form declarative sentences, they just fumble around in the emoji box on their smartphone screens, desperate to find some way of getting their inchoate thoughts across. And kids are responsible for this.

Thinking back, I recall that apropos of something perhaps slightly embarrassing, my friend and neighbor Sarah recently sent me a message containing nothing but three emoji:

I read this at the time as an amusing (and very compact) way to say "See no evil, hear no evil, speak no evil." I figured that she could in principle have typed out "Fear not, I am not a gossip, and no word of this will escape my lips," but had decided on something shorter and wittier.

In light of the *Telegraph* story, I now see that I should have been more concerned for her: Poor Sarah sent those monkeys because she is losing her capacity to form sentences! (She sees her young nieces fairly often; they must have corrupted her.)

The writer responsible for *The Telegraph*'s piffle, this dish of journalistic 💩, is Camilla Turner, who holds the title of education editor.

She fortified her argument with a grim-jawed quote from a fellow alarmist, Chris McGovern, who used to be a government adviser and now chairs something called the Campaign for Real Education. He said:

> There has unquestionably been quite a serious decline in young people's ability to use the English language and write properly punctuated English.
>
> We are moving in a direction of cartoon and picture language, which inevitably will affect literacy. Children will always follow the path of least resistance.
>
> Emoji convey a message, but this breeds laziness. If people think "all I need to do is send a picture," this dilutes language and expression.

Poppycock. Throwing in a smiley face 😃 or a monkey 🐒 or a picture of a saxophone 🎷 is neither a symptom of losing syntactic competence nor a cause of it. Essentially all emoji are just pictures of things that would be denoted in text by nouns; you still need to spell out verbs if you're going to actually say anything.

Haven't these hyperbole-mongers noticed that young people today write to each other more than young people have ever done in all of human history? Their texting, tweeting, WhatsApping, Snapchatting, Facebooking, and Instagramming may have psychological downsides (like cyber-bullying), but dropping the occasional pictographs into their prose is not going to strip them of the capacity to form sentences. Anyone who believes emoji are having even the slightest effect on English syntax is an utter 🤡.

Thinking about the Text

1. Geoffrey Pullum refutes the argument he saw in a newspaper that emoji use is "ruining people's grasp of English" (1), but he doesn't present any research or evidence to the contrary, other than his own personal experiences. How does he show that the **ARGUMENT** is faulty? What **EVIDENCE** does he present? Is his evidence persuasive? Why or why not?

2. Pullum claims that emoji are "just pictures of things that would be denoted in text by nouns" (12). Is that an accurate description? Look through your own recent texts—those you sent as well as those you received. Are all the emoji

representing nouns? What else might they be working as? Verbs? Adjectives? Are there any surprises in your results? If emoji can represent more than just nouns, how does that affect the strength of Pullum's argument?

3. Snarkiness is a central feature of Pullum's essay, but of course, the same ideas could be expressed in a more formal **STYLE** if the situation required it. Rewrite the paragraph that begins "Dependent on emoji!" (7) as you might expect to find it in a serious newspaper or journal in a way that retains all of the meaning that Pullum conveys in the original. Once you've rewritten the paragraph, reflect on what you did. What challenges did you face? How did you resolve them? Which version do you like better? Why?

4. Pullum inserts quite a few emoji in his essay. Some are quoted from actual text messages that he has received, some are referred to as examples, and two are actually meant to be read as part of the text; that is, they replace the spelled-out version of the respective words. What are those two emoji that stand in place of spelled-out words? How clear is the meaning of the sentences containing those emoji? How might the meaning have been different if he had spelled out those two words? Would his argument be better if those words were spelled out? Why or why not?

5. To rebut the assertion that emoji usage damages people's ability to communicate verbally, Pullum gives the example of stoplights, which are simple visual images that represent more complex messages. Indeed, our twenty-first-century world employs many such visual symbols. Take note of all the visual symbols (that aren't emojis) you encounter in the course of your daily routine. Make a list of what you've found and analyze each symbol according to what kinds of messages it conveys (purpose or function) and what visual features it uses (form). For example, stoplights perform the function of regulating movement in an efficient fashion, and they employ shape (usually round), color, and predictable placement in order to structure the message. Write up your observations in an essay that describes and **ANALYZES** your findings.

Blue-Collar Brilliance

MIKE ROSE

MY MOTHER, ROSE MERAGLIO ROSE (Rosie), shaped her adult identity as a waitress in coffee shops and family restaurants. When I was growing up in Los Angeles during the 1950s, my father and I would occasionally hang out at the restaurant until her shift ended, and then we'd ride the bus home with her. Sometimes she worked the register and the counter, and we sat there; when she waited booths and tables, we found a booth in the back where the waitresses took their breaks.

There wasn't much for a child to do at the restaurants, and so as the hours stretched out, I watched the cooks and waitresses and listened to what they said. At mealtimes, the pace of the kitchen staff and the din from customers picked up. Weaving in and out around the room, waitresses warned *behind you* in impassive but urgent voices. Standing at the service window facing the kitchen, they called out abbreviated orders. *Fry four on two*, my

MIKE ROSE (1944–2021) was a professor of education and information studies at UCLA. His work focused on teaching methods, on understanding people's engagement with the written word, and on bridging gaps between the academic and nonacademic worlds. Rose published numerous books, including *Why School? Reclaiming Education for All of Us* (2009) and *Back to School: Why Everyone Deserves a Second Chance at Education* (2012). This article was originally published in 2009 in the *American Scholar*, a magazine sponsored by the Phi Beta Kappa Society.

mother would say as she clipped a check onto the metal wheel. Her tables were *deuces*, *four-tops*, or *six-tops* according to their size; seating areas also were nicknamed. The *racetrack*, for instance, was the fast-turnover front section. Lingo conferred authority and signaled know-how.

Rosie took customers' orders, pencil poised over pad, while fielding questions about the food. She walked full tilt through the room with plates stretching up her left arm and two cups of coffee somehow cradled in her right hand. She stood at a table or booth and removed a plate for this person, another for that person, then another, remembering who had the hamburger, who had the fried shrimp, almost always getting it right. She would haggle with the cook about a returned order and rush by us, saying, *He gave me lip, but I got him*. She'd take a minute to flop down in the booth next to my father. *I'm all in*, she'd say, and whisper something about a customer. Gripping the outer edge of the table with one hand, she'd watch the room and note, in the flow of our conversation, who needed a refill, whose order was taking longer to prepare than it should, who was finishing up.

I couldn't have put it in words when I was growing up, but what I observed in my mother's restaurant defined the world of adults, a place where competence was synonymous with physical work. I've since studied the working habits of blue-collar workers and have come to understand how much my mother's kind of work demands of both body and brain. A waitress acquires knowledge and intuition about the ways and the rhythms of the restaurant business. Waiting on seven to nine tables, each with two to six customers, Rosie devised memory strategies so that she could remember who ordered what. And because she knew the average time it took to prepare different dishes, she could monitor an order that was taking too long at the service station.

Like anyone who is effective at physical work, my mother learned *to work smart*, as she put it, *to make every move count*. She'd sequence and group tasks: What could she do first, then second, then third as she circled through her station? What tasks could be clustered? She did everything on the fly, and when problems arose—technical or human—she solved them within the flow of work, while taking into account the emotional state of her co-workers. Was the manager in a good mood? Did the cook wake up on the wrong side of the bed? If so, how could she make an extra request or effectively return an order?

And then, of course, there were the customers who entered the restaurant with all sorts of needs, from physiological ones, including the emotions

Rosie solved technical and human problems on the fly.

that accompany hunger, to a sometimes complicated desire for human contact. Her tip depended on how well she responded to these needs, and so she became adept at reading social cues and managing feelings, both the customers' and her own. No wonder, then, that Rosie was intrigued by psychology. The restaurant became the place where she studied human behavior, puzzling over the problems of her regular customers and refining her ability to deal with people in a difficult world. She took pride in *being among the public*, she'd say. *There isn't a day that goes by in the restaurant that you don't learn something.*

My mother quit school in the seventh grade to help raise her brothers and sisters. Some of those siblings made it through high school, and some dropped out to find work in railroad yards, factories, or restaurants. My father finished a grade or two in primary school in Italy and never darkened the schoolhouse door again. I didn't do well in school either. By high school I had accumulated a spotty academic record and many hours of hazy disaffection. I spent a few years on the vocational track, but in my senior year I was inspired by my English teacher and managed to squeak into a small college on probation.

My freshman year was academically bumpy, but gradually I began to see formal education as a means of fulfillment and as a road toward making a living. I studied the humanities and later the social and psychological sciences and taught for 10 years in a range of situations—elementary school, adult education courses, tutoring centers, a program for Vietnam veterans who wanted to go to college. Those students had socioeconomic and educational backgrounds similar to mine. Then I went back to graduate school to study education and cognitive psychology and eventually became a faculty member in a school of education.

Intelligence is closely associated with formal education—the type of schooling a person has, how much and how long—and most people seem to move comfortably from that notion to a belief that work requiring less schooling requires less intelligence. These assumptions run through our cultural history, from the post–Revolutionary War period, when mechanics were characterized by political rivals as illiterate and therefore incapable of participating in government, until today. More than once I've heard a manager label his workers as "a bunch of dummies." Generalizations about intelligence, work, and social class deeply affect our assumptions about ourselves and each other, guiding the ways we use our minds to learn, build knowledge, solve problems, and make our way through the world.

Although writers and scholars have often looked at the working class, 10 they have generally focused on the values such workers exhibit rather than on the thought their work requires—a subtle but pervasive omission. Our cultural iconography promotes the muscled arm, sleeve rolled tight against biceps, but no brightness behind the eye, no image that links hand and brain.

One of my mother's brothers, Joe Meraglio, left school in the ninth grade to work for the Pennsylvania Railroad. From there he joined the Navy, returned to the railroad, which was already in decline, and eventually joined his older brother at General Motors where, over a 33-year career, he moved from working on the assembly line to supervising the paint-and-body department. When I was a young man, Joe took me on a tour of the factory. The floor was loud—in some places deafening—and when I turned a corner or opened a door, the smell of chemicals knocked my head back. The work was repetitive and taxing, and the pace was inhumane.

Still, for Joe the shop floor provided what school did not; it was *like schooling*, he said, a place where *you're constantly learning*. Joe learned the most

With an eighth-grade education, Joe (hands together) advanced to become supervisor of a G.M. paint-and-body department.

efficient way to use his body by acquiring a set of routines that were quick and preserved energy. Otherwise he would never have survived on the line.

As a foreman, Joe constantly faced new problems and became a consummate multi-tasker, evaluating a flurry of demands quickly, parceling out physical and mental resources, keeping a number of ongoing events in his mind, returning to whatever task had been interrupted, and maintaining a cool head under the pressure of grueling production schedules. In the midst of all this, Joe learned more and more about the auto industry, the technological and social dynamics of the shop floor, the machinery and production processes, and the basics of paint chemistry and of plating and baking. With further promotions, he not only solved problems but also began to find problems to solve: Joe initiated the redesign of the nozzle on a paint sprayer, thereby eliminating costly and unhealthy overspray. And he found a way to reduce energy costs on the baking ovens without affecting the quality of the paint. He lacked formal knowledge of how the machines under his supervision worked, but he had direct experience with them, hands-on knowledge, and was savvy about their quirks and operational capabilities. He could experiment with them.

Mike Rose started his research by observing —and by listening. Listening is a key part of thinking rhetorically; read more about it in Ch. 1.

In addition, Joe learned about budgets and management. Coming off the line as he did, he had a perspective of workers' needs and management's demands, and this led him to think of ways to improve efficiency on the line while relieving some of the stress on the assemblers. He had each worker in a unit learn his or her co-workers' jobs so they could rotate across stations to relieve some of the monotony. He believed that rotation would allow assemblers to get longer and more frequent breaks. It was an easy sell to the people on the line. The union, however, had to approve any modification in job duties, and the managers were wary of the change. Joe had to argue his case on a number of fronts, providing him a kind of rhetorical education.

Eight years ago I began a study of the thought processes involved in work 15 like that of my mother and uncle. I catalogued the cognitive demands of a range of blue-collar and service jobs, from waitressing and hair styling to plumbing and welding. To gain a sense of how knowledge and skill develop, I observed experts as well as novices. From the details of this close examination, I tried to fashion what I called "cognitive biographies" of blue-collar workers. Biographical accounts of the lives of scientists, lawyers, entrepreneurs, and other professionals are rich with detail about the intellectual dimension of their work. But the life stories of working-class people are few and are typically accounts of hardship and courage or the achievements wrought by hard work.

Our culture—in Cartesian fashion—separates the body from the mind, so that, for example, we assume that the use of a tool does not involve abstraction. We reinforce this notion by defining intelligence solely on grades in school and numbers on IQ tests. And we employ social biases pertaining to a person's place on the occupational ladder. The distinctions among blue, pink, and white collars carry with them attributions of character, motivation, and intelligence. Although we rightly acknowledge and amply compensate the play of mind in white-collar and professional work, we diminish or erase it in considerations about other endeavors— physical and service work particularly. We also often ignore the experience of everyday work in administrative deliberations and policymaking.

But here's what we find when we get in close. The plumber seeking leverage in order to work in tight quarters and the hair stylist adroitly handling scissors and comb manage their bodies strategically. Though work-related actions become routine with experience, they were learned at some point through observation, trial and error, and, often, physical or verbal assistance from a co-worker or trainer. I've frequently observed novices talking to themselves as they take on a task, or shaking their head or hand as if to erase an attempt before trying again. In fact, our traditional notions of routine performance could keep us from appreciating the many instances within routine where quick decisions and adjustments are made. I'm struck by the thinking-in-motion that some work requires, by all the mental activity that can be involved in simply getting from one place to another: the waitress rushing back through her station to the kitchen or the foreman walking the line.

The use of tools requires the studied refinement of stance, grip, balance, and fine-motor skills. But manipulating tools is intimately tied to knowledge of what a particular instrument can do in a particular situation and do better than other similar tools. A worker must also know the characteristics of the material one is engaging—how it reacts to various cutting or compressing devices, to degrees of heat, or to lines of force. Some of these things demand judgment, the weighing of options, the consideration of multiple variables, and, occasionally, the creative use of a tool in an unexpected way.

In manipulating material, the worker becomes attuned to aspects of the environment, a training or disciplining of perception that both enhances knowledge and informs perception. Carpenters have an eye for length, line, and angle; mechanics troubleshoot by listening; hair stylists are attuned to shape, texture, and motion. Sensory data merge with concept, as when an auto mechanic relies on sound, vibration, and even smell to understand what cannot be observed.

Planning and problem solving have been studied since the earliest 20 days of modern cognitive psychology and are considered core elements in Western definitions of intelligence. To work is to solve problems. The big difference between the psychologist's laboratory and the workplace is that in the former the problems are isolated and in the latter they are embedded in the real-time flow of work with all its messiness and social complexity.

Much of physical work is social and interactive. Movers determining how to get an electric range down a flight of stairs require coordination, negotiation, planning, and the establishing of incremental goals. Words, gestures, and sometimes a quick pencil sketch are involved, if only to get the rhythm right. How important it is, then, to consider the social and communicative dimension of physical work, for it provides the medium for so much of work's intelligence.

Given the ridicule heaped on blue-collar speech, it might seem odd to value its cognitive content. Yet, the flow of talk at work provides the channel for organizing and distributing tasks, for troubleshooting and problem solving, for learning new information and revising old. A significant amount of teaching, often informal and indirect, takes place at work. Joe Meraglio saw that much of his job as a supervisor involved instruction. In some service occupations, language and communication are central: observing and interpreting behavior and expression, inferring mood and motive, taking on the perspective of others, responding appropriately to social cues, and knowing when you're understood. A good hair stylist, for instance, has the ability to convert vague requests (*I want something light and summery*) into an appropriate cut through questions, pictures, and hand gestures.

Verbal and mathematical skills drive measures of intelligence in the Western Hemisphere, and many of the kinds of work I studied are thought to require relatively little proficiency in either. Compared to certain kinds of white-collar occupations, that's true. But written symbols flow through physical work.

Numbers are rife in most workplaces: on tools and gauges, as measurements, as indicators of pressure or concentration or temperature, as guides to sequence, on ingredient labels, on lists and spreadsheets, as markers of quantity and price. Certain jobs require workers to make, check, and verify calculations, and to collect and interpret data. Basic math can be involved, and some workers develop a good sense of numbers and patterns. Consider, as well, what might be called material mathematics: mathematical functions embodied in materials and actions, as when a carpenter builds a cabinet or a flight of stairs. A simple mathematical act can extend quickly beyond itself. Measuring, for example, can involve more than recording the dimensions of an object. As I watched a cabinetmaker measure a long strip of wood, he read a number off the tape out loud, looked back over his shoulder to the kitchen wall, turned back to his task, took another measurement, and paused for a moment in thought. He was solving a problem involving the molding, and the measurement was important to his deliberation about structure and appearance.

In the blue-collar workplace, directions, plans, and reference books rely on illustrations, some representational and others, like blueprints, that require training to interpret. Esoteric symbols—visual jargon—depict switches and receptacles, pipe fittings, or types of welds. Workers themselves often make sketches on the job. I frequently observed them grab a

25

pencil to sketch something on a scrap of paper or on a piece of the material they were installing.

Though many kinds of physical work don't require a high literacy level, more reading occurs in the blue-collar workplace than is generally thought, from manuals and catalogues to work orders and invoices, to lists, labels, and forms. With routine tasks, for example, reading is integral to understanding production quotas, learning how to use an instrument, or applying a product. Written notes can initiate action, as in restaurant orders or reports of machine malfunction, or they can serve as memory aids.

True, many uses of writing are abbreviated, routine, and repetitive, and they infrequently require interpretation or analysis. But analytic moments can be part of routine activities, and seemingly basic reading and writing can be cognitively rich. Because workplace language is used in the flow of other activities, we can overlook the remarkable coordination of words, numbers, and drawings required to initiate and direct action.

If we believe everyday work to be mindless, then that will affect the work we create in the future. When we devalue the full range of everyday cognition, we offer limited educational opportunities and fail to make fresh and meaningful instructional connections among disparate kinds of skill and knowledge. If we think that whole categories of people—identified by class or occupation—are not that bright, then we reinforce social separations and cripple our ability to talk across cultural divides.

Affirmation of diverse intelligence is not a retreat to a softhearted definition of the mind. To acknowledge a broader range of intellectual capacity is to take seriously the concept of cognitive variability, to appreciate in all the Rosies and Joes the thought that drives their accomplishments and defines who they are. This is a model of the mind that is worthy of a democratic society.

Thinking about the Text

1. Mike Rose begins his **ANALYSIS** with a pair of extended examples and a brief personal narrative. Readers may not figure out until later what, exactly, he is analyzing. What is Rose's subject, and what is the question that directs his inquiry?

2. Because of the academically oriented prejudices that Rose mentions, you may never have read anything that focuses on the cognitive tasks involved in

blue-collar work. Were you surprised by anything that Rose said—or not? **REFLECT** on your own attitudes toward blue-collar work; in what ways did Rose confirm or challenge them? Describe your reactions and reflections.

3. Why might Rose have chosen to begin his analysis with the extended information about his mother and uncle, himself, and other members of his family? Do you find these **EXAMPLES** and **NARRATIVES** effective rhetorical strategies for introducing an analysis of this topic? Why or why not?

4. Rose is suggesting that blue-collar workers merit more recognition for the cognitive skills that they bring to their work, but that is not all he is arguing. What is the overarching **ARGUMENT** that Rose is making in his article? What **EVIDENCE** in the text supports your answer?

5. Conduct a brief interview with someone who works a blue-collar job—for example, a mechanic, a sewing-machine operator, a hairstylist, a restaurant server, a janitor or housekeeper, or a truck driver. Find out what factors someone needs to consider to perform the job successfully; in other words, what does the person have to be aware of while working? To keep the interview focused, start with one of the following questions: What effect does the weather have on what you do? (Heat, humidity, cold, and other weather elements often affect even indoor work.) What are the most common mistakes a beginner in your job might make? Write an **ANALYSIS** of the cognitive tasks involved in the person's ordinary workday. Use clear and precise language, and be sure to mention any insights that you gained.

"Coco," a Story about Borders and Love

JIA TOLENTINO

ONE WEEKEND LAST FALL, my boyfriend, Andrew, whose favorite movies include "Deliverance" and the original "Texas Chain Saw Massacre," went off to go see the Pixar movie "Coco," by himself, and came back in a delirium of happy, wistful tears. "What's going on with you?" I asked, watching him wheel his bike back into the living room. I hadn't moved from my permanent station behind my computer monitor, a hub for the ongoing erosion of my belief in human good. "You have to go to see 'Coco,'" he croaked. "You *have* to. It's, like, the best movie of all time."

I assumed that he was being hyperbolic, until a night in April when I invited three friends over to watch "Coco," all of us first-time viewers with high expectations. People we knew—people in their twenties and thirties, few of them with children—had been freaking out about "Coco" in group texts and random conversations, saying things like, "I cried so hard I started choking," and "I've watched it five times this month on airplanes." "Hey ppl over here getting drunk and watching Coco just fyi," I texted Andrew, who was still at the office. In return, I received a series of panicked instructions

---

JIA TOLENTINO is a staff writer for the *New Yorker*, where her work, in addition to reviews and cultural commentary, often involves deep investigations on topics such as youth vaping, abortion law, and sexual assault. She is author of *Trick Mirror* (2019), a collection of essays. In this 2018 article from the magazine, she reviews Pixar's animated feature film *Coco*.

to not start without him. "You have already seen it. . . ." I texted. "I DON'T CARE!!!!!!!" he texted back. "DON'T START WITHOUT ME!!!!"

We started without him. Andrew came home a third of the way into the movie, cracked a beer, and silently sat down on the floor of the living room to watch. By the end, every one of us was crying through a manic grin. "I told you," he said. "It's the best movie of all time."

In the weeks since that viewing, "Coco" love has continued to spread among my demographic—thanks, in part, to the movie's release on Netflix. "Coco" is unlike any film I can think of: it presents death as a life-affirming inevitability; its story line about grudges and abandonment makes you feel less alone. The protagonist, Miguel, is a twelve-year-old boy in the fictional Mexican town of Santa Cecilia—named for the patron saint of musicians— and he is trying to get out from under the shadow of his great-great-grandfather, who left his family to pursue a career as a musician. His wife, the ferocious Mamá Imelda, was left to take care of their young daughter, Coco. She instituted a permanent household ban on music and started making shoes.

We meet Coco as an old woman. Her daughter, Miguel's grandmother,   5 now runs the family and its shoemaking business with an iron *chancla*. Earnest, sweet Miguel teaches himself to play the guitar in the attic, watching and re-watching tapes of the bygone star Ernesto de la Cruz. On the Day of the Dead, he accidentally shatters a framed photograph on the family *ofrenda*, then spots a hidden detail in the picture, one that makes him suspect that his wayward ancestor was in fact de la Cruz himself. He sprints to the town mausoleum, hoping to borrow de la Cruz's guitar and prove the value of music to his family. Instead, the guitar turns Miguel invisible, and whisks him across a skybridge covered in thick, soft marigold petals that glow like lava. He falls to his knees in the petals, and then looks up to see a grand floating metropolis, confetti-colored in the darkness: the Land of the Dead.

The second and third acts of the movie are mostly set in this city of jubilant sugar-skull skeletons, where you exist only as long as you are remembered by the living. (You can cross over to the living world on the Day of the Dead, but only if your photo is on display.) Miguel joins up with a raggedy show-biz hustler named Héctor, who's desperate to get his picture back up on an *ofrenda*, and who says he can bring Miguel to de la Cruz. Héctor lives in a waterfront shantytown filled with people who are about to be forgotten; at one point, he begs a guitar for Miguel off an ill-tempered cowboy named Chicharrón, who vanishes as soon as Héctor finishes singing an old dirty song.

Eventually, Miguel realizes that Héctor is his real ancestor, and the movie sprints to a conclusion that's as skillfully engineered to produce waterworks as the montage at the beginning of "Up." But until the end, "Coco" is mostly, wonderfully, a mess of conflict and disappointment and sadness. Héctor seems to have failed everyone who takes a chance on him. Miguel's face, painted in skeleton camouflage, often droops as if he were a sad little black-and-white dog. "Coco" is animated by sweetness, but this sweetness is subterranean, bursting through mostly in tiny details: the way that both Mamá Imelda and Miguel's grandmother brandish shoes when they're angry; or how the daffy Xolo[1] dog that accompanies Miguel on his adventure is named Dante; or how the skeletons return to their city through the Day of the Dead's efficient T.S.A. system, declaring the churros and beer that their families gave them for their journey home.

Before "Coco" hit theaters, it was easy to doubt that the movie would present Mexican culture as expansively and gorgeously as it does, with such natural familiarity and respect. It is Pixar's nineteenth movie, but its first with a nonwhite protagonist; Lee Unkrich, the director and creator of the initial story, is white. The movie's working title was "Día de los Muertos," and, in 2013, Disney lawyers tried, absurdly, to trademark that phrase. But Unkrich and his team approached their subject with openness and collaborative humility: they travelled to Mexico, they loosened Pixar's typical secrecy to build a large network of consultants, and, after the trademark controversy,

Moviegoers wouldn't need to know this background in order to enjoy the film, but the information adds flavor to Tolentino's review. See more about including information in your review on pp. 338–41.

---

1. *Xolo*: A breed of small, hairless dog that is common in parts of Mexico and has been raised there for thousands of years. [Editor's note]

they asked several prominent critics to come onboard. "Coco" is the first movie to have both an all-Latino cast and a nine-figure budget. It grossed more than eight hundred million dollars worldwide, won two Oscars, and became the biggest blockbuster in Mexican history.

"Coco" is also a definitive movie for this moment: an image of all the things that we aren't, an exploration of values that feel increasingly difficult to practice in the actual world. It's a story of a multigenerational matriarchy, rooted in the past—whereas real life, these days, feels like an atemporal, structureless nightmare ruled by men. It's about lineage and continuity at a time when each morning makes me feel like my brain is being wiped and battered by new flashes of cruelty, as though history is being forgotten and only the worst parts rewritten. It feels like myth or science fiction to imagine that our great-great-grandchildren will remember us. If we continue to treat our resources the way we are treating them currently, those kids—if they exist at all—will live in a world that is ravaged, punishing, artificial, and hard.

This world is hard enough already: its technological conditions induce 　10 emotional alienation, and its economic ones narrow our attention to questions of individual survival. As it is, I haven't assembled the *ofrenda* I ought to. I barely feel like I'm taking adequate care of the people I love right now, and I mean the ones I know personally. I feel certain that I'm failing the people I don't know but that I love nonetheless—the people in our national community, and the people who are seeking to become a part of it.

"Coco" is a movie about borders more than anything—the beauty in their porousness, the absolute pain produced when a border locks you away from your family. The conflict in the story comes from not being able to cross over; the resolution is that love pulls you through to the other side. The thesis of the movie is that families belong together. . . . If justice is what love looks like in public, then love has started to seem like the stuff of children's movies, or maybe the stuff of *this* children's movie—something that doesn't make sense in the adult world, but should.

Thinking about the Text

1. Jia Tolentino's **REVIEW** of *Coco* deals with more than just the movie itself; she segues into comparing the world of *Coco* with her perception of reality in the twenty-first-century United States as viewed through the lens of her "ongoing

erosion of . . . belief in human good" (1). Is her comparison valid? What does it suggest about her criteria for evaluating the film? Should she have restricted her comments to the content of the movie? Why or why not? Explain your reasoning.

2. Tolentino's review might give the impression that a life of "lineage and continuity" (9) could only exist in the cartoon world of *Coco*, since she perceives her life very differently. How about you? Do you feel the effect of lineage and continuity in your daily activities and the choices you make, perhaps in the influence of family or culture? **REFLECT** on that phrase and describe what place, if any, lineage and continuity have on the ways that you live your life.

3. What might have been Tolentino's **PURPOSE** in beginning her review with the anecdote about her boyfriend's reaction to *Coco*? How, if at all, does the anecdote support Tolentino's review? Explain your reasoning.

4. Tolentino doubts "that our great-great-grandchildren will remember us" (9), and she implies that such an interruption of memory would be a result of our specific conditions in the here and now, but perhaps loss of historical memory is nothing new. How much do you know about any of your own great-great-grandparents? What kinds of historical conditions can interfere with knowing one's own lineage? Do you participate in any family or cultural practices that preserve the memory of your close or distant ancestors? Would you like to do more? less? Why or why not?

5. Tolentino describes *Coco* as full of sweetness that is "subterranean, bursting through mostly in tiny details" (7). Might that description also apply to ordinary, everyday noncinematic life? Think about your life this week and identify a few sweet details—perhaps a kind gesture, a bird or squirrel, sinking into a soft seat at the end of a long day, some small observation or sensation that might ordinarily go unnoticed—and write a **DESCRIPTION** of those sweet details and your responses to them.

It's 2018, and Gay Men Still Can't Give Blood in America

JOSH TRUJILLO & LEVI HASTINGS

Writer, cartoonist, and game designer JOSH TRUJILLO (right) writes in numerous genres with a broad array of themes, including fantasy, history, gaming, and LGBTQ issues. He is the creator of *Dodge City*, a graphic print series about the Jazz Pandas, a competitive dodge ball team; stories highlight the players' lives both on and off the court, and the series is notable for diverse characters and portrayals. Trujillo also writes the stories of *Love Machines*, a series of romance comics about the objects of our everyday lives and the roles of technology in our very human relationships. In a 2019 interview for the website *On Comics Ground*, Trujillo explains that "the thing [he finds] most interesting about *Love Machines* is how technology has always been a huge constant in our emotional and romantic lives. Smartphones have totally transformed the way people date and interact, just like telephones did a hundred years before." He tweets from @LostHisKeysMan.

LEVI HASTINGS (left), an illustrator, cartoonist, and visual artist, also works in a variety of genres and topics; his passions include natural science, history, travel, and Queer culture. He has done illustrations for HBO, *Buzzfeed*, *The Nib*, and many more companies and media outlets. Recent work includes *Spirit of Springer*, a nonfiction children's book about an orphaned orca who was rescued and reunited with her pod, and *Mayor Pete*, a children's biography of US Secretary of Transportation Pete Buttigieg. His *Twitter* is @LeviHastingsArt.

Trujillo and Hastings have published several collaborations. In 2016, they launched their well-researched historical fiction comic series *Declaration*, a gay romance of the Revolutionary War era. The following graphic essay was published in *The Nib*, a comics blog, in June 2018.

The 2016 Orlando shooting was a horrific attack against the queer community,

But Americans showed incredible support for the victims.

In America, and in most countries,
cis gay and bisexual men are discriminated against.

They're prevented from donating
precious, vital, life-saving plasma.

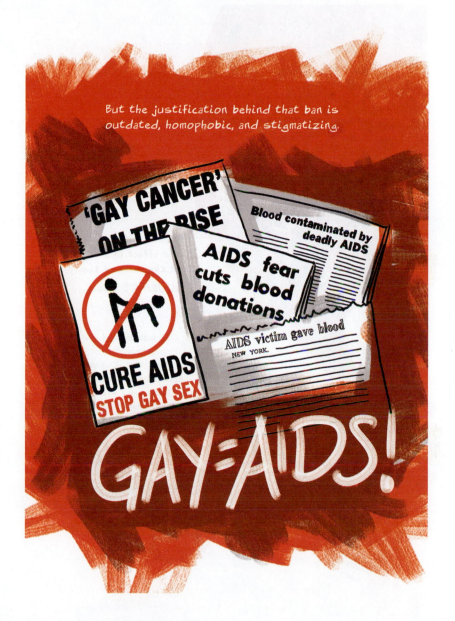

The FDA put this ban into effect in 1985, at the heart of the GRID/AIDS crisis.

It was based on a real fear that the disease could be transmitted through a blood transfusion.

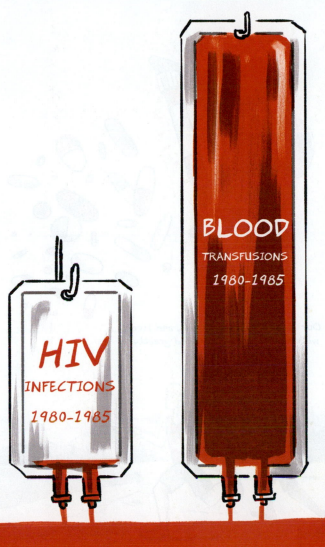

This was a small fraction of the 30 million blood transfusions that occurred without incident, but enough to create a panic.

Notice the color Trujillo and Hastings chose—not blood red, exactly, because that might have been too much, but a shade that contrasts well with black and is evocative of blood. Find advice for your color choices on pp. 774–75.

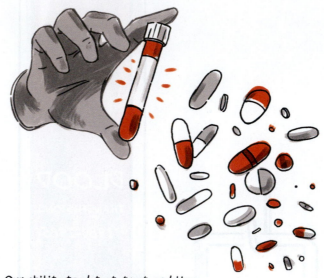

Our ability to detect, treat, and live with HIV/AIDS has improved greatly over the decades.

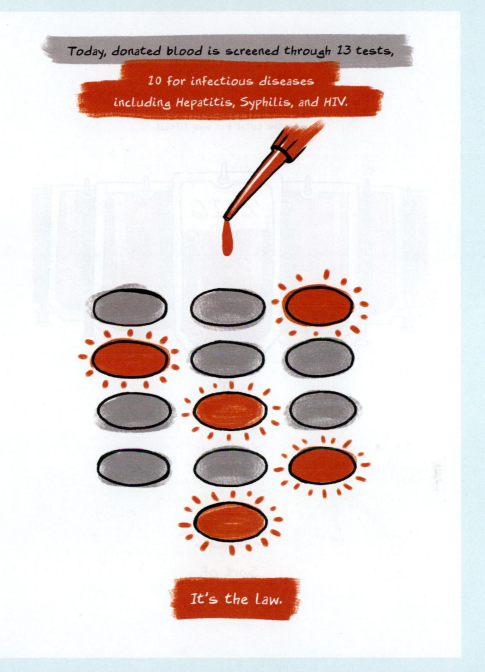

But the ban remained in effect.

Until in 2016, the year of the
Pulse nightclub massacre in Orlando,
when the total ban was lifted...

2016

Sort of.

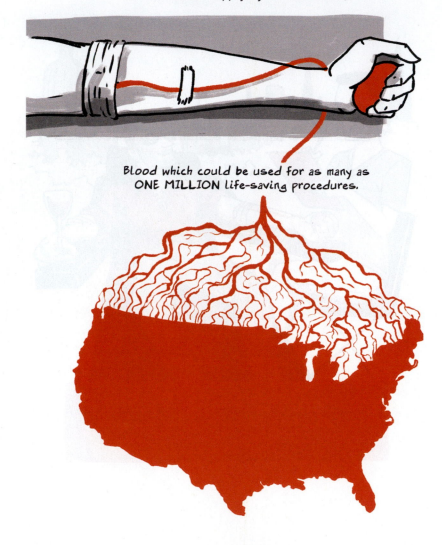

A 2014 Williams Institute study found that lifting the blood donation ban in the US could increase the blood supply by as much as 4%.

Blood which could be used for as many as ONE MILLION life-saving procedures.

By implementing individual risk assessment versus a blanket ban, the FDA can make an enormous difference in the health and well-being of all Americans.

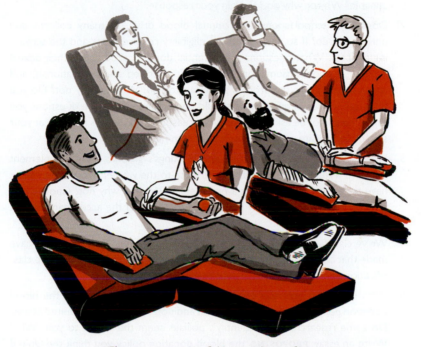

The gay community felt powerless after the Orlando shooting.

This policy change, though small, could be the first step towards empathy, compassion, and healing.

Thinking about the Text

1. Josh Trujillo and Levi Hastings are **PROPOSING** a change in the US policy for blood donation. What, exactly, are they proposing? Why? Is the proposal reasonable? Why or why not? Explain your response.

2. Does your school sponsor an annual blood drive, as many colleges and universities do? If so, investigate the eligibility requirements and the screening process. What questions are potential donors asked about their sexual activity, alcohol consumption, drug use (prescribed and recreational), and other habits? Does the process seem fair to you? Why or why not? Do you think other lines of questioning should be pursued? Are there questions you think should not be asked? Explain your reasoning. (If there is no drive at your school, investigate a blood drive in your community.)

3. How do the drawings in Trujillo and Hastings's graphic essay complement the text? What do the drawings contribute to the whole? Would you rather have read the text by itself as a prose essay? Why or why not? Choose one drawing and **ANALYZE** how it enhances (or doesn't) the accompanying text information.

4. We've classified this proposal under the theme Home. Why might we have made that choice? Identify one image in the essay that best supports the classification of Home and explain your reasoning for the choice.

5. With regard to gay male donors, Trujillo and Hastings mention the blood donation policies of several countries in addition to those of the United States. Do some research; which country's policies seem the fairest to you? Why? Write an essay **PROPOSING** the blood donation policy you think the United States should follow. Should it be similar to the US status quo or to the policy of one of another countries? Include **EVIDENCE** for your stance.

Why the Post Office Makes America Great

ZEYNEP TUFEKCI

I WAS TRANSPORTED RECENTLY TO A PLACE that is as enchanting to me as any winter wonderland: my local post office.

In line, I thought fondly of the year I came to this country from Turkey as an adult and discovered the magic of reliable mail service. Dependable infrastructure is magical not simply because it works, but also because it allows innovation to thrive, including much of the Internet-based economy that has grown in the past decade. You can't have Amazon or eBay without a reliable way to get things to people's homes.

Of course, infrastructure is also boring, so we get used to it and forget what a gift it truly is. I never do, maybe because I discovered it so late.

My first year in the United States was full of surprises. I remember trying to figure out if the 24-ounce glass of ice water the waitress placed in front of me was a pitcher, to be shared by the whole table. But where was the spout? I had expected some of what I encountered—I had seen enough movies, and came to this country expecting big cars and big houses and wide open spaces. I got used to gigantic glasses.

ZEYNEP TUFEKCI is a sociologist and assistant professor at the University of North Carolina, faculty associate at the Berkman Center at Harvard University, and author of *Twitter and Tear Gas: The Power and Fragility of Networked Protest* (2017). This *New York Times* essay was published in January 2016. Her newsletter is theinsight.org, and she tweets from @zeynep.

But I didn't expect the post office.   5

The first time I needed to mail something, I trekked over to my campus's post office, looking for the line to get my envelope weighed. The staff was used to befuddled international students like me, I suppose, and one clerk took my envelope without fuss, said "first class letter," and took my change.

Then I discovered some vending machines outside the office. People came and bought stamps. "So many people must be into stamp collecting," I thought to myself. Was that another weird American quirk? Otherwise, why would people waste money buying stamps in advance, without having their letters weighed?

Something I take for granted now just didn't occur to me: There were standardized rates, and you could just slap a stamp on your letter, drop it in a mailbox, and it would go to its destination.

I then encountered a visa service that asked me to mail in my passport. My precious, precious passport. With a self-addressed, stamped envelope for its return. I laughed at the audacity of the request. Despite being a broke student, I booked a plane trip. I couldn't envision putting my passport in the mail. I've since learned that this is a common practice, and I've even done it once or twice myself. But it still does not come easy to me.

I noticed that Americans were a particularly patriotic bunch: So many   10
of them had red flags on their mailboxes. Sometimes they would put those flags up. I presumed it was to celebrate national holidays I did not yet know about. But why did some people have their flags up while others did not? And why weren't they American flags anyway? As in Istanbul, where I grew up, I assumed patriotism had different interpretations and expressions.

The mystery was solved when I noticed a letter carrier *emptying* a mailbox. I was slightly unnerved: Was the mail being stolen? He then went over to another mailbox with the flag up, and emptied that box, too. I got my hint when he skipped the mailbox with the flag down.

Yes, I was told, in the United States, mail gets picked up from your house, six days a week, free of charge.

I told my friends in Turkey about all this. They shook their heads in disbelief, wondering how easily I had been recruited as a C.I.A. agent, saying implausibly flattering things about my new country. The United States in the world's imagination is a place of risk taking and ruthless competition, not one of reliable public services.

I bit my tongue and did not tell my already suspicious friends that the country was also dotted with libraries that provided books to all patrons free of charge. They wouldn't believe me anyway since I hadn't believed it myself. My first time in a library in the United States was very brief: I walked in, looked around, and ran right back out in a panic, certain that I had accidentally used the wrong entrance. Surely, these open stacks full of books were reserved for staff only. I was used to libraries being rare, and their few books inaccessible. To this day, my heart races a bit in a library.

Over the years, I've come to appreciate the link between infrastructure, innovation—and even ruthless competition. Much of our modern economy thrives here because you can order things online and expect them to be delivered. There are major private delivery services, too, but the United States Postal Service is often better equipped to make it to certain destinations. In fact, Internet sellers, and even private carriers, often use the U.S.P.S. as their delivery mechanism to addresses outside densely populated cities.

Almost every aspect of the most innovative parts of the United States, from cutting-edge medical research to its technology scene, thrives on publicly funded infrastructure. The post office is struggling these days, in some ways because of how much people rely on the web to do much of what they used to turn to the post office for. But the Internet is a testament to infrastructure, too: It exists partly because the National Science Foundation funded much of the research that makes it possible. Even some of the Internet's biggest companies, like Google, got a start from N.S.F.-funded research.

Infrastructure is often the least-appreciated part of what makes a country strong, and what makes innovation take flight. From my spot in line at the post office, I see a country that does both well; not a country that emphasizes one at the expense of the other.

15

Tufekci uses a light and entertaining tone to make an argument that is quite serious, and she uses a combination of appeals to get the job done. Find out more about using various kinds of appeals in Ch. 19.

Thinking about the Text

1. Zeynep Tufekci describes the relationship between infrastructure and innovation. What is that relationship? What examples does she provide to illustrate her point? **SUMMARIZE** her argument. Do you agree? Why or why not?

2. "To this day," confides Tufekci, "my heart races a bit in a library" (14). Do you share her reaction? How do you feel upon entering a library? Overwhelmed? Intimidated? Kid in a candy store? Scholarly? (If you haven't visited one in a while, do it now to refresh your memory.) Do you think a public library is an important element of infrastructure? Why or why not?

3. Tufekci employs personal **NARRATIVE** in support of an argument about US domestic policy. Is that rhetorical strategy an effective choice in this case? Why or why not?

4. Among the elements of everyday US life that surprised Tufekci when she arrived here were the large glasses of water provided free of charge to restaurant patrons, the post office, and the library. Take a look around at the ordinary parts of your life in the United States. Which of the things that you take for granted might be surprising to a newcomer? Why do you think so?

5. Tufekci points to the post office as a prime example of vital infrastructure. What else counts as infrastructure on a national and/or local level? List five examples. Choose one of those examples and write an essay describing how that infrastructure element could be expanded or enhanced in order to stimulate an innovation of some kind. Frame your essay as a **PROPOSAL** to state or local authorities supporting your infrastructure project.

My Life as an Undocumented Immigrant

JOSE ANTONIO VARGAS

Oᴺᴇ Aᴜɢᴜsᴛ ᴍᴏʀɴɪɴɢ nearly two decades ago, my mother woke me and put me in a cab. She handed me a jacket. *"Baka malamig doon"* were among the few words she said. ("It might be cold there.") When I arrived at the Philippines' Ninoy Aquino International Airport with her, my aunt and a family friend, I was introduced to a man I'd never seen. They told me he was my uncle. He held my hand as I boarded an airplane for the first time. It was 1993, and I was 12.

My mother wanted to give me a better life, so she sent me thousands of miles away to live with her parents in America—my grandfather (*Lolo* in Tagalog) and grandmother (*Lola*). After I arrived in Mountain View, Calif., in the San Francisco Bay Area, I entered sixth grade and quickly grew to love my new home, family and culture. I discovered a passion for language, though it was hard to learn the difference between formal English and American slang. One of my early memories is of a freckled kid in middle school asking me, "What's up?" I replied, "The sky," and he

---

JOSE ANTONIO VARGAS came to the United States from the Philippines at the age of twelve as an undocumented immigrant, a history he discloses in this 2011 essay from the *New York Times*. In 2020, he was named one of *Fortune*'s "40 under 40" most influential people in government and politics. His recent book, *White Is Not a Country* (2023), explores race and identities. He tweets from @joseiswriting.

and a couple of other kids laughed. I won the eighth-grade spelling bee by memorizing words I couldn't properly pronounce. (The winning word was "indefatigable.")

One day when I was 16, I rode my bike to the nearby D.M.V. office to get my driver's permit. Some of my friends already had their licenses, so I figured it was time. But when I handed the clerk my green card as proof of U.S. residency, she flipped it around, examining it. "This is fake," she whispered. "Don't come back here again."

Confused and scared, I pedaled home and confronted Lolo. I remember him sitting in the garage, cutting coupons. I dropped my bike and ran over to him, showing him the green card. *"Peke ba ito?"* I asked in Tagalog. ("Is this fake?") My grandparents were naturalized American citizens—he worked as a security guard, she as a food server—and they had begun supporting my mother and me financially when I was 3, after my father's wandering eye and inability to properly provide for us led to my parents' separation. Lolo was a proud man, and I saw the shame on his face as he told me he purchased the card, along with other fake documents, for me. "Don't show it to other people," he warned.

I decided then that I could never give anyone reason to doubt I was an 5 American. I convinced myself that if I worked enough, if I achieved enough, I would be rewarded with citizenship. I felt I could earn it.

I've tried. Over the past 14 years, I've graduated from high school and college and built a career as a journalist, interviewing some of the most famous people in the country. On the surface, I've created a good life. I've lived the American dream.

But I am still an undocumented immigrant. And that means living a different kind of reality. It means going about my day in fear of being found out. It means rarely trusting people, even those closest to me, with who I really am. It means keeping my family photos in a shoebox rather than displaying them on shelves in my home, so friends don't ask about them. It means reluctantly, even painfully, doing things I know are wrong and unlawful. And it has meant relying on a sort of 21st-century underground railroad of supporters, people who took an interest in my future and took risks for me.

Last year I read about four students who walked from Miami to Washington to lobby for the Dream Act, a nearly decade-old immigration bill that would provide a path to legal permanent residency for young people who have been educated in this country. At the risk of deportation—the Obama administration has deported almost 800,000 people in the last two years—they are speaking out. Their courage has inspired me.

There are believed to be 11 million undocumented immigrants in the United States. We're not always who you think we are. Some pick your strawberries or care for your children. Some are in high school or college. And some, it turns out, write news articles you might read. I grew up here. This is my home. Yet even though I think of myself as an American and consider America my country, my country doesn't think of me as one of its own.

My first challenge was the language. Though I learned English in the Philippines, I wanted to lose my accent. During high school, I spent hours at a time watching television (especially *Frasier*, *Home Improvement* and reruns of *The Golden Girls*) and movies (from *Goodfellas* to *Anne of Green Gables*), pausing the VHS to try to copy how various characters enunciated their words. At the local library, I read magazines, books and newspapers—anything to learn how to write better. Kathy Dewar, my high-school English teacher, introduced me to journalism. From the moment I wrote my first article for the student paper, I convinced myself that having my name in print—writing in English, interviewing Americans—validated my presence here.

The debates over "illegal aliens" intensified my anxieties. In 1994, only a year after my flight from the Philippines, Gov. Pete Wilson was re-elected in part because of his support for Proposition 187, which prohibited undocumented immigrants from attending public school and accessing other services. (A federal court later found the law unconstitutional.) After my encounter at the D.M.V. in 1997, I grew more aware of anti-immigrant sentiments and stereotypes: *they don't want to assimilate*, *they are a drain on society*. They're not talking about me, I would tell myself. I have something to contribute.

To do that, I had to work—and for that, I needed a Social Security number.... Using a fake passport, Lolo and I went to the local Social Security Administration office and applied for a Social Security number and card. It was, I remember, a quick visit. When the card came in the mail, it had my full, real name, but it also clearly stated: "Valid for work only with I.N.S. authorization."

When I began looking for work, a short time after the D.M.V. incident, my grandfather and I took the Social Security card to Kinko's, where he covered the "I.N.S. authorization" text with a sliver of white tape. We then made photocopies of the card. At a glance, at least, the copies would look like copies of a regular, unrestricted Social Security card. . . .

While in high school, I worked part time at Subway, then at the front desk of the local Y.M.C.A., then at a tennis club, until I landed an unpaid internship at *The Mountain View Voice*, my hometown newspaper. First I brought coffee and helped around the office; eventually I began covering city-hall meetings and other assignments for pay. . . .

Mountain View High School became my second home. I was elected to represent my school at school-board meetings, which gave me the chance to meet and befriend Rich Fischer, the superintendent for our school district. I joined the speech and debate team, acted in school plays and eventually became co-editor of *The Oracle*, the student newspaper. That drew the attention of my principal, Pat Hyland. "You're at school just as much as I am," she told me. Pat and Rich would soon become mentors, and over time, almost surrogate parents for me. . . . 15

[During my junior] year, my history class watched a documentary on Harvey Milk, the openly gay San Francisco city official who was assassinated. This was 1999, just six months after Matthew Shepard's body was found tied to a fence in Wyoming. During the discussion, I raised my hand and said something like: "I'm sorry Harvey Milk got killed for being gay. . . . I've been meaning to say this. . . . I'm gay."

I hadn't planned on coming out that morning, though I had known that I was gay for several years. With that announcement, I became the only openly gay student at school, and it caused turmoil with my grandparents. Lolo kicked me out of the house for a few weeks. Though we eventually reconciled, I had disappointed him on two fronts. First, as a Catholic, he considered homosexuality a sin and was embarrassed about having "*ang apo na bakla*" ("a grandson who is gay"). Even worse, I was making matters more difficult for myself, he said. I needed to marry an American woman in order to gain a green card.

Tough as it was, coming out about being gay seemed less daunting than coming out about my legal status. I kept my other secret mostly hidden.

While my classmates awaited their college acceptance letters, I hoped to get a full-time job at *The Mountain View Voice* after graduation. It's not that I didn't want to go to college, but I couldn't apply for state and federal financial aid. Without that, my family couldn't afford to send me.

But when I finally told Pat and Rich about my immigration "problem"— 20
as we called it from then on—they helped me look for a solution. At first,
they even wondered if one of them could adopt me and fix the situation
that way, but a lawyer Rich consulted told him it wouldn't change my legal
status because I was too old. Eventually they connected me to a new scholarship fund for high-potential students who were usually the first in their
families to attend college. Most important, the fund was not concerned with
immigration status. I was among the first recipients, with the scholarship
covering tuition, lodging, books and other expenses for my studies at San
Francisco State University.

As a college freshman, I found a job working part time at *The San
Francisco Chronicle*, where I sorted mail and wrote some freelance articles.
My ambition was to get a reporting job, so I embarked on a series of internships. First I landed at *The Philadelphia Daily News*, in the summer of 2001,
where I covered a drive-by shooting and the wedding of the 76ers star Allen
Iverson. Using those articles, I applied to *The Seattle Times* and got an internship for the following summer.

But then my lack of proper documents became a problem again. *The
Times*'s recruiter, Pat Foote, asked all incoming interns to bring certain
paperwork on their first day: a birth certificate, or a passport, or a driver's
license plus an original Social Security card. I panicked, thinking my documents wouldn't pass muster. So before starting the job, I called Pat and told
her about my legal status. After consulting with management, she called
me back with the answer I feared: I couldn't do the internship.

This was devastating. What good was college if I couldn't then pursue
the career I wanted? I decided then that if I was to succeed in a profession
that is all about truth-telling, I couldn't tell the truth about myself. . . .

For the summer of 2003, I applied for internships across the country.
Several newspapers, including *The Wall Street Journal*, *The Boston Globe*
and *The Chicago Tribune*, expressed interest. But when *The Washington Post*
offered me a spot, I knew where I would go. And this time, I had no intention
of acknowledging my "problem."

The *Post* internship posed a tricky obstacle: It required a driver's license. 25
(After my close call at the California D.M.V., I'd never gotten one.) So I spent
an afternoon at the Mountain View Public Library, studying various states'
requirements. Oregon was among the most welcoming—and it was just a
few hours' drive north.

Again, my support network came through. A friend's father lived in Portland, and he allowed me to use his address as proof of residency. Pat, Rich and Rich's longtime assistant, Mary Moore, sent letters to me at that address. Rich taught me how to do three-point turns in a parking lot, and a friend accompanied me to Portland.

The license meant everything to me—it would let me drive, fly and work. . . . My license, issued in 2003, was set to expire eight years later, on my 30th birthday, on February 3, 2011. I had eight years to succeed profession-ally, and to hope that some sort of immigration reform would pass in the meantime and allow me to stay.

It seemed like all the time in the world.

My summer in Washington was exhilarating. I was intimidated to be in a major newsroom but was assigned a mentor—Peter Perl, a veteran magazine writer—to help me navigate it. A few weeks into the internship, he printed out one of my articles, about a guy who recovered a long-lost wallet, circled the first two paragraphs and left it on my desk. "Great eye for details—awesome!" he wrote. Though I didn't know it then, Peter would become one more member of my network.

At the end of the summer, I returned to *The San Francisco Chronicle*.   30 My plan was to finish school—I was now a senior—while I worked for *The Chronicle* as a reporter for the city desk. But when *The Post* beckoned again, offering me a full-time, two-year paid internship that I could start when I graduated in June 2004, it was too tempting to pass up. I moved back to Washington.

About four months into my job as a reporter for *The Post*, I began feel-ing increasingly paranoid, as if I had "illegal immigrant" tattooed on my forehead—and in Washington, of all places, where the debates over immi-gration seemed never-ending. I was so eager to prove myself that I feared I was annoying some colleagues and editors—and worried that any one of these professional journalists could discover my secret. The anxiety was nearly paralyzing. I decided I had to tell one of the higher-ups about my situ-ation. I turned to Peter. . . . I told him everything: the Social Security card, the driver's license, Pat and Rich, my family.

Peter was shocked. "I understand you 100 times better now," he said. He told me that I had done the right thing by telling him, and that it was now our shared problem. He said he didn't want to do anything about it just yet. I had just been hired, he said, and I needed to prove myself. "When you've done enough," he said, "we'll tell Don and Len together." (Don Graham is the chairman of The Washington Post Company; Leonard Downie Jr. was then the paper's executive editor.) A month later, I spent my first Thanksgiving in Washington with Peter and his family.

In the five years that followed, I did my best to "do enough." I was promoted to staff writer, reported on video-game culture, wrote a series on Washington's H.I.V./AIDS epidemic and covered the role of technology and social media in the 2008 presidential race. I visited the White House, where I interviewed senior aides and covered a state dinner—and gave the Secret Service the Social Security number I obtained with false documents. . . .

It was an odd sort of dance: I was trying to stand out in a highly competitive newsroom, yet I was terrified that if I stood out too much, I'd invite unwanted scrutiny. I tried to compartmentalize my fears, distract myself by reporting on the lives of other people, but there was no escaping the central conflict in my life. Maintaining a deception for so long distorts your sense of self. You start wondering who you've become, and why.

In April 2008, I was part of a Post team that won a Pulitzer Prize for the 35 paper's coverage of the Virginia Tech shootings a year earlier. Lolo died a year earlier, so it was Lola who called me the day of the announcement. The first thing she said was, "*Anong mangyayari kung malaman ng mga tao?*"

What will happen if people find out?

I couldn't say anything. After we got off the phone, I rushed to the bathroom on the fourth floor of the newsroom, sat down on the toilet and cried.

In the summer of 2009, without ever having had that follow-up talk with top Post management, I left the paper and moved to New York to join *The Huffington Post.* . . .

While I worked at *The Huffington Post*, other opportunities emerged. My H.I.V./AIDS series became a documentary film called *The Other City*, which opened at the Tribeca Film Festival last year and was broadcast on Showtime. I began writing for magazines and landed a dream assignment: profiling Facebook's Mark Zuckerberg for *The New Yorker*.

The more I achieved, the more scared and depressed I became. I was 40 proud of my work, but there was always a cloud hanging over it, over me. My old eight-year deadline—the expiration of my Oregon driver's license— was approaching.

After slightly less than a year, I decided to leave *The Huffington Post*. In part, this was because I wanted to promote the documentary and write a book about online culture—or so I told my friends. But the real reason was, after so many years of trying to be a part of the system, of focusing all my energy on my professional life, I learned that no amount of professional success would solve my problem or ease the sense of loss and displacement I felt. I lied to a friend about why I couldn't take a weekend trip to Mexico. Another time I concocted an excuse for why I couldn't go on an all-expenses-paid trip to Switzerland. I have been unwilling, for years, to be in a long-term relationship because I never wanted anyone to get too close and ask too many questions. All the while, Lola's question was stuck in my head: What will happen if people find out?

Early this year, just two weeks before my thirtieth birthday, I won a small reprieve: I obtained a driver's license in the state of Washington. The license is valid until 2016. This offered me five more years of acceptable identification—but also five more years of fear, of lying to people I respect and institutions that trusted me, of running away from who I am.

I'm done running. I'm exhausted. I don't want that life anymore.

So I've decided to come forward, own up to what I've done, and tell my story to the best of my recollection. I've reached out to former bosses and employers and apologized for misleading them—a mix of humiliation and liberation coming with each disclosure. All the people mentioned in this article gave me permission to use their names. I've also talked to family and friends about my situation and am working with legal counsel to review my options. I don't know what the consequences will be of telling my story.

I do know that I am grateful to my grandparents, my Lolo and Lola, for 45
giving me the chance for a better life. I'm also grateful to my other family—the support network I found here in America—for encouraging me to pursue my dreams.

Vargas describes events that took place over a period of eighteen years. Learn the techniques he used to keep his narrative cohesive on pp. 203–4.

It's been almost 18 years since I've seen my mother. Early on, I was mad at her for putting me in this position, and then mad at myself for being angry and ungrateful. By the time I got to college, we rarely spoke by phone. It became too painful; after a while it was easier to just send money to help support her and my two half-siblings. My sister, almost 2 years old when I left, is almost 20 now. I've never met my 14-year-old brother. I would love to see them.

Not long ago, I called my mother. I wanted to fill the gaps in my memory about that August morning so many years ago. We had never discussed it. Part of me wanted to shove the memory aside, but to write this article and

Vargas has continued to advocate for immigration reform since the publication of this essay. At a political rally in December 2011, he raises a sign announcing his position—and raises his hand to ask politicians the hard questions that he argues must be addressed in order to change the conversation about immigration in America.

face the facts of my life, I needed more details. Did I cry? Did she? Did we kiss goodbye?

My mother told me I was excited about meeting a stewardess, about getting on a plane. She also reminded me of the one piece of advice she gave me for blending in: If anyone asked why I was coming to America, I should say I was going to Disneyland.

Thinking about the Text

1. Jose Antonio Vargas highlights issues about US immigration policy using details of his own experience, many of which are quite personal and probably difficult to admit. Point out three such details. What was your reaction to each of them? What is Vargas's **ARGUMENT** about immigration policy, and how do such details help him make that point?

2. Sprinkled throughout Vargas's narrative are bits of dialogue in Tagalog, the language of his Lolo and Lola. Given that he always provides the English translation, why might he have included the Tagalog? What function does it serve in his narrative?

3. How is Vargas's disclosure about his sexuality relevant to his point? Why might he have included it at all in telling about his immigrant experience? Support your response with evidence from the text.

4. Vargas **CONCLUDES** his narrative by recounting his mother's advice as he got on the plane: "If anyone asked why I was coming to America, I should say I was going to Disneyland" (48). Why do you think he ends this essay by mentioning Disneyland? What might he be implying? Did you find this ending effective— and if not, why not?

5. Vargas was fortunate to receive emotional and professional support from the teachers and employers to whom he disclosed his undocumented status. Imagine yourself in their place. How might you respond if one of your students or employees came to you admitting to being undocumented? What would you do, and why? What factors would need to be taken into consideration? Write an essay in which you respond to these questions.

The (Native) American Dream

TATÉ WALKER

IN THE MIDST of Colorado Springs' urban sprawl, Monycka Snowbird (Ojibwe) raises fowl, goats, rabbits, and indigenous plants to feed and make household products for her family and neighbors.

About 650 miles north in a sprawling rural landscape on the Cheyenne River reservation in South Dakota, Karen Ducheneaux (Lakota) and her *tiospaye*[1] are slowly building a series of ecodomes and straw bale buildings powered by solar, wind, and water in an effort to disconnect from pollutants of mind, body, and earth.

The two women represent a growing number of Native people and organizations in the United States both on and off tribal land committed to leading clean, sustainable, and culturally competent lives.

The efforts of individuals like these women, in addition to the prevalence of companies specializing in mainstreaming indigenous foods and

---

1. *Tiospaye*: Lakota word for the concept of "extended family," "deliberate family," and "the making of family." Membership presumes support for and commitment to the group. [Editor's note]

TATÉ WALKER (they/them) is a Lakota (Cheyenne River Sioux, South Dakota) writer, photographer/videographer, and Indigenous rights activist living in Phoenix. This article was published in 2015 in *Native Peoples: The Journal of the Heard Museum*. The Heard is an art museum in Phoenix founded in 1929 and dedicated to advancing American Indian art. Walker is the author of *Thunder Thighs and Trickster Vibes: Essays on Immigration, Gender, and Equality* (2016) and *The Trickster Riots* (2022). They tweet from @MissusTWalker.

Monycka Snowbird works in the yard.

Tiospaye. Walker doesn't define it, but context clues help you understand. Using a word or phrase from an additional language can be an effective choice; check out Ch. 33 to find out more.

non-profits committed to building energy efficient and sustainable housing in tribal communities, highlight the popularity and return of such lifestyles.

"Our people had this tiospaye system, where you really made a life with the people you felt close to, and had skills that complemented each other," says Ducheneaux. "We've spent generations at this point getting away from that beautiful system, and we're taught the only way to be successful is to follow the American dream, which is one of autonomy and being paid for your skills."

The American dream, Ducheneaux says, doesn't work on the reservation.

"It's not in our nature to turn our back on people who need us," she continues. "Our people without even realizing it sometimes are still living in a tiospaye system, because any success we've had as a people—success in material wealth—is because we can depend on each other."

Studies show food stability, affordability, and access is severely limited for Native communities. According to a report from the USDA's Economic Research Service released in December, just 25.6 percent of all tribal areas were within a mile's distance from a supermarket, compared with 58.8 percent of the total U.S. population.

The latest USDA data also shows 23.5 million people nationwide live in a food desert—that is to say, their access to a grocery store and healthy, affordable food is limited—and more than half of those people are low income. Many tribal communities and urban areas with high populations of Native people are considered food deserts.

Given the staggering rates of poverty, diseases like diabetes, and unem- 10 ployment for Natives nationwide—higher for those living on reservations—both Snowbird and Ducheneaux point to the many economic and health benefits of individuals creating their own energies, whether it's food, fuel and power, or social capital.

Returning to traditional roots in a literal sense is also what drives Snowbird, who has lived in Colorado Springs for more than 20 years. "We as indigenous people have gotten farther away from our traditional food sources than anyone else in this country, and I think that's why we have this sort of swelling epidemic of diabetes and obesity in Indian Country, because we're losing the knowledge of our traditional foods," says Snowbird, 40.

Some 440,000 people live in the Colorado Springs area, and Snowbird works with both Native and non-Native organizations throughout her region to educate and promote the benefits of urban food production, known in some places as backyard or micro farming. She leads educational classes for children and adults, including seed cultivation, plant recognition, harvesting, livestock butchering, and more.

"You can't be sovereign if you can't feed yourself," says Snowbird, borrowing a line from Winona LaDuke (Anishinaabe), an environmental activist and founder of Honor the Earth. "One of the ways colonizers controlled Indian people was to take our food sources away. Let's reclaim our food.

"We have to teach our kids it's not just about preserving our cultures and language; it's about restorative stewardship and about knowing where food comes from, who tribally it comes from," Snowbird says. "Indigenous food is medicine. And food brings everyone together." . . .

Snowbird learned to appreciate indigenous food systems from her father, 15 who hunted wild game and imparted an appreciation for knowing where your dinner comes from and how to prepare it beyond simply opening a box and heating up the contents.

But being known throughout Colorado Springs as "the Goat Lady" and earning a reputation as a knowledgeable indigenous educator didn't happen until a few years ago, when Snowbird spearheaded a city-wide movement to change and educate people on the local laws of urban food production.

Now Snowbird manages the Colorado Springs Urban Homesteading support group, which boasts roughly 1,200 members. Through that group, Snowbird leads several classes per season on animal husbandry, butchering, and more with her fiery brand of wit and know-how.

Perhaps closer to her heart, however, are the lessons she imparts to the city's urban Native youth. Colorado Springs School District 11, in which Snowbird's two daughters, ages 11 and 13, are enrolled, has the only Title VII Indian Education Program in the city.

"I talk to Title VII kids about what indigenous food is—that it's not just buffalo or corn," she explains. "I try to break it down for them in terms of what they ate at lunch that day, even if it was junk food."

Thanks in large part to Snowbird's efforts, the program has several 20 garden beds and a greenhouse growing traditional Native edibles, including Apache brown-striped sunflower seeds, . . . Pueblo chiles, and more.

"I come in sometimes and kids are bouncing off all the walls," Snowbird says. "But the moment you get their hands in the dirt, it's like all that contact with the earth just calms them."

The children also learn to grow, harvest and cook with chokecherries, prickly pears, beans, and other local vegetation.

"Starting the kids off with food lets us also discuss Indian issues without putting people on the defensive," Snowbird explains. "It's hard to get mad when you're talking about food."

Re-introducing and re-popularizing indigenous foods and traditional cooking, especially among Native youth, will help strengthen Native people and the communities they live in, Snowbird insists.

Snowbird admits maintaining a lifestyle committed to food sovereignty 25 can be hard on her tight budget. However, she says it helps her save and earn money in the long run. Snowbird is able to collect, grow, use and sell or barter with the milk, eggs, meat, vegetables, cleaning and toiletry items, and other useful goods produced on her property.

"I'm not completely self-sufficient by any means. But urban homesteading . . . is about as traditional as you can get," she insists. "It's living off the land within the radius of where you live and knowing the Creator has put what you need right where you are." . . .

For outsiders following along on Facebook as Ducheneaux and her family transition to living efficiently and sustainably, the process of building an ecodome and maintaining a traditional garden may have seemed as easy as digging a hole.

Weaving textiles and harvesting corn, two ways Snowbird practices sustainability.

Except that the hole in question—12 feet across and 4 to 6 feet deep in which the ecodome sits—took three months to dig out back in 2012, thanks to heavy rains and a landscape of gumbo.

"It was so much work," Ducheneaux recalls. "We had to move the gumbo out one wheelbarrow at a time."

But the effort, shared by about seven members of Ducheneaux's 30 tiospaye—including her mom, siblings, and their spouses, as well as volunteers—has been well worth it.

On 10 acres of family land on the Cheyenne River reservation, Ducheneaux and her family are creating the Tatanka Wakpala Model Sustainable Community. The family has funded the project with help from Honor the Earth and Bread of Life Church. . . .

The shell of the small, ecodome home—which the family learned to build via video and trial-by-error—is complete, and a garden featuring plants indigenous to the area produces hundreds of pounds of produce each year.

Considering hers is a reservation located within counties consistently listed as some of the poorest in the nation, and recognizing the tribe suffers from insufficient and inefficient housing where utility bills can reach into the high hundreds or more during the winter months, Ducheneaux hopes her family's model sparks a trend for other tribal members.

"We really believe that even people who aren't eco-friendly will be inspired by our use of wind and solar energy. We put up our own electric system and we'll never have to pay another utility bill," Ducheneaux says.

"We were waiting for the blueprint to drop in our laps. Then we realized 35 no one was going to do it for us, so we said we'd do it ourselves. We'll make mistakes and figure it out.". . .

"What we have going on out there is a desire to be more self-sufficient. When we sat around talking about this, we asked ourselves, 'What do we need?'" Ducheneaux explains. "We needed to start feeding ourselves and taking responsibility for our own food needs. . . . Not just growing food and raising animals, but going back to our Lakota traditions and treating the Earth respectfully by using what it gives us.". . .

Living in an urban or reservation setting provides those who want to live sustainably unique challenges, both Snowbird and Ducheneaux say.

"One of the challenges is being so far away from everything," Ducheneaux says of rural reservation life. "For a lot of our volunteers, it's eye-opening for them that the hardware store is a one-hour trip just in one direction."

Planning far ahead is key, Ducheneaux says.

Infrastructure, including a severe lack of Internet connectivity, weather, 40 and a disinterested tribal government can also be setbacks, although Ducheneaux notes the latter can benefit sustainability projects due to few, if any, restrictions on things like harvesting rainwater or land use.

For urban Natives, being disconnected from tribal knowledge—for instance, the indigenous names and uses of plants—is a major disadvantage, Snowbird said.

When someone in the community comes forward with that knowledge, it's often exploited for profit, and the people who would benefit most—namely Native youth—are left out.

"I always find it surprising how removed from the whole food process people are; they don't know or care where their food comes from," says Snowbird, who harvests edibles on hikes through the mountains or on strolls through downtown. She tries to combat this by giving eggs and other food produced on her property to those who wouldn't—or couldn't—normally buy organic in a supermarket.

"Pretty soon those people are asking me for more eggs and then we're talking about how they can get started with chickens in their backyard or growing herbs on their window sills," Snowbird says, adding those conversations eventually lead to discussions on indigenous issues, regardless of whether the person is Native or not. "We're trying to put the culture back in agriculture."

Thinking about the Text

1. Taté Walker highlights two projects that, according to one of their leaders, are "trying to put the culture back in agriculture" (44). What does that statement mean and what is its underlying concept? How well does Walker explain that concept? Why do you think so? Point to specific examples to support your conclusion.

2. Walker's interviewee Monycka Snowbird expresses surprise and dismay that people don't know or care where their food comes from. How much do you know about the plant (and perhaps animal) sources of what you eat? Would you, for example, recognize a potato plant? an avocado tree? Are you satisfied with your current level of knowledge? Does reading Walker's article motivate you to learn more about where your food comes from? Why or why not?

3. Without thinking about the original source of Walker's article, what impression do you have of its intended **AUDIENCE**? Point to **EVIDENCE** to support your reasoning. What might Walker have done differently if writing for a magazine or blog with a nearly all-Native readership or a large-circulation daily newspaper? Why do you think so? Explain your responses.

4. Much of the writing that promotes organic, locally sourced food emphasizes the health aspects of those choices, but Walker's interviewees take a broader approach—the health aspects of communities and the environment itself. What are some of the most serious problems facing your local community? Might a project based on any of the practices described by Walker serve to address one or more of these problems? If so, how? Describe what you envision might happen. If not, why not? Discuss your ideas with classmates.

5. Walker's article focuses on Indigenous communities in Colorado and South Dakota. Not so long ago, however, virtually every region of the now United States was occupied by Indigenous communities that derived their foods, depending on climate and geographical conditions, in the ways that Snowbird and Ducheneaux describe. What are/were the traditional foods of the area where you live? What did the Native people of your region plant? How were meals prepared from these foods? Write a **REPORT**; do **RESEARCH** using library sources, museums, online sources, and perhaps interviews with older relatives or neighbors. Be sure to appropriately document all of the sources you find.

Contesting Standardized English

MISSY WATSON

CONSIDER ALL THAT WE MISS when we require just one variety of a language, just one set of discourse conventions, when we stop listening or stop reading because listening or reading takes too much work. And consider which communities such exclusion benefits and which communities it hurts.

For nearly half a century, fields like applied linguistics, sociolinguistics, teaching English as a second language, second language writing, new literacy studies, composition and rhetoric, and education have revealed a wealth of research on the nature of language and literacy, discoveries that help expose just how nonsensical, fundamentally impossible, and downright unjust it is to exclude all other language varieties from public and academic discourse in order to safeguard and perpetuate standardized English. (I have intentionally used *standardized English* rather than *Standard English* throughout this article in order to indicate that there isn't actually a language we might call "Standard English" so much as there is a version of English that we actively standardize.)

MISSY WATSON is assistant professor of composition studies at City College of New York, where her research focuses on composition pedagogies, translingual writing, and related topics. This 2018 essay was published in *Academe*, the magazine of the American Association of University Professors, an organization with more than 45,000 members across the United States.

All dialects are linguistically equal and capable of meeting communicative needs. Languages and dialects spoken by individuals are multiple, intermingling, and (thus) always changing. Despite our instinct to preserve, homogenize, and standardize just one variety, no single variety is *actually* superior, we don't *actually* need a single homogeneous variety of language in order to communicate effectively, and, even if we wanted to (and we shouldn't), we can't *actually* stop languages, including standardized English, from changing.

We teachers and scholars have observed that our students are already linguistically diverse. Indeed, our students bring with them an abundance of useful and sophisticated linguistic and rhetorical resources that we should be tapping into, supporting, and strengthening. However, some of us have yet to recognize that the linguistic and rhetorical repertoires of some students are indeed useful and sophisticated; these students' lack of fluency in standardized English is the measurement by which we deem them deficient instead.

Meanwhile, we know that our students' linguistic and educational backgrounds continue to expand and that acquiring English as an additional language and standardized English as an additional dialect can take years or a lifetime, not semesters. It is nearly impossible for some individuals to gain native-like proficiency in another language (especially when they have learned the language after what linguists call the "critical period" in childhood). We are also acutely aware that language and identity are inextricably linked and that societal attitudes about language (especially about which languages are to be considered inferior) affect the lived experiences and material realities of language communities. We understand that errors in speech and writing are inevitable in many native and nonnative English speakers, no matter how many years of instruction and practice they've had. Many people across our nation and globe will not or cannot attain proficiency in standardized English; their choice to pursue—or not to pursue—mastery of standardized English, however, is not indicative of the inherent superiority of standardized English or the intellectual capabilities (or lack thereof) of speakers.

Research tells us that standardized English was historically (and continues to be) modeled after the speech of privileged white communities and that it remains one of many tools used to maintain social and racial hierarchies. We've learned that our preferences for standardized English, and for any language variety for that matter, are socially constructed. And we understand that standardized English undeniably harms individuals in emotional, psychological, social, and material ways.

Scholars have traced how standardized English works to exclude groups from public discourse, education, and employment opportunities. We've come to recognize that assimilation and eradication efforts have not succeeded in leveling the playing field. We're now well aware of the potentially devastating effects of demanding that so-called nontraditional students assimilate to standardized English and "standard" academic discourse, especially at the expense of their home languages, discourses, and identities. Yet, even when we respect their language differences and encourage them to preserve their full linguistic repertoires in contexts beyond our classroom walls, we, as teachers, harm students' senses of identity and community by telling them their other languages are not welcome in academic spaces.

We can no longer justify resorting to enforcing this oppressive variety (in composition courses and beyond) with claims that it's in our students' best interest for us to teach and assess only standardized English. The myth that standardized English will save students becomes especially apparent when we examine research in sociology and critical race studies that demonstrates how race, not the learning of standardized English, is the biggest factor in determining one's socioeconomic status and employment opportunities. Race—not employability, not intellect, not educability—determines stratification in rates of literacy and educational achievement.

Composition and Standardized English

I certainly play my part in perpetuating standardized English and the harms that come with it. I'm doing it right now with my use of standardized English in the writing of this essay. I regularly preach to my graduate students the need to adopt more informed and more inclusive views of language and literacy, and while I have much to say about how I do infuse different approaches and dispositions into my composition classrooms, I find myself, semester after semester, struggling to combat, reimagine, and revise my implicit and explicit enforcements and endorsements of standardized English.

And of course I'm struggling. There are lots of pragmatic reasons why. Historically, that's what composition classes like the ones I teach are typically centered around: teaching and assessing standardized English. And, after all, fostering mastery of standardized English has long been one of the

Missy Watson takes a clear position on her topic, and also offers a generous explanation of other points of view. Find out more about how to do that on pp. 170–71.

10

expected outcomes of higher education at large, which systematizes standardized English's superiority in our institutional structures, presenting relentless roadblocks to those who push back. It's difficult enough to raise awareness and persuade others that a problem actually exists (which, of course, many have tried to do for nearly fifty years).

Making the situation more complicated, most students are already accustomed to the expectation that they learn standardized English, and many are comfortable with that expectation and want such instruction. Employers and everyday citizens across the globe will continue to judge and discriminate against those who do not successfully use standardized English; students know this, and we're expert at reminding them of it. And, truth be told, we enforce standardized English partly because we ourselves are steeped in and benefit from the tradition of doing so: standardized English is what we learned in school and is what we've been trained to use and teach.

Some of my fellow composition teachers have other concerns. I've heard objections such as, "I barely have time to cover the curriculum at my college, much less infuse new approaches to language diversity," or "I myself don't have time to learn about how to treat writing and language differently, and my institution doesn't support professional development," or "Taking such radical approaches in my classroom could cost me my job." These are reasonable stances, highlighting the varied costs for teachers who work against the tide. Yet they are all the more reason for all of academe to begin taking a closer look at the prospect of—and, indeed, to begin taking more responsibility for—contesting the precedence of standardized English. No single teacher or discipline should alone bear the weight of this complicated dilemma. This should be a professional concern, across disciplines and campuses.

Standard Language Ideology

Perhaps the reality that standardized English works to oppress as well as to empower is still news to some professionals in higher education. Collectively, we've certainly been far better at focusing only on the benefits of learning and using standardized English. And perhaps that is one reason why we have not yet faced this issue in solidarity.

But what of those teacher-scholars like me, who have long known the reality of standardized English and still enforce it? Why do we do it? Why do we hesitate to fight standardized English even though we have long known of the damages such enforcement can cause? Of the fact that it only exists because it is tied to, authorized by, and serves people in power? Of the ways it more often serves as a *gate* rather than a *key* to success?

We do it because standard language ideology is massive and feels 15 impenetrable. Drawing on scholarship by linguists James Milroy and Rosina Lippi-Green, I have come to a working definition of *standard language ideology* as the unquestioned belief system that assigns the written language variety of a privileged group as standard (and superior) and all others nonstandard (and inferior), a worldview uncritically assumed neutral and commonsensical but used as an instrument for social stratification and maintaining the interests of privileged groups.

Standard language ideology is deeply entrenched in the perspectives of the masses in the United States. For the most part, those individuals and groups who are the most subjugated through its dominance subscribe to it just as much as the privileged white groups who most benefit from it. Until standard language ideology is combatted on a large scale across public settings and our students' future employers come to accept other varieties of language, we reason, we had better just help our students learn the language of power.

We wouldn't say such things if we were talking about racism, classism, sexism, ableism, homophobia, or xenophobia—that these ideologies are just too big to overcome, that they're too ingrained in the worldviews of our citizens and in the structures of society, that we ought to just settle for working *with them* rather than *against them*.

We wouldn't say, at least not in modern times, that it's in the best interest of every woman, person of color, LGBTQ person, immigrant, and working-class individual to just assimilate to the ways of upper-middle-class, hetero, able-bodied white men in power.

Of course, we know that many marginalized groups have long had to work within the constraints of such norms and dominant discourses. But, no, we don't make such demands in the face of such exclusion and oppression. Instead, we fight it, in ways big and small.

Yet, most of us across the disciplines are inclined to say, without pause 20 or hesitation, that it's in our students' best interest to master standardized English. We say that diverse groups of people should either eradicate their language differences or get darn good at switching them off in order to function in public settings without having to face discrimination.

The Politics of English

Why do we see language as a more acceptable basis for discrimination than characteristics such as race, class, gender, sexuality, and ability? Is it because language is considered a mere habit or practice that can be learned and reshaped rather than a part of our physiology, psychology, and identity? Are our pragmatic concerns more powerful than the harms caused by standard language ideology?

Are we too steeped in standard language ideology ourselves? As authorities on standardized English who, frankly, make our living perpetuating standard language ideologies, are we in too deep to reimagine our professional identities, to redefine the substance of what we do? And why are we so uncomfortable with even pondering these questions? Is it simply too unbelievable, too painful to consider that our best intentions for improving the lives and opportunities available to our students by enforcing standardized English may be, in a larger scheme, part of a problem we now must face?

To be fair, in today's globalized world, where occasions for cross-cultural communication increase daily, awareness of standard language ideology has widened, and larger communities of scholars and teachers across the globe work more explicitly to address and combat it. Many have already begun chipping away at standard language ideology, and we can and will continue to do just that.

I also believe, though, that we must continue working toward more unity on this as a problem facing higher education. The full politics of English, including standard language ideology, is an issue with which all professionals in academe must contend. We must join forces in revising the purposes of higher education, redefining the role standardized English plays within it, redesigning course outcomes and curricula, reimagining pedagogy, and retraining our community of professionals across the disciplines about how to better address the linguistic diversity at all of our campuses.

We must also disseminate our knowledge about standard language ideology and the harms it causes as widely as we can. We must share with the public, all educators, and all students what we have come to know about the politics of standardized English. And we must further examine how standard language ideology manifests itself in individuals, classrooms,

25

colleges and universities, and other public spaces across and beyond our communities and nation so that we'll be better equipped to combat it.

To start, we must confront our own privileging of standardized English and the judgments we ourselves make about the language differences of our students, our colleagues, our neighbors.

We have for too long remained complacent, turning a blind eye to the harms caused by the very language variety we're compelled to uphold. Let's get busy undoing that.

Thinking about the Text

1. Missy Watson poses this question: "Why do we see language as a more acceptable basis for discrimination than characteristics such as race, class, gender, sexuality, and ability?" (21). How does she answer her question? Summarize her **ARGUMENT**. Is it persuasive? Why or why not? Explain your reasoning, and point to examples from the essay to support your response.

2. Watson is a teacher who admits to struggling with her own classroom practices and assumptions about standardized English. How, if at all, does her admission affect her **AUTHORITY** to address an audience of her peers on the topic? Do you think she should have omitted mentioning that she struggles with the issue? Why or why not?

3. Watson, a university professor, is writing in a professional journal for an **AUDIENCE** of other teachers. What might she have had to do differently if she were presenting the same arguments to an audience of students? What examples or explanations, if any, would she have omitted? What else might she have wanted to include? She concludes with a proposal—a challenge, really—for her audience. How, if at all, would the challenge be different for a student audience?

4. Would your attitude toward writing a paper change if you didn't have to be concerned about following the conventions of standardized English? Might you be able to express yourself more clearly in a variety of English that more closely resembles your usual way of speaking or thinking? Might you want to include words or phrases from another language? Another dialect of English? How might your writing be different? To **REFLECT** on these questions, think about your experiences writing at school over the years. Consider your formal

and informal experiences with learning the rules of standardized English, your assessment of your language abilities, and your level of comfort with different varieties of English.

5. Watson calls on educators to redefine the role of standardized English and redesign course outcomes and the ways that writing is taught and evaluated. Suppose that your school is considering Watson's proposed actions and is soliciting input from students. Write a letter to the administration taking a **STANCE**. Consider addressing the following questions in your letter: How important do you consider competence in standardized English to be for your life and career plans? In the classes you've taken so far, is there too much emphasis on standardized English? too little emphasis? Have you ever felt singled out or discriminated against for your use of language (including your **DIALECT**, your pronunciation, or any other feature)? Have you ever felt that your academic advancement has been hindered by your language use? Have you ever wanted to learn more about the many dialectal varieties of English?

The Internet Is Not Ruining Grammar

JESSICA WILDFIRE

MILLENNIALS CATCH A LOT OF FLAK—for their selfies, their avocado toast, and their unconventional spelling. I work at a university, and I can't go a week without hearing someone complain about how the internet has corrupted English.

"Nobody cares about proofreading anymore," one professor told me a few days ago. "Smartphones have ruined our students."

Young people's grammar is practically the only thing you can get faculty to agree on these days. "Oh, they can't spell or punctuate at all," I hear. It's the ultimate echo chamber.

Grammarians have published hundreds of books and op-eds declaiming the end of language as we know it. All because of one evil technology. On top of that, I've gotten more than one email from Grammarly reps wanting me to adopt their app for my classroom. They promise to magically remove errors from my students' writing.

But not so fast. What if I *want* them to make "errors"? What if I want them to play around with language? 5

JESSICA WILDFIRE is (presumably) the *nom de plume*, or pen name, of a writer and teacher—an "unfluencer," as her bio states—who publishes essays on issues of grammar, gender, self-development, popular culture, and more; the image that always accompanies her writing may or may not resemble the actual author. This essay first appeared on *Medium* in August 2018. She also writes a *Substack* newsletter and tweets from @JessicaLexicus.

Language Is Always Changing

Here's the truth: Young people aren't breaking the rules. The rules are changing. As linguists know, language lives in a constant flux. You can't pin it down. Even what we think of as a single language has several varieties—dialects, regionalisms, accents.

Each variety has its own standards and ways of deviating from them. People cross back and forth between language borders, sneaking words and rules across customs.

You can't build walls between languages and their varieties any more than you can hope to build a wall between two countries. You can try, but it won't work. As poet Robert Frost said:

> Something there is that doesn't love a wall,
> That sends the frozen-ground-swell under it,
> And spills the upper boulders in the sun;
> And makes gaps even two can pass abreast.

You can't build walls around languages, and you can't keep them from morphing. Language is like water. The internet has dissolved all kinds of barriers over recent decades. It's also ushering in new ways of communicating, including new modes of grammar.

Welcome to the Period

We don't even really understand most of our silly rules. They didn't always 10 exist. They evolved. For starters, consider the period. This bit of punctuation has been around a while, first originating in the third century with Greek philosopher Aristophanes and becoming more common in the 15th century thanks to Italian printer and publisher Aldus Manutius. They work for me. I like periods. They're handy.

But let's not fool ourselves into believing they're timeless. Our use of periods has changed a helluva lot since their invention. Of course, they have their uses. When we're writing an email or a report, they help us end our sentences.

But guess what? If you end a text with a period, that means you're pissed off. It's why so many people drop them from messages on their phones and on social media. Online, the meaning of a period changes.

Americans have lived in crisis mode for centuries when it comes to punctuation and spelling. English courses for freshmen in college began appearing in earnest around the turn of the 20th century, in part because everyone was freaking out about students' spelling and grammar.

Since then, things have stayed pretty much the same. No better, no worse. And there's nothing extra we can or should do about it. Let language play.

How We Learn Grammar

The average American feels entitled to correct the grammar in every tweet they see. And yet they probably have no idea how we even learn grammar. Put simply, we acquire the rules by *living* them. Not by learning them. Not through worksheets. Or tests. Most humans have all the grammatical knowledge they need before they even finish elementary school. 15

Kids know how to construct sentences.

The problem is written punctuation. Again, we don't learn that by drills or memorizing rules. Almost every study in education, linguistics, and writing points to the same conclusion: We learn to punctuate by reading. Intuitively.

Honestly, do you really understand every single piece of logic that dictates when a sentence ends? Can you give a perfect definition of a sentence? I'll bet you can't. The best grammar guides in the world can't.

If there's one thing I'd like people to understand, it's this: You can never teach grammar by explaining it.

The internet doesn't cause bad grammar. Bad schooling does. Bad explanations do. And we accomplish nothing through hysterics. All our testing of students has done nothing but make things worse. 20

What a lot of people consider bad grammar isn't bad at all. Just different.

Usage Matters Most

A handful of snobs have always tried to tell everyone else how to write and speak. Look back at the history of English and you'll find hundreds of guides on how to use language "properly." These "experts" took rules from other languages—like Latin—and forced them on English. That's where we get the absurd warning against ending sentences with prepositions.

In Latin, it's actually impossible to end a sentence with a preposition. English allows you to.

So do it.

Apply this idea to social media and you'll understand what's happening. People who communicate online, with phones, are developing their own usage conventions. Ones that make sense to them. 25

These conventions include simplified, alternate spellings. Abbreviations. Emojis. And innovations in punctuation.

It's not about error in the old-school sense. Languages have always evolved, and curmudgeons have always whined about it. Roman school teachers did, just like your grandparents do now.

Different World, Different Rules

Nearly a decade ago, linguist David Crystal published a book titled *Txting: The Gr8 Db8*. He wrote it in response to all those doomsayers announcing the start of the apocalypse shortly after the launch of Twitter. Crystal's book gathered mounds of evidence to show how young people, or internet users in general, understand grammar.

Many of us believe students use text-speak in their academic writing now because they don't know any better. Yet studies by linguists have shown that most students actually *do* know how to switch back and forth. If they use Twitterisms, they're doing so intentionally. Or because they're in a hurry.

Not because they're stupid. Or uneducated. 30

As linguists already know, this is how people grow up in multilingual environments. They don't sit in classrooms memorizing rules, correcting sentences, and filling out conjugation tables. They talk on the street. They watch movies. They sing along to their favorite songs. They make mistakes. Over and over again.

Language standardization is important. But not for its own sake.

Yes, standardized rules help people understand each other better. But we need to stop treating every single deviation from standard English as a sin—especially online. It's not. Instead, we should educate everyone about the malleability of language and how grammars change situationally and over time. It's a lot harder than being a traditionalist, but maybe it's worth a shot.

We agree. It's *not* about "errors in the old school sense." Still, we have a whole chapter about polishing and editing your writing. It's about navigating what's expected in academic writing. Check out Ch. 35.

Thinking about the Text

1. Jessica Wildfire boldly asserts "Let language play" (14). What does she mean by that? Who is the **AUDIENCE** she is trying to persuade? Why? Do you agree? Why or why not?

2. According to Wildfire, periods in text messages are used differently than periods in longer prose. In texts, she notes, a period indicates anger. Do you agree with her assessment? Why or why not? How do you read a period in a text message? What factors might influence your interpretation (length of the message, how well you know the sender, etc.)? Why?

3. We don't actually know who Wildfire is—not her real name or where she teaches, her academic background, or anything other than the cryptic phrases she uses in her online bios. We take it on faith that the accompanying image truly depicts the author. Does the lack of concrete information inter-fere with her ability to speak with **AUTHORITY** on the topic of grammar rules and grammar learning? Why or why not? Explain your reasoning.

4. Regardless of where or how you were previously schooled, by the time you've reached the writing class you're taking now, you have surely encountered some rules of English grammar. Wildfire advocates eliminating the explicit teaching of grammar, **ARGUING** that such instruction simply isn't effective and that students will learn grammar rules naturally, "by living them" (15). Do you agree? Why or why not? Explain your reasoning.

5. As Wildfire notes, people who use their phones a lot for written communica-tions "are developing their own usage conventions" (25). What usage conven-tions are you developing? Probably you are conscious of some of them, while others are more automatic and unnoticed. Look over your texts, posts, and other online communications, and spend a day or two paying attention to what conventions you use in each communication and what your reasons are in that specific moment. Then write a brief personal usage guide similar to what you might find in a handbook or style guide. Include punctuation, capital-ization, spelling, abbreviations, emoji use, and any other factors you consider relevant.

My Brain Is in a War It Will Lose: Writing with Huntington's Disease

CARRIE JADE WILLIAMS

(start voice controls)

(capital) **I regularly trespass** (period)(capital) **In secret and not I** (apostrophe) **m not literally breaking in anywhere** (comma) **but my mind wanders** (period)(capital) **Daydreamer** (comma) **would be the polite term people use when they mean I** (apostrophe) **m now seriously forgetful** (period)(new paragraph)

I readjust the headset, make sure the microphone is right in front of my mouth and talk the computer to life because my words literally have power.

"Open document," I say, and the screen obeys, presenting a document that records my words in text.

(indent)(capital) **Gratitude creeps in when I'm not expecting it** (comma) **because without this** (capital) **Assistive** (capital) **Technology** (capital) **I would officially be irrelevant now** (period)(capital) **Silenced** (period)(capital) **Forgotten** (period)(capital) **Because** (capital) **I can no longer type** (period)(capital) **Or hold a pen** (period)(capital) **Or sometimes get my words out** (period)

5

CARRIE JADE WILLIAMS began writing at age thirty-one when she received a diagnosis for Huntington's disease, a rare degenerative disorder. Seven months later, she won the 2020 Bodley Head/*Financial Times* Essay Prize for this essay. Her *Instagram* is @carriejadewrites.

I speak the words on to the page. The computer translates and I become one with the page. Something that was once so easy, speed-typing words, sending emails, working, living, now reduced to a laborious task that requires concentration, determination and technology.

I can still communicate, I think, *I still have so much to say.*

The day I was handed my diagnosis I'd never even heard of it. As the news seeped in, it wasn't death that frightened me, or even dying, it was being a burden, being irrelevant.

"Your genetic test showed something," the neurologist had said. "Unfortunately you have something called Huntington's disease."

At the time I'd been relieved. I'd never heard of Huntington's disease so I naively presumed it couldn't be that bad. Sensing my positivity, he quickly extinguished it.

"Imagine Parkinson's meets ALS meets Alzheimer's, in one disease—that's what you have."

In the moments that followed I learnt there was no cure. Very few treatments. That I was terminal. That my brain, slowly being destroyed by this disease, was in a war that it would lose. In the weeks that followed I refused to even discuss Assistive Tech, let alone accept I needed it. Until typing became so challenging I had to admit defeat.

That memory haunts me every time I sit down at this desk and slide the headset over my ears. I'm grateful for the technology, for the ability to still communicate, but there are also those moments that chisel away at my self-esteem, because when I look at the page I see another challenge: that once this is finished I will need to edit it. Remove the voice commands. Pretend I didn't need them. Make them fit your world.

(indent)(capital) **You fight infections** (period)(capital) **Fight cancer** (period) (capital) **But** (capital) **Huntington** (apostrophe) **s disease is like moving into a town where you go to fade** (period)(capital) **And everyone wants to leave** (period)(new paragraph)

I tell the computer to save my work and prepare my body to stand. I think the thought *stand* but know that my body will only obey when it wants to. I need a break.

(indent)(capital) **For me buying chocolate has become a political act** (period) (capital) **Not any old chocolate** (period)(capital) **It has to be** (capital) **Swiss chocolate** (period)(capital) **Silky** (period)(capital) **Smooth** (period)(capital)

Ideally from(capital) **Marks and** (capital) **Spencer**[1] **because somehow that makes me feel even more indulgent** (period)(new paragraph)

As so frequently happens in M&S I'm stood between two women in the queue. Shopping basket lady who I bet owns a labradoodle. She looks like the type. Not that I think there's anything wrong with labradoodles, or labradoodle owners, but with every inch of my temporal lobe gobbled up by this disease comes a darker sense of humour that sometimes only I understand.

Mrs Labradoodle has done her weekly shop. Freshly squeezed orange juice, pastries and pasta sauce placed skilfully on the conveyor belt. I watch her. I watch her knowing that I will never be her age. I am 31 and if I make it to 35, I'll be doing well, so watching her at what I guess is around 55 I remind myself to let go of the breath I'm holding.

I place the chocolate bar down, fumble with my purse and pay. My political act complete. See, when people talk to me about Switzerland, they don't mean skiing. They are politely asking if I'd considered Dignitas. The Euthanasia clinic. I know they think they are being compassionate but all I hear is, "if I were forced to live your life, I'd choose death." When I'm still living, albeit differently, my neurodiversity doesn't equate to me as making my life valueless, it just means things have changed. I eat that Swiss chocolate because I'm determined to live.

Back home, I face the computer. My work littered with the commands　20
that I'm forced to use. I start to edit, to erase my disability. It's like playing hide and seek: the structures that make my work mine are forced to hide in a forest, replaced by what the neuroaverage world wants. Full stops. Question marks. They want me to pretend that I can press those keys on my laptop just like everyone else.

(indent)(capital) **And** (capital) **I do it** (period)(capital) **I want to fit in** (period)(capital) **Desperate to be accepted** (period)(capital) **But somehow** (comma) **with all the pretending** (comma) **editing and hiding** (comma) **instead of celebrating my disability** (comma)(capital) **I** (apostrophe) **m left questioning why inclusivity includes everyone** (comma) **but women like me** (period)(capital) **Neurodiverse** (period)(capital) **Brain damaged** (period) (capital) **Disabled** (period)(new paragraph)

1. *Marks and Spencer*: A major British retail chain selling clothes, home products, and groceries. It promotes itself as offering exclusive selections and luxury food items. [Editor's note]

Assistive Technology isn't perfect. My bank still isn't fully accessible; like so many things online, accessibility is an afterthought, the poor relation. Even though there are so many of us, people like me who need information to be presented a little differently to welcome us into the community.

(indent)(capital) **The way** (capital) **I experience the world co** (dash) **exists with** (capital) **Assistive** (capital) **Tech** (period)(capital) **It keeps the world open for me** (comma) **but without pressure and accountability most things online remain out of reach** (period)(new paragraph)

"Delete bracket, replace word, symbol." I may be a wilted flower by the standards of the world, one that must accept that the life I'd planned for will no longer be a reality, but I'm still in charge of my laptop, my words that dance across the page and speak the same language as the world.

The process of removing myself from the page is time-consuming, and 25 although I try to see myself in the blank page around the words, all I see is where I need to be erased to make the world accept me. (capital) **Gone**, becomes (invisible me) **Gone**.

Once completed, as I hold the page, I can't help but feel betrayed. When my work is finished, edited, and polished, although it ends up digestible for the world, it somehow does so by making my experience less.

(end voice controls)

Carrie Jade Williams reflects on her circumstances and on her writing, and her reflections help make her essay sharp and insightful. Learn more about applying reflection to your own writing on pp. 119–121.

Thinking about the Text

1. Carrie Jade Williams principally **NARRATES** her struggle to write given the limitations placed on her by Huntington's disease, but she does share one additional personal detail—her penchant for Swiss chocolate. What does that chocolate mean to Williams and why is it so important to tell us about it?

2. How would you describe the **TONE** of Williams's essay? Point to specific passages to support your response. Williams expresses anger and bitterness as well as hopeful determination—a combination that could be quite incompatible. How successfully does Williams convey those conflicting feelings in her essay? What observations did you make in order to arrive at your responses?

3. Williams intersperses paragraphs of polished prose with paragraphs that show the keyboarded commands of her dictation, including instructions for

text appearance (placing a comma, capitalizing a letter) that most people type out with their fingers and generally take for granted. Which paragraphs does Williams select for showing in the dictated, unedited form? Is there a pattern or common element to those paragraphs? Why might Williams have chosen those paragraphs and not others? How does this **DESIGN** of contrasting elements of the text relate to Williams's main argument? Explain your reasoning.

4. How have you responded emotionally to Williams's essay? Does anything that she says resonate with your own experiences or with what you may have learned from other people in your life? If you could meet Williams, what might you like to tell her or ask her? How might your conversation go?

5. Although few people have to exert as much effort into expressing themselves in writing as Williams does, everyone struggles, each in our own way, to produce a work of writing that is, in her words, "edited, polished, [and] digestible for the world" (26). What steps do you follow in order to get from the first hazy ideas to a polished and world-ready work? What are your specific struggles? Are they physical? emotional? something else? Do you struggle with technology limitations? What technologies do you use? Pencil? Laptop? Tablet? Phone? A braille writer? Voice-activated dictation? Adaptive devices? Assistive tech? Screen enhancements? Do you require quiet and isolation in order to focus? Do you thrive on noise and/or distractions? Write an essay describing your writing process, its challenges, and your creative solutions. You may want to use one or more **NARRATIVE** examples to enliven your writing.

Credits

ILLUSTRATIONS

TEXT

About the Authors

 **ANDREA A. LUNSFORD** is Professor Emerita of English at Stanford University and has also taught at the University of British Columbia, The Ohio State University, and the Bread Loaf School of English. Her scholarly interests include rhetorical theory, women and the history of rhetoric, collaboration, style, and technologies of writing. She's received the Braddock and Shaughnessy awards for her research on audience and classical rhetoric, and the CCCC Exemplar Award. She is currently completing work on *The Norton Anthology of Rhetoric and Writing*.

 **MICHAL BRODY** is a linguist and independent scholar. She was a founding faculty member of the Universidad de Oriente in Yucatán, Mexico. Her scholarly work centers principally on language pedagogy and politics in the United States and Mexico, as well as on sociolinguistic research on Yucatec Maya. She's a coauthor of *The Little Seagull Handbook* and *Let's Talk with Readings*, and she curates the *Let'sTalkLibrary*, the online readings component of *Let's Talk*. Brody is a 2008 inductee in the Chicago LGBT Hall of Fame.

 **LISA EDE** was Professor Emerita of English at Oregon State University, where she directed the Center for Writing and Learning and taught courses in composition, rhetoric, and literacy studies. She received the Braddock and Shaughnessy awards for her research on audience and classical rhetoric. Her books include *Situating Composition: Composition Studies and the Politics of Location* and (with Andrea A. Lunsford) *Writing Together: Collaboration in Theory and Practice*, among others.

JESSICA ENOCH is Professor of English and Director of the Academic Writing Program at the University of Maryland. Her recent publications include *Domestic Occupations: Spatial Rhetorics and Women's Work*; *Mestiza Rhetorics: An Anthology of Mexicana Activism in the Spanish-Language Press, 1887–1922* (coedited with Cristina Devereaux Ramírez); *Women at Work: Rhetorics of Gender and Labor* (coedited with David Gold); and *Retellings: Opportunities for Feminist Research in Rhetoric and Composition Studies* (coedited with Jordynn Jack).

BEVERLY J. MOSS is Associate Professor and Director of Second-Year Writing in the Department of English at The Ohio State University, where she teaches in the Rhetoric, Composition, and Literacy program, and is Director of the Bread Loaf Teacher Network for the Middlebury Bread Loaf School of English. Her research and teaching interests focus on community literacy, composition theory and pedagogy, and writing center theories and practices. Her books include *Literacy across Communities* and *A Community Text Arises: A Literate Text and a Literacy Tradition in African-American Churches*.

CAROLE CLARK PAPPER has spent four decades teaching writing and rhetoric. Prior to retiring from Hofstra University, where she directed the University Writing Center, she served for many years as the Director of the Ball State University Writing Program (winner of the CCCC Certificate of Excellence 2006–2007). Her continuing scholarly interests include visual literacy, composition theory and pedagogy, and writing center theories and practices.

KEITH WALTERS is Professor Emeritus of Applied Linguistics at Portland State University, where he taught courses in sociolinguistics, discourse analysis, and professional communication. Much of his research has focused on issues of language and identity in Tunisia, where he served as a Peace Corps volunteer, and in the Arab world more broadly. He's a coauthor of two other textbooks, *Everything's an Argument with Readings* and *What's Language Got to Do with It?* Prior to teaching at PSU, he taught in the Linguistics Department at the University of Texas at Austin and in the English Department at The Ohio State University. Most recently, he was a Fulbright scholar in the English Department at Bethlehem University in the West Bank.

About the Alphabet

IF YOU GREW UP IN THE UNITED STATES, the alphabet song may be one of the first things you learned to sing: *a - b - c - d - e - f - g / h - i - j - k - l - m - n - o - p / q - r - s / t - u - v / w - x / y and z / Now I know my abc's / Next time won't you sing with me?* And maybe you had a set of alphabet blocks, twenty-six little letters you could use to make words of your own. Combined, those letters yield everything from the word "Google" to the complete modernized works of Shakespeare. So alphabets are versatile, and perhaps that's part of their fascination. In our grandmothers' day, young women often made alphabet samplers, using fancy stitches to create the letters. Earlier, in medieval times, scribes labored to create highly ornate letters to adorn manuscripts whose words were "illuminated" by the intricate letters, often done in silver and gold.

We had these illuminated letters in mind when we asked Carin Berger to create a modern-day illuminated alphabet for this book. You'll see the results in every chapter, each of which begins with one of the letters Berger created. To us, they represent our old alphabet blocks, our grandmothers' samplers, and the illuminated letters that still dazzle us after many hundreds of years. But look again and you'll see that these letters are also striking images. And instead of being decorated with precious silver and gold leaf, our letters are decorated with bits of everyday text—maps, comics, stationery, receipts, school papers, checks, and so on. In our alphabet, old and new, low tech and high tech, word and image come together to create evocative, timely letters for our book.

And just as modern-day typefaces have names, so too does our alphabet. We call it Author.

The Norton Writer's Prize

*I have something to say to the world, and I have taken
English 12 in order to say it well.*

—W. E. B. DU BOIS

The Norton Writer's Prize recognizes outstanding original nonfiction by undergraduates. All entries are considered for possible publication in Norton texts—in fact, many of the essays that appear in this book were nominated for the prize.

The contest is open to students age 17 and above who are enrolled in an accredited 2- or 4-year college or university. Three cash prizes of $1,000 apiece are awarded annually for coursework submitted during the academic year, one in each of the following three categories:

- Writing by a first-year student in a 2- or 4-year college or university
- Writing by a student in a 2-year college or university
- Writing by a student in a 4-year college or university

Submissions must be between 1,000 and 3,000 words in length. Literacy narratives, literary and other textual analyses, reports, profiles, evaluations, arguments, memoirs, proposals, multimodal pieces, and other forms of original nonfiction will be considered if written by a student age 17 or above in fulfillment of an undergraduate course requirement at an eligible institution. Entries submitted in accordance with the Official Contest Rules will be considered for all applicable prizes, but no more than one prize will be awarded to any single entry.

For full contest rules, eligibility, and instructions on how to enter or nominate students, please visit **wwnorton.com/norton-writers-prize**. For questions, please email us at **composition@wwnorton.com**.

Current and former students of individuals acting as judges are not eligible to enter or win, and any entry recognized by any of the judges will be automatically disqualified. Employees of W. W. Norton & Company, Inc. ("Sponsor"), including Sponsor's corporate affiliates and subsidiaries, as well as such individuals' children and persons living in any of their households are not eligible to enter; nor are authors published by Sponsor, children of Sponsor's authors, previous contest winners (including runners-up) and persons living in their respective households. Void where prohibited. Must be 17 or older at the time of entry. Other restrictions apply.

Author / Title Index

Note: Page numbers in *italics* indicate figures.

Glossary / Index

Note: This glossary / index defines key terms and concepts and directs you to pages in the book where you can find specific information on these and other topics. Please note the words set in SMALL CAPITAL LETTERS are themselves defined in the glossary / index. Page numbers in *italics* indicate figures.

of a source without commenting on its value; an *evaluative annotation* gives an opinion about the source along with a description of it. Features: complete bibliographic information • a brief SUMMARY or DESCRIPTION of each work • evaluative comments (for an evaluative bibliography) • some indication of how each source will inform your RESEARCH • a consistent and concise presentation

ANTECEDENT, 739–43 The NOUN or PRONOUN to which a pronoun refers: Maya lost her wallet.

APA STYLE, 569, 625–72 A system of DOCUMENTATION used in the social sciences. APA stands for the American Psychological Association.

APPENDIX A section at the end of a written work for supplementary material that would be distracting in the main part of the text.

ARGUING A POSITION, 154–94 A GENRE that uses REASONS and EVIDENCE to support a CLAIM. Features: an explicit POSITION • a response to what others have said or done • useful background information • a clear indication of why the topic matters • good REASONS and EVIDENCE • attention to more than one POINT OF VIEW • an authoritative TONE and STANCE • an appeal to readers' values

ARGUMENT, 405–75 Any text that makes a CLAIM supported by REASONS and EVIDENCE.

ARTICLE The word "a," "an," or "the," used to indicate that a NOUN is indefinite (a writer, an author) or definite (the author).

ATTRIBUTION BIAS, 94–95, 524 The tendency to think that our motivations for believing what we believe are objectively good while thinking that those who we disagree with have objectively wrong motivations.

AUDIENCE, 34–35 Those to whom a text is directed—the people who read, listen to, or view the text. Audience is a key part of any RHETORICAL SITUATION.

AUTHORITY, 521 A person or text that is cited as support for a writer's ARGUMENT. A structural engineer may be quoted as an authority on

CLAUSES: When the United States holds a presidential election once every four years, citizens should vote.

COMPOUND-COMPLEX SENTENCE, 710 Two or more MAIN CLAUSES plus one or more SUBORDINATE CLAUSES: When the United States holds a presidential election once every four years, citizens should vote, but voter turnout is often disappointing.

COMPOUND SENTENCE, 706–8 Two or more MAIN CLAUSES joined by a comma and a COORDINATING CONJUNCTION or by a semicolon: The United States holds a presidential election once every four years, but voter turnout is often disappointing.

CONCLUSION The way a text ends, a chance to leave an AUDIENCE thinking about what's been said. Five ways of concluding a college essay: reiterating your point, discussing the implications of your ARGUMENT, asking a question, referring back to your OPENING, or proposing some kind of action.

CONFIRMATION BIAS, 95–96, 98, 524 The tendency to favor and seek out information that confirms what we already believe and to reject and ignore information that contradicts those beliefs.

CONTEXT, 35–36 Part of any RHETORICAL SITUATION, conditions affecting the text such as

what else has been said about a topic; social, economic, and other factors; and any constants such as due date and length.

COORDINATING CONJUNCTION, 707–8, 730, 732 One of these words—"and," "but," "or," "nor," "so," "for," or "yet"—used to join two elements in a way that gives equal weight to each one (bacon <u>and</u> eggs; pay up <u>or</u> get out).

COUNTERARGUMENT, 438, 441 In ARGUMENT, an alternative POSITION or objection to the writer's position. The writer of an argument should not only acknowledge counterarguments but also, if at all possible, accept, accommodate, or refute each counterargument.

COUNT NOUN A word that names something that can be counted (one book, two books). *See also* NONCOUNT NOUN

CREDIBILITY, 422–33 The sense of trustworthiness that a writer conveys through the text.

DIALECT, 36, 693–703 Varieties of LANGUAGE that are spoken by people in a particular region, social class, or ethnic group.

DICTION, 675 Word choice.

DOCUMENTATION, 562–69 Publication information about the sources cited in a text. The documentation usually appears in an abbreviated form in parentheses at the point of CITATION or in an endnote or a footnote. Complete documentation usually appears as a list of WORKS CITED or REFERENCES at the end of the text. Documentation styles vary by discipline. *See also* MLA STYLE and APA STYLE.

DOMINANT IMPRESSION, 463 The overall effect created through specific details when a writer describes something.

DRAFTING, 113–14 The process of putting words on paper or screen. Writers often write several drafts, REVISING each until they achieve their goal or reach a deadline. At that point, they submit a finished final draft.

E

EDITING, 116, 723–66 The process of fine-tuning a text—examining each word, phrase, sentence, and paragraph—to be sure that the text is correct and precise and says exactly what the writer intends. *See also* common errors; DRAFTING; PROOFREADING; REVISION

ELLIPSIS, 552, 754–755 Three spaced dots (. . .) that indicate an omission or a pause.

EMOTIONAL APPEALS, 421–22 Ways that authors appeal to an AUDIENCE's emotions, values, and beliefs by arousing specific feelings — for example, compassion, pity, sympathy, anger, fear. *See also* ETHICAL APPEALS; LOGICAL APPEALS

ESSENTIAL ELEMENT, 761–62 A word, PHRASE, or CLAUSE with information that is necessary for understanding the meaning of a sentence: French is the only language that I can speak.

ETHICAL APPEALS, 422–25 Ways that authors establish CREDIBILITY and AUTHORITY to persuade an AUDIENCE to trust their ARGUMENTS — by showing that they know what they're talking about (for example, by citing trustworthy SOURCES), demonstrating that they're fair (by representing opposing views accurately and even-handedly), and establishing COMMON GROUND. *See also* EMOTIONAL APPEALS; LOGICAL APPEALS

EVIDENCE, 427–33, 453–73 In an ARGUMENT, the data you present to support your REASONS. Such data may include statistics, calculations, EXAMPLES, ANECDOTES, QUOTATIONS, case studies, or anything else that will convince your readers that your reasons are compelling. Evidence should be sufficient (enough to show that the reasons have merit) and relevant (suitable to the argument you're making).

H

HASHTAG, 6, 686, 804, 808 A metadata tag created by placing a number sign (#) in front of a word or unspaced phrase (for example, #Black-LivesMatter), used in social media to mark posts by **KEYWORD** or theme and make them searchable by these tags. Also used to add commentary on a web text outside of the text itself.

HELPING VERB, 751 A **VERB** that works with a **MAIN VERB** to express a tense and mood. Helping verbs include "do," "have," "be," and **MODALS**: Elvis <u>has</u> left the building. Pigs <u>can</u> fly.

I

IMRAD, 55, 289, 773 Acronym representing sections of scientific reports conveying information: introduction (asks a question), methods (tells about experiments), results (states findings), and discussion (tries to make

can stand alone as a sentence: She sang. The world-famous soprano sang several arias.

MAIN VERB, 751 The verb form that presents the action or state. It can stand alone or be combined with one or more HELPING VERB. For example: My dog might have buried your keys. Leslie Jones is a comedian. Alexa was wearing a gown by Milly. The agent didn't appear old enough to drive.

MEDIUM, 767–68 A means for communicating—for example, in print, with speech, or online. *See also* DESIGN

MEMOIR, 468 A GENRE that focuses on something significant from the writer's past. Key features include good story, vivid details, and clear significance.

MISINFORMATION, 4, 92–101, 492 False or inaccurate information that may or may not be intended to deceive (lies, on the other hand, are always told deliberately).

MIXED CONSTRUCTION, 733–36 A sentence that starts out with one structure and ends up with another one: Although bears can be deadly is not a good reason to avoid camping altogether.

MLA STYLE, 569–624 A system of DOCUMENTATION used in the humanities. MLA stands for the Modern Language Association.

MODAL, 763 A HELPING VERB—such as "can," "could," "may," "might," "must," "ought to," "should," "will," or "would"—that does not change form for person or number and indicates probability or necessity.

MODE, 788–90 A way of conveying a message. Writing often uses multiple modes: linguistic, audio, visual, spatial, and/or gestural. *See also* STRATEGIES FOR SUPPORTING AN ARGUMENT, which are also referred to as modes.

MULTIMODAL WRITING, 788–809 Writing that uses more than one MODE of expression, including some combination of words, images, audio, video, links, and so on. Sometimes called "multimedia writing."

N

NARRATION, 468–70 A STRATEGY for presenting information as a story, for telling "what happened." It is a pattern often associated with fiction, but it shows up in all kinds of writing. When used in a REVIEW, a REPORT, or another academic GENRE, narration is used to support a point—not merely to tell an interesting story for its own sake. Narration can serve as the organizing principle for a paragraph or whole text.

NARRATIVE, 195–233 A GENRE that tells a story for the PURPOSE of making a point. Features: a clearly identified event • a clearly described setting • vivid, descriptive details • a consistent POINT OF VIEW • a clear point. *See also* LITERACY NARRATIVE

NARRATIVE SEQUENCING, 468–70 A STRATEGY FOR SUPPORTING AN ARGUMENT and a feature of Black discourse in which speakers link concrete narratives in a sequence that helps to convey their point. Narrative sequencing can make points feel less abstract than they would be if made without narrative examples in an argument.

NONCOUNT NOUN, 747–48 A word that names something that cannot be counted or made plural with certain modifiers or units: information, rice.

NONESSENTIAL ELEMENT, 761–62 A word, phrase, or CLAUSE that gives additional information but that is not necessary for understanding the basic meaning of a sentence: I learned French, which is a Romance language, online. Nonessential elements should be set off by commas.

NOUN A word that refers to a person, place, animal, thing, or idea (director, Stephen King, forest, Amazon River, tree frog, notebook, democracy).
> noncount, 747–48

novels, in MLA style in-text documentation, 575
NPR, 795
NPR Research News, 483

O

Oakland Promise, 294–96, *295*, *296*, 300, 301, 318
Obama, Barack, *32*, 165
object case, 743–45
observations
> as evidence, 429–30
> in field research, 506–7
> participant observation, 506

O'Connor, Diane, 716
"of" / "have," 763
Ohtani, Shohei, 42, *42*
older sources, 492–94
Olson, Ted, 22
One Billion Rising, 135, *136*
The Onion, 98
online sources
> avoiding plagiarism, 568
> evaluating, 520–27
> keeping track of, 515–16
> in lists of references (APA style), 637, 639–40, 646–48
> in works cited (MLA style), 598–99

op-ed, in works cited (MLA style), 591–92

OPENING, 714–17 The way a text begins, which plays an important role in drawing an AUDIENCE in. Some ways of opening a college essay: with a dramatic statement, a vivid image, a provocative question, an ANECDOTE, or a startling CLAIM.
> online, 716–17
> sentences, 714–17

"or," 707–8
oral forms of knowledge
> as field research, 505
> as sources, 497

oral presentations, in works cited (MLA style), 605–6
Oregon State University, Fisheries and Wildlife Club, 794, *794*

ORGANIZATION, 55–58, 113–14 The STRATEGIES a writer uses to arrange their writing so that they present ideas to readers in a clear and logical way. Strategies include presenting the most important information first followed by minor points; presenting what happened first to last (chronologically); and offering general information before specifics.
> chronological, 202
> general to specific, 57
> IMRAD, 55
> spatial, 320
> of summary / response essays, 86

organizing
> analyses, 275–76
> arguments, 179–80
> drafts, 113–14
> narratives, 223
> oral presentations, 810–12
> proposals, 394
> reflections, 126–27
> reports, 300–301, 319–20
> reviews, 358–59

Osaka, Naomi, 407–8, *408*

OUTLINING, 112 A process for GENERATING IDEAS AND TEXT or for examining a text. An informal outline simply lists ideas and then numbers them in the order that they will appear; a working outline distinguishes support from main ideas by indenting the former; a formal outline is arranged as a series of headings and indented subheadings, each on a separate line, with letters and numerals indicating relative levels of importance.

P

page numbers
    APA style, 652
    MLA style, 607
    works without, 578
papers from conference proceedings
    in lists of references (APA style), 645
    in works cited (MLA style), 597–98
paralipsis, 435

PARAPHRASE, 548–50, 554–56, 558–61 To reword a text in about the same number of words but without using the word order or sentence structure of the original. Paraphrasing is generally called for when a writer wants to include the details of a passage but does not need to quote it word for word. As with QUOTING and SUMMARIZING, paraphrasing requires DOCUMENTATION. *See also* PATCHWRITING
    deciding whether to quote, paraphrase, or summarize, 549–50
    signal phrases and, 558–59

parentheses, in keyword searches, 504
"parlor" metaphor (Burke), 8

PARTICIPANT OBSERVATION, 506 A form of observation in field research that operates on the principle that researchers can learn about a subject by doing (participating in it) as well as by watching.

PASSIVE VOICE, 689–90 When a VERB is in the passive voice, the subject is acted upon: A gift was given to Oliver.

PATCHWRITING, 566–67 PARAPHRASES that lean too heavily on the words or sentence structure of the source, adding or deleting some words, replacing words with synonyms, altering the syntax slightly—in other words, not restating the passage in fresh language and structure.

Patel, Eboo, 422–24, *423*
pathos, *See* EMOTIONAL APPEALS
peer review, *See* response
Pepper Dem Ministries (PDM), 467, *467*
periodicals, documenting, 495–96
    in working bibliographies, 519
    in works cited (MLA style), 585–92

PERIODIC SENTENCE, 712–13 A sentence that delays the main idea, expressed in a MAIN CLAUSE, until after details given in phrases and SUBORDINATE CLAUSES. *See also* CUMULATIVE SENTENCE

periods, 553, 729, 731–32
personal experience
    as evidence, 432
    insights coming from, 14
    as support for an argument, 466
personal interviews, in works cited (MLA style), 605
perspectives. *See also* POINT OF VIEW
    in arguments, 168–69
    considering multiple perspectives, 9–10, 57, 436–38, 524
persuasion, 5. *See also* RHETORIC
Pettitte, Andy, 251–52

Q

REGISTER, 693–94 Varieties of LANGUAGE associated not with particular people or users but with a particular activity or occupation—like soccer or chemical engineering.

REITERATION, 472–74 A STRATEGY for SUPPORTING AN ARGUMENT that uses the repetition of a keyword, phrase, image, or theme throughout a text to drive home a point.

RELATIVE PRONOUN A PRONOUN, such as "that," "which," "who," "whoever," "whom," and "whomever," that introduces a SUBORDINATE CLAUSE: The professor who gave the lecture is my adviser.

REPORT, 287–333 A writing GENRE that presents information to inform readers on a subject. Features: a topic carefully focused for a specific AUDIENCE • definitions of key terms • trustworthy information • effective ORGANIZATION and DESIGN • a confident, informative TONE. *See also* IMRAD; PROFILE

RESEARCH, 477–672 The process of gathering information from reliable SOURCES to help in making decisions, supporting ARGUMENTS, solving problems, becoming more informed, and so on. *See also* FIELD RESEARCH

SECONDARY SOURCE, 490–91 An ANALYSIS or interpretation of a PRIMARY SOURCE. In writing about the Revolutionary War, a researcher would probably consider the Declaration of Independence a primary source and a textbook's description of how the document was written a secondary source.

SIGNAL PHRASE, 558–59, 754, 756–57 A phrase used to attribute quoted, paraphrased, or summarized material to a source, as in "she said" or "he claimed."

SIGNIFYING, 474–75 A STRATEGY FOR SUPPORTING AN ARGUMENT by underscoring something true or important through humor, satire, and indirection.

SIGNPOST LANGUAGE, 146 Words and phrases meant to help listeners follow an oral presentation. Some functions of signpost language include introducing or concluding a presentation ("My topic today is . . ."), providing an overview ("I will make three major points"), or marking TRANSITIONS ("My third and final point is . . .").

SIMPLE SENTENCE, 706 A single MAIN CLAUSE, which contains at least a SUBJECT and a VERB. The main clause must stand alone: Citizens vote. The United States holds a presidential election once every four years. For sentences with more than a single main clause, *see* COMPOUND SENTENCE; COMPOUND-COMPLEX SENTENCE; COMPLEX SENTENCE.

SIMPLE SUBJECT, 747, 748 The word that determines the form of the VERB: The young farmer from Ten Barn Farm has the best tomatoes at the market. The simple subject is "farmer," a singular NOUN; for that reason, the verb "has" is singular.

SINGULAR "THEY," 725, 742–43 The use of "they," "them," and "their" to refer to a person whose gender is unknown or not relevant to

SPATIAL ORGANIZATION, **320** A way of ordering a text that mirrors the physical arrangement

VERB, 746–52 A word that expresses an action (dance, talk) or a state of being (be, seem). A verb is an ESSENTIAL ELEMENT of a sentence or CLAUSE. Verbs have four forms: base form (smile), past tense (smiled), past participle (smiled), and present participle (smiling). *See also* HELPING VERB; IRREGULAR VERB; TENSE

VISUAL ANALYSIS, 260–67 A GENRE of writing that examines an image, video, or some other visual text and how it communicates a message to an AUDIENCE. Features: a DESCRIPTION of the visual • some contextual information • attention to any words • close ANALYSIS of the

W

WIKI A website format, often consisting of
many linked pages on related topics, that
allows readers to add, edit, delete, or otherwise
change the site's content.

WORKING BIBLIOGRAPHY, 518–19 A record of all
sources consulted during research. Each entry
provides all the bibliographic information
necessary for correct DOCUMENTATION of each
source, including author, title, and publication information. A working bibliography is a
useful tool for recording and keeping track of
sources.

WORKS CITED, 579–609, 617 The list of full
bibliographic information, for all the sources
cited in the text, which appears at the end of a
researched text prepared in MLA STYLE. *See also*
bibliographies

MLA DOCUMENTATION DIRECTORY

APA DOCUMENTATION DIRECTORY

Menu of Readings ∽

Readings by Genre ∽

Analysis

Argument

*Student writing